A HISTORY OF PSYCHOLOGY

ORIGINAL SOURCES AND CONTEMPORARY RESEARCH

A HISTORY OF PSYCHOLOGY

ORIGINAL SOURCES AND CONTEMPORARY RESEARCH

Ludy T. Benjamin, Jr.

Texas A & M University

McGRAW-HILL BOOK COMPANY

New York St. Louis San Francisco Auckland Bogotá Caracas
Colorado Springs Hamburg Lisbon London Madrid Mexico
Milan Montreal New Delhi Oklahoma City Panama Paris San Juan
São Paulo Singapore Sydney Tokyo Toronto

This book was set in Times Roman by The College Composition Unit
in cooperation with Ruttle Shaw & Wetherill, Inc.
The editors were James D. Anker and John M. Morriss;
the designer was Carla Bauer;
new illustrations were done by Wellington Studios, Ltd.
the production supervisor was Denise L. Puryear.
Project supervision was done by The Total Book.
R. R. Donnelley & Sons Company was printer and binder.

A HISTORY OF PSYCHOLOGY:

Original Sources and Contemporary Research

2 3 4 5 6 7 8 9 0   DOCDOC   8 9 2 1 0 9 8

ISBN   0-07-004561-5
ISBN   0-07-004562-3

Library of Congress Cataloging-in-Publication Data

A History of psychology: original sources and contemporary research/
  edited by Ludy T. Benjamin, Jr.
    p. cm.
  Includes bibliographies and index.
  ISBN 0-07-004562-3: ISBN 0-07-004561-5 (pbk.)
  1. Psychology—History. I. Benjamin, Ludy T., (date)
BF81.H58 1988   87–20591
150'.9—dc19   CIP

ABOUT THE EDITOR

Ludy T. Benjamin, Jr., is Professor of Psychology at Texas A & M University, where he teaches graduate and undergraduate courses in the history of psychology. His published works include nine books and more than fifty articles in scholarly journals. His historical research has included works on psychology's public image, the development of the first American laboratories, applied psychology, the psychology of women, and the early organizations of American psychologists. Among his books are *Psychology* (1987), and *Teaching History of Psychology: A Handbook* (1981).

Benjamin was elected a Fellow of the American Psychological Association (APA) in 1981 and has served as president of two of APA's divisions, including the Division on the History of Psychology. Currently he serves as a member of the Board of Advisors of the Archives of the History of American Psychology, as a member of the Oral History Advisory Committee of the APA, and as Historian of the Eastern Psychological Association. In 1984 he received a Distinguished Teaching Award from Texas A & M University and in 1986 the prestigious Distinguished Teaching Award from the American Psychological Foundation.

This book is dedicated to

Harry Kirke Wolfe
1858–1918

As an inspiration for students in psychology
he had no peer

CONTENTS

PREFACE

This book is a reader in the history of psychology that covers the field from Descartes and the rise of modern science through the neobehaviorism of the 1950s. It is unlike any previous reader treating the history of psychology in that it combines primary and secondary sources. Primary sources are original material authored by the figures whose work is the subject matter of a history of psychology course, individuals such as Pinel, Locke, J. S. Mill, Broca, Fechner, Wundt, Darwin, James, Watson, and Freud. Works by each of those individuals and by many others, a total of twenty-four selections, are included in this book. Secondary sources are the studies written by historians of science and psychology about the individuals and ideas that are the primary sources. In short, primary source material was written by historical figures such as Freud or Darwin, whereas secondary source material was written about such primary work. There are thirty-seven secondary source articles included in this reader.

The idea for this book grew out of my own classes in the history of psychology, both undergraduate and graduate, which I have been teaching for seventeen years. Like most faculty, I have used a textbook in teaching those courses because of the integration provided by such books. However, I have two important goals for my classes that cannot be met with the standard textbooks. First, I want my students to read some of the actual primary sources. I want them to know what Galton said and how he said it. It is not enough that they read *about* the marvelous way William James had with words; I want them to read James. Second, I want my students to understand that the history of psychology is an active research specialty in psychology, that the information they are reading in their textbook is the result of some historian's painstaking efforts to reconstruct the past, and that those efforts go on every day. They will not learn that by reading about the work of Sokal or Henle or Leary or Samelson in their textbook; they need to read the actual words of those historians.

Those two goals represent the principal rationale for this book, that is, a collection of both primary source literature in the history of psychology and historical research in psychology done within the past twenty years. There are, however, other objectives that I wish to accomplish with this book. These objectives can best be introduced historically by reviewing the development of the research specialty of the history of psychology.

History of psychology as a research specialty is a recent development, dating to around 1965. That date is especially important because it marks the beginning of the

American Psychological Association's Division on the History of Psychology (Division 26); the founding of the Archives of the History of American Psychology at the University of Akron, now the single largest assemblage of manuscript collections in psychology; and the establishment of the *Journal of the History of the Behavioral Sciences,* the first journal devoted largely to research in the history of psychology, as well as other fields in the social sciences. With the special interest group, the increased archival collections, and the journal has come improved historical scholarship, showing a sophistication not prevalent prior to 1960. Modern researchers recognize the significance of such issues as presentism, historicism, and the role of the social history of science. They use a variety of sources, such as archival records and oral histories, and of techniques, such as prescriptive analysis and citation analysis. Partly this enhanced quality, and quantity, of historical research in psychology is due to the influx of historians of science into the field of behavioral science. But this research also represents the work of psychologists who have left their original specialties to pursue careers in historical work. One of the goals of this book is to make the reader aware of (1) the issues one deals with in doing historical research, (2) the sources available for this research, and (3) the techniques historians of psychology are using. This goal is partially accomplished in the opening chapter of this reader, which is a collection of five articles on these topics, written by historians of psychology. However, this kind of material is also dispersed throughout the reader, embedded in the context of the chapter topics—for example, a citation analysis investigating Wundt's influence in the United States, a prescriptive analysis of Descartes's ideas, and a comparative study of Fechner biographies.

Another objective of the book is to provide some coverage, where possible, of material that is often omitted from the standard history of psychology textbooks. Thus in the chapter on functionalism, a secondary source article examines the influence of Darwin and the functional psychologists on issues of sex differences and the psychology of women. As another example, the chapter on physiological roots of psychology includes a selection on phrenology and relates it to the nineteenth-century emphasis on the cortical localization of function.

The final objective of this book, and one of the most important, was to assemble some of the most significant literature in the history of psychology. Thus the primary source readings are taken from Darwin's *Origin,* James's *Principles,* Freud's *Interpretation of Dreams,* and John Stuart Mill's *System of Logic.* These selections are lengthy enough that the reader should get a good flavor of the style and substance of the work. Further, the secondary source articles are selected to represent some of the most important historical scholarship in the field. These studies have radically changed our views of Wundt's psychology, of the development of psychoanalysis, and of the spread of behaviorism.

This book is intended for use in history of psychology classes at the upper undergraduate and graduate levels. It is designed to be used as a supplement to one of the existing textbooks in the history of psychology and is broad enough in its coverage so that it can be used with any of a number of the leading textbooks. However, some instructors may find it satisfactory to use it alone.

The book is organized into sixteen chapters. The first chapter, as noted earlier, discusses the issues and methods of history of psychology research. The remaining fifteen chapters correspond to chapter titles frequently found in history of psychology textbooks, for example, British Empiricism, Functionalism, Behaviorism, Gestalt Psychology. Each chapter begins with an introduction that provides (1) a historical context for the selections included in the chapter, and (2) some information about the importance of the selections for the topic at hand.

Approximately half of the selections are adapted in some way, and that is especially true of the primary source material because a number of those selections are excerpts from books. The source note for each selection indicates whether it has been reprinted in full or adapted. In some selections when portions were omitted, the footnotes in the remaining portions were renumbered for clarity. The numbers for those footnotes have been placed in parentheses indicating their renumbering.

The organization of topics in this book and the selection of some of the readings have benefited from the capable advice of my colleagues in the history of psychology field. I want to acknowledge the very helpful assistance of Wolfgang Bringmann, Darryl Bruce, William Cronan-Hillix, David Leary, and Alfred Raphelson in reviewing a draft of this book. I owe a special debt to Michael M. Sokal for his very careful reading of the chapter introductions in this book, and for the multitude of suggestions he provided. Because I have not always followed the advice of the scholars, they cannot be held responsible for any faults in the final product. I am certain, however, that this book is significantly better because of their counsel.

I am pleased to acknowledge the excellent work of Ann Grogg who served as copy editor on the manuscript, Sydney Ellen Schultz who prepared the detailed index, and Annette Bodzin who was the project supervisor. I also want to give special thanks to my editor at McGraw-Hill, James D. Anker, whose interest in the history of psychology and in me helped bring this book into being. Of course, I owe a very special debt to the many authors and publishers who have allowed me to reprint their work in this book.

This book, like most endeavors in my life, has been a family effort. My daughters Melissa and Melanie and my wife Priscilla spent many hours checking sources in the library, photocopying, acquiring permissions, and reading galleys. Their substantial assistance was instrumental in the completion of this book, and I gratefully acknowledge their work.

Finally, I want to thank the many students from my history of psychology classes whose enthusiasm for the subject has made this project, and my involvement in the field, a labor of love. I hope this collection of readings will both instruct and inspire other students with the fascination and intrigue that are part of psychology's history.

Ludy T. Benjamin, Jr.

A HISTORY OF PSYCHOLOGY

ORIGINAL SOURCES AND CONTEMPORARY RESEARCH

CHAPTER 1

RESEARCH IN THE HISTORY OF PSYCHOLOGY

As noted in the preface to this book, history of psychology as a research specialty is approximately twenty-five years old. In that twenty-five years, history of psychology interest groups have formed, such as Division 26 of the American Psychological Association (a group of psychologists interested in the history of their field) and Cheiron: The International Society for the History of the Behavioral and Social Sciences (a group of historians, including psychologist-historians, of the social and behavioral sciences). Cheiron has a European counterpart that is one of a number of such organizations to emerge abroad in the past decade.

Specialty journals have been created in that twenty-five years, such as the *Journal of the History of the Behavioral Sciences,* which is published in the United States, and similar publications in Spain, Italy, Germany, and other countries. Historians of psychology also publish their work in a variety of historical journals of longer standing such as *Isis* (the quarterly publication of the History of Science Society), the *Journal of the History of Ideas,* and the *American Historical Review*.

Graduate programs have been established to train students in the theory, methods, and content of the history of psychology. The best known of these is the University of New Hampshire, which offers the doctoral degree in the history of psychology. Other traditional programs in the history of science, for example at the Universities of Chicago and Pennsylvania, also allow students to specialize in the history of behavioral science.

Archival sources in psychology have grown enormously, led by the Archives of the History of American Psychology, the single largest collection of unpublished materials in psychology, located at the University of Akron (see Benjamin, 1980; Popplestone & McPherson, 1976). In recent years psychologists have become more conscious of the value of archival materials, and efforts to preserve such materials have become more commonplace (see Sokal & Rafail, 1982). The manuscript collections of individual psychologists are more frequently being systematically preserved, as are the collections of organizations such as the American Psychological Association (whose archives are in the Library of Congress) and the Psychonomic Society (whose archives are in the collection at Akron).

With the formation of special groups drawing individuals together with common research interests, the establishment of new journal outlets to publish their research, the formation of new doctoral programs to train students in the new specialty, and the rapid growth of archival collections providing a rich data base for the new research, the history of psychology has emerged as a recognized research specialty in the fields of psychology and the history of science. It is a research specialty that has been created jointly by psychologists shifting from their original field of training (e.g., cognition, development, personality) to historical research and by historians of science shifting to psychology from the more traditional research areas of the natural sciences and medicine.

Science and practice (the application of that science) are both forms of behavior that psychologists have found interesting to study in their historical contexts. Thus studying the history of psychology means studying its evolution as a science and as a means of applying that science. Historians of science are also interested in those issues, and they have brought with them the research methods of their discipline and a propensity to look at the history of psychology in a broader context of culture, geography, politics, and economics.

This chapter is intended to provide a brief introduction to some of the methods and issues that are part of research in the history of psychology. Much of what will be said here is true for historical research in any field; however, the discussions in this chapter will be focused largely on the history of psychology. It is not the intent of this chapter to make the reader skilled in historiography, the methods of history. Rather, it is hoped that these selections will provide an awareness of critical issues in historical interpretation and the methods that underlie history. That awareness will help lead to an appreciation of the secondary source material in Chapters 2 through 16 which utilizes those methods and addresses those issues.

The first selection, by the historian of anthropology George W. Stocking, Jr., treats the issue of *presentism*—interpreting the past in the context of the present. According to Stocking (1965), presentist histories result in "anachronism, distortion, misinterpretation, misleading analogy, neglect of context, [and] oversimplification of process" (p. 215). He contrasts presentism with a view he labels *historicism*—an understanding of the past in its own context and for its own sake. The presentist approach is evident in all historical fields but seems especially problematic in the history of the behavioral sciences. Stocking discusses the reasons for its prevalence in psychology and how the pitfalls of that approach might be avoided.

The second selection, by the sociologist Gian Sarup, treats the topic of intellectual history, or what is often called the history of ideas. Sarup (1978) distinguishes between *anticipations* and *foundations* in the history of ideas:

> Anticipations are those antecedent ideas that have likeness to but not developmental ties with, later modes of thought. They are historically isolated instances of foreshadowing. Foundations, on the other hand, are the actual beginnings of later concepts and theories in the sense that the growth of thought is relatively continuous and the lines of influence are traceable. (p. 478)

Without an understanding of this distinction, the researcher is likely to mistake old ideas for new ones, failing to grasp the significance of the latter. Sarup draws on a number of examples in the history of ideas in psychology to clarify this distinction. Like the issue of presentism, it is an important lesson to learn for historical interpretation.

In the third selection, Mary Henle argues for the value of reading primary sources as a guard against historical distortion. Using a number of examples in the history of psychology literature, she illustrates how errors of interpretation can easily occur when the reader depends solely on secondary sources. In other words, those who want to know what William James said must read James himself. Two examples of Henle's historical work appear in Chapters 8 and 16.

Originally trained in the field of animal learning, Thomas C. Cadwallader, the author of the fourth selection, now works almost exclusively in the history of psychology. His article deals with the unique values of doing archival research. Those values are richly illustrated by examples drawn from his own research, principally on two figures in the early history of American psychology, Charles S. Peirce and Christine Ladd-Franklin.

The final selection is by Marion White McPherson, the cofounder, with John Popplestone, of the Archives of the History of American Psychology. McPherson is an authority on the history of psychological testing and the techniques of oral history; the latter is the subject of this selection. Oral histories as historical data continue as an issue of controversy in historiography. In this brief article, she discusses the values and limitations of this method. (See Benjamin [1981] for a description of the principal psychology oral history collections in the United States and Canada.)

The issues and methods discussed in this chapter will be evident in the chapters that follow. The use of archival sources is characteristic of virtually every example of historical research presented in this book. Oral history material will also be found in several articles. The importance of primary source material is also illustrated in several selections, as, for example, in Arthur L. Blumenthal's reinterpretation of Wilhelm Wundt and Lesley A. Diehl's research on G. Stanley Hall. Deborah J. Coon's article on Edwin B. Twitmyer and Ivan Pavlov raises Sarup's distinction between anticipations and foundations.

In addition, other historical issues and methods are treated as well. There is an example of a method known as *prescriptive analysis,* a few examples of the use of a quantitative technique known as *citation analysis,* and several studies looking at biography as history. Finally, most of the historical research presented in this volume illustrates (1) a keen awareness of the necessity to understand psychology's past for its own sake (historicism) and (2) a recognition that psychology has not evolved in a vacuum, that it is the product of complex forces within psychology as well as the cultural, political, economic, and geographic forces external to psychology (a view of historical writing usually called *external history*). Thus in reading these selections from contemporary research in the history of psychology, the reader should better appreciate the content through understanding the methods and issues involved in that research.

REFERENCES

Benjamin, L. T. (1980). Research at the Archives of the History of American Psychology: A case history. In J. Brozek & L. J. Pongratz (Eds.), *Historiography of modern psychology*. Toronto: C. J. Hogrefe, pp. 241–251.

Benjamin, L. T. (1981). *Teaching history of psychology: A handbook*. New York: Academic Press.

Popplestone, J. A., & McPherson, M. W. (1976). Ten years of the Archives of the History of American Psychology. *American Psychologist, 31,* 533–534.

Sarup, G. (1978). Historical antecedents of psychology: The recurrent issue of old wine in new bottles. *American Psychologist, 33,* 478–485.

Sokal, M. M., & Rafail, P. (1982). *A guide to the manuscript collections in the history of psychology and related areas*. Millwood, NY: Kraus.

Stocking, G. W., Jr. (1965). On the limits of 'presentism' and 'historicism' in the historiography of the behavioral sciences. *Journal of the History of the Behavioral Sciences, 1,* 211–218.

On The Limits of 'Presentism' and 'Historicism' in the Historiography of the Behavioral Sciences

George W. Stocking, Jr.

Although the April editorial on "Policy and Its Implementation" outlined the basic objectives of this journal, its frankly limited scope and purpose did not allow extended consideration of certain broader questions of motive and method in the historiography of the behaviorial sciences. Perhaps this was as it should have been. The "grass roots" impulses which produced the JHBS [*Journal of the History of the Behavioral Sciences*] were numerous, and express themselves in a variety of historiographical approaches. Furthermore, history itself is in many respects the most undisciplined of disciplines. There have been many attempts to codify historical method (*e.g.,* 9; 6) and to define the philosophical presuppositions of historical inquiry (*e.g., 5; 13*). But Clio, putative mother of many of the behavioral sciences (16; *cf.* 2), still drapes herself in skirts as varied as the progeny who once abandoned and now return to them. For all this, however, history remains a discipline of sorts, and one to which all the makers of this journal are at least avocationally committed. While we cannot assume and do not seek a consensus of motive and method, it is still appropriate to discuss these problems systematically. If we can neither prescribe nor proscribe historiographical points of view, we can at least define them and argue their relative merits.

With due regard for the oversimplification which ideal-typical analysis involves, let us proceed by setting up a series of dichotomies which may be subsumed under two alternative orientations toward historiography. If subtler analysis should destroy the neat dualism of the model, well and good. It may nevertheless serve as a polemical starting point. Consider then the following alternatives: "context" and "analogue"; "process" and "sequence"; "emergence" and "agency"; "thinking" and "thought"; "reasonableness" and "rationality"; "understanding" and "judgment"; "affective" and "utilitarian"; "historicism" and "presentism". Their explication will, I hope, flow from the ensuing argument. At this point, however, let us leap directly to the alternative orientations under which I will subsume them: in each case, the first term seems to me to characterize the attempt "to understand the past for the sake of the past"; the second, to characterize the study of "the past for the sake of the present."

The last two phrases are of course Herbert Butterfield's (3, p. 16). He used them a generation ago in a critique entitled *The Whig Interpretation of History,* which he defined as "the tendency in many historians to write on the side of Protestants and Whigs, to praise revolutions provided they have been successful, to emphasize certain principles of progress in the past and to produce a story which is the ratification if not the glorification of the present" (3, p. v). According to Butterfield, the whig interpretation introduces itself into historical writing as a principle of abridgment. Faced with the massive complexity of historical particularity, the general historian falls victim to the "historian's 'pathetic fallacy,'" "abstracting things from their historical context and judging them apart from their context—estimating them and organizing the historical study by a system of direct reference to the present." The whig historian reduces the mediating process by which the totality of an historical past produces the totality of its consequent future to a search for the origins of certain

Adapted from Stocking, G. W., Jr. (1965). On the limits of 'presentism' and 'historicism' in the historiography of the behavioral sciences. *Journal of the History of the Behavioral Sciences, 1,* 211–218. Copyright © 1965 by the Clinical Psychology Publishing Company. Adapted and reprinted by permission of the publisher.

expressing value judgments as contrasted w stating facts.

present phenomena. He seeks out in the past phenomena which seem to resemble those of concern in the present, and then moves forward in time by tracing lineages up to the present in simple sequential movement. When this abridging procedure is charged with a normative commitment to the phenomena whose origins are sought, the linear movement is "progress" and those who seem to abet it are "progressive". The result is whiggish history. Because it is informed by a normative commitment, its characteristic interpretive mode is judgment rather than understanding, and history becomes the field for a dramatic struggle between children of light and children of darkness. Because it wrenches the individual historical phenomenon from the complex network of its contemporary context in order to see it in abstracted relationship to analogues in the present, it is prone to anachronistic misinterpretation. Because it assumes in advance the progressive character of historical change, it is less interested in the complex processes by which change emerges than in agencies which direct it, whether they be great men, specific deterministic forces, or the "logic" of historical development itself.

Whiggish history is a variety of what I would call generally "presentism" in historical study. Butterfield offers no neat phrase to characterize its alternative, but for present purposes I would suggest the term "historicism". Now "historicism" is a word that has been used with a variety of meanings (10), which often have an underlying or explicit epistemological charge. By deliberately using it rather loosely, without epistemological commitment, I am of course to some extent sacrificing analytic subtlety to polemical convenience. Nevertheless, some term is necessary, and "historicism" conveys rather well the essential quality of the commitment to the understanding of the past for its own sake. This essence should already be generally evident, but we can make it more explicit—and at the same time relate this whole discussion more directly to the problems of the historiography of the be-

havioral sciences—by briefly explicating several of the dichotomies mentioned above: "thinking" and "thought"; "reasonableness" and "rationality"; understanding" and "judgment".

What I have to suggest in regard to the first two pairs of alternatives has been admirably stated in Joseph Levenson's *Confucian China and Its Modern Fate,* an extended essay on the *historicization* of a world view: the process by which a traditional and absolutistic *weltanschauung* becomes historical and relativistic under the impact of Western culture. In discussing this process, Levenson treats with a subtle and delicate hand the ways in which iconoclasts "relegate traditional ideas to the past" and traditionalists "transform traditional ideas in the present"—an "apparently paradoxical transformation-with-preservation" which depends on "a change in the thinker's alternatives." For, as Professor Levenson suggests, "a thought includes what its thinker eliminates; an idea has its particular quality from the fact that other ideas, expressed in other quarters, are demonstrably alternatives" (11, pp. xiii–xiv). Levenson goes on to quote the British philosopher of history, R. G. Collingwood, to suggest a logical principle by which such change may be understood: "a body of knowledge consists not of 'propositions', 'statements' or 'judgments'... but of these together with the questions they are meant to answer" (11, pp. xv, *cf.* 4). Levenson concludes that an "idea, then, is a denial of alternatives and an answer to a question" (11, p. xxii), and that intellectual history is the history of men *thinking* rather than the history of *thought* (11, p. 212).

In a general consideration of the problem of history and value, Levenson later comments on the alternatives of "reasonableness" and "rationality": "Absolutism is parochialism of the present, the confusion of one's own time with the timeless, a confusion of the categories of reasonable and rational." The historian, however, asks "not whether something is true or good, but why and where and to what end it came to be enacted or expressed.'' He goes beyond ''assessment of his subject's thought as rationally (timelessly and abstractly) perhaps erratic. He proceeds to analyse why, nevertheless, that thought was not ridiculous...but reasonable—in spite of or because of imperfect rationality.'' For ''reasonableness relates to the questions put by the subject's time...[to which] his ideas are answers'' (12, p. 87). It is in some context such as this, rather than in any explicitly epistemological framework, that I would like to pose the dichotomy between judgment and understanding (*cf.* 1, pp. 138–144): understanding is the attempt, by whatever means, to get at the ''reasonableness'' of what might otherwise be *judged* as falling short of some present or absolute standards of ''rationality.''

At this point, the reader may well ask ''what has all this to do with the work of our journal?'' In the first place I would suggest—in a frankly provocative, but open-minded spirit—that each of these orientations will tend to find its natural adherents among the historiographers of the behavioral sciences, and that each orientation carries with it a characteristic motivational posture. The orientation of the historian approaching the history of the behavioral sciences will tend to be ''historicist'' and his motivational posture ''affective.'' Presentism is by no means a dead issue in the historical fraternity, and historians are undeniably conditioned in a thousand subtle ways by the present in which they write. But in general, the historian approaches the past rather in the spirit of the mountain climber attacking Everest—''because it is there.'' He demands no more of it than the emotional satisfaction which flows from understanding a manifestation of the changing human self in time. The approach of the professional behavioral scientist, on the other hand, is more likely to be whiggish or, more broadly, ''presentist,'' and his motivational posture ''utilitarian.'' He may share the historian's emotional satisfaction, but he tends to demand of the past something more: that it be related to and even useful for furthering his professional activities in the on-going present. Thus the April

editorial emphasizes the utility of historical study as ''a way to implement interdisciplinary cooperation.''

Leaving aside for now the relative merits of the postures of these frankly ideal-typical practitioners, it is important to note that there is a sort of implicit whiggish presentism virtually built into the history of science and by extension, into the history of the behavioral sciences. However disillusioned we may have become with the idea of progress in other areas, however sophisticated in the newer philosophy of science, most of us take it for granted that the development of science is a cumulative ever-upward progress in rationality. Indeed George Sarton, long-time doyen of historians of science, described his study as ''the only history which can illustrate the progress of mankind'' because ''the acquisition and systematization of positive knowledge are the only human activities which are truly cumulative and progressive'' (15, p. 5). For Sarton, the history of mathematics was a whiggish progress unmarred by tory backslidings, ''an endless series of victories of the human mind, victories without counterbalancing failures, that is, without dishonorable and humiliating ones, and without atrocities'' (14, p. 13). In view of the occasionally strident scientism and also of the residual reformism of the behavioral sciences, it is hardly surprising that their historiography should manifest various signs of whiggish presentism. The careful reader will find a number in the first issues of our journal. In a general and impersonal way, one may note that antiquarianism can flow from a presentist orientation just as well as from a know-nothing historicism. Starting from whiggish assumptions about progress, the historian can become rather pedantically involved in the search for ''firsts'' and ''founders''—for the agents of cumulative forward progression. Or one may note how the search for analogues, for precursors of modernity, can produce its all too revealing shocks of recognition disappointed—as, for instance, when scientist X, who otherwise anticipated so much of our current thinking, is found to have an "insufficient appreciation" of some point which is today obvious.

Fortunately, however, the history of science provides us with other models than the "chroniclers of an incremental process." In recent years there has been, in the words of Thomas Kuhn, a "historiographic revolution in the study of science." Rather than searching out "the permanent contributions of an older science to our present vantage," historians have begun to attempt "to display the historical integrity of that science in its own time" (8, pp. 2–3). Although this revolution is still "in its early stages," Kuhn's own brilliantly controversial *Structure of Scientific Revolutions* is a clear indication that historicism, though it may have come late to the history of science, is by no means irrelevant to it. True, Kuhn's book is imperfectly historicist in its focus on the inner development of science to the deliberate neglect of the role of "technological advance or of external social, economic and intellectual conditions" (8, p. xii), and, one might add, the variety of national cultural traditions within which scientific development takes place. But however much some more traditional historians may have balked at its nomothetic language and its attempt to generalize the course of scientific development, Kuhn's approach to the internal development of science is informed by a spirit which is clearly historicist, in the sense in which I have used the term.

Kuhn's central concept is that of "paradigm"—an articulated set of assumptions about "the fundamental entities of which the universe is composed," the nature of their interaction "with each other and with the senses," the types of questions "which may legitimately be asked about such entities" and the techniques to be employed in seeking answers to these questions (8, pp. 4–5). In short, the paradigm functions as a disciplinary *world view*—which, as Kuhn points out, is culturally transmitted and sustained by a set of social institutions. Prior to the establishment of its first consensual paradigm, a science

tends to be a chaos of competing schools, each of which feels "forced to build [its] field anew from its foundations" (8, p. 13). Once accepted, the paradigm is the basis for the puzzle-solving mop-up work of "normal science", which serves primarily to complete the articulation of the paradigm. Scientific revolutions occur when anomalies "produced inadvertently by a game played under one set of rules" require for their assimilation the "elaboration of another set"—the creation of a new paradigm based on different assumptions, asking different questions, and suggesting different answers (8, p. 52). Without further elaborating, or necessarily accepting, the specifics of Kuhn's analysis, I would suggest that this approach does encourage us to see a body of knowledge as a set of propositions "together with the questions they are meant to answer," to understand the "reasonableness" of points of view now superseded, to see historical change as a complex process of emergence rather than a simple linear sequence—in short, to understand the science of a given period in its own terms.

Quite aside from the question of its general utility, Kuhn's schematization suggests further reason for the presentism of many historiographers of the behavioral sciences. Precisely because the behavioral sciences are for the most part in Kuhn's terms "pre-paradigmatic," their historiography is more open to certain vices of presentism than that of science generally. When there is no single framework which unites all the workers in a field, but rather competing points of view or competing schools, historiography simply extends the arena of the competition among them. At its most neutral, the result is the sterile tracing of theoretical lineages which is served up in "history of theory" courses in many behavioral science departments. As the degree of partisan involvement and historiographical effort increases, the author may attempt to legitimize a present point of view by claiming for it a putative "founder" of the discipline. Or he may sweep broadly across the history of a discipline, brushing out whigs and tories in the nooks and crannies of every century (17, 18). Inevitably the sins of history written "for the sake of the present" insinuate themselves: anachronism, distortion, misinterpretation, misleading analogy, neglect of context, oversimplification of process.

But does this mean that the history of the behavioral sciences should be written purely and simply "to understand the past for the sake of the past?" I think not. It may well be that such understanding exists only as a kind of historical Holy Grail—never to be found by sinful man, but enlightening the scholar who dedicates himself to the search. Or one may argue, as indeed Professor Levenson does, that the historian *must* "articulate his own [present] standards in order to find the rationale of his subjects', in order— by raising the question he could never recognize if he lacked his own convictions—to find what made it reasonable for the earlier generation to violate the later historian's criteria of rationality" (12, p. 89). But beyond such limitations which historicism would impose upon itself, there are compelling reasons for a much more active presentism in the historiography of the behavioral sciences. Precisely because most of us are practicing behavioral scientists, we are, and indeed must be, interested in *thought* as well as *thinking,* in *rationality* as well as *reasonableness*—not in absolutistic terms, but in the context of on-going attempts to develop generalized explanations of human behavior at the highest level that present knowledge permits. The case for an enlightened presentism in a particular area of the behavioral sciences has been so well put by Dell Hymes that I would like to quote from him at some length:

> There exists, indeed, not only a subject matter for a history of linguistic anthropology, but also a definite need. To my mind, there is a general need in the current study of language for codification, articulation as well as exploration. From a humanistic viewpoint, such work might be seen as the reconstitution of a general philology. In strictly anthropological terms, such work might be seen as the framing of a provisional general theory of language and culture. In either case, the work of crit-

icism and interpretation would have to draw for perspective equally as much on the history, or development, of the study of language as on a survey of current knowledge and research. History and systematics would be interdependent.

Reasons for this are familiar to students of intellectual history, and the combination seems often to have occurred. . . . I mention the matter here out of a strong sense of its timeliness and importance for anthropology. To the degree that we have lacked an active knowledge of the history of our field, we have been limited by lack of some of the perspectives that have not been transmitted to us, and by the partialness of some of those that have. A critical history can help us regain the one and transcend the other. In my own work I have sometimes felt that progress in understanding was but the recapture of perspective that had been lost.

Certainly a case can be made for an intellectual discontinuity in American linguistic anthropology during this century, such that some important work of preceding generations has become unintelligible, its meaning having to be recaptured by special study. I say this not out of overestimation of the worth of earlier work. Much of its content has been permanently superseded, and its neglect thus to some extent justified. But historical interpretation and critique of earlier periods has the two-edged value of regaining and transcending (mentioned above), and I say this, not as an historian, but as a practitioner, of the field in question. I would identify the situation in this way. Our most recent, still continuing, period has been dominated by reaction against an earlier perspective considered too sweeping, too ambitious in scope, too weak in data and method. In outline caricature, the devolution from generalizations of bold scope has been first to drop the generalizations, and then the scope. Very narrow definitions of linguistics, affecting anthropology, have come to the fore. By enabling us to put in full perspective many of our problems and assumptions, historical study will help change the situation in two respects. In some ways the consequence will be to depart in a much more thoroughgoing way from earlier work, since the departure will be not simply a contraction, but a fresh start. In other ways the consequence will be to renew earlier periods by renewing attention to problems posed in them. Ideally, the fresh start will harness the technical and empirical advances of the latest period to the broad sense of scope and relevance of its predecessors (7, pp. 60–61).

Perhaps one might generalize this argument in terms of the "pre-paradigmatic" state, the a-historical orientation, and the historically conditioned disciplinary fragmentation of the behavioral sciences. Because they are pre-paradigmatic, the various competing schools of the present and of the past exist in a sense contemporaneously. But because they have on the whole such notoriously short historical memories, the behavioral sciences of the present have very little awareness that their predecessors were in many instances asking questions and offering answers about problems which have by no means been closed. And because of the disciplinary fragmentation of approaches which were in the past often much more integrated, there may be fruits of interdisciplinary cooperation which are as easily picked in the past as in the present. In short, there are in a pre-paradigmatic situation tremendous problems of defining what the positive increments in our knowledge of human behavior actually have been. There is also a tremendous field in which the seeker of serendipity may indulge himself.

But precisely because in the history of the behavioral sciences there are legitimate and compelling reasons for studying "the past for the sake of the present," it is all the more important to keep in mind the pitfalls of a presentist approach. And beyond this I would argue that the utilities we are seeking in the present are in fact best realized by an approach which is in practice if not in impulse "affective" and "historicist." E. B. Tylor may speak to present anthropologists, but they will be better able to understand him if they are able to distinguish between the questions he asked which have long since been answered, the questions which are still open, and the questions which we would no longer even recognize as such. As I have suggested elsewhere, Tylor's central anthropological problem, in its simplest terms, was to "fill the gap between Brixham Cave and European Civilization without introducing the hand of God" (17)—that is, to show that human culture was, or might have been, the result of a natural evolutionary development. No anthropologist today would question the fact that culture was, in a broad sense, the product of an evolutionary development. That question has been answered. On the other hand, the question of filling in gaps is still very much open, and although our methods of approaching this problem are perhaps quite different, Tylor may still have something to say to us. However, the question of the hand of God, which greatly exercized a number of Tylor's contemporaries, and therefore Tylor, we would not even regard as a question. As Professor Levenson suggests, to approach Tylor in these terms requires a standpoint in the present. But it also requires that we know what the questions were to which Tylor's ideas were answers, and the alternatives which his answers were designed to exclude.

What is involved here, if I may turn to my own uses a distinction which Professor Levenson made in a somewhat different context, is the difference in intonation between the "historically (really) significant" and the "(merely) historically significant"—"between an empirical judgment of fruitfulness in time and a normative judgement of aridity in the here and now" (12, p. 85). "By abjuring judgment," by approaching the past "with an even-handed allocation of historical significance," the historian may be able to create out of "the nothing of the *historically* significant" something of value and utility in the present, something "historically *significant*" (12, p. 90). But to do this requires an approach in terms of context, process, emergence, thinking and reasonableness. Indeed, it is the burden of this essay that this goal requires an affective, historicist orientation which attempts "to understand the past for the sake of the past." By suspending judgment as to present utility, we make that judgment ultimately possible.

REFERENCES

1 Bloch, Marc. *The Historian's Craft*. New York: Alfred A. Knopf, 1961.

2 Bryson, Gladys. "The Emergence of the Social Sciences from Moral Philosophy," *International Journal of Ethics*, XLII (1932), 304–322.

3 Butterfield, Herbert. *The Whig Interpretation of History*. London: G. Bell and Sons, Ltd., 1963 [1931].

4 Collingwood, R. G. *An Autobiography*. London: Oxford University Press, 1939.

5 Collingwood, R. G. *The Idea of History*. New York: Oxford University Press, 1956 [1946].

6 Gottschalk, Louis. *Understanding History: A Primer of Historical Method*. New York: Alfred A. Knopf, 1960 [1950].

7 Hymes, Dell. "Notes Toward a History of Linguistic Anthropology," *Anthropological Linguistics*, 5 (1963), 59–103.

8 Kuhn, Thomas. *The Structure of Scientific Revolutions*. Chicago: University of Chicago Press, 1962.

9 Langlois, C. V., and C. Seignobos. *Introduction to the Study of History*. Translated by G. G. Berry. London: Duckworth, 1898.

10 Lee, D. E., and R. N. Beck, "The Meaning of 'Historicism'", *American Historical Review*, LIX (1954), 568–577.

11 Levenson, Joseph. *Confucian China and Its Modern Fate*, Vol. I: *The Problem of Intellectual Continuity*. Berkeley: University of California Press, 1958.

12 Levenson, Joseph. *Confucian China and Its Modern Fate*. Vol. III: *The Problem of Historical Significance*. Berkeley: University of California Press, 1965.

13 Meyerhoff, Hans, ed. *The Philosophy of History in Our Time*. Garden City, N. Y.: Doubleday and Co., 1959.

14 Sarton, George. *The Study of the History of Mathematics*. Cambridge: Harvard University Press, 1936.

15 Sarton, George. *The Study of the History of Science*. Cambridge: Harvard University Press, 1936.

16 Small, Albion W. *Origins of Sociology*. Chicago: University of Chicago Press, 1924.

17 Stocking, George W., Jr. "'Cultural Darwinism' and 'Philosophical Idealism' in E. B. Tylor: A Special Plea for Historicism in the History of Anthropology," *Southwestern Journal of Anthropology*, (1965) (in press).

18 Stocking, George W., Jr. Review of Margaret T. Hodgen, *Early Anthropology in the Sixteenth and Seventeenth Centuries*, *Isis*, LV (1964), 454–455.

Historical Antecedents of Psychology: The Recurrent Issue of Old Wine in New Bottles

Gian Sarup

It is not infrequent to find textbook writers and researchers introducing a scientific concept or theory with a few prefatory remarks about its philosophical lineage. Atomic physics may be pushed back to Democritus, and theories of ev-

Sarup, G. (1978). Historical antecedents of psychology: The recurrent issue of old wine in new bottles. *American Psychologist, 33*, 478–485. Copyright © 1978 by the American Psychological Association. Reprinted by permission of the publisher and the author.

olution to Anaximander. And psychological literature, despite its attitude toward philosophical connections as largely vestigial, has its share of attempts to identify the genesis of its problems and ideas in the reflections of earlier philosophers. In the social psychology of attitudes alone, one comes across observations to the effect that the blueprint of the Yale Communication Program was contained in Aristotle's *Rhetoric* (e.g., Jones & Gerard, 1967, p. 433), and that

Festinger's theory of cognitive dissonance has its germinal source in Peirce's (1877/1951) views on the motivating character of doubt (Tedeschi & Lindskold, 1976, p. 212). While symbolizing a much-needed historical concern, many of such linkages, which tend to become routinized over time, are fraught with possibilities for false attribution of credit in the history of ideas.

Since psychology, like several other sciences, emerged as a distinct discipline from the primordial network of philosophy, many of its current ideas and systems have their roots in philosophical thought. A line of distinguished scholars like Brett, Murphy, Boring, Flugel, R. I. Watson, Wolman, and others have patiently teased out many of these philosophical strands in psychology. However, the corpus of philosophical thought also contains numerous observations that have varied similarities but no demonstrable connection with subsequent developments in psychology. Any time such ideas are viewed as intellectual origins of a contemporary idea in psychology on the basis of their precedence and resemblance alone, we are failing to heed a critical distinction between *anticipations* and *foundations* in the history of ideas. Anticipations are those antecedent ideas that have likeness to, but not developmental ties with, later modes of thought. They are historically isolated instances of foreshadowing. Foundations, on the other hand, are the actual beginnings of later concepts and theories in the sense that the growth of thought is relatively continuous and the lines of influence are traceable. A recognition of the difference between anticipations and foundations can be considered an essential part of the historical sophistication without which the psychologist "mistakes old facts and old views for new, and...remains unable to evaluate the significance of new movements and methods" (Boring, 1950, p. ix). This article is an attempt to explicate this distinction and its implications with the help of case materials from psychological literature.

ANTICIPATIONS

The nature of anticipations may be discussed in the context of a controversy surrounding the intellectual sources of Festinger's theory of cognitive dissonance. Attempts have been made to date the idea of dissonance as an unpleasant tension seeking resolution, back to earlier writings. Elms (1972), for instance, tells us that the central idea of dissonance and other consistency theories is hardly a new one, and although he has "not come across specific mention of it in Plato or Aristotle,...amateur or professional cogitators have dabbled with the concept of psychological consistency for centuries" (p. 220).

More specifically, Tedeschi, Schlenker, and Bonoma (1971) have traced the origins of the concept of dissonance to an 1877 essay by C. S. Peirce and observed that Festinger's theory was "not much of a step to extend Peirce's thesis to the conditions that cause doubt" or dissonance. Peirce's essay, "The Fixation of Belief," was influential

> not only as a milestone in the history of philosophy, and particularly the American school of pragmatism, but also in clearly traceable way in the subsequent psychological thought of William James, John Dewey, Edward Tolman, and Leon Festinger. Peirce argued that men are motivated to attain a state of belief and to avoid a state of doubt. Doubt was considered to be an uncomfortable state, an irritant, from which men sought relief. When a man is in a state of belief, the cognitive basis for habit exists, since, given the proper circumstances, he will know how to act. For Peirce, the sole object of individual inquiry was the settlement of doubted opinions, to attain beliefs, and thus restore a comfortable state of mind (Tedeschi, Schlenker & Bonoma, 1971, p. 685).

Likewise, Crawford (1976) finds Festinger's 1957 statement of dissonance theory a less than precise formulation of a notion that is found in the passing observations of earlier thinkers. To illustrate, he quotes Alexander Bain (1880) to have postulated that "contrary statements, opinions or appearances operate on the mind as a painful jar, and stimulate a corresponding desire for reconciliation."

Notwithstanding the striking similarity shared by the antecedent ideas of Peirce and Bain with the basic thesis of dissonance theory, it is in order to ask for evidence supporting the direct or indirect paths of influence from earlier conceptions to Festinger's formulation. There is no mention of any of the figures in the Peirce-James-Dewey-Tolman chain nor of Bain in the references or in the index of Festinger's (1957) *A Theory of Cognitive Dissonance*. That Peirce's observations on the dynamics of doubt were merely anticipatory in relation to the basic hypothesis of dissonance theory seems plausible for the additional reason that there is not even a passing mention of Dewey, James, or Peirce, much less an acknowledgment of them as "the main sources from which . . . my ideas have come," in Tolman's (1952) autobiography either. Thus, the lack of factual support for the alleged intermediary nexus renders the indirect impact of Peirce on Festinger quite dubious.

But, as the absence of citation of earlier works does not rule out their impact on a recent formulation, there is always the likelihood, in this instance, that the ideas of Peirce and Bain had so pervaded the intellectual scene that Festinger could not have escaped their subliminal influence. This kind of argument based on endless possibilities defies systematic scrutiny. The issue of derivations becomes subject to vindication or refutation only when it is predicated on specific and delimited lines of influence.

In the foreword to his book *A Theory of Cognitive Dissonance,* Festinger has provided a short account of the circumstances under which the central ideas of his theory were conceived and formulated. While working on a "propositional integration" of the work in the area of communication and social influence, Festinger and his associates were greatly intrigued by the findings of a study by Prasad (1950) that rumors following an earthquake in India tended to predict further catastrophes. Festinger and his colleagues wondered why the people in the villages, where tremors were felt but not much damage had occurred, would be given to "anxiety-provoking" rumors of worse disasters to come, when one would ordinarily expect them to invent and circulate rumors with reassuring meanings. Then it occurred to them that such rumors were really anxiety-*justifying,* rather than anxiety-provoking, in the sense that for the people who were frightened as a result of the earthquake, rumors of impending doom "served the function of giving them something to be frightened about" and provided these people with "information to fit with the way they already felt."* It was this exciting hunch that sired the eventual formalization of the concept of dissonance as a psychologically uncomfortable tension that results from nonfitting cognitions and seeks resolution through cognitive additions and adjustments (Festinger, 1957, pp. v–ix).

Denying the widely-held notion that the theory of cognitive dissonance may have stemmed from physiological doctrines of homeostasis, Festinger (quoted in Evans, 1976, p. 326) has recently reiterated, "No, I do not think so. In the introduction to that book [*A Theory of Cognitive Dissonance*] I really state specifically and accurately how it arose, but I guess nobody believes it. Or else, nobody reads introductions to books!" Although quite a few psychologists (e.g., Aronson, 1972; McGuire, 1973, p. 451; Sahakian, 1974) have accepted the

---

* Heider (1944) had observed that "just as a good unit requires or is produced by the fact that its members are similar, so a good fear *requires* or is produced by danger in the environment" (p. 372, italics added). It is likely that Festinger was acquainted with Heider's thinking before or around the time (1951–?) he was engaged in resolving the puzzle of "anxiety-provoking" rumors. To my knowledge, the earliest reference in Festinger's work to this paper by Heider is to be found in a paper by Festinger and Hutte (1954) that was received in the editorial office of the *Journal of Abnormal and Social Psychology* in June 1953.

role played by the paradoxical findings of Prasad in the genesis of dissonance theory, it could be argued that the puzzle presented by the postdisaster spread of rumors was more of a catalytic occasion than a genetic source of Festinger's thinking. The theoretical tradition that served as groundwork for his ideas was that of the dynamics of psychological fields and cognitive systems with characteristic themes of equilibrium and balance, as formulated by Lewin and Heider. Festinger's studentship under Lewin and his exposure to Heider's *The Psychology of Interpersonal Relations* (cited as an unpublished manuscript in *A Theory of Cognitive Dissonance*) are more plausible sources of dissonance theory than the observations of Peirce and Bain, regardless of the latter's antecedence and resemblance to Festinger's core ideas.

Perhaps another instance of an anticipation mistaken for a foundation is to be seen when certain insights of Schopenhauer are claimed as the historical origins of Freud's ideas about the dynamics of motivated forgetting and its clinical significance (Procter-Gregg, 1956; MacKinnon & Dukes, 1962). In *The World as Will and Idea* (1819/1883), Schopenhauer had stated:

> The expression of the origin of madness . . . will become more comprehensible if it is remembered how unwillingly we think things which powerfully injure our interests, wound our pride, or interfere with our wishes; with what difficulty do we determine to lay such things before our own intellect for careful and serious investigation; how easily, on the other hand, we unconsciously break away or sneak off from them again; how on the contrary, agreeable events come into our minds of their own accord. . . . In that resistance of the will to allowing what is contrary to it to come under the examination of the intellect lies the place at which madness can break in upon the mind. (p. 168)

Conscious of overlaps between his thinking and Schopenhauer's views, Freud (1925/1959) thought it fit to note in his autobiographical study that "the large extent to which psychoanalysis coincides with the philosophy of Schopenhauer—not only did he assert the dominance of the emotions and the supreme importance of sexuality but he was even aware of the mechanism of repression—is not to be traced to my acquaintance with his thought. I read Schopenhauer very late in my life" (pp. 59–60). Unless one chooses to see repression at work in Freud's disclaimer or one demonstrates the indirect influence of Schopenhauer early in Freud's career, the character of Schopenhauer's reflections remains anticipatory.

Citation of earlier works by a thinker does not necessarily establish their status as historical foundations of his own thoughts. Very often, a theorist may even quote from an illustrious predecessor to legitimate his independently formulated or otherwise-derived ideas. In his *Psychopathology of Everyday Life,* Freud (1904/1938) noted that Nietzsche had well understood the process of motivated forgetting, and then quoted one of Nietzsche's aphorisms—"'I have done that,' says my Memory. 'I could not have done that,' says my Pride and remains inexorable. Finally, my Memory yields" (p. 103). About 20 years later, Freud (1925/1959) stressed that he did not borrow his ideas on repression or other points from Nietzsche, "another philosopher whose guesses and intuitions often agree in the most astonishing way with the laborious findings of psychoanalysis" (p. 60).

Operationally, an antecedent idea, which is similar to a later concept, remains an anticipation *until* the developmental continuity between the two is demonstrated through a specification of influence paths. In this sense, all anticipations within a broad intellectual tradition (e.g., American psychology or Western thought) are *potential* cases of foundations or historical roots. Yet to ignore the fact that not all anticipations terminate as foundations invites a situation wherein allegations of intellectual derivations tend to increase with marked gains in the popularity of an idea or theory. Often at work is an attributional process in which the theoretical partisanship of the writer interacts with the varied similarity between an antecedent idea and a subsequent one to produce judgments of banality and originality. Therefore, until a set of ideas has been shown to have *continuity,* besides similarity and priority, in relation to later developments, it is advisable to call it a case of anticipation and suspend one's judgment of the later formulation as "nothing new," a rehash, or an extension.

FOUNDATIONS

A clear-cut example of a historical foundation is suggested by Schlenker's (1974) observation that some of Spinoza's insights served as the basic components in Heider's *p-o-x* theory of cognitive balance. In Heider's system, a triadic situation involves relations between a reference person, *p,* and another person, *o,* and between the two persons and an object, *x.* These relations between the three entities are either of the sentiment type (liking, love, respect, etc., as experienced or perceived to exist by *p*) or of the unit type (similarity, proximity, membership, causality, etc., as perceived by *p*). Further, sentiment and unit relations are positive or negative. A triadic situation in the life space of *p* strives toward a balanced state in which "the perceived units and experienced sentiments coexist without stress," a state in which all three relations are positive or two of the three relations are negative and one positive. The theory enables one to predict from the knowledge of the signs of any two relations the character of the third sentiment or unit relation. For example,

> the case in which one positive and one negative relation is given, e.g., [*p* dislikes *o*] and [*o* owns *x*], there is tendency for the third to be negative, for only in this way can balance be obtained. Thus, *p* tends to dislike something his adversary *o* ... owns. Or, should *p* like *o,* he would tend to share *o*'s negative feelings about *x.* (Heider, 1958, p. 206)

Although Spinoza did not explicitly deal with the concept of balance, several of his propositions on the origin and nature of feelings depicted situations that have an underlying harmony. The rise of positive or negative affect toward an entity is *consistent* with the organism's perception of the entity as promotive or obstructive of the objects of his tendency toward fuller life. The situations depicted in Spinoza's postulates often involve three entities similar to those of Heider and are also defined in terms of the subject's perceptions and experience. The following propositions are representative of the several contained in Part III of Spinoza's *Ethics* (1677/1936) and are highly evocative of the balanced triads discussed by Heider:

> Proposition XVI. Simply from the fact that we conceive that a given object has some point of resemblance with the other object, which is wont to affect the mind pleasurably or painfully, although the point of resemblance be not the efficient cause of the said emotions, we shall still regard the first-named object with love or hate (p. 141).

> Proposition XXII. If we conceive that anything pleasurable affects some object of our love, we shall be affected with love toward that thing. Contrariwise, if we conceive that it affects an object of our love painfully, we shall be affected with hatred toward it (p. 145).

> Proposition XXIV. If we conceive that anyone pleasurably affects an object of our hate, we shall feel hatred toward him also. If we conceive that he painfully affects the said object, we shall feel love toward him (p. 147).

In his seminal paper on social perception and phenomenal causality, Heider (1944) had noted that "Spinoza's treatise 'On the origin and nature of emotions' in his *Ethics* is the most thoroughly worked out system" for understanding the influence of causal attributions on emotional reactions. Heider (1958) further acknowledged the relevance of Spinoza's system for the balance theory in his chapter on sentiments. He draws on Spinoza's views to provide an organismic context for the seemingly "detached" sentiments of his theory. Since "there is the danger that sentiments will be seen as automatic reactions to the unit organization of a situation without otherwise being related to significant processes within the person," Heider devotes several pages to discussing how these difficulties can be overcome by integrating his balance hypothesis within an organismic point of view represented by Spinoza, Koffka, Köhler, and others (Heider, 1958, pp. 212–216).

To assert that one of the historical roots of the balance theory goes back to Spinozan philosophy is not to lessen the accomplishment of Heider. His articulation of the notion of balance, lying dormant in Spinoza's *Ethics,* was uniquely perceptive. It enabled him to derive unit, especially causal, relations from sentiments (e.g., "if the attitudes toward a person and an event are similar, the event is easily ascribed to the person") as reciprocals to Spinoza's deduction of sentiments from unit relations. Also important was his broadening of the scope of unit relations in terms of the Gestaltist principles of perceptual grouping.

Far more challenging than the simple case of the Spinozan underpinnings of the balance theory has been the attempt to trace the beginnings of Freud's conception of mind to Herbartian psychology—an instance of a historical foundation in which the network of influences between the two sets of ideas has been charted in all its complexity by a number of devoted scholars over the years.

The seminal influence of Herbart's psychological ideas on Freud's theorizing has been the subject of repeated assertions since early in this century. Karpinska (1914) followed by Dorer (1932) and, recently, Glicklhorn (1960) have sought to document a Herbartian imprint upon Freud's concepts. Boring (1950), while recognizing that the major source of Freud's ideas is to be found in the French tradition of psychopathology, has cautioned that other sources like Leibnitz, Herbart, and Brentano should not be ignored in the process of gaining historical perspective on Freud's dynamic psychology. After describing Herbart's conception of ideas as active, varying in clearness, given to self-preservation, and inclined to resist inhibition by opposing ideas, Boring (1950) views Herbart as "a dynamic psychologist, fitting a line of succession from Leibnitz

to Freud" (p. 255). Wolman (1968) has more explicitly asserted Herbart's considerable influence on Freud's thinking and has listed several concepts and principles from Herbart's "energetic" theory that are substantially recapitulated in psychoanalysis. For Herbart,

> every idea is identical with a self-preservation act of the soul and a self-preservation act involves discharge of energy. Since energy is imperishable (The Law of Preservation of Energy), no idea can completely disappear. An idea inhibited by another idea does not perish; since it has lost some energy, it sinks below the "threshold of consciousness" (Schwelle des Bewusstseins). This is the process of repression (Verdrängung). The reappearance of repressed ideas meets resistance (Widerstand) offered by the already established "masses of ideas" (Vorstellungsmassen). (Wolman, 1968, p. 42)

And inhibited ideas strive to rise above the threshold of consciousness either through the weakening of ideas established in consciousness or through combination with other repressed ideas to overcome the resistance that was formerly too strong (Herbart, 1834/1891).

Notwithstanding Herbart's predominantly cognitive stance as shown in his derivation of desires and emotions from ideational dynamics, Freud's theory remains distinctively reminiscent of the Herbartian conceptualization of mental functioning. However, as resemblances and antecedence are not determinative of the foundational stature of a given set of antecedent ideas, one has to examine the structure of hypothesized linkages between the "source" and the "receiver" before a plausible case of impact is accepted as convincing. Figure 1 is a summary presentation of the direct and indirect paths of influence that need to be examined in determining the Herbartian ramifications in Freud's system.

Freud is reported to have studied during his Gymnasium years Lindner's *Textbook of Empirical Psychology by Genetic Method* (cited in Jones, 1953), which the author had described as a compendium of Herbartian psychology. The book contained a detailed discussion of the conflict between stronger and weaker ideas in try-

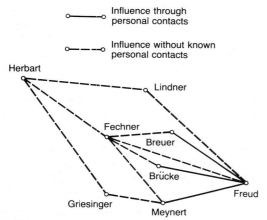

FIGURE 1
Influence paths between J. F. Herbart and S. Freud.

ing to push each other out of consciousness and of the indestructibility of the repressed ideas with their struggle to reenter the conscious under conditions of weakened resistance or combined assertion (Anderson, 1962; Jones, 1953).

Fechner's psychology, with its central concepts of conservation of mental energy and psychological thresholds, was directly built on Herbart's system (Boring, 1950, p. 261; Jones, 1953, p. 374). Fechner's analogy of mind to an iceberg that is nine-tenths submerged and whose course is determined not only by surface winds but also by deep undercurrents was a continuation of the emphasis accorded by Herbart to the unconscious processes.

Freud, in turn, was directly influenced by Fechner's ideas, which is evident in his acknowledgement that he "was always open to the ideas of G. T. Fechner and . . . also followed that thinker upon many important points" (Freud, 1925/1959, p. 59), such as in the "principle of constancy" and in the concept of mental topography. As regards Fechner's *indirect* influence on Freud, Jones has noted that "Fechner exercised an important influence on Brücke, . . . on Meynert, . . . and on Breuer," and Freud had worked with all three of these persons at different times during his early career.

According to Jones (1953, p. 42), Brücke's

elaboration of the Herbartian-Fechnerian principles of conservation and transformation of energy and his conception of attraction and repulsion as two basic kinds of energy found their echo in Freud's characterization of psychoanalysis in its dynamic aspect. It has to be noted that Brücke was a teacher of Freud at the University of Vienna. And Breuer, who held Fechner in very high regard and who had worked closely with Freud, must have constituted another link between Fechner and Freud (Jones, 1953, pp. 233, 377).

Meynert, a critical link in the last two chains between Herbart and Freud, was a recipient of Herbartian ideas not only through Fechner's work but also through Griesinger, the Berlin psychiatrist who was a strict follower of Herbart. Meynert is reported by Jones (1953, p. 376) to have been a careful student of Griesinger. And Freud, who had worked with Meynert at the General Hospital in Vienna, recalled in his biography that he, while still a student, had been greatly struck by Meynert's work and personality (Freud, 1925/1959, p. 10). Meynert's views on the direction of affect in terms of "attack" and "defense," and his use of the words *inhibiting* and *pressing back* point to his intermediary role between Herbart and Freud (Jones, 1953, pp. 375–376).

The foregoing discussion of the linkages in Figure 1 shows to a reasonable degree the partial grounding of the Freudian system in Herbartian ideas. The basic premises of conservation of mental energy and of active unconscious processes in Herbartian psychology are certainly far more than anticipations to Freud's system. However, this is not to suggest that Herbart had a definite notion of psychoanalysis or that psychoanalysis was simply an improvisation on Herbartian themes. As was noted in the Spinoza-Heider case, to identify elements of Herbartian psychology as one set of foundations of Freud's framework is not to ignore the vast and substantive changes introduced by Freud in reconceptualizing these ideas on the basis of his clinical work and insights.

SOME ISSUES IN THE SEARCH FOR HISTORICAL ROOTS

More often than in the physical sciences, theorizing in psychology is built upon firsthand ideas about human functioning. Given the immediacy of psychological experience and our stake in others' actions, it could be argued that basic insights into human behavior at the level of broad principles are quite likely to be products of independent reflection and observation. The recurrence of themes like the role of desire in cognitive processes, the quest for certainty, bodily accompaniments to emotions, etc., in the writings of philosophers, psychologists, and others testifies as much to the unusual potential for parallel insights in the domain of psychological inquiry as to the historical continuity of these ideas. The origins of psychological concepts and theories need not lie in efforts to develop the known ideas of others, much less in market pressures to rename what has already been proposed. And, notwithstanding the increasingly organized character of the psychological enterprise, the very nature of psychology's subject matter will remain conducive to independent conceptions of why we behave the way we do and will substantially add to the number of parallelisms that upon scrutiny will not be seen to terminate as foundations.

The multiplicity of nonterminating anticipations resulting from psychology's special potential for independent discoveries and the complexity of influence patterns in the case of foundations are characteristic of the task that faces the psychologist-historian in his disentangling of lineages in the development of ideas. Yet the difficulty of the task cannot be reason for being less than circumspect in suggesting anticipations for historical roots of psychological ideas. More autobiographical materials (e.g., the *History of Psychology in Autobiography* series) and studies of intellectual development (e.g., Cohen, 1977; Evans, 1976) would prove an invaluable resource for students of history to determine the course of ideas across and within generations of thinkers.

Contemporary formulations with a distinct history need not be in the nature of old wine in new bottles. After the initial assimilation, borrowed ideas are at times transformed to such an extent that their foundational value is virtually reduced to simple sources of inspiration. Concepts have a way of acquiring new meanings and significance when they are implicated in a system of wider and richer reference. If this kind of emergent uniqueness is lost sight of, then every achievement of modern science would be viewed as the giving of "technical" names to ideas of ancient origin. Whitehead was essentially correct when he remarked that "to come very near to a true theory, and to grasp its precise application, are two very different things, as the history of science teaches us. Everything of importance has been said before by somebody who did not discover it" (quoted in Merton, 1958, p. 457).

Relatedly, Young (1966) has warned that the retrospective tracking of a topical idea's roots sensitizes us to notice far too many "modern rings" in antecedent ideas. The usual tendency in the backward pursuit of sources is to neglect the context of the writings of earlier periods, with the result that "the near mention (and often the apparent mentioning based on what is really no more than a verbal similarity—pun) of a conception is hailed as discovery, and history... degenerates into the search for anticipations: 'Is A buried in B's grave?'" (Young, 1966, p. 19). It is important to realize that similarities between an antecedent idea and a subsequent one have to be determined not only by examining the ideas discretely but also in terms of the theoretical contexts in which they are enmeshed.

Even when an early idea is shown to be a legitimate foundation, its impact may not have been entirely salutary on subsequent developments. British associationist philosophers have contributed richly to the psychology of learning, but their work, with its bias toward sensations, also lulled psychology into the dead end of mental chemistry. However, unlike foundations, whose consequences have to be analyzed, a forerunner hardly bears any responsibility if a current preoccupation with his anticipations turns out to be less than a breakthrough. Commenting on the impasse faced after years of work carried out in the tradition of the "one-way" and "one-step" model of communication, Carolyn Sherif (1976) has cautioned that "Aristotle really should not share the blame for what happened in research on communication, despite the fact that it is considered scholarly to attribute the formula [Who says what to whom with what effect] to that worthy Greek" (p. 333).

The issue of anticipations versus foundations is not solely confined to philosophical antecedents that usually antedate psychological formulations by long time spans. Increasingly worthy for scrutiny are the "suspected" antecedents of a very recent idea to be found in somewhat less recent or even contemporaneous sources in psychology itself and in related sciences. What, for instance, could be the relationship of Sherif's (1936) ideas on the normative definition of ambiguous situations and of Hyman's (1942) work on self-evaluation by comparison with reference groups to Festinger's (1954) theory of social comparison processes? Or, could it be said that Newcomb's (1948) formulation of reference groups is partly traceable through Sherif to the symbolic interactionist tradition of C. H. Cooley, G. H. Mead, and W. I. Thomas, with their concepts of primary groups, significant others, selective affinity, imaginative sociability, attitudes as the psychological representations of social norms, etc.?

Compared to the ideas with an effectively continuous history, the ideas that have been sporadically anticipated generally have a greater title to originality. But their originality in the sense of historical or functional independence from past thinking is no guarantee of their validity or enduring significance. Dissonance theory, which can rightly claim a large measure of originality, has at times been questioned for its worth beyond an outburst of research fertility. The question of what does an idea *really* amount to in the scheme

of things is largely independent of its novelty or ancient heritage.

Instant genealogies of ideas are a tricky business, more so when they represent a "gesture to the pre-experimental literature as a sort of literary gloss before getting down to the serious part of an article" (Young, 1966, p. 17). Antecedence is always compelling, resemblances are suggestive, and the impulse for closure is hard to restrain. In this seductive setting for idea attributions, the distinction between anticipations and foundations should be a corrective to mistaking old views for new, a check on ignoring the uniqueness of new movements, and yet an aid in discerning the continuity of ideas on surer grounds.

REFERENCES

Andersson, O. *Studies in the prehistory of psychoanalysis.* Norstedts, Sweden: Svenska Bokforlaget, 1962.

Aronson, E. *The social animal* (1st ed.). San Francisco: W. H. Freeman, 1972.

Bain, A. *The emotions and the will* (3rd ed.). London: Longmans Green, 1880.

Boring, E. G. *A history of experimental psychology* (2nd ed.). New York: Appleton-Century-Crofts, 1950.

Cohen, D. *Psychologists on psychology: Modern innovators talk about their work.* New York: Taplinger, 1977.

Crawford, T. J. Theories of attitude change. In B. Seidenberg & A. Snadowsky (Eds.), *Social psychology: An introduction.* New York: Free Press, 1976.

Dorer, M. *Historische Grundlagen der Psychoanalyse.* Leipzig, Germany: Meiner, 1932.

Elms, A. C. *Social psychology and social relevance.* Boston: Little, Brown, 1972.

Evans, R. I. *The making of psychology: Discussions with creative contributors.* New York: Knopf, 1976.

Festinger, L. A theory of social comparison processes. *Human Relations,* 1954, *7,* 117–140.

Festinger, L. *A theory of cognitive dissonance.* Stanford, Calif.: Stanford University Press, 1957.

Festinger, L., & Hutte, H. A. An experimental investigation of the effect of unstable interpersonal relations in a group. *Journal of Abnormal and Social Psychology*, 1954, *49*, 513–522.

Freud, S. The psychopathology of everyday life. In A. A. Brill (Ed. and trans.), *The basic writings of Sigmund Freud*. New York: Modern Library, 1938. (Originally published, 1904)

Freud, S. An autobiographical study. In J. Strachey (Ed. and trans.), *The standard edition of the complete works of Sigmund Freud* (Vol. 20). London: Hogarth Press, 1959. (Originally published, 1925)

Glicklhorn, J. R. *Sigmund Freud's akademische Laufbahn im Lichte der Dokumente*. Munchen, Germany: Urban and Schwarzenberg, 1960.

Heider, F. Social perception and phenomenal causality. *Psychological Review*, 1944, *51*, 358–374.

Heider, F. *The psychology of interpersonal relations*. New York: Wiley, 1958.

Herbart, J. F. [*A textbook in psychology, an attempt to found the science of psychology on experience, metaphysics, and mathematics*] (N. J. Smith, trans.). *New York: Appleton, 1891. (Originally published, 1834)*

Hyman, H. H. The psychology of status. *Archives of Psychology*, 1942, No. 269.

Jones, E. *The life and work of Sigmund Freud* (Vol. 1). New York: Basic Books, 1953.

Jones, E. E., & Gerard, H. B. *Foundations of social psychology*. New York: Wiley, 1967.

Karpinska, L. Von. Ueber die Psychologischen Grundlagen des Freudismus. *Internationale Zeitschrift für Psychoanalyse*, 1914, *2*, 305–326.

MacKinnon, D. W., & Dukes, W. F. Repression. In L. Postman (Ed.), *Psychology in the making: History of selected problems*. New York: Knopf, 1962.

McGuire, W. J. The yin and yang of progress in social psychology: Seven koan. *Journal of Personality and Social Psychology*, 1973, *26*, 446–456.

Merton, R. *Social theory and social structure* (rev. ed.). New York: Free Press, 1958.

Newcomb, T. N. Attitude development as a function of reference groups. In M. Sherif, *An outline of social psychology*. New York: Harper & Row, 1948.

Peirce, C. S. The fixation of belief. In M. H. Fisch (Ed.), *Classic American philosophers*. New York: Appleton-Century-Crofts, 1951. (Originally published in *Popular Science Monthly*, 1877)

Prasad, J. A comparative study of rumors and reports in earthquakes. *British Journal of Psychology*, 1950, *41*, 129–144.

Procter-Gregg, N. Schopenhauer and Freud. *Psychoanalytic Quarterly*, 1956, *25*, 197–214.

Sahakian, W. S. *Systematic social psychology*. New York: Chandler, 1974.

Schlenker, B. R. Social psychology and science. *Journal of Personality and Social Psychology*, 1974, *29*, 1–15.

Schopenhauer, A. [*The world as will and idea*, Vol. 3] (R. B. Haldane & J. Kemp, trans.). London: Routledge & Kegan, 1883. (Originally published, 1819)

Sherif, C. W. *Orientation in social psychology*. New York: Harper & Row, 1976.

Sherif, M. *The psychology of social norms*. New York: Harper & Row, 1936.

Spinoza, B. *Philosophy of Benedict de Spinoza* (R. H. M. Elwes, trans.). New York: Tudor, 1936. (Originally published, 1677)

Tedeschi, J. T., & Lindskold, S. *Social psychology: Interdependence, interaction, and influence*. New York: Wiley, 1976.

Tedeschi, J. T., Schlenker, B. R., & Bonoma, T. V. Cognitive dissonance: Private ratiocination or public spectacle? *American Psychologist*, 1971, *26*, 685–695.

Tolman, E. C. Edward Chace Tolman. In E. G. Boring, H. S. Langfeld, H. Werner, & R. M. Yerkes (Eds.), *A history of psychology in autobiography* (Vol. 4). New York: Russell & Russell, 1968. (Originally published, 1952)

Wolman, B. The historical role of Johann Friedrich Herbart. In B. Wolman (Ed.), *Historical roots of contemporary psychology*. New York: Harper & Row, 1968.

Young, R. M. Scholarship and the history of the behavioural sciences. *History of Science*, 1966, *5*, 1–51.

A Whisper from a Ghost

Mary Henle

In the course of one of his Travels, Gulliver was in the enviable position of being able to call up and converse with figures long dead. I quote:

> Having a Desire to see those Ancients, who were most renowned for Wit and Learning, I set apart one Day on purpose. I proposed that *Homer* and *Aristotle* might appear at the Head of all their Commentators....I had a Whisper from a Ghost, who shall be nameless, that these Commentators always kept in the most distant Quarters from their Principals in the lower World, through a Consciousness of Shame and Guilt, because they had so horribly misrepresented the Meaning of those Authors to Posterity.... *Aristotle* was out of all Patience with the Account I gave him of *Scotus* and *Ramus,* as I presented them to him; and he asked them whether the rest of the Tribe were as great Dunces as themselves.

It may be added parenthetically that these were no ordinary Dunces; the logic of Ramus was influential for more than a hundred years, until the Port-Royalists took over.

In psychology, we have only a few generations of authors to misrepresent to posterity, but we have done so with a thoroughness that could have impressed Gulliver. I would like to illustrate the point with some examples of the treatment of a few major figures in the recent history of psychology. My account will be limited to figures whose work is available in English, so that the primary sources would be as easy for American readers to obtain as secondary ones. On the whole, I will avoid naming my secondary sources, since the problem with which I am concerned is widespread; I am interested in a trend, not in individuals. Only widely used secondary sources will be considered.

I will, however, mention by name the most famous writer of our contemporary secondary sources, E. G. Boring, whose histories have long been considered standard. Boring, it will be recalled, was a student and then a junior colleague of E. B. Titchener until 1918. As published and unpublished correspondence shows, he remained in touch with Titchener until the latter's death. He might thus be expected to be an authoritative source on Titchener, although he candidly admits that "Titchener alive did not always confirm the author's [Boring's] interpretation of his views" (Boring 1933:33). I will confine myself to three instances which suggest that Titchener had reason to have misgivings about Boring's interpretations of his views.

In Boring's discussion of the subject matter of Titchenerian psychology, one finds the sentence: "No wonder Titchener could conclude (posthumously, 1929) that introspective psychology deals solely with sensory materials" (1933:19). Titchener was certainly an impressive personality, but posthumous conclusions are too much to expect even of so towering a figure. As early as 1914 (the year of Boring's doctorate at Cornell), Titchener publicly expressed the wish that he could deal solely with sensory materials. Feelings stood in the way of such a simplification, and Titchener wrote: "I only wish that I could see my way clear to" the "reduction of affection to organic sensation" (1914:12–13 n.32). It is hard to believe that Boring was ignorant of this paper. He could easily have known that Titchener was actively engaged in the effort to reduce feelings to sensory data some ten years before the publication of the posthumous book. He did know that Nafe's research of 1924, by identifying "affective pressures," settled the matter for Titchener (Boring 1933:18). Indeed, Titchener wrote to Boring about how to observe these affective pressures (Boring 1937:476). But even apart from these considerations, if Boring had paid a little attention to the dates by which the posthumously published chapters were written, he would not have had to ascribe to Titchener conclusions from beyond the grave. If we cannot trust Boring on a matter of simple chronology, we need to be wary in connection with substantive matters.

I come to one of these: Boring's discussion of the context theory of meaning, Titchener's theory that meaning is carried by a context of images and sensations that cluster around a sensory or imaginal core. This discussion appears in an article of 1942, but since Boring allowed it to be reprinted in a collection of his papers published in 1963, it seems safe to conclude that he did not later take serious issue with it. I will quote a single sentence, though there are other things in the passage in question that would perhaps not have appealed to Titchener. "If the core is a face, then a name may be sufficient context" (1963:104). The interesting thing about this passage is not that Boring adopts a context theory, but that he says he does, but doesn't get it right. A perceived face is no mere bundle of sensory data; it has meaning. It is not a sensory core but a meaningful percept. In connection with what is perhaps Titchener's most famous theory, Boring is committing the stimulus error—for Titchener, the worst error a psychologist can commit.

One final example: In a paper presented to the American Psychological Association in 1967, Boring speaks of "Titchener's . . . shift toward behaviorism even before behaviorism began" (1969:21). It is the "facts of nature" and "the inexorable Zeitgeist" that nudge Titchener into a kind of behaviorism in 1910 (1969:30). What is the basis for this new interpretation?

Titchener's "behaviorism," to be found in the *Text-book,* apparently consists in his bringing meaning "under the scrutiny of psychology" (Boring 1969:26), and in the recognition that meaning need not be carried consciously, from which Boring concludes that "context is carried unconsciously" (1969:29). What Titchener actually says in the passage under consideration (1910:369) is that "meaning may be carried in purely physiological terms." He rejects what he calls the invention of "an unconscious mind to give coherence and continuity to the conscious" (1910:40). If we do so, he warns, "we voluntarily leave the sphere of fact for the sphere of fiction." Thus it cannot be correct to speak of the "forces that were pressing Titchener toward the acceptance of unconscious psychological processes" (Boring 1969:32). What he is speaking of is physiological processes, and there is no change in his position in this regard. His first book, *An Outline of Psychology* (1896), presents the position of psychophysical parallelism, which is maintained in the *Text-book.*

These passages seem to me not only *not* to show a drift by Titchener toward behaviorism, but also to misinterpret behaviorism. Surely behaviorism is something other than the recognition of physiological processes with no conscious counterpart. Furthermore, not being conscious seems to be equated by Boring with "the unconscious"; but the early behaviorists were certainly no more friendly to this concept as it was then (and is now) used than they were to a context theory of meaning. With regard to the involvement of meaning in Titchener's alleged behaviorism, it may be noted that it was not until the 1950s that the behaviorists became seriously interested in problems of meaning.

It is interesting to consider some of the things Titchener was saying about behaviorism in the years after he himself was said by Boring to have become a behaviorist. His reply to Watson's so-called Behavioristic Manifesto of 1913 was given before the American Philosophical Society on April 3, 1914, and published that year. In this paper, in which we see Titchener at his polemical best, he remarks: "Watson is asking us, in effect, to exchange a science for a technology. . . . Watson's behaviorism can never replace psychology because the one is technological, the other scientific" (1914:14).

Ten years later, in a letter to Watson himself, Titchener says:

It is quite true that the logic of the behaviorists is muddled; both Roback and I myself have pointed this out in print. The strength of the movement lies not in its fundamental logic but in its laboratory performance. (Cited by Larson and Sullivan 1965:348)

Boring suggests that the shift to behaviorism in Titchener's thinking "occurred without his knowledge of what was happening to his own thought" (1969:31). Even apart from the evidence reviewed, I find it hard to admit so large a discrepancy between what he thought and what he thought he thought in a man of Titchener's logic, clarity, and consistency.

Let us now turn to the treatment of behaviorism in a secondary source. Here is a quotation from another distinguished historian of psychology in an article on John B. Watson. He cites a number of comments about Watson written during the 1950s:

> The most laudatory of all is from one who looks at Watson's work from the standpoint of logic and the history of science. Bergmann writes:
> Second only to Freud, though at a rather great distance, John B. Watson is, in my judgment, the most important figure in the history of psychological thought during the first half of the century... although the attention he receives now, in the fifties, is perhaps not as great as it was in the twenties and thirties.... Among psychologists the sound core of Watson's contribution has been widely accepted; his errors and mistakes have been forgotten.... Watson is not only an experimental *psychologist*... he is also...a systematic thinker...a *methodologist*. In this latter area he made his major contribution.

What did Bergmann really say? For the full text, the reader is referred to the *Psychological Review* of 1956; here it will suffice to supply a bit of the context of this correct quotation.

As an experimental psychologist, Bergmann describes Watson as "fairly distinguished no doubt but without transcendent distinction." He sees Watson also as a social philosopher, a metaphysician, and a methodologist. How is he regarded in these roles? This is what Bergmann says:

> His social philosophy is, in my opinion, deplorable. His metaphysics is silly....His metaphysics... has a core both true and important. The trouble there was that Watson, unsubtle and, I fear, also very ignorant in philosophical matters, did not know how to state the true and commonsensical core without at the same time asserting a lot of patent nonsense. (1956:266)

Watson's greatness must therefore lie in his role as a methodologist. Bergmann continues:

> As I see him, Watson is above all a completer and a consummator—the greatest, though not chronologically the last, of the Functionalists.... The one methodological contribution of Watson which is specifically his own is merely a footnote—though, I insist, a most important one—to the methodological ideas of the Functionalists. (1956:267–268)

This footnote, which, according to Bergmann, has earned Watson such a high place in the history of the psychology of this century, is the thesis of methodological behaviorism.

This somewhat expanded account of the quotation from Bergmann gives an entirely different impression of his view of Watson from the quotation as previously presented. Indeed, if the contribution of a mere footnote to functionalism places Watson second only to Freud, one wonders about the security of Freud's own position in the history of our science.

I have a trunkful of misinterpretations of Gestalt psychology by highly regarded writers, some of which I have discussed elsewhere (Henle 1977). Instead of them, for my final example, I will turn to one of the most widely used sources in theories of personality, and I will look in it for the treatment of Kurt Lewin, contenting myself with one or two issues.

In the text I have selected, difficulties arise from the beginning: "The separation of the person from the rest of the universe is accomplished by drawing an enclosed figure. The boundary of the figure defines the limits of the entity known as the person.''

What is wrong with this apparently straightforward statement? Only that it contains an outdated conception of the motoric, Lewin's term for the perceptual and motor regions. It is true that Lewin's revision of this concept appears in a rather out-of-the-way place, in his foreword to a monograph by Robert Leeper (1943); Lewin himself never had the opportunity to incorporate it into a book of his own. But since Leeper's monograph appears in the bibliography of our text, the authors might be assumed to be familiar with this important change. And important it is: it makes of the motoric a functional rather than a phenomenal concept and thus removes an inconsistency from Lewin's theory.

Here is another statement from the same source that reveals a serious difficulty: "The hollow man was replenished with psychological needs, intentions, hopes, and aspirations. The robot was transformed into a living human being. The crass and dreary materialism of behaviorism was replaced by a more humanistic picture of people." This is all very nice, but it has nothing to do with Lewin. What are these needs that fill the hollow man? The authors themselves admit that Lewin gives no list. What are these fine hopes and aspirations? What is the specific nature of this humanistic picture? It is quite clear that Lewin does not tell us. Indeed, his neglect of the contents of personality suggests that Lewin was not interested in developing a theory of personality. He was, it seems to me, doing something different, working out a metatheory— but that is a matter that is not relevant for our present purposes. (See Henle 1978.) It *is* relevant to expect those who discuss Lewin in the context of personality theory to notice his neglect of content. It should not be dismissed as "an unfortunate oversight," as one author did; it should be used as a clue to what Lewin was really doing. It could help us to appreciate his contribution.

I could continue indefinitely with these and ad-ditional secondary sources, with their additional distortions. The point seems clear: if we want to know what somebody said, it seems wiser to read the original than to trust to what somebody else said he said.

If Gulliver could see Commentators as a Tribe of Dunces, what would he call those whose erudition rests upon the Commentaries of these Dunces?

REFERENCES

Bergmann, G. (1956). The contribution of John B. Watson. *Psychological Review, 63,* 265–276.

Boring, E. G. (1933). *The physical dimensions of consciousness.* New York: Century.

Boring, E. G. (1937). Titchener and the existential. *American Journal of Psychology, 50,* 470–483.

Boring, E. G. (1963). *History, psychology, and science: Selected papers.* New York: Wiley.

Boring, E. G. (1969). Titchener, meaning and behaviorism. In D. L. Krantz (Ed.), *Schools of psychology: A symposium.* New York: Appleton-Century-Crofts.

Henle, M. (1977). The influences of Gestalt psychology in America. *Annals of the New York Academy of Sciences, 291,* 3–12.

Henle, M. (1978). Kurt Lewin as metatheorist. *Journal of the History of the Behavioral Sciences, 14,* 233–237.

Larson, C. A., & Sullivan, J. J. (1965). Watson's relation to Titchener. *Journal of the History of the Behavioral Sciences, 1,* 338–354.

Leeper, R. W. (1943). *Lewin's topological and vector psychology: A digest and a critique.* Eugene: University of Oregon.

Titchener, E. B. (1896). *An outline of psychology.* New York: Macmillan.

Titchener, E. B. (1910). *A Text-book of psychology.* New York: Macmillan.

Titchener, E. B. (1914). On "Psychology as the behaviorist views it." *Proceedings of the American Philosophical Society, 53,* 1–17.

Titchener, E. B. (1929). *Systematic psychology: Prolegomena.* New York: Macmillan.

Unique Values of Archival Research

Thomas C. Cadwallader

I don't think I'm going out on a limb when I predict that when a history of the history of psychology is written some centuries into the future, that it will be recognized that around 1960—about a hundred years after the modern era of psychology began with the publication of Fechner's *Elements of Psychophysics,* and about 2300 years after the writing of what appears to be the first history of psychology, Aristotle's *De Anima*— the second phase of the history of psychology began. The decade of the 1960's was a decade of foundings if there ever was one: the division of the History of Psychology of the American Psychological Association, the *Journal of the History of the Behavioral Sciences,* the Cheiron Society, the Ph.D. program in the history of psychology at the University of New Hampshire, the Archives of the History of American Psychology, the summer institutes in the history of psychology. And I certainly would be remiss if I didn't note that most of those foundings were, in one way or another, associated with Robert I. Watson, Sr.

One of the features of the second phase of the history of psychology which I believe will distinguish it from the first is the increasing use of archival materials. Archival materials in the narrow sense are those materials which pertain to an institution and which are officially preserved by the institution (28). Such materials may well concern individual members, employees, students or other persons associated with the institution in some capacity. Many universities, especially the older ones, have archives, as do governmental agencies and some scholarly and scientific societies.

Archival materials in a broader sense include

a variety of materials that may bear upon some facet of history and which have been assembled into a collection which is housed in some institution—usually a library. I will confine present examples of archival materials to those concerning individuals. In this case, archival materials may take the form of *any* materials that a person may leave behind, or have been collected by others, and which may provide additional information about his professional or private life, his ideas or his publications. The most obvious examples are unpublished writings: manuscripts which were not published, drafts of published papers or books, correspondence, notebooks, notes, annotated books and papers, diaries and the like. Other sorts of materials may supply a missing piece of a puzzle: a scrap book, ticket stub, passport, bill, newspaper clipping, photograph or similar items which may show where the individual was at a critical point in his life or where he may have gotten an important idea. Such items, diverse as they may be, are all subsumed under the phrase "manuscript collection," which may also include some or, potentially at least, all of the individual's published writings. While the variety of archival materials that may be available is extensive, it is the unpublished writings (in the broad sense) that typically are the most fruitful for the historian's examination. The increasing application of archival research to questions in the history of psychology has been due to the fact that archival research does have certain unique values.

Before going further, I do want to emphasize that archival research is but one mode of historical research. There are certain kinds of questions or topics for which archival research may not be necessary. For example, research based solely on published materials may be completely adequate for some questions or topics; our own work (8) on the ancient physiological psychology contained in *The Edwin Smith Surgical Papyrus*

Adapted from Cadwallader, T. C. (1975). Unique values of archival research. *Journal of the History of the Behavioral Sciences, 11,* 27–33. Copyright © 1975 by the Clinical Psychology Publishing Company. Reprinted by permission of the publisher.

(4) is based entirely on published materials. Moreover, when archival research is necessary or useful, it should be used in conjunction with other existing source materials to help answer the question or to deal with the topic under investigation. Thus, in addition to archival materials one should draw upon such materials as published books or papers (secondary as well as primary), audio- or video-taped materials or personal interviews as may be appropriate.

The views presented in this paper, along with the examples cited, are drawn largely from the author's historical research done over the past several years. The archival research has been done primarily in Houghton Library, Harvard's rare book and manuscript library, where the Charles S. Peirce and William James papers are housed; in the Harvard University Archives in Widener Library; in the Manuscripts Room at Columbia University's Butler Library where the Ladd-Franklin papers are located; in the Manuscript Division of the Library of Congress where the Cattell papers are kept and in the Archives of the National Academy of Sciences. Other collections have been drawn upon to a lesser extent.

Now to some of the unique values of archival research. The order of listing has no significance; the numbers are nominal, not ordinal.

1. Unsuspected facets of history may be uncovered. Although Charles Peirce had been elected to the National Academy of Sciences (N.A.S.) in 1877, and although we have argued Peirce was the ''first modern American psychologist'' (7), he was elected as a physicist and astronomer. James McKeen Cattell, in 1901, was the first person to be elected as a psychologist, despite the greater eminence of William James. There are a series of letters among the Peirce and James papers at Harvard, the Cattell papers at the Library of Congress and records in the Archives of the N.A.S., which reveal a fascinating story of how psychology was accepted by the N.A.S. and how Cattell, James, Dewey, Royce and other psychologists were elected. While the complete story awaits further investigation, the following account is of sufficient intrinsic interest to warrant mention as an example. One of the most interesting items is a letter which Peirce addressed to James (22). Peirce apparently had second thoughts about sending it and did not send it, for it is among the Peirce papers, not the James papers, at Harvard. There is no comparable letter among the James papers addressed to William, but there is one to Mrs. William James (23) on the subject. Both letters were meant to explain why Cattell rather than James had been nominated, but the one to William was much more blunt. In it Peirce stated plainly that Cattell's work was of the sort that the other members of the Academy could clearly recognize as science. On the other hand, James's work, Peirce feared, might be considered as belonging to the ''Department of Literature.''

Peirce also wrote to Cattell (21) after the latter's nomination and said that while he couldn't guarantee Cattell's election, he predicted that he would be elected. Peirce followed his prediction with a very moving statement as to how he and Cattell should be allies in getting James into the Academy. This, incidentally, wasn't an easy task; for it took two years and included some interesting maneuvering on Peirce's part—but that's another story for another time.

2. The genesis of ideas may be uncovered or at least suggested. The publication of a paper or book is usually the final stage of a process that may have had a long and roundabout route before reaching its final form. Earlier versions of a paper, say, may reveal the sources from which the paper came. Notes and notebooks also may reveal the input which led to the development of ideas.

I suppose that if one were asked what psychological concepts to associate with William James, there would be a fairly high probability that one would say, ''habit and stream of consciousness.'' What follows is not intended as an account of how James got interested in these two concepts, but rather as an example of intriguing possibilities. During his student days at Harvard, on November 25, 1864, James began a large, indexed notebook ("Index Rerum"; [14]) to which he added at least as late as 1889 (with a reference [14, Appendix p. 30] to the second Heft of Münsterberg's *Beiträge*). In this notebook James kept notes from lectures, discussions and his reading on a wide variety of subjects. Entries were either by subject, in which case the source is cited, or by the name of the individual, in which case the views of the individual are noted. Peirce's views are recorded in both manners—some under "Peirce" and some under certain subjects. It is in the first manner that Peirce's views on habit are recorded (14, p. Pe.). Unfortunately the entry is not dated. It appears to be an early one, however, judging from its position on the page, by its content, and by the "hand" in which it is written. Hopefully it will prove datable, but that remains to be seen. Habit was one of Peirce's central concerns and discussions of it may be found among his writings from at least the 1860s until shortly before his death in 1914. Is it possible that Peirce importantly influenced James with respect to the concept of habit as he did with other concepts, notably pragmatism? At this point I cannot say, but it is a fascinating possibility to explore.

Let me interrupt with another interesting point gleaned from this early notebook of James. In our 1972 A.P.A. paper (7) in which we presented evidence for considering Peirce rather than James to be the first "modern" American psychologist, my wife and I reviewed the material which indicated that James did not know of Wundt until his 1867–1868 European trip. Additional corroboration of this point comes from the finding that the earliest of Wundt's papers to be mentioned in James's notebook (14, p. Wu) is to an 1869 one (32).

Now to return to the second concept well associated with James—the stream of consciousness. Here the possibility of another input from Peirce to James is from a roundabout source. Among the Peirce papers is a letter written by John Dewey to Paul Weiss, dated October 1, 1931 (9). Weiss was preparing a biography of Peirce at the time for the *Dictionary of American Biography* (30). Judging from the contents of Dewey's letter, he was responding to a request for reminiscences of Peirce. Dewey had been Peirce's student and a member of his Metaphysical Club at Johns Hopkins from 1882–1884. Recalling those days, Dewey wrote, "Peirce was then talking about, as it comes back to me now, what James later came to call the stream of consciousness" (9).

3. Archival research may reveal unsuspected personal influences. Boring and Boring, in their paper, "Masters and pupils among the American psychologists," cite Christine Ladd-Franklin as one of those few psychologists "who seem to have had no principal psychological teacher in the pre-Ph.D. days" (3, p. 531). They also cite her as one of the individuals "who acknowledged the intellectual influence of older savants who were not psychologists" (3, p. 528). The Borings then cite C.S. Peirce as the savant who influenced Ladd-Franklin but who was not a psychologist. But of course Peirce *was* a psychologist (and thus it is an interesting question as to why Boring and other historians of psychology failed to recognize him as such). Indeed at the very time Ladd-Franklin was his student at Hopkins—ostensibly in logic—Peirce was an active experimental psychologist (6) and was in fact investigating problems in color vision. He had begun his work on color at least by 1877 (19) and was to continue his interest for many years (24). We have found much evidence showing that Ladd-Franklin was exposed to Peirce's views on psychology. For example, among the Peirce papers are Ladd-Franklin's lengthy handwritten notes (15) on Peirce's 1880 paper, "The Algebra of Logic" (20), which begins with two pages of pure, and very modern, psychology. Ladd-Franklin comments on the psychology portion of that paper as well as on the remainder.

Ladd-Franklin's first paper in psychology was that on the horopter in the first issue of the *Amer-*

ican Journal of Psychology in November 1887 (16). We have found in one of Peirce's notebooks (18, p. 131) a citation of Wundt's *Physiologische Psychologie* on the horopter. We have also found among the Ladd-Franklin papers the letter to Ladd-Franklin from G. Stanley Hall in early 1887 telling her about his plans for his new journal and soliciting a manuscript from her (12). Thus Hall knew of her interest in psychology at that time. Will more correspondence be found to give an earlier "fix" on Ladd-Franklin's direct involvement with psychology? Will a firm basis for a link between Peirce's and Ladd-Franklin's interest in visual processes be found? Time may tell.

4. While everyone knows that academic and professional politics play a major role in shaping personal careers and otherwise influencing history, it is rare for such influences to be mentioned in published form. Archival materials are practically the only source of information on this sort of matter. We all know why John B. Watson left academia, went into advertising, and made a not-so-small fortune (and probably more than a few of us have wished, at one time or another, that we might "fail" so splendidly). That Watson's continued exile from professional psychology may have been due to the deliberate efforts of some individuals is suggested by finding among the Ladd-Franklin papers copies of her vigorous letters to prominent psychologists protesting against any connection with professional psychology by Watson in light of his behavior.

5. The last example to be given of the unique value of archival research is its ability to round out the picture of the personal side of an individual. Charles Peirce is often portrayed as a crotchety, eccentric individual who was hard to get along with, but one sees from an examination of his papers, and especially his diaries, that he was a very tender and loving husband. Only a few years before his death, when he was quite ill and in considerable pain from cancer, and living in very real poverty, Peirce wrote to Arnold, Constable and Co., asking them to recover his wife's

parasol with their best green silk. He reminded them of the handsome job they had done on the parasol some years before and asked that they again give it their most careful attention (26). On another occasion Peirce recorded in his diary that his wife was gravely ill. His entry ended: "God, if she is taken let me not remain one hour" (25, entry for December 27, 1905).

I have presented some of what seem to me to be unique values of archival research and some examples from my own research. I would like, now, to call attention to the best examples of archival research I have found to date. These are among the writings of Max H. Fisch. Fisch is Professor of Philosophy, Emeritus, at the University of Illinois and is, in addition to being the leading Peirce scholar, an historian of science. He also has the benefit (from our perspective at least) of having taken a graduate minor in psychology at Cornell in the days of Titchener. Fisch's painstaking pursuit of answers to certain questions and of topics demonstrates the value of archival research to a degree so far beyond anything I could say, that I hope you will remember to read Fisch if you forget everything else written here.

In his paper "Was there a Metaphysical Club in Cambridge?" (10), Fisch brings the archival method of research to a fine edge, slicing away the doubts raised by contradictory statements by some of its supposed members (and collated by Wiener [31]), and gently dissecting out evidence that enables him to conclude that there indeed had been such a club. Fisch's paper, "Peirce's Arisbe: The Greek influence in his later life" (11), is the finest example of historical writing I have ever encountered. It draws upon an enormous background of materials—published and archival—and relates a story as absorbing as any novel. Whether or not one is interested in Peirce or in seeing the fruits of the archival method in finest form, a reading of this paper will be well rewarded in terms of its sheer beauty. The papers of Max Fisch show archival research at its best.

If historians of psychology use archival materials as effectively and judiciously as Fisch does, then the history of psychology will be very much clearer than it presently is.

What is required for the history of psychology, as for the history of any discipline or for history in general to be done well, is the incorporation of archival research into the tool bag of its investigators. Much of the history of psychology is locked in recesses accessible only by archival research. To the extent to which archival research does become part of the methodology of historians of psychology, then the history of psychology will come closer and closer to the goals of recounting the development of psychology as it occurred, describing those variables—environmental, social, personal and intellectual—bearing on it, and pointing to its influences on contemporary and future psychology.

REFERENCES

1 *The American Archivist*. Washington: Society of American Archivists. Vol. 1, 1938; continuing. Quarterly.

2 Boring, E. G. Psychologists' letters and papers. *Isis*, 1967, *58*, 103–107.

3 Boring, M. D., and Boring, E. G. Masters and pupils among the American psychologists. *American Journal of Psychology*, 1948, *61*, 527–534. Reprinted in Boring, E. G. *History, psychology, and science*. Edited by R. I. Watson and D. T. Campbell. New York: Wiley, 1963, pp. 132–139.

4 Breasted, J. H. *The Edwin Smith surgical papyrus*. Chicago: University of Chicago Press, 1930. 2 vols.

5 Burnette, O. L., Jr. *Beneath the footnote. A guide to the use and preservation of American historical sources*. Madison: Society Press, State Historical Society of Wisconsin, 1969.

6 Cadwallader, T. C. Charles S. Peirce (1839–1914): The first American experimental psychologist. *Journal of the History of the Behavioral Sciences*, 1974, *10*, 291–298.

7 Cadwallader, T. C., and Cadwallader, J. V. America's first modern psychologist: William James or Charles S. Peirce? *Proceedings of the 80th Annual Convention, American Psychological Association, 1972*, pp. 773–774.

8 Cadwallader, T. C., Semrau, L. A., and Cadwallader, J. V. Early physiological psychology: Circa 3000 B. C. *Proceedings of the 79th Annual Convention, American Psychological Association, 1971*, pp. 719–720.

9 Dewey, J. Letter to Paul Weiss, October 1, 1931. Ms. L 123, Charles S. Peirce Papers, Houghton Library, Harvard University.

10 Fisch, M. H. Was there a Metaphysical Club in Cambridge? In E. C. Moore and R. S. Robin (Eds.) *Studies in the philosophy of Charles Sanders Peirce*. (Second Series) Amherst: University of Massachusetts Press, 1964, pp. 3–32.

11 Fisch, M. H. Peirce's Arisbe: The Greek influence in his later life. *Transactions of the Charles S. Peirce Society*, 1971, *7*, 187–210.

12 Hall, G. S. Letter to Christine Ladd-Franklin, January 29, 1887. Franklin Papers, Manuscripts Room, Butler Library, Columbia University.

13 Hamer, P. M. *A guide to archives and manuscripts in the United States*. New Haven: Yale University Press, 1961.

14 James, W. Notebook: Index Rerum. James Papers, Houghton Library, Harvard University. Call number: b MsAm 1092 U.

15 Ladd[-Franklin], C. Notes on C. S. Peirce's "On the algebra of logic" [see Ref. (20) below.], Ms. L. 237, Charles S. Peirce Papers, Houghton Library, Harvard University.

16 Ladd-Franklin, C. A method for the experimental determination of the horopter. *American Journal of Psychology*, 1887, *1*, 99–111.

17 *National Union Catalog: Manuscript Collections*. Washington: Library of Congress. 10 vols. (continuing).

18 Peirce, C. S. Notebook, Ms. 1156. [Entries from c. 1865 to c. 1874]. Charles S. Peirce Papers, Houghton Library, Harvard University.

19 Peirce, C. S. Note on the sensation of color. *American Journal of Science*, 1877, 3rd series, *13*, 247–251.

20 Peirce, C. S. On the algebra of logic. *American Journal of Mathematics*, 1880, *3*, 15–57. Reprinted in Ref. (27) vol. 3, para. 154–251.

21 Peirce, C. S. Letter to J. McK. Cattell, March 18, 1901. Container 35, J. McK. Cattell Papers, Library of Congress.

22 Peirce, C. S. Draft letter to William James, [c. April 4, 1901]. Ms. L 224, Charles S. Peirce Papers, Houghton Library, Harvard University.

23 Peirce, C. S. Letter to Alice James [Mrs. William James], April 12 [1902]. Letter No. 752, James Papers, Houghton Library, Harvard University.

24 Peirce, C. S. The color system. Paper presented at the meetings of the National Academy of Sciences, April 15–17, 1902. Cited in National Academy of Sciences. *Report for the year 1902.* Washington: Government Printing Office, 1903. P. 13.

25 Peirce, C. S. Diary entry for December 27, 1905. Ms. 1622, Charles S. Peirce Papers, Houghton Library, Harvard University.

26 Peirce, C. S. Draft letter to Arnold, Constable and Co., June, 1911. Ms. L 25, Charles S. Peirce Papers, Houghton Library, Harvard University.

27 Peirce, C. S. *Collected Papers.* Cambridge: Harvard University Press. Vols. 1–6 ed. by C. Hartshorne and P. Weiss, 1931–1935. Vols. 7 and 8 ed. by A. W. Burks, 1958.

28 Schellenberg, Theodore R. *Modern archives, principles and techniques.* Chicago: University of Chicago Press, 1956.

29 Tursman, R. (Ed.) *Studies in philosophy and in the history of science: Essays in honor of Max Fisch.* Lawrence, Kansas: Coronado, 1970.

30 Weiss, P. Charles S. Peirce. *Dictionary of American Biography,* 1934, *14,* 398–403. Reprinted in R. J. Bernstein (Ed.) *Perspectives on Peirce.* New Haven: Yale University Press, 1965, pp. 1–12.

31 Wiener, P. P. *Evolution and the founders of pragmatism.* Cambridge: Harvard University Press, 1949.

32 Wundt, W. Über die Entstehung räumlicher Gesichtswahrnehmungen. *Philosophische Monatshefte,* 1869, *3,* 225–247.

Some Values and Limitations of Oral Histories

Marion White McPherson

Referents for the term oral history are so variable that description is more applicable than definition and elaborating the meaning becomes a sequence of "generally this...but in some instances that..." Typically, the label refers to reminiscences delivered verbally and recorded on a tape recorder, but due to the limited durability of tapes, the accounts are usually transcribed and preserved in typescript form. The final products are more often documentary than oral. The interviewees are usually individuals with high visibility but many narrators are less distinguished people who were "on the scene" during activities deemed to be important. The

McPherson, M. W. (1975). Some values and limitations of oral histories. *Journal of the History of the Behavioral Sciences, 11,* 34–36. Copyright © 1975 by the Clinical Psychology Publishing Company. Reprinted by permission of the publisher.

designation "oral historian" is applied not to the individual who relates the historical data but to the professional who solicits them. The purpose of collecting these chronicles is to augment the public ledger, and they have been referred to as submerged history (4) or as the raw material from which history is written (6).

The emergence of the technique resulted from technological developments which created a need for oral histories and facilitated them. Advances in communication and travel diluted the written record. Telephone calls and personal visits became more prevalent than detailed and elaborate correspondence. Such practices may be efficient but they fragment the evidence.

Talking about one's experiences requires less time and effort than writing about them; as a result, oral histories tend to be lengthy and to be rapidly verbalized. Audio recording devices supplied a means of coping with this productivity and exact reproduction was publicized as the most distinctive aspect of the technique. Such fidelity is flaunted in spite of the fact that most typescripts are not replicas of the original narratives. The failure to develop a carbon is often due to the observation that a tape recorder may inhibit a narrator, usually just at the point at which disclosures are about to become confessional, confidential or critically controversial. When about to secure the most sensitive data, an interviewer may agree to shut off the tape recorder.

Another factor which alters the documentation is a conviction about the invalidity of histories. In order to correct mistakes, unidentified but nevertheless presumed present, as well as to create a more literary product, the tape is edited. Initially the oral historian may delete ungrammatical content, sometimes so extensively that the finished product has polish, but little of the flavor of unrehearsed reminiscence. The typescript is then sent to the interviewee with the assumption that modifications will be made solely in the interest of accuracy. These indictments and the remedies prevail even though there is no systematic assessment of the comparative validity of different forms of record compilation. All types of reports are subject to errors and, in fact, dispute about the authenticity of the printed word is prevalent among scientists and historians!

Doubt about the validity of oral histories has led to certain prescriptions for taking them. The mandates are often contradictory. Oral historians are admonished to let the interviewer lead, but not dominate. They are told to be simultaneously directive and nondirective. The principal must be permitted to relate the story as he perceives it, and yet he must be quizzed. Presumably, interrogation, particularly of a variety which implies sophistication about the topic under discussion, will serve both to counteract distortions of memory and to make the narrator more truthful. A few oral historians take this ad-

monition with such seriousness that they go into the interview believing that they—not the respondents—are the experts. When this occurs unfamiliar data may be interpreted as false and the history degraded.

A precise assessment of the merits of an oral history program is impossible. Contemporaries are not in a position to judge what historians of the future will and will not need. One quantifiable aspect is financial, which is likely to be high. Expenses include reimbursement for the oral historian(s) and stenographer(s). The former must come to know the narrator, his research, publications, educational and occupational background. He must be reimbursed for travel as well as for the time required to tape the history and to supervise its transcription. Forty to sixty hours is a reasonable estimate of the amount of time required for the first typing of most interviews. The initial monitoring of transcriptions requires approximately twice the recording time. A minimum of two drafts of the typescript is essential. Finally, the document must be indexed and catalogued.

In spite of their ambiguous worth, oral history programs are popular. Annual Oral History Conferences are held and each attracts 100 to 150 professionals for a three day session. Rosters of oral histories abound. By 1971, 23,115 persons had been interviewed, 52,264 interview hours recorded and 398,556 pages of typescript completed (5).

The strategy is commonly conceded to have been crystallized in 1948 into a program at Columbia University by Allen Nevins (6). It has been adopted by many professions—anthropology, history, folklore, journalism, fiction writing and political science. In spite of an intense intrigue with interviewing, psychology has not been very active, and certainly not dominant.

This neglect does not vitiate the discipline's claim to one of the forefathers, David P. Boder, who in 1946 interviewed 80 residents of displaced person camps for French, Italian, Swiss or German nationals (2). The interviews, conducted in the chosen language of individual narrators, were recorded in German, Russian, Yiddish, Polish, French or "some Baltic and Balkan languages." The 120 hours of narratives were personally translated by Boder and many of the interviews were published verbatim in 1949 in a book entitled *I Did Not Interview the Dead* (3). Boder conceived of this collection of "topical autobiographies" as one phase of a study of "the impact of catastrophe," but his label did not catch on and both the term oral history and nonpsychologists dominate the present scene.

REFERENCES

1 Anonymous. 'Aural' historians plan association. *Oral History Association Newsletter,* 1973, *7,* No. 2.

2 Boder, D. P. Application for Research Grant to National Institutes of Health, M582C2, 2/19/54. In *D. P. Boder Museum File,* Archives of the History of American Psychology, Akron, Ohio.

3 Boder, D. P. *I did not interview the dead.* Champaign-Urbana: University of Illinois Press, 1949.

4 Hand, W. D. The folklorist in oral history. In E. I. Dixon (Ch.) Definitions of oral history. In E. I. Dixon and J. V. Mink (Eds.), *Proceedings of the First National Colloquium on Oral History.* Los Angeles: Oral History Association, Inc., 1967, 5–34.

5 Shumway, G. L. *Oral History in the United States, A directory.* New York: Oral History Association, Inc., 1971.

6 Starr, L. M. What is oral history? In E. I. Dixon (Ch.) Definitions of oral history. In E. I. Dixon and J. V. Mink (Eds.), *Proceedings of the First National Colloquium on Oral History.* Los Angeles: Oral History Association, Inc., 1967, 5–34.

CHAPTER 2

DESCARTES AND THE RISE OF MODERN SCIENCE

The Renaissance, which began in the fourteenth century and lasted through the early part of the seventeenth century, started in Italy and spread to the rest of Europe. It represented a revival of interest in, and new approaches to, art, literature, and knowledge, including science. It was the era of Michelangelo and Da Vinci, of Shakespeare and Chaucer, and of Copernicus and Galileo. Its importance for science is that the late Renaissance marked an end to the dominance of *rationalism,* a philosophy that sought knowledge through reason and common sense. Replacing rationalism was a belief that knowledge should be acquired through observation and experimentation, a philosophy that marked the beginning of the *scientific method*. Psychology, as an experimental science, would grow from the post-Renaissance developments in philosophy and from physiological studies of the nervous system and sensory mechanisms.

A new world view emerged from the Renaissance, most significantly due to the work of Galileo Galilei (1564–1642). For Galileo, the universe was composed of matter in motion; atoms of one object would come into contact with atoms of another object, causing movement or a change in the second object. This view of the world was known as *mechanism,* and because it conceived of the universe as a giant machine, it implied that lawful explanations of the universe were possible. Like any machine, the universe would operate in an orderly way, and if so, then its operation could be understood by discovering the laws that governed it. This order and lawfulness meant that actions in the universe could be predicted by understanding the causal relationships within the world. Such a view was an especially important advance for science.

But if humans were part of the universe, could not they also be viewed as machines? Yes, according to French philosopher and mathematician René Descartes (1596–1650), who extended the mechanistic view to human behavior. Descartes viewed both the body and part of the mind as machines, capable of interacting with one another in such a way that not only did the mind influence the body but also the body was capable of influencing the mind. This idea, radical at the time, provided an excellent explanation for involuntary (reflexive) behavior and voluntary behavior. In adding human actions to the mechanistic world view, Descartes was arguing that human behavior was lawful and that its causes could be understood. He also localized the functions of the mind in the brain, whereas some earlier views had assigned certain mental processes, such as emotion, to organs such as the liver and heart.

Descartes was also a rationalist, interested in the nature of the human mind. He proposed that it consisted of two kinds of ideas: *innate ideas,* such as self and God, and *derived ideas,* which are acquired through experience in the world. These concepts would be studied by a group of British philosophers over the next two hundred years as they sought to understand how the mind acquires its knowledge. But that is the subject of the next chapter; this chapter will focus on Descartes, with special attention to his view of mind and body as it relates to the search for evidence of a material world.

Two selections are presented in this chapter. The first was written by Descartes and published as the sixth meditation in his *Meditations on First Philosophy* (1641). For Descartes, meditation was a tool to study the mind. It was an introspective technique, that is, an inward looking, but it should not be assumed to be the same as the method of introspection that would dominate the early years of experimental psychology. Descartes's meditation did not involve a reductionistic approach to the mind, certainly not with respect to innate ideas; nor did he try to build his understanding of mind on the collective introspections of others. The selection in this chapter is an excellent example of the meditative method and rationalism used by Descartes as he examined the existence of the material world. In it the reader will discover some of his views on sensation, imagination, and memory and their relation to his mind-body distinction.

The second selection was written by a historian of psychology, Robert I. Watson (1909–1980), who was the founder and first editor of the *Journal of the History of the Behavioral Sciences*. In the 1960s, Watson proposed a method to study the history of psychology that he called *prescriptive analysis* (see Watson, 1967). It was an approach in the tradition of intellectual history, meaning the history of ideas. Watson selected eighteen dimensions that he believed described the philosophy, content, and methodology of various approaches to psychology. These dimensions, or *prescriptions* as he called them, could be used to describe the major psychological schools (such as behaviorism or psychoanalysis) or the psychological views of an individual. These eighteen prescriptions were arranged in contrasting pairs such as empiricism-rationalism, inductivism-deductivism, mechanism-vitalism, and monism-dualism. Schools or individuals would not be investigated in terms of all eighteen prescriptions. Rather, the analysis would occur only for those issues on which the school or individual took a stance. In the end, psychological systems could be described in terms of their most salient features. Thus on the dimension of molarism-molecularism, Gestalt psychology (see Chapter 16) would be described as molar because of its holistic approach to the study of consciousness ("the whole is different from the sum of its parts"), whereas the structural school of psychology (see Chapter 8) would be labeled molecular because of its atomistic approach to psychology, an attempt to reduce consciousness to its most basic elements.

Watson (1967) proposed that prescriptions could provide a classification system and conceptual framework that could be used historically. Ultimately he saw prescriptive analysis as a tool for studying the psychology of discovery—an important historical activity.

In the article in this chapter, Watson (1971) uses his system of prescriptive analysis to present the psychological views of Descartes. The article provides a brief understanding of Watson's method of analysis and an excellent exposition of Descartes's psychological views. Watson compares Descartes with other intellectual giants of the early seventeenth century, such as Francis Bacon, Galileo Galilei, William Harvey, and Thomas Hobbes, and concludes that Descartes "was the most significant contributor to the psychology that was to be.... And it was Descartes, more than any other, who provided the background and formed the problems that were to become salient for psychology" (p. 223). It is for those reasons that the work of René Descartes is singled out for emphasis in this chapter.

REFERENCES

Watson, R. I. (1967). Psychology: A prescriptive science. *American Psychologist, 22,* 435–443.

Watson, R. I. (1971). A prescriptive analysis of Descartes' psychological views. *Journal of the History of the Behavioral Sciences, 7,* 223–248.

The Existence of Material Things:
The Real Distinction of Mind and Body

René Descartes

It remains for me to examine whether material things exist. I already know at least the possibility of their existence, in so far as they are the subject-matter of pure mathematics, since in this regard I clearly and distinctly perceive them. For God is undoubtedly able to effect whatever I am thus able to perceive; and I have never decided that anything could not be done by him, except on the ground that it would involve contradiction for me to perceive such a thing distinctly. Further, when I am occupied with material objects, I am aware of using the faculty of imagination; and this seems to imply that they exist. For when I consider carefully what imagination is, it seems to be a kind of application of the cognitive faculty to a body intimately present to it—a body, therefore, that exists.

To explain this, I begin by examining the difference between imagination and pure understanding. For instance, when I imagine a triangle, I do not just understand that it is a figure enclosed in three lines; I also at the same time see the three lines present before my mind's eye, and this is what I call imagining them. Now if I want to think of a chiliagon, I understand just as well that it is a figure of a thousand sides as I do that a triangle is a figure of three sides; but I do not in the same way imagine the thousand sides, or see them as presented to me. I am indeed accustomed always to imagine something when I am thinking of a corporeal object; so I may confusedly picture to myself some kind of figure; but obviously this picture is not a chiliagon, since it is in no way different from the one I should form if I were thinking of a myriagon, or any other figure with very many sides; and it in no way

helps me to recognise the properties that distinguish a chiliagon from other polygons. If now it is a pentagon that is in question, I can understand its figure, as I can the figure of a chiliagon, without the aid of imagination; but I may also imagine this very figure, applying my mind's eye to its five sides and at the same time to the area contained by them; and here I clearly discern that I have to make some special effort of mind to imagine it that I do not make in just understanding it; this new mental effort plainly shows the difference between imagination and pure understanding.

I further consider that this power of imagination in me, taken as distinct from the power of understanding, is not essential to the nature of myself, that is, of my mind; for even if I lacked it, I should nevertheless undoubtedly still be the selfsame one that I am; it seems, therefore, that this power must depend on some object other than myself. And if there is a body to which the mind is so conjoined that it can at will apply itself, so to say, to contemplating it, then I can readily understand the possibility of my imagining corporeal objects by this means. The difference between this mode of consciousness and pure understanding would then be simply this: in the act of understanding the mind turns as it were towards itself, and contemplates one of the ideas contained in itself; in the act of imagining, it turns to the body, and contemplates something in it resembling an idea understood by the mind itself or perceived by sense. I can readily understand, I say, that imagination could be performed in this way, if a body exists; and since there does not occur to me any other equally convenient way of explaining it, I form from this the probable conjecture that the body exists. But this is only probable; and, in spite of a careful investigation of all points, I can as yet see no way of

Descartes, R. (1641). *Meditationes de prima philosophia.* Adapted from E. S. Haldane and G. R. T. Ross (Trans.), *The philosophical works of Descartes.* Cambridge: Cambridge University Press, 1911, pp. 185–199.

arguing conclusively from the fact that there is in my imagination a distinct idea of a corporeal nature to the existence of any body.

Besides that aspect of body which is the subject-matter of pure mathematics, there are many other things that I habitually imagine— colours, sounds, flavours, pain, and so on; but none of these are so distinctly imagined. In any case, I perceive them better by way of sensation, and it is from thence that they seem to have reached my imagination, by the help of memory. Thus it will be more convenient to treat of them by treating of sense at the same time; I must see whether I can get any certain argument in favour of the existence of material objects from the things perceived in the mode of consciousness that I call sensation.

I will first recall to myself what kinds of things I previously thought were real, as being perceived in sensation; then I will set out my reasons for having later on called them in question; finally I will consider what to hold now.

In the first place, then: I had sensations of having a head, hands, feet, and the other members that make up the body; and I regarded the body as part of myself, or even as my whole self. I had sensations of the commerce of this body with many other bodies, which were capable of being beneficial or injurious to it in various ways; I estimated the beneficial effects by a sensation of pleasure, and the injurious, by a sensation of pain. Besides pain and pleasure, I had internal sensations of hunger, thirst, and other such appetites; and also of physical inclinations towards gladness, sadness, anger, and other like emotions. I had external sensations not only of the extension, shapes, and movements of bodies, but also of their hardness, heat, and other tangible qualities; also, sensations of light, colours, odours, flavours, and sounds. By the varieties of these qualities I distinguished from one another the sky, the earth, the seas, and all other bodies.

I certainly had some reason, in view of the ideas of these qualities that presented themselves

to my consciousness (*cogitationi*), and that were the only proper and immediate object of my sensations, to think that I was aware in sensation of objects quite different from my own consciousness: viz. bodies from which the ideas proceeded. For it was my experience (*experiebar*) that the ideas came to me without any consent of mine; so that I could neither have a sensation of any object, however I wished, if it were not present to the sense-organ, nor help having the sensation when the object was present. Moreover, the ideas perceived in sensation were much more vivid and prominent, and, in their own way, more distinct, than any that I myself deliberately produced in my meditations, or observed to have been impressed on my memory; and thus it seemed impossible for them to proceed from myself; and the only remaining possibility was that they came from some other objects. Now since I had no conception of these objects from any other source than the ideas themselves, it could not but occur to me that they were like the ideas. Further, I remembered that I had had the use of the senses before the use of reason; and I saw that the ideas I formed myself were less prominent than those I perceived in sensation, and mostly consisted of parts taken from sensation; I thus readily convinced myself that I had nothing in my intellect that I had not previously had in sensation.

Again, I had some reason for holding that the body I called "*my* body" by a special title really did belong to me more than any other body did. I could never separate myself entirely from it, as I could from other bodies. All the appetites and emotions I had, I felt in the body and on its account. I felt pain, and the titillations of pleasure, in parts of *this* body, not of other, external bodies. Why should a sadness of the mind follow upon a sensation of pain, and a kind of happiness upon the titillation of sense? Why should that twitching of the stomach which I call hunger tell me that I must eat; and a dryness of the throat, that I must drink; and so on? I could give no account of this except that nature taught me so; for there is no likeness at all, so far as I can see, between the twitching in the stomach and the volition to take food; or between the sensation of an object that gives me pain, and the experience (*cogitationem*) of sadness that arises from the sensation. My other judgments, too, as regards the objects of sensation seemed to have been lessons of nature; for I had convinced myself that things were so, before setting out any reasons to prove this.

Since then, however, I have had many experiences that have gradually sapped the faith I had in the senses. It sometimes happened that towers which had looked round at a distance looked square when close at hand; and that huge statues standing on the roof did not seem large to me looking up from the ground. And there were countless other cases like these, in which I found the external senses to be deceived in their judgment; and not only the external senses, but the internal senses as well. What [experience] can be more intimate than pain? Yet I had heard sometimes, from people who had had a leg or arm cut off, that they still seemed now and then to feel pain in the part of the body that they lacked; so it seemed in my own case not to be quite certain that a limb was in pain, even if I felt pain in it. And to these reasons for doubting I more recently added two more, of highly general application. First, there is no kind of sensation that I have ever thought I had in waking life, but I may also think I have some time when I am asleep; and since I do not believe that sensations I seem to have in sleep come from external objects, I did not see why I should believe this any the more about sensations I seem to have when I am awake. Secondly, I did not as yet know the Author of my being (or at least pretended I did not); so there seemed to be nothing against my being naturally so constituted as to be deceived even about what appeared to myself most true. As for the reasons of my former conviction that sensible objects are real, it was not difficult to answer them. I was, it seemed, naturally impelled to many courses from which reason dissuaded me;

so I did not think I ought to put much reliance on what nature had taught me. And although sense-perceptions did not depend on my will, it must not be concluded, I thought, that they proceed from objects distinct from myself; there might perhaps be some faculty in myself, as yet unknown to me, that produced them.

But now that I am beginning to be better acquainted with myself and with the Author of my being, my view is that I must not rashly accept all the apparent data of sensation; nor, on the other hand, call them all in question.

In the first place, I know that whatever I clearly and distinctly understand can be made by God just as I understand it; so my ability to understand one thing clearly and distinctly apart from another is enough to assure me that they are distinct, because God at least can separate them. (It is irrelevant what faculty enables me to think of them as separate.) Now I know that I exist, and at the same time I observe absolutely nothing else as belonging to my nature or essence except the mere fact that I am a conscious being; and just from this I can validly infer that my essence consists simply in the fact that I am a conscious being. It is indeed possible (or rather, as I shall say later on, it is certain) that I have a body closely bound up with myself; but at the same time I have, on the one hand, a clear and distinct idea of myself taken simply as a conscious, not an extended, being; and, on the other hand, a distinct idea of body, taken simply as an extended, not a conscious, being; so it is certain that I am really distinct from my body, and could exist without it.

Further, I find in myself powers for special modes of consciousness, e.g. imagination and sensation; I can clearly and distinctly understand myself as a whole apart from these powers, but not the powers apart from myself—apart from an intellectual substance to inhere in; for the essential (*formali*) conception of them includes some kind of intellectual act; and I thus perceive that they are distinct from me in the way aspects (*modos*) are from the object to which they belong. I also recognise other powers—those of local motion, and change of shape, and so on; these, like the ones I mentioned before, cannot be understood apart from a substance to inhere in; nor, therefore, can they exist apart from it. Clearly these, if they exist, must inhere in a corporeal or extended, not an intellectual substance; for it is some form of extension, not any intellectual act, that is involved in a clear and distinct conception of them. Now I have a passive power of sensation—of getting and recognising the ideas of sensible objects. But I could never have the use of it if there were not also in existence an active power, either in myself or in something else, to produce or make the ideas. This power certainly cannot exist in me; for it presupposes no action of my intellect, and the ideas are produced without my co-operation, and often against my will. The only remaining possibility is that it inheres in some substance other than myself. This must contain all the reality that exists representatively in the ideas produced by this active power; and it must contain it (as I remarked previously) either just as it is represented, or in some higher form. So either this substance is a body—is of corporeal nature—and contains actually whatever is contained representatively in the ideas; or else it is God, or some creature nobler than bodies, and contains the same reality in a higher form. But since God is not deceitful, it is quite obvious that he neither implants the ideas in me by his own direct action, nor yet by means of some creature that contains the representative reality of the ideas not precisely as they represent it, but only in some higher form. For God has given me no faculty at all to discern their origin; on the other hand, he has given me a strong inclination to believe that these ideas proceed from corporeal objects; so I do not see how it would make sense to say God is not deceitful, if in fact they proceed from elsewhere, not from corporeal objects. Therefore corporeal objects must exist. It may be that not all bodies are such as my senses apprehend them, for this sensory apprehension is in many ways obscure and con-

fused; but at any rate their nature must comprise whatever I clearly and distinctly understand—that is, whatever, generally considered, falls within the subject-matter of pure mathematics.

There remain some highly doubtful and uncertain points; either mere details, like the sun's having a certain size or shape, or things unclearly understood, like light, sound, pain, and so on. But since God is not deceitful, there cannot possibly occur any error in my opinions but I can correct by means of some faculty God has given me to that end; and this gives me some hope of arriving at the truth even on such matters. Indeed, all nature's lessons undoubtedly contain some truth; for by nature, as a general term, I now mean nothing other than either God himself, or the order of created things established by God; and by *my* nature in particular I mean the complex of all that God has given *me*.

Now there is no more explicit lesson of nature than that I have a body; that it is being injured when I feel pain; that it needs food, or drink, when I suffer from hunger, or thirst, and so on. So I must not doubt that there is some truth in this. Nature also teaches by these sensations of pain, hunger, thirst, etc., that I am not present in my body merely as a pilot is present in a ship; I am most tightly bound to it, and as it were mixed up with it, so that I and it form a unit. Otherwise, when the body is hurt, I, who am simply a conscious being, would not feel pain on that account, but would perceive the injury by a pure act of understanding, as the pilot perceives by sight any breakages there may be in the ship; and when the body needs food or drink, I should explicitly understand the fact, and not have confused sensations of hunger and thirst. For these sensations of thirst, hunger, pain, etc., are simply confused modes of consciousness that arise from the mind's being united to, and as it were mixed up with, the body.

Moreover, nature teaches me that my body has an environment of other bodies, some of which must be sought for and others shunned. And from the wide variety of colours, sounds, odours, flavours, degrees of hardness, and so on, of which I have sensations, I certainly have the right to infer that in the bodies from which these various sense-perceptions arise there is corresponding, though perhaps not similar, variety. Again, from the fact that some of these perceptions are pleasant to me and others unpleasant, it is quite certain that my body—or rather myself as a whole, who am made up of body and mind—can be variously affected for good or ill by bodies in its environment.

There are many other beliefs which may seem to be lessons of nature, but which I really derive not from nature but from a habit of inconsiderate judgment; e.g. that a region is empty if there is no occurrence in it that affects my senses; that if a body is (say) hot, it has some property just like my idea of heat; that in a white or green object there is the same whiteness or greenness as in my sensation, and in a sweet or bitter body the same flavour as I taste, and so on; that stars and towers and other distant bodies have just the size and shape they manifest to my senses; and the like. But to avoid an indistinct view of this matter, I must define here more accurately just what I mean by a lesson of nature. I am using "nature" here in a more restricted sense than the complex of everything that God has given me. For this complex includes much that belongs only to the mind—e.g. my seeing that what is once done cannot be undone, and the rest of what I know by the light of nature; I am not speaking here about this. Again, it includes much that has regard only to the body, e.g. a downward tendency; this again I am not now discussing. I am concerned only with what God has given to me considered as a compound of mind and body. It is a lesson of my "nature", in this sense, to avoid what gives me a sensation of pain, and pursue what gives me a sensation of pleasure, and so on. But it does not seem to be also a lesson of nature to draw any conclusion from sense-perception as regards external objects without a previous examination by the understanding; for knowledge of the truth about them seems to belong to the mind alone, not to the composite whole.

Thus, a star has no more effect on my eye than the flame of a small candle; but from this fact I have no real, positive inclination to believe it is no bigger; this is just an irrational judgment that I made in my earliest years. Again, I have a sensation of heat as I approach the fire; but when I approach the same fire too closely, I have a sensation of pain; so there is nothing to convince me that something in the fire resembles heat, any more than the pain; it is just that there must be something in it (whatever this may turn out to be) that produces the sensations of heat or pain. Again, even if in some region there is nothing to affect the senses, it does not follow that there is no body in it. I can see that on these and many other questions I habitually pervert the order of nature. My sense-perceptions were given me by nature properly for the sole purpose of indicating to the mind what is good or bad for the whole of which the mind is a part; and to this extent they are clear and distinct enough. But I use them as if they were sure criteria for a direct judgment as to the essence. of external bodies; and here they give only very obscure and confused indications.

I have already examined sufficiently the reason why, in spite of God's goodness, my judgments are liable to be false. But a new problem arises here about the objects that nature shows me I ought to seek or shun; and also as regards the errors I seem to have observed in internal sensations. For instance, a man is deceived by the pleasant taste of some food, and swallows the poison concealed within it. But what his nature impels him to desire is what gives the food its pleasant taste; not the poison, of which his nature knows nothing. All that can be inferred from this is that his nature is not omniscient; and this is not surprising, for a man is a finite thing and his nature has only a finite degree of perfection.

But we quite often go wrong about the things that nature does impel us towards. For instance, sick men long for drink or food that would soon be harmful to them. It might be said that they go wrong because their nature is corrupted; but this does not remove the problem. A sick man is no less God's creature than a healthy man; and it seems just as absurd that God should give him a nature that deceives him.

Now a clock built out of wheels and weights, obeys all the laws of "nature" no less exactly when it is ill-made and does not show the right time, than when it satisfies its maker's wishes in every respect. And thus I may consider the human body as a machine fitted together and made up of bones, sinews, muscles, veins, blood, and skin in such a way that, even if there were no mind in it, it would still carry out all the operations that, as things are, do not depend on the command of the will, nor, therefore, on the mind. Now, if, for instance, the body is suffering from dropsy, it has the dryness of the throat that normally gives the mind the sensation of thirst; and this disposes its nerves and other parts to taking drink, so as to aggravate the disease. But I can easily recognise that this is just as "natural" as it is for a body not so affected to be impelled by a similar dryness of the throat to take drink that will be beneficial to it.

Of course, if I consider my preconceived idea of the use of a clock, I may say that when it does not show the right time it is departing from its "nature". Similarly, if I consider the machine of the human body in relation to its normal operations, I may think it goes astray from its "nature" if its throat is dry at a time when drink does not help to sustain it. But I see well enough that this sense of "nature" is very different from the other. In this sense, "nature" is a term depending on my own way of thinking (a cogitatione mea), on my comparison of a sick man, or an ill-made clock, to a conception of a healthy man and a well-made clock; it is something extrinsic to the object it is ascribed to. In the other sense, "nature" is something actually found in objects; so this conception has some degree of truth.

"It may be a merely extrinsic application of a term when, considering a body that suffers from dropsy, we call its nature corrupted because it has a dry throat and yet has no need of drink. But if we consider the compound, the mind united to the body, it is not just a matter of terms; there is a real fault in its nature, for it is thirsty at a time when drink would be hurtful to it. So the question remains: how is it that the divine goodness does not prevent 'nature' (in this sense) from deceiving us?"

I must begin by observing the great difference between mind and body. Body is of its nature always divisible; mind is wholly indivisible. When I consider the mind—that is, myself, in so far as I am merely a conscious being—I can distinguish no parts within myself; I understand myself to be a single and complete thing. Although the whole mind seems to be united to the whole body, yet when a foot or an arm or any other part of the body is cut off I am not aware that any subtraction has been made from the mind. Nor can the faculties of will, feeling, understanding and so on be called its parts; for it is one and the same mind that wills, feels, and understands. On the other hand, I cannot think of any corporeal or extended object without being readily able to divide it in thought and therefore conceiving of it as divisible. This would be enough to show me the total difference between mind and body, even if I did not sufficiently know this already.

Next, I observe that my mind is not directly affected by all parts of the body; but only by the brain, and perhaps only by one small part of that—the alleged seat of common sensibility. Whenever this is disposed in a given way, it gives the same indication to the mind, even if the other parts of the body are differently disposed at the time; of this there are innumerable experimental proofs, of which I need not give an account here.

I observe further that, from the nature of body, in whatever way a part of it could be moved by another part at some distance, that same part could also be moved in the same way by intermediate parts, even if the more distant part did nothing. For example, if ABCD is a cord, there is no way of moving A by pulling the end D that could not be carried out equally well if B or C in the middle were pulled and the end D were not moved at all. Now, similarly, when I feel pain in my foot, I have learnt from the science of physic that this sensation is brought about by means of nerves scattered throughout the foot; these are stretched like cords from there to the brain, and when they are pulled in the foot they transmit the pull to the inmost part of the brain, to which they are attached, and produce there a kind of disturbance which nature has decreed should give the mind a sensation of pain, as it were in the foot. But in order to reach the brain, these nerves have to pass through the leg, the thigh, the back, and the neck; so it may happen that, although it is not the part in the foot that is touched, but only some intermediate part, there is just the same disturbance produced in the brain as when the foot is injured; and so necessarily the mind will have the same sensation of pain. And the same must be believed as regards any other sensation.

Finally, I observe that, since any given disturbance in the part of the brain that directly affects the mind can produce only one kind of sensation, nothing better could be devised than that it should produce that one among all the sensations it could produce which is most conducive, and most often conducive, to the welfare of a healthy man. Now experience shows that all the sensations nature has given us are of this kind; so nothing can be found in them but evidence of God's power and goodness. For example: when the nerves of the foot are strongly and unusually disturbed, this disturbance, by way of the spinal cord, arrives at the interior of the brain; there it gives the mind the signal for it to have a certain sensation, viz. pain, as it were in the foot; and this arouses the mind to do its best to remove the cause of the pain, as being injurious to the foot. Now God might have so made human na-

ture that this very disturbance in the brain was a sign to the mind of something else; it might have been a sign of its own occurrence in the brain; or of the disturbance in the foot, or in some intermediate place; or, in fact, of anything else whatever. But there would be no alternative equally conducive to the welfare of the body. Similarly, when we need drink, there arises a dryness of the throat, which disturbs the nerves of the throat, and by means of them the interior of the brain; and this disturbance gives the mind the sensation of thirst, because the most useful thing for us to know in this whole process is that we then need drink to keep healthy. And so in other cases.

From all this it is clear that in spite of God's immeasurable goodness, man as a compound of body and mind cannot but be sometimes deceived by his own nature. For some cause that occurs, not in the foot, but in any other of the parts traversed by the nerves from the foot to the brain, or even in the brain itself, may arouse the same disturbance as is usually aroused by a hurt foot; and then pain will be felt as it were in the foot, and there will be a "natural" illusion of sense. For the brain-disturbance in question cannot but produce always the same sensation in the mind; and it usually arises much more often from a cause that is hurting the foot than from another cause occurring somewhere else; so it is in accordance with reason that it should always give the mind the appearance of pain in the foot rather than some other part. Again, sometimes dryness of the throat arises not, as usual, from the fact that drink would be conducive to bodily health, but from some contrary cause, as in dropsy; but it is far better that it should deceive us in that case, than if it always deceived us when the body was in good condition. And so generally.

This consideration is of the greatest help to me, not only for noticing all the errors to which my nature is liable, but also for readily correcting or avoiding them. I know that all my sensations are much more often true than delusive signs in matters regarding the well-being of the body; I can almost always use several senses to examine the same object; above all, I have my memory, which connects the present to the past, and my understanding, which has now reviewed all the causes of error. So I ought not to be afraid any longer that all that the senses show me daily may be an illusion; the exaggerated doubts of the last few days are to be dismissed as ridiculous. In particular, this is true of the chief reason for doubt—that sleep and waking life were indistinguishable to me; for I can now see a vast difference between them. Dreams are never connected by memory with all the other events of my life, like the things that happen when I am awake. If in waking life somebody suddenly appeared and directly afterwards disappeared, as happens in dreams, and I could not see where he had come

from or where he went, I should justifiably decide he was a ghost, or a phantasm formed in my own brain, rather than a real man. But when I distinctly observe where an object comes from, where it is, and when this happens; and when I can connect the perception of it uninterruptedly with the whole of the rest of my life; then I am quite certain that while this is happening to me I am not asleep but awake. And I need not have the least doubt as to the reality of things, if after summoning all my senses, my memory, and my understanding to examine them I have no conflicting information from any of these sources. But since practical needs do not always leave time for such a careful examination, we must admit that in human life errors as regards particular things are always liable to happen; and we must recognise the infirmity of our nature.

A Prescriptive Analysis of Descartes' Psychological Views

Robert I. Watson

METHODOLOGICAL PRESCRIPTIONS AT THE BEGINNING OF MODERN SCIENCE

In the Seventeenth Century there was no universally accepted scientific method with experiments and observations methodologically similar being conducted by those interested in science. It almost seemed as if there were as many methods as there were people who thought and wrote about scientific matters. Lacking guidance from a scientific paradigm, each man worked out his particular way of coming to terms with the older speculative traditions.

It was not unnatural that Descartes, and his contemporaries Bacon and Hobbes, each would

Adapted from Watson, R. I. (1971). A prescriptive analysis of Descartes' psychological views. *Journal of the History of the Behavioral Sciences, 7,* 223–248. Copyright © 1971 by the Clinical Psychology Publishing Company. Adapted and reprinted by permission of the publisher.

believe that his particular intellectual formulation was the result of the methods he used. A dogmatic methodism, a belief that technique had an inherent quality of insuring success, was especially prominent in Descartes.

From our vantage point, we can see that along with the others of this time, Descartes had two sets of choices to make—one concerning what was considered to be the major source of knowledge, to follow the rational or the empirical prescription and the other concerning the priority to be given either to general principles or of individual facts, to follow the deductive or the inductive prescription.

Rationalism, his choice in one of these pairs, is a concept with many shades and variations of meaning. In its broadest sense, rationalism is the belief that in thinking logically a man's mind works the same way as does the universe, making it possible that ultimately man can understand everything, just as he understood in Descartes' time simple mathematical or physical problems. In the present context, the more specific meaning intended is that of an adherent to the rationalistic prescription who finds the primary, if not the exclusive, source of knowledge to lie in reason.

If, on the other hand, one follows the empirical prescription, knowledge is found in experience. Experience, however, does not come from the senses alone, a narrower doctrine that came to be known as sensationalism. In addition to analysis of sensory experience, often some form of introspective analysis was accepted by the empiricist. To use the formulation of John Locke, the first great modern adherent to empiricism, "reflection" by which we are informed concerning the workings of our minds is operative in addition to the effect of experience. Empiricism, although only counter-dominant, was never completely dormant, and was to receive a strong impetus from the success of the emerging experimental method.

During the period now under consideration, the rationalistic prescription was dominant. Apart from this being a heritage from the past, in earlier periods as well as at the beginning of the modern age, rationalism lent itself more readily than did empiricism to support of religious doctrines since rationalism in lay and religious matters reinforced one and other in their common insistence upon independence from sense perception.[1] This helps to account for the adoption and adaptation of Greek rationalistic systems by Christian theologians. Rationalistic dominance received further support from the increased scope and precision that new mathematical discoveries were beginning to provide at this time. Such was the inspiration of mathematics to the men of this age, that, after Descartes, if a particular philosophical or scientific issue could not be solved mathematically, it would at least be treated in the "spirit of mathematics." What is this spirit? It was to arrive at what were considered to be unchallengeable premises and

then proceed to elaborate them by deductive reasoning.

Deductive Rationalism and Descartes

Descartes was deeply interested in the problem of finding precisely the right method to obtain knowledge and thereby to bring about an essential reform. Descartes' solution was intertwined with his conviction of the certainty of the operations of mathematics. The solution of uniting method and mathematics came in a revelation in a very literal sense. It occurred as part of a dream on St. Martin's Eve, 10 November, 1619. One of the insights it gave him was that of applying algebra to geometry—the basic conception of analytic geometry. In effect, this unites algebra to spatial relationships. But it was more than a mathematical advance, tremendous though it was, that occurred that night. There was also another insight—that the method of mathematics could be extended to other fields of knowledge. His aim, however, was not to produce a mathematical interpretation of the universe, but rather to develop a point of view in likeness of mathematics in the way described a moment ago. His first task became the rationalistic one of finding self-evident truths, and once these were established, his second task would be to deduce the other truths that they implied. As did the men of the Middle Ages, he wanted to begin with accepted truths. There was to be this difference: they had begun with accepted truths based on religious pronouncements; he wished to begin with accepted truths based on reasoning.

It is unnecessary with this audience to trace Descartes' sceptical journey to the bed rock of "I think, therefore I am" and his triumphant return with his beloved basic principles, now not matters of mere belief but rationally established truths. One consequence, however, must be indicated. Descartes thereafter was to have a profound faith in the ability of reason to discover the true principles of any problem which he chose to investigate. Never thereafter did he waver in this conviction, never did he even consider that reason might be inadequate for any task to which it legitimately be put (on which ground he excluded little besides revealed dogma).

Descartes supported his rationalism by insisting that the clear, compelling, not to be doubted, and inevitable principles are innate. Before we experience the ideas of God, self, the axioma of mathematics, the figure of the triangle, we have the corresponding ideas. God simultaneously established laws of nature and endowed our minds with them so that, provided we used the right method, we would arrive at them. The innateness of ideas is stated time and again. It is variously spoken of as "certain primary germs of truth implanted by nature"; "naturally existent"; and "imprinted...in our minds."

Ideas are not created by the process of thought; rather, they are *discovered* as the content of thought. A clear indication is given when Descartes was challenged by a critic to explain how a man would have an idea of God if he were to be born without the use of his senses and therefore without sensory experience. Descartes answered that he would not only have an idea of God and self, but, since he lacked sense experiences, he would hold them in an even more purified and clear fashion because these ideas existed for him without the adulteration of sense experience. Sources of error found in everyday sensory experience serve to stifle knowledge of innate ideas, a handicap from which a person born without sense would not suffer.

Descartes' earlier statements about innate ideas had given his critics the impression that he was saying that we are born with them in ready-made, complete form. Under their criticism, he modified his view to say that what he meant by innate ideas is the potentiality of thought that is actualized by experience. Innate ideas are not always present; rather, we have the capacity of summoning up such ideas.[2] When we are exposed to extraneous things, it is the faculty of thinking, not those extraneous things them-

selves, that transmit ideas to our minds. They transmit something which gives "the mind occasion to form these ideas, by means of an innate faculty." An innate idea is a "propensity." To drive home the point, he argued that, just as generosity or disease may run in families, so, too, there may be a familial disposition for certain ideas. Neither ideas nor any other innate characteristic appears full-blown, they await experience to bring them out. Formulation in terms of propensity was something which was later to lend itself readily to adaptation for use in discussing nature versus nurture.

Inept as they are, Descartes held that sense experiences are of some use since they provide the occasions for the arousal of our innate ideas of mathematical entities and other simple natures. The role of perception is that of bringing innate ideas to consciousness. The mind then discovers ideas which it already implicitly possessed.

Descartes' position on innateness of basic principles is in agreement with his dualistic separating of mind and body. In thinking the mind may function entirely independent of body. When the mind functions in this independent fashion, it has pure ideas, i.e., pure activities as contents of thought without any dependence for their truth upon the world of objects. As would Kant after him, Descartes held that the mind provided the ground for certain structuring principles which were therefore *a priori.*

Knowledge of truth and falsity comes from thinking alone. The senses contribute to the materials of thought but neither sensation alone nor imagination alone could ever assure us of their truth value. Thinking must intervene. Sensory experiences, as he warns again and again, are fallible, and because sensory experiences are omnipresent, it is no easy task for the judgments made by the human mind to be free from their erroneous impressions. This, he admits, makes it hard to follow the rules of correct thinking which occupied so much of his attention in the *Rules for the Direction of the Mind,* and *Dis-*

course of the Method of Rightly Conducting the Reason. But with faithful adherence to these rules, one can do so, Descartes had no doubt. It follows that his was to be a deductive procedure, the beginning of investigation with already formulated principles.

Descartes gives a clear summary statement of how he would use this deductive method, in order to find further principles in his short statement, *Rules for the Direction of the Mind*. Besides intuition, he says, the other fundamental operation of the mind is deduction. Intuition had supplied the first principles of truth safeguarded as to their validity by the already familiar test of clarity so that knowledge comes first from intuition. Deduction that follows is the process of making inferences from this certain knowledge. It is the process whereby the mind allows inferences to be drawn from basic principles in successive steps. These remote deductively derived conclusions have the characteristic of being derived step by step, which intuitive truths do not have.

Descartes relied primarily on deduction but in the broader sense made evident in earlier discussion. No more than to Bacon was deduction as he conceived it dependent upon the Aristotelian syllogism which is useful only in restating that which is already discovered. This dependence upon deduction is not exclusive. He specifically denied the charge that he always deduced particular truths from universal propositions. Instead he said, he always started with particular propositions as he indicated in replying to a critic; he argued that in order to discover the truth, we should always start with particular notions, in order to arrive at general conceptions subsequently, though we may also proceed in the reverse way, after having discovered the universals, deduce other particulars from them. Thus in teaching a child the elements of geometry, we shall certainly not make him understand the general truth that *"when equals are taken from equals the remainders are equal,"* or that *"the whole is greater that its parts,"* unless we show him examples in particular cases. The minds'

knowledge then, is such that general propositions are formed from particulars and Descartes cannot be said to exclude induction. Nevertheless, beyond a certain irreducible minimum, he preferred to depend upon deduction.

Descartes, did not, as legend would have it, believe that all physics could be deduced from first principles. "We cannot determine by reason how big these pieces of matter are, how quickly they move, or what circles they describe...(this) is a thing we must learn from observation. Therefore, we are free to make any assumptions we like about them so long as all the consequences agree with experience."[3] Hypotheses must be framed and experiments must be used in order to select from among competing equally deductively and rationally plausible interpretations.

The intellect's unaided powers were not enough, "experiments (are) necessary to me in order to justify and support my reasoning." Descartes would experiment—but only to fill out the details, to show from among the alternatives, the way God actually did produce certain effects or to demonstrate from among the possible alternatives the one God has chosen to produce. Experiment, therefore, had a subordinate but acknowledged place in his scheme. As he conceived it, the more advanced the knowledge became, the more necessary experiments became. It not unexpectedly follows that experiment is stressed by Descartes in connection with biological and physiological problems.

To some slight extent, Descartes practiced what he preached. There is evidence that he did make some observations, collected some specimens, and made vivisections.[4] Moreover, he, himself, exhibited his method by exercises in optics and geometry appended for that purpose to the *Discourse*. Neither in these studies nor anywhere else did Descartes, or any other person for that matter, employ his method in all of its details. Instead, he behaved as did other scientists: he discovered experimentally the equality of the sines of the angles of incidence and of refraction in 1626 and only later did he fit it into the deductive proofs of the *Dioptric* first published in 1637.

Looking back over Descartes' rationalistic and deductive system from our vantage point, shows it to be open to serious qualification and criticism. An unvarying system in which each step is laid out in advance may be suitable for exposition of scientific procedures in general terms for the interested reader. It is not a method of scientific discovery because there is no one method of scientific investigation, there are many.

Descartes' method is that of the philosophical system builder rather than that of the scientist. He rejected experimental proof if it could not be assimilated into his system. This explains how he could be so blind as not to be content with Harvey's demonstration that the heart was a contractible muscle and insisted, instead, that the heart was a heated container as it was called for to be by his primary principles. Similarly, after praising Galileo for freeing himself of the errors of the schools and for using mathematics, Descartes went on to say "...he has merely sought reasons for certain particular effects without having considered the first causes of nature; and thus he has built without a foundation."[5] He was criticizing Galileo for not having "theoretical" i.e., "metaphysical" presuppositions as a "foundation," for his work, a standpoint that we see to be its precise strength.

The clarity and distinctness of the postulates followed, Descartes held, are important in any deductive system. But then and now, one can argue that they do not tell the whole story. Dependence on self-evident truths is not characteristic of scientific advance. In fact, regarding postulates as tentative, not certain, to be discarded when they disagree with observations or experiments, is a lesson scientists had to learn many times over the centuries. In this methodological sense, Galileo was right and Descartes wrong. In Descartes' hands, the hypothetic-deductive method of Galileo lost its hypothetical to retain only its deductive character.

Despite their defects, Descartes' rational and deductive analysis of the order of nature following mathematical methods was one of the most influential ideas of the Seventeenth Century. It over-shadowed by far Bacon and his adherence to induction and empiricism. With such different views neither could have appreciated the significance of the work of the other. They could not see, as we do from our vantage point, that induction and deduction, and rationalism and empiricism could and would be integrated in the course of scientific endeavour.

DUALISM AND DESCARTES

Against the general scientific background of the early Seventeenth Century and Descartes' methodological and attitudinal conceptions and presuppositions it now becomes appropriate to examine his way of regarding the relationship between mind and body and the nature of mind itself.

Before Descartes, body and mind had not been seen clearly as opposing entities. Influences by Aristotle, medieval theologians had conceived living bodies as so imbued with soul that no chasm between soul and body could be seen. It was Descartes who established for all of those who came after to see, the distinction between a spiritual mind and a mechanistic body. Indeed, a sharply defined dualism was a problem that he did much to create.

Descartes conceived of two substances—thought, whose essential character is thinking, and extension (matter), whose essential quality is extensiveness (length, width and depth). With the distinction asserted, it becomes necessary to show how he arrived at this conception.

Cartesian dualism followed directly from his deductive search for certainty. Acceptance of his dictum, "I think therefore I am," made thinking separate from matter, since in the course of his search for certainty, it will be remembered, matter had been recovered at a separate later step.

A host of other arguments supported his absolute distinction between mind and body: matter can easily be divided into parts, while mind cannot: the mind, the independent substance, can "act independently of the brain: for certainly the brain can be of no use in pure thought...''; mind moves the body since "the most certain and most evident" experience makes us "immediately aware of its doing so";[6] and the mind and body can exist apart from one another, and therefore are distinct and separate.

But one argument, above all, was to be important for the future of psychology. This was a distinction between an objective and subjective prescription first given scientific sponsorship by Galileo and to be known from the day of Boyle and Locke[7] as the distinction between primary and secondary qualities.[8]

Without too much attention to the matter, the scholastic philosophers of the past had assumed that in sense perception the mind was directly in touch with real things.[9] To them, things were entities having "qualities" that were inherent in objects. So long as science was content to remain Aristotelian with things being just what they appeared to be, with water being wet, the fire hot, there was no problem. But now Galileo had begun to uncover a new universe, a particular pitch was a certain number of vibrations and water was material particles in motion. The sound of the string, the coolness and wetness of the water, seemed no longer to be properties of water itself. But whence came these properties? The answer was that it must be the mind that heard the sound or felt the water.

This issue was brought into sharp focus by both general scientific developments and by a specific relevant distinction made by Galileo. During these early modern days measurements had been made of weight, size and motion almost to the exclusion of heat, color and sound. The fascination that their mathematical manipulation had for the scientist of the day made the former seem somehow more real than the latter. In the interest of clarifying the nature of the scientific task by setting the limits of physical science and in furthering his mathematical *a priorism,* Galileo

made a sharp distinction between the objective and mathematical and the subjective and sensitive world. Discussions occurred in the setting of a consideration of Aristotle's contention that motion is the cause of heat. This Galileo denied, saying that an object or substance has shape, quantity, and motion, and only these. These are the "primary qualities"; they cannot be separated from things. But warmth, (and by a logical extension a color, a taste, a sound and a smell) do not inevitably accompany objects. These are, Galileo said, "mere names, having their location only in the responsive body...." If the sensing persons were taken away, these qualities would no longer exist. These "secondary qualities" do not have the status of physical reality. Take away the sensing person and these qualities disappear. In short, they are qualities of sensation, not of things; they are subject rather than object. They have no reality apart from experience. To Galileo, their subjectivity meant that they are to be banished from natural science.

Galileo had made a highly novel contribution which served to place physical science on a more methodologically objective footing. In the interest of *methodological* objectivity in the physical sciences Galileo was arguing that a *contentual* subjectivity existed concerning the psychology that was to be. Objectivity was being denied to sensory experiences since they were not external to the individual. Instead, sensory experiences were subjective, occurring only within an individual. There is no question that this distinction, useful though it may have been at the time, prolonged the period before psychology was to emerge as a science since the "subjectivity" of sense qualities has been a problem to be overcome ever since.

What was merely a methodological distinction for Galileo, became for Descartes an argument for a dualism of two worlds. In support of the immateriality of the mind, he happily enlisted the distinction between primary and secondary qualities and phrased it that odors, smells, and tastes became mere sensation, "existing in...(one's) thought.'' Bodies exist only in the shape and motion. He goes so far as to say that sensations represent nothing outside of our minds.[10] They are not in the objects, but in our minds. Instead of sensible qualities residing in bodies, actually it is quite possible that sensible qualities and the objects are not at all similar. In approaching fire and first feeling heat, then moving still closer and feeling pain, far from compelling one to believe that ''heat'' and ''pain'' are somehow in the fire itself, on the contrary, suggests that they are not. The upshot, then was that secondary qualities were relegated to the mind of the perceiver while primary qualities were the properties of nature and the features of the world requiring mechanical explanation and, to be, by definition, the only essential properties, of the scientific concern.

A rigid separation of body and mind, contrasted and separated entities, was insisted on by Descartes. All reality of the human being, Descartes was saying, is either spatial (body) or conscious (mind). The relationship is disjunctive; what is spatial is not conscious, what is conscious is not spatial. It follows that mind or body each can be studied without reference to the other. The physical world, including body and its mathematically measureable relationships, is in one realm, the mind with its thoughts, sensations and free will is in another. The body's behavior is determined by mechanistic laws, but in the mind there is purpose and freedom of will, making a person's actions subject to praise and blame. As distinguished from body, man's mind then cannot be reduced to an aspect of a mechanical system because man's mind transcends the material world and the efficient causality which governs therein.

Descartes' dualism had important implications for the sciences in general and for psychology in particular. Matter, including body, was to be treated mathematically and explained mechanically. The two substance view, mind and matter, simplified physical science by means of what it excluded, while at the same time, it introduced a major problem for psychology. From

the present perspective the effect of dualism was more pernicious than helpful. The dualistic view of psychology, so firmly established by Descartes, was to dominate even into the twentieth century. Ever since Descartes, psychologists have had the problem of dealing with the relation between mind and body. Descartes, himself, offered one solution.

While laboring mightily to separate mind and body, Descartes was acutely aware there was an interaction and union between them. Evidence, so prevalent in nature, that he could not ignore it, attested that the mind influences the body and the body influences the mind. His answer was to postulate a point of interaction—the pineal gland. His choice of what is now known to be a vestigial organ of no functional significance whatsoever, was based entirely on speculative reasoning. The gland's location, deep in the center of the brain, was seen as befitting its central role, while its uniqueness among brain structures in not being divided into hemispheres served to emphasize its unitary nature.

With a point of interaction selected on these grounds, Descartes proceeded to speculate on how it acted to bring about interaction of body and mind. He postulated that the slightest movement of the pineal gland can alter the flow of the animal spirits, and, reciprocally, the animal spirits can alter movements of the gland. According to its direction of inclination, animal spirits are thereby directed which serves to bring about responses in that region. The sources of stimulation for these inclinations of the pineal gland are not only external sense impressions, but also those arising from the two internal senses, the natural appetites (hunger, thirst and the like), and passions (love, hate, fear, etc.).

Selecting a point of interaction, any point of interaction, however, created the necessity of explaining how mind, a non-material substance, can influence a material body, and *vice versa*. The mind, answered Descartes, directs the *course* of motion flowing through the body without in any way altering the *volume* of motion. In his opinion, this way of understanding the relationship did no violence to the separation of the mental and physical, since, as he saw it, the mind did not exert a physical force. The weakness of this argument is all too obvious today, since we realize this explanation violates that which came to be called the principle of the conservation of momentum. Altering direction is just as much a result of physical energy as is alteration of quantity. Descartes has raised a problem of how the mind and body influenced one another, but had by no means solved it.

He also considered the general nature of the union of mind and body. That there is, in his opinion, a union, he leaves no doubt. This union is not accidental, Descartes insisted.[11] "Accidental," to Descartes, meant something that which, if absent, would still not destroy the object, such as man's clothing which is "accidental" to the man. The relationship is much closer than, say, that of a sailor to a ship. Pain is felt by the mind when the body is hurt which is a more intimate relation than the concern the sailor feels when his ship is damaged. The union of mind and body, it would seem, is an integral one for Descartes.

Although related to body, mind possesses a unity denied to body. If one takes away a part of the body, the body is decreased, but this does not thereby take away part of the mind. Moreover, corporeal objects can be subdivided into parts which is not the case with mind. Instead, mind is united with all parts of the body so as to form a whole. This is to say, the mind is united with an integrated assemblage of organs, which, precisely because the organs are interrelated, makes for a kind of unity.

It now becomes appropriate to focus upon the mind as affected by the body, rather than the reverse, which has been discussed in considering prescriptive influences from physiological problems. Perception, imagination and passion are prominent themes which he uses in this connection.

Sensing has three aspects: (1) the effect on the motions of the bodily organs by external objects; (2) the mental result as in the perception of pain,

color or sound, and the like, due to an intermixture of mind and body; and (3) "judgment" made on the basis of the past experiences with things sensed. Since the first has already been discussed in the setting of his physiology, it is the second and third aspects that receive attention. Descartes contends that the first and second aspects, just mentioned, cannot be false. It is the third aspect of judgment which, if not used reflectively, brings about errors which only understanding, and mature understanding at that, can correct.

By introducing the aspect of judgment into discussion of "sense," it is apparent that Descartes is using "sensing" in a manner similar to others who would refer to "perception" of things, that is, the "sensing" of external objects, of hunger, thirst and other natural appetites. In order to avoid terminological confusion the term "perception" will be used hereafter. It is also evident that some perceptions go beyond the body since judgment, which is of the mind, has been introduced in explaining the third level of sensing. As he put it elsewhere, perception is not by sense alone, but involves preconceived opinion exercised upon the sensed object.

Imagination is also related to body. In imagining, the mind contemplates a material form, as distinguished from understanding when the mind employs itself alone. Imagination is not essential since with understanding, but without imagination, one can still find truth. Imagination is sometimes useful, he admits, as a supplemental aid when one is considering material things. The difference between understanding and imagination is shown by the fact that images are produced without contribution on the part of the person and, indeed, sometimes against his will, neither of which characterize understanding.

Much of philosophy before Descartes had emphasized an interest in the contemplative and intellectual, rather than in the active and emotional. In considering "passions" in some detail, Descartes struck a heretofore long neglected note. He was one of the earliest attempts to isolate and to understand the primary constituents of emotional life.

As Descartes conceived the "passions" they concerned more than what we call emotions. "Passion" is derived from the so-called passivity of the mind, a term introduced to stand in contrast with the mind's own initiation of activity through understanding. Passions of the mind, then, arise from bodily movements. The brain was their physiological seat. Descartes admitted that the heart, then accepted by many as their center, is affected by the passions, but that this is a mistake arising from the close connection between animal spirits and blood.

In the broadest sense, every conscious state that arises in the mind occasioned by bodily movements, is a passion. Passions, he indicated, were of three kinds: perceptions referable to the external world, such as the light of a torch and the sound of a bell; appetitive perceptions referable to the body, such as hunger, thirst and other appetites, and perceptions referable to the mind, such as anger and joy. These last, the emotions as such, are those on which Descartes concentrated, that is, those "... perceptions, feelings or emotions of the soul (mind) which we specifically relate to it, and which are caused, maintained and fortified by some movement of the animal spirits." These "passions of the mind," the emotions, are those which are referred to the mind alone in the sense that their effects are felt there. For the passions, there is usually no known proximate cause to which they can be attributed as is the case with the perceptions and the appetites. Sadness, a passion, is experienced in the mind itself, and even though, as in all perceptions, there is a physical cause, it cannot be attributed directly to some definite object.

Surprisingly enough, Descartes had a considerable amount to say about the external indices of the passions. He took the position that we can learn about the passions from study of external behavior. He comments on such matters as the effect of the passions on changes of color, in blushing and pallor of the face, and on trembling, languor, fainting, laughter, crying and sighing.

Although objects moving the body are innumerable, he conceived that the passions they excite, affect us only in a limited number of basic ways. His analysis caused him to arrive at six primary passions—admiration (wonder), love, hatred, desire, joy and sadness. Wonder is the intellectual passion, all of the rest are forms of "desire." He was now using this latter term in a broader sense than for the passion of desire itself. Passions, whenever they incite to action, become desires in this broader sense.

Primary passions give rise to related secondary passions. To admiration are related the secondary passions of esteem, contempt, generosity, pride, humility, veneration and disdain. Passions of desire (in the narrower sense) include hope, fear, jealousy, confidence, courage, and cowardice, while from joy and sadness arise derision, envy, anger, shame, regret and joyfulness.

The passions of joy and sadness are the vehicles for his advancing a theory of pleasure and pain. Joy is agreeableness, while sadness is disagreeableness. Pleasure and pain are the predecessors of these passions and serve to produce them. Feelings of pleasure occur when experiencing that which is beneficial, and pain when experiencing that which is harmful.

Joy and sadness come from a consciousness of self-perfection or imperfection. The passions function to incite the mind to consent to "actions which may serve to maintain the body, or to render it in some manner perfect." This call for personal fulfillment and maturity contains more than a hint of what we would today call a self-actualizing approach to personality.

THE MIND AND DESCARTES

At long last, the problem of mind, the salient issue of the emerging psychology, is at hand. The conceptions of the mind's structure, its faculties, its relations to will, the problem of objectivity and primary and secondary qualities will be of major concern. But before considering them, something must be said about the use of meditation as the method for the study of mind.

MEDITATION AS A METHOD FOR THE STUDY OF MIND

It is instructive to compare meditation, as Descartes used it, to the method of introspection which was to be so characteristic of later psychology. From our temporal perspective the classic introspective method has proven to be a cooperative enterprise drawing upon the work of many men in an effort to find the structure of mind. It has been found to proceed by analysis of the contents of this structure into parts according to one schema or another.

In spite of his faith in reason, Descartes clearly took an impatient view about learning from the introspections of others. Meditation was not a collective enterprise. He denied categorically that we need to borrow observations from others concerning the passions because, as he put it, we feel them ourselves. Moreover, Cartesian meditation did not lend itself to molecular analysis of mental states into component parts or aspects. Innate ideas, for example, once achieved, were given to consciousness in all their self-contained unity from which Descartes then proceeded without any attempt to analyse them. So on both counts, Cartesian meditation was dissimilar to the later method of introspection that was to be the dominant method in psychology for a considerable period of time.

THE STRUCTURE OF MIND

Descartes clearly regarded the mind as a substance as previous discussion attests. It was he, along with Hobbes, who made the conception of mind as substance, structure or content prominent on the modern scene. Although the same substance in each case Descartes considered the mind to show different structural emphases—mind as thought, mind as ideas, mind as consciousness and mind as self-consciousness.

Mind as Thought

Time and again, Descartes stressed that mind is identical with thinking. As he put it, "the human mind...is a thinking thing, and not extended in length, width, and depth, nor participating in anything pertaining to body." Thought is not a process but a substance, immaterial though it may be. He meant it quite literally when he called it a "thing." The ideational content of the mind, discussed later as still another view, will bring this out even more clearly.

When Descartes wished to be especially precise about thinking as a spiritual substance, or "single agency," he would refer to "understanding" rather than thinking. When the mind is engaged in understanding, the body is an intruder. In these instances, sense, imagination, and memory serve but to obscure and falsify the intuition of ideas of basic principles or their deductive elaboration, giving further support to his contention that a man born without sense would have the greatest appreciation of these ideas. In this restricted meaning, the mind is almost no more than a passive spectator in the world of objects, encapsulated, self-contained and static.

In addition to this narrow meaning just considered in which the mind is in contact with basic principles, Descartes used thinking more broadly to refer to all of which we are consciously aware, including not only "understanding" but also will, imagination and sense, and memory. This broader view comes about when mind in interaction with body is considered. In this perspective, the mind is related to objects—and relation to objects is expressed through the body. The brain, not involved in understanding, now comes into use.

All perceptions, images, emotions and volitions then are related to thinking and aspects of thinking. The mind senses, imagines, remembers, feels emotions and carries out acts of will.

The traditional Aristotelian distinction between sensitive and a rational soul, between sensing and imagining in contrast to thinking, is no longer operative. In effect, the sensitive soul is merged with the thinking mind.

While mind as thinking is fundamental for Descartes, several subsidiary views are discernible in which mind is conceived as ideas, as consciousness and as self-consciousness.

Mind as Ideas

Ideas make up the content of this mind substance for Descartes. There are three kinds of ideas. Above all are the ideas which arise directly from the mind—the innate ideas, those basic, most-certain principles, which are the supreme achievement of the mind.

There are also ideas that form a link between the mind and natural objects, the ideas the mind has through sense, memory and imagination. An idea may represent in the mind an object in the world which is its cause. It is not the eye that sees but the mind, although through the intervention of the brain. Ideas of the mind relating to objects, may also be false. Ideas may or may not conform to external reality. Indeed, a major source of human error is to forget that ideas do not always conform to external objects.

Another category of ideas are those manufactured by the mind, such as ideas of imaginary objects which makes sleepers and madmen have ideas of objects which do not exist. We all, he asserts, experience ideas of the mind as being within the mind itself.[12] Such are the passions, the feelings of joy, anger and the like, and perceptions of volition, that is awareness of oneself as willing.

Ideas are not to be confused with images which arise from motion imparted to the senses. Ideas arise from the mind uninfluenced by the body, except as it serves as the instigator to trigger their appearance. But what is sensed cannot give rise to the idea itself and there is no direct correspondence between sensing and ideation.

Mind as Consciousness

The mind underlies consciousness; it is not identical with consciousness. Consciousness is a substance, a thing, an aspect of the structure *of* the mind. Regarding it as a function was yet to appear. The concept of consciousness as substance is neatly illustrated by Descartes' two types of memory—memory of material things leaving traces of preceding excitations on the brain and memory of mental things which leave permanent traces in consciousness itself.

Thought in the extended sense (as differentiated from understanding) covers everything in us of which we are immediately conscious. Ideas in this context are the forms of thoughts. Ideas are immediate awareness of what the mind perceives. Ideas include willing and fearing, for example, since in so doing one perceives, one wills, or one fears.

Awareness is an awareness of consciousness. Despite his acceptance of the potentiality of innate ideas, nothing exists in the mind of which it is not conscious. This follows because the mind contains only thought. Indeed we must be conscious of thought for it to exist. Even infants, he argues, are conscious of their thoughts, although afterwards, they might not remember them. An unconscious mind would have been a contradiction in terms for Descartes. In fostering the prescription of conscious mentalism, he did so without even the slightest consideration of a mental life of which one is unaware, i.e., an unconscious mentalism.

Mind as Self-Consciousness

In advancing his "*cogito ergo sum*" Descartes had made self-consciousness his primary datum. He could conceive of the world being nonexistent and of not having a body, but he could conceive of not having a mind which is unaware of itself. Indeed the criterion of truth for things other than the mind is that it be as clear and distinct as that of the mind's own existence.

The mind thinks and it is conscious of itself. Knowledge of self is immediate, and occurs whenever a person first asks himself that particular question, claimed Descartes. The very moment that there is awareness in consciousness, he added, that instant there is awareness of one's own existence.

Descartes also used self-consciousness as an explanatory concept. For example, the continuity of personal identity is used to characterize the waking state and distinguish it from that of sleeping. Self-consciousness also relates to self-evaluation. Self-blame and esteem arise in his opinion through exercise of free will and the control or lack of it we have over our volition. It is for these reasons that a man can be praised or blamed.

Although only a beginning, a concept of unity or self can be found to be emerging in Descartes. The unity of the mind is at the same time the unity of the self. The arguments for unity of mind then become arguments for unity of self as well, although this is a point he did not make explicit.

An important caution must be offered concerning his accounts of mind. Although they were to lead psychologists with different aims and presuppositions than his own toward the particular perspectives just given, Descartes' aim, in contrast, was essentially philosophical, or to be more specific, epistemological. He wished to demonstrate unequivocally that we are thinking beings.

The Faculties of Mind

A conception of mental phenomena as processes or activities, the functional prescription as it shall be called, was also discernible in his thinking although mind as content, the contentual prescription dominated. The functional conception was a tradition traceable at least as far back as Augustine, for whom memory, will and imagination of the mind were to be attributed to their respective faculties, powers or agencies. Faculties were supposed to produce the various mental activities of which human beings were prone. Faculty psychology was a forerunner of functional psychology insofar as it conceived of the mind as having specifiable function or functions.

Descartes specifically claimed authorship of the view that the mind consists of only one thing, the "faculty" of thinking. The mind has unity so that faculties are not parts of that mind since it is one and the same mind which employs itself in these faculties. They are, as he put it, "...modes of thinking peculiar to themselves...."

The substantial nature of mind, "...a thing that thinks..." made it relatively easy for Descartes to espouse a faculty point of view. Hence, his easy reference after the above quoted words to go on "...or a thing that has in itself the faculty of thinking."

The faculties useful in cognition are stated by Descartes somewhat casually and inconsistently. One account he gave called for thinking in the form of understanding and imagination, sense and memory. Of these, only understanding can give the truth; the others are auxiliary. Thinking, already familiar as a "...power...(that is) purely spiritual," uses the bodily-based faculties by applying itself to them or it may cooperate and thus use them. Elsewhere, feeling and willing are also treated as faculties by Descartes. Discussion of willing will be indicative of will as a power.

Will and Its Freedom

Speaking generally two extreme positions may be discerned concerning the freedom of the will. There is the view that, since man possesses a non-material mind or spiritual soul endowed with the power of free choice, he transcends the material world and, therefore, the system of causality. There is the opposed view that would extend the scientific conception of the material universe to include man, in which free will would be seen as an epiphenomenon and freedom of will denied. Between these extremes there is a number of views which would offer qualification and elaborations.

Descartes accepted clearly and unequivocally the reality of the freedom of the will. After stating that all men possess the faculty of willing, he went on to say that it is the power of choosing or not choosing to do a thing. In another place, he referred to judging or refraining from judging as an act of will, which, he adds, is under our control. There is freedom of the will, then, shown in choosing or judging.

This freedom is evident, innate, and found by self-examination claimed Descartes. The very capacity to apply methodic doubt, the starting point of his method, he holds, is evidence of this freedom. In doubting all things, he perceived liberty to do so to exist. Man's freedom of will is received from God. Man's will is free in the same sense and from the same source in God as are miracles, since in both instances, there is a suspension of causality.

But what is the relation of the will to the mind? Despite his repeated references to understanding as the only function of mind, a position that has been accepted as his up to this point, when dealing with the relation of mind to will, he introduces the latter as a faculty. Besides understanding, he now says, there is also the will, in contradiction to his position that mind is pure thought. Statements to the contrary were, he now argues, a matter of emphasis; will is also of the mind. He was perhaps influenced in acceptance of this position by the Church, for to follow its dictates, he had to accept both the will as influencing the mind and its freedom.

His position concerning will as a faculty of the mind is made especially clear when we examine the question of the cooperation and conflict of the will and the understanding. In a setting of considerations of man's ability to distinguish between the true and the false, he argues that error arises from misapplication of the will which consists of extending it beyond understanding. Understanding does not cause errors, incorrect exercise of one's will does. Will exceeds understanding in that we can will many things that we do not understand and therefore err. If we understand (which is God given), we cannot err in willing, but if we do not understand and will nevertheless, we can commit error.

The relation of the will to the passions is important to Descartes because to show how to control the passions is Descartes' didactic and moral aim for considering them. The first step toward this control is to understand them which he believed his book on the passions to give. When passions are aroused, we can divert ourselves until the agitation calms and then, and only then, should we make a judgement as to what is to be done. Then the freely acting mind can influence the workings of the bodily machine by the process of willing which can cause the pineal gland to incline in the manner necessary for the appropriate bodily action.

As distinguished from the passion or desire, will is that which gives or withholds consent to desire. In this context, the principal effect of the passions is to incite the mind to will. The agitation of the animal spirits, especially if it be violent, is of the body, and, just as a clap of thunder must be heard whether we want to or not, so too the mind cannot completely control the passions. The will, however, can quickly gain control of the passions by not permitting their effects to proceed further than the first beginnings. Through the will, the hand that rose to strike in anger can be restrained before the blow is struck; running away in fear can be stopped after the first involuntary movements. Most actions originate with the will, reflex responses being a major class of exceptions. The activity of the will, or rather its failure yet to act, is shown in involuntary action described earlier in connection with the functioning of the nervous system.

In sum, the mind is free since it initiates action through the will and thus transcends causality. Since to be free is to be without laws, Descartes was denying that there can be a science of psychology. The material world was rigidly determined. Physical processes and everything about animals and the bodies of men fall within this material world. The one exception was the human mind which has volition.

Methodological and Contentual Objectivity-Subjectivity

To his successors, Descartes was to be a rich source for various combinations of methodological and contentual objectivity and subjectivity. His conception of matter as extension furthered an objective quantitative science and opened the way to a view of man as a machine. Through his concept of an animal as an automaton and more specifically, through his concept of reflex action, Descartes contributed to the beginnings of both physiological and animal psychology. It was this sort of thinking that led a modern commentator, Randall, to say that Descartes "... held to a thoroughly mechanistic biology and psychology."[13] This is true for the latter only if one is thinking of psychology today. It is not true for the centuries between, during which psychology was conceived to be the study of mind. In historical perspective, the psychological side to the story is to prove to be quite a different matter. A non-mechanistic phase in the history of psychology was about to be entered upon because of Descartes. His contentually subjective position concerning the mind, was to dominate in psychology well into the first years of the Twentieth Century. Although Descartes insisted on a contentual subjectivity for the mind, in so doing, he was searching for a methodological objectivity and, hence, his view should not be confused with "subjectivism" in this sense. He wanted desperately to attain a truth comparable to the impersonal truth of mathematics. He wished to distinguish the reality of consciousness from the world "outside" of which consciousness is not a part. In consciousness, we each are alone with ourselves. Reality, including other persons, is reached only by an inference, a step in itself that emphasized the distance between subject and object.

Descartes' *Meditations*, as Husserl[14] asserts, is the prototype of philosophical reflection in that he turned within himself for immediate experience. In so doing, he fostered the phenomenological approach which calls for mind to be studied in precisely this fashion.

Descartes must be given credit for a consistent, maintained attempt to examine "the sheer facts of experience" as MacLeod[15] put it recently. Just prior to the quotation MacLeod had explained that two German words, *"Erlebnis"* and *"Erfahrung,"* give a convenient distinction that the English word "experience" does not convey. *"Erlebnis"* refers to present experience, that which is immediately given without reference to origin; *"Erfahrung"* refers to an accumulation of experiences. This makes it possible to speak of Descartes as stressing experience in the sense of "Erlebnis" without implying he was empirical, i.e., depending upon accumulated experience as the source of knowledge which, as is very obvious, he was not. As a consequence of this emphasis, he contributed to a phenomenological point of view. Those who came after Descartes could find in him support for that which they wished to stress, whether it be contentual objectivity or subjectivity or methodological objectivity or subjectivity.

NOTES

Unless otherwise noted, citations to Descartes are the works in Elizabeth S. Haldane & G. R. T. Ross (Trans.), *The philosophical works of Descartes.* (2 vols.) Cambridge: University Press, 1911.

(1) Reichenbach, H. *The rise of scientific philosophy.* Berkeley, Calif.: University of California Press, 1951.

(2) Descartes, R. *Notes directed against a certain programme.* (1648) p. 443.

(3) Descartes, R. *Principles of philosophy.* (1644) In V. Cousin (Ed.), *Oeuvres,* Vol. 3, Paris: Levrault, 1824.

(4) Haldane, Elizabeth S. *Descartes, his life and times.* New York: Dutton, 1905.

(5) Descartes, R. *Letter to Mersenne,* March 1638. In *Oeuvres et lettres.* (Intro. by A. Bridoux.) Paris: Gallimard, 1953, p. 996.

(6) Descartes, R. *Letter to Arnauld.* (1648) In N. K. Smith (Trans.), *Descartes' philosophical writings.* London: Macmillan, 1952, pp. 280–281.

(7) It would seem that the actual term, "primary" and "secondary" in this context was introduced by Robert Boyle in 1666 in his "Origin of Forms and Qualities According to the Corpuscular Philosophy." T. Birch (Ed.), *Works,* Vol. 3, London: Johnson, *et al.* 1773. (1666) Details are given in Sir William Hamilton's edition of the *Works of Thomas Reid, D. D.* (Edinburgh: Machlachlan & Stewart, 1863) Vol. II, p. 825, Note D.

(8) Galileo, G. *Il Saggiatore.* (1623) Quoted in Joan W. Reeves, *Body and mind in Western thought.* London: Penguin Books, 1958, Question 48.

(9) Willey, B. *Seventeenth century background.* London: Chatto & Windus, 1934.

(10) Descartes, R. *Principles of philosophy.* (1644) IX.

(11) Descartes, R. Letter to Regius. (1641) In N. K. Smith (Trans.), *Descartes' philosophical writings.* London: Macmillan, 1952, pp. 269–270.

(12) Haldane, Elizabeth S. *Descartes, his life and times.* New York: Dutton, 1905.

(13) Randall, J.H., Jr., *The career of philosophy: from the Middle Ages to the Enlightenment.* New York: Columbia University Press, 1962, p. 381.

(14) Husserl, E. *Cartesian meditations: an introduction to phenomenology.* The Hague: Nijhoff, 1964. (1936)

(15) MacLeod, R. B. Phenomenology: a challenge to experimental psychology. In T. Wann (Ed.), *Behaviorism and phenomenology: contrasting bases for modern psychology.* Chicago: University of Chicago Press, 1964, pp. 47–78.

BRITISH EMPIRICISM

In the previous chapter, Descartes's meditation illustrates that author's attempt to know the contents of the mind, with a special emphasis on innate ideas. Indeed, he stressed reason over perception and innate ideas over experience. Such views classify him as a *rationalist,* which has led the historian of psychology Thomas Leahey (1987) to call Descartes a paradoxical figure. Leahey notes the contrast between Descartes's rationalism and his mechanism, the latter view ultimately supporting an empirical psychology.*

In contrast to the notion of innate ideas and knowledge by reason stood the British *empiricists,* a group of philosophers who spanned a period of approximately two hundred years, beginning with John Locke (1632–1704). Locke rejected the notion of innate ideas and argued forcefully that all ideas were derived from experience. Resurrecting Aristotle's notion of *tabula rasa,* Locke described how experience would write on the blank slate, thus filling the mind with its ideas. Although all ideas were derived from experience, they were not all derived from direct sensory experience; some were the products of the mind from the processes of reflection, or what Locke called the internal operations of the mind. Thus, one could know a rose from direct sensory experience—its aroma, color, texture. But it was also possible to "experience" the rose when it was not present by reflecting on these earlier experiences. These ideas of reflection were not derived from any sensory contact of the moment.

---

* Although mechanism and rationalism might seem to be unlikely philosophical partners, they have co-existed in great thinkers other than Descartes. For example, Issac Newton (1642–1727) developed a mechanistic view of the world using rationalist methods in his *Philosophiae Naturalis Principia Mathematica* (1687).

Unlike Descartes, Locke was more interested in how the mind works, that is, how it acquires knowledge, than in what it actually knows. He studied that question for twenty years, writing and rewriting his most important work for psychology, *An Essay Concerning Human Understanding,* which was finally published in 1690. Many historians use the publication of that book to mark the formal beginning of British empiricism.

The first selection in this chapter is an excerpt from Locke's *Essay.* In it he discusses the nature and extent of knowledge, including his descriptions of *simple* and *complex ideas* and *primary* and *secondary qualities.* Simple ideas are derived from either sensory experience or reflection, but complex ideas are the product only of reflection. Primary and secondary qualities are distinguished as follows. Primary qualities are sensory qualities that exist in an object, such as the thorny shape of a rose stem or the whiteness of a feather. Secondary qualities exist in the experiencing individual and are not a part of the object itself, for example, the pain experienced from the rose thorn or the tickle from the feather. That is, the pain is not part of the rose thorn, nor is the tickle part of the feather. Instead, these qualities of sensory experience are part of the individual. Locke's distinction between primary and secondary qualities was especially important for a science of psychology because it recognized experience that was independent of the physical objects of the world. In essence, these secondary qualities were products of the mind, and as such were the very basis of psychological study.

Empiricism continued through the work of George Berkeley (1685–1753), especially in terms of observations on sensory systems such as vision. Berkeley disagreed with Locke's distinction between primary and secondary qualities, arguing that only the latter could really be known to exist. For Berkeley, all knowledge was dependent on the experiencing individual, and qualities of objects existed only as perceived.

Berkeley was followed by David Hartley (1705–1757) and David Hume (1711–1776), whose principal interests were in learning, or what they called *association.* They were particularly interested in how ideas became associated with one another to form the complex ideas about which Locke had written. Both men emphasized contiguity as a fundamental law of association; that is, ideas that were adjacent to one another in space or time were likely to be associated with one another. They sought to determine the limits of contiguity in forming associations.

Continuing in the empiricist-associationist tradition were the Mills, father James Mill (1773–1836) and his son John Stuart Mill (1806–1873). James Mill recognized that some associations were formed more easily than others and that some were more lasting. His extremely mechanical view of the mind described a set of factors that determined the strength and durability of associations.

John Stuart Mill extended his father's work on association, but his most important work for psychology was *A System of Logic,* published in 1843. It is the source for the second selection in this chapter. In his book, Mill argues for the feasibility of a science of psychology (in his words, a "science of human nature"). That was a hotly debated question in Mill's time, as many agreed with Auguste Comte that there could be no science of the mind because the mind could not study its own processes (Hothersall, 1984). Although Mill acknowledged that psychology was, in his time, an inexact science, he believed it was as precise as some sciences, such as astronomy, and worthy of study. He also proposed a related field of study that he labeled *ethology,* or the science of the formation of character. This field was to discover the individual and social factors that developed individual character, or what we might describe today as *personality.* (Mill's use of the word *ethology* should not be confused with its contemporary usage as a naturalistic approach to the study of animal behavior.)

From Locke to John Stuart Mill, the approaches to studying the mind enjoyed an evolution that deepened the emphases of empiricism and mechanism. The British empiricists stressed the role of sensations, the nature of ideas, how these ideas were acquired, and how more complex ideas were formed through associations. These areas of inquiry would form the basis of the study of consciousness in the experimental psychology about to take shape in Germany, the subject of Chapters 6 and 7.

There are two secondary source selections in this chapter, one dealing with Locke, the other with J. S. Mill. The article on Locke by Martha E. Moore-Russell examines the social and political forces that surrounded Locke and the writing of his *Essay.* She uses what she calls a *person-in-society approach* to describe how she thinks Locke's philosophy was determined by his interpretation of the socio-political world around him. In writing this article, she has made use of a number of sources, including several of Locke's works that were never published.

The other article, by the University of New Hampshire historian of psychology David E. Leary, describes the fate and influence of J. S. Mill's proposed science of ethology. Leary notes that Mill's ethology proposal, published as part six of his *System of Logic,* seems to have been ignored in historical accounts. This article traces its influence up to 1940 and describes its culmination in the field of social anthropology.

REFERENCES

Hothersall, D. (1984). *History of psychology.* New York: Random House.
Leahey, T. H. (1987). *A history of psychology: Main currents in psychological thought* (2d ed.). Englewood Cliffs, NJ: Prentice-Hall.

On the Extent of Human Knowledge

John Locke

1. Knowledge, as has been said, lying in the perception of the agreement or disagreement of any of our ideas, it follows from hence, That,

First, we can have knowledge no further than we have *ideas*.

2. Secondly, That we can have no knowledge further than we can have *perception* of that agreement or disagreement. Which perception being: 1. Either by *intuition,* or the immediate comparing any two ideas; or, 2. By *reason,* examining the agreement or disagreement of two ideas, by the intervention of some others; or, 3. By *sensation,* perceiving the existence of particular things: hence it also follows:

3. Thirdly, That we cannot have an *intuitive knowledge* that shall extend itself to all our ideas, and all that we would know about them; because we cannot examine and perceive all the relations they have one to another, by juxta-position, or an immediate comparison one with another. Thus, having the ideas of an obtuse and an acute angled triangle, both drawn from equal bases, and between parallels, I can, by intuitive knowledge, perceive the one not to be the other, but cannot that way know whether they be equal or no; because their agreement or disagreement in equality can never be perceived by an immediate comparing them: the difference of figure makes their parts incapable of an exact immediate application; and therefore there is need of some intervening qualities to measure them by, which is demonstration, or rational knowledge.

4. Fourthly, It follows, also, from what is above observed, that our *rational knowledge* cannot reach to the whole extent of our ideas: because between two different ideas we would examine, we cannot always find such mediums as we can connect one to another with an intuitive knowledge in all the parts of the deduction; and wherever that fails, we come short of knowledge and demonstration.

5. Fifthly, *Sensitive knowledge* reaching no further than the existence of things actually present to our senses, is yet much narrower than either of the former.

6. Sixthly, From all which it is evident, that the *extent of our knowledge* comes not only short of the reality of things, but even of the extent of our own ideas. Though our knowledge be limited to our ideas, and cannot exceed them either in extent or perfection; and though these be very narrow bounds, in respect of the extent of All-being, and far short of what we may justly imagine to be in some even created understandings, not tied down to the dull and narrow information that is to be received from some few, and not very acute, ways of perception, such as are our senses; yet it would be well with us if our knowledge were but as large as our ideas, and there were not many doubts and inquiries *concerning the ideas we have,* whereof we are not, nor I believe ever shall be in this world resolved. Nevertheless, I do not question but that human knowledge, under the present circumstances of our beings and constitutions, may be carried much further than it has hitherto been, if men would sincerely, and with freedom of mind, employ all that industry and labour of thought, in improving the means of discovering truth, which they do for the colouring or support of falsehood, to maintain a system, interest, or party they are once engaged in. But yet after all, I think I may, without injury to human perfection, be confident, that our knowledge would never reach to all we might desire to know concerning those ideas we have; nor be able to surmount all the difficulties, and resolve all the questions that might arise concerning any of them. We have the

From Locke, J. (1690). *An essay concerning human understanding.* Adapted from A. C. Fraser (Trans.), Oxford: Clarendon Press, 1894, pp. 190–225.

ideas of a *square,* a *circle,* and *equality;* and yet, perhaps, shall never be able to find a circle equal to a square, and certainly know that it is so. We have the ideas of *matter* and *thinking,* but possibly shall never be able to know whether [any mere material being] thinks or no; it being impossible for us, by the contemplation of our own ideas, without revelation, to discover whether Omnipotency has not given to some systems of matter, fitly disposed, a power to perceive and think, or else joined and fixed to matter, so disposed, a thinking immaterial substance: it being, in respect of our notions, not much more remote from our comprehension to conceive that GOD can, if he pleases, superadd to matter *a faculty of thinking,* than that he should superadd to it *another substance with a faculty of thinking;* since we know not wherein thinking consists, nor to what sort of substances the Almighty has been pleased to give that power, which cannot be in any created being, but merely by the good pleasure and bounty of the Creator. For [I see no contradiction in it, that the first Eternal thinking Being, or Omnipotent Spirit, should, if he pleased, give to certain systems of created senseless matter, put together as he thinks fit, some degrees of sense, perception, and thought; though, as I think I have proved, lib. iv. ch. 10, § 14, &c., it is no less than a contradiction to suppose matter (which is evidently in its own nature void of sense and thought) should be that Eternal first-thinking Being. What certainty of knowledge can any one have, that some perceptions, such as, v.g., pleasure and pain, should not be in some bodies themselves,] after a certain manner modified and moved, as well as that they should be in an immaterial substance, upon the motion of the parts of body: Body, as far as we can conceive, being able only to strike and affect body, and motion, according to the utmost reach of our ideas, being able to produce nothing but motion; so that when we allow it to produce pleasure or pain, or the idea of a colour or sound, we are fain to quit our reason, go beyond our ideas, and attribute it wholly to the good pleasure of our Maker. For,

since we must allow He has annexed effects to motion which we can no way conceive motion able to produce, what reason have we to conclude that He could not order them as well to be produced in a subject we cannot conceive capable of them, as well as in a subject we cannot conceive the motion of matter can any way operate upon? I say not this, that I would any way lessen the belief of the soul's immateriality: I am not here speaking of probability, but knowledge; and I think not only that it becomes the modesty of philosophy not to pronounce magisterially, where we want that evidence that can produce knowledge; but also, that it is of use to us to discern how far our knowledge does reach; for the state we are at present in, not being that of vision, we must in many things content ourselves with faith and probability: and in the present question, about the Immateriality of the Soul, if our faculties cannot arrive at demonstrative certainty, we need not think it strange. All the great ends of morality and religion are well enough secured, without philosophical proofs of the soul's immateriality; since it is evident, that he who made us at the beginning to subsist here, sensible intelligent beings, and for several years continued us in such a state, can and will restore us to the like state of sensibility in another world, and make us capable there to receive the retribution he has designed to men, according to their doings in this life. [And therefore it is not of such mighty necessity to determine one way or the other, as some, over-zealous for or against the immateriality of the soul, have been forward to make the world believe. Who, either on the one side, indulging too much their thoughts immersed altogether in matter, can allow no existence to what is not material: or who, on the other side, finding not *cogitation* within the natural powers of matter, examined over and over again by the utmost intention of mind, have the confidence to conclude—That Omnipotency itself cannot give perception and thought to a substance which has the modification of solidity. He that considers how hardly sensation is, in our thoughts, reconcilable to extended matter; or existence to anything that has no extension at all, will confess that he is very far from certainly knowing what his soul is. It is a point which seems to me to be put out of the reach of our knowledge: and he who will give himself leave to consider freely, and look into the dark and intricate part of each hypothesis, will scarce find his reason able to determine him fixedly for or against the soul's materiality. Since, on which side soever he views it, either as an *unextended substance,* or as a *thinking extended matter,* the difficulty to conceive either will, whilst either alone is in his thoughts, still drive him to the contrary side. An unfair way which some men take with themselves: who, because of the inconceivableness of something they find in one, throw themselves violently into the contrary hypothesis, though altogether as unintelligible to an unbiased understanding. This serves not only to show the weakness and the scantiness of our knowledge, but the insignificant triumph of such sort of arguments; which, drawn from our own views, may satisfy us that we can find no certainty on one side of the question: but do not at all thereby help us to truth by running into the opposite opinion; which, on examination, will be found clogged with equal difficulties. For what safety, what advantage to any one is it, for the avoiding the seeming absurdities, and to him unsurmountable rubs, he meets with in one opinion, to take refuge in the contrary, which is built on something altogether as inexplicable, and as far remote from his comprehension? It is past controversy, that we have in us *something* that thinks; our very doubts about what it is, confirm the certainty of its being, though we must content ourselves in the ignorance of what *kind* of being it is: and it is in vain to go about to be sceptical in this, as it is unreasonable in most other cases to be positive against the being of anything, because we cannot comprehend its nature. For I would fain know what substance exists, that has not something in it which manifestly baffles our understandings. Other spirits, who see and know

the nature and inward constitution of things, how much must they exceed us in knowledge? To which, if we add larger comprehension, which enables them at one glance to see the connexion and agreement of very many ideas, and readily supplies to them the intermediate proofs, which we by single and slow steps, and long poring in the dark, hardly at last find out, and are often ready to forget one before we have hunted out another; we may guess at some part of the happiness of superior ranks of spirits, who have a quicker and more penetrating sight, as well as a larger field of knowledge.]

But to return to the argument in hand: our knowledge, I say, is not only limited to the paucity and imperfections of the ideas we have, and which we employ it about, but even comes short of that too: but how far it reaches, let us now inquire.

7. The affirmations or negations we make concerning the ideas we have, may, as I have before intimated in general, be reduced to these four sorts, viz. identity, co-existence, relation, and real existence. I shall examine how far our knowledge extends in each of these:

8. *First,* as to *identity* and *diversity.* In this way of agreement or disagreement of our ideas, our intuitive knowledge is as far extended as our ideas themselves: and there can be no idea in the mind, which it does not, presently, by an intuitive knowledge, perceive to be what it is, and to be different from any other.

9. *Secondly,* as to the second sort, which is the agreement or disagreement of our ideas in *co-existence,* in this our knowledge is very short; though in this consists the greatest and most material part of our knowledge concerning substances. For our ideas of the species of substances being, as I have showed, nothing but certain collections of simple ideas united in one subject, and so co-existing together; v.g. our idea of flame is a body hot, luminous, and moving upward; of gold, a body heavy to a certain degree, yellow, malleable, and fusible: for these, or some such complex ideas as these, in men's minds, do these two names of the different substances, flame and

gold, stand for. When we would know anything further concerning these, or any other sort of substances, what do we inquire, but what *other* qualities or powers these substances have or have not? Which is nothing else but to know what *other* simple ideas do, or do not co-exist with those that make up that complex idea?

10. This, how weighty and considerable a part soever of human science, is yet very narrow, and scarce any at all. The reason whereof is, that the simple ideas whereof our complex ideas of substances are made up are, for the most part, such as carry with them, in their own nature, no *visible necessary* connexion or inconsistency with any other simple ideas, whose co-existence with them we would inform ourselves about.

11. The ideas that our complex ones of substances are made up of, and about which our knowledge concerning substances is most employed, are those of their secondary qualities; which depending all (as has been shown) upon the primary qualities of their minute and insensible parts; or, if not upon them, upon something yet more remote from our comprehension; it is impossible we should know which have a *necessary* union or inconsistency one with another. For, not knowing the root they spring from, not knowing what size, figure, and texture of parts they are, on which depend, and from which result those qualities which make our complex idea of gold, it is impossible we should know what *other* qualities result from, or are incompatible with, the same constitution of the insensible parts of gold; and so consequently must always co-exist with that complex idea we have of it, or else are inconsistent with it.

12. Besides this ignorance of the primary qualities of the insensible parts of bodies, on which depend all their secondary qualities, there is yet another and more incurable part of ignorance, which sets us more remote from a certain knowledge of the co-existence or *inco-existence* (if I may so say) of different ideas in the same subject; and that is, that there is no discoverable connexion between any secondary quality and those primary qualities which it depends on.

13. That the size, figure, and motion of one body should cause a change in the size, figure, and motion of another body, is not beyond our conception; the separation of the parts of one body upon the intrusion of another; and the change from rest to motion upon impulse; these and the like seem to have *some connexion* one with another. And if we knew these primary qualities of bodies, we might have reason to hope we might be able to know a great deal more of these operations of them one upon another: but our minds not being able to discover any connexion betwixt these primary qualities of bodies and the sensations that are produced in us by them, we can never be able to establish certain and undoubted rules of the *consequence* or *co-existence* of any secondary qualities, though we could discover the size, figure, or motion of those invisible parts which immediately produce them. We are so far from knowing *what* figure, size, or motion of parts produce a yellow colour, a sweet taste, or a sharp sound, that we can by no means conceive how *any* size, figure, or motion of any particles, can possibly produce in us the idea of any colour, taste, or sound whatsoever: there is no conceivable connexion between the one and the other.

14. In vain, therefore, shall we endeavour to discover by our ideas (the only true way of certain and universal knowledge) what other ideas are to be found constantly joined with that of *our* complex idea of any substance: since we neither know the real constitution of the minute parts on which their qualities do depend; nor, did we know them, could we discover any necessary connexion between them and any of the secondary qualities: which is necessary to be done before we can certainly know their necessary co-existence. So, that, let our complex idea of any species of substances be what it will, we can hardly, from the simple ideas contained in it, certainly determine the necessary co-existence of any other quality whatsoever. Our knowledge in all these inquiries reaches very little further than our experience. Indeed some few of the primary qualities have a necessary dependence and vis-

ible connexion one with another, as figure necessarily supposes extension; receiving or communicating motion by impulse, supposes solidity. But though these, and perhaps some others of our ideas have: yet there are so few of them that have a visible connexion one with another, that we can by intuition or demonstration discover the co-existence of very few of the qualities that are to be found united in substances: and we are left only to the assistance of our senses to make known to us what qualities they contain. For of all the qualities that are co-existent in any subject, without this dependence and evident connexion of their ideas one with another, we cannot know certainly any two to co-exist, any further than experience, by our senses, informs us. Thus, though we see the yellow colour, and, upon trial, find the weight, malleableness, fusibility, and fixedness that are united in a piece of gold; yet, because no one of these ideas has any evident dependence or necessary connexion with the other, we cannot certainly know that where any four of these are, the fifth will be there also, how highly probable soever it may be; because the highest probability amounts not to certainty, without which there can be no true knowledge. For this co-existence can be no further known than it is perceived; and it cannot be perceived but either in particular subjects, by the observation of our senses, or, in general, by the necessary connexion of the ideas themselves.

15. As to the incompatibility or repugnancy to co-existence, we may know that any subject may have of each sort of primary qualities but one particular at once: v.g. each particular extension, figure, number of parts, motion, excludes all other of each kind. The like also is certain of all sensible ideas peculiar to each sense; for whatever of each kind is present in any subject, excludes all other of that sort: v.g. no one subject can have two smells or two colours at the same time. To this, perhaps will be said, Has not an opal, or the infusion of *lignum nephriticum,* two colours at the same time? To which I answer, that these bodies, to eyes differently placed, may at the same time afford different colours: but I take liberty also to say, that, to eyes differently placed, it is different parts of the object that reflect the particles of light: and therefore it is not the same part of the object, and so not the very same subject, which at the same time appears both yellow and azure. For, it is as impossible that the very same particle of any body should at the same time differently modify or reflect the rays of light, as that it should have two different figures and textures at the same time.

On the Science of Human Nature

John Stuart Mill

CHAPTER III
THAT THERE IS, OR MAY BE, A SCIENCE OF HUMAN NATURE

§ 1. It is a common notion, or at least it is implied in many common modes of speech, that the thoughts, feelings, and actions of sentient beings are not a subject of science, in the same strict

From Mill, J. S. (1843). *A system of logic, ratiocinative and inductive, Being* a *connected view of the principles of evidence and the methods of scientific investigation.* New York: Harper & Brothers, pp. 586–596. (8th edition, 1900).

sense in which this is true of the objects of outward nature. This notion seems to involve some confusion of ideas, which it is necessary to begin by clearing up.

Any facts are fitted, in themselves, to be a subject of science which follow one another according to constant laws, although those laws may not have been discovered, nor even be discoverable by our existing resources. Take, for instance, the most familiar class of meteorological phenomena, those of rain and sunshine. Scientific inquiry has not yet succeeded in ascertaining the order of antecedence and consequence among these phenomena, so as to be able, at least in our regions of the earth, to predict them with certainty, or even with any high degree of probability. Yet no one doubts that the phenomena depend on laws, and that these must be derivative laws resulting from known ultimate laws, those of heat, electricity, vaporization, and elastic fluids. Nor can it be doubted that if we were acquainted with all the antecedent circumstances, we could, even from those more general laws, predict (saving difficulties of calculation) the state of the weather at any future time. Meteorology, therefore, not only has in itself every natural requisite for being, but actually is, a science; though, from the difficulty of observing the facts on which the phenomena depend (a difficulty inherent in the peculiar nature of those phenomena), the science is extremely imperfect; and were it perfect, might probably be of little avail in practice, since the data requisite for applying its principles to particular instances would rarely be procurable.

A case may be conceived, of an intermediate character, between the perfection of science and this its extreme imperfection. It may happen that the greater causes, those on which the principal part of the phenomena depends, are within the reach of observation and measurement; so that if no other causes intervened, a complete explanation could be given not only of the phenomena in general, but of all the variations and modifications which it admits of. But inasmuch as other, perhaps many other causes, separately insignificant in their effects, co-operate or conflict in many or in all cases with those greater causes, the effect, accordingly, presents more or less of aberration from what would be produced by the greater causes alone. Now if these minor causes are not so constantly accessible, or not accessible at all, to accurate observation, the principal mass of the effect may still, as before, be accounted for, and even predicted; but there will be variations and modifications which we shall not be competent to explain thoroughly, and

our predictions will not be fulfilled accurately, but only approximately.

It is thus, for example, with the theory of the tides. No one doubts that Tidology (as Dr. Whewell proposes to call it) is really a science. As much of the phenomena as depends on the attraction of the sun and moon is completely understood, and may, in any, even unknown, part of the earth's surface, be foretold with certainty; and the far greater part of the phenomena depends on those causes. But circumstances of a local or casual nature, such as the configuration of the bottom of the ocean, the degree of confinement from shores, the direction of the wind, etc., influence, in many or in all places, the height and time of the tide; and a portion of these circumstances being either not accurately knowable, not precisely measurable, or not capable of being certainly foreseen, the tide in known places commonly varies from the calculated result of general principles by some difference that we can not explain, and in unknown ones may vary from it by a difference that we are not able to foresee or conjecture. Nevertheless, not only is it certain that these variations depend on causes, and follow their causes by laws of unerring uniformity; not only, therefore, is tidology a science, like meteorology, but it is, what hitherto at least meteorology is not, a science largely available in practice. General laws may be laid down respecting the tides, predictions may be founded on those laws, and the result will in the main, though often not with complete accuracy, correspond to the predictions.

And this is what is or ought to be meant by those who speak of sciences which are not *exact* sciences. Astronomy was once a science, without being an exact science. It could not become exact until not only the general course of the planetary motions, but the perturbations also, were accounted for, and referred to their causes. It has become an exact science, because its phenomena have been brought under laws comprehending the whole of the causes by which the phenomena are influenced, whether in a great or only in a trifling degree, whether in all or only in some cases, and assigning to each of those causes the share of effect which really belongs to it. But in the theory of the tides the only laws as yet accurately ascertained are those of the causes which affect the phenomenon in all cases, and in a considerable degree; while others which affect it in some cases only, or, if in all, only in a slight degree, have not been sufficiently ascertained and studied to enable us to lay down their laws; still less to deduce the completed law of the phenomenon, by compounding the effects of the greater with those of the minor causes. Tidology, therefore, is not yet an exact science; not from any inherent incapacity of being so, but from the difficulty of ascertaining with complete precision the real derivative uniformities. By combining, however, the exact laws of the greater causes, and of such of the minor ones as are sufficiently known, with such empirical laws or such approximate generalizations respecting the miscellaneous variations as can be obtained by specific observation, we can lay down general propositions which will be true in the main, and on which, with allowance for the degree of their probable inaccuracy, we may safely ground our expectations and our conduct.

§ 2. The science of human nature is of this description. It falls far short of the standard of exactness now realized in Astronomy; but there is no reason that it should not be as much a science as Tidology is, or as Astronomy was when its calculations had only mastered the main phenomena, but not the perturbations.

The phenomena with which this science is conversant being the thoughts, feelings, and actions of human beings, it would have attained the ideal perfection of a science if it enabled us to foretell how an individual would think, feel, or act throughout life, with the same certainty with which astronomy enables us to predict the places and the occultations of the heavenly bodies. It needs scarcely be stated that nothing approaching to this can be done. The actions of individuals could not be predicted with scientific accuracy, were it only because we can not foresee the whole of the circumstances in which those individuals will be placed. But further, even in any given combination of (present) circumstances, no assertion, which is both precise and universally true, can be made respecting the manner in which human beings will think, feel, or act. This is not, however, because every person's modes of thinking, feeling, and acting do not depend on causes; nor can we doubt that if, in the case of any individual, our data could be complete, we even now know enough of the ultimate laws by which mental phenomena are determined, to enable us in many cases to predict, with tolerable certainty, what, in the greater number of supposable combinations of circumstances, his conduct or sentiments would be. But the impressions and actions of human beings are not solely the result of their present circumstances, but the joint result of those circumstances and of the characters of the individuals; and the agencies which determine human character are so numerous and diversified (nothing which has happened to the person throughout life being without its portion of influence), that in the aggregate they are never in any two cases exactly similar. Hence, even if our science of human nature were theoretically perfect, that is, if we could calculate any character as we can calculate the orbit of any planet, *from given data;* still, as the data are never all given, nor ever precisely alike in different cases, we could neither make positive predictions, nor lay down universal propositions.

Inasmuch, however, as many of those effects which it is of most importance to render amenable to human foresight and control are determined, like the tides, in an incomparably greater degree by general causes, than by all partial causes taken together; depending in the main on those circumstances and qualities which are common to all mankind, or at least to large bodies of them, and only in a small degree on the idiosyncrasies of organization or the peculiar history of individuals; it is evidently possible with regard to all such effects, to make predictions which will *almost* always be verified, and general propositions which are almost always true. And whenever it is sufficient to know how the great majority of the human race, or of some nation or class of persons, will think, feel, and act, these propositions are equivalent to universal ones. For the purposes of political and social science this *is* sufficient. As we formerly remarked, an approximate generalization is, in social inquiries, for most practical purposes equivalent to an exact one; that which is only probable when asserted of individual human beings indiscriminately selected, being certain when affirmed of the character and collective conduct of masses.

It is no disparagement, therefore, to the science of Human Nature, that those of its general propositions which descend sufficiently into detail to serve as a foundation for predicting phenomena in the concrete, are for the most part only approximately true. But in order to give a genuinely scientific character to the study, it is indispensable that these approximate generalizations, which in themselves would amount only to the lowest kind of empirical laws, should be connected deductively with the laws of nature from which they result; should be resolved into the properties of the causes on which the phenomena depend. In other words, the science of Human Nature may be said to exist in proportion as the approximate truths, which compose a practical knowledge of mankind, can be exhibited as corollaries from the universal laws of human nature on which they rest; whereby the proper limits of those approximate truths would be shown, and we should be enabled to deduce others for any new state of circumstances, in anticipation of specific experience.

The proposition now stated is the text on which the two succeeding chapters will furnish the comment.

CHAPTER IV
OF THE LAWS OF MIND

§ 1. What the Mind is, as well as what Matter is, or any other question respecting Things in themselves, as distinguished from their sensible manifestations, it would be foreign to the purposes of this treatise to consider. Here, as throughout our inquiry, we shall keep clear of all speculations respecting the mind's own nature, and shall understand by the laws of mind those of mental Phenomena; of the various feelings or states of consciousness of sentient beings. These, according to the classification we have uniformly followed, consist of Thoughts, Emotions, Volitions, and Sensations; the last being as truly states of Mind as the three former. It is usual, indeed, to speak of sensations as states of body, not of mind. But this is the common confusion, of giving one and the same name to a phenomenon and to the approximate cause or conditions of the phenomenon. The immediate antecedent of a sensation is a state of body, but the sensation itself is a state of mind. If the word Mind means any thing, it means that which feels. Whatever opinion we hold respecting the fundamental identity or diversity of matter and mind, in any case the distinction between mental and physical facts, between the internal and the external world, will always remain, as a matter of classification; and in that classification, sensations, like all other feelings, must be ranked as mental phenomena. The mechanism of their production, both in the body itself and in what is called outward nature, is all that can with any propriety be classed as physical.

The phenomena of mind, then, are the various feelings of our nature, both those improperly called physical and those peculiarly designated as mental; and by the laws of mind, I mean the laws according to which those feelings generate one another.

§ 2. All states of mind are immediately caused either by other states of mind, or by states of body. When a state of mind is produced by a state of mind, I call the law concerned in the case a law of Mind. When a state of mind is produced directly by a state of body, the law is a law of Body, and belongs to physical science.

With regard to those states of mind which are called sensations, all are agreed that these have for their immediate antecedents, states of body.

Every sensation has for its proximate cause some affection of the portion of our frame called the nervous system, whether this affection originates in the action of some external object, or in some pathological condition of the nervous organization itself. The laws of this portion of our nature—the varieties of our sensations, and the physical conditions on which they proximately depend—manifestly belong to the province of Physiology.

Whether the remainder of our mental states are similarly dependent on physical conditions, is one of the *vexate questiones* in the science of human nature. It is still disputed whether our thoughts, emotions, and volitions are generated through the intervention of material mechanism; whether we have organs of thought and of emotion, in the same sense in which we have organs of sensation. Many eminent physiologists hold the affirmative. These contend that a thought (for example) is as much the result of nervous agency, as a sensation; that some particular state of our nervous system, in particular of that central portion of it called the brain, invariably precedes, and is presupposed by, every state of our consciousness. According to this theory, one state of mind is never really produced by another: all are produced by states of body. When one thought seems to call up another by association, it is not really a thought which recalls a thought; the association did not exist between the two thoughts, but between the two states of the brain or nerves which preceded the thoughts: one of those states recalls the other, each being attended in its passage by the particular state of consciousness which is consequent on it. On this theory the uniformities of succession among states of mind would be mere derivative uniformities, resulting from the laws of succession of the bodily states which cause them. There would be no original mental laws, no Laws of Mind in the sense in which I use the term, at all; and mental science would be a mere branch, though the highest and most recondite branch, of the science of physiology. M. Comte, accordingly, claims the scientific cognizance of moral and intellectual phenomena exclusively for physiologists; and not only denies to Psychology, or Mental Philosophy properly so called, the character of a science, but places it, in the chimerical nature of its objects and pretensions, almost on a par with astrology.

But, after all has been said which can be said, it remains incontestable that there exist uniformities of succession among states of mind, and that these can be ascertained by observation and experiment. Further, that every mental state has a nervous state for its immediate antecedent and proximate cause, though extremely probable, can not hitherto be said to be proved, in the conclusive manner in which this can be proved of sensations; and even were it certain, yet every one must admit that we are wholly ignorant of the characteristics of these nervous states; we know not, and at present have no means of knowing, in what respect one of them differs from another; and our only mode of studying their successions or co-existences must be by observing the successions and co-existences of the mental states, of which they are supposed to be the generators or causes. The successions, therefore, which obtain among mental phenomena, do not admit of being deduced from the physiological laws of our nervous organization; and all real knowledge of them must continue, for a long time at least, if not always, to be sought in the direct study, by observation and experiment, of the mental successions themselves. Since, therefore, the order of our mental phenomena must be studied in those phenomena, and not inferred from the laws of any phenomena more general, there is a distinct and separate Science of Mind.

The relations, indeed, of that science to the science of physiology must never be overlooked or undervalued. It must by no means be forgotten that the laws of mind may be derivative laws resulting from laws of animal life, and that their truth, therefore, may ultimately depend on physical conditions; and the influence of physiological states or physiological changes in altering or counteracting the mental successions, is one of the most important departments of psychological study. But, on the other hand, to reject the resource of psychological analysis, and construct the theory of the mind solely on such data as physiology at present affords, seems to me as great an error in principle, and an even more serious one in practice. Imperfect as is the science of mind, I do not scruple to affirm that it is in a considerably more advanced state than the portion of physiology which corresponds to it; and to discard the former for the latter appears to me an infringement of the true canons of inductive philosophy, which must produce, and which does produce, erroneous conclusions in some very important departments of the science of human nature.

§ 3. The subject, then, of Psychology is the uniformities of succession, the laws, whether ultimate or derivative, according to which one mental state succeeds another; is caused by, or at least, is caused to follow, another. Of these laws some are general, others more special. The following are examples of the most general laws:

First. Whenever any state of consciousness has once been excited in us, no matter by what cause, an inferior degree of the same state of consciousness, a state of consciousness resembling the former, but inferior in intensity, is capable of being reproduced in us, without the presence of any such cause as excited it at first. Thus, if we have once seen or touched an object, we can afterward think of the object though it be absent from our sight or from our touch. If we have been joyful or grieved at some event, we can think of or remember our past joy or grief, though no new event of a happy or painful nature has taken place. When a poet has put together a mental picture of an imaginary object, a Castle of Indolence, a Una, or a Hamlet, he can afterward think of the ideal object he has created, without any fresh act of intellectual combination. This law is expressed by saying, in the language of Hume, that every mental *impression* has its *idea*.

Secondly. These ideas, or secondary mental states, are excited by our impressions, or by other ideas, according to certain laws which are called Laws of Association. Of these laws the first is, that similar ideas tend to excite one another. The second is, that when two impressions have been frequently experienced (or even thought of) either simultaneously or in immediate succession, then whenever one of these impressions, or the idea of it, recurs, it tends to excite the idea of the other. The third law is, that greater intensity in either or both of the impressions is equivalent, in rendering them excitable by one another, to a greater frequency of conjunction. These are the laws of ideas, on which I shall not enlarge in this place, but refer the reader to works professedly psychological, in particular to Mr. James Mill's *Analysis of the Phenomena of the Human Mind,* where the principal laws of association, along with many of their applications, are copiously exemplified, and with a masterly hand.

These simple or elementary Laws of Mind have been ascertained by the ordinary methods of experimental inquiry; nor could they have been ascertained in any other manner. But a certain number of elementary laws having thus been obtained, it is a fair subject of scientific inquiry how far those laws can be made to go in explaining the actual phenomena. It is obvious that complex laws of thought and feeling not only may, but must, be generated from these simple laws. And it is to be remarked, that the case is not always one of Composition of Causes: the effect of concurring causes is not always precisely the sum of the effects of those causes when separate, nor even always an effect of the same kind with them. Reverting to the distinction which occupies so prominent a place in the theory of induction, the laws of the phenomena of mind are sometimes analogous to mechanical, but sometimes also to chemical laws. When many impressions or ideas are operating in the mind together, there sometimes takes place a process of a similar kind to chemical combination. When impressions have been so often experienced in conjunction, that each of them calls up readily and instantaneously the ideas of the whole group, those ideas sometimes melt and coalesce into one another, and appear not several ideas, but one; in the same manner as, when the seven prismatic colors are presented to the eye in rapid succession, the sensation produced is that of white. But as in this last case it is correct to say that the seven colors when they rapidly follow one another *generate* white, but not that they actually *are* white; so it appears to me that the Complex Idea, formed by the blending together of several simpler ones, should, when it really appears simple (that is, when the separate elements are not consciously distinguishable in it), be said to *result from,* or *be generated by,* the simple ideas, not to *consist* of them. Our idea of an orange really *consists* of the simple ideas of a certain color, a certain form, a certain taste and smell, etc., because we can, by interrogating our consciousness, perceive all these elements in the idea. But we can not perceive, in so apparently simple a feeling as our perception of the shape of an object by the eye, all that multitude of ideas derived from other senses, without which it is well ascertained that no such visual perception would ever had existence; nor, in our idea of Extension, can we discover those elementary ideas of resistance, derived from our muscular frame, in which it has been conclusively shown that the idea originates. These, therefore, are cases of mental chemistry; in which it is proper to say that the simple ideas generate, rather than that they compose, the complex ones.

With respect to all the other constituents of the mind, its beliefs, its abstruser conceptions, its sentiments, emotions, and volitions, there are some (among whom are Hartley and the author of the *Analysis*) who think that the whole of these are generated from simple ideas of sensation, by a chemistry similar to that which we have just exemplified. These philosophers have made out a great part of their case, but I am not satisfied that they have established the whole of it. They have shown that there is such a thing as mental chemistry; that the heterogeneous nature of a feeling A, considered in relation to B and C, is

no conclusive argument against its being generated from B and C. Having proved this, they proceed to show, that where A is found, B and C were, or may have been present, and why, therefore, they ask, should not A have been generated from B and C? But even if this evidence were carried to the highest degree of completeness which it admits of; if it were shown (which hitherto it has not, in all cases, been) that certain groups of associated ideas not only might have been, but actually were, present whenever the more recondite mental feeling was experienced; this would amount only to the Method of Agreement, and could not prove causation until confirmed by the more conclusive evidence of the Method of Difference. If the question be whether Belief is a mere case of close association of ideas, it would be necessary to examine experimentally if it be true that any ideas whatever, provided they are associated with the required degree of closeness, give rise to belief. If the inquiry be into the origin of moral feelings, the feeling for example of moral reprobation, it is necessary to compare all the varieties of actions or states of mind which are ever morally disapproved, and see whether in all these cases it can be shown, or reasonably surmised, that the action or state of mind had become connected by association, in the disapproving mind, with some particular class of hateful or disgusting ideas; and the method employed is, thus far, that of Agreement. But this is not enough. Supposing this proved, we must try further by the Method of Difference, whether this particular kind of hateful or disgusting ideas, when it becomes associated with an action previously indifferent, will render that action a subject of moral disapproval. If this question can be answered in the affirmative, it is shown to be a law of the human mind, that an association of that particular description is the generating cause of moral reprobation. That all this is the case has been rendered extremely probable, but the experiments have not been tried with the degree of precision necessary for a complete and absolutely conclusive induction.

It is further to be remembered, that even if all which this theory of mental phenomena contends for could be proved, we should not be the more enabled to resolve the laws of the more complex feelings into those of the simpler ones. The generation of one class of mental phenomena from another, whenever it can be made out, is a highly interesting fact in psychological chemistry; but it no more supersedes the necessity of an experimental study of the generated phenomenon, than a knowledge of the properties of oxygen and sulphur enables us to deduce those of sulphuric acid without specific observation and experiment. Whatever, therefore, may be the final issue of the attempt to account for the origin of our judgments, our desires, or our volitions, from simpler mental phenomena, it is not the less imperative to ascertain the sequences of the complex phenomena themselves, by special study in conformity to the canons of Induction. Thus, in respect to Belief, psychologists will always have to inquire what beliefs we have by direct consciousness, and according to what laws one belief produces another; what are the laws in virtue of which one thing is recognized by the mind, either rightly or erroneously, as evidence of another thing. In regard to Desire, they will have to examine what objects we desire naturally, and by what causes we are made to desire things originally indifferent, or even disagreeable to us; and so forth. It may be remarked that the general laws of association prevail among these more intricate states of mind, in the same manner as among the simpler ones. A desire, an emotion, an idea of the higher order of abstraction, even our judgments and volitions, when they have become habitual, are called up by association, according to precisely the same laws as our simple ideas.

§ 4. In the course of these inquiries, it will be natural and necessary to examine how far the production of one state of mind by another is influenced by any assignable state of body. The commonest observation shows that different minds are susceptible in very different degrees to the action of the same psychological causes. The idea, for example, of a given desirable object will excite in different minds very different degrees of intensity of desire. The same subject of meditation, presented to different minds, will excite in them very unequal degrees of intellectual action. These differences of mental susceptibility in different individuals may be, first, original and ultimate facts; or, secondly, they may be consequences of the previous mental history of those individuals; or, thirdly and lastly, they may depend on varieties of physical organization. That the previous mental history of the individuals must have some share in producing or in modifying the whole of their mental character, is an inevitable consequence of the laws of mind; but that differences of bodily structure also co-operate, is the opinion of all physiologists, confirmed by common experience. It is to be regretted that hitherto this experience, being accepted in the gross, without due analysis, has been made the groundwork of empirical generalizations most detrimental to the progress of real knowledge.

It is certain that the natural differences which really exist in the mental predispositions or susceptibilities of different persons are often not unconnected with diversities in their organic constitution. But it does not therefore follow that these organic differences must in all cases influence the mental phenomena directly and immediately. They often affect them through the medium of their psychological causes. For example, the idea of some particular pleasure may excite in different persons, even independently of habit or education, very different strengths of desire, and this may be the effect of their different degrees or kinds of nervous susceptibility; but these organic differences, we must remember, will render the pleasurable sensation itself more intense in one of these persons than in the other; so that the idea of the pleasure will also be an intenser feeling, and will, by the operation of mere mental laws, excite an intenser desire, without its being necessary to suppose that the desire itself is directly influenced by the physical peculiarity. As in this, so in many cases, such differences in the kind or in the intensity of the physical sensations as must necessarily result from differences of bodily organization, will of themselves account for many differences not only in the degree, but even in the kind, of the other mental phenomena. So true is this, that even different *qualities* of mind, different types of mental character, will naturally be produced by mere differences of intensity in the sensations generally; as is well pointed out in the able essay on Dr. Priestley, by Mr. Martineau, mentioned in a former chapter:

"The sensations which form the elements of all knowledge are received either simultaneously or successively: when several are received simultaneously, as the smell, the taste, the color, the form, etc., of a fruit, their association together constitutes our idea of an *object;* when received successively, their association makes up the idea of an *event.* Any thing, then, which favors the associations of synchronous ideas will tend to produce a knowledge of objects, a perception of qualities; while any thing which favors association in the successive order, will tend to produce a knowledge of events, of the order of occurrences, and of the connection of cause and effect: in other words, in the one case a perceptive mind, with a discriminate feeling of the pleasurable and painful properties of things, a sense of the grand and the beautiful will be the result: in the other, a mind attentive to the movements and phenomena, a ratiocinative and philosophic intellect. Now it is an acknowledged principle, that all sensations experienced during the presence of any vivid impression become strongly associated with it, and with each other; and does it not follow that the synchronous feelings of a sensitive constitution (*i.e.,* the one which has vivid impressions) will be more intimately blended than in a differently formed mind? If this suggestion has any foundation in truth, it leads to an inference not unimportant; that where nature has endowed an individual with great original susceptibility, he will probably be distinguished by fondness for natural history, a relish for the beautiful and great, and moral enthusiasm; where there is but a mediocrity of sensibility, a love of science, of abstract truth, with a deficiency of taste and of fervor, is likely to be the result."

We see from this example, that when the general laws of mind are more accurately known, and, above all, more skillfully applied to the detailed explanation of mental peculiarities, they will account for many more of those peculiarities than is ordinarily supposed. Unfortunately the reaction of the last and present generation against the philosophy of the eighteenth century has produced a very general neglect of this great department of analytical inquiry; of which, consequently, the recent progress has been by no means proportional to its early promise. The majority of those who speculate on human nature prefer dogmatically to assume that the mental differences which they perceive, or think they perceive, among human beings, are ultimate facts, incapable of being either explained or altered, rather than take the trouble of fitting themselves, by the requisite processes of thought, for referring those mental differences to the outward causes by which they are for the most part produced, and on the removal of which they would cease to exist. The German school of metaphysical speculation, which has not yet lost its temporary predominance in European thought, has had this among many other injurious influences; and at the opposite extreme of the psychological scale, no writer, either of early or of recent date, is chargeable in a higher degree with this aberration from the true scientific spirit, than M. Comte.

It is certain that, in human beings at least, differences in education and in outward circumstances are capable of affording an adequate explanation of by far the greatest portion of character; and that the remainder may be in great part accounted for by physical differences in the sensations produced in different individuals by the same external or internal cause. There are, however, some mental facts which do not seem to admit of these modes of explanation. Such, to take the strongest case, are the various instincts of animals, and the portion of human nature which corresponds to those instincts. No mode has been suggested, even by way of hypothesis, in which these can receive any satisfactory, or even plausible, explanation from psychological causes alone; and there is great reason to think that they have as positive, and even as direct and immediate, a connection with physical conditions of the brain and nerves as any of our mere sensations have. A supposition which (it is perhaps not superfluous to add) in no way conflicts with the indisputable fact that these instincts may be modified to any extent, or entirely conquered, in human beings, and to no inconsiderable extent even in some of the domesticated animals, by other mental influences, and by education.

Whether organic causes exercise a direct influence over any other classes of mental phenomena, is hitherto as far from being ascertained as is the precise nature of the organic conditions even in the case of instincts. The physiology, however, of the brain and nervous system is in a state of such rapid advance, and is continually bringing forth such new and interesting results, that if there be really a connection between mental peculiarities and any varieties cognizable by our senses in the structure of the cerebral and nervous apparatus, the nature of that connection is now in a fair way of being found out. The latest discoveries in cerebral physiology appear to have proved that any such connection which may exist is of a radically different character from that contended for by Gall and his followers, and that, whatever may hereafter be found to be the true theory of the subject, phrenology at least is untenable.

CHAPTER V
OF ETHOLOGY, OR THE SCIENCE OF THE FORMATION OF CHARACTER

§ 1. The laws of mind as characterized in the preceding chapter, compose the universal or abstract portion of the philosophy of human nature; and all the truths of common experience, constituting a practical knowledge of mankind, must, to the extent to which they are truths, be results or consequences of these. Such familiar maxims, when collected a *posteriori* from observation of life, occupy among the truths of the science the place of what, in our analysis of Induction, have so often been spoken of under the title of Empirical Laws.

An Empirical Law (it will be remembered) is a uniformity, whether of succession or of coexistence, which holds true in all instances within our limits of observation, but is not of a nature to afford any assurance that it would hold beyond those limits; either because the consequent is not really the effect of the antecedent, but forms part along with it of a chain of effects flowing from prior causes not yet ascertained, or because there is ground to believe that the sequence (though a case of causation) is resolvable into simpler sequences, and, depending therefore on a concurrence of several natural agencies, is exposed to an unknown multitude of possibilities of counteraction. In other words, an empirical law is a generalization, of which, not content with finding it true, we are obliged to ask, why is it true? Knowing that its truth is not absolute, but dependent on some more general conditions, and that it can only be relied on in so far as there is ground of assurance that those conditions are realized.

Now, the observations concerning human affairs collected from common experience are precisely of this nature. Even if they were universally and exactly true within the bounds of experience, which they never are, still they are not the ultimate laws of human action; they are not the principles of human nature, but results of those principles under the circumstances in which mankind have happened to be placed. When the Psalmist "said in his haste that all men are liars," he enunciated what in some ages and countries is borne out by ample experience; but it is not a law of man's nature to lie; though it is one of the consequences of the laws of human nature, that lying is nearly universal when certain external circumstances exist universally, especially circumstances productive of habitual distrust and fear. When the character of the old is asserted to be cautious, and of the young impetuous, this, again, is but an empirical law; for it is not because of their youth that the young are impetuous, nor because of their age that the old are cautious. It is chiefly, if not wholly, because the old, during their many years of life, have generally had much experience of its various evils, and having suffered or seen others suffer much from incautious exposure to them, have acquired associations favorable to circumspection; while the young, as well from the absence of similar experience as from the greater strength of the inclinations which urge them to enterprise, engage themselves in it more readily. Here, then, is the *explanation* of the empirical law; here are the conditions which ultimately determine whether the law holds good or not. If an old man has not been oftener than most young men in contact with danger and difficulty, he will be equally in-

cautious; if a youth has not stronger inclinations than an old man, he probably will be as little enterprising. The empirical law derives whatever truth it has from the causal laws of which it is a consequence. If we know those laws, we know what are the limits to the derivative law; while, if we have not yet accounted for the empirical law—if it rests only on observation—there is no safety in applying it far beyond the limits of time, place, and circumstance in which the observations were made.

The really scientific truths, then, are not these empirical laws, but the causal laws which explain them. The empirical laws of those phenomena which depend on known causes, and of which a general theory can therefore be constructed, have, whatever may be their value in practice, no other function in science than that of verifying the conclusions of theory. Still more must this be the case when most of the empirical laws amount, even within the limits of observation, only to approximate generalizations.

The Philosopher and Society: John Locke and the English Revolution

Martha E. Moore-Russell

Most studies of John Locke's thought follow what might be called the Platonic tradition, in which the content of philosophy is identified with a transcendent realm of ideal forms. Systematic philosophers have hunted for the formal consistency within and between his works in order to make unitary statements about this thought. And historians have looked for connections between the man and some ethereal cloud of disembodied ideas existing in the culture. Whether it is called the *Zeitgeist,* the intellectual milieu, or the

climate of opinion, the characterization is the same. Ideas are given a life of their own, rising up out of an intellectual heritage, reflecting the times, and living on to influence the thought of a future age. In the words of Basil Willey, for example, "Locke summed up in his work the doctrines and assumptions of the seventeenth century, and his great influence imposed them bodily on the eighteenth as unquestionable truths."[1]

There is a great deal of insight and wisdom in the Platonic view. Locke did borrow from contemporary currents of thought, and there is probably consistency, at some level of analysis, which unifies his thinking on various subjects. But as an explanation of his intellectual development, this view is incomplete. It leaves out the

Moore-Russell, M. E. (1978). The philosopher and society: John Locke and the English revolution. *Journal of the History of the Behavioral Sciences, 14,* 65–73. Copyright © 1978 by the Clinical Psychology Publishing Company. Reprinted by permission of the publisher and the author.

influence of social and political factors, and it does not consider how Locke changed ideas in using them. What I hope to accomplish is to redress the impersonality of the traditional approach. In its extreme form, it looks at cognition as a frozen slice of form and logic. It takes philosophy out of the head of a thinking human being and endows it with properties which have little to do with social and political life. The point of view I shall advance is not an alternative to the history of ideas, but rather an attempt to formulate the psychology of that historical process. I take the view that philosophy, like all thinking, takes place in the person and that the way in which social and political life influences the person is through his efforts to understand it. I will call this approach the "person-in-society" approach. So, instead of examining the cogency and internal consistency of Locke's philosophy, I will look at it as one man's construction of his social and political context.

In particular, I will analyze some works which Locke never published. They were written between 1660 and 1664, some three decades before the publication of the celebrated *Essay Concerning Human Understanding* (1690) and the *Treatises of Government* (1690). The first part of the present article analyzes two tracts concerned with the power of the government to determine the ceremonial aspects of religious worship.[2] The objective is to make three points: first, that one of the central functions of the tracts (which concern an otherwise abstract issue) was to make sense out of the social and political turmoil following the English Revolution and the restoration of the Stuart monarchy in 1660; second, that the tracts contain both the traditional Scholastic ideas derived from his classical Oxford education, and the beginnings of the modern view expressed in his major works three decades later; and finally, that the former presupposed the passing feudal system of society while the latter presupposed the modern one. Loosely speaking, what I mean by "modern view" is the essential idea of British liberalism and empiricism: that the individual has within himself the power to act on his own and in his own right.

The second part of this article analyzes eight essays on the law of nature where Locke recognized the contradictions between the social structure presupposed by his traditional views and the society in which he perceived himself.[3] The objective of this part will be to show that in his efforts to understand his social and political context, Locke formulated the epistemological issue of the *Essay,* the issue of innate ideas versus sense perception as the basis of knowledge. I will also endeavor to point out the implications of the person-in-society approach for some current interpretations of Locke's epistemology and political theories.

In the tracts on government, what seems to have been most disturbing to Locke about the Revolution was the disintegration of a familiar social structure. In seventeenth-century England, a system which presumed duty and conscience as the basis of civil society gave way to one based upon the voluntary consent of rational individuals acting each in his own right.[4] Individual initiative became important as a component of social life. But in 1660, Locke saw individual initiative as the ambitious self-interest which had caused an extended crisis in human affairs.[5] Referring to the previous eighteen years of civil war and social disorder, Locke wrote:

> I no sooner perceived myself in the *world* but I found myself in a storm, which hath lasted almost hitherto,... And I would men would be persuaded to be so kind to their *religion,* their *country* and *themselves* as not to hazard again the substantial blessings of *peace* and *settlement* in an overzealous contention about things which they themselves confess to be little and at most are but indifferent.[6]

Of special interest in the tracts are Locke's contradictory assumptions about the structure of society. One structure that he presumed to exist was composed of the continuous hierarchy of authority of feudal society. The other was composed of dissociated individuals. The assumption of individuals, each having the power to act in his own right, underlies his views on reason, will, and Christian piety. He believed that each man was an entire authority unto himself in religious and moral matters; that each man possessed an autonomous will directed by personal ambitions; and that each was the center of an active "inner worship of the heart."[7] Immediately following the Restoration and what appeared to be an uncertain peace, Locke constructed contemporary history in these terms. Because of the civil disasters which he attributed to man's individualistic nature, he argued for the absolute and arbitrary power of the government. "Allowing every man by nature as large a liberty as he himself can wish," he wrote, "[I] shall yet make it appear that whilst there is society, government and order in the world, rulers still must have the power of all things indifferent."[8]

Human reason appeared to Locke to be fragmented into isolated centers of cognition like Descartes's solitary *cogito*. Each had the power by itself of apprehending, or misapprehending, truth. And this view of a fragmented human rationality is central to his understanding of the social and political turmoil. According to Locke, the Revolution had been caused by the diversity and pugnacity of men's personal opinions. "Indeed," he wrote, "[I have] observed that almost all those tragical revolutions which have exercised Christendom these many years have turned upon this hinge."[9] Opinions, he said, men took to themselves with as little thought as they took their wives, defending both for no other reason than that they were theirs. When civil laws had not had the "luck to square with a man's private judgment," they lost their moral force. And even though England was exhausted from the clash of opinions and arms, there was hardly anyone who could participate in controversies without imagining his own interests to be seriously at stake.[10] Even Locke would not have his own understanding, "the noblest part," imposed upon. He asserted the right to hold his own opinion and to

dissent from others' defense of Christian liberty.[11] So Locke felt a kinship with those of his contemporaries who were aggressively opinionated in matters of religion and politics.

Just as human understanding was fragmented into as many opinions as there were men, so too was the human will. Locke observed that men were possessed of "ambitious thoughts and discontented minds, the greatest part not satisfied with their own condition." To them liberty meant a "liberty for ambition to pull down well-framed constitutions, that out of its ruins they [might] build themselves fortunes."[12] Once again, what is of interest is the view of an ambitious, *self-centered* will.

Christian piety was solitary and assertive too. Locke stated that while some held the view that divine worship was the same thing as religion, it was "more correctly understood as being the actions of the inner virtues." The inner depths of the soul were a shrine dedicated to God's worship, completely hidden from the eyes of other men. Each soul had the power to express itself in certain outward performances, such as public prayer, acts of thanksgiving, and the singing of psalms. And the outward acts of the soul's inner powers were required because God was not satisfied with the "silent and almost furtive form of worship alone."[13]

So it was that, in his views on reason, will, and piety, Locke expressed an atomistic and instrumental conception of the human faculties. But in the tracts, he also stated the contradictory view of a unitary rationality. This was "right reason" according to Stoic philosophy, or the law of nature. And it was superior to any one man's simple reason. It was delivered to men as a rule and pattern of living. This universal law, "the foundation of all moral good and evil," was known merely by the light of reason implanted in men. It provided the mutual understanding through which social order maintained itself.[14]

What is significant about the law of nature as a construction of society is that it described the stable structure of an agrarian, feudal society which was based upon duty and conscience. Being universal and eternal, it referred to a system in which ultimate authority rested beyond any one man's ability to change it. For the most part, men agreed on fundamentals, and the culture was fairly homogeneous. All of this had been a fairly reasonable construction of reality, in Christendom, before the spiritual individualism of the Reformation and the emergence of contentious Protestant sects. The feudal construction of society does appear in the tracts on government, but it is explicitly examined in eight essays on the law of nature written at about the same time. So let us examine these essays, and the way in which they show Locke's efforts to understand the revolutionary changes in society as he saw them.

The main point of the essays is that the law of nature can be known, and that all men are obliged to obey it. But Locke's argument on its behalf is not convincing. He failed to resolve the contradictions which presented themselves in his own reasoning between the feudal social structure described in the law of nature, and the fragmented, pluralistic, mercantile society in which he lived. In his own estimation, the law of nature was not explanatory, but he asserted it nonetheless, saying, "In spite of these objections we maintain that the binding force of the law of nature is perpetual and universal."[15]

One of the contradictions Locke uncovered concerned the supposed orderliness dictated by the law of nature, on the one hand, and the apparent disorder in the world of experience, on the other. Referring to the order dictated by the law of nature, Locke wrote that it was by God's order "that the heaven revolves in unbroken rotation, the earth stands fast and the stars shine, and it is He who has set the bounds even to the wild sea and prescribed to every kind of plants the manner and periods of germination and growth; it is in obedience to His will that all living things have their own laws of birth and life."[16] Citing Aristotle's *Nicomachean Ethics* as his authority, Locke wrote that everything had a special kind of work it was designed to perform

and that "the proper function of man is acting in conformity with reason, so much so that man must of necessity perform what reason prescribes."[17]

Yet, in spite of the supposed universal rationality of human nature, Locke noted that most people live as though there were no rational ground in life at all. Some men, he wrote:

> brought up in vice, can scarcely distinguish between good and evil, because a bad way of life, becoming strong by lapse of time, has established barbarous habits, and evil customs have perverted matters of principle.... For how few there are who in matters of daily practise or matters easy to know surrender themselves to the jurisdiction of reason or follow its lead, when, either led astray by the violence of passions or being indifferent through carelessness or degenerate through habit, they follow the inducements of pleasure or the urges of their base instincts rather than the dictates of reason.[18]

Here Locke attributed the crisis in society to the disparate urges of self-centered hedonism; as a concept of motivation, these drives had causal power in the mechanical sense, as opposed to the traditional sense of formal cause. In the quoted passage, there is the construction of society as a social arrangement in which men surrendered themselves in conformity with reason. Alongside is that of a society composed of independent and self-interested individuals. But only the latter seemed to explain the disordered state of affairs in society. To the extent that self-interested individualism had caused the social and political upheaval in mid-seventeenth-century England, the law of nature referred to an arrangement which existed only in the society's collective memory.

The second contradiction that Locke uncovered concerned the supposed innateness of the law, on the one hand, and the apparent lack of consensus about the law, on the other. Locke's nativism followed the Aristotelian notion that man's nature was acting in conformity with the rational principle, and the Cambridge Platonist notion that the law was an inward law, given.

Yet, he noted, "there are some who make no use of the light of reason but prefer darkness."[19] Furthermore, even the most rational did not absolutely agree as to what the law was, since it was about this law that the parties of men contended so fiercely. As Locke saw it, there was a problem, "If indeed natural law is discernible by the light of reason, why is it that not all people who possess reason have knowledge of it?"[20]

In subsequent essays Locke tried to reconcile an innate understanding of first principles with the independence of mind he felt in himself and in others. In the second essay, he stated vaguely "that there is some sort of truth...a man can attain by himself and without the aid of another."[21] Then, he reversed his earlier position on the innateness of the law, even though innateness would be "an easy and very convenient way of knowing."[22] Instead, he said that it would be sufficient for his purposes to prove that a man could attain knowledge if he made proper use of his faculties; whereupon he asserted that sense perception was the basis of knowledge.[23]

> But since we are searching now for the principle and origin of the knowledge of this law and for the way in which it becomes known to mankind, I declare that the foundation of all knowledge is derived from those things which we perceive through the senses. From these things, then, reason and the power of arguing, which are distinctive marks of man, advance to the notion of the maker of these things (there being no lack of arguments in this direction such as are necessarily derived from the matter, motion and visible structure and arrangement of this world) and at last they conclude and establish for themselves as certain that some Deity is the author of all these things. As soon as this is laid down, the notion of a universal law binding on all men necessarily emerges.[24]

With respect to the previous quotation, I would like to pause to consider some of the implications of the person-in-society approach I have advanced for traditional interpretations of Locke's philosophy. Up until this point in his thinking, Locke had not stated, nor even assumed, a materialist ontology underlying his psychology. Yet historians have often said that his psychology took its formal structure from the mechanical theories of seventeenth-century science, and that, in its mature form around 1690, it was the philosophical counterpart of Newton's *Principia* (1687). Still another interpretation is that Locke's political philosophy was a rationalization of the Glorious Revolution of 1688.[25]

Except for the coincidence of events around 1690, these interpretations leave much unaccounted for. As we have seen, Locke had begun to formulate the individualistic theories of his later liberalism more than two decades before the Glorious Revolution. And he had begun to do so when society was given up to anarchy, divine-right monarchy being seen as the only solution. In this situation, Locke could not have anticipated the *constitutional* monarchy which his mature political theories are supposed to have justified. Furthermore, we have Locke's own testimony that an individualistic view of society explained the social and political events of the time, while the universalist view did not. In addition, we have seen that Locke had formulated an atomistic, mechanical view of human nature before he had assimilated the materialist philosophy of the experimental scientists.[26] There is no a priori reason why a construction of the physical world in terms of forces and pieces of matter in motion is prior to a construction of the social and political world in terms of powers and divided individuals. What seems clear is that Locke's mechanical theories of human nature were a construction of experience, and not merely ideas appropriated from the scientific milieu. The fact that there is a formal similarity between scientific and political theories in this period is simply an insufficient explanation of either.

Another interpretation, which does account for the complex interrelationships between seventeenth century thought and their social and political context, is as follows. Elementaristic and mechanical conceptions of matter, intellect, and society made sense in the seventeenth century. *Varieties* of mechanical views were formulated by men of affairs such as Locke, as they interacted in the material and social world they were creating. So Locke's intellectual achievement was at once personal and social. What he did was to adapt various contemporary ideas in order to construct a veridical representation of the society in which he participated. He filled out the fine detail of this representation in a densely articulated cognitive structure in which epistemology, political philosophy, even ethics and theology, intertwined in a complex network of ideas. The power of autonomous individuals, which he had perceived in 1660 to have caused a violent revolution, was perceived in 1690 as the basis of a reasonable government by consent. By then, Locke and many of his contemporaries had more or less come to terms with the exercise of individual initiative in society.

Let me return to some further considerations on the essays on the law of nature. In the essays, sense-empiricism was a convincing argument of positive knowledge because it gave the capacity for understanding to the individual. It explained how he was able to figure out a moral plan of action for himself. In the fourth essay, "Can Reason Attain the Knowledge of Natural Law through Sense-Experience? Yes." Locke remarked that some men had proved that there was a deity from the testimony of the conscience, and some had proved it from the innate idea of God, but neither of these proofs derived its force from men's inborn faculties. Arguing on behalf of man's capacity to attain knowledge by himself, Locke stated that the senses introduced the ideas of objects into the deep recesses of the mind. Then, reason could advance to things unknown by arguing from one thing to another in a definite and fixed order of propositions. From the beauty, order, array, and motion of objects, the mind could undoubtedly infer that there must be a powerful and wise creator who had a just and inevitable command over man. And the mind could infer the rule of his duty from his own constitution and faculties.[27]

These statements are significant for the underlying assumptions about the structure of society. There is, on the one hand, the idea of an a priori principle of duty enforced by the conscience. This notion presumed a society in which men interacted predictably with one another because they shared a mutual understanding of each other's given role and status. On the other hand, the epistemological assumptions of sense-empiricism, *viz.*, that the mind is ontologically isolated from the object of knowledge, and that each man attains knowledge by himself, presumed a society of independent individuals. In such an arrangement, individual initiative was presumed to determine each man's status. The fact that the mixture is unreconciled suggests that social relations were uncertain in the years following the Revolution, when Locke wrote these essays. Or perhaps it suggests only that Locke was unsure as to the basis of social relations. His uncertainty is further evidenced in the fluctuating status he gives to innate ideas, for in spite of his flat rejection of innate ideas in the fourth essay referred to earlier in this article, Locke switches his view yet again when he writes that the precepts of nature are imprinted on the soul and "the same in everyone of us."[28]

So, to sum up and conclude, taking the point of view of the person-in-society we have said that the development of Locke's philosophic thought is a psychological question and does not belong exclusively to a Platonic realm of ideas. It was one man's active, complex, and often contradictory construction of seventeenth-century life. The tracts on government and the essays on the law of nature argue unconvincingly for a disintegrating system of social interaction based upon mutual understanding. This construction had been appropriate to small agrarian communities where members agreed on the presence of an unalterable hierarchy of authority. But Locke's argument on behalf of this view is not convincing. Throughout the tracts and essays he had noted ways in which men had not acted accordingly, but had acted on their own initiative and in their own interest. To him, the English Revolution had been a "most unhappy lesson" because it had shown how disruptive ambitious self-interest could be.

NOTES

1 Basil Willey, *The Seventeenth Century Background* (London: Chatto & Windus, 1946), p. 291.

2 John Locke, *Two Tracts on Government,* ed. Philip Abrams (Cambridge: University Press, 1967).

3 John Locke, *Essays on the Law of Nature,* ed. W. von Leyden (Oxford: Clarendon Press, 1958).

4 In *Society and Puritanism in Pre-Revolutionary England* (London: Secker & Warburg, 1964), pp. 381–418, Christopher Hill has advanced the thesis that there was a transition between 1590 and 1642 from a civil society based upon conscience enforced through the taking of oaths to one based upon interest. And C. B. MacPherson has advanced the view that English political thought in the seventeenth to the nineteenth centuries has assumed a society of disconnected individuals; MacPherson's interpretation emphasizes the possessive quality of individualism in Locke's *Treatises* as evidence of a market economy in the seventeenth century. See his *The Political Theory of Possessive Individualism: Hobbes to Locke* (Oxford: Clarendon Press, 1962), pp. 194–262.

5 The English Revolution may have been the most cataclysmic single event of what many historians have come to view as a period of general "crisis" throughout Europe. H. R. Trevor-Roper has argued, for example, that it was the most violent of the mid-century power struggles between the Renaissance monarchies and the gentry classes, and that it owed its particular severity to the fact that the English Court was the most overgrown, most obstinate, and yet the frailest in Europe. See "The General Crisis of the Seventeenth Century," in *Crisis in Europe, 1560–1660,* ed. Trevor Aston (Garden City, N.Y.: Doubleday, 1965), pp. 100–102. According to E. J. Hobsbawm, the Revolution erupted because the conditions and structure of feudal or agrarian society stood in the way of the revolutionizing forces of capitalism. It was, he believes, the first complete bourgeois revolution from which modern capitalism emerged, and consequently, it was the most dramatic incident of the general European crisis. See "The Crisis of the Seventeenth Century," ibid., pp. 29, 33, 57. More recently, Lawrence Stone has advanced the thesis that the Revolution was brought about by the rise of social tensions between traditional power elites:

between Puritans and Anglicans, between the landed classes and the Crown, and between new London mercantile interests and the entrenched commercial oligarchy. See his *The Causes of the English Revolution,* 1529–1642 (New York: Harper & Row, 1972), p. 30.

6 John Locke, "Preface to the Reader," in *Two Tracts on Government,* p. 119. Hereinafter cited as "Preface."

7 John Locke, "Whether the civil magistrate may incorporate indifferent things into the ceremonies of divine worship and impose them on the people: Confirmed," trans. from the Latin text by Philip Abrams, in *Two Tracts on Government,* p. 214. Hereinafter cited as "Second Tract."

8 John Locke, "Question: Whether the civil magistrate may lawfully impose and determine the use of indifferent things in reference to religious worship." In *Two Tracts on Government,* ibid., p. 123.

9 Ibid., p. 160.

10 "Second Tract," p. 210.

11 "Preface," p. 122.

12 Ibid., p. 121.

13 "Second Tract," p. 212.

14 Ibid., p. 222.

15 John Locke, "Is the Binding Force of the Law of Nature Perpetual and Universal? Yes," in *Essays on the Law of Nature,* p. 193.

16 John Locke, "Is There a Rule of Morals, or Law of Nature Given to Us? Yes," in *Essays on the Law of Nature,* p. 109.

17 Ibid., p. 113.

18 Ibid., p. 115.

19 Ibid., p. 115.

20 Ibid., pp. 111–115.

21 John Locke, "Can the Law of Nature Be Known by the Light of Nature? Yes, in *Essays on the Law of Nature,* p. 123.

22 Ibid., p. 127.

23 Ibid., p. 131.

24 Ibid., p. 133.

25 Christopher Hill, for example, summarizes Locke's place in history as follows: "Locke began as a political supporter of Shaftesbury, and followed him into political exile. Yet he was no democrat, and happily accepted 1688 as the revolution to end revolutions. He and Isaac Newton were the backroom boys of the Whig Junto. Locke associated with the scientists, and attempted in his *Es-*

say Concerning Human Understanding, to establish a materialist psychology that would reconcile science and Christianity.'' *The Century of Revolution, 1603–1714* (Edinburgh: Thomas Nelson, 1961), p. 295. The atomism, mechanism, and materialism of the experimental scientists of the Oxford ''experimental philosophical clubbe'' is exemplified in the work of Robert Boyle. See, for example, his *The Excellency and Grounds of the Mechanical Hypothesis* (London, 1674).

26 In addition to lack of evidence that Locke had assimilated the materialism of Boyle and the other Oxford experimentalists, it appears that he was more inclined in his medical studies to a Paracelsian approach in terms of reactions, substances, and principles than toward the mechanical ap-

proach. And we also know that he did not join the experimental work of exponents of the mechanical philosophy until around 1662, although Boyle had returned to Oxford from travels on the Continent in 1660. See Kenneth Dewhurst, *John Locke (1632–1704), Physician and Philosopher: A Medical Biography* (London: Wellcome Historical Medical Library, 1963), pp. 4–8. The genesis of Locke's interest and involvement in the Oxford ''experimental philosophical clubbe'' is a study that would be worth doing.

27 John Locke, ''Can Reason Attain the Knowledge of Natural Law through Sense-Experience? Yes,'' in *Essays on the Law of Nature,* pp. 149–155.

28 John Locke, ''Can the Law of Nature Be Known from the General Consent of Men? No,'' in *Essays on the Law of Nature,* p. 167.

The Fate and Influence of John Stuart Mill's Proposed Science of Ethology

David E. Leary

The years between 1840 and 1940 constituted an important period in the history of the human sciences. During this period, under the impulse of cataclysmic social events and the inspiration of rapid development in the physical and biological sciences, the previously existing ''moral sciences'' underwent radical development, and other new human sciences were proposed and formulated for the first time. In the early part of this crucial period in the history of the modern human sciences, few works were as important as John Stuart Mill's *System of Logic* (1843), which culminated in the well-known Book VI, entitled ''On the Logic of the Moral Sciences.''[1] This work attempted to bring rigorous thinking to the human sciences, especially as regards methods and standards of proof. It was both an indication

Leary, D. E. (1982). The fate and influence of John Stuart Mill's proposed science of ethology. *Journal of the History of Ideas, 43,* 153–162. Copyright © 1982 by the Journal of the History of Ideas. Reprinted by permission of the publisher and the author.

of, and an influence upon, the developing self-consciousness with which nineteenth-century investigators sought to bring human affairs within the purview of strictly scientific procedures. Going through numerous editions—eight in Mill's own lifetime—the work was a best seller for the rest of the nineteenth century.

No matter what the impact of the work as a whole, however, and of Book VI in particular, its central proposal regarding the development of a science of human character seems to have been virtually ignored, and thus Mill's plea for a science of Ethology, as he called it, seems to have been one of the many nineteenth-century proposals which did not pass the test of history. This paper is an attempt to answer the question, whatever became of Mill's Ethology? This will not be an entirely antiquarian question if in answering it we can detect an important influence on the development of the human sciences. And indeed it is the thesis of this paper that we can locate such an influence.

I. MILL'S PROGRAM AND ITS INITIAL FAILURE

In Chapter 5 of Book VI in his *Logic,* Mill argued that there was a great need for a "science of the formation of character." This science, which he termed Ethology, would be the science of human nature which Psychology itself could not provide. According to his suggested division of labor, Psychology would be the science for discovering the universal laws of mind, whereas Ethology would be the science entrusted with the task of explaining particular individual minds, or characters, according to the general laws provided by Psychology. Ethology too would have its laws, but they would be derivative; that is, they would be deduced from the universal laws of Psychology.

In Mill's view, any individual character, or the collective character of any group of people, must be explained in terms of the application of universal laws to particular circumstances. The reason people differ is not that they operate according to different principles. The principles—for Mill, the laws of association—are the same for all; but differences arise from the circumstances in which people find themselves. Ethology is the science which seeks to explain the practical, or circumstantial, application of the general laws of mind. Being a true science, its laws are necessarily universal. But its applications to individual cases will never be exact for the simple reason that we can never fully determine all the factors which have entered into a given person's life history. The goal which Mill proposed, therefore, was that Ethology be developed to a point where the best possible predictions could be made regarding the "tendencies" which different characters would exhibit in certain circumstances. Only when this was done could the moral and social sciences be developed to any degree of theoretical and practical utility.

Mill's proposed science of Ethology was well known since his *Logic* was widely read for decades, but though the *Logic* went through a number of editions in which various parts were changed, the section on Ethology was never essentially modified or further developed. His own attempt to develop a science of Ethology was never made. As he wrote to Alexander Bain in late 1843, "I do not know when I shall be ripe for beginning 'Ethology.' The scheme has not assumed any definite shape with me yet."[2] In fact, as Bain reports, Mill's scheme "never came to anything; and he seems shortly to have dropped thinking of it."[3] And with this failure to develop an Ethology, Mill had also to give up his hope of writing a work on Sociology because he was convinced that "there is no chance, for [a science of] Social Statics at least, until the laws of human character are better treated."[4] Since the development of Sociology had been a major goal of Mill's, we can only conclude that he met with insuperable difficulties in trying to develop his Ethology.

It is not too difficult to pinpoint some of the specific problems that Mill encountered. For one thing, the possibility of a deductive science of Ethology depended upon the prior existence of an apodictic, systematic Psychology. In his *Logic* Mill had been very confident about the existence of such a science. We may reasonably assume that Mill soon discovered how unreasonably sanguine that opinion was. Secondly, not only was Mill overly confident about the state of certainty which Psychology could offer, but beyond that he had in mind a grossly inadequate Psychology; his brand of associationism was in its last days. His own protégé, Alexander Bain, whom he soon acknowledged as his superior in psychological matters, was instrumental in bringing about the transformation of Psychology in Britain from an introspective to a biological science. Whereas Mill thought of psychological laws in terms of the interaction of ideas, Bain and the next generation became aware of the vast amount of recent research on the brain and nervous system and were beginning to realize the need to integrate this new knowledge into the science of Psychology. And with the advent of the age of Darwin, psychological thinking was increasingly done not only by employing biological metaphors but also by utilizing biological factors. These developments were in marked contrast to Mill's approach in the *Logic,* in which organismic factors played a very negligible role.[5] Mill's psychology was excessively intellectualistic. He spoke of the laws of *mind,* whereas any viable science of character, as Gordon Allport has pointed out, must "account for the galaxy of human interests, motives, conflicts, and passions which are the essential forces in the formation of character."[6]

Finally, Mill's proposed methodology proved to be impracticable. A deductive science which also claimed to deal with the empirical events of everyday life was simply impossible. Even if an adequate Psychology had been in existence, it is difficult to imagine how one could simply deduce a science of human character. One's deductions would always have to be made with an eye on the type of human character to be explained. Mill himself recognized this fact and subsequently allowed for the necessity of arriving inductively at some kind of empirical propositions regarding the human character-types that were then to be explained deductively. Nevertheless his proposed methodology still depended too heavily upon deduction rather than upon empirical observation.

In summary, then, the development of a science of character demanded a more systematic, more biological, more emotionally oriented, and more empirical psychology. In addition to these four weaknesses in Mill's program, there were two other reasons why his program got so little initial response. One was that the first attempt to implement this program was a dismal failure, even according to its author, Alexander Bain.[7] This failure was even more notable because Bain had supplied the needs of Mill's program by developing a more systematic, biological, and empirical psychology which gave particular attention to non-intellectual and specifically emotional factors.[8] Unfortunately, Bain, like Mill, presented his Ethology as an alternative to Phrenology. In 1843, when Mill first proposed Ethology,

it was reasonable to criticize Phrenology which was still near the peak of its popularity. But by 1861, when Bain published *On the Study of Character, Including an Estimate of Phrenology,* Mill's derogatory opinion of Phrenology was widely accepted, and there was no longer any need to argue the case of Ethology in relation to the success or failure of Phrenology. Therefore, when Bain devoted over one half of his book to an extended and detailed attack on Phrenology, it did little to make his work appealing or relevant.

The final factor involved in the initial failure of Mill's Ethology was the turning of British social thought in the 1860s toward increasingly developmental concerns and away from the "Social Statics" which Mill had hoped to base upon his Ethology. Under the influence of evolutionism, ethnologists and anthropologists turned their attention to questions pertaining to the origins and historical development of different social groups. In addition, also influenced by the new mode of thought, they formulated their answers to these questions in terms of assumed differences in racial and physical factors rather than in terms of social learning, or character formation, which Mill espoused. Thus, Mill's program was not only impracticable as he designed it, and inadequate as Bain formulated it, it was also irrelevant to the concerns of the succeeding generation of social scientists.[9]

II. A. F. SHAND'S REVISION AND DEVELOPMENT OF ETHOLOGY

For thirty-five years after Bain's book there was much discussion about character and character formation in England, but the major part of this discussion was couched in moralistic, educational, and inspirational works on how to raise and train children. Although some of these works made reference to Mill's Ethology, none of them constituted a real attempt to develop Mill's program. Rather, these references were simply made in an attempt to gain respectability for the study of character at hand.[10] In addition to these literary and educational treatises on character formation, an effort was made during this period to study character in a more scientific fashion. But again Mill's lead was not followed. Instead, it was Francis Galton who set the standard for the quantitatively-oriented anthropometric studies of these decades.[11]

Such was not the case in France. There, where the works of Mill and Bain had been made known through the works of Hippolyte Taine and Théodule Ribot,[12] l'éthologie was pursued in more or less conscious imitation of Mill's original program. I say "more or less" because there was criticism as well as enthusiasm for the science of character in France. Furthermore, France's literary tradition of studying le caractère, represented by La Bruyère,[13] had a definite influence on the French ethological movement. Nonetheless, especially in response to the work of Ribot, a number of French authors in the 1890s devoted themselves to the study of character. The works which resulted were conscious attempts to develop a science of character along the general lines suggested by Mill. The leaders of this "school," whose ethological works eventually blended into the tradition of French medico-developmental psychology, were Frédéric Paulhan, Alfred Fouillée, and Paulin Malapert.[14]

For the purposes of this paper, the major importance of these French writers is that they provided the tangible historical link between John Stuart Mill's proposal of Ethology in 1843 and Alexander F. Shand's revision and development of Ethology at the turn of the century. For it was through his reading of these French authors in the mid-1890s that Shand, an English gentleman-scholar, was inspired to assume the challenge of fulfilling Mill's program. The first major result of this inspiration was a seminal article published in 1896 in the journal Mind. In this article, entitled "Character and the Emotions," Shand presented a programmatic statement of the basic premises of his new Ethology.[15] This statement met with general approval, especially among

Shand's friends, such as G. F. Stout, William McDougall, and Edward Westermarck. But Shand was such a perfectionist that he continued revising the details of his argument and did not publish his book on The Foundations of Character until 1914.[16] Even then he fully intended to revise and expand this work, but the war years intervened and he never got around to it in subsequent years.

Shand made a number of changes in Mill's original program. Some of his changes were inspired by his reading of the French ethologists; for instance, Shand rejected excessive reliance on deduction and moved away from Mill's intellectualistic model of character. But so far as Shand was concerned the most important positive contribution of the French was the notion of organization or system, which he utilized in rethinking the basic psychological foundation of character. For although the work of the French ethologists had persuaded him of the necessity of an emotionalistic model of character, he became convinced that the psychology of his time, including that of the French, provided no adequate theory of emotion. To develop a more adequate basis for his Ethology, Shand used the concept of organization or system to help him distinguish between emotions and sentiments. According to this distinction, which he based on both observation and speculation, emotions are the basic human tendencies, considered separately. Sentiments, on the other hand, are complex, organized systems of these basic tendencies. These sentiments, Shand maintained, form over time, as the originally independent emotions become patterned through experience into the basic systems of behavioral and cognitive tendencies. These systems are the basis of character. Such is Shand's theory in a nutshell, although he worked it out in considerably greater detail.

Shand was aware that further research might necessitate a revision of his theory of the sentiments; and he knew that his book did not offer the final word on character. In fact, he conceived his work, as its title indicates, as merely a "foundation'' for the science of Ethology: it was only intended, he said, to be ''a map or plan...to guide us.'' Yet it turned out to be a very useful map. The theory of sentiments which he presented in his 1896 article drew immediate attention and was soon made widely known through its adoption in G. F. Stout's popular textbook, *A Manual of Psychology*.[17] Then in 1903, Stout invited Shand, as the leading expert on the subject, to contribute a chapter on the emotions to his *Groundwork of Psychology*.[18] And in 1908, William McDougall placed Shand's theory of sentiment at the center of his own theory of character and social behavior in his immensely influential *Introduction to Social Psychology*.[19] The publication of Shand's book in 1914 brought similar attention to his more fully developed theory of character. Then, as noted above, the war years interfered with normal activity. Although the demand was sufficient to warrant two later editions of the book, in 1920 and 1926, Shand never published his planned sequel. Yet G. F. Stout, writing in 1936, was still confident that Shand's general plan was ''comprehensive, original, and capable of being worked out in detail.'' However, he had to report that unfortunately ''successors have not hitherto been found to carry forward the investigation which he began.'' Stout suggested that the reason for this was undoubtedly that ''the interest of psychologists had been diverted into other channels.'' But he was certain that when ''they do take up Shand's problem they will find that his book fulfills the promise of its title and supplies foundations on which they can build.''[20]

III. SHAND'S ETHOLOGY AND THE CONCEPTUAL FOUNDATIONS OF SOCIAL ANTHROPOLOGY

Stout's final judgment seems overly optimistic today. Shand's work had already influenced psychologists and anthropologists before 1936, and it was never to do so again. But the nature of that previous influence was significant. As regards the psychological study of character, Shand affected the thinking of subsequent psychologists by his stress upon the emotive aspects of character. Allport, for instance, credits Shand with ''his recognition of systematized emotional dispositions as the functional units of which the personality (or as he prefers to call it, the character) is composed.''[21] And as regards the anthropological study of social organization, Shand provided a theory of character which served as the psychological underpinning of the new social anthropology which arose in the third decade of the twentieth century. For in the 1920s, after sixty years of emphasis upon evolutionary and racial approaches to social arrangements, A. R. Radcliffe-Brown and Bronislaw Malinowski led a movement back toward a ''Social Statics'' which, as Mill had envisioned, was based upon the conception of character as a product of social learning and emotional ties rather than racial inheritance and animal instinct. For both of them, Shand's ethological theory of character provided an important conceptual foundation.

In 1906, ten years after Shand's article on character, Radcliffe-Brown began his original field work in the Andaman Islands. He completed it in 1908, the year William McDougall published his *Introduction to Social Psychology,* in which Shand's theory of sentiments played a central explanatory role. Radcliffe-Brown did not complete the writing and rewriting of his monograph on *The Andaman Islanders* until 1914 (the same year in which Shand's book appeared), and it was not published until 1922.[22] Despite the delay, however, the central ideas in Radcliffe-Brown's book were still fresh and novel in the early 1920s. In fact, they signalled a new turn in British anthropological thought—away from the evolutionary and individual psychological approaches of Haddon and Rivers and toward a Durkheimian conception of society as an integrated system of institutions, customs, and beliefs.[23] Radcliffe-Brown did not seek to understand this social system in terms of its developmental history, nor simply in terms of its dependence upon the fullfillment of some supposedly innate individual needs. Rather, he sought to understand the significance of social institutions, customs, and beliefs by first determining their contemporary meaning to the people themselves and then by referring to their social effects. Finally, he attempted to understand the function of each institution, custom, and belief in relation to the entire system of institutions, customs, and beliefs. In working all this into a unified theory, Radcliffe-Brown relied heavily upon Shand's concept of character, or sentiment, as he found it expressed in McDougall's *Introduction to Social Psychology*.[24] Thus, according to Radcliffe-Brown, the characters of the Andamanese—i.e., their customs and beliefs—were based upon the formation of certain sentiments; and these sentiments in turn were formed through the experience of customs and beliefs in childhood. Hence, the maintenance of social order was dependent upon the learning of particular patterns of emotions constituting sentiments which in turn regulated the characteristic social behavior and beliefs of a given people. In this way, with Radcliffe-Brown's new approach to anthropology, Mill's hope of founding a science of "Social Statics" upon a science of human character, or Ethology, came to a belated fruition.[25]

At approximately the same time, Bronislaw Malinowski adopted Shand's concept of sentiment into his own developing system of thought. An admirer of both Shand and McDougall, Malinowski freely admitted his debt to Shand in his 1927 classic, *Sex and Repression in Savage Society*.[26] Although his relation to Shand was clear even before this time, *Sex and Repression* revealed the full extent of his allegiance. As with Radcliffe-Brown, the theory of the sentiments provided the basic foundation of Malinowski's understanding of culture and society. As he wrote, "Mr. Shand's theory of sentiments will always remain of paramount importance for the sociologist, since social bonds as well as cultural values are sentiments standardized under the influence of tradition and culture." Again, as with Radcliffe-Brown, there is the closed, reciprocal relation between sentiments and social arrangements. Sentiments are formed in certain social contexts; and certain social contexts are perpetuated by these related sentiments. The importance given to Shand's theory is indicated by the fact that Malinowski saw repressed sexual needs (à la psychoanalytic theory) as merely a special case subsumed under the rubric of sentiment. "We see, therefore," Malinowski concluded, "that the theory to which we must attach our results in order to put them on a sound theoretical basis is Shand's theory of the sentiments, and that instead of speaking of a 'nuclear complex' we should have to speak of the family sentiments, of kinship ties, typical of a given society."[27] This is how Malinowski explained the customs and beliefs of the Trobriand Islanders in 1927, near the beginning of a very productive career in anthropology.

In the years ahead, Malinowski, like Radcliffe-Brown, would change idioms to a certain extent. As Radcliffe-Brown gradually spoke more of "interest" and "value," so Malinowski came to speak of "needs" and "satisfaction" rather than "sentiment."[28] But the original conceptual framework is still clearly visible in their later works; and that framework, as we have seen, was at least partially the result of an intellectual tradition stretching from Mill and Bain, through the French ethologists, to Shand, through McDougall, to Radcliffe-Brown and Malinowski. And from the tutelage of Radcliffe-Brown and Malinowski came an entire generation of anthropologists who by 1940 had firmly established the vigorous new field of social anthropology.

NOTES

1 John Stuart Mill, *A System of Logic: Ratiocinative and Inductive*, 2 vols., repr. of 8th rev. ed. (1872), in *Collected Works*, ed. J. M. Robson, 18 vols. to date (Toronto, 1963–), vols. VII–VIII (1973–74). In Mill's time the term "moral sciences" referred to all the

sciences dealing with the mental, behavioral, and social aspects of human life.

2 John Stuart Mill, *The Early Letters of John Stuart Mill,* ed. Francis E. Mineka (1963), in *Collected Works,* VIII, 617.

3 Alexander Bain, *John Stuart Mill: A Criticism with Personal Recollections* (London, 1882), 78.

4 Mill, *Early Letters, op. cit.,* 613.

5 Mill's non-organismic approach is particularly noteworthy since he proposed his Ethology as an alternative to Phrenology, a discipline which admitted a biological assessment, and the possibility of an hereditarian explanation, of character. The fact that Mill, a political and social liberal committed to expeditious social change, favored an environmentalist explanation of character is not surprising, but it does place his thought squarely within a tradition which was losing strength in mid-nineteenth century Britain. The place of Phrenology was soon taken by more reputable and lasting biological sciences. See Robert M. Young, *Mind, Brain and Adaptation in the Nineteenth Century* (Oxford, 1970).

6 Gordon W. Allport, *Personality: A Psychological Interpretation* (New York, 1937), 87.

7 Bain admitted the failure of his *On the Study of Character, Including an Estimate of Phrenology* (London, 1861) in his *Autobiography* (London, 1904), 260.

8 Bain had developed his psychology in *The Senses and the Intellect* (London, 1855) and *The Emotions and the Will* (London, 1859).

9 The concerns of the post-Millian generation, as well as the correlative limitations of British social theory which constituted the general context of the initial failure of Mill's Ethology, have been investigated by J. W. Burrow, whose analysis develops the earlier insights of Noel Annan and, especially, Talcott Parsons. See J. W. Burrow, *Evolution and Society: A Study of Victorian Social Theory* (Cambridge, Eng., 1966); Noel Annan, *The Curious Strength of Positivism in English Political Thought* (London, 1959); and Talcott Parsons, *The Structure of Social Action* (New York, 1937), esp. Part I. Also relevant is Reba N. Soffer, *Ethics and Society in England: The Revolution in the Social Sciences, 1870–1914* (Berkeley, 1978). Leslie Stephen's treatment of Mill's thought in *The En-glish Utilitarians* (3 vols. [London, 1900], III) is equally enlightening. Finally, when I speak about the influence of "evolutionism" on ethnology and anthropology it should be clear that this influence was exerted by Lamarckian and Spencerian thought as much as, and in many cases more than, Darwinian thought. Indeed, it was Lamarckian thought that helped mediate between the environmentally "social" and the genetically "racial," whereas Spencer influenced evolutionary social thought well before Darwin proposed his theory in 1859.

10 E.g., cf. Alexander Stewart, *Our Temperaments: Their Study and Their Teaching* (London, 1887), 12.

11 E.g., cf. Francis Galton, [Address to the Anthropological Section of the British Association for the Advancement of Science], *Nature,* 2 (1877), 344–47; and L. S. Hearnshaw, *A Short History of British Psychology, 1840–1940* (New York, 1964), 56–66.

12 Hippolyte A. Taine, *Histoire de la Littérature anglaise,* 4 vols. (Paris, 1863–64); and Théodule Ribot, *La Psychologie anglaise contemporaine* (Paris, 1870).

13 Jean de La Bruyère, *Les Caractères de Théophraste, Traduits du Grec: avec les Caractères ou les Moeurs de ce Siècle* (Paris, 1688), trans. Jean Stewart (Baltimore, 1970).

14 The relevant works of Théodule Ribot are "Les bases affectives de la personnalité," *Revue philosophique,* 18 (1884), 138–72; "Les bases intellectuelles de la personnalité," *ibid.,* 410–66; "Sur les diverses formes du caractère," *Revue philosophique,* 34 (1892), 480–500; and "Les caractères anormaux et morbides," *Année philosophique,* 2 (1895), 1–17. The works of the French school of ethologists include Bernard Pérez, *Le Caractère de l'Enfant à l'Homme* (Paris, 1892), Frédéric Paulhan, *Les Caractères* (Paris, 1893), Alfred Fouillée, *Le Tempérament et le Caractère (Paris, 1895),* Frédéric Queyrat, *Les Caractères et l'Education morale* (Paris, 1896), Albert Levy, *La Psychologie du Caractère* (Paris, 1896), Paulin Malapert, *Les Eléments du Caractère et leurs Lois de Combinaison* (Paris, 1897), and Paulin Malapert, *Le Caractère* (Paris, 1902).

15 A. F. Shand, "Character and the Emotions," *Mind,* 5 (1896), 203–26.

16 A. F. Shand, *The Foundations of Character: Being a Study of the Tendencies of the Emotions and Sentiments* (London, 1914).

17 G. F. Stout, *A Manual of Psychology*, 2nd rev. ed. (London, 1901), Bk. 4, ch. 9.

18 A. F. Shand, "The Sources of Tender Emotion," in G. F. Stout, *The Groundwork of Psychology* (London, 1903), ch. 16.

19 W. McDougall, *An Introduction to Social Psychology* (London, 1908), ch. 5.

20 G. F. Stout, "Alexander Faulkner Shand (1858–1936)," *Proceedings of the British Academy,* **22** (1963), 403, 407. Stout's obituary (pp. 401–07) is the best extant biography of Shand.

21 Allport, *Personality, op. cit.,* 88–89.

22 A. R. Radcliffe-Brown, *The Andaman Islanders* (Cambridge, Eng., 1922).

23 For general background information regarding A. C. Haddon and W. H. R. Rivers, cf. T. K. Penniman, *A Hundred Years of Anthropology,* 3d rev. ed. (London, 1965). Regarding the Durkheimian conception of society, cf. Steven Lukes, *Émile Durkheim: His Life and Work* (New York, 1972). Since Durkheim was a very important influence on both Radcliffe-Brown and Malinowski, and since Durkheim also stressed both system and sentiment, it is pertinent to wonder about the possibility of an intellectual tie between Durkheim, the French ethologists, and Shand. However, I have not been able to establish any positive relationship.

24 *Ibid.,* chs. 5 & 6.

25 Incidentally, George Stocking has drawn my attention to the fact that, as a student, Radcliffe-Brown would have read Mill's proposal of Ethology in the Moral Sciences Tripos at Cambridge University. Thus, in addition to his knowledge of Shand's version of Ethology, he would have had direct access to the original Millian program.

26 B. Malinowski, *Sex and Repression in Savage Society* (London, 1927), 175–78, 240–42, 247–50, 259.

27 *Ibid.,* 177.

28 E.g., A. R. Radcliffe-Brown, "On Social Structure" (1940), in *Structure and Function in Primitive Society: Essays and Addresses* (New York, 1952), 188–204; and B. Malinowski, "A Scientific Theory of Culture" (1941), in *A Scientific Theory of Culture and Other Essays* (Chapel Hill, 1944), 1–144.

CHAPTER 4

THE PHYSIOLOGICAL ROOTS
OF PSYCHOLOGY

The emergence of experimental psychology in the nineteenth century was, to a large extent, the melding of questions from the field of philosophy and methods from the field of physiology. The previous two chapters considered the modern philosophical antecedents of psychology, principally in terms of mechanism and empiricism. In this chapter the focus is on the physiological origins of psychology, largely the work of the nineteenth century. That century was a time of great progress in physiology, particularly with respect to an understanding of the workings of the nervous system.

In 1811, the Scottish anatomist Charles Bell (1774–1842) privately published a booklet in which he stated that the spinal cord was made up of two kinds of nerves—*sensory* (in the dorsal portion of the cord) and *motor* (in the ventral part of the cord). Eleven years later the French physiologist François Magendie (1783–1855) published a similar statement in a French scientific journal, laying claim to the discovery. That claim of priority angered Bell and his supporters. Magendie countered that he had never read Bell's booklet, which seems likely because Bell is said to have distributed the copies only to select friends. This incident has been judged, with the passage of time, to be one of independent discovery, and the controversy resolved to some extent by labeling the specificity of spinal function as the Bell-Magendie Law.

That discovery was an important one for several reasons. First, it added substantially to the view that specificity existed throughout the nervous system, that is, that different parts of the brain and spinal cord controlled different functions. Second, the work of Bell and Magendie on the spinal cord identified separate sensory and motor systems—separate systems for interpreting stimuli and initiating responses (of obvious importance to the soon-to-be stimulus-response psychologies).

Extending the work on nerve function, the German physiologist Johannes Müller (1801–1858) discovered what would become known as the *doctrine of specific nerve energies*. Müller wrote that there were five kinds of nerves, each type corresponding to a particular sensory system. Thus, visual nerves carried only visual information. For example, the optic nerve can be artificially stimulated by pressure on the eyeball. With this pressure, and the eyes closed, the subject will "see" things (light, color, perhaps movement) because the excitation of visual nerve fibers results in visual perception, regardless of the actual source of stimulation (in this case not light, but mechanical pressure).

Müller was also interested in the speed of nerve conduction. He concluded that nerve impulses were so instantaneous that they could never be measured. Yet a few years later his countryman, Hermann von Helmholtz (1821–1894), using a motor nerve from a frog's leg, was able to measure the speed of conduction and found it to be much slower than imagined (around 50 to 90 meters per second). Helmholtz's discovery meant that mental processes were not instantaneous and that the time required for mental actions might be measured. F. C. Donders (1818–1889), a Dutch physiologist, would pursue such mental measurements (more about him later).

As mentioned earlier, one idea that was gaining popularity in the nineteenth century was that different brain areas served different functions, an idea known as *cortical localization of function*. A French surgeon Pierre Flourens (1794–1867), whose work partially supported cortical localization though he did not, systematically removed portions of animal brains to observe the subsequent effects on the behavior of those animals. His studies convinced him that the cerebrum was responsible for higher mental processes such as perception, memory, and reasoning, while the cerebellum controlled such functions as the coordination of movement. The work of Flourens was extended by another French surgeon, Paul Broca (1824–1880), whose clinical autopsy method allowed him to locate specific functional areas within the cerebrum. Examining the brains of individuals who had lost their ability to speak, Broca found damage in a particular area of the frontal lobe of the cerebrum, an area he believed was responsible for producing speech. Today, neuroscientists refer to that part of the brain as Broca's Area.

Still later in the nineteenth century, researchers began to use mild amounts of electric current to stimulate the neurons of the brain artificially, demonstrating that certain motor and perceptual responses could be reliably produced from stimulation of particular brain areas. There was accompanying research, particularly in the physiology of the sensory systems, that greatly increased our knowledge of perception, especially in the visual and auditory systems—for example, discoveries in color vision, depth perception, sound perception, and touch sensitivity. These studies of sensory physiology, of fundamental importance for the new science of psychology, were largely stimulated by the emphasis the empiricists placed on the senses in acquiring knowledge.

In short, philosophers had debated the workings of the mind for centuries—questions about the nature of perception, of reason, of learning. The physiologists of the nineteenth century were well equipped in terms of technological and conceptual advances to begin answering those questions, and they did so by reducing the mind to its neurological substrate. Later chapters will have more about that reductionism.

The initial article in this chapter is Paul Broca's account of his famous patient Leborgne (also known as Tan). Leborgne was unable to speak for the final twenty-one years of his life. After Leborgne's death, Broca's autopsy of his patient's brain revealed a lesion in the left frontal lobe. Broca presented his important finding at a meeting of the Paris Anthropological Society, during which he allowed the members to see Leborgne's brain, preserved in a jar.

Whereas the Broca article exemplifies the work on cortical localization of function, the second selection, by Hermann von Helmholtz, deals with the work in sensory physiology. This selection, on visual perception, is taken from Helmholtz's classic work, *Handbook of Physiological Optics* (1856–1866).

The remaining three articles in this chapter were authored by historians of psychology and psychiatry. Raymond E. Fancher's article is on phrenology, a controversial side trip in the history of psychology that has been variously called the first systematic scientific program of behavioral research (see O'Donnell, 1985), the first applied psychology (as a precursor of mental testing), and the first physiological psychology. Phrenology was a natural extension of the ideas of cortical localization of function, but it did not hold up to scientific scrutiny (see Bakan, 1966; Boring, 1950; Walsh, 1976). Fancher tells the interesting tale of Franz Joseph Gall (1758–1828) as leader of the phrenological movement and of the work of Flourens in discrediting that movement.

Other cases of scientific rejection in the realm of physiology are provided in the article by Jacques M. Quen, who describes the fate of three methods (Mesmerism, Perkinism, and acupuncture) used to treat medical and psychological disorders in the nineteenth century. This article is also interesting for its rejection of Thomas Kuhn's (1970) theory of scientific revolutions in accounting for the development of these three areas and for its claims about the nature of scientific acceptance-rejection. Kuhn (1970) has argued that scientific discovery *begins* with an awareness of anomaly, a recognition that nature and scientific expectation are at odds. But Quen claims that with regard to Mesmerism, Perkinism, and acupuncture, discovery *stopped* with a recognition of the anomaly.

The final article in this chapter is a discussion by Elizabeth Scarborough of citation analysis as a tool in historical research. She uses the 1868 mental chronometry study of F. C. Donders as a case study. Donders's work on reaction time as a measure of the speed of mental events has been rediscovered by researchers interested in the topic because of the contemporary use of mental chronometry techniques by cognitive psychologists (see, for example, Moyer & Bayer, 1976; Paivio, 1980).

REFERENCES

Bakan, D. (1966). The influence of phrenology on American psychology. *Journal of the History of the Behavioral Sciences, 2,* 200–220.

Boring, E. G. (1950). *A history of experimental psychology* (2d ed.). New York: Appleton–Century–Crofts.

Kuhn, T. (1970). *The structure of scientific revolutions* (2d ed.). Chicago: University of Chicago Press.

Moyer, R. S., & Bayer, R. H. (1976). Mental comparisons and the symbolic distance effects. *Cognitive Psychology, 8,* 228–246.

O'Donnell, J. M. (1985). *The origins of behaviorism: American psychology, 1870–1920.* New York: New York University Press.

Paivio, A. (1980). On weighing things in your mind. In P. W. Jusczyk & R. M. Klein (Eds.), *The nature of thought: Essays in honor of D. O. Hebb.* Hillsdale, NJ: Lawrence Erlbaum, pp. 133–154.

Walsh, A. A. (1976). Phrenology and the Boston medical community in the 1830s. *Bulletin of the History of Medicine, 50,* 261–273.

On the Speech Center

Paul Broca

A TWENTY-ONE-YEAR CASE OF APHEMIA PRODUCED BY THE CHRONIC AND PROGRESSIVE SOFTENING OF THE SECOND AND THIRD CONVOLUTIONS OF THE SUPERIOR PORTION OF THE LEFT FRONTAL LOBE

On 11 April 1861 there was brought to the surgery of the general infirmary of the hospice at Bicêtre a man named Leborgne, fifty-one years old, suffering from a diffused gangrenous cellulitis of his whole right leg, extending from the foot to the buttocks. When questioned the next day as to the origin of his disease, he replied only with the monosyllable *tan,* repeated twice in succession and accompanied by a gesture of his left hand. I tried to find out more about the antecedents of this man, who had been at Bicêtre for twenty-one years. I questioned his attendants, his comrades on the ward, and those of his relatives who came to see him, and here is the result of this inquiry.

Since youth he had been subject to epileptic attacks, yet he was able to become a maker of lasts, a trade at which he worked until he was thirty years old. It was then that he lost his ability to speak and that is why he was admitted to the hospice at Bicêtre. It was not possible to discover whether his loss of speech came on slowly or rapidly or whether some other symptom accompanied the onset of this affliction.

When he arrived at Bicêtre he had already been unable to speak for two or three months. He was then quite healthy and intelligent and differed from a normal person only in his loss of articulate language. He came and went in the hospice, where he was known by the name of

"Tan." He understood all that was said to him. His hearing was actually very good, but whenever one questioned him he always answered, "Tan, tan," accompanying his utterance with varied gestures by which he succeeded in expressing most of his ideas. If one did not understand his gestures, he was apt to get irate and added to his vocabulary a gross oath ["Sacré nom de Dieu!"] ... Tan was considered an egoist, vindictive and objectionable, and his associates, who detested him, even accused him of stealing. These defects could have been due largely to his cerebral lesion. They were not pronounced enough to be considered pathological, and, although this patient was at Bicêtre, no one ever thought of transferring him to the insane ward. On the contrary, he was considered to be completely responsible for his acts.

Ten years after he lost his speech a new symptom appeared. The muscles of his right arm began to get weak, and in the end they became completely paralyzed. Tan continued to walk without difficulty, but the paralysis gradually extended to his right leg; after having dragged the leg for some time, he resigned himself to staying in bed. About four years had elapsed from the beginning of the paralysis of the arm to the time when paralysis of the leg was sufficiently advanced to make standing absolutely impossible. Before he was brought to the infirmary, Tan had been in bed for almost seven years. This last period of his life is the one for which we have the least information. Since he was incapable of doing harm, his associates had nothing to do with him any more, except to amuse themselves at his expense. This made him angry, and he had by now lost the little celebrity which the peculiarity of his disease had given him at the hospice. It was also noticed that his vision had become notably weaker during the last two years. Because he kept to his bed this was the only aggravation one could notice. As he was not incontinent, they changed his linen only once a week; thus the diffused cellulitis for which he was brought to the hospital on 11 April 1861 was not recognized by the attendants until it had made considerable progress and had infected the whole leg....

The study of this unfortunate person, who could not speak and who, being paralyzed in his right hand, could not write, offered some difficulty. His general state, moreover, was so grave that it would have been cruel to torment him by long interviews.

I found, in any case, that general sensitivity was present everywhere, although it was unequal. The right half of his body was less sensitive than the left, and that undoubtedly contributed to the diminished pain at the site of the diffuse cellulitis. As long as one did not touch him, the patient did not suffer much, but palpation was painful and the incisions that I had to make provoked agitation and cries.

The two right limbs were completely paralyzed. The left ones could be moved voluntarily and, though weak, could without hesitation execute all movements. Emission of urine and fecal matter was normal, but swallowing was difficult. Mastication, on the other hand, was executed very well. The face did not deviate from normal. When he whistled, however, his left cheek appeared a little less inflated than his right, indicating that the muscles on this side of the face were a little weak. There was no tendency to strabismus. The tongue was completely free and normal; the patient could move it anywhere and stretch it out of his mouth. Both of its sides were of the same thickness. The difficulty in swallowing... was due to incipient paralysis of the pharynx and not to a paralysis of the tongue, for it was only the third stage of swallowing that appeared labored. The muscles of the larynx did not seem to be altered. The timbre of the voice was natural, and the sounds that the patient uttered to produce his monosyllable were quite pure.

Tan's hearing remained acute. He heard well the ticking of a watch but his vision was weak. When he wanted to see the time, he had to take the watch in his left hand and place it in a peculiar position about twenty centimeters from his right eye, which seemed better than his left.

The state of Tan's intelligence could not be exactly determined. Certainly he understood almost all that was said to him, but, since he could express his ideas or desires only by movements of his left hand, this moribund patient could not make himself understood as well as he understood others. His numerical responses, made by opening or closing his fingers, were best. Several times I asked him for how many days had he been ill. Sometimes he answered five, sometimes six days. How many years had he been in Bicêtre? He opened his hand four times and then added one finger. That made 21 years, the correct answer. The next day I repeated the question and received the same answer, but, when I tried to come back to the question a third time, Tan realized that I wanted to make an exercise out of the questioning. He became irate and uttered the oath, which only this one time did I hear from him. Two days in succession I showed him my watch. Since the second hand did not move, he could distinguish the three hands only by their shape and length. Still, after having looked at the watch for a few seconds, he could each time indicate the hour correctly. It cannot be doubted, therefore, that the man was intelligent, that he could think, that he had to a certain extent retained the memory of old habits. He could understand even quite complicated ideas. For instance, I asked him about the order in which his paralyses had developed. First he made a short horizontal gesture with his left index finger, meaning that he had understood; then he showed successively his tongue, his right arm, and his right leg. That was perfectly correct, for quite naturally he attributed his loss of language to paralysis of his tongue.

Nevertheless there were several questions to which he did not respond, questions that a man of ordinary intelligence would have managed to answer even with only one hand. At other times he seemed quite annoyed when the sense of his answers was not understood. Sometimes his answer was clear but wrong—as when he pretended to have children when actually he had none. Doubtless the intelligence of this man was seriously impaired as an effect either of his cerebral lesion or of his devouring fever, but obviously he had much more intelligence than was necessary for him to talk.

From the anamnesis and from the state of the patient it was clear that he had a cerebral lesion that was progressive, had at the start and for the first ten years remained limited to a fairly well-circumscribed region, and during this first period had attacked neither the organs of motility nor of sensitivity; that after ten years the lesion had spread to one or more organs of motion, still leaving unaffected the organs of sensitivity; and that still more recently sensitivity had become dulled as well as vision, particularly the vision of the left eye. Complete paralysis affected the two right limbs; moreover, the sensitivity of these two limbs was slightly less than normal. Therefore, the principal cerebral lesion should lie in the left hemisphere. This opinion was reinforced by the incomplete paralysis of the left cheek and of the left retina, for, needless to say, paralyses of cerebral origin are crossed for the trunk and the extremities but are direct for the face....

The patient died on 17 April [1861]. The autopsy was performed as soon as possible—that is to say, after 24 hours. The weather was warm but the cadaver showed no signs of putrefaction. The brain was shown a few hours later to the Société d'Anthropologie and was then put immediately into alcohol. It was so altered that great care was necessary to preserve it. It was only after two months and several changes of the fluid that it began to harden. Today it is in perfect condition and has been deposited in the Musée Depuytren....

The organs destroyed are the following: the small inferior marginal convolution of the temporal lobe, the small convolutions of the insula, and the underlying part of the striate body, and, finally, in the frontal lobe, the inferior part of the transverse frontal convolution and the posterior part of those two great convolutions designated as the second and third frontal convolutions. Of the four convolutions that form the superior part of the frontal lobe, only one, the superior and most medial one, has been preserved, although not in its entirety, for it is softened and atrophied, but nevertheless indicates its continuity, for, if one puts back in imagination all that has been lost, one finds that at least three quarters of the cavity has been hollowed out at the expense of the frontal lobe.

Now we have to decide where the lesion started. An examination of the cavity caused by the lack of substance shows at once that the center of the focus corresponds to the frontal lobe. It follows that, if the softening spread out uniformly in all directions, it would have been this lobe in which the disease began. Still we should not be guided solely by a study of the cavity, for we should also keep an eye on the parts that surround it. These parts are very unequally softened and cover an especially variable extent. Thus the second temporal convolution, which bounds the lesion from below, exhibits a smooth surface of firm consistency; yet it is without doubt softened, though not much and only in its superficial parts. On the opposite side on the frontal lobe, the softened material is almost fluid near the focus; still, as one goes away from the focus, the substance of the brain becomes gradually firmer, although the softening extends in reality for a considerable distance and involves almost the whole frontal lobe. It is here that the softening mainly progressed and it is almost certain that the other parts were affected only later.

If one wished to be more precise, he could remark that the third frontal convolution is the one that shows the greatest loss of substance, that not only is it cut transversely at the level of the anterior end of the Sylvian fissure but it is also completely destroyed in its posterior half, and that it alone has undergone a loss of substance equal to about one-half of its total. The second or middle frontal convolution, although deeply affected, still preserves its continuity in its innermost parts; consequently it is most likely that the disease began in the third convolution....

Anatomical inspection shows us that the lesion was still progressing when the patient died. The lesion was therefore progressive, but it progressed very slowly, taking twenty-one years to destroy a quite limited part of the brain. Thus it is reasonable to believe that at the beginning there was a considerable time during which degeneration did not go past the limits of the organ where it started. We have seen that the original focus of the disease was situated in the frontal lobe and very likely in its third frontal convolution. Thus we are compelled to say, from the point of view of pathological anatomy, that there were two periods, one in which only one frontal convolution, probably the third one, was attacked, and another period in which the disease gradually spread toward other convolutions, to the insula, or to the extraventricular nucleus of the corpus striatum.

When we now examine the succession of the symptoms, we also find two periods, the first of which lasted ten years, during which the faculty of speech was destroyed while all other functions of the brain remained intact, and a second period of eleven years, during which paralysis of movement, at first partial and then complete, successively involved the arm and the leg of the right side.

With this in mind it is impossible not to see that there was a correspondence between the anatomical and the symptomological periods. Everyone knows that the cerebral convolutions are not motor organs. Of all the organs attacked, the corpus striatum of the left hemisphere is the only one where one could look for the cause of the paralysis of the two right extremities. The second clinical period, in which the motility changed, corresponds to the second anatomical period, when the softening passed beyond the limit of the frontal lobe and invaded the insula and the corpus striatum.

It follows that the first period of ten years, clinically characterized only by the symptom of aphemia, must correspond to the period during which the lesion was still limited to the frontal lobe.

Concerning the Perceptions in General

Hermann von Helmholtz

The sensations aroused by light in the nervous mechanism of vision enable us to form conceptions as to the existence, form and position of external objects. These ideas are called *visual perceptions*. In this third subdivision of Physiological Optics we must try to analyze the scientific results which we have obtained concerning the conditions which give rise to visual perceptions.

Perceptions of external objects being therefore of the nature of ideas, and ideas themselves being invariably activities of our psychic energy, perceptions also can only be the result of psychic energy. Accordingly, strictly speaking, the theory of perceptions belongs properly in the domain of psychology. This is particularly true with respect to the mode of the mental activities in the case of the perceptions and with respect to the determination of their laws. Yet even here there is a wide field of investigation in both physics and physiology, inasmuch as we have to determine, scientifically as far as possible, what special properties of the physical stimulus and of the physiological stimulation are responsible for the formation of this or that particular idea as to the nature of the external objects perceived. In this part of the subject, therefore, we shall have to investigate the special properties of the retinal images, muscular sensations, etc., that are concerned in the perception of a definite position of the observed object, not only as to its direction but as to its distance; how the perception of the form of a body of three

From Helmholtz, H. von (1860). *Handbuch der Physiologischen Optik* Volume 3. In J. P. C. Southall (Trans.), *Handbook on physiological optics*. Rochester, NY: Optical Society of America, 1924–1925, vol. 3, pp. 1–6. Copyright © 1962. Reprinted by permission of the publisher.

dimensions depends on certain peculiarities of the images; and under what circumstances it will appear single or double as seen by both eyes, etc. Thus, our main purpose will be simply to investigate the material of sensation whereby we are enabled to form ideas, in those relations that are important for the perceptions obtained from them. This problem can be solved entirely by scientific methods. At the same time, we cannot avoid referring to psychic activities and the laws that govern them, as far as they are concerned with the perception of the senses. But the discovery and description of these psychic activities will not be regarded as an essential part of our present task, because then we might run the risk of losing our hold of established facts and of not adhering steadily to a method founded on clear, well-recognized principals. Thus, for the present at least, I think the psychological domain of the physiology of the senses should be kept separate from pure psychology, whose province really is to establish as far as possible the laws and nature of the processes of the mind.

Still we cannot altogether avoid speaking of the mental processes that are active in the sense-perceptions, if we wish to see clearly the connection between the phenomena and to arrange the facts in their proper relation to one another. And hence, to prevent any misconception of the plan I have in mind, I intend to devote the latter part of this chapter to a discussion of the conclusions which I think can be inferred with respect to these mental processes. And yet we know by experience that people very seldom come to any agreement as to abstract questions of this nature. The keenest thinkers, philosophers like Kant for instance, have long ago analyzed these relations correctly and demonstrated them, and yet there is no permanent and general agreement about them among educated people. And, therefore, in the subsequent chapters devoted specially to the theory of the visual perceptions, I shall endeavour to avoid all reference to opinions as to mental activity, as involving questions that always have been, and perhaps always will be, subjects of debate between the

various metaphysical schools; so as not to distract the reader's attention from those facts about which an agreement may possibly be reached, by wrangling over abstract propositions that are not necessarily involved in the problem before us.

Here I shall merely indicate at the outset certain general characteristics of the mental processes that are active in the sense-perceptions, because they will be constantly encountered in connection with the various subjects to be considered. Without some previous explanation of their general significance and wide range of activity, the reader might be apt in some special case to regard them as paradoxical and incredible.

The general rule determining the ideas of vision that are formed whenever an impression is made on the eye, with or without the aid of optical instruments, is that *such objects are always imagined as being present in the field of vision as would have to be there in order to produce the same impression on the nervous mechanism, the eyes being used under ordinary normal conditions*. To employ an illustration which has been mentioned before, suppose that the eyeball is mechanically stimulated at the outer corner of the eye. Then we imagine that we see an appearance of light in front of us somewhere in the direction of the bridge of the nose. Under ordinary conditions of vision, when our eyes are stimulated by light coming from outside, if the region of the retina in the outer corner of the eye is to be stimulated, the light actually has to enter the eye from the direction of the bridge of the nose. Thus, in accordance with the above rule, in a case of this kind we substitute a luminous object at the place mentioned in the field of view, although as a matter of fact the mechanical stimulus does not act on the eye from in front of the field of view nor from the nasal side of the eye, but, on the contrary, is exerted on the outer surface of the eyeball and more from behind. The general validity of the above rule will be shown by many other instances that will appear in the following pages.

In the statement of this rule mention is made of the ordinary conditions of vision, when the visual organ is stimulated by light from outside; this outside light, coming from the opaque objects in its path that were the last to be encountered, and having reached the eye along rectilinear paths through an uninterrupted layer of air. This is what is meant here by the normal use of the organ of vision, and the justification for using this term is that this mode of stimulation occurs in such an enormous majority of cases that all other instances where the paths of the rays of light are altered by reflections or refractions, or in which the stimulations are not produced by external light, may be regarded as rare exceptions. This is because the retina in the fundus of the firm eyeball is almost completely protected from the actions of all other stimuli and is not easily accessible to anything but external light. When a person is in the habit of using an optical instrument and has become accustomed to it, for example, if he is used to wearing spectacles, to a certain extent he learns to interpret the visual images under these changed conditions.

Incidentally, the rule given above corresponds to a general characteristic of all sense-perceptions, and not simply to the sense of sight alone. For example, the stimulation of the tactile nerves in the enormous majority of cases is the result of influences that affect the terminal extensions of these nerves in the surface of the skin. It is only under exceptional circumstances that the nerve-stems can be stimulated by more powerful agencies. In accordance with the above rule, therefore, all stimulations of cutaneous nerves, even when they affect the stem or the nerve-centre itself, are perceived as occurring in the corresponding peripheral surface of the skin. The most remarkable and astonishing cases of illusions of this sort are those in which the peripheral area of this particular portion of the skin is actually no longer in existence, as, for example, in case of a person whose leg has been amputated. For a long time after the operation the patient frequently imagines he has vivid sensations in the foot that has been severed. He feels exactly the places that ache on one toe or the other. Of course, in a case of this sort the stimulation can

affect only what is left of the stem of the nerve whose fibres formerly terminated in the amputated toes. Usually, it is the end of the nerve in the scar that is stimulated by external pressure or by contraction of the scar tissue. Sometimes at night the sensations in the missing extremity get to be so vivid that the patient has to feel the place to be sure that his limb is actually gone.

Thus it happens, that when the modes of stimulation of the organs of sense are unusual, incorrect ideas of objects are apt to be formed; which used to be described, therefore, as *illusions of the senses*. Obviously, in these cases there is nothing wrong with the activity of the organ of sense and its corresponding nervous mechanism which produces the illusion. Both of them have to act according to the laws that govern their activity once for all. It is rather simply an illusion in the judgment of the material presented to the senses, resulting in a false idea of it.

The psychic activities that lead us to infer that there in front of us at a certain place there is a certain object of a certain character, are generally not conscious activities, but unconscious ones. In their result they are equivalent to a *conclusion,* to the extent that the observed action on our senses enables us to form an idea as to the possible cause of this action; although, as a matter of fact, it is invariably simply the nervous stimulations that are perceived directly, that is, the actions, but never the external objects themselves. But what seems to differentiate them from a conclusion, in the ordinary sense of that word, is that a conclusion is an act of conscious thought. An astronomer, for example, comes to real conscious conclusions of this sort, when he computes the positions of the stars in space, their distances, etc., from the perspective images he has had of them at various times and as they are seen from different parts of the orbit of the earth. His conclusions are based on a conscious knowledge of the laws of optics. In the ordinary acts of vision this knowledge of optics is lacking. Still it may be permissible to speak of the psychic acts of ordinary perception as *unconscious conclusions,* thereby making a distinction of some sort between them and the common so-called conscious conclusions. And while it is true that there has been, and probably always will be, a measure of doubt as to the similarity of the psychic activity in the two cases, there can be no doubt as to the similarity between the results of such unconscious conclusions and those of conscious conclusions.

These unconscious conclusions derived from sensation are equivalent in their consequences to the so-called *conclusions from analogy*. Inasmuch as in an overwhelming majority of cases, whenever the parts of the retina in the outer corner of the eye are stimulated, it has been found to be due to external light coming into the eye from the direction of the bridge of the nose, the inference we make is that it is so in every new case whenever this part of the retina is stimulated; just as we assert that every single individual now living will die, because all previous experience has shown that all men who were formerly alive have died.

But, moreover, just because they are not free acts of conscious thought, these unconscious conclusions from analogy are irresistible, and the effect of them cannot be overcome by a better understanding of the real relations. It may be ever so clear how we get an idea of a luminous phenomenon in the field of vision when pressure is exerted on the eye; and yet we cannot get rid of the conviction that this appearance of light is actually there at the given place in the visual field; and we cannot seem to comprehend that there is a luminous phenomenon at the place where the retina is stimulated. It is the same way in case of all the images that we see in optical instruments.

On the other hand, there are numerous illustrations of fixed and inevitable associations of ideas due to frequent repetition, even when they have no natural connection, but are dependent merely on some conventional arrangement, as, for example, the connection between the writ-

ten letters of a word and its sound and meaning. Still to many physiologists and psychologists the connection between the sensation and the conception of the object usually appears to be so rigid and obligatory that they are not much disposed to admit that, to a considerable extent at least, it depends on acquired experience, that is, on psychic activity. On the contrary, they have endeavoured to find some mechanical mode of origin for this connection through the agency of imaginary organic structures. With regard to this question, all those experiences are of much significance which show how the judgment of the senses may be modified by experience and by training derived under various circumstances, and may be adapted to the new conditions. Thus, persons may learn in some measure to utilize details of the sensation which otherwise would escape notice and not contribute to obtaining any idea of the object. On the other hand, too, this new habit may acquire such a hold that when the individual in question is back again in the old original normal state, he may be liable to illusions of the senses.

Facts like these show the widespread influence that experience, training and habit have on our perceptions. But how far their influence really does extend, it would perhaps be impossible to say precisely at present. Little enough is definitely known about infants and very young animals, and the interpretation of such observations as have been made on them is extremely doubtful. Besides, no one can say that infants are entirely without experience and practice in tactile sensations and bodily movements. Accordingly, the rule given above has been stated in a form which does not anticipate the decision of this question. It merely expresses what the result is. And so it can be accepted even by those who have entirely different opinions as to the way ideas originate concerning objects in the external world.

Gall, Flourens, and the Phrenological Movement

Raymond E. Fancher

GALL AND THE PHRENOLOGICAL MOVEMENT

For all the controversy [Franz Joseph] Gall [1758–1828] generated, everyone agreed he was a brilliant brain anatomist. He examined the brains of humans and animals alike, and introduced several new dissection techniques. He showed that the brain and spinal cord are composed of just two basic kinds of substance: the pulpy *gray matter* which occupies the outer surface or cortex of the brain, the inner part of the spinal cord, and several discrete locations within the brain; and a *white matter* which consists of billions of fibers connecting the various gray areas. He also showed that the two halves of the brain are interconnected by stalks of white matter called *commissures,* and that the white fibers originating in the spinal cord cross over in the lower brain from one side to the other. This means that sensation ascending the spinal cord from one side of the body stimulates the brain on the opposite side, and that movement on one side of the body is initiated by brain activity on the opposite side. All of these fundamental facts about the nervous system are still taught today at the outset of any course on neurology.

More important for psychology were Gall's comparative studies of different kinds of brains. He examined the brains of different kinds of animals, children, elderly and brain damaged people, as well as normal adults. These studies showed, in a general but convincing way, that the higher mental functions of an organism were directly related to the size and intactness of its *cortex,* the mass of gray matter on the outer surface of the brain. Larger amounts of intact cortex were generally associated with more intelligent organisms. No one before Gall had shown so clearly that brain size paralleled mental development.

This demonstration of a relationship between mind and brain was accepted even by Gall's severest critics. Combined with his anatomical studies, it should have earned him a secure and respected place in the history of science. Unfortunately for his reputation, however, he embedded these noncontroversial ideas within a larger theory that came to be called *phrenology.** Not content to stop with the bare assertion that the mind was localized somewhere and somehow in the brain, phrenology held that discrete psychological "faculties" were localized in specific small parts of the brain. Furthermore, Gall believed that bumps and indentations on the surface of the skull provided accurate measures of the underlying brain parts, and hence of the different faculties.

Phrenology was a curious mixture, combining some keen observations and insights with an inappropriate scientific procedure. Because of its transparent flaws, it quickly attracted the scorn of most of the scientific establishment. When Gall failed to win the respectful attention of professional scientists, he presented phrenology in spectacular lectures and demonstrations directed at laymen. These won him a wide popular following and a handsome income, but of course this only intensified the negative reaction among scientists. An English scientist typified this reaction when he called phrenology "that sinkhole of human folly and prating coxcombry."

According to Gall's autobiography, the foundations of his curious science were laid by an observation he made as a schoolboy. He noticed a

From Fancher, R. E. (1979). *Pioneers of psychology.* New York: W. W. Norton, pp. 44–59. Copyright © 1979 by W. W. Norton and Co. Reprinted by permission of the publisher.

---

* The actual word "phrenology" (literally, "science of the mind") was neither coined nor used by Gall, but by one of his students. The term has come to be so closely identified with Gall, however, that it will be used here to denote his general theory.

number of schoolfellows whom he did not believe to be as bright as himself, but who nevertheless got better grades because they were better memorizers. As he thought about each of these exasperating rivals, he realized that they all shared in common the feature of large, protuberant eyes.

This first observation of a correlation between a physical and a psychological characteristic took on theoretical significance for Gall many years later, as he was conducting his comparative anatomical studies of the brain.* Those studies showed, of course, that behavioral differences between species were matched by differences in their brain structure. Since the most distinctive behavioral characteristic of humans was their higher mental functioning, and their most distinctive brain feature was their highly developed cortex, Gall concluded that the cortex was the seat of the higher functions. The non-cortical brain structures, which vary proportionately less than the cortex across species, were postulated to underlie the activities necessary for life itself, such as respiration, digestion, or locomotion.

Gall went further by noting that human beings differ not only from other species by virtue of their higher mental faculties, but also *within themselves* in the distribution of those faculties. Some people are more intelligent than others, more honest, more amorous, or have better memories. Since all of these personality characteristics are localized in the cortex, reasoned Gall, personality differences between human beings ought to be reflected by differences in their cortexes.

Here his childhood observation seemed relevant. Gall hypothesized that there must be a particular part of the cortex, lying directly behind the eyes, that is responsible for the faculty of "verbal memory." People whose brains are characterized by unusual development of this brain part must also have unusual memories for names and facts. Furthermore, their eyes will be pushed out by the highly developed brain tissue, thus accounting for their protuberance in people with good memories.

If the capacity for verbal memory were localized in one circumscribed region of the brain, it seemed reasonable to assign other higher faculties to other locations. Differences in personality endowment should be mirrored by differences in the development of the corresponding brain regions. Theoretically, a person's entire character could be mapped simply by noting the relative sizes of the different regions. This was the fundamental hypothesis of Gall's phrenology.

As he sought ways to confirm his basic hypothesis, Gall was faced with the problem of how to measure differences in brain configuration. X-rays had not yet been discovered, and the procedure of opening someone's skull was too drastic to be used except in extraordinary circumstances. Undaunted, Gall resorted to a secondary hypothesis. Just as the brain part responsible for verbal memory can cause the eyes to protrude, so highly developed regions in other parts of the cortex should cause measurable irregularities in the surrounding skull. *Craniometry,* or measurement of the physical dimensions of the skull, should lead to inferences about the dimensions of the underlying cortex. Gall's method of investigation was to seek correlations between skull measurements and personality traits.

Once embarked upon his program, Gall found it easy to develop hypotheses. Sometimes chance encounters helped, as when he "discovered" that the region determining sexual response is in the

---

* The general idea that psychological characteristics may be reflected in physical features was not original to Gall, but was very popular in his time. The art of *physiognomy*—the reading of a person's character in his physical features—had been effectively advocated by the mystic Johann Kaspar Lavater (1741–1801) in the late eighteenth century, and remained influential through much of the nineteenth. In 1836, for example, the young student Charles Darwin was almost rejected for the post of naturalist aboard H.M.S. *Beagle* because the captain thought his nose was inappropriately shaped for a seafarer. Later in the century, the Italian criminologist Cesare Lombroso (1831–1901) published a highly influential physiognomic theory of the "criminal type," part of which still persists today in the myth that evil-doers must be shifty-eyed and sneering.

back of the neck. He was attending to one of his patients, whose habitual behavior earned her the posthumous title of "Gall's Passionate Widow." In the midst of an hysterical fit, she threw herself backwards with great force. Gall caught her to keep her from falling, and as he did so he supported the back of her neck with his hand. He immediately noticed that her neck was thick and hot, leading him to suspect that the structure at the base of her brain, the *cerebellum,* must be unusually well-developed and the source of her most prominent characteristic. Observations on other people satisfied Gall all too easily that well-developed necks were generally associated with heightened sexual motivation.

It is easy to laugh at such episodes, but it should be emphasized that there was nothing inherently improper about Gall's theory. In fact, it had a certain naive plausibility, and was testable by direct observation. Gall's major problems arose because of the slipshod way he made those observations, and because of his inability to modify his theory in accordance with data that did not confirm it.

Essentially, there were three crucial defects in his theory. First, the assumption that the shape of the skull accurately reflects the underlying brain was false. This obviously invalidated the phrenologists' claim that they could read character by measuring the skull. It did not invalidate the more basic hypothesis of a relationship between brain configuration and personality, however.

A second major defect lay in Gall's choice of psychological units to describe differences in personality. Since he wanted to account for psychological differences among people, he had to have a basic system of dimensions on which they could vary. The problem of describing variations in the physical characteristics of the brain was simple and straightforward compared with that of describing personality variations. Indeed, psychologists to the present day differ about the nature of the most basic dimensions of personality. Gall, however, unquestioningly adopted the

view that all human variability in character can be accounted for by differing combinations of twenty-seven specific "faculties." The memory differences indicated by bulging eyes, for example, were reflections of differences in the "Faculty of attending to and distinguishing Words; Recollection of Words, or Verbal Memory." The heightened sexuality of people with large cerebellums was due to the "Faculty of Amativeness." Other faculties in Gall's scheme included "acquisitiveness," "reverence," "benevolence," "secretiveness," and "mirthfulness." His phrenological program consisted of finding specific brain regions, or "organs," to correspond to the twenty-seven different faculties.

Of course the twenty-seven faculties Gall selected were completely arbitrary. He had no evidence that his list of faculties was any more basic than a list anyone else could devise. It is now generally recognized that personality characteristics such as "reverence" or "acquisitiveness" are not simple givens, but are the complex results of many factors interacting with one another. Several years after Gall's original formulation, his students found it necessary to add even more faculties to the list. One such typical phrenological configuration is given here in Figure 1. But no amount of manipulation could salvage the faculty approach to psychology, and so long as phrenology lacked an adequate system for describing psychological characteristics, it could never hope to account adequately for differences in human personality.

Even the inadequacy of its psychological assumptions did not discredit phrenology as much as its third fatal defect: the feckless methods by which its hypotheses were usually tested. Gall always maintained that his theory was grounded in observation, a statement that was literally true but that did not reflect the arbitrariness with which some observations were emphasized while others were conveniently ignored. Any positive evidence was unquestioningly and enthusiastically hailed; negative evidence was explained away.

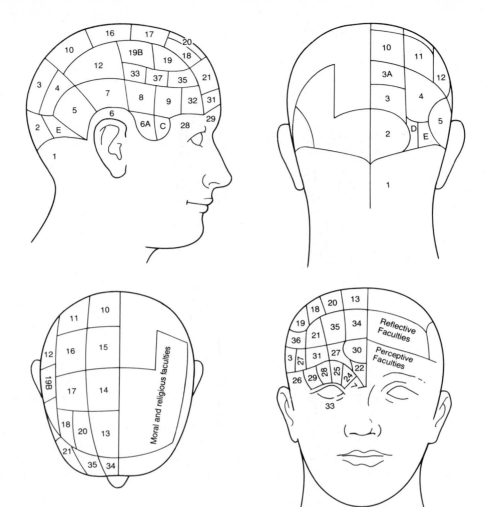

FIGURE 1
A typical phrenological configuration.

1. Amativeness.
2. Philoprogenitiveness.
3. Inhabitiveness.
3.A. Continuitiveness.
4. Adhesiveness.
D. Marriage or Union for Life.
5. Defensiveness.
E. The Centre of Energy.
6. Destructiveness.
6.A. Alimentiveness.
C. Bibativeness.
7. Secretiveness.
8. Acquisitiveness.
9. Constructiveness.
10. Self-Esteem.

11. Approbativeness.
12. Cautiousness.
13. Benevolence.
14. Reverence.
15. Firmness.
16. Conscientiousness.
17. Hope.
18. Marvellousness.
19. Love of the Picturesque.
19.B. Sublimity.
20. Imitation
21. Mirthfulness.
22. Individuality.
23. Form.
24. Size.

25. Weight.
26. Color.
27. Locality.
28. Number.
29. Order.
30. Eventuality.
31. Time.
32. Tune.
33. Verbal Memory.
34. Comparison.
35. Causality.
36. Graveness.
37. Gayness.
38. Awe.

Gall's treatment of the "organ of acquisitiveness" is a good case in point. He located this region after he had befriended a gang of lower class boys, who sometimes did errands for him. Having won their confidence, Gall noted that the boys varied greatly in their attitudes toward petty theft. Some openly admitted to thieving and bragged about their profits, while others were indifferent or expressed an active dislike of their larcenous companions. When Gall just happened to investigate the boys' heads he was astonished, he assures us, to find that the inveterate thieves had long prominences just above and to the front of the ears. The heads of the boys actively opposed to thievery were flat in that region, while the indifferent group had intermediate sized bumps there.

With little effort, Gall found other examples of people with large organs of acquisitiveness who also had marked inclinations to steal. One of the more memorable was a repeatedly-jailed young man who finally gained an almost psychotherapeutic—if somewhat slanderous—insight into his own nature, according to Gall: "As he felt incapable of resisting temptation, he wished to learn the trade of *tailor;* because, as he said, he might then indulge his inclination with impunity." Another case was a mentally retarded young man with a small and unsymmetrical skull and retreating forehead, whose only well-developed feature was the organ of acquisitiveness. An incorrigible thief, this poor soul seemed to Gall to offer "conclusive proof" of his theory, since the activity of the boy's organ of acquisitiveness "was not balanced by the action of other parts," and the propensity to thievery was able to emerge with unmitigated strength.

Though this case was conclusive proof to Gall, his mention of the potential "balancing action" of other brain parts highlights a dodge that he was only too quick to employ in other, less convenient cases. An individual with a huge organ of acquisitiveness but no thieving propensities could be explained away by invoking a large counteractive organ of "benevolence," for example. With twenty-seven or more independently varying faculties to work with, an almost infinitely large number of combinations existed to explain away any anomalous cases.

This was just one of the dubious strategies Gall employed in his analysis of two eminent Viennese gentlemen who led exemplary lives until middle age, despite large bulges of acquisitiveness. Then they both became insane, and when hospitalized, "they wandered all over the hospital, from morning till night, picking up whatever they could lay their hands on—straw, rags, clothes, wood," which they carefully concealed in their shared apartment. There, they stole from each other. Gall easily accounted for their changed behavior by asserting that up until their insanity, their acquisitive tendencies had been held in check by other well developed faculties of a more socialized nature. Then their insanity affected *just* the organs of those higher faculties, permitting the acquisitive tendencies to gain the upper hand. Gall summarized, "The case of these two persons proves, that a man, whose intellect is not quite too feeble, may, in health, overcome the unfortunate impulses of certain organs." Between the counterbalancing effects of many faculties, and "illness" that arbitrarily interfered with some faculties but not with others, Gall could "prove" anything he chose.

If Gall himself was cavalier in his treatment of evidence, he attracted followers who raised such tendencies almost to an art form. When a cast of the right side of Napoleon's skull indicated a phrenological analysis markedly at variance with the emperor's known characteristics, the phrenologists unhesitatingly replied that his true personality was reflected on the left side— a cast of which was conveniently missing. When Descartes's skull was examined, it was found to be exceptionally small in the parts associated by phrenology with the rational faculties. The phrenologists retorted that Descartes's rationality had always been overrated.

Not surprisingly, such tactics made phrenologists the butt of many jokes in the scientific community. According to one story, a noted phrenologist was offered an opportunity to examine the preserved brain of the great physicist Laplace. When the brain of a recently deceased imbecile was secretly substituted for Laplace's, it had no effect on the phrenologist's glowing description of the brain's qualities. A widely circulated scientific joke had it that Gall's own skull, which was preserved following his death and placed on exhibition at the Musée de l'Homme in Paris, was twice as thick as the average.

The scientific establishment responded to phrenology with more than jokes, however. Several individuals recognized that phrenological hypotheses were potentially significant and scientifically testable, even if the phrenologists' own uncontrolled observations were inadequate tests. Foremost among these was a young Frenchman named Pierre Flourens (1794–1867), who conducted a series of experiments in the 1820s that appeared to settle the question of localization of functions in the brain once and for all. Actually, however, they merely presented one side of a classic scientific controversy that remains alive today.

FLOURENS AND THE DISCREDITING OF PHRENOLOGY

It is difficult to think of two scientists working in the same area whose personalities and careers diverged more sharply than Gall and Flourens. Whereas Gall was always an outsider, never accepted by orthodox scientists, Flourens epitomized the man of the Establishment. A scientific prodigy who received his medical degree and published his first scientific paper at age nineteen, Flourens was the special protégé of Georges Cuvier (1769–1832), known as "The Dictator of Biology," and the most celebrated scientist in France. Cuvier's endorsement guaranteed that Flourens's work would be greeted enthusiastically, though it was good enough to stand out on its own.

Appalled by the shoddy methods of the phrenologists, Flourens determined to study the functions of the brain strictly by *experiment,* that is, by the systematic manipulation of the brains of animals, and the careful comparison of their behavior with that of control animals whose brains

had not been altered. Experimental techniques promised much more precision and control over the variables than the simple naturalistic observation that Gall usually employed.

The specific technique Flourens employed was the *ablation,* or surgical removal, of certain small parts of the brain, followed by observation of the subject's behavior after recovery from the operation. Most brain tissue does not regenerate after removal. Thus if specific functions are observed to be permanently missing or altered following an ablation, then the ablated brain tissue may be assumed to be involved in the normal production of those functions.

Flourens did not invent the ablation technique, but he refined it to a new degree. His predecessors had failed to obtain conclusive results for two general reasons. First, they did not cleanly excise clearcut brain regions, but merely pinched, pricked, or compressed parts of the brain. Since brain tissue is spongy in texture, it was seldom possible to determine precisely which parts of the brain were injured by these procedures, and to what extent. Thus any resulting behavior change could not be related to precisely localized brain lesions. Secondly, most of Flourens's predecessors were poor surgeons whose animals did not live long following their operations. It was often impossible to determine how much of their altered behavior was the result of specific ablations, and how much was caused by simple shock from the surgical trauma. Gall, who recognized the anti-phrenological bias of these early experimentalists, had some justification when he called them "mutilators" and dismissed their work as too sloppy to challenge his ideas. It was, of course, a case of the kettle calling the pot black.

Flourens was a much more formidable antagonist for Gall because of his extraordinary skill as a surgeon. Working on the small brains of birds and rabbits as well as dogs, he was able to ablate precisely determined, small portions of the brain. Rather than pinching or pricking the tissue, he completely removed thin slices from various locations. He carefully nursed his subjects following their operations, and so long as they were not missing a brain part necessary for life itself they usually survived. Flourens always waited until the animals had recovered as much as possible before drawing conclusions from his observations, making sure that the effects were the result of ablated brain tissue and not of post-operative complications.

Flourens set out to test Gall's hypotheses by ablating areas supposedly related to specific faculties. Since he worked with animals, he could not test those faculties that are uniquely human, such as verbal memory. But Gall had argued that many features of animal brains are similar to those of humans, including the "organ of amativeness," the cerebellum. Some of Flourens's earliest and most widely known studies involved ablation of this region. He found something quite different from what phrenology predicted, as evidenced by the following description of a dog whose cerebellum he had excised:

> I removed the cerebellum in a young but vigorous dog by a series of deeper and deeper slices. The animal lost gradually the faculty of orderly and regular movement. Soon he could walk only by staggering in zigzags. He fell back when he wanted to advance; when he wanted to turn to the right he turned to the left. As he made great efforts to move and could no longer moderate these efforts, he hurled himself impetuously forward, and did not fail to fall or roll over. If he found an object in his path, he was unable to avoid it, no matter what means he took; he hurled himself right and left; nevertheless he was perfectly well; when one irritated him he tried to bite; in fact, he bit any object one presented to him when he could reach it, but often he could no longer direct his movements with precision so as to reach the object. He had all his intellectual faculties, all his senses; he was only deprived of the faculty of co-ordinating and regularizing his movements.*

This is a classic description of a cerebellar lesion, scarcely to be improved upon even after years of further research. Flourens demonstrated conclusively that the function of the cerebellum is to or-

ganize and integrate the many small individual movements that must be combined in a flexible yet systematic way to constitute any purposive behavior. Even a simple act like walking requires the proper ordering of thousands of individual muscular movements. This integrating function of the cerebellum was a far cry from "amativeness," of course, and this disconfirmation of a specific phrenological localization was a severe blow to Gall's reputation.

Flourens also ablated tissue from the cortical lobes, the region implicated by Gall in the higher faculties. As sections were progressively removed, animals gradually lost the use of all their senses, and their capacity for voluntary action. Thus a totally decorticated pigeon was kept alive by force feeding and other ministrations by Flourens, but seemed totally insensitive to visual and auditory stimulation and never once initiated a movement that was not directly elicited by prodding. As Flourens concluded, "Picture to yourself an animal condemned to perpetual sleep, and deprived even of the faculty of dreaming during this sleep; such, almost exactly, had become the state of this pigeon whose cerebral hemispheres I had removed." In his view, the animal had lost its *will* along with its cortex.

Flourens believed this finding disproved phrenology. It was true, of course, that he had shown positive evidence of a kind of brain localization. Cortical and cerebellar ablations yielded very different effects, indicating that the two brain parts serve different functions. But *within* the cortex or cerebellum, the functions seemed to Flourens to be evenly distributed. All of the various sensory and voluntary functions tended to disappear *together* as increasingly larger sections of cortex were ablated. If the functions were precisely localized in specific regions, as the phrenologists believed, one would have expected more specificity in the effects of small lesions—or at least so argued Flourens.

Actually, Flourens's logic on this point was far from unassailable, since it held good only if the dimensions of the small ablated regions corresponded precisely to the dimensions of a par-

*Quoted in J. M. D. Olmsted, "Pierre Flourens." In E. A. Underwood (Ed.), *Science, medicine, and history.* New York: Oxford University Press, 1953, Volume 2, pp. 290–302.

ticular cerebral "organ." Flourens himself described the tissue he removed as "slices," however. Assuming phrenology to be correct, a "slice" could remove tissue from several cerebral organs at once, and result in a *general* lowering of functions as Flourens in fact observed. Gall eagerly seized upon this in his criticism of Flourens: "He mutilates all the organs at once, weakens them all, extirpates them all at the same time." This was a cogent criticism, for Flourens did in fact miss important effects of cortical localization—though quite unlike those predicted by phrenology—because he removed tissue from several functionally distinct areas at once.

Flourens struck a somewhat more damaging blow to phrenology by his observation that animals sometimes recovered all or part of their lost functions with the passage of time. Phrenology held that the several organs covered the *entire* cortex and determined behavioral characteristics by their relative sizes. Accordingly, ablation ought to alter the relative sizes permanently, and there should be no return to the original condition following recovery. Flourens showed that there is much more plasticity to the brain than phrenology assumed, especially if the experimental animal was young and the original ablation relatively small. Researchers to the present day have been very interested in exploring the limits of this plasticity, in determining when and how recovery from brain damage is most likely to occur.

In summary, Flourens's experiments suggested conclusions about brain function that were quite different from phrenological theory. He had found evidence for a kind of localization of functions, but only of very general functions in the large anatomical divisions of the brain. Thus the cerebellum mediated motor coordination, while the cortex seemed the seat of "will." Within each division these specific functions—or *actions propres,* as Flourens called them—

were evenly distributed, however. The *actions propres* bore scant similarity to the variegated faculties of the phrenologists.

Flourens's conception of the brain emphasized the integration among its separate parts. While each major part had its *action propre,* it also seemed functionally connected with the other parts. Injury to the cortex, for example, impaired the will and thus altered the kinds of movements that were voluntarily initiated; the cerebellum, which had to integrate the movements, was thus influenced as well. Conversely, deficiencies in motor coordination caused by injury to the cerebellum were perceived by the will, and influenced the volitional urges arising in the cortex. Thus, Flourens believed the separate brain parts were components of a single, harmonious, integrated system, manifesting an *action commune* that overrode and controlled their individual *actions propres.* In a conception more reminiscent of Descartes than of Gall, Flourens believed the brain and nervous system to be the seat of an integrated and harmonious soul.

His view was eagerly accepted by most of the scientific community. Phrenological hypotheses had been clearly repudiated by his findings on the cerebellum and the recovery of functions, and the cortex seemed to be the undifferentiated organ of a general "will." The question of localized functions within the cortex *seemed* conclusively answered in the negative.

But there was the one crucial flaw in Flourens's experiments. By taking undifferentiated slices from the cortexes of animals whose brains were relatively small to begin with, he had failed to discover the differentiations of function that were there. This error went undetected for many years, until brain researchers returned their attention to the highly developed human cortex and its relation to a uniquely human function, that of language.

Case Studies in Nineteenth Century Scientific Rejection: Mesmerism, Perkinism, and Acupuncture

Jacques M. Quen

In 1774, Franz Anton Mesmer found that patients got better when he treated them with magnets. Mesmer postulated a universal, magnetic, ethereal fluid with energic qualities, as the active agent. Later, he called his treatment Animal Magnetism. In the years following, he achieved a remarkable notoriety and fame for successfully treating numerous patients in Austria and France. Within ten years of its discovery, Animal Magnetism was a matter of serious controversy in the French medical community. In 1784, a French royal commission, headed by American Ambassador Benjamin Franklin, published a report that exposed Mesmer's theory of the physical basis of his method as fallacious, and accounted for its effectiveness as due to the subject's "imagination." The report appears to have stopped further medical investigation of the phenomenon until much later.

In 1795, Elisha Perkins, a founding member of the Connecticut Medical Society and President of the Windham County Medical Society, discovered a treatment for painful conditions utilizing a simple knife blade. By February of the following year he had obtained a government patent on two metal rods of secret composition, one colored silver, the other gold. This was probably the first patent for a medical device issued in the new country. The rods were called Perkins's Metallic Tractors and sold for about 25 Continental Dollars. Lady Oxholm, the wife of a Danish diplomat, took a pair of the Tractors back to Denmark, where the royal physicians tested them, published an enthusiastic report, and named the method Perkinism. Perkins, meanwhile, was cited by the state medical society for having

Quen, J. M. (1975). Case studies in nineteenth century scientific rejection: Mesmerism, Perkinism, and acupuncture. *Journal of the History of the Behavioral Sciences, 11,* 149–156. Copyright © 1975 by the Clinical Psychology Publishing Company. Reprinted by permission of the publisher.

gleaned up from the miserable remains of animal magnetism, a practice, consisting of stroking with pointed metallic instruments, the pained parts of human bodies; giving out that such strokings will radically cure the most obstinate pain to which our frame is incident . . . causing false reports to be propagated of the effects of such strokings. . . .

The following year, having failed to appear before them and to vindicate himself, Perkins was expelled from the Society. He died in the 1799 New York epidemic while trying to cure cases of Yellow Fever with his Tractors. A detailed history of Elisha Perkins and his method is presented elsewhere.[1] His son, Benjamin D. Perkins, went to England in 1797 to establish a base for Perkinism and the sale of Perkins's Metallic Tractors.

England became the locus of as intense a controversy as had occurred earlier in America. During this time, *Terrible Tractoration,* described by its American author, Thomas Green Fessenden ("Christopher Caustic"), as "a satirical effusion in Hudibrastic verse," appeared in defense of Perkinism.[2] During this same period, Dr. John Haygarth of Bath, conducted experiments using fake Tractors made of bone, wax and wood, painted to resemble the genuine ones. Using first the spurious and then the genuine Tractors, Haygarth and his colleagues achieved striking therapeutic responses in chronically disabled patients. He proved that the composition of the Tractors was of no significance, that Perkins's theory of excess "electroid" being drained off was without foundation, and that the therapeutic effects were dependent upon the "imagination" of the patient. In answer, Perkineans pointed to the Tractors' effectiveness on animals (barring sheep, whose greasy coats interfered with the action of the Tractors) as proof that the method did not depend on the "imagination" for its effectiveness.

The patients selected for Haygarth's experiments were largely people for whom conventional medical treatments had been ineffective.

> Robert Thomas, aged 43...with a rheumatick affection of the shoulder, which rendered his arm perfectly useless...so far recovered [after fake Tractor treatment] that he could carry coals, etc. and use his arm sufficiently to assist the nurse; yet previous to the use of the spurious Tractors he could no more lift his hand than if a hundred weight were upon it or a nail driven through it.[3]
>
> Thomas Ellis...had been incapable of walking without support, or feeding himself, for four months.... He now began to mend so fast that he could comb his hair very readily, and...[ten days after starting fake Tractor treatments]...he put on his jacket and walked across the ward without a stick or the least assistance.[4]
>
> Edmund Williams...with *stillicidum urinae* [urinary dribbling]....The man was a poor and feeble subject, and appeared to be impressed with the idea that nothing would be serviceable to him but he was "willing to try anything"...[after several fake Tractor treatments]...a bystander asked him "if he thought himself mended?" He replied he would soon answer his question and upon sitting down, suddenly exclaimed, "yes, I am better." It was demanded of him how he knew it? "When I used to sit down (said the man) there was always a spirt of water thrown from me, but now I can prevent it." The experiment was two or three times repeated, and the same result; in fact, the patient absolutely regained in great measure the power of retention afterwards.[5]

These remarkable cures by fake Tractor treatment were matched by the reported effects of genuine Tractors, including the cure of epilepsy, of acute insanity, and the increased speed of healing of scalds and wounds. Once they had proved that Perkins's theory was fallacious and that the actual effects were a function of the "imagination," Haygarth and his colleagues abandoned interest.[6]

By the end of the first decade of the nineteenth century, Perkinism appeared to have been pretty well forgotten in America and England, except for its immortalization in Byron's *English Bards and Scotch Reviewers* (1809):

> What varied wonders tempt us as they pass!
> The Cow-pox, Tractors, Galvanism, Gas,
> In turns appear to make the vulgar stare,
> Till the swoll'n bubble bursts—and all is air.

In 1970, two historians of psychiatry, Eric T. Carlson and Meribeth M. Simpson, at Cornell University Medical College, published a study of Mesmerism and Perkinism,[7] which was concerned with the similarities in the histories of these two treatment methods. The Franklin Commission was cited as "not interested in the possible use of animal magnetism and dismissed the fact that it did produce effects along with their dismissal of the specious theory on which it rested."[8] Carlson and Simpson concluded their study with:

> Mesmer's elegant clinic with its impressive paraphernalia and Perkins's simple, if expensive Tractors were dismissed equally by the majority of the men of science. Mesmer and Perkins had drawn in similar fashion on popular theories of physics of their day in order to explain their therapeutic successes, but once the true sources of their cures, imagination and suggestion became apparent, the whole matter was pushed aside. The powers of suggestion had been dramatically demonstrated, but for legitimate medicine there seemed no way to put this curious weapon to use.[9]

The third method to be considered is nineteenth century Western acupuncture, whose history begins somewhat earlier. In 1693, 14 years after he had been in Japan as the Dutch East India Company medical officer, Ten Rhyne published a book describing his experiences with acupuncture. In 1727, *A History of Japan,* the English translation of a book by Englebert Kaempfer, a physician attached to the Dutch embassy in Japan in 1691–92, described nine acupuncture points in the abdomen. Little notice was taken of either of these by the Western medical profession of the time. It was a French physician, Berlioz, who first published, in 1816, a description of acupuncture experiments that he had been conducting since 1810.[10] In 1821, an English physician, James Morss Churchill, published a small pamphlet describing his encouraging clinical experiences.[11] Soon there was a stream of articles in the Western medical literature, describing the successful use of acupuncture for painful musculoskeletal conditions, but without a theory to account for the action.

Common sewing needles were used in the early nineteenth century, frequently with a tab of sealing wax on the end so that they would be easier to push and wouldn't get lost in the patient's body. The needles were inserted directly into the painful area and relief would follow shortly.

Following the introduction of acupuncture, many new uses were developed for the needle as a surgical instrument. Needles were used to drain ganglia and edematous tissue, to clot blood in arterial aneurysms, and as electrodes to stimulate specific paralyzed muscles. Experiments were described in which drowned kittens were resuscitated, after complete cardiac arrest, by direct acupuncture into the heart.

Western physician acupuncturists offered almost no theories to account for the therapeutic results. Direct acupuncture of the painful area was used almost exclusively in the early and mid-nineteenth century with no acknowledgement or apparent awareness of the oriental method or rationale. The Chinese rarely insert the needle at the site of the pain. In 1871, *Lancet* published an article describing the traditionally successful use of direct acupuncture at the Leeds Infirmary.[12] In 1879, Dumontpallier, a physician at La Pitié, experimented with acupuncture at the contralateral site of pain. He found this to be quite effective, but again, no reference was made to the Chinese practice.[13] In 1892, William Osler, in his textbook of medicine, recommended direct acupuncture as an excellent specific treatment for lumbago, adding that the standard "bonnet pin" would do quite nicely.[14]

Imported into America in 1825,[15] acupuncture stimulated some clinical trial, but no lasting interest. It was not until the early 1970's that reports of acupuncture anesthesia in major surgery in Mainland China aroused great excitement in America. Soon the medical literature contained letters suggesting that the anesthetic effect was due to hypnosis or, in effect, the "imagination." The Chinese pointed out that since it was used successfully on their laboratory animals one could rule out both "imagination" and faith in Chairman Mao. The modern Chinese, however, have yet to offer a substantial theory for its action. In the West, the Melzack-Wall "gate control theory" has been invoked.[16] This theory maintains that there is a cell in the substantia gelatinosa of the spinal cord (thalamus, reticular substance, *etc.*) which, when stimulated, "acts like a gate" closing the pathways for pain. One could alternatively say that the "imagination" acts like a gate closing the pathways to pain. Recently, Wall has come out with a statement that acupuncture anesthesia is due to hypnosis or suggestion.[17]

In nineteenth century England, John Elliotson, who is perhaps best known for his interest in and active support of Mesmerism and phrenology, was one of the early English physician acupuncturists. Discussing the mystery surrounding the mode of action of acupuncture, he pointed out,

> It is neither fear nor confidence; since those who care nothing about being acupunctured, and those who laugh at their medical attendant for proposing such a remedy, derive the same benefit, if their case is suitable, as those who are alarmed and those who submit to it with faith. Neither is it counter-irritation; since the same benefit is experienced when not the least pain is occasioned, as when pain is felt. Galvanism, likewise fails to explain; because although the needle becomes oxidated and affords galvanic phenomena while in the body, these phenomena bear no proportion to their benefit, [they] equally take place when acupuncture is practised upon a healthy person, and do not take place when needles of gold or silver are employed, which, however, are equally efficacious with a needle of steel.[18]

As if addressing himself to the question of why these treatment methods were rejected, John Renton, a Scots physician, wrote of acupuncture in 1830:

The utility of a specific is very readily suspected, when its infallibility is given out for the removal of too many diseases, and more particularly of those between which no analogy can be traced. And when, moreover, no satisfactory explanation can be afforded of the *modus operandi* of the reagent, professional persons, unhappily for the interests of medical science, are too apt to reason upon the authenticity of the facts averred, instead of adopting the more simple and direct method of determining their value by subjecting them to the fact of further experience. Indeed the different attempts which have been made to account (as by electricity for example) for the various physical and physiological phenomena produced by acupuncturation, have been very injurious to the successful diffusion of the practice; and accordingly, we find that the very rapidity and perception of the cures have acted as causes of why the efficacy of the remedy has been doubted, and that its boasted recoveries have been imputed more to mental reaction—that is, to impressions acting upon the patient's mind from a fancied and mystical confidence in the use of the means employed,—than to any real good effects resulting from the operation itself.[19]

Was the rejection of these three treatment methods based on simple selfish economics? Requiring no scientific training or knowledge, their widespread acceptance might have threatened the livelihood of the practicing physician. Although this might have affected the reaction of some, it was not mentioned in contemporary correspondence, and it could not have been a significant factor for the nonphysician scientists.

It was a confirmed observation, in the history of each method, that patients, who had not been relieved by conventional medical treatments, were relieved by these therapies. What factors in the medical and scientific communities determined the responses to these phenomena?

Gunther Stent says that some scientific discoveries are premature because their "implications cannot be connected by a series of simple logical steps to canonical, or generally accepted knowledge."[20] He cites, as one example:

[Michael Polanyi's 1914–1916] theory of the adsorption of gases on solids which assumed that the force attracting a gas molecule to a solid surface depends only on the position of the molecule, and not on the presence of other molecules, in the force field. In spite of the fact that Polanyi was able to provide strong experimental evidence in favor of his theory, it was generally rejected.... it was also considered so ridiculous by the leading authorities of the time that Polanyi believes that continued defense of his theory would have ended his professional career if he had not managed to publish work on more palatable ideas. The reason for the general rejection of Polanyi's adsorption theory was that at the very time he put it forward the role of electrical forces in the architecture of matter had just been discovered. Hence there seemed to be no doubt that the adsorption of gases must also involve an electrical attraction between the gas molecules and the solid surface. That point of view, however, was irreconcilable with Polanyi's basic assumption of the mutual independence of individual gas molecules in the adsorption process. It was only in the 1930's, after a new theory of cohesive molecular forces based on quantum-mechanical resonance rather than on electrostatic attraction had been developed, that it became conceivable gas molecules could behave in the way Polanyi's experiments indicated they were actually behaving. Meanwhile Polanyi's theory had been consigned so authoritatively to the ashcan of crackpot ideas that it was rediscovered only in the 1950's.[21]

Polanyi, in 1963, said, "This miscarriage of the scientific method could not have been avoided.... There must be at all times a predominantly accepted scientific view of the nature of things, in the light of which research is jointly conducted by members of the community of scientists. A strong presumption that any evidence which contradicts this view is invalid must prevail. Such evidence *has to be disregarded,* even if it cannot be accounted for, in the hope that it will eventually turn out to be false or irrelevant [emphasis added]."[22] Stent's comment on Polanyi's position is that it "is a view of the operation of science rather different from the one commonly held, under which acceptance of authority is seen as something to be avoided at all costs. The good scientist is seen as an unprejudiced man with an open mind who is ready to embrace any new idea supported by the facts. The history of science shows, however, that its practitioners do not appear to act according to that popular view."[23]

With the advance of quantum physics, parallels between physical theories and the social and behavioral sciences become increasingly evident. Such a parallel is found between the physicist Polanyi's concept of the nature of scientific progress and an observation of Erik Erikson's in the development of psychoanalysis as a science. In a footnote to a statement on the unconscious concomitants of prejudice, Erikson says:

> As for [Jung's archetype] theory, we may note in passing that the first conceptual controversies in psychoanalysis throw light on the problem of identity in the initial stages of a science. . . . [Jung's] scientific rebellion . . . led to ideological regression and (weakly denied) political reaction. This phenomenon—as similar ones before and after—had its group psychological counterpart in reaction within the psychoanalytic movement: *as if in fear of endangering a common group identity based on common scientific gains, psychoanalytic observers chose to ignore not only Jung's interpretations but the facts he observed* [emphasis added].[24]

In exploring the fundamental question of this study, Thomas Kuhn's theory of the structure of scientific revolutions must be considered.[25] Kuhn says, "Discovery commences with the awareness of anomaly, *i.e.*, with the recognition that nature has somehow violated the paradigm-induced expectations that govern normal science. It then continues with a more or less extended exploration of the area of anomaly. And it closes only when the paradigm theory has been adjusted so that the anomalous has become the expected."[26] In regard to the three treatment methods discussed, we could say that the commencement of discovery stopped with the awareness of the anomaly. [Kuhn's the-

ory does not take into account the reaction of the apocryphal farmer who, upon seeing a giraffe for the first time, concluded, "There ain't no sech animal!"]

Kuhn's primary concern is with the elucidation of the nature of scientific revolutions and, consequently, he considers only those anomalies which are not ignored and which lead to the revision of paradigms. Polanyi, Stent, and Erikson deal with a class of anomalies which the scientific community needs to, or wants to ignore, while Kuhn deals with the class which have a persistent irritant effect until integrated into a new paradigm. The former group of anomalies seems to require that the individual making the observation provide the theory, or some acceptable rationale, for them. When this is rejected or discredited, as it was with Mesmerism and Perkinism, the phenomena are met with "selective inattention" by the scientific community. Nineteenth century Western acupuncture, receiving no theoretical explanation, was ignored by those who needed a "normal science" rationale to allow themselves to acknowledge or use it. We see, then, a group psychological mechanism for rejection of those anomalies which do not demand an explanation.

One might also note that Kuhn's view is sequential and prospective. He does not deal with the retrospective aspect of a revolution, that is, the need to define itself as distinctly different from what had gone before, the need to reject more than is necessary, to ensure no contamination from the unacceptable past. To extend the suggested anthropomorphic analogy of Erikson, the efforts of a new science to individuate and to establish a distinctive identity, are much like those of the developing child who feels he "must" be negativistic to establish his own identity, separate and distinct from the parents and siblings.

The absence of a scientifically orthodox theory of the mode of action, and the consequent implication of the "imagination," are the outstanding traits of these three therapies. Carlson and Simpson pointed out the relationship between the implication of imagination and the loss of investigative interest in Mesmerism and Perkinism. Renton makes it clear that this was the case with acupuncture in 1830. What is the connecting link? What made the study of the "imagination" and its use for healing an area of scientific disrespectability? Was it related to political, economic, or other social ferment of the time? There had long been a medical awareness that "passions" could induce disease states; why was there no room in the contemporary medical or scientific conception of reality for an "imagination" that could treat or heal?

Our present knowledge of this problem is inadequate to provide a single answer to explain all three cases satisfactorily. Each of them, despite major similarities, is quite different from the other two. Mesmerism (hypnotism) has an uneasy position in clinical medicine today. Despite its use and a revival of interest by psychoanalysts, physicians, and psychologists, it is still avoided by the majority in the mental health professions as a treatment modality, even in an adjunctive role. Acupuncture is dealt with as a novel plaything in current medical literature, and speculation is rife among those who have no clinical or laboratory experience with it as to its "probable" mode of action. Perkinism, with the best documented record of therapeutic effectiveness and safety, is quite dead (except, perhaps, for the current use of copper bracelets).

It would be foolish to argue that these three nineteenth century treatment modalities should be revived and incorporated unchanged into the contemporary medical armamentarium. However, it would be more than foolish to continue to turn our backs on the fact that these and other treatment methods, rejected by the scientific medical community, provided relief and palliation for many people who did not benefit from "normal science" medical treatment. Something was utilized, with remarkable therapeutic efficacy, by the patients who responded to these anomalous methods.

Why was nineteenth century medicine unable to distinguish between fallacious theory and therapeutic fact? Are we really better able to do so in the mid-twentieth century? Much more work must be done in studying what determines which therapeutic modes a medical community (or a society) will accept and which it will reject. We can no longer afford to repeat the mistakes of the past, if ever we could. It is more than merely desirable that serious and genuine efforts be made to understand why our scientists avoided broader study of the effective therapeutic phenomena in the "anomalous" methods of Mesmerism, Perkinism, and acupuncture. This preliminary report highlights a broad area of ignorance of the sociology and psychology of medical community mechanisms for the evaluation of potential treatment methods.

NOTES

1 Quen, Jacques M. "Elisha Perkins, physician, nostrum-vendor, or charlatan?" *Bulletin of the History of Medicine,* 1963, *37,* 159–166. See also Jacques M. Quen, "A study of Dr. Elisha Perkins and Perkinism." Unpublished M. D. thesis, Department of the History of Medicine, Yale University Medical School, 1954.
2 Quen, Jacques M. "Perkinism and Terrible Tractoration." *Journal of the History of Medicine and Allied Sciences,* 1964, *19,* 296–297.
3 Haygarth, John. *Of the Imagination as a Cause and as a Cure of Disorders of the Body.* (Bath: R. Cruttwell, 1801), 2nd edition, pp. 6–8.
4 *Ibid.,* pp. 8–9.
5 *Ibid.,* pp. 16–17.
6 To appreciate the complexity of Haygarth's view, his book should be read. The opening paragraph says, "That faculty of the mind which is denominated the Imagination...has not wholly escaped the notice of medical writers but merits their further investigation. This slight Essay may, perhaps, incite others to prosecute the inquiry more fully, in order to extend the power of physicians to prevent and cure the maladies of mankind (P. 1)." However, the thrust of the book is as I have characterized it above.
7 Carlson, Eric T., and Simpson, Meribeth M. "Perkinism vs. Mesmerism." *Journal of the History of the Behavioral Sciences,* 1970, *6,* 16–24.
8 *Ibid,* p. 19.
9 *Ibid.,* p. 23.

10 Berlioz, L. V. J. *Mémoires sur les Maladies Chroniques, les Évacuations Sanguines, et l'Acupuncture.* (Paris: Croullebois, 1816).

11 Churchill, James Morss. *A Treatise on Acupuncturation.* (London: Simkin and Marshall, 1822).

12 Teale, T. Pridgin, "On the relief of pain and muscular disability by acupuncture." *Lancet,* 1871, *1,* 567–568.

13 Dumontpallier, *Sur L'Analgesie Thérapeutique Locale, déterminée par l'irritation de la region similaire du cote oppose du corps.* (Paris, 1879) reported in "Dumontpallier on the cure of pain by acupuncture at a distance" in the *London Medical Record,* 1880, *8,* 6–7.

14 Osler, William. *The Principles and Practice of Medicine.* (New York: Appleton, 1892), p. 282. See also p. 820 for acupuncture in cases of sciatica.

15 Morand, M. J. *Memoir on Acupuncturation.* (Trans. by B. Franklin Bache) Philadelphia: Robert Desilver, 1825).

16 Matsumoto, Teruo, "Acupuncture and U. S. medicine." *Journal of the American Medical Association,* 1972, *220,* 1010. See also Burton, Charles, "Is there a scientific basis for acupuncture?" *Medical Tribune,* 1972, *31,* 5.

17 Reported in *Medical Tribune,* 1973, *31,* 13.

18 Elliotson, John, "Acupuncture," in *The Cyclopaedia of Practical Medicine,* Ed. by John Forbes, Alexander Tweedie, John Conolly, and thoroughly revised by Robley Dunglison. (Philadelphia: Lea & Blanchard, 1850) 4 vols. Vol. I, pp. 54–56, p. 56.

19 Renton, John, "Observations on acupuncture." *Edinburgh Medical & Surgical Journal,* 1830, *34,* 100–107, p. 101.

20 Stent, Gunther, "Prematurity and uniqueness in scientific discovery." *Scientific American,* 1972, December, 84–93, p. 84.

21 *Ibid.,* p. 86.

22 Polanyi, Michael, "The potential theory of adsorption: Authority in science has its uses and its dangers." *Science,* 1963, *141,* 1010–1013, p. 1012.

23 Stent, *op. cit.,* fn. 22, p. 88.

24 Erikson, Erik H., "Ego development and historical change: clinical notes." In *Identity and the Life Cycle,* in the series *Psychological Issues,* Vol. 1, No. 1. (New York: International Universities Press, 1959) p. 31, fn. 7.

25 Kuhn, Thomas S., *The Structure of Scientific Revolutions.* (2nd ed.) *International Encyclopedia of Unified Science,* Vol. 2, No. 2. (Chicago: University of Chicago Press, 1970).

26 *Ibid.,* pp. 52–53.

Citation Analysis as a Tool in Historical Study:
A Case Study Based on F. C. Donders and Mental Reaction Times

Elizabeth Scarborough

The present study represents an effort to apply a controlled, quantitative method to assess the current status of a significant scientific paper: a work of F. C. Donders, the Dutch physiologist, on mental reaction time (Donders, 1868a). The study was based on an examination of the frequency of citation of this paper in current psychological literature.

Goodman [Scarborough], E. S. (1971). Citation analysis as a tool in historical study: A case study based on F. C. Donders and mental reaction times. *Journal of the History of the Behavioral Sciences, 7,* 187–191. Copyright © 1971 by the Clinical Psychology Publishing Company. Reprinted by permission of the publisher.

A characteristic of contemporary science (which in part prompted this study) is its ahistorical orientation. One consequence of this orientation Derek J. de Solla Price has labeled the "immediacy factor," the more frequent citation of recent papers relative to earlier ones. Price holds that this factor is "responsible for the well-known phenomenon of papers being considered obsolescent after a decade" (Price, 1965, p. 513). Nevertheless, it was noted that two recent papers (Posner & Mitchell, 1967; Smith, 1968) did cite the 100-year-old study of Donders. These papers reflect a revival of interest in the problem area examined by Donders and the possibility of the current usefulness of the method which he devised.

Donders' approach to "mental chronometry" involved the identification of three types of reaction times. The a-reaction refers to a situation having one signal and one response and is known as the *simple* reaction. The b-reaction involves several signals and several responses, the *discrimination-plus-choice* reaction. The c-reaction is less complex, again with several signals, but requiring a response to only one specified signal within the array. The c-reaction may therefore be called the *discrimination* reaction.

Donders demonstrated that the time required for making each of these responses could be measured. He proposed that by subtracting a, the simple reaction, from c, the discrimination reaction, it was possible to measure the speed of the mental process required for making the discrimination, that is, the time necessary to identify one of a certain set of changes in the environment. By subtracting c from b, one could obtain a measure of the time taken to select the correct response. Quite reasonably, Donders' approach became known as the subtractive method.

The present study attempted to determine the extent to which mid-twentieth-century investigators of reaction time, choice behavior and mental chronometry did in fact recognize and use the pioneering work of Donders.

METHOD

The Posner and Mitchell (1967) and Smith (1968) papers were used as a starting point. All references cited by those two papers were examined to determine which ones also cited Donders. Of these references, those which did cite Donders were used for further examination. The references for each of these "second order" articles were then checked for their citation of Donders. Therefore a paper which cited Donders enlarged the population by adding its reference list to the original lists taken from Posner and Mitchell and Smith.*

In this way, a list of 132 references was compiled. (Twenty-nine of the references were cited by two or more of the papers examined.) Of these, 14 were unavailable to the investigator. Three were unpublished papers by authors whose addresses are unknown (not listed in APA Directory). Four were unpublished papers by authors who failed to respond to a letter requesting their reference lists. Five were references dealing with statistical matters pertinent to a theory being developed in one of the papers that cited Donders (LaBerge, 1962). One was an incorrect reference and not traceable, and one was a 1928 reference to an unavailable journal.

RESULTS

Twelve reference lists from the population of 132 were found to include Donders' 1868 paper. The sources and relationship between them are shown in Table 1.

Posner and Mitchell (1967) dealt directly with Donders in reporting a series of studies which represent efforts to extend the subtractive method to the analysis of depth of processing in simple classification tasks.

Smith (1968) also treated Donders extensively in an analysis of major theoretical positions on choice reaction time. He assessed the influence of Donders' subtraction method on current theory and pointed out the dependence of current theory on Donders' postulate that the latent period is filled with a sequence of events.

---

* Five references which did cite Donders were exceptions to this procedure. Boring (1950; 1963) and Woodworth (1938; 1954) are books dealing with history and experimental psychology and include content far beyond the scope of Donders' problem. The Cattell (1947) reference is a reprint of an article originally published in 1886. Inclusion of Cattell's references would therefore have confounded the results by introducing into the population papers which were contemporaneous of Donders rather than reflective of his historical influence.

Table 1.
References Citing Donders' 1868 Paper (Arrows Indicate Source of Reference.)

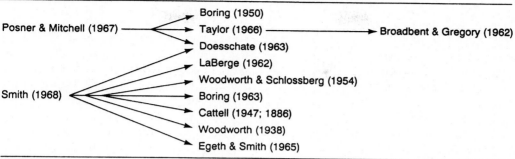

Taylor's (1966) experiment used Donders' b- and c-reactions and introduced another method of fractionating the two-choice response as a test of additivity of component latencies.

The relationship between differences in b- and c-reactions as a function of S-R compatibility was demonstrated by Broadbent and Gregory (1962).

LaBerge (1962) gave credit to Donders in discussing choice behavior when he referred to "a situation traditionally labeled the disjunctive reaction" followed by a reference which cited the 1868 paper.

Cattell (1947) compared his own data on time taken up by cerebral operations to Donders' data on time for b and c reactions.

Doesschate (1963) discussed the history of reaction-time measurements, giving considerable attention to Donders' contribution and describing the apparatus used by Donders to demonstrate the possibility of measuring the duration of individual mental processes such as discrimination and selection.

Both Boring (1950; 1963) and Woodworth (1938; 1954) considered Donders' work in its historical context. The unpublished paper by Egeth and Smith (1965) was not available for study by the investigator, though the authors did send their list of references, indicating that they did cite Donders.

It is noted that five of the 12 references concern the direct use of Donders' method and findings (Broadbent & Gregory, 1962; Cattell, 1947; Posner & Mitchell 1967; Smith, 1968, Taylor, 1966). Five references deal with Donders in the historical sense of evaluating his contribution to late nineteenth-century research (Boring, 1950; 1963; Doesschate, 1963; Woodworth, 1938; 1954). One reference makes only passing mention of Donders' method (LaBerge, 1962).

In addition to the twelve references which were identified by the procedure given above, three other papers also cited Donders and serve to point up the extent of his influence at the present. In the same journal issue in which the Doesschate (1963) paper appeared, an article by Shouten (1963) described a complex electronic system designed to carry out routine measuring operations automatically, thereby greatly facilitating research on reaction time. This system was named the DONDERS, to honor the physiologist who first demonstrated the possibility of measuring duration of reaction times.

In response to a letter requesting unpublished papers appearing in the reference population of this study, Sternberg sent the writer two additional papers, each of which he delivered during the summer of 1968. In both of these papers Sternberg discussed Donders' work. The paper delivered in the United States (Sternberg, 1968a) cited the German version (Donders, 1868a), the better known of the papers whereby Donders communicated his work. Sternberg used Donders' subtraction method as a reference procedure for experiments on the retrieval of information from human memory and further proposed a check on the validity of the method. The second paper (Sternberg, 1968b) was presented at the Donders Centenary Symposium on Reaction-Time held at the Instituut Voor Perceptie Onderzoek, Eindhoven, Netherlands, August, 1968. Here Sternberg cited the Dutch version of Donders' paper (1868b) and proposed a new method for using reaction-time measurements to study stages of information processing.

DISCUSSION

It appears that after a period of several decades of neglect, wide use is currently being made of F. C. Donders' methods, terminology and findings (see review of studies in Posner & Mitchell, 1967; Smith, 1968; Sternberg, 1968a). In terms of its reflection in the problems being investigated, Donders' 1868 work continues to exert influence on one area of psychological research and may justifiably be identified as a classic paper, using Price's (1965) definition based on frequency of citation and long life.

The "immediacy factor," however, is evident. Although a large number of studies are identified by Posner and Mitchell (1967) and Smith (1968) as being directly concerned with investigating Donders' phenomena and using and testing his methods, only a very few of these gave credit to Donders as the originator of the concepts being used. This may be viewed as an example of the "ahistorical" nature of current research writing.

Several explanations may account for the failure of current researchers to cite Donders. During the 1950's and 1960's there was no English translation of his 1868 works. (This situation has now been remedied due to the inclusion of such a translation in the proceedings of the Donders Centenary Symposium: Koster, 1969.) Another possible explanation lies in the fact that the subtractive method has become so much a part of the common knowledge of researchers that it is no longer deemed necessary to identify its originator. A further possibility is that present writers are more concerned with getting on with their immediate research interests and the citation of secondary sources is simply a way of expediting their work.

Nevertheless, the Donders' 1868 paper stands presently as an exception to the "immediacy" factor. Boring and Woodworth, both well-known to twentieth-century experimental psychologists, preserved Donders' contributions. With the revival of interest in cognitive psychology in the 1950's, researchers recognized the fruitfulness of Donders' approach, which appears now in a new context focussed on choice behavior and the processing of information.

The significance of this study lies not only in the data provided concerning Donders' current influence and the nature of research writing, but also in that it illustrates a methodological approach which might serve as a useful tool in historical study. Citation analysis is being recognized as a valuable procedure for obtaining data in a systematic fashion. The process lends itself to computerization and is being pursued on a large scale by the Institute for Scientific Information in Philadelphia, Pennsylvania. The Science Citation Index developed there, however, does not yet include the social sciences.*

The technique used in this study is admittedly tedious. It requires extensive library facilities and does not insure exhaustive coverage. It does, however, provide a way of moving through a content area and assessing the current influence of a historical work in a relatively efficient manner.

---

*Ed. note: The Institute for Scientific Information now publishes a Social Science Citation Index, and new computer programs have eased the labor of the research tool described in this article.

REFERENCES

Boring, E. G. *A history of experimental psychology.* (2nd ed.) New York: Appleton-Century-Crofts, 1950.

Boring, E. G. *History, psychology, and science: Selected papers.* (Ed. by R. I. Watson & D. T. Campbell) New York: Wiley, 1963.

Broadbent, D. E., & Gregory, M. Donders' B- and C-reactions and S-R compatibility. *Journal of Experimental Psychology,* 1962, *63,* 575–578.

Cattell, J. McK. *Psychological research.* Lancaster, Pa.: Science Press, 1947. (1886)

Doesschate, G. ten. Notes on the history of reaction time experiments. *Philips Technical Review,* 1963, *25,* 75–80.

Donders, F. C. Die Schnelligkeit psychischer Processe. *Archiv für Anatomie und Physiologie,* 1868, 657–681. (a)

Donders, F. C. Over de snelheid van psychische processen. *Onderzoekingen gedaanin het Physiologisch Laboratorium der Utrechtsche Hoogeschool,* 1868–69, Tweede reeks, II, 92–120. (b)

Egeth, H., & Smith, E. E. Categorization time and parallel vs. sequential processing of memorial information. Unpublished manuscript, University of Michigan, 1965.

Koster, W. D. (Ed.) *Attention and performance II.* Amsterdam: North Holland, 1969.

LaBerge, D. A recruitment theory of simple behavior. *Psychometrika,* 1962, *27,* 375–396.

Posner, M. I., & Mitchell, R. F. Chronometric analysis of classification. *Psychological Review,* 1967, *74,* 392–409.

Price, D. de S. Networks of scientific papers. *Science,* 1965, *149,* 510–515.

Schouten, J. F., & Domberg, J. The "DONDERS," an electronic system for measuring human reactions. *Philips Technical Review,* 1963, *25,* 64–74.

Smith, E. E. Choice reaction time: An analysis of the major theoretical positions. *Psychological Bulletin,* 1968, *69,* 77–110.

Sternberg, S. Inferring the organization of cognitive events from reaction-time: Some scanning processes in active memory. Paper presented at Symposium on Research in Cognitive Psychology, City University of New York, June 7, 1968. (a)

Sternberg, S. The discovery of processing stages: Extensions of Donders' method. Based on paper presented at the Donders Centenary Symposium on Reaction-Time held at the Instituut Voor Perceptie Onderzoek, Eindhoven, Netherlands, August, 1968. (b)

Taylor, D. H. Latency components in two-choice responding. *Journal of Experimental Psychology,* 1966, *72,* 481–487.

Woodworth, R. S. *Experimental psychology.* New York: Holt, 1938.

Woodworth, R. S., & Schlosberg, H. *Experimental psychology.* (Rev. ed.) New York: Holt, 1954.

CHAPTER 5

THE FRENCH CLINICAL TRADITION

For many decades, the public's prototypical image of a psychologist has been that of a professional involved in the treatment or counseling of clients (see Benjamin, 1986; Wood, Jones, & Benjamin, 1986). And now, for the first time in psychology's history, that image proves to be an accurate one for most psychologists (Stapp, Fulcher, & Wicherski, 1984). Contemporary students possess this clinical image of the field as well and often are surprised in taking a history of psychology course to learn that it is largely about the history of experimental psychology. There are a number of reasons for this narrowness of focus in the history of psychology.

First, many members of the founding generation of psychology as a science were interested in consciousness of the normal mind rather than in psychopathology. It was not that the abnormal mind seemed less interesting; rather, the emphasis on normality stemmed from a reasoned belief that studying normal individuals would lead more rapidly to an understanding of the workings of the mind.

Second, the field of mental illness was a medical field, dominated for centuries by the somatic view that held that psychological disturbances resulted from organic causes. The somatic view would begin to be replaced in the nineteenth century by the psychic view that regarded mental illness as a result of psychological causes, often the result of learning and experience. The tremendous impact of Sigmund Freud's work (see Chapter 15) hastened the acceptability of the psychic view.

Third, the profession of clinical psychology, at least in the United States, is a recent phenomenon. Almost no doctoral programs in clinical psychology existed before World War II, and very small numbers of psychologists were actually heavily involved in clinical work before that time. Further, those that were engaged in clinical psychology functioned chiefly as mental testers; their jobs typically involved assessment and diagnosis, not some kind of psychotherapy. Many of those early clinicians were women, who likely chose that field of psychology when they found the doors of academe closed to them because of their sex.

Fourth, clinical psychology is an applied field, and, as such, it is viewed by many as lying outside the field of scientific psychology. Historically, clinical psychology has been associated with such objectionable notions as demon possession, the occult, and bizarre therapies, and with treatments difficult to evaluate scientifically, such as hypnosis and psychoanalysis. These areas were objectionable for different reasons, but all have added to the scientist's distrust of clinical work.

The topic of psychopathology is an ancient one, dating to the beginnings of speculation about human nature (see Jackson, 1969; Simon, 1972; Simon & Weiner, 1966). This field involved more than just speculation about mental disorders; it included a variety of prescribed treatments as well. In the nineteenth century, when experimental methods were brought to bear on the study of the normal mind, there were those who sought to apply those same methods to the study of psychopathology. One of the pioneers in the field of experimental psychopathology was Emil Kraepelin (1856–1926), a German psychiatrist, who took his medical degree at Leipzig where he studied with Wilhelm Wundt, the founder of the science of psychology (see Chapter 7). Applying methods he learned from Wundt, Kraepelin studied a variety of mental disorders. His research led to his development, in 1883, of the first comprehensive taxonomy of psychological disorders, grouping disorders as neuroses and psychoses and naming disorders such as paranoia and manic-depressive psychosis.

Another Wundt student, Lightner Witmer (1867–1956), an American from Philadelphia, returned to his native city to establish the first psychological clinic in the United States in 1896 (see O'Donnell, 1979). That clinic was involved in diagnosis, treatment, and research, and its cases and research were reported regularly in Witmer's own journal, *The Psychological Clinic*. Similar clinic-research facilities were soon opened in conjunction with a number of hospitals, and these clinics were frequently headed by psychologists trained in the new experimental psychology.

Obviously a history of psychopathology is beyond the scope of this book. Limited treatment is provided in this chapter and in Chapter 15 (psychoanalysis). For more comprehensive coverage, the reader should consult one or more of the following sources: Alexander & Selesnick (1966), Maher & Maher (1985), Reisman (1966), and Zilboorg (1941). This chapter will focus on views of psychopathology in France in the eighteenth and nineteenth centuries, principally through the work of Philippe Pinel and Jean Martin Charcot.

The tradition of neurological research in France is strong (recall the discussion of Magendie, Flourens, and Broca in the previous chapter). That tradition, in combination with its progressive views on the treatment of the mentally ill, has made France a country of historical significance in clinical psychology.

Two of the most familiar historical images of treatment of the mentally ill are provided in the eighteenth-century engravings and paintings showing the deplorable conditions at the infamous mental asylum in London known as Bedlam (actually St. Mary of Bethlehem Hospital) and the humane unchaining of the insane in the Bicêtre and Salpêtrière asylums of Paris. The latter accomplishment was due to Philippe Pinel (1745–1826), a French psychiatrist.

The somatic view of mental illness held that because mental disorders were the result of physical causes, they were, in the main, nontreatable. Thus, mental patients were essentially imprisoned, often in chains. Pinel was one of a handful of eighteenth-century physicians who questioned a solely organic interpretation of mental illness and one of the first to put his beliefs to practice. In 1793, in the midst of the French Revolution, he became director of the Bicêtre Asylum and within several months had acquired permission from the asylum's governing board to begin removing the chains from some of the inmates. One of the first inmates to be unchained was an English army officer who had been hospitalized for forty years: "no one had dared to come close to him after the day when, in an attack of fury, he had killed a guard. After two years of remaining calm, following his liberation from the chains, the officer was allowed to leave the hospital" (Zilboorg, 1941, p. 323).

Pinel believed in the possibility of successful treatment, but he acknowledged that recovery was impossible under the conditions he found when he arrived at the Bicêtre Asylum. In addition to removing the chains, Pinel ordered changes in the behavior of his staff and guards: "No man was allowed to strike a maniac even in his own defence. No concessions however humble, nor complaints nor threats were allowed to interfere with the observance of this law. The guilty was instantly dismissed from the service" (Pinel, 1806, pp. 90–91). Not only did a number of patients recover sufficiently to be released from the asylum, but the health and quality of life improved dramatically for the inmates. For example, of the 261 patients admitted in the two years before Pinel arrived at the Bicêtre, 152 died within a year of admission, a death rate of 58 percent. In the first two years of Pinel's directorship that rate had dropped to 12 percent (Hothersall, 1984).

Such successes enhanced Pinel's reputation with the Paris hospitals' governing board which, in 1795, appointed him to head La Salpêtrière, an asylum for insane women that housed one of the largest patient populations in all of Europe. Pinel instituted similar changes with similar success in that institution as well, and remained there until his death at age 83. His funeral was an important state affair, attended by the leading political and medical figures of France, and by some of the former patients at the Bicêtre and La Salpêtrière.

Gregory Zilboorg (1941), a historian of medicine, has written that the essence of Pinel's contribution was that his reorganization of hospital procedures made psychotherapy possible. The fame of his success spread to other countries, causing a revolution in care of the mentally ill in the beginning of the nineteenth century. Without a doubt Pinel's humanitarian practices constitute one of the major landmarks in the history of psychopathology. The first selection in this chapter is an excerpt from Pinel's *Treatise on Insanity* (1801), describing some of his hospital practices.

Jean Martin Charcot (1825–1893) was born the year before Pinel's death. As a medical student, Charcot studied at the Salpêtrière Asylum and in 1862, after pursuing a private medical practice, accepted a staff position at that famous hospital. He spent the rest of his life in research and treatment there. By 1870 he had achieved international fame as a neurologist, working on diseases such as poliomyelitis, multiple sclerosis, and epilepsy. Hundreds of Europe's best medical students and physicians flocked to Paris to study with Charcot, among them a 29-year-old Viennese doctor named Sigmund Freud. (Charcot's relationship to Freud is discussed in one of the selections in this chapter and in the introduction to Chapter 15.)

The Salpêtrière population was a treasure house for a student of psychopathology. In the 1870s, Charcot chose to focus on patients he diagnosed as suffering from hysteria, a disorder that was of little interest to his medical colleagues, many of whom viewed hysteria as a patient's pretense of mental illness. But Charcot considered it a serious affliction and spent much of his career at Salpêtrière developing a classification of types of hysteria and working on methods of treatment. He was a flamboyant character, theatrical in his lectures and often given to overstatement. Not surprisingly, he was frequently the center of controversy. The second selection in this chapter is Charcot's description of male hysteria, excerpted from his *Clinical Lectures on Certain Diseases of the Nervous System* (1873).

The two secondary source articles also deal with Charcot. The first is by H. F. Ellenberger, a renowned authority on the history of psychiatry. His article provides a detailed look at Charcot's career at Salpêtrière, including the rapid demise of his confidence and influence toward the end of his life. The final selection from Frank J. Sulloway's biography of Freud (acknowledged by many historians as the best biography ever authored on Freud), describes the four and one-half months Freud spent in Charcot's clinic. The emphasis is on Freud's view of the work of Charcot, and its inclusion here is intended to show the importance of the French clinical tradition as an influence on psychoanalysis.

REFERENCES

Alexander, F. G., & Selesnick, S. T. (1966). *The history of psychiatry*. New York: Harper & Row.

Benjamin, L. T. (1986). Why don't they understand us? A history of psychology's public image. *American Psychologist, 41,* 941–946.

Hothersall, D. (1984). *History of psychology*. New York: Random House.

Jackson, S. W. (1969). Galen—on mental disorders. *Journal of the History of the Behavioral Sciences, 5,* 365–384.

Maher, B. A., & Maher, W. B. (1985). Psychopathology: II. From the eighteenth century to modern times. In G. A. Kimble & K. Schlesinger (Eds.), *Topics in the history of psychology*, Volume 2. Hillsdale, NJ: Erlbaum, pp. 295–329.

Maher, W. B., & Maher, B. A. (1985). Psychopathology: I. From ancient times to the eighteenth century. In G. A. Kimble & K. Schlesinger (Eds.), *Topics in the history of psychology*, Volume 2. Hillsdale, NJ: Erlbaum, pp. 251–294.

O'Donnell, J. M. (1979). The clinical psychology of Lightner Witmer: A case study of institutional innovation and intellectual change. *Journal of the History of the Behavioral Sciences, 15*, 3–17.

Pinel, P. (1806). *A treatise on insanity*. Sheffield: W. Todd. (Originally published in 1801.)

Reisman, J. M. (1966). *The development of clinical psychology*. New York: Appleton-Century-Crofts.

Simon, B. (1972). Models of mind and mental illness in ancient Greece: II. The Platonic model. *Journal of the History of the Behavioral Sciences, 8*, 389–406.

Simon, B., & Weiner, H. (1966). Models of mind and mental illness in ancient Greece: I. The Homeric model. *Journal of the History of the Behavioral Sciences, 2*, 303–314.

Stapp, J., Fulcher, R., & Wicherski, M. (1984). The employment of 1981 and 1982 doctoral recipients in psychology. *American Psychologist, 39*, 1408–1423.

Wood, W., Jones, M., & Benjamin, L. T. (1986). Surveying psychology's public image. *American Psychologist, 41*, 947–953.

Zilboorg, G. A. (1941). *A history of medical psychology*. New York: Norton.

Treating the Insane

Philippe Pinel

AN INSTANCE ILLUSTRATIVE OF THE ADVANTAGE OF OBTAINING AN INTIMATE ACQUAINTANCE WITH THE CHARACTER OF THE PATIENT

A man, in the vigour of life, confined at Bicêtre, fancied himself to be a king, and always spoke with the voice of command and authority. He had been for sometime at the Hôtel Dieu, where blows and other indignities, received from the keepers, had greatly exasperated his fury. Thus rendered suspicious and unmanageable, it was extremely difficult to fix upon a proper method of treating him. To have recourse to coercive means might still further aggravate his disorder, whilst condescension and acquiescence appeared likely to confirm him in his chimerical pretensions. I determined to wait the further development of his character, and taking advantage of any favourable circumstance that might happen. I was not long kept in suspence. He one day wrote a letter to his wife full of passionate expressions, accusing her with great bitterness of prolonging his detention, in order to enjoy her own entire liberty. He moreover threatened her with all the weight of his vengeance. Before this letter was sent off, he gave it to read to another patient, who reproved his passionate conduct, and remonstrated with him in a friendly manner, for endeavouring, as he did, to make his wife miserable. This remonstrance was kindly received. The letter was not sent, and another, replete with expressions of esteem, was substituted in its place. Mr. Poussin, the governor, saw in the effects of this friendly advice, the evident symptoms of a favourable change which was about to take place. He immediately availed himself of the occa-

From Pinel, P. (1801). *Traite medico-philosophique sur l'alienation mentale, ou la manie.* Adapted from D. D. Davis (Trans.), *A treatise on insanity.* Sheffield: W. Todd, 1806, pp. 191–264.

sion, and went to the maniac's apartment, where, in the course of conversation, he led him by degrees to the principal subject of his delirium. "If you are a sovereign," observed the governor, "why do you not put an end to your detention; and wherefore do you remain here, confounded with maniacs of every description?" He repeated his visits daily, when he assumed the tone of friendship and kindness. He endeavoured from time to time to convince him of the absurdity of his pretensions, and pointed out to him another maniac, who had for a long time indulged in the conviction that he was invested with sovereign power, and on that account, was now become an object of derision. The maniac was soon shaken in his convictions. In a short time he began to doubt his claim to sovereignty; and, at last, he was entirely convinced of his pretensions being chimerical. This unexpected revolution was accomplished in the course of a fortnight, and after a few months' longer residence in the house, this respectable husband and father was restored to his family.

A CASE OF CONVALESCENT INSANITY AGGRAVATED BY NEGLECT OF ENCOURAGING THE PATIENT'S TASTE FOR THE FINE ARTS

The gloomy and irritable character of maniacs, even when convalescent, is well known. Endowed, in most instances, with exquisite sensibility, they resent with great indignation the slightest appearances of neglect, contempt or indifference, and they forsake for ever what they had before adopted with the greatest ardour and zeal. A sculptor, a pupil of the celebrated Lemoin, was defeated in his endeavours to be admitted a member of the academy. From that moment he sunk into a profound melancholy, of which the only intermissions consisted in invectives against his brother, whose parsimony he supposed had arrested his career. His extravagance and violence rendered it necessary to confine him for lunacy. When conveyed to his apartment, he gave himself up to all the extravagances of maniacal fury. He continued in that state for several months. At length a calm succeeded, and he was permitted to go to the interior of the hospital. His understanding was yet feeble, and a life of inactivity was not a little irksome to him. The art of painting, which he had likewise cultivated, presented its renascent attractions to him, and he expressed a desire of attempting portrait painting. His inclination was encouraged and gratified and he made a sketch of the governor and his wife. The likeness was striking; but incapable of much application, he fancied that he perceived a cloud before his eyes. He allowed himself to be discouraged by a conviction of his insufficiency to emulate the models of fine taste, of which the traces were not yet effaced from his memory. The talent which he had discovered, his disposition to exercise it, and the probability of rescueing for his country the abilities of so promising a youth, induced the board of Bicêtre to request of him a pledge of his genius; leaving to him the choice of his subject, that his imagination might not be cramped. The convalescent, as yet but imperfectly restored, shrunk from the task which was thus imposed upon him; requested that the subject might be fixed upon, and that a correct and proper sketch might be given him for a model. His application was evaded, and the only opportunity of restoring him to himself and to his country was thus allowed to escape. He felt exceedingly indignant; considered this omission, as an unequivocal mark of contempt; destroyed all the implements of his art; and with angry haughtiness declared, that he renounced for ever the cultivation of the fine arts. This impression upon his feelings so unintentionally communicated, was so profound, that it was succeeded by a paroxysm of fury of several months' continuance. To this violence again succeeded a second calm. But now the brilliant intellect was for ever obscured, and he sunk irrecoverably into a sort of imbecility and reverieism, bordering upon dementia. I ordered

him to be transferred to the hospital infirmary, with a view of trying the effects of a few simple remedies, combined with the tonic system of regimen. Familiar and consolatory attentions to him, and such other assistance as his case appeared to suggest, were recurred to, more as they were dictates of humanity than as probable means of recovery. His taste for the fine arts, with his propensity to exertion of any kind, had for ever disappeared. Ennui, disgust with life, his gloomy melancholy and apathy made rapid progress. His appetite and sleep forsook him, and a colliquative diarrhea put an end to his degraded existence.

AN ATTEMPT TO CURE A CASE OF MELANCHOLIA PRODUCED BY A MORAL CAUSE

The fanciful ideas of melancholics are much more easily and effectually diverted by moral remedies, and especially by active employment, than by the best prepared and applied medicaments. But relapses are exceedingly difficult to prevent upon the best founded system of treatment. A working man, during an effervescent period of the revolution, suffered some unguarded expressions to escape him, respecting the trial and condemnation of Louis XVI. His patriotism began to be suspected in the neighborhood. Upon hearing some vague and exaggerated reports of intentions on the part of government agents to prosecute him for disloyalty, he one day betook himself in great tremour and consternation to his own house. His appetite and sleep forsook him. He surrendered himself to the influence of terror, left off working, was wholly absorbed by the subject of his fear; and at length he became fully impressed with the conviction that death was his unavoidable fate. Having undergone the usual treatment at the Hotel Dieu, he was transferred to Bicêtre. The idea of his death haunted him night and day, and he unceasingly repeated, that he was ready to submit to his impending fate. Constant employment at his trade, which was that of a tailor, appeared to me the most probable means of diverting the current of his morbid thoughts. I applied to the board for a small salary for him, in consideration of his repairing the clothes of the other patients of the asylum. This measure appeared to engage his interest in a very high degree. He undertook the employment with great eagerness, and worked without interruption for two months. A favourable change appeared to be taking place. He made no complaints nor any allusions to his supposed condemnation. He even spoke with the tenderest interest of a child of about six years of age, whom it seemed he had forgotten, and expressed a very great desire of having it brought to him. This awakened sensibility struck me as a favourable omen. The child was sent for, and all his other desires were gratified. He continued to work at his trade with renewed alacrity, frequently observing, that his child, who was now with him altogether, constituted the happiness of his life. Six months passed in this way without any disturbance or accident. But in the very hot weather of Messidore, (June and July) year 5, some precursory symptoms of returning melancholy began to show themselves. A sense of heaviness in the head, pains of the legs and arms, a silent and pensive air, indisposition to work, indifference for his child, whom he pushed from him with marked coolness and even aversion, distinguished the progress of his relapse. He now retired into his cell, where he remained, stretched on the floor, obstinately persisting in his conviction, that there was nothing left for him but submission to his fate. About that time, I resigned my situation at Bicêtre, without, however, renouncing the hope of being useful to this unfortunate man. In the course of that year, I had recourse to the following expedient with him. The governor, being previously informed of my project, was prepared to receive a visit from a party of my friends, who were to assume the character of delegates from the legislative body, dispatched to Bicêtre to obtain information in regard to Citizen..., or upon his innocence, to pronounce upon him a sentence of acquittal. I then concerted with three other physicians whom I engaged to person-

ate this deputation. The principal part was assigned to the eldest and gravest of them, whose appearance and manners were most calculated to command attention and respect. These commissaries, who were dressed in black robes suitable to their pretended office, ranged themselves round a table and caused the melancholic to be brought before them. One of them interrogated him as to his profession, former conduct, the journals which he had been in the habits of reading, and other particulars respecting his patriotism. The defendant related all that he had said and done; and insisted on a definitive judgement, as he did not conceive that he was guilty of any crime. In order to make a deep impression on his imagination, the president of the delegates pronounced in a loud voice the following sentence. ''In virtue of the power which has been delegated to us by the national assembly, we have entered proceedings in due form of law, against Citizen... : and having duly examined him, touching the matter whereof he stands accused, we make our declaration accordingly. It is therefore, by us declared, that we have found the said Citizen...a truly loyal patriot; and, pronouncing his acquittal, we forbid all further proceedings against him. We furthermore order his entire enlargement and restoration to his friends. But inasmuch as he has obstinately refused to work for the last twelve months, we order his detention at Bicêtre to be prolonged six months from this present time, which said six months he is to employ, with proper sentiments of gratitude, in the capacity of tailor to the house. This our sentence is entrusted to Citizen Poussin, which he is to see executed at the peril of his life.'' Our commissaries then retired in silence. On the day following the patient again began to work, and, with every expression of sensibility and affection, solicited the return of his child. Having received the impulse of the above stratagem, he worked for some time unremittingly at his trade. But he had completely lost the use of his limbs from having remained so long extended upon the cold flags.

His activity, however, was not of long continuance; and its remission concurring with an imprudent disclosure of the above well intended plot, his delirium returned. I now consider his case as absolutely incurable.

THE EFFECTS OF THE COLD AND WARM BATH, AND ESPECIALLY OF THE BATH OF SURPRISE, IN THE CURE OF MANIACAL DISORDERS

A young gentleman, twenty-two years of age, of a robust constitution, was deprived of part of his property by the revolution. He gave way to melancholy, began to look forward to futurity with extreme despondency, and lost his sleep. He was, at length, seized by violent maniacal fury. He was put upon the treatment for acute mania, in the town of his department. With his hands and feet tied he was suddenly immersed in the cold bath. Notwithstanding the violence with which he resisted this treatment, it was practiced upon him for some time. His delirium chiefly consisted in supposing himself to be an Austrian general, and he commonly assumed the tone and manner of a commander. During the process of bathing his fury was greatly exasperated by the mortifying consideration that his rank was neglected and despised. His disorder becoming more and more aggravated by this method, his relations came to the determination to convey him to Paris to be under my care. Upon my first interview with him he appeared exceedingly enraged. To conciliate his favour and obtain his good opinion, I felt the necessity of assenting to his illusive ideas. The bath was never mentioned to him. He was treated with mildness and put upon a diluent regimen, with the liberty of walking at all hours in a pleasant garden. The amusement which he derived from this liberty, exercise and familiar conversation, in which from time to time I engaged him, gradually induced a state of calmness, and towards the end of a month he was not remarkable either for haughtiness or diffidence. In about three months his delirium had completely left him. But towards the autumn of that year, and the spring of

the succeeding, some threatening symptoms of a return of his disorder betrayed themselves in his manner and conduct. His looks became more animated, and he was unusually petulant and loquacious. In those circumstances I ordered him a gentle purge to be repeated at intervals, with frequent draughts of whey. He was continued upon this plan for a fortnight. I then advised him to take the warm bath. Not to rouse his former repugnance to bathing, this indication was suggested to him as a practice merely agreeable and conducive to cleanliness. By those means his paroxysms were prevented. To ascertain, however, the permanence of his cure he was detained at my house for a twelve month. Upon his departure he returned into the country, where, for the last two years, he has been occupied partly by literary pursuits, and partly by those of agriculture. No symptom of his delirium has since appeared.

"Cold bathing," says Mr. Haslam, "having for the most part been employed in conjunction with other remedies, it becomes difficult to ascertain how far it may be exclusively beneficial in this disease. The instances in which it has been separately used for the cure of insanity, are too few to enable me to draw any satisfactory conclusions. I may, however, safely affirm, that in many instances, paralytic affections have in a few hours supervened on cold bathing, especially when the patient has been in a furious state, and of a plethoric habit." Dr. Ferriar appears more decidedly favourable to the practice of bathing. In cases of melancholia he advises the cold, and in mania the warm bath. The only case, however, which he adduces in support of the practice must be acknowledged to be equivocal, inasmuch as it was treated, especially in its advanced stages, successively by opium, camphor, purgatives and electricity. General experiments of this nature are, perhaps, more calculated to perpetuate than to dissipate uncertainty. The real utility of bathing in maniacal disorders, remains yet to be ascertained. To establish the practice upon a solid foundation, it must be tried with constant and judicious reference to the different species of insanity. A raving female manic was put upon the use of the warm bath. She bathed twenty-five times, great debility was the immediate consequence, and her mania was shortly after succeeded by dementia. I am led to suppose, that the warm bath may be resorted to with more probability of success, as a preventative of approaching maniacal paroxysms.

It has been said, that the bath of surprise has been found a valuable remedy in some cases of insanity which had resisted the effects of the warm bath, the cold shower bath, and other remedies. This superiority of the unexpected application of cold water, has been ascribed to an interruption of the chain of delirious ideas, induced by the suddenness of the shock, and the general agitation of the system experienced from this process. It is well known that the enthusiast Van Helmont, has made some valuable remarks upon the durable effects of sudden immersion in cold water in some cases of mental derangement. His practice was to detain the patient in the bath for some minutes. It may be proper to observe, that this method, however successful in some instances, might in others be extremely dangerous, and that it can only be resorted to with propriety in cases almost hopeless, and where other remedies are ineffectual; such as in violent paroxysms of regular periodical mania, inveterate continued insanity, or insanity complicated with epilepsy.

Hysteria in the Male Subject

Jean Martin Charcot

Gentlemen: We shall study to-day hysteria in the male sex, and in order the better to compass the subject, we shall consider male hysteria more particularly in adolescent subjects, or such as are in the vigor of age and in full maturity, that is to say, in men of from twenty to forty years, and we shall give attention more especially to that intense, very pronounced form which corresponds to what is called in the female great hysteria, or hystero-epilepsy with mixed crises. If I have decided to take up this subject which I have touched upon many times already, it is because we have actually in our clinical service at the present time a truly remarkable collection of patients whom I shall cause to appear before you, and whom I shall study with you. I have for my object especially to make you recognize and prove by your senses the identity of the great neurosis in both sexes, for in the comparison which we shall make as we go on of the symptoms of hysteria major in the female and in the male, everywhere we shall have occasion to remark the most striking similarities, and here and there only, certain differences which as you will see, are of but secondary importance.

Moreover, this question of hysteria in the male subject is one of the questions regarded as of special interest at the present day. In France, during the last few years it has much occupied the attention of physicians. From 1875 to 1880 five inaugural dissertations on hysteria in the male were defended before the Faculty of Paris, and Klein, author of one of these theses written under the direction of Dr. Olivier, succeeded in compiling eighty cases of this affection. Since then the important publications of Bourneville and his pupils have appeared; of Debove, Raymond, Dreyfus and some others; and all these works tend to prove, among other things, that cases of male hysteria may be met with quite frequently in ordinary practice. Quite recently, male hysteria has been studied in America by Putnam and Walton, principally in connection with and as a sequel of traumatisms, and more especially of

From Charcot, J. M. (1873). *Leçons sur les maladies du système nerveux.* In E. P. Hurd (Trans.), *Clinical lectures on certain diseases of the nervous system.* Detroit: G. S. Davis, 1888, pp. 180–194.

railroad accidents. They have recognized, along with Page, who has also interested himself in this question in England, that many of those nervous accidents designated under the name of *railway spine,* and which, in his opinion, might better be called *railway brain,* are in reality, whether appearing in man or in woman, simply hysterical manifestations. It is easy, then, to understand the interest which such a question has to the practical mind of our confreres of the United States. The victims of railroad accidents quite naturally claim damages of the companies. The case goes into court; thousands of dollars are at stake. Now, I repeat, often it is hysteria which is at the bottom of all these nervous lesions. Those neuropathic states, so grave and so tenacious, which present themselves as the sequel of "collisions" of that kind, and which render their victims unable to work or pursue any regular occupation for months and for even years, are often only hysteria, nothing but hysteria. Male hysteria is then worthy of being studied and known by the medico-legalist, for he is often called upon to give his opinion, in matters concerning which great pecuniary interests are at stake, before a tribunal which would be likely to be influenced (and this circumstance renders his task the more difficult) by the disfavor which is still attached to the word hysteria on account of prejudices profoundly rooted. A thorough acquaintance not only with the disease, but also with the conditions under which it is produced, will be on such occasions the more useful from the fact that the nervous disorders often ensue without any traumatic lesion, and simply as a consequence of the psychical nervous shock resulting from the accident; frequently, moreover, they do not come on immediately after the accident, but some time afterwards, when, for instance, one of the victims of the collision, who may have been disabled by fracture of the leg, will have got well after being incapacitated for work for three or four months; another, perhaps, may have been suffering from nervous troubles which are des-

tined to prevent him from working for six months or a year, but which have not reached their full intensity. You see how delicate in such cases is the mission of the medical jurist, and it is this medico-legal side of the question which seems among our American confreres to have awakened a new interest in the study of hysterical neuroses heretofore a little neglected.

In proportion as the disease has been better studied and better known (as habitually happens in similar circumstances), cases become apparently more and more frequent, and at the same time, more easy of analysis. I just told you that four or five years ago, Klein, in his thesis, had collected eighty cases of hysteria in men; to-day, Batault who is preparing in our hospital service a special work on the subject, has been able to gather together 218 cases of the same kind, none of which belong to our clinic.

Male hysteria is, then, far from being rare. Indeed, gentlemen, if I were to judge from what I see every day among us, these cases are very often misunderstood, even by very distinguished physicians. It is granted that an effeminate young man may, after certain excesses, disappointments, deep emotions, present various phenomena of an hysterical nature, but that a vigorous mechanic, well developed, not enervated by an indolent or too studious mode of life, a fireman of a locomotive, for instance, never before emotional, at least in appearance, may, as the result of a railroad accident, a collision, a car running off from the track, become hysterical just like a woman—all this has never entered into the imagination of some people. Nothing, however, is better proved, and pathology must adjust itself to this new conception, which will hereafter take its place along with other propositions which are today received as demonstrated truths, after having long fought their way through scepticism, and often through ridicule.

There is a prejudice which doubtless contributes much to oppose the diffusion of right knowledge relative to hysteria in the male sex; I refer to the relatively false notion generally entertained of the clinical tableau of this neurosis in the female. In the male, in fact, the disease often presents itself as an affection remarkable by the permanence and tenacity of the symptoms which characterize it. In the female, on the contrary—and this is without doubt that which seems to constitute the capital difference between the two sexes in the estimation of anyone who does not thoroughly and radically know the disease in the female—what is generally believed to be the characteristic feature of hysteria is the instability, the mobility of the symptoms. In hysteria, it is said, observations of the disease in the female being naturally taken as the basis of this opinion, the phenomena are mobile, fugacious, and the capricious march of the affection is often interrupted by scenes of the most unexpected nature. Very well, but, gentlemen, this mobility, this fugaciousness is far from being a universal characteristic of hysteria, even in the female, as I have shown you by numerous examples.

Yes, even in females there are cases of hysteria with durable, permanent phenomena, extremely difficult to modify, and which sometimes resist all medical interference. Cases of this kind are numerous, very numerous, if, indeed, they do not constitute the majority. This is a point to which I shall return shortly. But for the moment I content myself by remarking, only, that the permanence of the hysterical symptoms in the male, and their tenacity often prevent the medical attendants from recognizing their true character. Some, in presence of phenomena which resist all therapeutic modifiers, will believe, I imagine, if there exist sensorial troubles with nervous crises simulating more or less the epileptic fit, that they have to do with an organic localized lesion (lesion en foyer), an intra-cranial neoplasm, or if it is a case of paraplegia, with an organic spinal lesion. Others will willingly admit, or will even affirm, that there can be no question in these cases of an organic alteration, but simply of a dynamic lesion; but in view of symptoms whose te-

nacity does not comport with the scheme which they have in mind of hysteria, they will think that they have before them a special disease, not yet described, and which merits a place by itself.

A mistake of this kind seems to me to have been committed by M. M. Oppenheim and Thomsen, of Berlin, in a memoir which contains, however, a great number of interesting facts, carefully observed, if not always well interpreted, at least according to my way of thinking. These gentlemen have observed hemi-anaesthesia, sensitive and sensorial, like in all points to that of hysterical patients, in seven observations similar to those of Putnam and Walton. These cases had to do with firemen, conductors, workingmen, victims of rail-road or other accidents, all of whom had sustained a blow on the head, a concussion, or a general shock. Alcoholism, lead-poisoning, etc., were not factors in these cases, and the fact was recognized that, according to every probability, there existed no organic lesion in these subjects.

We have here, then, a set of cases quite like those of Putnam and Walton, but differing from the latter in this respect that the German authorities are not willing to concede that these are cases of hysteria, which to their minds constitute something peculiar, some undefined, undescribed pathological state, demanding a new place in the nosological category. The principal arguments which Oppenheim and Thomsen adduce to the support of their thesis are the following: 1. The anaesthesia is obstinate; we do not see there those capricious changes which are characteristic(?) of hysteria. It lasts just as it is for months and for years. 2. Another reason is that the psychical state of the patient is not that of the hysterical. The troubles of this order in these patients have not the changing, mobile traits of hysterical manifestations. The patients are conspicuously depressed, melancholic after a permanent sort, and without great fluctuations in the degree of their melancholy.

It is impossible for me to agree with the conclusions of M. M. Oppenheim and Thomsen, and I hope to show you, gentlemen, 1, that the sensorial hysterical troubles may in the female, even, present a remarkable tenacity, and that in the male it is often so; 2, that in the male in particular, the depression and the melancholic tendency are most commonly observed in the most marked, the least contestable cases of hysteria. We do not indeed ordinarily observe in the male subject, although this is assuredly not a distinctive characteristic of the first order, those caprices, those changes of character and humor, which belong more commonly, but not necessarily, to the hysteria of the female.

But it is time, gentlemen, to bring to end these preliminary remarks, in order to come to the principal object of our lesson today. We shall proceed by clinical demonstration to study together in detail a certain number of perfectly characteristic cases of male hysteria. While thus engaged we shall bring to view the likeness and the differences that exist between the symptoms of hysteria observed in men and those with which we are familiar every day in the corresponding form of the disease in women. Lastly, I intend to present after the manner of a summary, certain general considerations on the great hysteria (hysteria major) as seen in the male sex.

But before coming to my subject proper, I desire briefly to remind you by two examples to what extent in the female the permanent symptoms of hysteria, the hysterical stigmata, as we are wont to call them for convenience, may show themselves fixed, tenacious, and consequently exempt from that proverbial mobility which has been attributed to them, and which some writers regard as characteristic of the disease. I shall not refer now to the six or eight subjects of great hysteria actually assembled in our wards. Certain of them have presented for months and even for years a simple or double anaesthesia which our best and most appropriate therapeutic modifiers can influence only for a few hours. I will limit myself to presenting to you two women who

are veritable veterans of hystero-epilepsy, and who now, being rid for several years of their great attacks, and discharged from the medical service, exercise in the hospital the functions of domestics. The first, L. by name, well known in the history of hystero-epilepsy, and noted for the "demoniacal" character which her convulsive crises presented, is to-day 63 years of age. She entered the Salpêtrière in 1846, and I have not ceased to have her under observation since 1871. At this time she was affected, as she is still to-day, with a right hemi-anaesthesia, complete, absolute, sensorial and sensitive, with ovaria on the same side, which, during this long period of fifteen years, has never been modified, *even temporarily,* whether by the action many times tried of aesthesiogenous agents, whether by the progress of age and the menopause. Six years ago, at the time when our attention was more particularly directed to the modifications which the visual field undergoes in the hysterical, we detected in this patient the existence in a marked degree of the classic contraction of the visual field, which was pronounced on both sides, but much more so on the right. The repeated examination once or twice every year since then has never failed to reveal the permanence of this contraction.

The other patient, Aurel by name, aged 62 years, and in whom the great seizures, replaced sometimes by certain symptoms of angina pectoris, have only ceased within a dozen of years, presented as far back as 1851, according to a precious note dated that very year, a left hemi-anaesthesia, complete and absolute, sensorial and sensitive, which, as you can observe for yourselves, exists this very day, after a lapse of 34 years. This patient has been under our observation for fifteen years, and never has the hemi-anaesthesia in question ceased to present itself during our often-repeated examinations. The double contraction of the visual field, very plain on both sides, but more pronounced on the left, which the campimetric examination has enabled us at the present time to find, already existed with her five years ago.

This is enough, I think, to show you how stable and permanent in these women are the stigmata of which no one would think of disputing the hysterical nature, and how little this corresponds to the notion, erroneous by reason of being carried too far, which is generally entertained of the evolution of the symptoms of the disease.

I come now to the study of our male hysterics.

Case I.—Rig..., aged 44 years, clerk in an oil factory, entered the Salpêtrière May 12, 1884, or about a year ago. He is a large strong man, of firm muscles; was formerly a cooper, and endured without fatigue arduous toil. The hereditary antecedents in this patient are very remarkable. His father is still living, aged 76 years. From the age of 38 to 44 the latter, by reason of disappointments and pecuniary losses, suffered *nervous attacks,* as to the nature of which the patient can give us but little information. His mother died at the age of 63, of asthma. His mother's *great uncle* was *epileptic,* and died in consequence of a fall into the fire during one of his fits. The *two daughters of this uncle* were also *epileptic.* Rig...has had seven brothers and sisters who have never had any nervous diseases. Four are dead; among the three living, one sister is asthmatic. He himself has had nine children, four of whom died young. Of the five who are still living, *one daughter fifteen years old has nervous crises; another, aged ten years, has attacks of hystero-epilepsy* which Dr. Marie has witnessed in this very place; *another daughter is feeble in intelligence;* lastly, two boys present nothing in particular to note.

In the personal antecedents we find the following facts: At the age of 19 or 20 years, the patient was attacked with acute articular rheumatism, without lesions of the heart. The last attack lasted six months, and it is, perhaps, to the rheumatism that we are to attribute the deformation of the hands, which we note in this patient. While a child, he was very timid, his sleep was troubled by dreams and nightmares, and besides he was addicted to somnambulism. He would often rise in the night-time and go to work, and the next morning he would be much surprised to find his job done. This state continued from 12 to 15 years. He married at 28 years of age. We do not find in his antecedents either syphilis or alcoholism, vices from which coopers are not always exempt. He came to Paris when 32 years old, working at first with his father, then employed as shop clerk in an oil refinery.

In 1876, when 32 years of age, he met with his first accident. He cut himself quite deeply with a razor which he was sharpening, as some people are in the habit of doing, by straping it back and forth on the front aspect of the fore arm. A vein was cut, and the blood spurted; under the influence of the hemorrhage and the fright, the patient lost consciousness and fell to the ground. He was a long time in recovering, remaining two months profoundly anaemiated, pale and without power to work.

In 1882, consequently about three years ago, he was lowering a barrel of wine into the cellar, when the cord which held it gave way; the barrel rolled down the stairway and would certainly have crushed him if he had not jumped to one side, he did not, however, save himself sufficiently to avoid a slight wound of the left hand. Despite the fright which he experienced, he was able to get up and help raise the cask. But five minutes afterward, he had an attack of loss of consciousness which lasted twenty minutes. Coming to himself, he was unable to walk, so weak had his limbs become, and he was taken home in a carriage. For two days, it was absolutely impossible for him to work; during the night his sleep was disturbed by frightful visions and interrupted by cries of: help! I am killed! He went over again in dreams the scene in the cellar. He had nevertheless resumed his work, when ten days after the accident, in the middle of the night, he had his first attack of hystero-epilepsy. Since this time, the attacks returned almost regularly every two months; and often in the interval, during the night, whether at the moment of the first sleep or about the time of waking, he would be profoundly disturbed by visions of ferocious animals.

Formerly as he came out of these fits, he remembered that he had been dreaming during the attack, a phenomenon which no longer exists. He imagined that he was in a dark forest pursued by robbers or frightful animals, or the scene of the cellar was acted over again, and he saw wine casks rolling upon him and threatening to crush him. He affirms that never, during these seizures, or in the interval, has he had dreams or hallucinations of a gay or agreeable character.

About this time, he went to St. Anne's Hospital for advice and treatment. The physicians there prescribed for him bromide of potassium, and this medicine (a fact to be noticed) has never had the least influence on the attacks, although administered for a long time till the organism was saturated with it. It was under these conditions that Rig..., was admitted to the Salpêtrière, and at his entrance we made note of the following state.

The patient is pale, anaemic, has but little appetite, especially for meat, to which he prefers acid foods; in short, the general condition is far from satisfactory. The *hysterical stigmata* in this patient are very well marked. They consist in *a double anaesthesia in patches* of great extent, for pain (pinching, pricking) and for cold. Sensorial anaesthesia in general does not exist, except to a very mild degree; taste and smell are normal; hearing is nevertheless quite perceptibly blunted, especially in the left ear; the patient hears no better when the sonorous object is applied to the cranium. As far as vision is concerned, the symptoms are much plainer, and alone suffice, in a measure, to enable us to affirm the hysterical nature of the affection. He presents, in fact, on both sides *a notable contraction of the visual field,* more marked, however, on the right. He distinguishes all the colors, but the visual field of the blue is more contracted than that of the red, and passes within the latter, a phenomenon when it is met with, which is quite characteristic, as far

as I know, of the visual field of hysterical patients; of this I have many times shown you examples. Lastly, to finish what I say of the permanent stigmata, there exist in Rig...*two hysterogenous* points, the one cutaneous, seated below the last right false ribs, the other deeper, in the popliteal space of the right side, at a point where the patient has a cyst, which is the seat of extreme pain of spontaneous origin. There does not exist in this patient any testicular point. Pressure exercised over the spasmogenous points, whether accidentally or voluntarily, produces all the phenomena of the hysterical aura; precordial pain, constriction of the neck, with the sensation of a ball, hissings in the ears, and beatings in the temples, these two last phenomena constituting, as you know, the cephalic aura. Those points whose excitation may provoke the attack with singular facility are, on the other hand, but feebly *spasm-checkers* (*spasmo-frenateurs*), that is to say, their excitation, even when intense and prolonged, arrests but imperfectly the attack in the process of evolution.

In the mental state of Rig..., today as in the past, it is always anxiety, fear, distress, that predominate. He cannot sleep in the dark; in full day he does not like to be alone; he is of excessive sensitiveness, and he experiences great fright at the sight or remembrance of certain animals, such as rats, mice, toads, which he often sees, moreover, in terrifying nightmares, or in hallucinations occurring when half asleep. He is always sad; "I am weary of myself," he says. He manifests a certain mobility of mind characterized by the fact that he can apply himself to nothing, and that he undertakes and abandons with the same facility five or six tasks at a time. He is intelligent and has a fair amount of education. He is, moreover, of a mild disposition, and totally devoid of vicious propensities.

The attacks are spontaneous or provoked. Whatever may be the manner of their origin, they always begin by a keen sensation of smarting or burning in the region of the spasmogenous points, to which succeed first a pain in the epigastrium, then the sensation of constriction of the neck and of a ball, finally the cephalic aura consisting of sibilant noises in the ears, and beatings in the temples. At this moment the patient loses consciousness and the *paroxysm* proper begins. It is divided into *four periods* which are quite clear and distinct. In the first, the patient executes certain epileptiform convulsive movements. Then comes the period of great gesticulations of salutation, which are of extreme violence, interrupted from time to time by an arching of the body which is absolutely characteristic, the trunk being bent bow fashion, sometimes in front (emprosthotonos), sometimes backward (opisthotonos), the feet and head alone touching the bed, the body constituting the arch. During this time the patient utters wild cries. Then comes the third period, called period of passional attitudes, during which he utters words and cries in relation with the sad delirium and terrifying visions which pursue him. Sometimes it is the woods, the wolves, or other frightful animals, sometimes it is the cellar, the stairway, the rolling cask. Finally he regains consciousness, recognizes the persons around him and calls them by name, but the delirium and hallucinations still continue for some time. He looks all around and under the bed for the black beasts which threaten him; he examines his arms, thinking to find there the bites of the animals which he thinks he has felt. Then he comes to himself, and the attack is over, although it is generally sure to be repeated a few minutes later, and so on, till after three or four successive paroxysms, the patient at last completely regains the normal state. Never during the course of these crises has he bitten his tongue or wet his bed.

For more than a year, Rig...has been subjected to treatment by static electrization, which, in cases of this kind, as you know, often gives us good results; we have prescribed at the same time all the tonics and reconstituents imaginable. Nevertheless, the phenomena which we have just described, the permanent stigmata and fits, persist just as they were, without appreciable changes; they seem, in short, having already existed almost three years, to be of the kind that undergo very slow modification. We have, however, certainly here, as you will all agree, a case of hystero-epilepsy with mixed crises (epileptiform hysteria) as clearly characterized as possible, and it is plain that the stability of the stigmata, on which we have sufficiently insisted, should not an instant stay our diagnosis.

To conclude this case, so perfectly typical, I will still further call your attention to certain particulars which the clinical analysis has disclosed. In the first place. I will mention particularly the nervous heredity, so strongly pronounced in his family: hysteria in the father (very probable at least); great uncle and cousins-german of the mother epileptic; two daughters, one of whom is hysterical, the other hystero-epileptic. You will frequently, gentlemen, meet with these conditions of heredity in the hysterical male patient, and find them, perhaps, more marked even than in the female.

I must remind you, moreover, how in our patient the hysterical manifestations were developed on the occasion and as the result of an accident which threatened his life. Could the traumatism which was the consequence of the accident (and it was nothing but a trifling wound of the finger) have sufficed of itself to cause the development of the nervous symptoms? This is possible, but I would not affirm it. It is always necessary, alongside of the traumatism, to take account of a factor which very probably has played a more important part in the genesis of these accidents than the wound itself. I refer to the terror experienced by the patient at the moment of the accident, and which found expression shortly afterwards in loss of consciousness followed by temporary paresis of the inferior extremities. This same psychical element is found, apart from the traumatism, in some of the cases described by Putnam, Walton, Page, Oppenheim and Thomsen, where its influence, often predominant, cannot be misunderstood.

Charcot and the Salpêtrière School

H.F. Ellenberger

The Salpêtrière School was strongly organized and headed by a powerful figure, that of the great teacher Jean Martin Charcot (1825–1893), a neurologist who had come belatedly to the study of certain mental phenomena. During the years 1870–1893, Charcot was considered to be the greatest neurologist of his time. He was the consulting physician of kings and princes and patients came to see him "from Samarkand and the West Indies." But celebrity had come to him after long years of incessant and obscure toil, and few of those who marveled at Charcot's extraordinary success realized that it was a belated one reached after many years of strenuous and unnoticed work.

No real biography of Charcot has been written as yet. Most accounts, such as Guillain's book (1), are based on necrologies and depict for the most part the Charcot of the brilliant years. Valuable memories have been recorded by his disciple Souques (2) and particularly by the Russian physician Lyubimov (3) who had been acquainted with Charcot for the last 20 years of Charcot's life.

Charcot was born in Paris, the son of a carriage-builder who, it was said, made carriages of great beauty and who was reputed to be more of an artist than an artisan. Very little is known about Charcot's childhood and youth. It is said that he was a cold, silent, shy, and aloof young man who had a speech impediment. He wore a black moustache (the story goes that his first rich patient was referred to him on the condition that he shave off his moustache). As an *interne* (medical resident), the young Charcot was assigned for some time to the Salpêtrière, an old hospital which, at that time, was mainly a medical poor-house for

four or five thousand old women. Charcot realized that this hospital sheltered numerous patients with rare or unknown neurologic diseases and would be a gold mine for clinical research. He kept this in mind while he was slowly pursuing his career as an anatomo-pathologist. As a young doctor, he was asked by one of his teachers to be physician and companion to a rich banker traveling to Italy, which gave him an opportunity of getting acquainted with Italy's artistic wealth (4). His medical career was rather slow and laborious. The turning point came in 1862 when, at the age of thirty-six, Charcot was appointed chief physician in one of the Salpêtrière's largest sections and took up his old plans with feverish activity. Case histories were taken, autopsies performed, laboratories opened, while he was building at the same time a team of devoted collaborators. He was inspired by Duchenne (de Boulogne), a neurologist of outstanding genius who had no official position and whom Charcot called his "Master in Neurology" (5, 6). Within eight years (1862–1870), Charcot made the discoveries that gave him his position of eminence.

In 1870, Charcot took on the supplementary charge of a special ward which the hospital administration had reserved for a fairly large number of women patients suffering from "convulsions." Some of them were epileptics others were hysterics who had learned to imitate epileptic crises. Charcot strove to discover means of distinguishing between hysterical and epileptic convulsions. He also started to investigate hysteria with the same method he used for organic neurologic diseases and, with his disciple Paul Richer, gave a description of the full blown hysterical crisis (the *grande hystérie*) (7).

In 1878, probably under the influence of Charles Richet, Charcot extended his interest to hypnotism, of which he undertook a purportedly

Ellenberger, H. F. (1965). Charcot and the Salpêtrière school. *American Journal of Psychotherapy, 19,* 253–267. Copyright © 1965 by *American Journal of Psychotherapy.* Reprinted by permission of the publisher.

scientific study (as he had done with hysteria), taking as subjects several of the most gifted of his female hysterical patients. He found that these subjects developed the hypnotic condition through three successive stages: "lethargy," "catalepsy," and "somnambulism," each stage showing very definite and characteristic symptoms. Charcot read his findings at the Académie des Sciences at the beginning of 1882 (8); it was, Janet said, a *tour de force* to have hypnotism accepted by the same Académie which thrice within the past century had condemned it under the name of magnetism. This resounding paper gave magnetism a new dignity, and this heretofore shunned subject became the topic of innumerable publications.

Among Charcot's most spectacular achievements were the investigations on traumatic paralysis (9) which he conducted in 1884 and 1885. In his time, paralysis was generally considered to result from lesions of the nervous system caused by an accident, although the existence of "psychic paralysis" had been postulated in England by B. C. Brodie (10) in 1837 and by Russel Reynolds (11) in 1869. But how could a purely psychologic factor cause paralysis without the patient's awareness of that factor and excluding the possibility of simulation?

Charcot had already analyzed the differences between organic and hysterical paralysis. In 1884, three men afflicted with a monoplegia of one arm consecutive to traumatism were admitted to the Salpêtrière. Charcot first demonstrated that the symptoms of that paralysis, while differing from those of organic paralysis, coincided exactly with the symptoms of hysterical paralysis. The second step was the experimental reproduction of similar states of paralysis under hypnosis. Charcot suggested to some hypnotized subjects that their arms would be paralyzed. The resulting hypnotic paralysis proved to have exactly the same symptoms as the spontaneous hysterical paralysis and the post-traumatic paralysis of the three male patients. Charcot was able to reproduce these conditions segment by seg-

ment, and he also suggested their disappearance in the reverse order. The next step was a demonstration of the effect of the trauma. Charcot chose easily hypnotizable subjects and suggested to them that in their waking state, as soon as they were slapped on the back, their arm would become paralyzed. When awakened, the subjects showed the usual post-hypnotic amnesia, and as soon as they were slapped on the back, they were instantly struck with a monoplegia of the arm of exactly the same type as the post-traumatic monoplegia. Finally, Charcot pointed out that in certain subjects living in a state of permanent somnambulism, hypnotic suggestion was not even necessary. They got paralysis of the arm after being slapped on the back, without special verbal suggestion. The mechanism of post-traumatic paralysis seemed thus to be demonstrated. Charcot assumed that the nervous shock following the trauma was a kind of hypnoid state analogous to hypnotism and therefore enabling the development of an autosuggestion of the individual. "I do not think that in any physiopathologic research it would often be possible to reproduce more accurately the condition which one has set oneself the task to study," Charcot concluded.

Charcot ranged the hysterical, post-traumatic, and hypnotic paralysis in the group of "dynamic paralysis" in contrast to "organic paralysis" resulting from a lesion of the nervous system. He gave a similar demonstration in regard to hysterical mutism and hysterical coxalgia. Here, too, he reported experimentally, by means of hypnotism, clinical pictures identical with the hysterical conditions. In 1892, Charcot distinguished "dynamic amnesia," in which lost memories can be recovered under hypnosis, from "organic amnesia" where this is impossible (12, 13).

In the last years of his life, Charcot realized that a vast realm existed between that of clear consciousness and that of organic brain physiology. His attention was drawn to "faith healing," and in one of his last articles (14), he stated that he had seen patients going to Lourdes and returning healed from their diseases. He tried to eluci-

date the mechanism of such cures and anticipated that an increased knowledge of the laws of
"faith healing" would result in great therapeutic
progresses.

There are many descriptions and pictures of
Charcot, but they pertain almost without exception to Charcot at his zenith around 1880 or to
the declining Charcot of the last years. The most
lively ones were given by Léon Daudet, who had
studied medicine at the Salpêtrière and whose father, the novelist Alphonse Daudet, had been
Charcot's intimate friend. Here is a condensed
excerpt of Léon Daudet's Memoirs (15, 16, 17)
describing Charcot:

> Charcot was a small, stout and vigorous man with
> a big head, a bull's neck, a low forehead, broad
> cheeks. The line of his mouth was hard and medi-
> tative. He was clean shaven and kept his straight
> hair combed back. He somewhat resembled Napo-
> leon and liked to cultivate this resemblance. His
> gait was heavy, his voice authoritative, somewhat
> low, often ironical and insisting, his expression ex-
> traordinarily fiery.
>
> A most learned man, he was familiar with the
> works of Dante, Shakespeare, and the great poets;
> he read English, German, Spanish and Italian. He had
> a large library full of strange and unusual books.
>
> He was very humane; he showed a profound com-
> passion for animals and forbade any mention of
> hunters and hunting in his presence.
>
> A more authoritarian man I have never known,
> nor one who could put such a despotic yoke on peo-
> ple around him. To realize this, one only had to see
> how he could, from his pulpit, throw a sweeping
> and suspicious glance at his students and hear him
> interrupt them with a brief, imperative word.
>
> He could not stand contradiction, however
> small. If someone dared contradict his theories, he
> became ferocious and mean and did all he could to
> wreck the career of the imprudent man unless he
> retracted and apologized.
>
> He could not stand stupidity. But his need for
> domination caused him to eliminate the more bril-
> liant of his disciples, so that in the end he was sur-
> rounded by mediocre people. As a compensation,
> he maintained social relationships with artists and
> poets and gave magnificent receptions.
>
> It was one of his favourite ideas that the share

of dream-life in our waking state is much more than
just "immense."

Many references to Charcot can be found in
the *Diary* of Edmond and Jules de Goncourt (18).
These two brothers were known for their biting
descriptions and seem to have been particularly
antagonistic to Charcot, whom they described as
follows:

> Charcot was an ambitious man, envious of any su-
> periority, showing a ferocious resentment against
> those who declined invitations to his receptions, a
> despot at the university, hard with his patients to
> the point of telling them bluntly of their impending
> death, but cowardly when he himself was ill. He
> was a tyrant with his children and compelled for
> instance his son Jean, who wanted to be a seafar-
> er, to become a physician. As a scientist, Charcot
> was a mixture of genius and charlatan. Most un-
> pleasant was his indiscretion in talking of his pa-
> tients' confidential matters.

The description given by the Russian physician Lyubimov (3) is so vastly different that one
can hardly believe it concerns the same person:

> Beside his extraordinary gift as a teacher, a scien-
> tist and an artist, Charcot was extremely humane,
> devoted to his patients and would not tolerate any-
> thing unkind being said about anyone in his pres-
> ence. He was a poised and sensible man, very cir-
> cumspect in his judgments, with a quick eye for
> distinguishing peoples' value. His family life was a
> harmonious and happy one; his wife, who was a
> widow with a daughter when he married her, helped
> him with his work and was active in charitable or-
> ganizations. He gave great care to the education of
> his son Jean who had spontaneously chosen to be
> a physician and whose first scientific publications
> were a great joy for his father. He enjoyed the de-
> votion of his students and of his patients, so that
> his patron saint's day, the Saint Martin on Novem-
> ber 11th, was celebrated with entertainments and
> rejoicing at the Salpêtrière.

One may wonder how Charcot gained that enormous prestige which he enjoyed in the years 1880
to 1890. Several reasons may be distinguished.
Firstly, the Salpêtrière was anything but an or-

dinary hospital. It was a city within a city in the seventeenth century style, consisting of about 45 buildings with streets, squares, gardens, and an old and beautiful church. It was also a place of historical fame: Saint Vincent de Paul had carried out there his charitable activities; it had later been converted by Louis XIV into an asylum for beggars, prostitutes, and the insane; it was also one of the places where the notorious September Massacres had taken place during the French Revolution and where Pinel had achieved his mental hospital reforms. It was also known from one episode in the classic novel *Manon Lescaut* by the Abbé Prévost. Its thousands of old women had inspired some of Baudelaire's poems. Before Charcot, the Salpêtrière had been little known to medical students, and physicians did not relish the thought of being appointed there. Charcot was now credited with being the scientific wizard who had turned this historical place into a Temple of Science.

That old-fashioned hospital with its antiquated buildings had no laboratories, no examination rooms, no teaching facilities. With his iron will—and with the help of his political connections—Charcot built a treatment, research, and teaching unit. He had carefully chosen his collaborators; he installed consulting rooms for ophthalmology, otolaryngology, and so on, as well as laboratories and a photographic service, later a museum for anatomo-pathology, and finally an outpatient service where men were also admitted, and a large auditorium. Among Charcot's disciples were Bourneville, Pitres, Joffroy, Cotard, Gilles de la Tourette, Meige, Paul Richer, Souques, Pierre Marie, Raymond, Babinski; there is hardly one French neurologist of that time who had not been Charcot's student. On that School, which was his creation, Charcot exerted an absolute domination. Each one of his lectures was carefully recorded by students and published in one or the other of several medical journals he had founded. There came a time when no one could be appointed at the Paris medical faculty without his sanction. The patriotic feeling contributed to Charcot's fame: He and Pasteur were to the French a proof of France's scientific genius, challenging Germany's alleged scientific superiority.

Charcot personified what the French call a "prince de la Science"; he was not only a man of high scientific reputation, but also a powerful and wealthy man. Through his marriage with a rich widow and the very high fees which he charged his patients, he was able to lead the life of the wealthy class. Aside from his villa in Neuilly, he had in 1884 acquired a splendid residence on the Boulevard Saint-Germain which had been decorated according to his own plans. It was a kind of private museum with Renaissance furniture, stained glass windows, tapestries, paintings, antiques, and rare books. He was himself an artist who did excellent drawings and was an expert in painting on china and enamel; he was a keen connoisseur of the history of art (19). He was also a master of French prose and had an exhaustive knowledge of French literature. An infrequent thing at his time, he also knew English, German, and Italian and showed a particular admiration for Shakespeare whom he often quoted in English, and for Dante whom he quoted in Italian. Every Tuesday night, he gave fastuous receptions in his splendid home to the *Tout-Paris* of scientists, politicians, artists, and writers. He was known to be the physician and sometimes the confident of kings and princes. Emperor Pedro II of Brazil, it was said, came to his home, played billiards with him, and attended his lectures at the Salpêtrière.

Charcot was also a very influential figure in English medical circles; at an international Congress which took place in London in 1881, his demonstration on the tabetic arthropathies was received with a storm of applause. He had many admirers in Germany, although he declined invitations to congresses in that country after the Franco-German war of 1870–1871. In Vienna, he was well acquainted with Meynert and Moritz Benedikt. Charcot was very popular in Russia where he had been called several times as consultant physician to the Czar and his family. Russian physicians welcomed him because he relieved them from their strong dependence on German scientists. According to Guillain (1), he arranged an unofficial encounter between Gambetta and the Grand Duke Nikolai of Russia, from which the Franco-Russian alliance was to issue. Charcot travelled extensively; every year he made a carefully planned journey to a different European country, visiting the museums, making drawings, writing travelogues.

Great as it was, Charcot's prestige was still enhanced by a halo of mystery which surrounded him, which had slowly grown after 1870 and reached its peak with his celebrated paper on hypnotism in 1882. He gained the reputation of being a great thaumaturgist. Instances of his quasi-miraculous cures are reported by Lyubimov (3):

> Many patients were brought to Charcot from all over the world, paralytics on stretchers or wearing complicated apparatuses. Charcot ordered the removal of these appliances and told the patients to walk. There was, for instance, a young lady who had been paralyzed for years. Charcot bade her stand up and walk, which she did under the astounding eyes of her parents and of the Mother Superior of the Convent in which she had been staying. Another young lady was brought to Charcot with a paralysis of both legs. Charcot found no organic lesion; the consultation was not yet over when the patient stood up and walked back to the door where the cabman, who was waiting for her, took off his hat in amazement and crossed himself.

In the eyes of the public, Charcot was the man who had explored the abysses of the human mind, hence his nickname "Napoleon of Neuroses." He had come to be identified with the discovery of hysteria, hypnotism, dual personality, catalepsy, and somnambulism. Strange things were said about his hold on the Salpêtrière's hysterical young women and about happenings there. Jules Claretie (20) relates that during a patients' ball at the Salpêtrière, it happened that a gong was inadvertently sounded, whereupon many hysterical women instantaneously fell into catalepsy and kept the attitudes in which they found themselves when the gong was sounded. Charcot was also the man whose searching gaze penetrated the depths of the past and who retrospectively interpreted works of art, giving

modern neurologic diagnoses on cripples represented by painters (21). He founded a journal, the *Iconographie de la Salpêtrière,* followed by the *Nouvelle Iconographie de la Salpêtrière,* probably the first journals to combine art and medicine. Charcot was also considered to have found a scientific explanation for demoniac possession which, he assumed, was nothing but a form of hysteria; he also interpreted this condition retrospectively in works of art (22). He was known for his collection of rare old works on witchcraft and possession, some of which he had reprinted in a book series titled *The Diabolical Library.*

All these features contributed to the incomparable fascination exerted by Charcot's *séances* at the Salpêtrière. Tuesday mornings were devoted to examining new, heretofore unseen patients in the presence of physicians and students who enjoyed seeing Charcot display his clinical acumen, the assurance and swiftness with which he was able to disentangle the most complicated case histories and arrive at a diagnosis, even of rare diseases. But the greatest attraction were his solemn lectures on Friday mornings, each of which had been prepared with the utmost care. The large auditorium was filled to capacity with physicians, students, writers and a curious crowd long before the beginning of the lectures. The podium was always decorated afresh with pictures and anatomic schemata pertaining to the day's lecture. Charcot, his bearing reminiscent of Napoleon or Dante, entered at ten o'clock, often accompanied by an illustrious foreign visitor and a group of assistants who sat down in the first rows. Amidst the absolute silence of the audience, he started speaking in a low pitch and gradually raised his voice, giving sober explanations which he illustrated with skillful colored chalk drawings on the blackboard. With an inborn acting talent, he imitated the behavior, mimicry, the gait, the voice of a patient afflicted with the disease he was talking about, after which the patient was brought in. The patient's entrance was sometimes also spectacular. When Charcot lectured on tremors, three or four women were introduced wearing hats with long feathers which, by their quivering made it possible to distinguish the specific characteristics of tremors in various diseases (23). The interrogation took the form of a dramatic dialogue between Charcot and the patient. Most spectacular were the lectures which he gave about hysteria and hypnotism. Another of Charcot's innovations was the use of photographic projections, a procedure which at that time was unusual for medical teaching. The lecture was concluded with a discussion of the diagnosis and a recapitulation stating the lecture's main points, and both were models of lucidity and concision. The lecture lasted for two hours, but the audience, it was said, never found it too long, even when it concerned rare organic brain diseases (4). Lyubimov points to the difference between Charcot's lectures and those of Meynert which he had also attended in Vienna and which left him exhausted and confused, whereas he left Charcot's lectures with a feeling of exhilaration.

It is easy to understand the spell-binding effect which Charcot's teaching exerted on laymen, on many physicians, and especially on foreign visitors such as Sigmund Freud, who spent four months at the Salpêtrière in 1885–1886. Other visitors were more skeptical. The Belgian physician Delboeuf, whose interest in Charcot's work had brought him to Paris in the same period as Freud, was soon assailed by the strongest doubts when he saw how carelessly experiments with hysterical patients were carried out. On his return to Belgium, he published a strongly critical account of Charcot's methods (24).

Those visitors who came to see Charcot in Paris for a short visit and were envious of him, were often unaware that he was surrounded by a host of powerful enemies. He was stamped as an atheist by the clergy and the Catholics (one of the reasons being that he had the nuns at the Salpêtrière replaced by lay nurses), but some atheists found him too spiritualist. He was publicly accused of charlatanism by the magnetists (25). He also had fierce enemies in political and society circles (as is obvious from the *Diary* of the Goncourt brothers). Among neurologists, some who had remained his admirers as long as he remained on the solid ground of neuropathology, deserted him when he shifted to the study of hypnotism and to spectacular experiments with hysterical patients. Lyubimov tells how the German neurologist Westphal expressed deep concern about the new turn taken by Charcot's research after visiting him in Paris. In America, he was attacked on the same grounds by Bucknill; Beard, while admitting that Charcot had made "serious mistakes," nonetheless proclaimed that he still respected him "as a man of genius and a man of honour" (26). Charcot also had to wage a continuous battle against the Nancy School in which he was steadily losing ground to his opponents. Bernheim sarcastically proclaimed that among thousands of patients whom he had hypnotized, only one displayed the three stages described by Charcot—a woman who had spent three years at the Salpêtrière.

Charcot also met with undying hatred on the part of some of his medical colleagues and particularly on the part of his former disciple Bouchard, an ambitious man 12 years his junior. Worse still, a few of his seemingly loyal disciples duped him by showing him more and more extraordinary manifestations which they rehearsed with patients and then demonstrated to him. It is true that many of his disciples never participated in such activities, but no one apparently dared warn him; he had been extremely cautious for a long time, but eventually La Rochefoucauld's maxim applied to him also: "deception always goes further than suspicion." According to Guillain, Charcot began to feel strong doubts toward the end of his life and was thinking of taking up again the entire study of hypnotism and hysteria, which death prevented him from doing. The secret enemy, who was so well acquainted with his medical condition and who for years sent him anonymous letters depicting his angina pectoris and announcing his impending death (23, 27) most likely belonged to the medical circle around Charcot.

The extreme opinions prevailing about Charcot, the fascination he exerted on the one hand, and the fierce enmities he aroused on the other, made it extremely difficult in his lifetime to make a true assessment of the value of his work and, contrary to expectations, the passing of time has not made this task much easier. It is therefore necessary to distinguish the various fields of his activity. First, it is often forgotten that Charcot, as an internist and anatomo-pathologist, made valuable contributions to the knowledge of pulmonary and kidney diseases and that his lectures on diseases of old age were for a long time a classic of what is now called "geriatrics." Second, in neurology, which was his "second career," he made outstanding discoveries upon which his lasting fame will undisputedly rest: delineation of disseminated sclerosis, amyotrophic lateral sclerosis ("Charcot's disease"), locomotor ataxia and its peculiar arthropathies ("Charcot's joints"), his work on cerebral and medullar localizations, on aphasia, and so on.

On the other hand, it is most difficult to evaluate objectively what could be called Charcot's "third career," that is, his exploration of hysteria and hypnotism. As happens with many scientists, he lost control of the new ideas which he had formulated and was carried away by the movement he had created.

Pierre Janet has well shown which were Charcot's methodologic errors in that field (28): The first was his excessive concern with delineating specific disease entities, chosing as model type those cases which showed as many symptoms as possible; he assumed that the other cases were incomplete forms. Since this method had proved fruitful for neurology, Charcot took it for granted that the same would hold true for mental conditions as well. He thus gave arbitrary descriptions of the *grande hystérie* and the *grand hypnotisme*. A second error was to oversimplify the descriptions of these disease entities in order to make them more intelligible to his students. A third fatal error was Charcot's lack of interest in his patients' backgrounds and in the ward life at the Salpêtrière. He hardly ever made rounds; he saw his patients in his hospital examination room while his collaborators, who had examined them, reported to him. Charcot never suspected that his patients were often visited and magnetized on the wards by incompetent people. Janet has shown that the alleged "three stages of hypnosis" were nothing but the result of training which Charcot's patients underwent at the hands of magnetizers. Seeing that the early history of magnetism and hypnotism was forgotten, Charcot—even more than Bernheim—believed that all the manifestations he noted in his hypnotized patients were new discoveries.

Another fact which from the start distorted Charcot's investigations in dynamic psychiatry was the peculiar collective spirit which pervaded the Salpêtrière. This closed community sheltered not only crowds of old women, but comprised also special wards for hysterical patients, some of them young, pretty, and cunning: nothing could be more eminently propitious to the development of mental contagion. These women were the star attractions, utilized to demonstrate clinical cases to the students and in Charcot's lectures given in the presence of the *Tout-Paris*. Due to Charcot's paternalistic attitude and his despotic treatment of students, his staff never dared contradict him; they therefore showed him what they believed he wanted to see. After rehearsing the demonstrations, they showed the subjects to Charcot who was careless enough to discuss their cases in the patients' presence. A most peculiar atmosphere of mental suggestion developed between Charcot, his collaborators, and his patients which would certainly be worthy of an accurate sociologic analysis.

Janet has pointed out that Charcot's descriptions of hysteria and hypnotism were based on a very limited number of patients. The *prima donna,* Blanche Wittmann, deserves more than an anecdotic mention. The role of patients in the elaboration of dynamic psychiatry has been all too neglected and would also be worthy of intensive investigation. Unfortunately, it is very difficult to gather relevant information in retrospect.

We know nothing of Blanche Wittmann's origin and background prior to her admission to the ward for hysterical patients at the Salpêtrière. According to Baudouin (29), she was young when she arrived there and rapidly became one of Charcot's most renowned subjects and was nicknamed *la reine des hystériques*. She was often exhibited to demonstrate the "three stages of hypnosis," of which she was not only the type, but the prototype, according to Frederick Myers who had seen her (30). Baudouin states that she is the woman in full hysterical crisis, depicted between Charcot and Babinski in Bouillet's famous painting; she can also be recognized in several pictures in the *Iconographie de la Salpêtrière* and elsewhere. She was authoritarian, capricious, and unpleasant toward the other patients and toward the personnel.

For some unknown reason, Blanche Wittman left the Salpêtrière and was admitted at the Hôtel-Dieu where she was investigated by Jules Janet, Pierre Janet's brother (31). After achieving the "first stage of hypnosis," that is, lethargy, Jules Janet modified the usual technique and saw the patient in a quite new condition: a new personality, "Blanche II," emerged, showing herself much more balanced than "Blanche I." The new personality disclosed that she had been permanently present and conscious, hidden behind "Blanche I," and that she was always aware of everything which occurred during the many demonstrations when she had acted out the "three stages of hypnosis" and was supposed to be unconscious. Myers noted that "it is strange to reflect for how many years the dumbly raging Blanche II has thus assisted at experiences to which Blanche I submitted with easy complacence."

Jules Janet kept Blanche Wittmann in her second state for several months and found that she was remarkably (and apparently lastingly) improved by his treatment. What later happened to Blanche Wittmann has been succinctly reported by Baudouin: She returned to the Salpêtrière where she was given a job in the photographic laboratory; later, when a laboratory of radiology was opened, she was employed there. She was

still authoritarian and capricious; she denied her past history and became angry when she was asked about that period of her life. Since the dangers of radiology were not yet known, she became one of the first victims of the radiologist's cancer. Her last years were a calvary which she crossed without showing the least hysterical symptom. She had to suffer one amputation after another and died a martyr of Science.

Coming back to Charcot's third career, it contributed more than anything else to his contemporary fame. The writer T. de Wyzewa (32), in an obituary he wrote on Charcot, said that in a few centuries his neurologic work may be forgotten, but that he would stand in the memory of mankind as the man who had revealed to the world an unsuspected realm of the mind. It is through that breakthrough, and not due to his literary works (which have remained unpublished) that Charcot exerted a powerful influence on literature. As stated by de Monzie (33), he was the starting point of a whole tradition of psychiatrically oriented writers such as Alphonse Daudet and his son Léon Daudet, Zola, Maupassant, Huysmans, Bourget, Claretie, and later Pirandello and Proust, not to speak of many authors of popular novels. Charcot himself was the model for a specific character in many novels and plays in the 1890's: the great scientist of world renown impavidly pursuing his uncanny research in the abyss of the human mind.

An American visitor who saw Charcot at the beginning of 1893 noticed that, while his intellectual strength was as lively as ever, his physical health was greatly shaken (34). He kept working feverishly until August 15, 1893, when he left for a vacation with two of his favorite disciples, Debove and Strauss, intending to visit the Vézelay churches. He died unexpectedly in his hotel room in the night of August 16 and was given a state funeral in Paris on August 19. In spite of the deluge of praise which was lavished on his memory, his fame soon waned. The publication of his complete works, which had been planned in 15 volumes, was abandoned after Volume 9 had appeared in 1894. According to Lyubimov, Charcot had left a considerable amount of literary works: memoirs, illustrated travelogues, critical studies on philosophic and literary works, all of which he did not want published in his lifetime. Lyubimov adds that Charcot's true personality could not be known before their publication. However, none of these writings have ever been printed. Charcot's son Jean (1867–1936), who had studied medicine to please his father, gave up this profession a few years later and made himself famous as a seafarer and explorer of the South Pole (35, 36). Charcot's precious library was donated by his son to the Salpêtrière (37) and gradually fell into the most pitiful state of neglect, as did the Musée Charcot.

The evil that men do lives after them;
The good is oft interred with their bones.

So it was with Charcot. It did not take long before his glory was transformed into the stereotype of the despotic scientist whose belief in his own superiority blinded him into unleashing a psychic epidemic. One year after Charcot's death, Léon Daudet, who had been a medical student on his ward, published a satirical novel, *Les Morticoles* (38), which gave fictitious names to prominent physicians and ridiculed the Paris medical world. Charcot was depicted under the name of "Foutange" and Bernheim was called "Boustibras"; faked hypnotical *séances* at the "HôpitalTyphus" with "Rosalie" (portraying Blanche Wittmann) were described in a caricatural manner. Another malevolent account of Charcot's Salpêtrière was later given by Axel Munthe (39) in his autobiographic novel *The Story of San Michele*.

Jules Bois, who was well acquainted with Charcot, relates that during the last months of his life, the old man expressed his pessimism in regard to the future of his work, which he felt would not survive him for long (40). In fact, less than ten years had elapsed before Charcot was largely forgotten and disowned by most of his disciples. His successor Raymond, while giving lip service to Charcot's work on neuroses, himself belonged to the organicist trend in neurology. One of Charcot's favorite disciples, Joseph Babinski, who had made himself known during Charcot's lifetime by his experiments in transferring hysterical symptoms with a magnet from one patient to another (41, 42) now became the main protagonist of a radical reaction against Charcot's concept of hysteria. Hysteria, he claimed, was nothing but the result of suggestion, and it could be cured by "persuasion" (42). The name "hysteria" itself was replaced by that of "pithiatisme" coined by Babinski. Guillain (1) reports that when he was a resident at the Salpêtrière in 1899, that is six years after Charcot's death, there still were a few of Charcot's hysterical female patients who would, for a small remuneration, act out for the students the full-fledged attack of the *grande hystérie*. But hysterical patients eventually disappeared from the Salpêtrière.

As years went by, Charcot's neurologic discoveries were taken for granted and his name became associated with a regrettable episode in the long history of the Salpêtrière. In 1925, his centennial was celebrated at the Salpêtrière with a strong emphasis on his neurologic achievements and a few rapid apologies about the *légère défaillance* (the slight lapse) which his work on hysteria and hypnotism had been. Psychoanalysts, however, praised him in that regard as a "precursor of Freud." In 1928, a group of Paris surrealists, in their endeavor to counteract all accepted ideas of their time, decided to celebrate the discovery of Charcot's hysteria, "the greatest poetical discovery of the end of the 19th century" (43).

Several years later, the author of the present [article], then a medical student at the Salpêtrière, met a very old woman patient who had spent almost her entire life there and had known Charcot and his school; she kept talking to herself and had hallucinations in which she was hearing all these men speaking in turn. These voices from the past, which had never been recorded but still resounded in the disturbed mind of that wretched old woman, were all that was surviving of the glory that had been Charcot's Salpêtrière.

REFERENCES

1 Guillain, G. *J. M. Charcot (1825–1893). Sa vie, son oeuvre.* Paris, Masson, 1955.
2 Souques, A. Charcot intime. *Press Méd.,* 33(I): 693–698, 1925.
3 Lyubimov, A. *Profesor Sharko, Nautshno-biograf-itshesky etiud.* St. Petersburg, Tip. Suvorina, 1894.
4 Levillain, F. Charcot et l'Ecole de la Salpêtrière. *Revue Encyclopédique,* 1894, pp. 108–115.
5 Guillain, G. L'Oeuvre de Duchenne (de Boulogne). *Etudes Neurologiques,* 3e série, Paris, Masson, 1929, pp. 419–448.
6 Guilly, P. *Duchenne (de Boulogne).* Thèse méd., Paris, 1936.
7 Richer, P. *Etudes cliniques sur l'hystéro-épilepie ou Grande Hystérie.* Paris, Delahaye & Lecrosnier, 1881 (with many pictures).
8 Charcot, J. M. Sur les divers états nerveux déterminés par l'hypnotisation chez les hystériques. *C. R. Acad. Sci.* 94(I): 403–405, 1882.
9 ———. *Oeuvres Complètes. Leçons sur les maladies du Système Nerveux,* 3. Paris, Progrès Médical, 1890, pp. 299–359.
10 Brodie, B. C. *Lectures illustrative of certain local nervous affections.* London, 1837.
11 Reynolds, R. Remarks on paralyses and other disorders of motion and sensation, dependent on ideas. *Brit. Med. J.,* 2: 493–485, 1869.
12 Charcot, J. M. Sur un cas d'amnésie rétro-antérograde, probablement d'origine hystérique. *Rev. Méd.* 12: 81–96, 1892.
13 Souques, A. *Rev. Méd.* 12: 267–400, 867–881, 1892. Follow-ups to Charcot (12).
14 Charcot, J. M. La Foi qui guérit. *Arch. Neurol.* 25: 72–87, 1893.
15 Daudet, Léon. *Souvenirs des milieux littéraires, politiques, artistiques et médicaux de 1885 à 1905.* 2e série: *Devant la douleur.* Paris, 1917, pp. 4–15.
16 ———. *Les Oeuvres et les Hommes.* Paris, Nouvelle Librairie Nationale, 1922, pp. 197–243.
17 ———. *Quand mon père vivait. Souvenirs inédits sur Alphonse Daudet.* Paris, Grasset, 1940, pp. 113–119.

18 De Goncourt, E. and J. *Journal. Mémoires de la vie littéraire.* Paris, Fasquelle & Flammarion, 4 vol., 1956 (see particularly vol. 3).
19 Meige, H. Charcot artiste. *Nouvelle Iconographie de la Salpêtrière,* 11: 489–516, 1898.
20 Claretie, J. *La Vie à Paris, 1881.* Paris, Havard, 1882, p. 128–129.
21 Charcot, J. M., and Richer, P. *Les Difformes et les malades dans l'art.* Paris, Lecrosnier & Babé, 1889.
22 ———. *Les Démoniaques dans l'art.* Paris, Delahaye & Lecrosnier, 1887.
23 Féré, Ch. J. M. Charcot et son oeuvre. *Revue des Deux Mondes.* 122: 410–424, 1894.
24 Delboeuf, J. De l'Influence de l'imitation et de l'éducation dans le somnambulisme provoqué. *Revue Philosophique.* 22: 146–171, 1886 (II).
25 Bué in *Le Magnétisme humain. Congrés International de 1889.* Paris, Georges Carré, 1890, pp. 333–334, 338–339.
26 Beard, G. M. *The Study of Trance, Muscle-Reading and Allied Nervous Phenomena in Europe and America, with a Letter on the Moral Character of Trance Subjects and a Defence of Dr. Charcot.* New York, 1882.
27 Hahn, G. Charcot et son influence sur l'opinion publique. *Revue des Questions Scientifiques,* 2e série, 6(II): 230–261, 353–379, 1894.
28 Janet, P. J. M. Charcot, son oeuvre psychologique. *Revue Philosophique,* 39: 569–604, 1895.
29 Baudouin, A. Quelques souvenirs de la Salpêtrière. *Paris-Méd.,* 15 (I) May 23, No. 21, X–XIII, 1925.
30 Myers, F. *Human personality and its survival of bodily death.* London, Longmans, Green & Co., 1903, vol. 1, p. 447.
31 Janet, J. L'Hystérie et l'hypnotisme, d'après la théorie de la double personnalité. *Revue Scientifique (Revue Rose),* 3e série, 15: 616–623, 1888.
32 *Le Figaro,* Tuesday, August 17, 1893.
33 De Monzie, A. Discours au Centenaire de Charcot. *Rev. Neurol.,* 32 (I), 1925 (special issue for Charcot's centennial).
34 Withington, C. F. A last glimpse of Charcot at the Salpêtrière. *Boston Med. and Surg. J.,* 129: 207, 1893.
35 Anonymous. *Jean-Baptiste Charcot.* Paris, Yacht-Club de France, 1937.
36 Dupouy, A. *Charcot.* Paris, Plon, 1938.

37 Charcot, J.-B. Discours prononcé à l'inauguration de la bibliothèque de son père. *Bull. Méd.*, vol. 21, Nov. 23, 1907.
38 Daudet, Léon. *Les Morticoles*. Paris, Charpentier, 1894.
39 Munthe, A. *The Story of San Michele*. New York, Duffin, 1929, Chapter XVII.
40 Bois, J. *Le Monde invisible*. Flammarion, s.d., pp. 185–192.

41 Babinski, J. *Recherches servant à établir que certaines manifestations hystériques peuvent être tranférées d'un sujet à l'autre sous l'influence de l'aimant*. Paris, Delahaye & Lecrosnier, 1886.
42 ———. Définition de l'Hystérie. *Rev. Neurol,* 9: 1074–1080, 1901.
43 Aragon & Breton. Le cinquantenaire de l'hystérie (1878–1928). *La Révolution Surréaliste*, 4: 20–22, 1928.

Charcot and Freud

Frank J. Sulloway

It was a decisive moment in Freud's life when he applied for and won a government-sponsored traveling fellowship open to the junior *Sekundarärzte* at the Vienna General Hospital. The fellowship, which was allotted to him in June of 1885 by the university's Faculty of Medicine, carried with it an automatic six-month leave of absence from his post at the hospital. In his proposal, Freud had announced his intention to study with Charcot in Paris. His narrow victory over his sole rival candidate—by thirteen votes to eight—was accomplished, so his friend Fleischl later told him, only upon "Brücke's passionate intercession, which had caused a general sensation."[1] Freud was in Paris from 13 October 1885 to 28 February 1886, and he spent seventeen of these twenty weeks in attendance at Charcot's clinic.

Jean Martin Charcot (1825–93) was then at the height of the varied medical career that had led him to the study of neurology, and his stature in French medicine was equaled only by that of the great Louis Pasteur.[2] Son of a carriage builder, Charcot had become by the 1880s a consulting physician to the most prominent royal families in Europe. And from all over the world ordinary patients and physicians flocked to the Salpêtrière

in Paris in order to seek his medical advice. Charcot was charismatic and authoritarian and enjoyed a legendary reputation even in his own lifetime. He was especially famed for the miraculous cures in which the power of his commandment alone repeatedly enabled paralytic individuals (no doubt largely hysterics) to throw off their crutches and walk.

Also a highly cultured man, Charcot was particularly at home with art and literature. He read widely in the English, German, Spanish, and Italian languages and enjoyed quoting Shakespeare and Dante, his two favorite authors, in their native tongues. In social circles he was also well known for the spectacular receptions and parties at his palatial home on the Boulevard Saint-Germain, where Freud himself was several times a guest (*Letters,* pp. 194–96, 206–8).

Almost every prominent French neurologist in the late nineteenth century studied at one time or another under Charcot at the famous Salpêtrière. This huge medical complex included some forty-odd buildings devoted largely to the care of older women. There Charcot had gradually built up numerous research laboratories in the various major medical disciplines. He had also created the necessary teaching facilities for instructing medical students about the many unique neurological disorders then common among the Salpêtrière's several thousand pa-

Adapted from Sulloway, F. J. (1979). *Freud: Biologist of the mind*. New York: Basic Books, 1979, pp. 28–35. Copyright © 1979 by Basic Books, Inc. Reprinted by permission of the publisher and the author.

tients. It is perhaps worth noting that Freud found the laboratory conditions at the Salpêtrière rather unsatisfactory for his own neuroanatomical needs—compared at least with what he was used to—and he eventually gave up, on this account, his plans to pursue anatomical studies of infantile brains while in Paris (Jones 1953: 210–11).

Like Freud, hundreds of other foreigners came yearly to visit this "Mecca of neurology" and to attend Charcot's famous Tuesday and Friday lectures on the subject of nervous diseases. The Tuesday lectures were extemporaneous and consisted of Charcot's on-the-spot diagnoses of ailing patients brought to him without prior consultation from the well-stocked wards of the Salpêtrière. It was an unforgettable performance about which Freud, in speaking of "the magic" of Charcot's great personality, later warmly reminisced in his Preface to the German translation of these lectures (Freud 1892–94, *S.E., I*: 135–36). In contrast to the Tuesday lectures, those given on Fridays were models of highly organized learning and lucidity; and Charcot rarely failed to keep his packed audience spellbound throughout the two hours that he customarily devoted to each major neurological disease.

Charcot had begun his medical career in pathological anatomy. As a young intern at the Salpêtrière, where he had served for a short time in the course of his medical training, he had been fascinated by the many strange and seemingly incurable neurological afflictions he had encountered there. He had vowed to himself then and there that he would someday return to study in more detail this neglected world of medical treasures; and in 1862, at the age of thirty-seven, he finally honored that vow, coming back to the Salpêtrière as head of one of its major divisions.

By 1870, Charcot was concentrating on the problem of how to distinguish hysterical from epileptic convulsions. With his disciple and assistant Paul Richer, he succeeded in providing a formal clinical description of the stages that, in his view, characterized the "hysterical crisis" (*grande hystérie*).

His approach, while extremely important in the scientific understanding of hysteria, was also symptomatic of the dubious "type" concept of disease then popular in French medicine. Although the type concept had formerly proved useful in Charcot's anatomically based neurological work, it later brought him into considerable discredit when he attempted to apply it to the more problematic phenomena of hysteria.

By 1878, Charcot had taken up the study of hypnotism—a bold step in his medical career, since in France, as elsewhere, the whole subject had been in considerable scientific disrepute for almost a century (ever since the debates over mesmerism in the 1780s). Four years later, in 1882, Charcot delivered a paper on hypnotism at the *Académie des Sciences* in which he personally endorsed the phenomenon of hypnotism as genuine and provided a detailed description of the hypnotic trance as occurring in three sequential stages ("lethargy," "catalepsy," and "somnambulism"). Charcot's paper created a sensation. It also brought about a complete reversal within France of the negative attitude in official science toward mesmerism or "animal magnetism"—a subject that the *Académie des Sciences* itself had twice formally condemned.[3]

By the mid-1880s, when Freud went to Paris to study with Charcot, the latter had just begun his famous researches on the subject of traumatic paralyses. In 1884 and 1885, Charcot had shown that these traumatic paralyses were distinct symptomatically from organic ones, and he had succeeded in *artificially* reproducing such non-organic paralyses with the use of hypnosis. He subsequently established a similar medical distinction between traumatic and organic amnesia. Before his death in 1893, Charcot's interests in the psychopathology of disease even caused him to consider the psychological mechanism of faith healing (Charcot 1893). It is no wonder, then, that the neurologist whose work on hypnotism and hysteria in the 1880s enthralled both the French medical community and a generation of novelists and playwrights eventually received the nickname "Napoleon of Neuroses" (Ellenberger 1970:95).

Charcot exerted an immediate and profound influence upon Freud, who later named his eldest son after this important figure in his life. His first personal impression of Charcot, whom Freud met a week after reaching Paris, readily conveys his fascination:

> At ten o'clock M. Charcot arrived, a tall man of fifty-eight [in fact, only a month shy of sixty], wearing a top hat, with dark, strangely soft eyes (or rather, one is; the other is expressionless and has an inward cast), long wisps of hair stuck behind his ears, clean shaven, very expressive features with full protruding lips—in short, like a worldly priest from whom one expects a ready wit and an appreciation of good living. . . . I was very much impressed by his brilliant diagnosis and the lively interest he took in everything, so unlike what we are accustomed to from our great men with their veneer of distinguished superficiality. (*Letters*, p. 175)

By the end of November (a month later), Freud was even more ecstatic in singing the praises of Charcot. "I think I am changing a great deal," he wrote to his future bride. "Charcot, who is one of the greatest physicians and a man whose common sense borders on genius, is simply wrecking all my aims and opinions. I sometimes come out of his lectures as from out of Notre Dame, with an entirely new idea about perfection. . . . Whether the seed will ever bear fruit, I don't know; but what I do know is that no other human being has ever affected me in the same way" (*Letters*, pp. 184–85).

It is nevertheless odd that, by the beginning of December, Freud was at the point of returning to Vienna, as Jones (1953:208) has reported on the basis of an unpublished letter to Martha Bernays. Freud's reasons seem to have been twofold: his inability to carry out his planned work on the anatomy of the brain and his disappointment over a lack of personal contact with Charcot, to whom Freud was just another face in a large crowd of foreign visitors. But fortu-

nately the idea occurred to Freud at about this time of offering his services to Charcot as German translator for the third volume of Charcot's *Leçons sur les maladies du système nerveux* (1887). In a formal letter of request to Charcot, Freud humorously commented, "Concerning my capacity for this undertaking it must be said that I only have motor aphasia in French but not sensory aphasia" (quoted in Jones 1953:209).

Charcot received Freud's proposal warmly. Thanks to the latter's proficiency as a translator, the German volume was published only seven months later—even before the French original— under the title *Neue Vorlesungen über die Krankheiten des Nervensystems insbesondere über Hysterie* (New Lectures on the Diseases of the Nervous System, Particularly on Hysteria, 1886). Charcot rewarded Freud's labors by giving him a complete leather-bound set of his works inscribed *"À Monsieur le Docteur Freud, excellents souvenirs de la Salpêtrière. Charcot"* (Freud library, New York). Finally, as a result of this translation arrangement, Freud entered into a much closer relationship with Charcot and his circle of personal friends and was soon invited to attend the splendid parties given by Charcot at his home.

It was, of course, Charcot's demonstrations concerning hysteria and hypnotism—many of which, Freud later recalled, had initially provoked in him and others "a sense of astonishment and an inclination to scepticism"—that really captured Freud's imagination during his four-and-a-half-month stay in Paris (*Autobiography*, 1925d, S.E., 20: 13). These dramatic demonstrations—particularly those of hypnotism—first revealed to Freud the remarkable circumstance that multiple states of consciousness could simultaneously coexist in one and the same individual without either state apparently having knowledge of the other. Charcot and his disciples had used such demonstrations not only for illustrating the psychogenic nature of hysterical paralyses but also as an aid to understanding the phenomenon of "split personality" (or *double conscience*). As Freud later commented about such hypnotic experiments: "I received the profoundest impression of the possibility that there could be powerful mental processes which nevertheless remained hidden from the consciousness of men" (*Autobiography*, 1925d, S.E., 20.:17; see also 1893*f, S.E., 3*:22).

With regard to the specific problem of hysteria, Charcot, who seems to have believed that the theory of *organic* nervous diseases was virtually complete, had accordingly begun full-time work upon this long-puzzling malady in the period immediately preceding Freud's visit to the Salpêtrière. Later, on the occasion of Charcot's death in 1893, Freud described what was known about this disease before Charcot's medical intervention, with the following words: "This, the most enigmatic of all nervous diseases, for the evaluation of which medicine had not yet found a serviceable angle of approach, had just then fallen into thorough discredit; and this discredit extended not only to the patients but to the physicians who concerned themselves with the neurosis. It was held that in hysteria anything was possible, and no credence was given to a hysteric about anything." Charcot's personal achievement in elucidating this protean disease, Freud added, was comparable to, but on a somewhat smaller scale than, Philippe Pinel's (1745–1826) famous liberation of the madmen from their chains at the Salpêtrière almost a century before. "The first thing that Charcot's work did," Freud said in summing up Charcot's medical revolution, "was to restore its dignity to the topic. Little by little, people gave up the scornful smile with which the patient could at that time feel certain of being met. She was no longer necessarily a malingerer, for Charcot had thrown the whole weight of his own authority on the side of the genuineness and objectivity of hysterical phenomena" ("Charcot," 1893*f, S.E., 3:*19).

A series of more specific medical discoveries had also soon emerged from Charcot's intensive work on hysteria. Three of these, in particular,

Freud later stressed as having profoundly affected his own thinking on the problem that, in many ways, launched him into his psychoanalytic career.

To begin with, Charcot had shown how the peculiar mechanism of traumatic-hysterical dysfunctions was to be understood from the remarkable fact that identical symptoms could be *induced artificially* by means of suggestions given to hysterical patients during a state of hypnosis. Furthermore, the analogy of hypnotically induced paralysis was all the more convincing as a key to such hysterical dysfunctions when one learned that these impairments were not always manifested immediately. Rather, the patient might return home apparently unharmed by a frightening experience, only to suffer a severe dysfunction several days or even weeks later.

In a like manner, Charcot had persuasively demonstrated that "hysterically prone" individuals could be put into a hypnotic trance and, without any suggestion at all, be induced to simulate paralytic dysfunctions after receiving a light blow to an arm or a leg. Charcot and his assistants explained this phenomenon by assuming that, in these patients, the power of external suggestion had simply been replaced by that of *auto*suggestion. All such subconscious hypnotic suggestions, Charcot believed, were dependent upon an idea or a series of ideas somehow isolated psychically from normal waking consciousness—the ego—and yet firmly planted within a second region of the mind in what he described as "the fashion of parasites" (Charcot 1887:335–37). Freud concluded: "[Charcot] succeeded in proving, by an unbroken chain of argument, that these paralyses were the result of ideas which had dominated the patient's brain at moments of a special disposition" (1893*f,* S.E., *3*:22). In other words, Charcot was the first to understand the hitherto hidden *mechanism* of hysterical phenomena, and he did so, moreover, in proto-Freudian terms.

Implicit in Charcot's first major medical generalization about hysteria was his second—namely, the *psychogenic nature of hysterical symptoms.* "M. Charcot was the first to teach us that to explain hysterical neurosis we must apply to psychology" (Freud 893c, *S.E., I*:171); and Freud also commented on how foreign Charcot's clinical and psychological approach to neurological problems had at first seemed to a physician like himself, trained in the Germanic tradition, with its emphasis on a physiological interpretation of symptoms.[4] At the same time, Freud encountered in Charcot's clinical emphasis a refreshing subordination of theory to medical facts. In one of his favorite anecdotes about Charcot, Freud tells how he once dared to contradict the master on some medical point with the remark: "But that can't be true, it contradicts the Young-Helmholtz theory"—to which Charcot unhesitatingly replied, "*La théorie, c'est bon, mais ça n'empêche pas d'exister* ['Theory is good; but it doesn't prevent things from existing']" (Freud 1893f, *S.E., 3*:13).

Freud deemed Charcot's third and last major contribution to the scientific understanding of hysteria to be his emphatic *rejection of the common notion that this disease is always caused by the female hysteric's disturbed sexual organization.* In his 1888 article "Hysteria" for Villaret's *Handwörterbuch der gesamten Medizin* (Encyclopedic Handbook of Medicine), Freud later exhibited the ironic imprint of Charcot's influence by giving as his principal argument against the sexual etiology of hysteria Charcot's own insistence that this disease could be found in children *before the onset of puberty* (a denial of infantile sexuality) and that severe cases were unquestionably found in the male sex. (Charcot had further fixed the ratio of male to female hysteria at roughly I:20. See Freud 1888b, *S.E., I*:50–51.)

In addition to working on his translation of Charcot's lectures while in Paris, Freud began an ingenious study on the psychogenic nature of traumatic hysterical paralyses. He later credited Charcot with the basic idea, but as Jones (1953:233) rightly points out, other contemporary ev-

idence indicates that the major inspiration, although implied in Charcot's overall teachings, was really Freud's own. Freud's idea was to show, using clinical material available to him at the Salpêtrière, that *hysterical* paralyses are largely independent of the regular anatomical distributions governing known instances of *organic* paralysis. For example, he observed that organic cerebral paralyses regularly affected a distal segment (the hand) more than they did a proximal one (the shoulder), but that in hysterical paralysis this was not always true (1893c, *S.E.,I*:162–63). In short, the functional lesions of hysterical paralysis appeared to follow a layman's notion of paralysis, not the laws of neuroanatomy. Hysteria, Freud concluded, "*behaves as though anatomy did not exist or as though it had no knowledge of it*" (*S.E., I*:169).

NOTES

(1) Unpublished letter to Martha Bernays, 23 June 1885; cited by Jones 1953:76.

(2) With the possible exception of Guillain (1955, trans. 1959), no adequate biographical treatment of Charcot yet exists. This surprising lacuna in the history of medicine is perhaps related to the sharp reversal of medical opinion after Charcot's death regarding the reliability of his famous researches on hypnotism and hysteria. The following account of his life and work relies heavily upon Ellenberger (1970:89–101), who has composed a brief but multifaceted portrait of Charcot on the basis of many scattered recollections by contemporaries who knew and worked with him. See also Jones (1953:185–86, 207–8, 226–29) for a more anecdotal account, based largely upon Freud's letters to his fiancée, Martha Bernays, written during his stay in Paris; and *Letters*, pp. 171–211.

(3) See Ellenberger (1970:57–85) and Darnton (1968) for informative treatments of the life of Franz Anton Mesmer and the subsequent history of the mesmerism and hypnotism movements.

(4) Preface to Freud's translation of Charcot's *Tuesday Lectures* (1892–94), *S.E., I*: 134–35.

REFERENCES

Charcot, J. M. (1887). *Lecons sur les maladies du systeme nerveux, faites a la Salpêtrière*, III. In *Oeuvres completes* (1888–94, 3).

Charcot, J. M. (1893). "La Foi qui guerit." *Archives de Neurologie, 25,* 72–87.

Darnton, R. (1968). *Mesmerism and the End of the Enlightenment in France.* Cambridge: Harvard University Press.

Ellenberger, H. F. (1970). *The Discovery of the Unconscious: The History and Evolution of Dynamic Psychiatry.* New York: Basic Books; London: Allen Lane.

Freud, S. (1888*b*). "Aphasia," "Gehirn," "Hysterie," and "Hysteroepilepsie." In *Handworterbuch der gesamten Medizin,* I. Edited by Albert Villaret. Stuttgart: Ferdinand Enke. (Unsigned; authorship uncertain.)

Freud, S. (1892–94). "Preface and Footnotes to the Translation of Charcot's *Tuesday Lectures*." In *Standard Edition, 1,* 131–143.

Freud, S. (1893*c*). "Some Points for a Comparative Study of Organic and Hysterical Motor Paralyses." In *Standard Edition, 1,* 157–172.

Freud, S. (1893*f*). "Charcot." In *Standard Edition, 3,* 9–23.

Freud, S. (1925*d*). *An Autobiographical Study.* In *Standard Edition, 20,* 3–70.

Freud, S. (1960*b*). *Letters of Sigmund Freud.* Selected and edited by Ernst L. Freud. Translated by Tania and James Stern. New York: Basic Books; London: Hogarth Press, 1961.

Guillain, G. (1955). *J. M. Charcot, 1825–1893: Sa vie, son oeuvre.* Paris: Masson et Cie. *Trans.:* Guillain (1959).

Jones, E. (1953). *The Life and Work of Sigmund Freud.* Vol. I: *The Formative Years and the Great Discoveries, 1856–1900.* New York: Basic Books; London: Hogarth Press.

CHAPTER 6

PSYCHOPHYSICS

Recall, from Chapter 3, John Locke's distinction between primary and secondary qualities. That distinction acknowledged the existence of experience that was independent of the physical objects of the world. As psychology sought to establish itself as a scientific discipline, it was important that human perception and physical stimulation not be perfectly correlated. If such a perfect relationship existed, meaning that changes in physical stimuli always resulted in similar changes in the perception of those stimuli, then it meant that perception (and, more broadly, psychology) and physical stimuli were the same. Under those circumstances there was no need for a special field of psychology; human perception would be wholly explained by the laws of the discipline of physics.

But how was it possible to compare the physical world with the psychological world? (The reader should recognize that question as a version of the centuries-old mind-body problem.) One answer to that question came to Gustav Theodor Fechner (1801–1887) on the morning of October 22, 1850, while he was lying in bed. He reasoned that the mind could be studied by recording an individual's reactions to known changes in physical stimulation. This approach, which Fechner labeled *psychophysics,* allowed the comparison of the psychological world and the physical world. Fechner made two important discoveries that were antecedent to the founding of experimental psychology. First, he demonstrated that there was not a one-to-one correspondence between changes in the physical world (stimuli) and changes in the psychological world (the perception of those stimuli). Second, he demonstrated that although the relationship between stimuli and perceptions was not linear, it was predictable; that is, the psychological and physical worlds are lawfully related.

This relationship had already been anticipated in the work of Ernst Weber (1795–1878), a German physiologist whose initial contributions on touch sensitivity were published in 1834. He studied the relative sensitivity of various areas of the skin through a technique he called the *two-point threshold.* In this method, two blunt needles were applied simultaneously to an area of the skin. Sometimes the two needles were close together, and other times they were far (perhaps 2 inches) apart. The subjects were blindfolded during the trials and asked to say whether they felt one or two points of stimulation on the skin. In more sensitive areas of the skin, the subjects reported feeling two points of stimulation even when the needles were close together. In this way, the differential sensitivity of the skin could be mapped.

Weber was also interested in muscle sensations, and he conducted a series of experiments in which subjects lifted small weights. The subjects were often asked to compare two weights to judge which one was heavier or lighter. By varying the difference in weight in these comparisons, Weber was able to discover the minimum weight change required for a subject to say another weight was heavier or lighter. This difference became known as the *difference threshold,* or *just noticeable difference* (jnd). Weber made an extremely important discovery in these weight studies, noting that although the size of the difference threshold between two weights differed according to the size of the weights, the ratio of the change in weight to the base weight was constant. He noted a similar constant relationship in his studies on the perception of tones, leading him to describe that relationship in a simple but profound formula that many psychologists still refer to as the first statement of a psychological law.

$$\frac{\Delta S}{S} = K$$

In this statement of Weber's Law, S equals a particular weight (or loudness of tone, or brightness of light), and ΔS equals the amount of change that must occur in S for the subject to perceive it as heavier (or louder in the case of sound, or brighter in the case of light). The letter K is a constant that is the same within any sensory dimension (such as weight perception) but has a different value for other sensory dimensions. For example, for lifted weights, K = .02; for brightness of light, K = .015; and for loudness of tone, K = .1. Take Weber's original work on weight as an example. For a weight of 30 grams, how much weight has to be added or subtracted before the subject can identify the new weight as heavier or lighter? Using the value of .1 for K and 30 for S, the equation can be solved for ΔS, which turns out to be 3. That is the value that has to be added to or subtracted from the standard weight for a reliable difference in weight to be perceived. Thus, a weight of 33 grams could be reliably perceived as heavier than a standard weight of 30 grams. That 3-gram difference is the difference threshold. If the standard weight was 90 grams instead of 30, then the difference threshold would be 9 grams (using Weber's formula, with K = .1).

For Weber, these studies were a means to understanding the physiology of sensory systems. It is not known whether Fechner was aware of the earlier work of Weber or not; some sources, such as Edna Heidbreder (1933) say that Fechner did not know of Weber's work until after he began his own studies. Whether he knew of Weber's studies or not, Fechner appreciated the value of such measurements for the study of the mind, and it led him to search for methods that would measure mental states as they corresponded to changes in the physical world. In 1860 he published one of the most important books in the history of psychology, *Elements of Psychophysics,* a treatise of such consequence that it has led some historians of psychology to name Fechner as the founder of scientific psychology (see Boring, 1950; Adler, 1977). This book laid out the conceptual issues in measuring the physical and psychological worlds, described a set of methods for undertaking that measurement, and reported Fechner's own psychophysical work, including a logarithmic law that predicted stimulus-perception relationships better than the earlier law of Weber. Fechner achieved better precision because he recognized that the values of physical stimuli increase at a much faster rate than the corresponding psychological perceptions. However, both laws held for only the intermediate range of stimuli and did not predict well when sensory values were extreme.

Fechner's 1860 book proved of great influence in psychology, both conceptually and methodologically, as evidenced by the late nineteenth-century work of Wilhelm Wundt and Hermann Ebbinghaus in Germany, and Charles S. Peirce and George Trumbull Ladd in the United States.

The selections in this chapter all deal with the work of Fechner. The initial article is an excerpt from Fechner's *Elements of Psychophysics* in which he discusses his ideas on mind and body that gave rise to psychophysics. He defines his concepts concerning stimuli and sensations and describes the concept and tasks of psychophysics. The selection was translated from the original German by Helmut Adler, a leading authority on Fechnerian psychology.

Following the primary source material by Fechner are two studies of his work authored by historians of psychology. The first of these articles was written by Edwin G. Boring (1886–1968) on the centennial of the publication of Fechner's classic book. Boring spent most of his career as professor of psychology at Harvard University. His book on the history of experimental psychology, published in 1929, established him as the foremost historian of psychology in America, a title he retained all his life. In the article reprinted here, Boring discusses the importance of Fechner's work for the founding of experimental psychology.

The second of the secondary source articles is authored by Marilyn E. Marshall of Carleton University in Canada. Among contemporary historians of psychology, she is generally acknowledged as one of the principal authorities on the life and work of Fechner (see Marshall, 1969, 1974a, 1974b). In her article, she writes about the use of biographical material as a tool in the history of science, comparing five different biographical studies of Fechner. This article is important, not only for what it says about Fechner but also for what it says about the relationship between biography and history.

REFERENCES

Adler, H. E. (1977). Vicissitudes of Fechnerian psychophysics in America. *Annals of the New York Academy of Sciences, 291,* 21–32.

Boring, E. G. (1950). *A history of experimental psychology* (2d ed.). New York: Appleton-Century-Crofts.

Heidbreder, E. (1933). *Seven psychologies.* New York: Appleton-Century-Crofts.

Marshall, M. E. (1969). Gustav Fechner, Dr. Mises, and the comparative anatomy of angels. *Journal of the History of the Behavioral Sciences, 5,* 39–58.

Marshall, M. E. (1974a). William James, Gustav Fechner, and the question of dogs and cats in the library. *Journal of the History of the Behavioral Sciences, 10,* 304–312.

Marshall, M. E. (1974b). G. T. Fechner: Premises toward a general theory of organisms. *Journal of the History of the Behavioral Sciences, 10,* 438–447.

Psychophysics and Mind-Body Relations

Gustav Theodor Fechner

I. GENERAL CONSIDERATIONS ON THE RELATION OF BODY AND MIND

While knowledge of the material world has blossomed in the great development of the various branches of natural science and has benefited from exact principles and methods that assure it of successful progress, and while knowledge of the mind has, at least up to a certain point, established for itself a solid basis in psychology and logic, knowledge of the relation of mind and matter, of body and soul, has up to now remained merely a field for philosophical argument without solid foundation and without sure principles and methods for the progress of inquiry.

The immediate cause of this less favorable condition is, in my opinion, to be sought in the following factual circumstances, which admittedly only make us seek their more remote origins. The relationships of the material world itself we can pursue directly and in accord with experience, as no less the relationships of the inner or mental world. Knowledge of the former, of course, is limited by the reach of our senses and their amplifications, and of the latter by the limitations of everyone's mind; still, these researches go on in such a way that we are able to find basic facts, basic laws, and basic relationships in each of the fields, information which can serve us as a secure foundation and starting point for inference and further progress. The situation is not the same in relating the material and mental worlds, since each of these two inextricably associated fields enters into immediate experience only one at a time, while the other remains hidden. At the moment when we are conscious of our feelings and thoughts, we are unable to perceive the activity of the brain that is associated with them and with which they are in turn associated—the material side is then hidden by the mental. Similarly, although we are able to examine the bodies of other people, animals, and the whole of nature directly in anatomical, physiological, physical, and chemical terms, we are not able to know anything directly about the minds that belong to the former nor of God who belongs to the latter, for the spiritual side is here hidden by the material. There thus remains great latitude for hypothesis and disbelief. Is there really anything revealed, we may ask, once the covers are lifted, and if so, what?

The uncertainty, the vacillation, the argument over these factual issues has so far not allowed us to gain a solid foothold or to find a point of attack for a theory of these relationships, whose factual basis is still in dispute.

And what can be the reason for this singular condition, in which body and mind can be observed, each for itself but never together, in spite of the fact that they belong to each other? Usually we can best observe things which belong together when they occur together. The inviolability of this aspect of the relationship between the mental and material worlds makes us suspect that it is fundamental, that it is rooted in their basic natures. Is there nothing similar that can at least illustrate these facts even though it cannot get to the root of the matter?

Admittedly, we can point to one thing or another. For example, when standing inside a circle, its convex side is hidden, covered by the concave side; conversely, when outside, the concave side is covered by the convex. Both sides belong together as indivisibly as do the mental and material sides of man and can be looked upon as analogous to his inner and outer sides.

From Fechner, G. T. (1860). *Elementen der psychophysik.* Adapted from H. E. Adler (Trans.), *Elements of psychophysics.* New York: Holt, Rinehart and Winston, 1966, pp. 1–18. Copyright © 1966 by Holt, Rinehart and Winston. Reprinted by permission of the publisher.

It is just as impossible, standing in the plane of a circle, to see both sides of the circle simultaneously as it is to see both sides of man from the plane of human existence. Only when we change our standpoint is the side of the circle we view changed, so that we now see the hidden side behind the one we had seen before. The circle is, however, only a metaphor and what counts is a question of fact.

Now, it is not the task or the intention of this work to enter into deep or penetrating discussions on the basic question of the relationship of body and mind. Let everyone seek to solve this puzzle—insofar as it appears to him as such—in his own way. It will therefore be without prejudice for what follows, if I state my opinion here in a few words, in order not to leave unanswered some possible questions about the general beliefs that formed the starting point of this inquiry and that for me, at least, still form the background. At the same time I am providing something to go by in this field of fluctuating ideas for those who are still seeking a point of view rather than believing that they have found one, even though what I say will not contain anything essential for further progress of this work. In view of the great temptation in starting a work such as this to lose oneself in voluminous and extensive discussions of this sort, and of the difficulty, by no means slight, of avoiding them completely, I hope that I will be forgiven if I limit myself here to the following brief exposition of my position.

To begin with, however, let me add a second illustrative example to the first. The solar system offers quite different aspects as seen from the sun and as observed from the earth. One is the world of Copernicus, the other the world of Ptolemy. It will always be impossible for the same observer to perceive both world systems simultaneously, in spite of the fact that both belong quite indivisibly together and, just like the concave and convex sides of the circle, are basically only two different modes of appearance of the same matter from different standpoints. Here again one needs but to change the point of view in order to make evident the one world rather than the other.

The whole world is full of such examples, which prove to us that what is in fact one thing will appear as two from two points of view; one cannot expect to find things the same from one standpoint and from the other. Who would not admit that it is always thus and cannot be otherwise? Only with respect to the greatest and most decisive example does one deny it or fail to think of it. That is the relationship of the mental and material worlds.

What will appear to you as your mind from the internal standpoint, where you yourself are this mind, will, on the other hand, appear from the outside point of view as the material basis of this mind. There is a difference whether one thinks with the brain or examines the brain of a thinking person. These activities appear to be quite different, but the standpoint is quite different too, for here one is an inner, the other an outer point of view. The views are even more completely different than were the previous examples, and for that reason the differences between the modes of their appearance are immensely greater. For the twofold mode of appearance of the circle or the planetary system was after all basically gained by taking two different external standpoints; whether within the circle or on the sun, the observer remained outside the sweep of the circles outside the planets. The appearance of the mind to itself, on the other hand, is gained from the truly inner point of view of the underlying being regarding itself, as in coincidence with itself, whereas the appearance of the material state belonging to it derives from a standpoint that is truly external, and not in coincidence.

Now it becomes obvious why no one can ever observe mind and body simultaneously even though they are inextricably united, for it is impossible for anyone to be inside and outside the same thing at one time.

Here lies also the reason why one mind cannot perceive another mind as such, even though one might believe it would be easiest to become aware of the same kind of entity. One mind, insofar as it does not coincide with the other, becomes aware only of the other's material manifestations. A mind can, therefore, gain awareness of another only through the aid of its corporeality, for the mind's exterior appearance is no more than its material nature.

For this reason, too, the mind appears always as unitary, because there exists only the one inner standpoint, whereas every body appears different according to the multitude of external standpoints and the differences among those occupying them.

The present way of looking at these phenomena thus covers the most fundamental relationships between body and mind, as any basic point of view should seek to do.

One more item: body and mind parallel each other; changes in one correspond to changes in the other. Why? Leibniz says: one can hold different opinions. Two clocks mounted on the same board adjust their movement to each other by means of their common attachment (if they do not vary too much from each other); this is the usual dualistic notion of the mind-body relation. It could also be that someone moves the hands of both clocks so that they keep in harmony; this view is occasionalism, according to which God creates the mental changes appropriate to the bodily changes and vice versa, in constant harmony. The clocks could also be adjusted so perfectly from the beginning that they keep perfect time, without ever needing adjustment; that is the notion of prestabilized harmony. Leibniz has left out one point of view—the most simple possible. They can keep time harmoniously—indeed never differ—because they are not really two different clocks. Therewith we can dispense with the common board, the constant adjustment, the artificiality of the original setting. What appears to the external observer as the organic clock with its movement and its works of organic wheels and levers (or as its most important and essential part), appears to the clock itself quite differently, as its own mind with its works of feelings, drives, and thoughts. No in-

sult is meant, if man here be called a clock. If he is called that in one respect, yet he will not be so called in every respect.

The difference of appearance depends not only on the difference of standpoint, but also on the differences among those that occupy it. A blind person does not see any of the exterior world from an external standpoint, though his position is just as favorable as that of a seeing person; and a nonliving clock does not see its interior in spite of its standpoint of coincidence, which is just as favorable as that of a brain. A clock can exist only as external appearance.

The natural sciences employ consistently the external standpoint in their considerations, the humanities the internal. The common opinions of everyday life are based on changes of the standpoints, and natural philosophy on the identity of what appears double from two standpoints. A theory of the relationship of mind and body will have to trace the relationship of the two modes of appearance of a single thing that is a unity.

These are my fundamental opinions. They will not clear up the ultimate nature of body and mind, but I do seek by means of them to unify the most general factual relationships between them under a single point of view.

However, as I mentioned before, it remains open to everyone to seek to effect the same end by another approach, or not to seek to accomplish it at all. Everyone's chosen approach will depend on the context of his other opinions. By arguing backwards, he will have to determine the possibility or impossibility of finding a suitable general relationship himself. At this point it is not important whether he wants to consider body and mind as only two different modes of appearance of the same entity or as two entities brought together externally, or to consider the soul as a point in a nexus of other points of essentially the same or of a different nature, or to dispense entirely with a fundamentally unitary approach. Insofar as an empirical relationship between body and mind is acknowledged and its empirical pursuit is allowed, there is no objection to trying even the most complicated kind of representation. In what follows we shall base our inquiry only on the empirical relationships of body and mind, and in addition adopt for use the most common expressions for the designation of these facts, though they are expressed more in the terms of a dualistic approach than my own monistic one. Translation from one to the other is easy.

This does not mean, however, that the theory which will be developed here will be altogether indifferent to the points of view on the basic relationships of body and mind and without influence upon them, for the contrary is true. Still, one must not confuse the effects that this theory may have some day—and that are partially beginning to take form even now—with the basis of this theory. This basis is indeed purely empirical, and every assumption is to be rejected from the start.

One may well ask whether the possibility of such a basis does not directly contradict the fact, with which we started, that the relationships of body and mind are outside the realm of experience. They are not, however, beyond experience altogether, for only the immediate relationships are beyond immediate experience. Our own interpretation of the general relation of body and mind already has had the support of common experiences with these relationships, even if they do not strike everyone who comes to this work with preconceived notions as necessary. What follows will show how we can draw quite as much on special experiences, which can serve us partly to orient ourselves in the area of meditated relationships and partly to provide a foundation for deductions regarding immediate relationships.

Indeed, we could not rest content with this general point of view, even if it were generally accepted. The proof, the fertility, and the depth of a universal law do not depend on the general principles but on the elementary facts. The law of gravitation and the molecular laws (which undoubtedly include the former) are elementary

laws; were they thoroughly known and the whole range of their implications exhausted, we would have a theory of the material world in its most general form. Similarly we must seek to form elementary laws of the relationship of the material and the mental world in order to gain a durable and developed theory instead of a general opinion, and we will only be able to do this, here as elsewhere, by building on a foundation of elementary facts.

Psychophysics is a theory that must be based on this point of view. More details follow in the next chapter.

II. THE CONCEPT AND THE TASK OF PSYCHOPHYSICS

Psychophysics should be understood here as an exact theory of the functionally dependent relations of body and soul or, more generally, of the material and the mental, of the physical and the psychological worlds.

We count as mental, psychological, or belonging to the soul, all that can be grasped by introspective observation or that can be abstracted from it; as bodily, corporeal, physical, or material, all that can be grasped by observation from the outside or abstracted from it. These designations refer only to those aspects of the world of appearance, with whose relationships psychophysics will have to occupy itself, provided that one understands inner and outer observation in the sense of everyday language to refer to the activities through which alone existence becomes apparent.

In any case, all discussions and investigations of psychophysics relate only to the apparent phenomena of the material and mental worlds, to a world that either appears directly through introspection or through outside observation, or that can be deduced from its appearance or grasped as a phenomenological relationship, category, association, deduction, or law. Briefly, psychophysics refers to the *physical* in the sense of physics and chemistry, to the *psychical* in the sense of experiential psychology, without referring back in any way to the nature of the body or of the soul beyond the phenomenal in the metaphysical sense.

In general, we call the psychic a dependent function of the physical, and vice versa, insofar as there exists between them such a constant or lawful relationship that, from the presence and changes of one, we can deduce those of the other.

The existence of a functional relationship between body and mind is, in general, not denied; nevertheless, there exists a still unresolved dispute over the reasons for this fact, and the interpretation and extent of it.

With no regard to the metaphysical points of this argument (points which concern rather more the so-called essence than the appearance), psychophysics undertakes to determine the actual functional relationships between the modes of appearance of body and mind as exactly as possible.

What things belong together quantitatively and qualitatively, distant and close, in the material and in the mental world? What are the laws governing their changes in the same or in opposite directions? These are the questions in general that psychophysics asks and tries to answer with exactitude.

In other words, but still with the same meaning: what belong together in the inner and outer modes of appearance of things, and what laws exist regarding their respective changes?

Insofar as a functional relationship linking body and mind exists, there is actually nothing to prevent us from looking at it and pursuing it from the one direction rather than from the other. One can illustrate this relationship suitably by means of a mathematical function, an equation between the variables x and y, where each variable can be looked upon at will as a function of the other, and where each is dependent upon the changes of the other. There is a reason, however, why psychophysics prefers to make the approach from the side of the dependence of the

mind on the body rather than the contrary, for it is only the physical that is immediately open to measurement, whereas the measurement of the psychical can be obtained only as dependent on the physical—as we shall see later. This reason is decisive; it determines the direction of approach in what follows.

The materialistic reasons for such a preference we need not discuss, nor are they meaningful in psychophysics, and the dispute between materialism and idealism over the essential nature of the dependency of one on the other remains alien and immaterial to psychophysics, since it concerns itself only with the phenomenal relationships.

One can distinguish immediate and mediated relationships of dependency or direct and indirect functions relating body and mind. Sensations are in a directly dependent relationship to certain processes in our brains as far as the one is determined by the other or has the other as its immediate consequence; but sensations are merely in a mediated relationship to the external stimulus, which initiates these processes only via the intervention of a neural conductor. All our mental activity has dependent upon it an immediate activity in our brain, or is accompanied immediately by brain activity, or else directly causes the activity, of which the effects then are transmitted to the external world via the medium of our neural and effector organs.

The mediated functional relationships of body and mind fulfill completely the concept of a functional relationship only under the supposition that the mediation enters into the relationship, since omission of the mediation leads to the absence of the constancy or lawfulness of the relationship of body and mind, which exists by virtue of this mediation. A stimulus then releases proper sensations only when a living brain does not lack the living nerves to transmit the effect of the stimulus to the brain.

As far as the psychic is to be considered a direct function of the physical, the physical can be called the carrier, the factor underlying the psychical. Physical processes that accompany or underlie psychical functions, and consequently stand in a direct functional relationship to them, we shall call psychophysical.

Without making any assumptions about the nature of psychophysical processes, the question of their substrate and form we may leave undecided from the start. There is a twofold reason why we may dispense with this question right away: first, because the determination of the general principles of psychophysics will involve the handling only of quantitative relations, just as in physics, where qualitative depend on earlier quantitative relationships; and second, because we will have to give no special consideration to psychophysical processes in the first part, under the plan of work which follows immediately.

By its nature, psychophysics may be divided into an outer and an inner part, depending on whether consideration is focused on the relationship of the psychical to the body's external aspects, or on those internal functions with which the psychic are closely related. In other words, the division is between the mediated and the immediate functional relationships of mind and body.

The truly basic empirical evidence for the whole of psychophysics can be sought only in the realm of outer psychophysics, inasmuch as it is only this part that is available to immediate experience. Our point of departure therefore has to be taken from outer psychophysics. However, there can be no development of outer psychophysics without constant regard to inner psychophysics, in view of the fact that the body's external world is functionally related to the mind only by the mediation of the body's internal world.

Moreover, while we are considering the regular relations of external stimulus and sensation, we must not forget that the stimulus, after all, does not awaken our sensations directly, but only via the awakening of those bodily processes within us that stand in direct relation to sensation. Their nature may still be quite unknown, the inquiry regarding their nature may be neglected for the present (as already stated), but the fact that

they do exist must be affirmed and referred to often, whenever it comes to the point of taking dead aim and following up those lawful relationships which are our immediate concern in outer psychophysics. Similarly, even though the body's activities, which are directly subject to the activity of our will and obey it, are still totally unknown, we should not forget that the effect of the will on the outer world can only be achieved via just such activities. We thus have implicitly to interpolate everywhere the unknown intermediate link that is necessary to complete the chain of effects.

Psychophysics, already related to psychology and physics by name, must on the one hand be based on psychology, and on the other hand promises to give psychology a mathematical foundation. From physics outer psychophysics borrows aids and methodology; inner psychophysics leans more to physiology and anatomy, particularly of the nervous system, with which a certain acquaintance is presupposed. Unfortunately, however, inner psychophysics has not profited so far from recent painstaking, exact, and valuable investigations in this field to the extent it should. Inner psychophysics undoubtedly will do this one day, once these investigations (and those from the different kind of attack on which this work is based) have succeeded to the point of reaching a common meeting ground, where they will be able to cross-fertilize each other. That this is not yet the case to any extent indicates only the incomplete state in which our theory finds itself.

The point of view from which we plan to attack our task is as follows: Even before the means are available to discover the nature of the processes of the body that stand in direct relation to our mental activities, we will nevertheless be able to determine to a certain degree the quantitative relationship between them. Sensation depends on stimulation; a stronger sensation depends on a stronger stimulus; the stimulus, however, causes sensation only via the intermediate action of some internal process of the body. To the extent that lawful relationships between sensation and stimulus can be found, they must include lawful relationships between the stimulus and this inner physical activity, which obey the same general laws of interaction of bodily processes and thereby give us a basis for drawing general conclusions about the nature of this inner activity. Indeed, later discussion will show that, in spite of all our ignorance of the detailed nature of psychophysical processes there exists, for those aspects which are concerned with the more important relationships of ordinary mental life, a basis which within limits already allows us to form certain and sufficient conceptions of the fundamental facts and laws which define the connection of outer to inner psychophysics.

Quite apart from their import for inner psychophysics, these lawful relationships, which may be ascertained in the area of outer psychophysics, have their own importance. Based on them, as we shall see, physical measurement yields a psychic measurement, on which we can base arguments that in their turn are of importance and interest.

III. A PRELIMINARY QUESTION

For the present the discussion of all obscure and controversial questions of inner psychophysics—and almost the whole of inner psychophysics at this time consists of such questions—will be postponed along with the discussion of inner psychophysics itself. Later experience will provide us with the means for the answers. Nevertheless, one of these questions will at least have to be touched upon briefly at the start. This point, which concerns the future of the whole of psychophysics, we take up now in order to answer it to the extent that it can be answered in general, leaving everything else for later discussion.

If we classify thinking, willing, and the finer esthetic feelings as higher mental activities, and sensations and drives as lower mental activities, then, at least in this world—leaving the question of the next world quite open—the higher mental activities can go on no less than the lower without involving physical processes or being tied to psychophysical processes. No one could think with a frozen brain. There can be just as little doubt that a specific visual sensation or auditory sensation can only come about because of specific activities of our nervous system. No one questions this. The idea of the sensory side of the mind is actually based on the conception that there exists an exact connection between it and corporeality. Great doubt exists, however, as to whether each specific thought is tied to just as specific a process in the brain and, if not, whether brain activity as a whole suffices for thinking and the higher mental activities in general, without the necessity for a special type or direction of physiological process in the brain in order for these processes to take place in a specific way and direction. Indeed, it seems that the essential difference between the higher and lower mental spheres (distinguished by some as soul and mind in their narrower senses) is sought precisely in this point.

If we now assume that the higher mental activities are really exempt from a specific relationship to physical processes, there would still be their general relationship, which may be granted to be real, and which would be subject to the consideration and investigation of inner psychophysics. This general relationship will, in any case, be subject to general laws, including common principles, still to be discovered. Indeed, their discovery should always remain the most important of the tasks of inner psychophysics. One of the next chapters . . . will lead us to a consideration of just such conditions.

A metaphor: thought may be regarded as part of the stream of bodily processes itself, and may be real only in terms of these processes, or it may need this stream only for steering as an oarsman steers his boat, raising only some incidental ripples with his oar. The conditions and laws of the river must be taken into account in both instances when the flow or progress of thought is concerned, though in each case from a quite different point of view, to be sure. Even the freest navigation* is subject to laws, as to the nature of the elements and the means that serve it. Similarly, psychophysics will find it necessary, in any case, to deal with the relationship of higher mental activity to its physical base. From what point of view, however, and to what extent, psychophysics will one day have itself to decide.

For the time being everyone should try to confine the conception and the scope of inner psychophysics as much as he can until the force and limitations of facts compel him to abandon the attempt. In my opinion, which as of now has to be considered as a mere opinion, there are no boundaries in this respect.

Indeed, I feel that the experience of harmony and melody, which undoubtedly have a higher character than single tones, is based on the ratios of the vibrations that themselves underlie the separate sensations, and that these ratios can change only in exact relationship to the manner in which the single tones are sounded together or follow one another. Thus, harmony and melody suggest to me only a higher relation, and not one lacking a special relationship of dependency between the higher mental sphere and its physical basis. Indeed everything seems to agree with this suggestion so easily pursued and extended. However, neither the pursuit nor even the assertion of this matter is relevant here at the start.

IV. CONCEPTS CONCERNING SENSATION AND STIMULUS

In the present incomplete state of psychophysical investigations, there would be little profit in an enumeration, definition, and classification of all the psychological conditions that could at some time form their subject matter. At first we shall occupy ourselves mainly with sensory experiences in the common meaning of the word

* Trans. Note: A reference to free navigation as a political problem—for example, free navigation on the Rhine.

experience, making use of the following distinctions in nomenclature.

I intend to distinguish between intensive and extensive sensations, depending on whether they concern the sensory perception of something whose magnitude can be judged intensively or extensively. For example, I shall include as an intensive sensation the sensation of brightness, as an extensive sensation the perception of a spatial extent by sight or touch; and accordingly I shall distinguish between the intensive and extensive magnitude of a sensation. When one object appears to us brighter than another, we call the sensation it arouses intensively greater; when it appears larger than another we call it extensively greater. This is merely a matter of definition and implies, as generally understood, no specific measure of sensation.

With every sensation whatsoever, intensive as well as extensive, magnitude and form may be distinguished, although in the case of intensive sensations magnitude is often called strength and form quality. With sounds, the pitch, even though it is a quality of the sound, has also a quantitative aspect insofar as we can distinguish a higher from a lower pitch.

E. H. Weber—and undoubtedly quite to the point—calls the spatial sense, or the capacity or sense whereby we arrive at extensive sensations (as the term is used here), a general sense. Those senses that give rise to intensive sensations he calls special senses. The former sensations cannot, like the latter, arise from the impression of single independent nerve fibers or their respective ramifications (sensory circles), but can do so only by a coordination of the impressions of several fibers, wherein the strength and quality of the impression as well as the number and arrangement of the nerve centers are essential to fix the size and form of the extensive sensation. His discussions of this matter are very apt contributions to the clarification of the general relationship of the senses. At present it suffices to have pointed out the foregoing difference in the circumstances on which intensive and extensive sensations depend. In fact, these brief preliminary discussions are intended only to introduce the discussion of appropriate measures of sensitivity and sensation, and therefore do not enter into the theory of sensations to any greater extent than this purpose warrants.

Because of their different natures and the different conditions upon which they depend, it is necessary to make a special examination of the laws governing extensive and intensive sensations. One might think that the magnitude of extensive sensations, or the extensive size of sensations, depended on the number of sensory circles stimulated, according to the same laws and corresponding to the way in which the magnitude of intensive sensations depends on the intensity of stimulation; but this is both incorrect to assume a priori and impossible to prove as yet. Our future investigations will preferably concern themselves, though not exclusively, with the intensive sensations, and in the main are so to be understood, unless the contrary is apparent from the added adjective *extensive* or from the context.

Next to the distinction between extensive and intensive sensations we may consider the distinctions between objective and common sensations and between the so-called positive and negative sensations. Objective sensations, such as sensations of light and sound, are those that can be referred to the presence of a source external to the sensory organ. Changes of the common sensations, such as pain, pleasure, hunger, and thirst, can, however, be felt only as conditions of our own bodies. For this relationship the reader is also referred to Weber's classic work in his treatise on touch and common sensations.

As positive and negative sensations it is usual to contrast such sensations as warmth and cold, pleasure and pain, which share the characteristic that the manner of their arousal or the relation to that which gives rise to them includes an antithesis. For example, the sensation of cold originates and increases through the withdrawal of heat, whereas warmth arises through the addition of heat. The sensation of pleasure is connected with a seeking of the cause of its arousal, just as dislike is connected with the opposite tendency.

While such designations as positive and negative sensations may be allowed in the usage of common language, one should not fail to note that the so-called negative sensations have nothing negative about them psychologically. They do not represent a lack, a lessening, a removal of sensations. On the contrary, they may be as violent, or even more so, than the so-called positive sensations, and are able to manifest themselves or give rise to just as strong positive effects on the body. For example, the sensation of freezing can cause a shaking of the whole body, and that of pain can cause crying besides other vigorous movements of the body.

The term *stimulus,* in its narrow sense, refers only to means of arousing the body, the excitation of intensive sensations. To the extent that stimuli belong to the outside world, they are external stimuli; insofar as they belong to the internal world of the body, they are internal stimuli. The former concept can be explained factually by recording external stimuli, such as light and sound; the latter concept will first need closer examination and may then perhaps be at least partially eliminated. A murmuring in our ears can start through the external influences of oscillations of the air, which a waterfall sends to our ears. A similar murmur can originate without outside influence through causes within our body. These are in general unknown; yet insofar as they produce the equivalent of the effect of an outside stimulus, they must be considered its equivalent. From this point of view it will often suit us to treat these unknown, but admittedly (according to their effects) factual, internal bodily sources of sensations under the same concepts, standpoints, and formulas as the external sources.

If the mind were affected only by external and internal excitations to the extent that their effects reach a specific part of the body, then all sensations would, as far as we grant their dependence on the body, be only results of activities of the body. Thus even the innermost conditions of the body would fall under the concept of stimuli. If, on the other hand, it is essentially the case that sensations are only accompanied by bodily activities in a functional relationship, it would not be proper to include such simultaneously conditioned sensations with directly determined sensations. Only those stimuli that serve to cause sensations should be included, if one does not wish to mix two different kinds of things. In the meanwhile we do not immediately have to come to a decision. These diverse opinions have no influence on our factual observations, as long as we consider the existence and magnitude of internal stimuli only according to their equivalent effects as compared to external stimuli and take them into account as such. At this time internal stimuli are an unknown x as to their location and quality, although they enter despite this limitation into the phenomenal sphere with a quantitative effect that is comparable to that of an external stimulus. The internal stimulus derives its name and value from this effect.

Some things, like weights, to which one would hesitate to give the meaning of stimulus in everyday life, will be classed as such without misgivings, as far as they give rise to tactile pressure, or weight, when lifted. On the other hand, a generalization of the word stimulus to the causes by which extensive sensations are evoked in us has its drawbacks, especially inasmuch as little clarity exists so far about these causes. We perceive, with our eyes closed, a black visual field of a certain extent, even without the addition of external causes, and, by specially focusing our attention, we can become conscious of a certain extent of our body surface, even without being touched by calipers or other instruments. Added outside stimulation partially sets the boundaries of these natural sensation fields, partially determines their form, and partially provides a basis for judging relative size and dis-

tance, without, however, giving rise to the sensation of space. This sensation seems to be rooted in the inborn coordination and organic connections of active nerves, or of their central endings although nothing certain has been decided about the matter so far. If it is still possible to talk of a stimulus in this connection, we could do so only with respect to the coordination of the internal excitation of these nerves. Since these, however, are probably conditions that occur simultaneously with the sensation, this expression [the sensation of space] would again become unsuitable. Experience can also, aided by movements, take part in the judging of extents—as some like to emphasize. This is not the place, however, to go any deeper into this still rather obscure matter, where only the definitions of words are concerned.

One can say, disregarding this obscurity and the question of the extent to which the term *stimulus* is appropriate, that the magnitude of the stimulus in intensive sensations is replaced in the extensive case by the number of active sensory circles insofar as the perceived extension decreases or increases as a dependent function. Thus, in relation to quantitatively dependent relationships, this number can be brought under a common, though rather general, point of view. One cannot assert in this way, however, that the law by which they are dependent is the same in both cases, or that the magnitude of the extensive sensation does not depend on other circumstances besides that number. Indeed, these points are themselves the object of important psychophysical investigations.

Under the application of most outer forces on which sensations are dependent, the sensation increases, after it once becomes noticeable, as the force acting on it is increased continually and in the same direction, and decreases with the lessening of the force continually until unnoticeable. With regard to some sensations, however, such as warmth and pressure on the skin, the organism is so constituted that a sensation arises only by reason of a difference from a given average or normal influence, such as the normal skin temperature or normal air pressure. This sensation then increases in both directions but with different characteristics, as a sensation of warmth or cold, pressure or tension, depending on whether one increases the influence above this point or reduces it below this point. In this case one would correctly regard as the stimulus, not the absolute magnitude of the acting force, but its positive or negative deviation from the point that divides the sensations of contrasting character, the point at which no sensation exists. We could call the former a positive, the latter a negative stimulus.

As far as the interrelationship of stimulus and sensation is to be considered, stimuli are always assumed to be effective under comparable circumstances, unless the contrary is expressly mentioned or can be seen from the context. This comparability can, however, be nullified by a different mode of stimulation, as well as by a differing condition of the subject or the organ at the time the stimulus impinges. The concept of differential sensitivity relates to this condition....

For the sake of brevity one says of a stimulus which evokes a sensation, as well as of a stimulus difference which is accompanied by a difference in sensations, that they are felt more strongly or weakly, according to whether the sensation or difference in sensations is stronger or weaker. This is also an expression that must be allowed to serve us without giving rise to misunderstanding.

Fechner: Inadvertent Founder of Psychophysics

Edwin G. Boring

Certainly the most interesting tool that science employs in its perpetual pursuit of knowledge is the scientist, with his enthusiasms, egoisms, and prejudices, his inevitable unconscious attitudinal orientation in the consensus of contemporary opinion, which we call the *Zeitgeist*. One wonders what science would be like if automation could take over completely. Are there mechanical equivalents for jealousy and pride and pigheadedness and insight, and those other interacting personal forces that contribute to contemporary truth in the scientific field?

Fechner never tried to found psychophysics or a new experimental psychology. He was, in his own estimation in those last forty-five years of his life, a philosopher, fighting what he regarded as the crass materialism of his day, the *Nachtansicht* or "night view," as he called it,

Boring, E. G. (1961). Fechner: Inadvertent founder of psychophysics. *Psychometrika, 26,* 3–8. Copyright © 1961 by the Psychometric Society. Reprinted by permission of the publisher.

and promoting the faith that mind and soul are the ultimates of reality, the *Tagesansicht* or "day view." This favoring of the clear philosophical vision in the day view as opposed to the materialistic darkness of the night view is Fechner's panpsychism, a faith that seems mystical to most modern scientists, partly because the German word *Seele* does not distinguish between mind and soul, between that which compares the sensory intensities of two lifted weights and whatever it is that persists after the body's death.

Let us take time to recall what Fechner did with the 86 years of his life between 1801 and 1887. At the age of 16 he went to Leipzig to study physiology, which in those days meant taking a doctorate in medicine. He stuck to physiology for only seven years and then turned to the study of physics and mathematics. He began work in this new field humbly, making his early reputation by the translation into German of French handbooks of physics and chemistry. At the age of 33, after some research in the new physics of electricity, he was made professor of physics at Leipzig; he held that post until 1839, when he resigned for reasons of poor health.

For 15 years he had been a physicist, but three other interests were emerging. Under the nom de plume of Dr. Mises, he provided scope for his humanistic interests by beginning a series of essays on various topics, the first of which was a satire on the current medical faith in the potency of iodine: *Proof that the Moon is Made of Iodine* (1821). Out of this side of Fechner's nature emerged his vigorous support of spiritualism as opposed to materialism: he wrote *The Little Book on Life after Death* in 1836. On the scientific side there was his growing interest in sense-physiology, and presently his papers on subjective colors and afterimages in 1838 and 1840. It must have been then that he permanently injured his eyesight by gazing too long at the sun through colored glasses.

There followed from 1839 to 1851 a dozen years of retirement in Leipzig. During the first three or four years he suffered from some form of psychoneurosis, and it would seem that this German academic never quite escaped from unusual seclusiveness as he lived on in Leipzig outside of the University. It was during this period that his concern with the "day view" of reality, with panpsychism, emerged. In 1848 he published *Nanna*, a volume named for the goddess of flowers, in which he argued for the mental life of plants. Then in 1851 came the *Zend-Avesta*, with a subtitle specifying that the volume was about the things of heaven and the life to come.

Actually this philosophical period of Fechner's life extended altogether over 43 years from 1836 to 1879, during which, in writing in 1861 on the problem of the soul, he remarked that he had already called four times to a sleeping world which had not awakened, and he was now calling a fifth time, and "if I live, I shall call yet a sixth and a seventh time, 'Steh! auf!' and always it will be the same 'Steh! auf!' " He did call twice more, the seventh in 1879 in the volume on the "day view and the night view."

Fechner's philosophy won him little respect among the scientists, nor any great acclaim by the philosophers. William James took him seriously, hailed the *Zend-Avesta* when he belatedly discovered it, told Bergson that Fechner "seems to me of the real race of prophets." James described Fechner's philosophy in *A Pluralistic Universe* [4] and related Fechner's views to his own. It was this excitement about spiritualism that pushed Fechner into psychophysics—strange parentage it was for psychophysics.

On that now famous morning of 22 October 1850, Fechner, lying in bed and puzzling how to do away with materialism, had the thought that, since conscious events are necessarily related to events in the brain—at least in the living person—an equation between the two systems would have the effect of identifying them and of abolishing the dualism, abolishing it in favor of a psychic monism which was what Fechner wanted. If he knew about Weber's law, he did not think about its relevance then. Later, however, he realized the significance of Weber's experiments and also of Daniel Bernoulli's contention in 1738 that *fortune morale* (psychic) is proportional to the logarithm of *fortune physique* (physical). Now Fechner thought: sensation is a function of its stimulus; you can measure stimuli, but how can you measure sensations? He concluded that sensory magnitude can be measured in terms of sensitivity, and he laid down the general outlines of his program in *Zend-Avesta,* the book about heaven and the future life. Imagine sending a graduate student of psychology nowadays to the Divinity School for a course in immortality as preparation for advanced experimental work in psychophysics! How narrow we have become!

After the publication of the *Zend-Avesta* Fechner had 14 years of intense activity in psychophysics, the first 9 of them in experimentation. After that came the epochal event, the publication of the *Elemente der Psychophysik* in two parts in 1860, the occasion that we celebrate today. It was the psychophysics, not the panpsychism, that attracted attention. Fechner's alleged measurement of sensation met with criticism and objection which indeed showed its importance in the current scientific belief that belonged to the mid-nineteenth century. History was now ready for a scientific psychology, but how can you become scientific unless you can measure your phenomena? Fechner's scheme was plausible and the need for sensory measurement led some to overlook its defects. He argued that sensation cannot be measured directly but can be indirectly. What you do is to measure sensitivity by determining differential thresholds; then, to find the magnitude of the sensation, you calculate the number of just noticeable differences (jnd) from zero sensation at the absolute threshold to the sensation that is being measured. Of course, this business of counting up jnd to measure a sensation met with the question: How do you know that all jnd are equal? And indeed, when measured by certain other scales, jnd may turn out not to be equal.

About 1865 Fechner turned from psychophysics to a new interest in experimental esthetics, publishing his classic in that field in 1876. The world, however, would not leave him free. Applause from some reinforced criticism from others, and Fechner was forced—for it was not easy for a German scholar to let criticism go unanswered—to reply to objections and to defend his measurement of sensation. He must have thought that he would himself have been content to go on crying to a sleeping world that the measurement of sensation had now made plausible man's grasp on immortality; but when the world at last awoke, it was to the wrong cry—unfortunately for Fechner, fortunately for us.

Tolstoy, speaking of History in his *War and Peace* and arguing for cultural determination—and thus indirectly against the importance of Great Men in the determination of History—remarked that "History, the unconscious, general hive-life of mankind, uses every moment of the life of kings as a tool for its own purposes.... A king is History's slave." History itself is the sum of the myriad of events that make it up, and ev-

ery one of these is caused, though there be so many that prediction from a knowledge of them becomes impossible. As to the Great, Tolstoy imagined a young cavalry commander who achieved high honor because, exuberant with good health, unaware of danger but without orders, he led his men at a gallop across the level plain in what turned out to be a successful charge. So with Fechner. He attacked the ramparts of materialism and was decorated for measuring sensation.

Scientists, for the most part, believe in the operation of deterministic causality between events, yet they also like in ordinary professional conversation to leave room for the originality of Great Men. There is a contradiction here. To see the Great Man's important contribution to thought as a consequence of the combination of commonly accepted knowledge, plus certain ideas or discoveries of other men, plus one or two coincidences of the kind of insight that brings thitherto unrelated ideas into useful connection, is largely to reduce greatness to a link in a complex causal chain. When the whole story is told of an invention or a discovery or the founding of a school, when as much attention is given to the antecedents as to the consequences of the great event, its greatness seems to diminish, its importance becomes less as it spreads over a broader range of activities and a longer span of time.

The case with Fechner goes about like this. The times were ready for scientists to get hold of mind by measuring it. Sensory thresholds had been determined as much as a hundred years before Fechner. The physiologists were already experimenting with sensation—Johannes Müller with specific nerve energies in 1826, Ernst Heinrich Weber with tactual sensibility in 1834. To contemporaneous thought Herbart had contributed the notion of the measurement of ideas, while denying the possibility of experimenting on them; and he had made Leibnitz's concept of the threshold well known. Lotze published his *Medical Psychology: The Physiology of the Mind* the year after Fechner's *Zend-Avesta*. It was in this setting that Fechner had on 22 October 1850 his important insight about measuring sensation and relating the measures of sensation to the measures of their stimuli.

Fechner's claim to originality of epoch-making magnitude lies in this insight. His claim to honor lies in his careful and laborious work through the decade of the 1850's, and the crucial character of the *Elemente* when it finally came out in 1860. He is credited with having given experimental psychology the three fundamental psychophysical methods still in constant use today, but actually the method of limits goes back to 1700 and may be said to have been formalized by Delezenne in 1827, whereas the method of constant stimuli was first used by Vierordt in 1852. Only the method of average error belongs to Fechner, and that only half, for he and his brother-in-law, A. W. Volkmann, developed it in the 1850's. What Fechner did in the *Elemente* was to present the case for sensory measurement and write the systematic handbook for psychophysics, a new field of scientific endeavor. In this sense he founded psychophysics as a field that is ancillary to the establishment of the philosophy of panpsychism.

It is conceivable that the *Elemente* might have fallen flat, as the laborious production of a queer old mystic in Leipzig who went to endless pains to prove a point that most wise men do not believe. The times, however, were ripe for psychophysics. Immediately the methods began to be used, and new facts began to accumulate, while the argument waxed about Fechner's interpretation of what it is that the methods do, about whether sensation had actually been measured after all.

In general, the greatness of Great Men is a subjective addition to history which posterity adds in order to understand history. History is continuous and sleek. Great Men are the handles that you put on its smooth sides. You have to simplify natural events in order to understand them, and science itself is forced to generalize in the interest of economy of thinking. Just so the history of science singles out events, schools, trends, and discoveries and eponymizes them,

that is to say, it names them for a central figure. Fechner has become the name for a change in the newly developing scientific psychology, for the gradual acceptance of the belief that the fleeting and evanescent mind-consciousness—can be measured. That had to happen before anything else could take place in respect of scales and measurement in the psychological sphere.

William James admired Fechner, the philosopher, but deplored Fechner, the psychophysicist. Almost everyone knows how he said, "But it would be terrible if even such a dear old man as this could saddle our science forever with his patient whimsies, and, in a world so full of more nutritious objects of attention, compel all future students to plough through the difficulties, not only of his own works, but of the still drier ones written in his refutation.... The only amusing part of it is that Fechner's critics should always feel bound, after smiting his theories hip and thigh and leaving not a stick of them standing, to wind up by saying that nevertheless to him belongs the *imperishable glory,* of first forming them and thereby turning psychology into an *exact science.* Well, say I, isn't that sort of glory as nearly imperishable as one could expect ever to get? But then, of course, James did not agree with Tolstoy. He thought that there are Great Men.

Only this year Henri Piéron has expressed a thought quite similar to James' except that Piéron and James are on opposite sides of the Fechner fence. Piéron wrote in concluding a centennial article about the importance of Fechner's psychophysics: "And thus the shade of Fechner does not cease in our day to hover over many American laboratories of experimental psychology which without doubt never hear tell of Fechner except when Stevens declares that nothing of Fechner's work remains." That is hardly fair to us Americans. Stevens' students hear about Fechner, and scattered over America are a small coterie of psychologists who seldom miss noting the date when 22 October comes around.

And now here are we celebrating the centenary of the *Elemente.* In complimenting Fechner we compliment ourselves, of course. A centenary is virtually a religious rite. We could not be pleasing Fechner now, even if he had justified his contribution to psychophysics by eventually finding himself immortal. What we need for our own use are symbols of our faith, our faith in science and measurement and quantification. It is right to hang Fechner's picture on the wall. It is a symbol of what we will to have important. It is right to be glad when your son is born on 22 October. It is right to atomize the smooth flow of History by the eponymy of great names. The scientist may be a determinist in his model-making, but as an active scholar and experimenter he needs more motivation than simple description and the generalization of observation can provide. He needs humor and reverence, as well as a little distortion of the complacency of history, to keep his prime-mover going, and what good is the scientific machine without a prime-mover?

It was given to Fechner to have the idea of measuring sensation independently of the measure of its material stimulus. In his own opinion he succeeded. Posterity doubts the validity of his procedure or even condemns it. Yet, if posterity has something better, it grew out of what Fechner provided. All honor then to the man who, resolved to achieve one goal, actually reached another, who because of his patient insistence remains the central figure at the absolute threshold at which measurement entered psychology. It may be said that he gave to sensations their magnitudes.

REFERENCES

1 Boring, E. G. *A history of experimental psychology,* (2nd ed.) New York: Appleton-Century-Crofts, 1950. Pp. 275–296.

2 Brett, G. S. *A history of psychology, III.* New York: Macmillan, 1921. Pp. 127–139.

3 Hall, G. S. *Founders of modern psychology.* New York: Appleton, 1912. Pp. 123–177.

4 James, W. *A pluralistic universe.* New York: Longmans Green, 1909. Pp. 131–177.

5 Kuntze, J. E. *Gustav Theodor Fechner.* Leipzig: Breitkopf and Härtel, 1892.

6 Lasswitz, K. *Gustav Theodor Fechner.* Stuttgart: Fromanns, 1896.

7 Murphy, G. *Historical introduction to modern psychology.* (2nd ed.) New York: Harcourt Brace, 1949. Pp. 84–92.

8 Perry, R. B. *Philosophy of the recent past.* New York: Scribners, 1926. Pp. 81–86.

9 Ribot, T. A. *German psychology of today.* (2nd ed.) New York: Scribners, tr. 1886. Pp. 134–187.

10 Titchener, E. B. *Experimental psychology.* Vol. II, pt. ii. New York: Macmillan, 1905. Pp. xx–cxvi.

11 Wundt, W. *Gustav Theodor Fechner.* Leipzig: Engelmann, 1901.

Biographical Genre and Biographical Archetype: Five Studies of Gustav Theodor Fechner

Marilyn E. Marshall

Shortly after the hero of Virginia Woolf's *Orlando* turns into a woman to a terrific blast of trumpets, Mrs. Woolf's fictional biography slows to an unusual crawl. She writes: "It was November. After November, comes December, then January, February, March and April. After April comes May. June, July, August follow. Next is September. Then October, and so behold, here we are back at November again, with a whole year accomplished" (Woolf, 1928, p. 172).

Mrs. Woolf admits that "this method of writing biography...is a little bare perhaps" (*ibidem,*

Marshall, M. E. (1980). Biographical genre and biographical archetype: Five studies of Gustav Theodor Fechner. *Storia e Critica Della Psicologia, 1,* 197–210. Copyright © 1980 by Marilyn Marshall. Reprinted by permission of the author.

p. 172) but what is the biographer to do if his subject, like Orlando, just sits down and merely thinks for twelve months? (*ibidem, p. 173*). "There is nothing for it but to recite the calendar, tell one's beads, blow one's nose, stir the fire, look out of the window, until she has done" (*ibidem*).

This fable for biographers[1] suggests that the sort of life which a biographical subject leads influences the character of the work which can be written about him. In what follows, I will consider several biographical studies of Fechner, a man who did little but think and write, not merely for months, but for years on end. My focus will be, first, on differentiating among the works to illustrate something of the range and variability of the biographies, and second, on suggesting that it is not only the life of the subject which influences the character of a biography, nor the well-discussed interaction between character of biographer and subject, but further, the expectations which biographers have of what the subject's life should have been. To what extent may our available portraits of Fechner be drawn to conform to the outlines of generalized models of what biography should be, of what the life of an important nineteenth century scientist should have been?

Table 1 contains an outline summary of five biographical studies of Fechner. These include the most comprehensive and interesting of the some twenty-five biographical and personal studies of which I am aware. They are listed in order of priority of publication, and this comes close to being an order according to weight as well. I have characterized each briefly, first according to the profession of the author and his relation to Fechner, and second according to the author's professed or apparent motive in writing the biography;[2] third is my estimate of the author's interpretational emphasis; finally, I have given the gist of the biographical technique used and the source materials referred to. I suggest these dimensions of classification because each may influence the kind of data, data arrangement, and interpretation of data

given by the authors; and each, consequently, affects the historian's use of the proffered material. I cannot talk here about each dimension for each biography, but will rather sample, sip, and taste in my narrative.

First, let me give you an idea of the kind of information on which I based these summary statements. With respect to Number 1, for example, to describe the author's motive tersely as "widow's wish" may strike you as unlikely, but Kuntze (1892) writes at the end of his Preface: "The decision to write the biography was not an easy one for me... Yet Fechner's widow did not cease to urge me, and to comply with her wishes I dared attempt the work" (Kuntze, 1892, p. 361). Kuntze, Fechner's nephew, lived in the Fechner household as a stepson for some 50 years, and was thus in an admirable position to supply details of Fechner's domestic life and habits. Indeed, all subsequent biographers are dependent on Kuntze for such information.

The one other biographical study to treat of Fechner's personality in any detail is Number 5, a psycho-historical example. I have referred to Hermann's (1926) motive as "didactic (scientific)" because his purpose is to show psychoanalytic constructs, and his own theory of scientific creativity, illustrated in (and explanatory of) the life and writings of Fechner. At this juncture, let me pursue a sample dilemma in the use of biography. The dilemma is the common one of finding two different interpretations of the same data by different biographers. The illustration will also serve to support my use of the term "psychoanalytic" to describe Hermann's interpretational emphasis, and my disapproving phrase, "highly selective," to modify Hermann's technique.

Hermann tells a story with a (to us) familiar ring and a familiar vocabulary. When Fechner was five, his youngest sister was born (a fact taken from Kuntze); the father baptized the new baby, and the next day the father died (another fact); Fechner, at five, was ripe for the resolution of the Oedipus conflict (permit me to call this theory); would the association of baby's birth and father's death not inhibit the later normal de-

Table 1.
Descriptive Summary of Five Fechner Biographies

Reference	Profession and relation to G. T. Fechner	Motive	Emphasis	Technique	Sources
Kuntze, J. E. *Gustav Theodor Fechner* (Dr. Mises). Leipzig: Breitkopf & Härtel, 1892, 316 pp.	German jurist, historian of law, Fechner's nephew	commemorative (personal), "widow's wish"	Christian, German nationalism	chronologically "interwoven" critical and personal, emphasis on latter	conversation over 50 years, Fechner's personal archive, knowledge of Fechner's work
Lasswitz, K. *Gustav Theodor Fechner*. Stuttgart, Fromann, 1896, 206 pp.	German historian of philosophy and science (atomism), author of imaginative (science) fiction; no personal relation indicated but responsible for a revival of Fechner's philosophical works after 1900	didactic (social)	wedding of natural science and Weltanschauung	sequential life and work first treated chronologically; Fechner's world picture is treated topically	the "life" part of a "life and work" derives from Kuntze; knowledge of Fechner's works
Wundt, W. *Gustav Theodor Fechner*. Leipzig: Engelmann, 1901. In Wundt, *Reden und Aufsätze*. Leipzig: Kröner, 1913, 89 pp.	German psychologist, colleague and friend of Fechner	commemorative (official) for Leipzig University and Royal Saxon Academy of Sciences	new foundation for psychological science and metaphysics	topical arrangement, on "The Origin of Life," on "Life and Consciousness," on "Psychophysics," etc.; addenda on "Personal memories," Fechner's relation to the philosophy of his time, "Fechner's philosophical method"	Fechner diary and archive available, but probably not used; knowledge of works and personal contact
Hall, G. S. "Gustav Theodor Fechner". In Hall, *Founders of American Psychology*. New York: D. Appleton & Co., 1912, 52 pp.	American psychologist, slight and ambivalent personal contact	didactic (descriptive historical)	science supplemented by myth	quasi-chronological account of life and works	almost completely derivative of Lasswitz and Wundt
Hermann, I. "Gustav Theodor Fechner. Eine psychoanalytische Studie über individuelle Bedingtheiten wissenschaftlicher Ideen". *Imago, XI*, 1926, 62 pp.	German analyst, author of articles and books on psychogenesis of scientific creativity	didactic (scientific)	psychoanalytic biography	highly selective look at highly selected works	Kuntze biography, Fechner's own writings

velopment of Fechner's libido, asks Hermann? Moreover would not the impressionable child be burdened with over-abundant guilt feelings? (Hermann, 1926). These questions are hypotheses in rhetorical clothing. Given the paucity of evidence which Hermann offers for the link between putative cause and effect, one is not surprised when Hermann shifts the scene abruptly in his next sentence to Leipzig, *nineteen* years later: "Then the mother decided to move to Leipzig... in order to remove Fechner from the influence of doubtful friends" (*ibidem,* p. 10). Please note, *en passant,* that the nineteen years which separated trauma from evidence of pathology and which Hermann ignores, were not, in Fechner's case, empty years of Orlando—like sitting and thinking.

Who were these questionable friends? One was Martin Schulze, and on and off he shared lodgings with Fechner. He was a quasi-mad young wanderer with bare feet and rucksack, a poet, a lover of nature, and a hater of the artificialities of society and intellectualism. He ended his days in an asylum around 1850. Fechner and Schulze tramped and camped together, met in the evenings together with a circle of close friends which included young Christian Weisse. Under Schulze's influence Fechner admits to becoming completely uninterested in science; Schulze made Fechner's occupation with science a burden and created an inner schism in his life. Fechner offers this information in a clever portrait which he wrote of Schulze, which Kuntze (1892) prints in one of his biographical chapters. Kuntze, however, titles this chapter "The Sinister Friend," on the basis of his own vivid memory of Schulze from the point of view of a small and terrified child, and from the widow's memory of Schulze's daemonic guise.

The title of that chapter is enough for Hermann! He has seen in Kuntze that the mother moved to Leipzig to save her son from an undesirable friend, that this friend exercised a sinister fascination over Fechner. Hermann insinuates forthwith, a homosexual relationship be-

tween Fechner and Schulze. He reaps further support for Fechner's homosexuality quoting from a letter written to Fechner by another friend, Rüffer: "You want to believe that you could mean something to me! Dear brother, you could not mean something to me, you do already, you have always done, and not just something, but much! It is strange, Müller is on the whole opener toward me than towards you....But for him I feel a different love than for you; the latter I would like to compare with the irresistible feeling with which a woman is attracted to a man. I feel that I must lean on your strength and on your character, so as not to lose my balance....Be assured that neither a Schulze, Nauwerk, nor a Weisse can love you as I do—not even Müller or Spielberg. See, a thousand ties hold me to you, the tenderest of which is that of a brother, because we embrace one mother with childlike love, and because your sisters are mine" (Hermann, 1926, p. 10; from Kuntze, 1892, p. 36).

Now Hermann copied this letter from Kuntze and placed it in his own text in conjunction with the sinister Schulze and the mother's move to Leipzig (Hermann, 1926, p. 10). But Hermann committed a distortion which could mislead the unwitting reader. He did not copy the letter in full. It is a quarrelmending letter which begins: "Although I felt ashamed after your letter and your generous offer to consider everything undone and to belong to me again with the old loyal friendship proven over seven years, this shame gave place to joy.... I think it was good that such a storm arose" (Kuntze, 1892, p. 36). The passage omitted by Hermann, I believe, offers two potentially important pieces of information: first, Rüffer was not a new Leipzig friend whom Fechner's mother might question out of ignorance, but one of seven years (and apparently adored by Fechner's mother as if he were her own son); second, the two friends had recently quarrelled. Perhaps some part of the effusive adoration expressed in the letter is explicable in terms of the recent emotional storm.

While Hermann takes Rüffer's letter as evidence of Fechner's homosexuality, connecting it with the idea of a sinister friend, Kuntze places the letter in an entirely different context. It is in a passage which tells of the play of Fechner, the child, turning into the academic activity of a maturing youth, of Fechner's magical attractiveness to his peers because of his readiness for fun and his rich ideas, of the fact that all his old school friends shared lodgings with him at one time or another'' (Kuntze, 1892, p. 35). Kuntze introduces the Rüffer letter, saying: "The era still stood under the sign of "friendship"; in each park a sentimental altar was erected to "friendship"; subjective intimacy reigned in the companionable life of feeling, and corresponding to this was the ability to pour out one's sentiments in letters'' (*ibidem*).

I submit that placed in the context given by Kuntze, Rüffer's letter may be interpreted as an expressive example of the subjective intimacy which was so much a part of the romantic ideal, as a Saxon counterpart to the extravagant expressions of love common to the Victorian period elsewhere, rather than as automatic evidence of homosexuality. Kuntze, under the widow's eye in 1892, would scarcely have printed the letter had he believed it indicated anything but friendship and the old student ideal, *inter amicos omnia communia*. Sexual maladaptation was, in Kuntze's world, simply not yet a part of the archetype of the great man, nor was the tracing of greatness to childhood woes a part of the biographical model which dominated the *genre*.

The fact that Kuntze and Hermann operated under two different models of what biography should be is illustrative of a change in the style of biography which occurred in the early twentieth century"[3] Of the five portraits outlined, only Hermann's may be considered a twentieth century work, in the sense that it attends specifically to the relation between the character of the man and his writings. Hermann's view is the Freudian one, that Fechner's works were effects of the dynamics of his personality formed by Fechner's early experiences. This is not the view of the usual nineteenth century biographer who is in-

terested in the man and his work, but rarely analyzes the relation between the two.[4] The biographies of Hall, Lasswitz, and Wundt present the image of Fechner retiring to his study to write, but we learn little of the relation between man and work. Even the voluminous chronicle of Kuntze, which actually *contains* the data necessary to a study of the relation between man and product, emphasizes neither this relationship nor the process of intellectual development, which is another characteristic of post-Freudian biography. To the contrary, Kuntze takes pains to establish an *anti*-developmentalist scheme for his biography, insisting that Fechner's ideas and gifts: "Were all so well developed in his youth that his life can hardly be considered as a progressive development, but rather as the actualization and sorting out of an already existing resource'' (Kuntze, 1892, p. 314).

All five of our portraits escape the twentieth century debunking trend in biography, which is traced by many historians to Lytton Strachey's *Eminent Victorians*. Though much earlier Cromwell advised Mr. Lely to paint him warts and all, and though biographers followed this lead toward realistic portraiture, it was not the wart on which attention was focused, and well through the nineteenth century the biographer was wont to block out disagreeable facts about his subject. Great men tended to be seen as uniformly good and virtuous men.

Of the violent countertrend in biography which occurred after the century's turn, one historian has written: "Biography became for a while a dance of impish glee around scores of broken altars. No eminence was safe as long as dynamite or crowbars were anywhere to be obtained, and the search for flaws became so relentless that the price of microscopes tripled'' (Johnson, 1937, p. 478). In one sense, Hermann's vision of Fechner's youthful homosexuality might be seen as consistent with this debunking trend, for it does erode the rather stiff and unidimensionally academic portraits of the earlier studies. But Hermann was not trying to bring Fechner down to the level of ordinary man by showing his warts. On the contrary, he was trying to enshrine him as a great man, on the theory that sexual maladaptation is a correlate of scientific creativity. To paraphrase Strachey, this may be not so much debunk as plain bunk.

Before turning altogether from the topic of debunking, let me draw your attention to the biographical study of G. Stanley Hall. Hall's portrait (1912) is uniformly complimentary in good nineteenth century style. When he writes of his personal contact with Fechner, it is as follows, blandly: "I lived near him for an academic year, and called occasionally (introduced by a card from Wundt), as a student who was trying to understand psycho-physics. Once our conversation drifted to Slade, and he told me of a solid wooden ring put over a solid spool-head much too big for it and of another wooden ring on the one upright leg of a tripod table, and also of a message written between two sealed slates, at which both he and his wife, who was always present at our interviews, shook their heads and expressed doubt. He sent me to Zöllner who showed me these things, and asked impressively how they could be done save in a space of more than three dimensions" (Hall, 1912, p. 167).

Now contrast this saltless porridge with Hall's account of the same events in a letter which he wrote to William James: "Fechner is a curiosity. His eyelids are strangely fringed and he has had a number of holes, square and round, cut, Heaven knows why, in the iris of each eye—and is altogether a bundle of oddities in person and manners. He has forgotten all the details of his *Psychophysik;* and is chiefly interested in theorizing how knots can be tied in endless strings, and how words can be written on the inner side of two slates sealed together. He . . . wants me to go to Zöllner and talk to him about American spiritualism, but I have not been. Fechner is tedious enough, and I hear Zöllner is more so" (James, 1920, p. 18). This is a more familiar and bumptious Hall, and it leaves little doubt that he entertained negative feelings about Fechner. But he left these out of his biographical portrait, for they were infra dig with respect to the portrai-

ture of the period, and to the sober celebratory spirit of *Founders*.

I have left until last the excellent biographical sketches of Lasswitz and Wundt, perhaps because they appear generally to be unproblematic. In them the author intrudes positively into the life and the work of his subject. In the case of Lasswitz, this is because his interpretational bias, to see in all of Fechner the attempt to wed science and metaphysics, coincides with Fechner's own ubiquitous aim. Lasswitz's motive, to offer a materialist dominated public a paragon of a spiritual leader (Lasswitz, 1896, p. 4), does not prevent him from exercising his skill as an historian of atomism. He writes comfortably and fluently about the physical foundations of Fechnerian philosophy, something which few others have accomplished (but see Schreier, 1979).

In the case of Wundt, too, his psychological bias proves an advantage, giving him a scientific context from which he offers superb, if general, critiques of Fechner's methods and materials. Furthermore, Wundt's own problems of advancement within the nineteenth century German academy sensitized him to several professional blows suffered by Fechner early in his career, which the intimate, Kuntze, fails altogether to mention. And though Wundt does not emphasize personality in this official biography, he manages at moments to bring the reader closer to the man, Fechner, than do his other biographers. One remarkable and uniquely Wundtian insight is that Fechner, who loved conversation and controversy, spoke of his ideas publicly only when they were perfected. For example, the entire *Kollektivmasslehre* was discovered by Wundt when he was ordering Fechner's papers after his death. "Nobody had known of the existence of this work, neither Frau Fechner nor any of his friends and colleagues, yet he had carried the plan with him for approximately twenty years and had been occupied with its elaboration for almost a decade" (Wundt, 1913, p. 315). Such are the fine moments in biography, when the skeleton of history begins to pick up flesh.

Though their treatments of Fechner are generally accurate with respect to the evidence of Fechner's own pen, Lasswitz and Wundt both reveal idiosyncratic biases which emerge in their evaluation of Fechner's response to spiritism, and they differ, consequently, in their treatment of Fechner's involvement in the famous Leipzig seances of 1877. Lasswitz, whose image of the great scientist embraces a natural interest in the poetic and mystical, describes Fechner as a zealous participant in the seances of the American medium, Henry Slade (Lasswitz, 1896, p. 106). Wundt, whose own participation in one such seance brought him much ire and grief (Marshall & Wendt, 1980), describes Fechner as an almost unwilling participant in the Slade affair (Wundt, 1913, p. 340). Both views are over-generalizations, for Fechner vacillated. He had indeed previously refused sittings with Slade and attended one without knowing that it was going to occur, but he also attended a second by design and with keen anticipation. Wundt's image of the great scientist took him further to portray Fechner, if not as a skeptic, at least as suspending judgment about the alleged facts of spiritism. Quoting a paragraph from Fechner's diary of 1877, Wundt writes that Fechner's impressions of Slade's performances were overwhelmingly unfavorable, indicating only slick conjuring (Wundt, 1913, pp. 340–341). But Wundt's selectivity in quotation is misleading, for Fechner continues, in the same passage, to say that in spite of his doubts he believes there is something in the facts of spiritism. Furthermore, after hearing the reports of J. F. C. Zöllner and W. Weber on their even more wonderful experiences with Slade, Fechner, on hearsay evidence from his admired colleagues, and in spite of his own earlier admonition that one should struggle against a spiritistic interpretation of Slade's phenomena, confessed that he had been convinced by the facts.

CONCLUSION

He who writes about the use of biography in history usually believes that biography somehow should be a part of the historical enterprise. In closing, this author wishes to make her view on this matter explicit. An important part of the task of the historian of psychology is the analysis of works—famous, infamous, remembered, and all-but-forgotten—which have tried to explain the nature of human experience and action. These writings are the artifacts left by centuries of creative intellectual effort. Most of the authors are now dead, and I agree with the literary critics who write that the work exists, but, "The tears shed or unshed, the personal emotions are gone and cannot be reconstructed" (Wellek, Warren, 1942–1956, p. 80). This suggests that the most intimate parts of the lives of scientists will remain outside the bounds of the task (and the capability) of the historian of science. Yet the historian's task can not end with an understanding of the content of individual works, for there is really no work or artifact an sich, no independent entity, which is its own sole context. Every work is severally determined by social, economic, cultural, and intellectual contexts, and it is necessary to know these in order to evaluate a single work with fidelity. Most frequently, it is biography, imperfect and incomplete though it be, which serves as the connecting link between scientific work and context. When available, it is thus indispensable as a tool in historical study.

Even should we grant that some of the meanings of some writings can be gleaned by studying the single work, any historian with a penchant for the study of intellectual development and change will be led eventually to compare several works by the same author. And as soon as two works by the same man are viewed side by side, the historical enterprise fades into the biographical. For one is then dealing with relations between ideas put forward over a greater or lesser time span, and the relation between these ideas may make sense only with reference to the development of personality, by which I mean the complex accumulation over time of special experiences, temperamental value biases, and traditions unique to individual people.

The use of biography in historical study is not unproblematic, however, and it was to a sampling of problems which this paper turned. By now, readers will recognize that this essay—this bagatelle—in no way represents an attempt at scholarly analysis of the Fechnerian biographical corpus. My remarks were aimed in a meta-biographical direction. That is, they were intended to show some characteristics of biography in general, and they should be construed as an invitation to extend the range of vision with which the historian of psychology views his biographical source materials. I would suggest that this extension of vision is salutary not only in the case of biographical material. The autobiography, the diary, the sermon, the essay, the letter, indeed, the scientific text itself, are in any period written according to particular commonly (if not consciously) accepted models which govern literary *genres* in particular periods; and an awareness of these particularities is necessary if the sources are to lead rather than to mislead scholarship.

Finally, when we deal with outstanding men, as we almost inevitably do in biography, we must also ask to what extent the painted biographical picture is a likeness of the particular man, and to what extent the portrait is merely a likeness of a generalized and temporally parochial, or individually idiosyncratic, model of what great men should be like. To my knowledge, there has been little systematic work done on the history of the concept of the great man in science or social science—nothing, at least, to compare with the study of the hero in literary history. It strikes me as a potentially exciting enterprise, and one which could benefit the sometimes fraught interface of biography and history.[5]

NOTES

1 This is Leon Edel's happy description in his very helpful *Literary Biography* (1957).
2 I have followed the two-fold classification suggested by Harold Nicolson (1927).
3 For a survey of these trends in English literature, see Johnson (1937).
4 For a discussion of this characteristic, see Fiedler (1952).
5 Such a study would lead to many questions of interest to both psychologists and historians, not least among these the extent to which the hero of literary history and the hero of science share attributes within a given period, or the extent to which the generalized biographical model may become a self-fulfilling prophecy for individual scientists, leading to what Ernst Kris (1953) calls "enacted biography".

REFERENCES

Edel, L. (1957). *Literary biography. The Alexander Lectures, 1955–1956.* Toronto: University of Toronto Press.

Fiedler, L. A. (1952). Archetype and signature: A study of the relationship between biography and poetry. *Sewanee Review, 60,* 253–273.

Hall, G. S. (1912). *Founders of American psychology.* New York: D. Appleton & Co.

Hermann, I. (1926). Gustav Theodor Fechner. Eine Psychoanalytische Studie über individuelle Bedingtheiten wissenschaftlicher Ideen. *Imago. Zeitschrift für Anwendung der Psychoanalyse auf den Geisteswissenschaften, 2,* 9–70.

James, H., ed. (1920). *The letters of William James.* Boston: The Atlantic Monthly Press.

Johnson, E. (1937). *One mighty torrent. The drama of biography.* New York: Macmillan, 1955.

Kris, E. (1953). *Psychoanalytic explorations in art.* London: Allen & Unwin.

Kuntze, J. E. (1892). *Gustav Theodor Fechner. Ein deutsches Gelebrtenleben.* Leipzig: Breitkopf & Härtel.

Lasswitz, K. (1896). *Gustav Theodor Fechner.* Stuttgart: Fromann, 1902.

Marshall, M. E., Wendt, R. A. (1980). Wundt spiritism and the nature of science. In *Wundt studies,* eds. W. Bringmann and R. Tweney (Göttingen: Hogrefe).

Nicolson, H. (1927). *The development of English biography. Hogarth Lectures, No. 4.* London: Hogarth.

Strachey, L. (1918). *Eminent victorians.* New York: G. P. Putnam's Sons.

Wellek, R., Warren, A. (1942–1956). *Theory of literature.* New York: Harcourt, Brace & World.

Woolf, V. (1928). *Orlando. A biography.* New York: Penguin Books, 1946.

CHAPTER 7

WILHELM WUNDT AND THE FOUNDING OF THE SCIENCE OF PSYCHOLOGY

Origins are rarely unequivocal, and the founding of the science of psychology is no exception. Some historians argue the priority of William James in founding the first laboratory of psychology at Harvard University in 1875. Others argue that James's laboratory was not a research laboratory but was used for demonstrational purposes in teaching physiology. We have already described the contributions of Gustav Theodor Fechner in the previous chapter, and in some psychological circles he is identified as the founder of experimental psychology. Certainly he brought the methods of measurement to the problems of the mind. But for most historians, the title of founder is given to Wilhelm Wundt (1832–1920). In recognition of Wundt's role in founding the science of psychology (see Ben-David & Collins, 1966), the American Psychological Association issued a commemorative medallion in 1979 with Wundt's portrait engraved on the front. The date marked the centennial of the founding of Wundt's psychology laboratory in Leipzig. The following year, the Twenty-Second International Congress of Psychology was held in Leipzig and another commemorative Wundt medallion was issued, this one made of Meissen porcelain.

Why is the founding honor awarded to Wundt? Thomas Leahey (1987) writes, "Wundt is the founder because he wedded physiology to philosophy and made the resulting offspring independent. He brought the empirical methods of physiology to the questions of philosophy and also created a new, identifiable role—that of psychologist, separate from the roles of philosopher, physiologist, or physician" (p. 182). John O'Donnell (1985) has referred to Leipzig as the place where psychology was initially manufactured, and argues that Wundt's central role in the development of modern psychology, "derives not from any scientific discovery that bears his name eponymously but rather from his heroic propagandizing for experimentalism'' (p. 16). Wundt's plans for psychology gestated for more than twenty years before the Leipzig laboratory was founded.

Wundt graduated from the University of Heidelberg in 1855, finishing at the top of his medical school class. After a short time in Berlin, where he worked with the famous physiologist, Johannes Müller, Wundt returned to Heidelberg to work as Helmholtz's assistant. There he published his first book, on muscular movements and sensations, in 1858. A second book followed in 1862 entitled *Contributions to the Theory of Sensory Perception.* It was in this book that Wundt laid out his plans for psychology, an experimental science that would uncover the facts of consciousness. At this time he was teaching a course on experimental physiology that included some psychological material. By 1867 the title of Wundt's course had become ''Physiological Psychology,'' and out of these lectures emerged his most important work, the *Principles of Physiological Psychology* (1873–1874). This work went through six editions in Wundt's lifetime and is clearly among the most important publications in the history of psychology. It was a compendium of all the research to that date related to Wundt's vision of an experimental psychology. In the preface to that work he made his vision clear, noting that it was his intention to establish psychology as a new domain of science.

In 1874 Wundt took a position at Zurich University, but he stayed there only a year before accepting a newly established professorship in philosophy at the University of Leipzig. There he would remain for the rest of his life, establishing the first psychological laboratory in 1879 and the first psychological journal, *Philosophische Studien,* two years later in 1881. It was the beginning of an academic Mecca for psychology that would draw students from all over Europe, particularly Germany and Austria, and from the United States and Canada. In his career, Wundt directed the doctoral theses of sixty-six students in psychology. That number included such famous individuals as Hugo Münsterberg, Edward Bradford Titchener, Charles Spearman, and Emil Kraepelin.

In the latter part of the nineteenth century, it was not uncommon for American students to go abroad for their graduate education (see Sokal, 1981). Of Wundt's psychology students, sixteen came from Canada and the United States, including Lightner Witmer, who founded the first psychological clinic in the United States at the University of Pennsylvania (see O'Donnell, 1979); Walter Dill Scott, who was one of the pioneers of industrial psychology (see Ferguson, 1976), Edward Wheeler Scripture, who would distinguish himself in speech pathology; Charles H. Judd, whom many consider to be the founder of educational psychology; Harry Kirke Wolfe, whose undergraduate psychology laboratory at the University of Nebraska produced an inordinately large number of graduates who went on to become eminent psychologists (see Benjamin & Bertelson, 1975; Benjamin, 1987), and James McKeen Cattell, who founded psychology laboratories at the University of Pennsylvania and Columbia University (see Sokal, 1980). The first two Americans to earn a doctoral degree in psychology from Wundt were Wolfe and Cattell, both graduating in 1886. Cattell and two other Americans who visited Wundt's laboratory, William James and G. Stanley Hall, are discussed in Chapter 10. (See Hillix & Broyles [1980] for an example of the academic lineage of Wundt in contemporary American psychology.)

For Wundt, psychology was the study of *immediate experience,* that is, experience devoid of any cultural, social, or linguistic interpretations. The more biased experience was called *mediate experience,* meaning it was mediated by these processes of learning. Immediate experience was basic, unfettered by learning, and this was the experience Wundt sought to study. His research sought to create experiences in a laboratory setting that could be repeated, independently verified by others, and were thus subject to systematic study. A principal method of study in Wundt's laboratory was *introspection,* an experimental form of self-observation. In employing this technique, he laid down explicit criteria for its use, including the requirement that stimulus variables be altered in various trials to discover how such manipulations affected the subject's experience. Introspective judgments were primarily quantitative in nature unlike the qualitative emphases of E. B. Titchener (see Chapter 8), and dealt mostly with sensory dimensions such as intensity and duration (Danziger, 1980). Other methods were also used, including the psychophysical techniques of Fechner and certain physiological procedures.

About half the research studies conducted in Wundt's laboratory were on sensory processes and perception, topics that occupied much of the early work in psychology (recall the empiricist emphasis on that area). But there were also studies of reaction time, learning (association), attention, and emotion.

Having defined the subject matter of psychology as the study of immediate experience, Wundt mapped out the goals of psychology as the analysis of experience into its component elements. Those elements were of two kinds: sensations and feelings. This atomistic approach sought to reduce experience to its most basic elements. But Wundt's plan was more than just the delineation of a psychological periodic table. In addition to determining what constituted an element of experience, he was also interested in discovering how these basic elements combined to form what he called psychical compounds.

Other emerging experimental psychologies developed in opposition to Wundtian psychology, at laboratories in Würzburg, Berlin, Frankfurt, and Vienna. Some argued with Wundt about the validity of his reductionistic approach, favoring instead an approach that analyzed experience at some more global level. Others dissented over methodological issues, for example, arguing for other introspective procedures. Still others argued about what topics were or were not appropriate to study in the fledgling science of psychology.

In the end, Wundt's psychology, and that of his contemporaries, was replaced by newer psychological approaches. Although parts of his psychological system exist in modern psychology (see the Blumenthal article in this chapter), we continue to remember him principally for his vision in seeing the promise of a science of psychology and then taking the giant steps required in the nineteenth century to establish the discipline. It is true that Wundt built on the work of those philosophers and physiologists who came before him, just as a mason mixes gravel and cement, but it was Wundt who fashioned those elements into the concrete blocks of psychology and laid them in place to form a new scientific structure.

The first selection in this chapter is from Wundt's *Outlines of Psychology,* which he published in 1896 and is one of the many Wundt works that have been translated into English. It deals with his descriptions of psychical elements and compounds and was intended as a concise statement of his approach to psychology. It is the primary source material for this chapter.

Knowledge of Wundt has increased substantially in the past decade. Partly this new vision was facilitated by the attention given to the Wundt laboratory centennial in 1979, but it is also the result of two other factors. First, historians of psychology have begun to read Wundt in the original German, rather than the English translations. Not only has this scholarship resulted in a new image of Wundt's theoretical system in psychology, but it has portrayed a depth of understanding and breadth of interest (e.g., his writings on culture, law, art, language, history, and religion) that has been missing from biographical and theoretical accounts of Wundt. Second, these historians have made much use of archival material in Germany associated with Wundt and his contemporaries. Our three secondary source articles in this chapter are examples of this new scholarship.

The first article is an archival study of Wundt, focusing particularly on the events surrounding the founding of the laboratory in 1879. It is authored by Wolfgang G. Bringmann, Norma J. Bringmann, and Gustav A. Ungerer, all of whom have contributed greatly to our understanding of Wundt and his role in psychology.

The second of these articles is by Arthur L. Blumenthal. One of the earliest articles of the new Wundt scholarship to emphasize the importance of the original German editions, it radically changed what the history books said about Wundt. An especially important part of this article is the section relating Wundt's ideas to contemporary psychology, particularly cognitive psychology, despite the fact that citations to Wundt's works are declining. This loss of Wundt's influence is evidenced in the citation analysis performed by Josef Brožek, an internationally known historian of psychology. This article is included as a second illustration (the other is in Chapter 4) of the use of citation analysis as a historiographic method. Not surprisingly, it finds that Wundt's *Principles of Physiological Psychology* is the most often cited of his works.

REFERENCES

Ben–David, J. &, Collins, R. (1966). Social factors in the origin of a new science: The case of psychology. *American Sociological Review, 31,* 451–465.

Benjamin, L. T. (1987). A teacher is forever: The legacy of Harry Kirke Wolfe, 1858–1918. *Teaching of Psychology, 14,* 68–74.

Benjamin, L. T., & Bertelson, A. D. (1975). The early Nebraska psychology laboratory, 1889–1930: Nursery for presidents of the American Psychological Association. *Journal of the History of the Behavioral Sciences, 11,* 142–148.

Danziger, K. (1980). The history of introspection reconsidered. *Journal of the History of the Behavioral Sciences, 16,* 241–262.

Ferguson, L. W. (1976). The Scott Company. *JSAS Catalog of Selected Documents in Psychology, 6,* 128 (Ms. 1397).

Hillix, W. A., & Broyles, J. W. (1980). The family trees of American psychologists. In W. G. Bringmann & R. D. Tweney (Eds.), *Wundt studies.* Toronto: C. J. Hogrefe, pp. 422–434.

Leahey, T. H. (1987). *A history of psychology: Main currents in psychological thought* (2d ed.). Englewood Cliffs, NJ: Prentice-Hall.

O'Donnell, J. M. (1979). The clinical psychology of Lightner Witmer: A case study of institutional innovation and intellectual change. *Journal of the History of the Behavioral Sciences, 15,* 3–17.

O'Donnell, J. M. (1985). *The origins of behaviorism: American psychology, 1870–1920.* New York: New York University Press.

Sokal, M. M. (1980). Graduate study with Wundt: Two eyewitness accounts. In W. G. Bringmann & R. D. Tweney (Eds.), *Wundt studies.* Toronto: C. J. Hogrefe, pp. 210–225.

Sokal, M. M. (1981). *An education in psychology: James McKeen Cattell's journal and letters from Germany and England, 1880–1888.* Cambridge, MA: MIT Press.

Psychical Elements and Compounds

Wilhelm Wundt

I. PSYCHICAL ELEMENTS

1. All the contents of psychical experience are of a composite character. It follows, therefore, that *psychical elements,* or the absolutely simple and irreducible components of psychical phenomena are the products of analysis and abstraction. This abstraction is rendered possible by the fact that the elements are in reality united in different ways. If an element, *a,* is connected in one case with the elements *b, c, d,* ... and in another case with *b', c', d',* ... it is possible to abstract it from all the other elements, because none of them is always united with it. If, for example, we hear a simple tone of a certain pitch and intensity, it may be located now in this direction, now in that, and may be heard at different times in connection with various other tones. But since the direction is not constant, or the accompanying tone in all cases the same, it is possible to abstract from these variable elements, and we have the single tone as a psychical element.

2. As a result of psychical analysis, we find that there are *psychical elements of two kinds,* corresponding to the *two factors* contained in immediate experience, namely, to the objective contents of experience and to the experiencing subject. The elements of the objective contents we call *sensational elements,* or simply *sensations:* such are a tone, or a particular sensation of heat, cold, or light, if in each case we neglect for the moment all the connections of these sensations with others, and also all their spacial and temporal relations. The subjective elements, on the other hand, are designated as *affective elements,* or *simple feelings*. We may mention as examples, the feelings accompanying sensations of light, sound, taste, smell, heat, cold, or pain, the feelings aroused by the sight of an agreeable or disagreeable object, and the feelings arising in a state of attention or at the moment of a volitional act. Such simple feelings are in a double sense products of abstraction: every such feeling is connected in reality with an ideational element, and is furthermore a component of a psychical process which occurs in time, during which the feeling itself is continually changing.

3. The actual contents of psychical experience always consist of various combinations of sensational and affective elements, so that the specific character of a given psychical process depends for the most part, not on the nature of its elements, so much as on their union into a composite psychical compound. Thus, the idea of an extended body or of a rhythm, an emotion, and a volition, are all *specific* forms of psychical experience. But their character as such is as little determined by their sensational and affective elements as are the chemical properties of a compound body by the properties of its chemical elements. *Specific* character and *elementary* nature of psychical processes are, accordingly, two entirely different concepts. Every psychical element is a specific content of experience, but not every specific content is at the same time a psychical element. Thus, spacial and temporal ideas, emotions, and volitional acts, are specific, but not elementary processes.

4. Sensations and simple feelings exhibit certain common attributes and also certain characteristic differences. They have in common *two determinants,* namely, *quality* and *intensity*. Every simple sensation and every simple feeling has a definite *qualitative* character that marks it off from all other sensations and feelings; and this quality must always have some degree of *intensity*. Our *designations* of psychical elements are based entirely upon their qualities; thus, we distinguish such sensations as blue, grey, yellow, warmth and cold, or such feelings as grave, cheer-

From Wundt, W. (1896). *Grundriss der Psychologie.* Leipzig: Engelmann. From C. H. Judd (Trans.), *Outlines of psychology.* New York: Gustav Sechert, 1902, pp. 32–41, 100–103.

ful, sad, gloomy, and sorrowful. On the other hand, we always express the differences in the intensity of psychical elements by the same quantitative designations, as weak, strong, medium strong, and very strong. These expressions are in both cases class-concepts which serve for a first superficial arrangement of the elements, and each expression embraces an unlimitedly large number of concrete elements. Language has developed a relatively complete stock of names for the qualities of simple sensations, especially for colors and tones. Names for the qualities of feelings and for degrees of intensity are far behind in number and precision. Certain attributes other than quality and intensity, such as distinctness and indistinctness, are sometimes classed with quality and intensity as fundamental attributes. But since clearness, obscurity, etc., . . . always arise from the interconnection of psychical compounds, they can not be regarded as determinants of psychical elements.

5. Made up, as it is, of the *two* determinants, quality and intensity, every psychical element must have a certain *degree of intensity* from which it is possible to pass, by continual gradations, to every other degree of intensity in the same quality. Such gradations can be made in only *two* directions: one we call *increase* in intensity, the other *decrease*. The degrees of intensity of every qualitative element, form in this way a single dimension, in which, from a given point, we may move in two opposite directions, just as from any point in a straight line. This fact in regard to intensity may be expressed in the general statement: *The various intensities of every psychical element form a continuity of one dimension.* The extremities of such a continuity we call the *minimal* and *maximal sensations,* or the *minimal* or *maximal feelings,* as the case may be.

In contrast with this uniformity in intensities, *qualities* have more variable attributes. Every quality may, indeed, be assigned a place in a definite continuity of similar qualities in such a way that it is possible to pass uninterruptedly from a given point in this continuous series to any other point.

But the various continuities of different qualities, which we may call *systems of quality,* exhibit differences both in the variety of possible gradations, and in the number of directions of gradation. With reference to these two kinds of variations in systems of quality, we may distinguish, on the one hand, *homogeneous* and *complex* systems, and on the other hand, *one-dimensional, two-dimensional,* and *many-dimensional* systems of quality. Within a homogeneous system, only such small differences are possible, that generally there has never arisen any practical need of distinguishing them by different names. Thus, we distinguish only *one* quality of pressure, of heat, of cold, or of pain, only *one* feeling of pleasure or of excitement, although, in intensity, each of these qualities may have many different grades. It is not to be inferred from this fact that in each of these systems there is really only *one* quality. The truth is that in these cases the number of different qualities is merely very limited; if we were to represent the system geometrically, we should probably never reduce it to a *single* point. Thus, for example, sensations of pressure from different regions of the skin show, beyond question, small qualitative differences which are great enough to make it possible for us to distinguish clearly any point of the skin from others at some distance from it. Such differences, however, as arise from contact with a sharp or dull point, or from a rough or smooth body, are not to be regarded as different qualities. They always depend on a large number of simultaneous sensations, and without the various combinations of these sensations into composite psychical compounds, the impressions mentioned would be impossible.

Complex systems of quality differ from those we have been discussing, in that they embrace a large number of clearly distinguishable elements between which all possible intermediate forms exist. In this class we must include the tonal system and color system, the systems of smells and tastes; and among the complex feeling systems we must include those which form the subjective complements of these sensational systems, such as the systems of tonal feelings, color feelings, etc. It is probable also that many systems of feelings belongs here, which are objectively connected with composite impressions, but are as feelings, simple in character; such are the various feelings of harmony or discord which correspond to various combinations of tones. The differences in the *number of dimensions* have been determined with certainty only in the case of two or three sensational systems. Thus, the tonal system is one-dimensional. The ordinary color system, which includes the colors and their transitional qualities to white, is two-dimensional; while the complete system of light sensations, which includes also the dark color-tones and the transitional qualities to black, is three-dimensional.

6. In regard to the relations discussed thus far, sensational elements and affective elements agree in general. They differ, on the other hand, in certain essential attributes which are connected with the fact that sensations are immediately related to objects, while feelings are immediately related to the subject.

1) When varied in a single dimension, sensational elements exhibit *pure qualitative differences,* which are always in the *same direction* until they reach the possible limits of variation, where they become *maximal differences*. Thus, in the color system, red and green, blue and yellow, or in the tonal system, the lowest and highest audible tones, are the maximal differences and are at the same time purely qualitative differences. Every affective element, on the contrary, when continuously varied in the proper direction of quality, passes gradually into a feeling of *opposite quality*. This is most obvious in the case of those affective elements which are regularly connected with certain sensational elements, as for example, tonal feelings or color feelings. As sensations, a high and low tone present differences that approach more or less the maximal differences of tonal sensation; the corresponding tonal feelings are opposites. In general, then, *series of sensational qualities are bounded at their extremes by maximal differences; series of affective qualities*

are bounded by maximal opposites. Between affective opposites is a middle zone, where the feeling is not noticeable at all. It is, however, frequently impossible to demonstrate this indifference-zone, because, while certain simple feelings disappear, other affective qualities remain, or new ones may arise. The latter case appears most commonly when the passing of the feeling into the indifference-zone depends on a change in sensations. Thus, in the middle of the musical scale, those feelings disappear which correspond to the high and low tones, but the middle tones have independent affective qualities of their own which appear clearly only when the other complicating factors are eliminated. This is to be explained by the fact that a feeling which corresponds to a certain sensational quality is, as a rule, a component of a complex affective system, in which it belongs at the same time to various dimensions. Thus, the affective quality of a tone of given pitch belongs not only to the dimension of pitch feelings, but also to that of feelings of intensity, and finally to the different dimensions in which the clang character of tones may be arranged. A tone of middle pitch and intensity may, in this way, lie in the indifference-zone so far as feelings of pitch and intensity are concerned, and yet have a very marked clang feeling. The passage of affective elements through the indifference-zone can be directly observed only when care is taken to abstract from other accompanying affective elements. The cases most favorable for this observation are those in which the accompanying elements disappear entirely or almost entirely. Wherever such an indifference-zone appears without complication with other affective elements, we speak of the state as *free from feelings,* and of the sensations and ideas present in such a state, as *indifferent*.

2) Feelings which have specific, and at the same time simple and irreducible quality, appear not only as the subjective complements of simple sensations, but also as the characteristic attendants of composite ideas or even of complex ideational processes. Thus, there is a simple tonal feeling which

varies with the pitch and intensity of tones, and there is also a feeling of harmony which, regarded as a feeling, is just as irreducible as the tonal feeling, but varies with the character of compound clangs. Still other feelings, which may in turn be of the most various kinds, arise from melodious series of clangs. Here, again, each single feeling taken by itself at a given moment, appears as an irreducible unit. Simple feelings are, then, much more various and numerous than simple sensations.

3) The various pure sensations may be arranged in a number of separate systems, between the elements of which there is no qualitative relation whatever. Sensations belonging to different systems are called *disparate*. Thus, a tone and a color, a sensation of heat and one of pressure, or, in general, any two sensations between which there are no intermediate qualities, are disparate. According to this criterion, each of the four special senses (smell, taste, hearing, and sight) has a closed, complex sensational system, disparate from that of the other senses; while the general sense (touch) contains four homogeneous sensational systems (sensations of pressure, heat, cold, and pain). All simple feelings, on the other hand, form a single interconnected manifold, for there is no feeling from which it is not possible to pass to any other, through intermediate forms or through indifference-zones. But here too we may distinguish certain systems the elements of which are more closely related, as, for example, feelings from colors, tones, harmonies and rhythms. These are, however, not absolutely closed systems, for there are everywhere relations either of likeness or of opposition to other systems. Thus, feelings such as those from sensations of moderate warmth, from tonal harmony, and from satisfied expectation, however great their qualitative differences may be, are all related in that they belong to the general class of "pleasurable feelings." Even closer relations exist between certain single affective systems, as, for example, between tonal feelings and color feelings, where the feelings from deep tones seem to be related to those from dark colors, and

feelings from bright colors to those from high tones. When in such cases a certain relationship is ascribed to the sensations themselves, it is probably due entirely to a confusion of the accompanying feelings with the sensations.

This third distinguishing characteristic shows conclusively that the source of the feelings is *unitary* while that of the sensations, which depend on a number of different, and in part distinguishable, conditions, is not unitary. Probably this difference in the character of the sources of feeling and sensations is directly connected, on the one hand, with the relation of the feelings to the unitary subject, and, on the other hand, with the relation of sensations to the great variety of *objects*.

6a. It is only in modern psychology that the terms "sensation" and "feeling" have gained the meanings assigned to them in the definitions above given. In older psychological literature these terms were sometimes used indiscriminatingly, sometimes interchanged. Even yet sensations of touch and sensations from the internal organs are called feelings by physiologists, and the sense of touch itself is known as the "sense of feeling." This corresponds, it is true, to the original significance of the word, where feeling is the same as touching, and yet, after the differentiation has once been made, a confusion of the two terms should be avoided. Then again, the word "sensation" is used even by psychologists to mean not only simple, but also composite qualities, such as compound clangs and spacial and temporal ideas. But since we have the entirely adequate word "idea" for such compounds, it is more advantageous to limit the word sensation to sense qualities which are psychologically simple. Finally the term "sensation" has sometimes been restricted so as to mean only those impressions which come directly from external sense stimuli. For the psychological attributes of a sensation, however, this circumstance is entirely indifferent, and therefore, such a definition of the term is unjustifiable.

The discrimination between sensational elements and affective elements in any concrete case is very much facilitated by the existence of indifference-zones in the feelings. Then again it follows from the fact that feelings range between opposites rather than mere differences, that feelings are much the more variable elements of our immediate experience. This changeable character, which renders it almost impossible to hold an affective state constant in quality and intensity, is the cause of the great difficulties that stand in the way of the exact investigation of feelings.

Sensations are present in all immediate experiences, but feelings may disappear in certain special cases, because of their oscillation through an indifference-zone. Obviously, then, we can, in the case of sensations, abstract from the accompanying feelings, but we can never abstract from sensations in the case of feelings. In this way two false views may easily arise, either that sensations are the *causes* of feelings, or that feelings are a particular species of sensations. The first of these opinions is false because affective elements can never be derived from sensations as such, but only from the attitude of the subject, so that under different subjective conditions the same sensation may be accompanied by different feelings. The second view, that feelings are a particular species of sensations, is untenable because the two classes of elements are distinguished, on the one hand by the immediate relation of sensations to objects and of feelings to the subject, and on the other hand, by the fact that the former range between maximal differences, the latter between maximal opposites. Because of the objective and subjective factors belonging to all psychical experience, sensations and feelings are to be looked upon as real and equally essential, though everywhere interrelated, elements of psychical phenomena. In the interrelation of the two groups of elements, the sensational elements appear as the more constant; they alone can be isolated through abstraction, by referring them to external objects. It follows, therefore, of necessity that in investigating the attributes of both kinds of elements, we must start with the sensations. Simple sensations, in the consideration of which we abstract from the accompanying affective elements, are called *pure sensations*. . . .

II. PSYCHICAL COMPOUNDS

1. By "psychical compound" we mean any composite component of our immediate experience which is marked off from other contents of this experience by characteristics peculiarly its own, in such a way that it is recognized as a relatively independent unity and is, when practical necessity demands it, designated by a special name. In developing such a name, language has followed the general rule that only *classes* and the most important *species* into which phenomena may be grouped shall have special designations. Thus such terms as idea, emotion, volitional act, etc., designate general classes of psychical compounds, such terms as visual idea, joy, anger, hope, etc., designate special species included in these classes. So far as these designations are based upon actual, distinguishing characteristics, they have a certain value for psychological analysis. But in granting this, we must avoid from the first, *two* presuppositions to which the existence of these names might easily mislead us. The first is, that a psychical compound is an absolutely independent content of immediate experience. The second is, that certain compounds, as for example, ideas, have the *nature of things*. The truth is that compounds are only *relatively* independent units. Just as they are made up of various elements, so they themselves unite to form a complete interconnection, in which relatively simple compounds may continually combine to form more composite ones. Then, again, compounds, like the psychical elements contained in them, are never things, but *processes* which change from moment to moment, so that it is only through deliberate abstraction, which is, indeed, indispensable for the investigation in many cases, that they can be thought of as constant at any given moment. . . .

2. All psychical compounds may be resolved into psychical elements, that is, into pure sensations and simple feelings. The two kinds of elements behave, however, in an essentially different manner, in keeping with the special properties of simple feelings. . . . The sensational elements found by such a resolution, always belong to one of the sensational systems already considered. The effective elements, on the other hand, include not only those which correspond to the pure sensations contained in the compounds, but also those due to the interconnection of the elements into a compound. The sys-

tems of sensational qualities, accordingly, remain the same, no matter how many varieties of compounds arise, while the systems of simple affective qualities continually increase. Furthermore, it is a general principle valid for all psychical compounds, whether they are composed of sensations only, of feelings only, or of combinations of both sensations and feelings, that *the attributes of psychical compounds are never limited to those of the elements that enter into them.* It is true rather that *new* attributes, peculiar to the compounds themselves, always arise as a result of the combination of these elements. Thus, a visual idea has not only the attributes of the light sensations and sensations of ocular position and movements contained in it, but it has also the attribute of spacial arrangement of the sensations, a factor not present in the elements themselves. Again a volition is made up not only of the ideas and feelings into which its single acts may be resolved, but there result also from the combination of these single acts, new affective elements which are specifically characteristic of the complex volition. Here, again, the combinations of sensational and affective elements are different. In the first case, on account of the constancy of the sensational systems, no new sensations can arise, but only peculiar *forms of their arrangement.* These forms are the *extensive spacial* and *temporal manifolds.* When, on the other hand, affective elements combine, *new simple feelings* arise, which unite with those originally present to make *intensive* affective units of composite character.

3. The classification of psychical compounds is naturally based upon the character of the ele-

ments that enter into them. Those composed entirely or chiefly of sensations are called *ideas,* those consisting mainly of affective elements, *affective processes.* The same limitations hold here as in the case of the corresponding elements. Although compounds are more the products of immediate discrimination among actual psychical processes than are the elements, still, there is in all exactness no pure ideational process and no pure affective process, but in both cases we can only abstract to a certain extent from one or the other component. As in the case of the two kinds of elements, so here, we can neglect the accompanying subjective states when dealing with ideas, but we must always presuppose some idea when giving an account of the affective processes.

We distinguish, accordingly, three chief forms of *ideas:* 1) intensive ideas, 2) spacial ideas, 3) temporal ideas; and three forms of *affective processes:* 1) intensive affective combinations, 2) emotions, 3) volitions. Temporal ideas constitute a sort of link between the two kinds of compounds, for certain feelings play an important part in their formation.

REFERENCES

Kant, Anthropologie, 2nd. Bk. Herbart, Textbook of Psychology, §68 and 95. (Differentiation of the concepts sensation and feeling in the present-day sense.)

Horwicz, Psychologische Analysen auf physiolog. Grundlage, 2 vols., 1872–1878.

Wundt, Ueber das Verhältniss der Gefühle zu den Vorstellungen, Vierteljahrsschr. f. wiss. Philos., III, 1879. (Also in Essays, 1885.)

The Establishment of Wundt's Laboratory: An Archival and Documentary Study

Wolfgang G. Bringmann, Norma J. Bringmann, and Gustav A. Ungerer

Traditionally, the academic year 1879–80 has been regarded as the period during which Wundt's laboratory became a reality. Researches at the Wilhelm Wundt Archive in Leipzig and the Dresden State Archive fully support this claim. All in all, the year 1879 was an auspicious one for Wundt. On January 1 of that year, his regular salary was increased by about twenty-five percent to 5,400 Marks annually (Fensch, 1977). On January 26, his son Max was born, who, like his sister Lorle before him, would serve as a research subject for his father's studies of language development.

AN IMPORTANT PETITION

Perhaps encouraged by events, Wundt submitted a petition to the Royal Saxon Ministry of Education on March 24, in which he requested a regular budget for the "establishment and support" of a collection of "psychophysical apparatus." Wundt's long letter to his superiors tells us a great deal about the development of his viewpoint concerning the function of a university laboratory.

> The undersigned had contemplated already at that time (1875) to connect psychophysical practica with his lectures . . . in order to instruct those of his students who were particularly interested in psychology in the techniques of conducting their own psychophysical research work. He believed, however, that he should carry out these plans only after he had convinced himself that such practical activities were desirable.

Adapted from Bringmann, W. G., Bringmann, N. J., & Ungerer, G. A. (1980). The establishment of Wundt's laboratory: An archival and documentary study. In W. G. Bringmann & R. D. Tweney (Eds.), *Wundt studies: A centennial collection.* Toronto: C. J. Hogrefe, pp. 123–159. Copyright © 1980 by C. J. Hogrefe. Adapted and reprinted by permission of the publisher and the author.

After having taught at Leipzig for nearly four years and having been able to stimulate interest in psychological research through the teaching of the seminar (*Psychological Society*), Wundt believed that the time had come to begin offering courses in psychological research techniques.

> Since the seminars on theoretical aspects of psychological research, taught by the undersigned, have attracted a significant enrollment, it has become ever clearer to him that they need to be supplemented by a practical introduction to the basic psychophysical research methods. (March 24).

In his petition Wundt also declared his willingness to donate his own collection of equipment to the university in exchange for an annual stipend of "600 Marks . . . for the establishment and maintenance of a set of psychophysical apparatus." Although the sum requested by Wundt was trifling, his request was denied due to "financial exigencies."

It almost looks as if Wundt had given up hope for his laboratory, because he did not offer his *Psychological Society* during the Summer Semester, as had been his habit since 1877. Instead he scheduled his seminar course in logic (*Logical Society*). However, in the Winter Catalogue for 1878–80, the psychological seminar was again listed (1879):

> *Psychological Society.* Monday 7–9 p.m. (*private and gratis*).

Since it was a *private* course, students needed Wundt's permission to enroll but the word *gratis* indicated that no fee was to be charged.

An Eyewitness Account

Information about what took place in this seminar during the Winter Semester of 1879–80 has been provided by an eyewitness—G. Stanley Hall (1840–1926). Hall is generally considered to be Wundt's first American student, although, having already received his doctorate at Harvard University, he was not formally enrolled at Leipzig. In Hall's autobiography, *Life and Confessions of a Psychologist* (1924), he comments:

> I also attended Wundt's seminary, in which his method was then to assign readings, expecting each to report in detail. He took incessant notes, so that in a sense we read for him; and I have thought this method was the key for the vast erudition which marks his publications (p. 204).

Despite his sarcasm, Hall was to copy the format of Wundt's seminar course in later years at Clark University, even including the Monday night schedule. Hall's report also indicates that the *Psychological Society* did not include any opportunities for practical psychological research.

THE LABORATORY

Wundt has provided considerable information about the early days of his laboratory, which will be quoted in chronological order. The earliest account is contained in another petition to the ministry, dated April 4, 1882, in which Wundt once again summarized the history of his institute.

> The undersigned began...to offer a practical seminar activity in addition to his theoretical seminar during the Winter Semester of 1879–80.

This practical seminar, as Wundt calls it to distinguish it from the *Psychological Society,* was not listed in the catalogue at all. Wundt provides the same information to the Austrian philosopher Jerusalem, who had inquired about the origin of Wundt's institute (1892):

> The main dates about the institute are quickly collected. In the Winter of 1879–80 it was opened first as a private undertaking. Stanley Hall and Max Friedrich... were the first participants.... Initially the institute had only *one* single room at its disposal. (February 2).

The official history of Wundt's laboratory, which he wrote on the occasion of the 500th anniversary of Leipzig University, is slightly more explicit (1909):

> Following the psychological seminars, which during the first semesters were held in the form of a colloquium, dealing with the topics of the formal lecture, individual students began to occupy themselves in this room in the Konvict with research investigations. (p. 1).

This interestingly suggests that the actual practical research of Wundt's institute was originated by his students. It is noteworthy that Wundt gives credit to his students for helping him to get his laboratory started. His comment may only have been a matter of courtesy on his part. On the other hand, Wundt may have known what most teachers of psychology eventually discover. It is dangerous to inspire students with your ideas about research or practical professional services, because they will eventually expect you to practice what you preach. While these and other accounts of the early laboratory vary, it is clear that Wundt regarded the inofficial practical research activities as the actual beginning of his institute. The practical research activities took place in the classroom on the third floor of the *Konvikt* building which had been assigned to Wundt in the summer of 1876.

Although G. Stanley Hall was eager to minimize his association with Wundt, he provides independent support for the existence of Wundt's laboratory in his autobiography (1924):

> ...Wundt at Leipzig...had only lately been elected full professor there...and his laboratory was but little organized....I participated as subject in several of the experiments. But as the laboratory was open only in the afternoon and especially because I felt it necessary to ground myself in physiology, I left Wundt and spent most of the day in the laboratory of Professor Ludwig, who gave me a problem in myology working with me a great deal.... Wundt was an indefatigable worker and we rarely saw him outside the laboratory, although, even here he spent little time and did little work.... He impressed me as rather inept in the use of his hands. (p. 205).

While Hall is obviously biased in almost all that he has to say about Wundt and his small laboratory, he nevertheless confirms its independent existence. His comparison with Ludwig's Physiological Institute is meaningless, when one considers that Carl Ludwig (1816–1895) had come to Leipzig a decade before Wundt and was able to move in a special laboratory building which had been constructed at the cost of nearly 200,000 Marks (Stieda, 1909).

Dissertation Research

According to Wundt, the first research project completed under his supervision in the laboratory was the dissertation of Max Friedrich on *The duration of simple and complex apperceptions* (1881).... Friedrich, who was by training a mathematician and not a philosopher, acknowledged that his work was carried out "under the direction of Professor Dr. Wundt." The preliminary research was begun in "early December" of 1879 and Wundt, Hall and Friedrich were the first participants. The data collection continued in early January of 1880 and ended along with the winter semester in early March. Despite Hall's claims that Wundt did not spend much time in the laboratory, we discover that he participated in the data collection on no less than 16 occasions between January 17 and March 5. We also find that Hall participated in the data collection only on an irregular basis. In conclusion, an approximate date can be fixed for the beginning of the actual work in Wundt's laboratory in the *Konvikt*. The earliest time is "early December," the latest suitable date would be January 17, when Wundt, Hall, Tischer and Friedrich participated as experimental subjects.

MY PSYCHOPHYSICAL LABORATORY

It has been suggested by Boring that Wundt was not really aware of the establishment of his laboratory, and that he chose the 1879 date randomly many years later when he was writing the history of his institute (Boring, 1965). Nothing could be further from the truth, as we can learn from a letter of recommendation written by Wundt for

Hall on June 18, 1880. Hall used this letter in securing his appointment at Johns Hopkins University, and a copy has been found in the papers of Coit Gilman (1831–1908). Wundt penned the recommendation in Latin letters rather than in the traditional German script which he used for most of his writing (1880a):

> I have come to know Dr. G. Stanley Hall well through frequent personal contact during his extended stay in Leipzig as a man of comprehensive philosophical knowledge, great scientific interests and solid independent judgment. In particular Mr. Hall has been able to gain a rare knowledge of the German scientific literature not only in psychology but also in the related subjects of sensory- and neurophysiology.

As far as Hall's participation in the laboratory is concerned, Wundt states generously:

> He has participated in the work of my psychophysical laboratory during the winter semester of 1879–80 and the summer semester of 1880 with great industry and success. (June 18).

Additional evidence that Wundt regarded his "humble" facilities on the third floor of the *Konvikt* as a laboratory can be found in correspondence between Wundt and Kraepelin dated August 4 and October 14, 1880.

EXPANSION AND RECOGNITION

The Philosophical Studies

Once Wundt had his own laboratory facilities in which his students were conducting independent psycho-physical research, it comes as no surprise that he soon founded his own journal, the *Philosophical Studies*. Considerable new information about the origin of Wundt's journal has been discovered in his correspondence with the noted psychiatrist Emil Kraepelin (1880b):

> Your comment about a journal of psychology, which you regard as desirable has much interested me, especially since I have had similar ideas.... I have currently a number of investigations on the time sense ...

for which I do not yet have a place of publication.... The best physiological journals pursue other interests as a rule, and a philosophical journal...does not have the necessary space for such topics.... If the project should become reality in any form, I would like to count on your collaboration. (August 4).

Wundt later elaborated some of his plans for such a project to Kraepelin (1880c):

The plan of a psychological journal, which you suggested, has come closer to realization. After due deliberation, I think it would be best to extend the scope of the journal to the whole field of psychology and related subject areas.... I also think it would be best if the journal would initially print only original research...and not reviews of other research. (October 14).

Wundt had apparently talked to his publisher and many details were already worked out (1880d):

The individual issues are to appear in an informal order...and the publication is to depend on available material. The publisher has declared himself willing to provide an honorarium of 40 Marks and 40 reprints of each article. I would like to bring out articles in the first issue which represent the different fields which the journal is to cover. (December 17, 1880).

Wundt announced his plans to publish "*Psychological Studies*" in January of 1881. The main purpose of the new journal was to publish experiments "which over the last several years have been carried out in my laboratory." The title of the journal was already changed by August 4 of the same year to *Philosophische Studien*. It seems possible that the change in title was due to the fact that a journal called *Psychologische Studien* was already in existence, and, moreover, dealt with the obnoxious topic of spiritism and other parapsychological phenomena (Wundt, 1927). The first number of the *Philosophische Studien,* containing a long article by Wundt on psychological methods and the Friedrich dissertation, was published in October of 1881. The first volume, however, was not completed until 1883.

Institute for Experimental Psychology

By April, 1882, Wundt felt sufficiently confident of the solid accomplishments of his laboratory to compose yet another petition for university support of his work. The lengthy missive began with a history of the laboratory (1882):

Already at that time (1875), the undersigned had contemplated the eventual foundation of a seminar for experimental psychology, in which students could be instructed through practica in carrying out their own research. However, he had thought it best to delay specific petitions in this direction until his teaching at the university had produced the conditions necessary for such a seminar activity. Accordingly, the undersigned started a practical seminar program about two years ago during the winter semester of 1879–80 and in publicly announced practica beginning with the summer semester of 1880.

Wundt also reported that he had supported the experimental work of his students out of his own pocket. Thus, he had been forced to limit the areas in which research could be carried out to those for which his personal research equipment was suitable. He had apparently been able to attract quite a few students.

To these practica in experimental psychology a larger number of students than the undersigned had originally expected have been attracted. These include not only students who are specializing in philosophy. Many students in the sciences and mathematics have actively participated in the psycho-physical research as well.

Wundt also mentioned that he had supervised a significant number of dissertations which were published in his own journal.

As far as the achievements of the Seminar for Experimental Psychology during the last two years are concerned, the undersigned would like to mention several pertinent dissertations, which were accepted by the College of Arts and Sciences and which have been published in the *Philosophical Studies* by him. (April 4).

Wundt also complained that the large anatomical drawings, which he had initially obtained as lecture illustrations for small classes, were totally inappropriate for his big lecture classes which exceeded 250 students. Finally, Wundt asked the Royal Ministry of Culture and Public Education to add the *"Institute of Experimental Psychology"* to the number of academic institutes of Leipzig University. He also requested approval of an annual budget of 900 Marks for this institute.

This letter contains a whole chapter of psychological history. Wundt used the name *Institute* for the first time as a synonym for *Seminar*. His eloquent petition, however, was only partially successful. The Ministry thanked him for his efforts, refused the establishment of a regular budget, but agreed to provide the requested 900 Marks for the current year. Official recognition was not mentioned.

A Famous Visitor

Recognition of a somewhat different type came late in the fall in the form of a personal visit by William James (1840–1910), who had just returned from a trip to Prague to see Carl Stumpf (1882):

> I stayed in Berlin a week, in Leipzig five days, in Liege two and a half days with Delboeuf. In each place I heard all the university lectures that I could and spoke with several of the professors. From some I got very good hints as to how not to lecture. Helmholtz, for example, gave me the very worst lecture I ever heard in my life except one (that one was by our most distinguished American mathematician). The lecture I heard in Prague from Mach was on the same elementary subject as Helmholtz's and one of the most artistic lectures I ever heard. Wundt in Leipzig impressed me very agreeably personally. He has a ready smile and is entirely unaffected and unpretending in his manner. I heard him twice and was twice in his laboratory. He was very polite but showed no desire for further acquaintance. (November 26).

James' letter makes it very clear that Wundt's laboratory was in full existence at that time. His comments about Wundt's accessibility are in agreement with the observations of Hall, who in 1879 had found Wundt "very accessible and free to talk about everything." One also gains the impression that James is somewhat unhappy about his favorable impression of Wundt, because he was certainly familiar with Stumpf's intense personal dislike of Wundt and his work.

Call to Breslau

Wundt was considered for an appointment at Breslau University, as we discover in a letter from his friend Siegfried Brie (1883):

> The news in your letter surprised me to a high degree. It is the first word that they have thought of me in Breslau. Here, I heard only a short time ago that Paulssen in Berlin or Windelband in Strassburg had been recommended. Everyone here is of the opinion that the Prussian government does not like to call anyone from Leipzig... because in Prussia the system of academic calls seems to have been replaced by bureaucratic promotions. It would be a joy for my wife and myself to renew our friendship with you and your family, since we have no one as close as you in Leipzig. You know, of course, that my working conditions here in Leipzig are not the best. It is also doubtful if the Saxon government will make an effort to keep me.

His friend's letter had placed Wundt in a difficult position. Wundt and his family enjoyed their friendship with the Brie family, but were not all that eager to leave Leipzig, as we find out in the next section of the letter.

> I very much doubt that any personal activity on my side will help the call. Secondly, I am in these matters a fatalist. I prefer to let events approach me and if they do not work out, I regard it as proof that they should not have occurred at all. (January 27).

Nevertheless, the formal call was received and communicated by Wundt to his superiors together with a list of conditions which could help him decide to stay in Leipzig.

Reward and Recognition

The first bonus for deciding not to leave his position in Leipzig was a nearly forty percent raise in salary from 5400 to 7500 Marks a year (Fensch, 1977). In addition, the local administrators in Leipzig were instructed to:

> place the immediately adjacent small auditorium at his (Wundt's) disposal in addition to the room, which he has used until now in the *Konvikt* building, and to carry out the minor changes in construction according to his wishes.

The minor changes desired by Wundt were, in fact, quite substantial as we can see in the drawings submitted by the architect and approved by the University. A total of 1614 Marks was expended to turn two old classrooms and a hallway into quite a respectable laboratory. The following changes were made (Drucker, 1883):

(a) The hallway area in front of classroom number V on the third floor of the *Konvikt* building was separated by walls and turned into an office-waiting room. Part of it was to be used as a darkroom.

(b) The new classroom, which had been assigned to Wundt (Number III) on the same floor was divided into two workrooms by the construction of a dividing wall.

(c) Storm windows and screens were installed on all windows.

(d) The walls and ceilings were painted with waterbase paint. All woodwork was painted with oil paint.

(e) Connections for gas light were installed in all rooms and hallways and all rooms were connected with electrical lines.

(f) Three new cabinets, five tables and 12 cane-bottom chairs were added to the existing furnishings of the laboratory. (August 1).

Altogether the enlarged laboratory of Wundt consisted of two large (Rooms 1 and 7) and five small rooms (2, 3, 4, 5 and 6) providing approx-

FIGURE 1
Floorplan of Wundt's Leipzig laboratory.

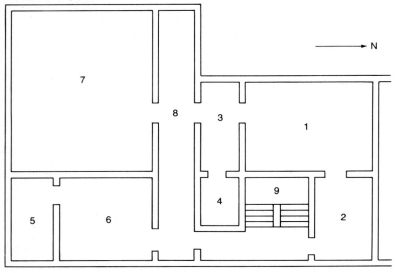

1. Classroom # 5	4. Darkroom	7. Classroom # 4
2. Conference room	5. Workroom (Laboratory)	8. Hallway
3. Waiting room	6. Workroom (Laboratory)	9. Staircase

imately 1000 square feet of space (Bringmann & Ungerer, 1980). Incidentally, the original storage room, which had been assigned to Wundt in 1876 (Fensch, 1977), now served as his university office (Room 1), except for a small section (Rooms 3 and 4) which was used as darkroom and for equipment storage.

The assignment and equipment of a permanent home for the laboratory was followed on June 26, 1883 by the inclusion of Wundt's Laboratory among the *regular* academic institutes of Leipzig University (Fensch, 1977). The new seminar was called *Institute for Experimental Psychology*. It also received a regular annual budget at that time. The Winter Catalogue of Leipzig University for 1883–1884 contains the information that Wundt's private laboratory had officially become the 26th institute or seminar of the university (1883–84):

> 26. *Institute for Experimental Psychology (Convict Building)*, Professor Dr. Wilhelm Wundt, Director, 6 Goethestra ße. Cand math. G. Lorenz, Famulus, 6 Salomonstra ße.

REFERENCES

Boring, E. G. On the subjectivity of important historical dates: Leipzig 1879. *Journal of the History of the Behavioral Sciences*, 1965, 1, 5–10.

Bringmann, W., & Ungerer, G. A. An archival journey in search of Wilhelm Wundt. In L. Pongratz & J. Brozek (Eds.) *Historiography of Psychology*. Göttingen: Hogrefe, 1980.

Drucker, R. Personal communication, October 31, 1979.

Fensch, D. Zur Rolle Wilhelm Wundt's bei der Institutionalisierung der Psychologie in Leipzig. *Psychologie-Historische-Manuskripte*, 1977, 1, 60–66.

Friedrich, M. Über die Apperceptionsdauer bei einfachen und zusammengesetzten Vorstellungen. *Philosophische Studien*, 1883 (1881), 1, 38–77.

Hall, G. S. *Life and confessions of a psychologist*. New York: Appleton, 1924.

Stieda, W. *Die Entwicklung der Universität Leipzig in ihrem tausendsten Semester*. Leipzig: Hirzel, 1909.

Wundt, E. *Wilhelm Wundts Werk*. München: Beck, 1927.

Wundt, W. Letter of recommendation for G. S. Hall, June 18, 1880a. (Clark U.).

Wundt, W. to E. Kraepelin, August 4, 1880b. (Tübingen U.).

Wundt, W. to E. Kraepelin, October 14, 1880c. (Tübingen U.).

Wundt, W. to E. Kraepelin, December 17, 1880d. (Tübingen U.).

Wundt, W. to Ministry of Education, April 4, 1882.

Wundt, W. to W. Jerusalem, February 2, 1892. (Tübingen U.).

Wundt, W. *Das Institut für experimentelle Psychologie*. Leipzig: Hirzel, 1909.

A Reappraisal of Wilhelm Wundt

Arthur L. Blumenthal

Approximately 100 years ago, in an era of intellectual ferment, events of marked consequence took place in the history of psychology. It was in the decade of the 1870s that the first handbook of experimental psychology ap-

Blumenthal, A. L. (1975). A reappraisal of Wilhelm Wundt. *American Psychologist, 30,* 1081–1088. Copyright © 1975 by the American Psychological Association. Reprinted by permission of the publisher and the author.

peared, followed soon by the founding of the first formal laboratory of experimental psychology. Both were the achievements of Wilhelm Wundt, ever since recognized as experimental psychology's great patron, though later barred from any role that might remotely resemble sainthood. Soon after the wave of "new" psychologists spread out from Wundt's laboratory, a series of intellectual revolutions largely erased from memory the content of Wundtian psychological theory.

Now that the movement set in motion by Wundt has come through its first century, it would seem fitting to mark the centenary by briefly turning back, reexamining psychology's historical foundations, and paying homage to the founding father. There is, however, another reason for review, being less ceremonial and clearly more interesting. To put it simply, the few current Wundt-scholars (and some do exist) are in fair agreement that Wundt as portrayed today in many texts and courses is largely fictional and often bears little resemblance to the actual historical figure (cf. Blumenthal, 1970; Bringmann, Balance, & Evans, 1975; Mischel, 1970).

Naturally, it might be suspected that the above radical statement is only the nit-picking of a few antiquarians obsessed with minor matters of interpretation. But alas, such is not the case. These are claims about the very fundamentals of Wundt's work, often asserting the opposite of what has been a standard description prevailing over much of the past century. Yet, if popular historical accounts of Wundt are in need of serious correction, then one might again ask whether Wundt still turns out to be irrelevant and of little interest. This article is addressed to that question, and its answers will, I suspect, contain some surprises for many readers.

There is another question that immediately follows upon these claims. It is, How could such historical misinterpretations have arisen? This is surely a fascinating question but one requiring separate treatment. For the moment merely take note that Wundtian anecdotes have long been passed down from author to author without worthy recourse to original sources, and, also, that it is common in intellectual history for later schools of thought to foster distortions and misinterpretations of earlier ones—psychology, of course, offering numerous opportunities. For now, let us examine the fundamentals of Wundt's psychology that have, for better or worse, been disguised or lost in the course of history's machinations.

WUNDT'S METHOD

The basic premise in Wundtian psychology is that the only certain reality is immediate experience. Proceeding from this premise, Wundt had accepted the following goals for all science: the construction of explanations of experience and the development of techniques for objectifying experience. By the latter, he meant that the scientist attempts to communicate and reproduce his experiences in others in standardized ways; thus it becomes possible to perform tests that lead to public agreement about phenomena and to agreement about their explanation. This was commonplace for Wundt and is found at the outset of many of his texts.

In the natural sciences, as Wundt continues, it is the attributes of experience derived from external objects and energies that are subjected to tests, explanations, and public agreement. But in the case of psychology, it is the attributes of experience derived from the processes of the experiencing subject that are made the object of tests, explanations, and public agreement. These psychological entities include experienced memory and perceptual capacities, fluctuations of attention or alertness, ranges of our sensitivities, etc. In the jargon of today, we would without hesitation say "human information-processing capacities."

Yet it is this subtle division between the physical and the psychological sciences that has led to innumerable textbook treatments of Wundt as a mind-body dualist, and that is one of history's glaring distortions. For if you read Wundt, in almost any of his texts, you will discover that his rejection of mind-body dualism is as emphatic a statement on the matter as you are likely ever to encounter. He often said that psychology cannot be defined as the science of the mind because there are no objects called "minds" that are distinct from objects called "bodies," a scenario that appears repeatedly in his works.

Although physiologists and psychologists study one and the same organism, Wundt viewed them as analyzing and objectifying different experiences derived from different vantage points. This is now usually called the "double-aspect" resolution of the mind-body problem. And Wundt's use of the phrase "psychophysical parallelism" referred to this same view, though again it unfortunately led many later reviewers to the mind-body–dualism interpretation. Rather, it referred to the separate orientations of physiology and psychology where it is separate *methodologies,* in the sense of separate types of observations, that here run in parallel.

Another serious problem of misinterpretation concerns Wundt and *introspection.* Contrary to frequent descriptions, Wundt was not an introspectionist as that term is popularly applied today. The thrust behind his entire experimental program was the claim that progress in psychology had been slow because of reliance on casual, unsystematic introspection, which had led invariably to unresolvable debates. In several books and monographs (in particular, 1888 and 1907) Wundt argued that armchair introspection could, in principle, never succeed, being a logical impossibility as a scientific technique. The 1907 monograph was a severe critique of the Würzburg psychologists for their return to an earlier style of unverifiable introspection.

Wundt promoted the cause of experimental psychology more through accomplishments in his laboratory than through polemics. From its outset, the Wundtian program followed the general conceptions of experimental science and the requirement that private experience be made public and replicable, in this case for the study of perception, attention, memory, etc. To be sure, there were some disagreements, conflicting data, and unsupported speculations in those days, just as there are today.

Wundt's adherence to the canons of experimental procedure was so strict that, in fact, it sharply limited his use of experiments in psychology. Thus, in the case of most "higher" mental processes such as language or concept formation, he felt that true experiments were not feasible. Instead, these topics must, he argued, be studied through techniques of historical and naturalistic

observation and also of logical analysis. This Wundt did by examining the social-cultural products of human mental activity, making logical inferences about the underlying processes. In the case of language, for example, he went deeply into the technical study of linguistics (Blumenthal, 1970). So in these ways, a large part of Wundt's psychological work is not experimental.

WUNDT'S THEORETICAL SYSTEM

But so far these are methodological matters and do not speak to the essence of Wundt's psychological theory. What emerged as the paradigm psychological phenomenon in his theoretical system would now be described as selective volitional attention. It is why he identified his psychology as "voluntaristic" to distinguish it from other schools (see especially Wundt, 1896b). He did not use the label "structuralist" which was proffered and perpetuated by Titchener and James.

Mischel (1970) has recently surveyed Wundt's writings, detailing Wundt's grounding in volitional-motivational processes. Yet it was with apparent forceful impact on later historical interpretation that Titchener (1908) had given short shrift to this theme, at the very heart of Wundtian psychology, because of the overtones of continental idealist philosophy in notions of volition. Titchener's longest period of formal education came at Oxford, and not surprisingly he maintained certain biases toward the British empiricist-sensationist tradition, even though that tradition was anathema to Wundt's views, and more than any other topic the brunt of Wundt's polemical writings.

Without giving supportive citation, Boring (1950) states that Wundt had opposed the implication of an active volitional agent in psychology. But now Mischel (1970) with extensive citation has shown, on the contrary, that volition-motivation is a central, primary theme in Wundt's psychology. Briefly, that theme runs as follows: To explain a volitional act on the basis of its motives is different from the explanation of occurrences in the physical sciences, and "volitional activities are the type in terms of which all other psychological phenomena are to be construed" (Wundt, 1908, Vol. 3, p. 162).

Wundt's studies of volition, in turn, amounted to an elaborate analysis of selective and constructive attentional processes (often summarized under the term *apperception*), which he localized in the brain's frontal lobes. Other psychological processes (perceptions, thoughts, memories) are, according to Wundt, generally under the control of the central attentional process.

It is on this basis that Wundt claimed another point of separation between psychology and physics—a difference between psychological and physical causality (see especially, Wundt, 1894). In the case of physics, actions and events obey inviolable laws; but in the case of psychosocial phenomena, actions are *made* by an active agent with reference to rule systems.

Wundt acknowledged the principle of the conservation of energy and, consequently, the theoretical possibility of reducing psychological observations to physiological or physical descriptions. Still, he argued, these physical sciences would then describe the act of greeting a friend, eating an apple, or writing a poem in terms of the laws of mechanics or in terms of physiology. And no matter how fine-grained and complicated we make such descriptions, they are not useful as descriptions of psychological events. Those events need be described in terms of intentions and goals, according to Wundt, because the actions, or physical forces, for a given psychological event may take an infinite variety of physical forms. In one notable example, he argued that human language cannot be described adequately in terms of its physical shape or of the segmentation of utterances, but rather must be described as well in terms of the rules and intentions underlying speech. For the ways of expressing a thought in language are infinitely variable, and language is governed by creative rules rather than fixed laws (Wundt, 1900–1920).

MECHANISM OR ORGANISM?

These distinctions lead to a related and consistent theme in Wundt's writings concerning what he called "the false materialization of mental processes," which he found prevalent in other schools of psychology, especially associationism. His reactions against associationism were directed mostly at the form it had assumed in mid-19th-century Germany in Herbart's psychology.

Herbart, you may recall, had atomized mental processes into elemental ideas that became associated into compounds according to classical associationist descriptions. Wundt considered that approach to be a mere primitive analogy to systems of physical mechanics, and he argued at length that those systems teach little about the interrelations of psychological processes (Wundt, 1894). For those systems were oblivious to what he felt was the essential distinction between psychological and physical causality; they portrayed mental processes as if they were a "mere field of billiard balls" colliding and interacting with each other, where central control processes are lacking.

Boring's widely repeated assertion that Wundt turned to chemistry for his model seems clearly inaccurate to the serious reader of Wundt. However, the Wundtian mental-chemistry cliché did become popular among later textbook writers. Wundt did in his early years make brief, passing references to J. S. Mill's use of a chemical analogy to describe certain perceptual processes, namely, that one cannot determine the quality of water (i.e., "wetness") from the separate qualities of oxygen and hydrogen. Similarly, the qualities of a perception are not directly given in its underlying elements.

But Wundt points out that this analogy does not go far enough, and by the end of the century he is describing it as a false analogy because the chemical synthesis is, in the final analysis, wholly determined by its elements while the psychological synthesis is "truly a new formation, not

merely the result of a chemical-like formation."
And, "J. S. Mill's discussion in which the mental formation is conceived as a 'psychic chemistry' leaves out its most significant aspect—the special creative character of psychic syntheses" (Wundt, 1902, p. 684). What the chemical analogy lacks is the independent, constructive, attentional process which in the psychological case is the source of the synthesis.

Wundt did, of course, write chapters on elementary sensory-perceptual processes and elemental affective processes, but with the emphasis on *process*. And he acknowledged that a major part of any scientific methodology involved analysis of a system into component processes. Further, he stressed that these elements were to be taken as hypothetical constructs. Such elemental processes would never actually be observed, he thought, in pure isolation but would always be aspects or features of larger images or configurations.

Here Wundt used the German word *Gebilde*. For a translation, the dictionary (*Cassell's*) gives us the following choices: either "creation," "product," "structure," "formation," "system," "organization," "image," "form," or "figure." But in the few English translations of Wundt, we find the word "compound," unfortunately again suggesting the analogy to chemistry. "Compound" is a conceivable choice, but in the context of Wundt's configurational system it seems not the best term. Another example: Wundt's "whole or unified mental impression" (*Gesamtvorstellung*) is unfortunately translated as "aggregate ideas."

In the following note in an obscure book, published in 1944, Wundt's own son, Max Wundt, rebutted the caricature of his father's work as a psychology of mental elements:

> One may follow the methodologically obvious principle of advancing from the simple to the complicated, indeed even employing the approach that would construct the mind from primitive mechanical elements (the so-called psychology of mental elements). In this case, however, method and phenomena can become grossly confused.... Whoever in particular ascribes to my father such a conception could not have read his books. In fact, he had formed his scientific views of mental processes in reaction against a true elementistic psychology, namely against that of Herbart, which was dominant in those days. (p. 15)

To confound matters further, the later movement toward holism in Gestalt psychology placed Wundt in a contrastive position and again portrayed him as an elementalist and associationist in ways not characteristic of his intentions. True, there is always a chapter titled "Associations" in Wundt's texts—but it is a far cry from the serial linkages of atomistic ideas found among many associationists. Wundt's "associations" are "structural integrations," "creative syntheses," "fusions," and "perceptual patternings."

Wundt's later students, including Sander, Krueger, and Volkelt, renamed their school *Ganzheit* psychology or roughly "holistic psychology," and throughout the 1920s and 1930s the old Wundtian institute at Leipzig was a center for theorists with a holistic bent. Wundt's journal, the *Psychologische Studien,* which had ceased publication upon his retirement, was then reactivated with the title, *Neue Psychologische Studien*. It was the central organ of the *Ganzheit* psychologists; however, its articles primarily followed Wundt's interests in the "higher" mental processes and hence were mostly nonexperimental investigations.

Werner (1948) has written that Wundt represented the halfway mark in the transition from Herbart's atomism to the Gestaltist's holism. But from the point of view of Wundt's voluntaristic psychology, the essential central control processes were of no more primacy to the Gestaltists than to Herbart—both conceived a rather passive organism, one that is controlled by external or independent forces such as the a priori self-organizing qualities of sensory fields. Both, in sharp contrast to Wundt, appealed to physics for models and theories.

MODERN RECONSTRUCTIONS

Now to describe Wundt's psychology in more detail, and to consider its present relevance, I want to outline some six current trends that could be viewed as reconstructions of Wundtian psychology in modern clothing:

First, Wundt's central emphasis on volitional processes bears noteworthy resemblance to the modern work on "cognitive control" as found, for example, in extensive research by Gardner, Klein, Holzman, and their associates (cf. Gardner, Holzman, Klein, Linton, & Spence, 1959). Both traditions used notions of different styles of attention deployment to explain a variety of perceptual and thought processes (sometimes even involving the same materials, e.g., the Müller-Lyer illusion).

The recent research, employing factor analyses of a variety of performance tasks, has determined two independent variables of cognitive control, which Gardner et al. call "field-articulation" and "scanning." These can be defined, as well, simply by substituting a similar description found in Wundt's psychology texts, as follows: First, in corresponding order, is Wundt's mental "clearness" process that concerns the focusing or emphasizing of a single item of experience. Wundt described this as "apperceptive synthesis" where variations from broad to narrow syntheses may occur. The second variable is a mental "distinctiveness" process which is the marking off of an item of experience from all others. Wundt described this as "apperceptive analysis," a relating and comparing function. The discovery and testing of nearly identical attention deployment factors in recent times occurred independently of the old Wundtian psychology. And too, the recent studies make frequent use of elaborate personality theories that were unavailable to Wundt.

Second, detailed comparisons have been made recently between the development of psycholinguistics in the 1960s and that of Wundtian psycholinguistics at the turn of the century (Blumenthal, 1970). Both the modern transformational grammarians after Chomsky and the Wundtian psycholinguists at the turn of the century trace their notions of language back to the same historical sources (e.g., to Humboldt). The psycholinguistic issues debated in the 1960s often parallel those debated at the turn of the century, such as the opposition between taxonomic and generative descriptions of language. Very briefly, Wundt's analysis of language usage depicts the transformation of simultaneous configurations of thought into sequential representations in language symbols by means of the scanning activities of attention (Wundt, 1900–1920, Vol. 1).

A *third* reconstruction concerns abnormal psychology. Among his students, the one who maintained the longest intellectual association with Wundt was the psychiatrist Emil Kraepelin (see Fischel, 1959). Kraepelin's (1919) attentional theory of schizophrenia is an application of Wundtian psychology, an explanation of schizophrenias as abnormalities of the attention deployment (apperception) process. It conceives certain abnormalities of behavior as resulting from flaws in the central control process that may take the form of either highly reduced attentional scanning, or highly erratic scanning, or extremes of attentional focusing. Kraepelin proposed that abnormalities in simple perceptual tests should show up in schizophrenic individuals corresponding to these particular control-process distortions.

The modern attentional theory of schizophrenia is a direct revival of the Kraepelinian analysis, as noted, for example, in an extensive review by Silverman (1964). As in the Kraepelinian descriptions, abnormalities of behavior result from disruptions of the central attentional processes where there is either highly reduced or highly erratic attentional scanning and focusing. And these mental changes, again, are indicated by divergent performances in simple perceptual tests.

Fourth is Wundt's three-factor theory of affect, which was developed by analogy to his formulations of multidimensional descriptions of certain areas of sensory experience. For the description of emotional experience, he used these three bipolar affective dimensions: *pleasant versus unpleasant, high arousal versus low arousal,* and *concentrated attention versus relaxed attention.* Wundt had adopted the first two dimensions from earlier writers on the topic of emotion. The third dimension reflects his characteristic emphasis on the process of attention.

Around the turn of the century, an intensive sequence of investigations to relate these dimensions to unique bodily response patterns did not meet with popular success. However, years later, when factor analysis became available, statistical studies of affective and attitudinal behavior again yielded factors that parallel those of Wundt rather closely (cf. Burt, 1950; Osgood, Suci, & Tannenbaum, 1957; Schlosberg, 1954; and several others reviewed by Strongman, 1973). Osgood's three dimensions are described as "good-bad," "active-passive," and "strong-weak." Schlosberg's dimensions are "pleasantness-unpleasantness," "high-low activation," and "attention-rejection."

Emotions and affects held an important place in Wundt's system because they were postulated as the constituents of volition. Further, Wundt suggested that almost every experience (perception, thought, or memory) has an affective component. Thus, affect became the basis for his explanation of pattern recognition: a melody, for instance, produces a very similar emotional configuration as it is transformed to other keys or played on other instruments. Wundt speculated that affect was the by-product of the act of apperceptive synthesis, and as such it was always on the periphery of consciousness. That is, we can never focus our attention upon an emotion, but can only focus on objects or memories that produce an emotional aura in immediate experience.

Fifth, the study of selective attention has been at the core of much of the recent work on human information processing (e.g., Broadbent, 1958; Kahneman, 1973; Moray, 1970; Neisser, 1967). It is impossible here to relate this highly complex

field to the early Wundtian psychology other than to note the prominence of attention in both and that the time variable is central to both. Space permits mention of only two examples:

The seminal investigations of Sperling (1960) concerning perceptual masking are one example. Sperling took direct inspiration from Wundt's 1899 monograph on the use of tachistoscopes in psychological research in which Wundt came to the following three conclusions about the perception of extremely brief stimuli: (1) the effective duration of a percept is not identical with the duration of the stimulus—but rather reflects the duration of a psychological process; (2) the relation between accuracy of a perception and stimulus duration depends on pre- and postexposure fields (which may induce what we now call masking); and (3) central processes, rather than peripheral sense organ aftereffects, determine these critical times. Wundt's observations spurred a body of early research, and those early data are now relevant to a large body of similar modern investigations.

Perhaps the most frequently employed technique in Wundt's laboratory was that of reaction-time measurement. This was the direct adoption of a program suggested earlier by Donders (1868–1869). Essentially, inferences were made about human information-processing capacities on the basis of measured performance times under systematically varied performance conditions. This program has now, in post-mid-20th century, been widely and successfully revived. It is well illustrated, for instance, in the seminal studies of Sternberg (1970) on the attentional scanning of immediate-memory images, in which Sternberg draws the relation between his work and the earlier Donders program.

For a *sixth* and final comparison, I must refer to what Wundt called his deepest interest, which resulted in a 10-volume work titled *Völkerpsychologie: Eine Untersuchung der Entwicklungsgestze von Sprache, Mythus, und Sitte.* An English version of this title could be *Cultural Psychology: An Investigation of the Developmental Laws of Lan-*

*guage, Myth, and Morality.** Appearing from 1900 through 1920, this series contains two books on language, three on myth and religion, one on art, two on society, one on law, and one on culture and history. If there is a current work by another author that is conceptually close to these volumes, it is Werner's (1948) *Comparative Psychology of Mental Development,* today read in some circles of developmental psychologists.

Following Wundt, Werner described an *organismic* psychology that is in opposition to *mechanistic* psychologies. He also drew parallels, as did Wundt, between the development of individuals and of societies. And Werner acknowledged indebtedness to Wundt. But in Wundt's *Völkerpsychologie* there is, again, greater emphasis on volitional and attentional processes in the analysis of the development of human culture; he theorized that those central mental processes had emerged as the highest evolutionary development, and that they are the capacities that set men above other animals. It is the highly developed selective-attention capacities that, as he claimed, enabled mankind to make a consistent mental advance and to develop human culture. For without these capacities, men would forever be at the mercy of sporadic thoughts, memories, and perceptions.

WUNDT'S HISTORICAL CONTEXTS

Wundt was not a mere encyclopedist or compiler of volumes, contrary to many descriptions. It was typical of him, however, always to compare and to contrast his system with other schools of thought, ancient and modern. Perhaps in that

---

* *Völkerpsychologie* has also been translated as "folk psychology," "psychology of peoples," and "ethnic psychology." Wundt quite deliberately avoided the terms *sociology* and *anthropology* because they were then heavily identified with the mid-19th-century positivism of Auguste Comte and related Anglo-French trends, which Wundt opposed. Some later writers on the history of psychology erroneously stated that the *Völkerpsychologie* is available in English translation. They apparently mistook a different and simpler one-volume work that E. Schaub (1916) translated as *Elements of Folk Psychology*.

sense he could be considered an encyclopedist. True, most of his works begin with a long recital of his antecedents and the antecedents of rival positions.

Wundt's motivation for scholarly productivity should not be surprising, considering the strong family traditions that lay behind him (and that went unrecognized by most historical writers). Recent researchers (Bringmann et al., 1975) claim that no other German intellectual has a family tree containing as many ancestors engaged in intellectual pursuits. On his father's side were historians, theologians, economists, and geographers. On his mother's side were natural scientists and physicians. Two of his ancestors had been rectors of the University of Heidelberg.

To conclude, I wish to draw an outline of the streams of history in which Wundt lived and worked. Historians have often defined a few broad, alternating cultural epochs in the 19th century. At some risk in using a much-abused word, one might call each a "zeitgeist"—a time that favored a particular cultural style. These periods begin with the dominant romanticism and idealism early in the century, largely a German-inspired ethos shared by Kant, Humboldt, Schopenhauer, Goethe, Hegel, and Fichte, to mention a few. In that era, philosophy, science, religion, and art were often combined into something called "nature-philosophy." Such an integration was exemplified in the pantheistic writings of Gustav Fechner, an exotic latecomer to the romantic movement and an important source of inspiration for Wundt. (In several ways, Wundt's 10-volume *Völkerpsychologie* reflects the spirit of the old nature-philosophy.)

Around the mid-19th century, a positivist and materialist movement grew dominant by vigorously rejecting the previous idealism. There then appeared the influential Berlin Physical Society, the mechanistic psychology of Herbart, the behavioristic linguistics of the so-called *Junggrammatiker* linguists, and Comtean positivist sociology, among other examples across the disciplines. At the peak of this movement, academicians became methodology conscious to the extreme. The taxonomic methods of biology were imported into the social sciences. There was often a downgrading of "mentalism" in favor of "physicalism" and "environmentalism."

Then, toward the end of the 19th century came a resurgence of the romanticist-idealist outlook, particularly in continental Europe. It has been described either as neoromanticism, neoidealism, or neo-Kantianism. H. Stuart Hughes (1958) has provided a summarization in his influential book, *Consciousness and Society: The Reorientation of European Social Thought, 1890–1930*. At around the time of World War I, this movement went into sharp decline, being displaced by a rebirth and rise in popularity of positivism and behaviorism which subsequently dominated many intellectual circles well into the 20th century.

Wundt's psychology rose and fell with the late-19th-century neoidealism. His core emphasis on volition and apperception comes straight from the earlier German idealist philosophy. It is not surprising that this should be so, for as a youth he was deeply inspired by the romanticist-idealist literature and nature-philosophy (Wundt, 1920). Certainly his intellectual development also included the influence of mid-19th-century positivism, especially in his promotion of experimental psychology. Yet, during that positivist period, he had remained largely unrecognized as a psychological theorist. The popular success of his theoretical system seems coordinated with the beginnings of neoidealist reorientations, and his system became fully formed in the *Grundriss* of 1896 (and later editions; Wundt, 1896a).

But unfortunately for Wundt, zeitgeist support disappeared rapidly in the early 20th century; definitions of psychology were then changing, and his works were soon meaningless to a newer generation. Few, especially outside Germany, understood any more what the old term *apperception* had once referred to.

Strange as it may seem, Wundt may be more easily understood today than he could have been just a few years ago. This is because of the current milieu of modern cognitive psychology and of the recent research on human information processing. Yet this new understanding does require serious study of Wundt in the original German. Most current textbook summaries of Wundt grew out of a time when early behaviorist and positivist movements were eager to encourage a break with the past, hence giving understandably little effort to careful description of the enormous body of writings they were discarding. Simplistic historical accounts resulted.

Today much of the history of Wundt remains to be told, both of his personal development and of his psychological system. It is well worth telling.

REFERENCES

Blumenthal, A. L. *Language and psychology: Historical aspects of psycholinguistics.* New York: Wiley, 1970.

Boring, E. G. *A history of experimental psychology.* New York: Appleton-Century-Crofts, 1950.

Bringmann, W. G., Balance, W., & Evans, R. B. Wilhelm Wundt 1832–1920: A biographical sketch. *Journal of the History of the Behavioral Sciences,* 1975, *11,* 287–297.

Broadbent, D. *Perception and communication.* New York: Pergamon, 1958.

Burt, C. The factorial study of emotions. In M. Reymert (Ed.), *Feelings and emotions.* New York: McGraw-Hill, 1950.

Donders, F. Over de snelheid van psychische processen. *Tweede Reeks,* 1868–1869, II, 92–120. (Trans. by W. Koster as On the speed of mental processes, In *Acta Psychologica,* 1969, *30,* 412–431.)

Fischel, W. Wilhelm Wundt und Emil Kraepelin. *Karl Marx Universität Leipzig, Beiträge zur Universität Geschichte,* 1959, *1.*

Gardner, R. W., Holzman, P. S., Klein, G. S., Linton, H., & Spence, D. P. Cognitive control: A study of individual consistencies in cognitive behavior. *Psychological Issues,* 1959, Monograph 4.

Hughes, H. S. *Consciousness and society: The reorientation of European social thought, 1890–1930.* New York: Knopf, 1958.

Kahneman, D. *Attention and effort*. Englewood Cliffs, N.J.: Prentice-Hall, 1973.

Kraepelin, E. *Dementia praecox and paraphrenia* (Trans. by M. Barclay from selected writings of Kraepelin). Chicago, Ill.: Chicago Medical Book, 1919.

Mischel, T. Wundt and the conceptual foundations of psychology. *Philosophical and Phenomenological Research*, 1970, *31*, 1–26.

Moray, N. *Attention*. New York: Academic Press, 1970.

Neisser, U. *Cognitive psychology*. New York: Appleton-Century-Crofts, 1967.

Osgood, C., Suci, G., & Tannenbaum, P. *The measurement of meaning*. Urbana: University of Illinois Press, 1957.

Schlosberg, H. Three dimensions of emotion. *Psychological Review*, 1954, *61*, 81–88.

Silverman, J. The problem of attention in research and theory in schizophrenia. *Psychological Review*, 1964, *71*, 352–379.

Sperling, G. The information available in brief visual presentations. *Psychological Monographs*, 1960, *74* (11, Whole No. 498).

Sternberg, S. Memory-scanning: Mental processes revealed by reaction-time experiments. In J. Antrobus (Ed.), *Cognition and affect*. Boston, Mass.: Little, Brown, 1970.

Strongman, K. T. *The psychology of emotion*. New York: Wiley, 1973.

Titchener, E. B. *The psychology of feeling and attention*. New York: Macmillan, 1908.

Werner, H. *The comparative psychology of mental development*. New York: Science Editions, 1948.

Wundt, M. *Die Wurzeln der deutschen Philosphie in Stamm und Rasse*. Berlin: Junker und Dunnhaupt, 1944.

Wundt, W. Selbstbeobachtung und innere Wahrnehmung. *Philosophische Studien*, 1888, *4*, 292–309.

Wundt, W. Ueber psychische Kausalität und das Prinzip des psychophysichen Parallelismus. *Philosophische Studien*, 1894, *10*, 1–124.

Wundt, W. *Grundriss der Psychologie*. Leipzig: Engelmann, 1896 (10th ed., 1911). (Trans. by C. Judd of 1896 and 1907 editions as *Outlines of psychology*.) (a)

Wundt, W. Ueber die Definition der Psychologie. *Philosophische Studien*, 1896, *12*, 1–66. (b)

Wundt, W. Zur Kritik tachistokopischer Versuche. *Philosophische Studien*, 1899, *15*, 287–317.

Wundt, W. *Völkerpsychologie: Eine Untersuchung der Entwicklungsgesetze von Sprache, Mythus, und Sitte* (10 vols.). Leipzig: Engelmann, 1900–1920.

Wundt, W. *Grundzüge der physiologischen Psychologie* (Vol. 2). Leipzig: Engelmann, 1902 (5th ed.).

Wundt, W. Ueber Ausfrageexperimente und ueber Methoden zur Psychologie des Denkens. *Psychologische Studien*, 1907, *3*, 301–360.

Wundt, W. *Logik* (3 vols.). Leipzig: Engelmann, 1908.

Wundt, W. *Erlebtes und Erkanntes*. Stuttgart: Krohner, 1920.

The Echoes of Wundt's Work in the United States, 1887–1977: A Quantitative Citation Analysis

Josef Brožek

INTRODUCTION

The present study was born in the context of the anticipated celebrations of the centennial of 'scientific' psychology, officially set for 1979–1980. However, its aim was (and is) to contribute new factual

Brožek, J. (1980). The echoes of Wundt's work in the United States, 1887–1977: A quantitative citation analysis. *Psychological Research, 42*, 103–107. Copyright © 1980 by Springer-Verlag. Reprinted by permission of the publisher.

information, not to join the chorus of Wundt's admirers or critics. The information presented here is quantitative in character and will be supplemented by a qualitative analysis of the context in which Wundt's works were being cited. In regard to methodology (cf. Woodward 1980, section on quantitative history), the present study is a continuation of the earlier analyses of the reverberations of F.C. Donders' 1868 paper on the rapidity of mental processes (Brožek 1970), and of translations of psychological publications into the languages of Yugoslavia, examined as an indicator of the politico-cultural 'climate' (Brožek 1972).

The initial aim of this study was to characterize, quantitatively, the changes over time in the frequency of citation of Wundt's works in an American psychological journal with a long, uninterrupted publication record. As it turned out, several other issues could be treated quantitatively: The 'rank of merit' of Wundt's book length publications; citation of the original editions versus the translations of Wundt's books; citation of individual editions of books published in more than one edition; and citation of Wundt's journal articles. The present report will be limited to the first two topics, i.e., the decline in Wundt's impact on American psychology, and the relative 'weight' of Wundt's individual publications. A more comprehensive, detailed, and thoroughly documented account is being published elsewhere (Brožek 1980).

PROCEDURES

Notes on the author, title, the volume and page on which a reference was made to Wundt, and the context in which this was done constituted the 'raw material' for this study. The information was collected by perusing, page by page, the first 90 volumes of the *American Journal of Psychology*.

It became readily apparent that the material was heterogenous and that for the purpose of analysis relatively homogenous sub-samples had to be defined. First, book notes and book reviews, including reviews of Wundt's works, although interesting in their own right, were set aside. This was also true of a rare article by a non-American; a series of papers constituting a manual for a laboratory course in physiological psychology; articles on terminology; articles specifically devoted to Wundt; specialized bibliographies including Wundt's works; biographies and obituaries; mentions of Wundt in numerous briefer necrologues; theoretico-historical articles; discussions of Wundt's ideas, at times lengthy, and containing

a plethora of citations dealing with apperception, attention, creative synthesis, history of reflex action, space perception, and the three-dimensional theory of feeling; allusions to Wundt in the text without citation of a specific reference; Wundt's works listed in bibliographies appended to a paper without page citation and/or not referred to specifically in the text or footnotes.

WUNDT'S FAME: THE RATE OF DECAY

In defining the sub-sample used in the study of the trend in the citation frequency of Wundt's publications, additional restrictions were imposed. To begin with, only papers reporting experimental studies were considered. Not without some hesitation, a few papers dealing with apparatus and a rare paper which was observational but not experimental were omitted. In addition, we excluded citations repeated in the same article and bearing on the same issue, and Wundt's works cited solely as a source of information about studies performed by other investigators.

The citation frequencies of Wundt's works in the experimental papers published in the first 90 volumes of the *American Journal of Psychology* are indicated in Table 1. The frequencies are given for each 10 and 30 volumes. For the 30-volume intervals the frequencies are expressed in percentages as well.

When the total span of time is considered, the citation frequencies (column 2) obtained for the nine 10-volume intervals show a distinct decrease. The slight upturn in the interval between the 81st and 90th volume reflects, for the most part, an increased interest of American psychologists in the psychology of language.

The decline of Wundt's glory is seen clearly when the citation frequencies are cumulated over larger segments of time. Of the total number of citations in the specified sample (N=130), 72.3 percent were cited in the first 30 volumes, 20.0 percent in the next 30 volumes, and 7.7 percent in the last 30 volumes.

Table 1.
Citations of Wundt's books in experimental papers published in the *American Journal of Psychology* in the years 1887–1977, by 10 and 30 volumes

Volumes	f_{10}	Volumes	f	Percentage	f_{10}
1–10	31	1–30	94	72.3	31.3
11–20	25				
21–30	38				
31–40	11	31–60	26	20.0	8.7
41–50	11				
51–60	4				
61–70	1	61–90	10	7.7	3.3
71–80	3				
81–90	6				
	130			100%	

f_{10} = average frequency for 10-volume intervals.

Column 2 of Table 1 indicates that the frequencies are fairly uniform over substantial periods of time. Consequently, the changes in citation frequencies may be viewed as discontinuous, i.e., as changes in 'level.' These levels are represented in the last column of Table 1 by the average citation frequencies for 10-volume intervals, calculated for volumes 1–30, 31–60, and 61–90.

THE RELATIVE SIGNIFICANCE OF WUNDT'S BOOK-LENGTH PUBLICATIONS

Combining experimental and non-experimental articles published in the *American Journal of Psychology* over a period of 90 years, we obtain a total of 231 citations of Wundt's books. The breakdown is indicated in Table 2. The last column of the table expresses the frequency of citation of a given work as a percentage of the total number of book citations.

The most widely cited work, by far, is Wundt's *The Principles of Physiological Psychology (Grundzüge der physiologischen Psychologie)*, accounting for 61.1 percent of all the citations of Wundt's books. The citation analysis clearly brings out that the *Grundzüge* has been Wundt's bestseller! This is no surprise, yet the citation analysis yields informative, quantitative 'weight' factors. By con-

Table 2.
Wundt's books, original and translated into English, cited in experimental and non-experimental articles published in the *American Journal of Psychology*, 1887–1977.

Abbreviated titles	N	Percentage
Grundzüge[1]	141	61.1
Vorlesungen[2]	34	14.7
Grundriss[3]	16	6.9
Völkerpsychologie	8	3.5
Beiträge[4]	7	3.0
Einführung[5]	6	2.6
Essays	5	2.2
Logik	5	2.2
Kleine Schriften	4	1.7
Elemente[6]	3	1.3
Ethik	1	0.4
Fechner[7]	1	0.4
Total	231	100.0

[1] Grundzüge der physiologischen Psychologie (Principles of Physiological Psychology)
[2] Vorlesungen über die Menschen- und Tierseele (Lectures on Human and Animal Psychology)
[3] Grundriss der Psychologie (Outlines of Psychology)
[4] Beiträge zur Theorie der Sinneswahrnehmung (Contributions to the Theory of Sensory Perception)
[5] Einführung in die Psychologie (An Introduction to Psychology)
[6] Elemente der Völkerpsychologie (Elements of Folk Psychology)
[7] Gustav Theodor Fechner: Rede zur Feier seines 100-jährigen Geburtstages

trast, the 10 volumes of *Völkerpsychologie* (3.5 percent) have had little echo in American psychology, as judged from the sample of the journal literature covering a period of 90 years.

Long after the *Grundzüge* come the long-lived *Lectures on Human and Animal Psychology*, with 14.7 percent, followed by the *Outlines of Psychology (Grundriss der Psychologie)* with 6.9 percent of the citations.

The remaining publications, noted in Table 2, are cited with low frequencies. The percentages range from 3.5 down to 0.4.

SYNOPSIS

As is true of all the historiographic methods, citation analysis has its advantages and its limitations. In the present study we have used this approach to examine the changes in citation rates and the relative importance of Wundt's book-length publications. Data on the citations of individual editions when more than one edition of a given work were available, as well as citations of the original German versions and the American translations, will be presented elsewhere (Brožek 1980). In contrast to the books, the citation frequency of Wundt's journal articles has been very low. For the purpose of these analyses citation data have been pooled across a period of 90 years.

The *Grundzüge der physiologischen Psychologie* was by far the most frequently cited work. In contrast, the *Völkerpsychologie* fared poorly.

Citation analysis is particularly informative when we are concerned with an objective assessment of changes over time. The data have indicated clearly a distinct decline of Wilhelm Wundt's impact on American psychology, with 72.3 percent of citations in experimental papers falling into the first 30 volumes, 20.0 percent into the middle 30 volumes, and 7.7 percent into the last 30 volumes of the *American Journal of Psychology*.

REFERENCES

Brožek, J. (1970) Citation 'longevity' as criterion of significance: F.C. Donders (1868) and the timing of mental operations. Proc. 78th Annu. Conv. APA 787–788.

Brožek, J. (1972) Quantitative explorations in the history of psychology in Yugoslavia: Translations. Psychol. Rep. 31:397–398.

Brožek, J. (1980) Wundt in America. In: Brožek, J., Pongratz, L.J. (eds.) Contemporary historiography of psychology. Toronto: C. J. Hogrefe.

Donders, F. C. (1868) Die Schnelligkeit psychischer Prozesse. Arch. Anat. Physiol. wiss. Med. 6:657–681.

Woodward, W.R. (1980) Toward a critical historiography of psychology. In: Brožek, J., Pongratz, L.J. (eds.) Contemporary historiography of psychology. Toronto: C. J. Hogrefe.

CHAPTER 8

E. B. TITCHENER AND STRUCTURALISM

The previous chapter noted that nearly a quarter of Wundt's doctoral students in psychology were from North America. These psychologists returned to transform American psychology from philosophical discourse to an experimental science, and they did so by founding psychology laboratories at the University of Pennsylvania (1887), University of Nebraska (1889), Columbia University (1890), Catholic University (1891), Cornell University (1891), Harvard University (1891), Yale University (1892), Stanford University (1893), University of Minnesota (1894), Smith College (1895), University of California (1896), Wesleyan University (1897), New York University (1900), and Northwestern University (1900). Although these new laboratories were founded by Wundt's students, who used the various scientific methods they had learned in their study at Leipzig, the brand of psychology practiced at those universities was not readily identified with Wundt's conceptual position. Instead, a very narrow version of Wundtian psychology in the United States was largely, but not exclusively, represented in the psychology of his British student, Edward Bradford Titchener (1867–1927), who arrived at Cornell University in Ithaca, New York, in 1893.

The laboratory at Cornell had been founded two years earlier, as noted above, by another of Wundt's students, Frank Angell, who left after a year to begin a similar laboratory at Stanford University. Titchener began to build his laboratory in the Leipzig tradition and soon established himself as one of the foremost psychologists in the United States. In the thirty-five years of his professional career he wrote more than two hundred articles and books and trained more than fifty doctoral students in his brand of psychology. Many of those students would found laboratories of their own (for example, Margaret Floy

Washburn at Vassar College, and Walter B. Pillsbury at the University of Michigan).

Titchener would name his system of psychology *structuralism* because of its emphasis on discovering the elemental structure of consciousness. Conceptually, that focus of his system was similar to one of the goals of Wundtian psychology, although Wundt never used the label *structuralism* to refer to his psychology. Indeed, Wundt was not the atomist that most histories of psychology have described him to be (recall the selection from Wundt in the previous chapter and the article by Blumenthal in that same chapter). For the past sixty years, textbooks on the history of psychology have been treating the psychological systems of Wundt and Titchener as if they were the same (see Leahey, 1981), often discussing them together in a chapter entitled "Structuralism." Titchener may have contributed to that confusion, as some authors have suggested, by his selective translations of Wundt's writings. Indeed, most of the Wundt read by American psychologists in the early part of the twentieth century was the Wundt that was translated by Titchener and his colleagues.

Before he went to Leipzig, Titchener was schooled at Oxford University in the traditions of British associationism. His extremely reductionistic approach to the study of consciousness can be traced to those influences. In essence, his system of psychology represented only the bottom level of Wundtian psychology in a hierarchy that sought to explain mental processes fully. For Wundt, such explanation required an understanding of the processes of apperception and creative synthesis. He recognized that there was more to consciousness than an aggregate of sensory and emotional elements. The previous chapter includes some of Wundt's (1896) thoughts on these issues:

> The actual contents of psychical experience always consist of various combinations of sensational and affective elements, so that the specific character of a given psychical process depends for the most part, not on the nature of its elements, so much as on their union into a composite psychical compound. (p. 33)

Wundt studied psychical elements as part of his systematic approach to psychology, but he recognized the importance of higher-order processes and wrote much about their role in understanding consciousness. There is a more holistic nature to his system, a fact recognized by his students who succeeded him at Leipzig, who named their psychology *Ganzheit psychology,* roughly translated as holistic psychology. Do not misread these comments to mean that Wundt was a Gestalt psychologist (see Chapter 16). He was not; but his system had more in common with the Gestalt approach than has been traditionally believed.

As indicated earlier, Titchener defined his psychology in the narrowest of terms. He rejected child psychology, abnormal psychology, and any studies on animals. His experimental science was built largely on *introspection,* a technique that proved to be of little use in those areas of study. It was narrower still, in comparison to Wundt, because of Titchener's adherence to positivism, for he agreed with Auguste Comte that unobservable processes had no place in science. Whereas Wundt sought to explain consciousness by invoking some hypothetical mental processes, Titchener avoided the mentalistic dilemma by focusing his efforts on a purely descriptive science.

But American psychology was not satisfied with description. Influenced by the pragmatism of Charles S. Peirce and John Dewey, and the evolutionary ideas of Charles Darwin, many American psychologists were asking questions about the why of consciousness. As Rand B. Evans (1972) has described it, these other psychologists were interested in the questions of what consciousness *is for,* whereas Titchener was interested in what conscious *is.* It was this difference in approach that led Titchener to label the opposition's views as *functionalism* (see Chapter 11) because of its emphasis on the functions of consciousness, as contrasted to his emphasis on the structure of consciousness.

Cornell became the stronghold for this descriptive psychology, protecting its purity from the infidels that made up most of American psychology. Titchener's disagreements led him to abandon the American Psychological Association (founded in 1892), to which most of his colleagues belonged, and to form his own organization in 1904, usually referred to as "The Experimentalists" or "Titchener's Experimentalists" (see Boring, 1967). The annual meetings of this group were essentially by invitation only. It was another attempt by Titchener to deal with psychology exclusively on his own terms.

Few of Titchener's students became disciples, although many continued to espouse the appropriate ideas in his presence (E. G. Boring may have been his most loyal student.) When Titchener died of a brain tumor at age 60, structuralism died with him. His system of psychology is not a part of contemporary psychology; his many research articles, so carefully conceived and executed, are no longer cited in the literature. Current references to him are almost always of a historical nature. But these statements are not meant to imply that his legacy is nonexistent. He was a model scientist when psychology needed such models to break its bonds with philosophy. That contribution was manifested in several ways, but is nowhere more evident than in the success of Titchener's four volumes of *Experimental Psychology.*

Those books were published between 1901 and 1905. Two were for the psychology instructor and two for the student. Two volumes dealt with quantitative studies, and two focused on qualitative studies. Collectively they were known as "The Manuals" or "Titchener's Manuals." And they were used to train an entire generation of American psychology students, not just those at Cornell, in the methods of this new science. Titchener was an excellent scientist who modeled and communicated the integrity of scientific investigation better than any psychologist of his day. His manuals certainly rank among the most important books in the history of psychology. Oswald Külpe, a psychologist who frequently battled Titchener on theoretical grounds, called Titchener's *Experimental Psychology* "the most erudite psychological work in the English language" (Boring, 1950, p. 413).

The initial selection in this chapter is from Titchener's *Text-book of Psychology,* which he published in 1910. It begins with a discussion of Titchener's distinction between mind and consciousness and continues with a discussion of the method of psychology (introspection) and the scope of psychology.

The second selection is by Mary Henle, a historian of psychology and an authority on Gestalt psychology. It asks the question, "Did Titchener commit the stimulus error?" and analyzes the inconsistencies in Titchener's system related to his use of introspection. This article also speculates on some of the changes in Titchener as a psychologist in the last decade of his life—a period in which significant theoretical changes were under way in Titchener's thinking.

Those changes are described in the third selection by the historian of psychology Rand B. Evans, the acknowledged authority on Titchener. Drawing from correspondence and unpublished manuscripts, as well as from published sources, Evans builds a convincing case for Titchener's "lost system" that represented both conceptual and methodological changes from his earlier views.

There is much in the way of new scholarship in the history of psychology to help us recognize the similarities and differences in the systems of Titchener and Wundt. This chapter and the previous one are intended to portray this new knowledge.

REFERENCES

Boring, E. G. (1950). *A history of experimental psychology* (2d ed.). New York: Appleton-Century-Crofts.

Boring, E. G. (1967). Titchener's experimentalists. *Journal of the History of the Behavioral Sciences, 3,* 315–325.

Evans, R. B. (1972). E. B. Titchener and his lost system. *Journal of the History of the Behavioral Sciences, 8,* 168–180.

Leahey, T. H. (1981). The mistaken mirror: On Wundt's and Titchener's psychologies. *Journal of the History of the Behavioral Sciences, 17,* 273–282.

Wundt, W. (1896). *Outlines of psychology.* New York: Gustav Sechert.

The Method and Scope of Psychology

Edward Bradford Titchener

§ 5. MENTAL PROCESS, CONSCIOUSNESS AND MIND

The most striking fact about the world of human experience is the fact of change. Nothing stands still; everything goes on. The sun will someday lose its heat; the eternal hills are, little by little, breaking up and wearing away. Whatever we observe, and from whatever standpoint we observe it, we find process, occurrence; nowhere is there permanence or stability. Mankind, it is true, has sought to arrest this flux, and to give stability to the world of experience, by assuming two permanent substances, matter and mind: the occurrences of the physical world are then supposed to be manifestations of matter, and the occurrences of the mental world to be manifestations of mind. Such an hypothesis may be of value at a certain stage of human thought; but every hypothesis that does not accord with the facts must, sooner or later, be given up. Physicists are therefore giving up the hypothesis of an unchanging, substantial matter, and psychologists are giving up the hypothesis of an unchanging, substantial mind. Stable objects and substantial things belong, not to the world of science, physical or psychological, but only to the world of common sense.

We have defined mind as the sum-total of human experience considered as dependent upon the experiencing person. We have said, further, that the phrase 'experiencing person' means the living body, the organised individual; and we have hinted that, for psychological purposes, the living body may be reduced to the nervous system and its attachments. Mind thus becomes the sum-total of human experience considered as dependent upon a nervous system. And since hu-

man experience is always process, occurrence, and the dependent aspect of human experience is its mental aspect, we may say, more shortly, that mind is the sum-total of mental processes. All these words are significant. 'Sum total' implies that we are concerned with the whole world of experience, not with a limited portion of it; 'mental' implies that we are concerned with experience under its dependent aspect, as conditioned by a nervous system; and 'processes' implies that our subject-matter is a stream, a perpetual flux, and not a collection of unchanging objects.

It is not easy, even with the best will possible, to shift from the common-sense to the scientific view of mind; the change cannot be made all in a moment. We are to regard mind as a stream of processes? But mind is personal, my mind; and my personality continues throughout my life. The experiencing person is only the bodily organism? But, again, experience is personal, the experience of a permanent self. Mind is spatial, just as matter is? But mind is invisible, intangible; it is not here or there, square or round.

These objections cannot be finally met until we have gone some distance into psychology, and can see how the scientific view of mind works out. Even now, however, they will weaken as you look at them. Face that question of personality. Is your life, as a matter of fact, always personal? Do you not, time and again, forget yourself, lose yourself, disregard yourself, neglect yourself, contradict yourself, in a very literal sense? Surely, the mental life is only intermittently personal. And is your personality, when it is realised, unchanging? Are you the same self in childhood and manhood, in your working and in your playing moods, when you are on your best behaviour and when you are freed from restraint? Surely, the self-experience is not only intermittent, but also composed, at different times, of very different factors. As to the other question: mind is, of course, invisible, because sight is mind; and mind is intangible, because touch

From Titchener, E. B. (1910). *A textbook of psychology.* New York: Macmillan, pp. 15–30. Copyright © 1910 by Macmillan Publishing Company. Reprinted by permission of the publisher.

is mind. Sight-experience and touch-experience are dependent upon the experiencing person. But common sense itself bears witness, against its own belief, to the fact that mind is spatial: we speak, and speak correctly, of an idea in our head, a pain in our foot. And if the idea is the idea of a circle seen in the mind's eye, it is round; and if it is the visual idea of a square, it is square.

Consciousness, as reference to any dictionary will show, is a term that has many meanings. Here it is, perhaps, enough to distinguish two principal uses of the word.

In its first sense, consciousness means the mind's awareness of its own processes. Just as, from the common-sense point of view, mind is that inner self which thinks, remembers, chooses, reasons, directs the movements of the body, so is consciousness the inner knowledge of this thought and government. You are conscious of the correctness of your answer to an examination question, of the awkwardness of your movements, of the purity of your motives. Consciousness is thus something more than mind; it is "the perception of what passes in a man's own mind";[1] it is "the immediate knowledge which the mind has of its sensations and thoughts."[2]

In its second sense, consciousness is identified with mind, and 'conscious' with 'mental.' So long as mental processes are going on, consciousness is present; as soon as mental processes are in abeyance, unconsciousness sets in. "To say I am conscious of a feeling, is merely to say that I feel it. To have a feeling is to be conscious; and to be conscious is to have a feeling. To be conscious of the prick of the pin, is merely to have the sensation. And though I have these various modes of naming my sensation, by saying, I feel the prick of a pin, I feel the pain of a prick, I have the sensation of a prick, I have the feeling of a prick, I am conscious of the feeling; the thing named in all these various ways is one and the same."[3]

The first of these definitions we must reject. It is not only unnecessary, but it is also misleading, to speak of consciousness as the mind's awareness of itself. The usage is unnecessary, because, as we shall see later, this awareness is a matter of observation of the same general kind as observation of the external world; it is misleading, because it suggests that mind is a personal being, instead of a stream of processes. We shall therefore take mind and consciousness to mean the same thing. But as we have the two different words, and it is convenient to make some distinction between them, we shall speak of mind when we mean the sum-total of mental processes occurring in the life-time of an individual, and we shall speak of consciousness when we mean the sum-total of mental processes occurring *now*, at any given 'present' time. Consciousness will thus be a section, a division, of the mind-stream. This distinction is, indeed, already made in common speech: when we say that a man has 'lost consciousness,' we mean that the lapse is temporary, that the mental life will shortly be resumed; when we say that a man has 'lost his mind,' we mean—not, it is true, that mind has altogether disappeared, but certainly that the derangement is permanent and chronic.

While, therefore, the subject-matter of psychology is mind, the direct object of psychological study is always a consciousness. In strictness, we can never observe the same consciousness twice over; the stream of mind flows on, never to return. Practically, we can observe a particular consciousness as often as we wish, since mental processes group themselves in the same way, show the same pattern of arrangement, whenever the organism is placed under the same circumstances. Yesterday's high tide will never recur, and yesterday's consciousness will never recur; but we have a science of psychology, as we have a science of oceanography.

§ 6. THE METHOD OF PSYCHOLOGY

Scientific method may be summed up in the single word 'observation'; the only way to work in science is to observe those phenomena which form the subject-matter of science. And observation implies two things: attention to the phenomena, and record of the phenomena; that is, clear and vivid experience, and an account of the experience in words or formulas.

In order to secure clear experience and accurate report, science has recourse to experiment. An experiment is an observation that can be repeated, isolated and varied. The more frequently you can *repeat* an observation, the more likely are you to see clearly what is there and to describe accurately what you have seen. The more strictly you can *isolate* an observation, the easier does your task of observation become, and the less danger is there of your being led astray by irrelevant circumstances, or of placing emphasis on the wrong point. The more widely you can *vary* an observation, the more clearly will the uniformity of experience stand out, and the better is your chance of discovering laws. All experimental appliances, all laboratories and instruments, are provided and devised with this one end in view: that the student shall be able to repeat, isolate and vary his observations.

The method of psychology, then, is observation. To distinguish it from the observation of physical science, which is inspection, a looking-at, psychological observation has been termed introspection, a looking-within. But this difference of name must not blind us to the essential likeness of the methods. Let us take some typical instances.

We may begin with two very simple cases. (1) Suppose that you are shown two paper discs: the one of an uniform violet, the other composed half of red and half of blue. If this second disc is rapidly rotated, the red and blue will mix, as we say, and you will see a certain blue-red, that is, a kind of violet. Your problem is, so to adjust the proportions of red and blue in the second disc that the resulting violet exactly matches the violet of the first disc. You may repeat this set of observations as often as you like; you may isolate the observations by working in a room that is free from other, possibly disturbing colours; you may

vary the observations by working to equality of the violets first from a two-colour disc that is distinctly too blue, and secondly from a disc that is distinctly too red. (2) Suppose, again, that the chord c-e-g is struck, and that you are asked to say how many tones it contains. You may repeat this observation; you may isolate it, by working in a quiet room; you may vary it, by having the chord struck at different parts of the scale, in different octaves.

It is clear that, in these instances, there is practically no difference between introspection and inspection. You are using the same method that you would use for counting the swings of a pendulum, or taking readings from a galvanometer scale, in the physical laboratory. There is a difference in subject-matter: the colours and the tones are dependent, not independent experiences: but the method is essentially the same.

Now let us take some cases in which the material of introspection is more complex. (1) Suppose that a word is called out to you, and that you are asked to observe the effect which this stimulus produces upon consciousness: how the word affects you, what ideas it calls up, and so forth. The observation may be repeated; it may be isolated,—you may be seated in a dark and silent room, free from disturbances; and it may be varied,—different words may be called out, the word may be flashed upon a screen instead of spoken, etc. Here, however, there seems to be a difference between introspection and inspection. The observer who is watching the course of a chemical reaction, or the movements of some microscopical creature, can jot down from moment to moment the different phases of the observed phenomenon. But if you try to report the changes in consciousness, while these changes are in progress, you interfere with consciousness; your translation of the mental experience into words introduces new factors into that experience itself. (2) Suppose, again, that you are observing a feeling or an emotion: a feeling of disappointment or annoyance, an emotion of anger or chagrin. Experimental control is still possible; situations may be arranged, in the psychological laboratory, such that these feelings may be repeated, isolated and varied. But your observation of them interferes, even more seriously than before, with the course of consciousness. Cool consideration of an emotion is fatal to its very existence; your anger disappears, your disappointment evaporates, as you examine it.

To overcome this difficulty of the introspective method, students of psychology are usually recommended to delay their observation until the process to be described has run its course, and then to call it back and describe it from memory. Introspection thus becomes retrospection; introspective examination becomes *post mortem* examination. The rule is, no doubt, a good one for the beginner; and there are cases in which even the experienced psychologist will be wise to follow it. But it is by no means universal. For we must remember (*a*) that the observations in question may be repeated. There is, then, no reason why the observer to whom the word is called out, or in whom the emotion is set up, should not report at once upon the first stage of his experience: upon the immediate effect of the word, upon the beginnings of the emotive process. It is true that this report interrupts the observation. But, after the first stage has been accurately described, further observations may be taken, and the second, third and following stages similarly described; so that presently a complete report upon the whole experience is obtained. There is, in theory, some danger that the stages become artificially separated; consciousness is a flow, a process, and if we divide it up we run the risk of missing certain intermediate links. In practice, however, this danger has proved to be very small; and we may always have recourse to retrospection, and compare our partial results with our memory of the unbroken experience. Moreover, (*b*) the practised observer gets into an introspective habit, has the introspective attitude ingrained in his system; so that it is possible for him, not only to take mental notes while the observation is in progress, without interfering with consciousness, but even to jot down written notes, as the histologist does while his eye is still held to the ocular of the microscope.

In principle, then, introspection is very like inspection. The objects of observation are different; they are objects of dependent, not of independent experience; they are likely to be transient, elusive, slippery. Sometimes they refuse to be observed while they are in passage; they must be preserved in memory, as a delicate tissue is preserved in hardening fluid, before they can be examined. And the standpoint of the observer is different; it is the standpoint of human life and of human interest, not of detachment and aloofness. But, in general, the method of psychology is much the same as the method of physics.

It must not be forgotten that, while the method of the physical and the psychological sciences is substantially the same, the subject-matter of these sciences is as different as it can well be. Ultimately, as we have seen, the subject-matter of all the sciences is the world of human experience; but we have also seen that the aspect of experience treated by physics is radically different from the aspect treated by psychology. The likeness of method may tempt us to slip from the one aspect to the other, as when a textbook of physics contains a chapter on vision and the sense of colour, or a text-book of physiology contains paragraphs on delusions of judgment; but this confusion of subject-matter must inevitably lead to confusion of thought. Since all the sciences are concerned with the one world of human experience, it is natural that scientific method, to whatever aspect of experience it is applied, should be in principle the same. On the other hand, when we have decided to examine some particular aspect of experience, it is necessary that we hold fast to that aspect, and do not shift our point of view as the enquiry proceeds. Hence it is a great advantage that we have the two terms, introspection and inspection, to denote observation taken from the different standpoints of psychology and of physics.

The use of the word introspection is a constant reminder that we are working in psychology, that we are observing the dependent aspect of the world of experience.

Observation, as we said above, implies two things: attention to the phenomena, and record of the phenomena. The attention must be held at the highest possible degree of concentration; the record must be photographically accurate. Observation is, therefore, both difficult and fatiguing; and introspection is, on the whole, more difficult and more fatiguing than inspection. To secure reliable results, we must be strictly impartial and unprejudiced, facing the facts as they come, ready to accept them as they are, not trying to fit them to any preconceived theory; and we must work only when our general disposition is favourable, when we are fresh and in good health, at ease in our surroundings, free from outside worry and anxiety. If these rules are not followed, no amount of experimenting will help us. The observer in the psychological laboratory is placed under the best possible external conditions; the room in which he works is fitted up and arranged in such a way that the observation may be repeated, that the process to be observed may stand out clearly upon the background of consciousness, and that the factors in the process may be separately varied. But all this care is of no avail, unless the observer himself comes to the work in an even frame of mind, gives it his full attention, and is able adequately to translate his experience into words.

§ 7. THE SCOPE OF PSYCHOLOGY

If mind is the sum-total of human experience considered as dependent upon the experiencing person, it follows that each one of us can have direct acquaintance only with a single mind, namely, with his own. We are concerned in psychology with the whole world of human experience; but we are concerned with it solely under its dependent aspect, as conditioned by a nervous system; and a nervous system is a particular thing, possessed by a particular individual. In strictness, therefore, it is only his own mind, the experience dependent upon his own nervous system, that each of us knows at first-hand; it is only to this limited and individual subject-matter that the method of experimental introspection can be directly applied. How, then, is a scientific psychology possible? How can psychology be anything more than a body of personal beliefs and individual opinions?

The difficulty is more apparent than real. We have every reason to believe, not only in general that our neighbours have minds like our own, that is, are able like ourselves to view experience in its dependent aspect, but also in detail that human minds resemble one another precisely as human bodies do. Within a given race there is much apparent diversity of outward form: differences in height and figure, in colour of hair and eyes, in shape of nose and mouth. We notice these differences, because we are obliged in everyday life to distinguish the persons with whom we come in contact. But the resemblances are more fundamental than the differences. If we have recourse to exact measurements, we find that there is in every case a certain standard or type to which the individual more or less closely conforms and about which all the individuals are more or less closely grouped. And even without measurement we have evidence to the same effect: strangers see family likenesses which the members of the family cannot themselves detect, and the units in a crowd of aliens, Chinese or Negroes, look bewilderingly alike.

Now all of our main social institutions rest upon the assumption that the individuals of whom society is composed possess minds, and possess minds that are of the same sort. Language, religion, law and custom,—they one and all rest upon this assumption, and they one and all bear testimony that the assumption is well grounded. Would a man invent language in order to talk to himself? Language implies that there are more minds than one. And would the use of a common speech be possible if minds were not essentially alike? Men differ in their command of language, as they differ in complexion, or in liability to disease; but the general use of language testifies to a fundamental likeness of mental constitution in us all.

Hence the psychologist is fully justified in believing that other men have minds of the same kind as his own, and in basing psychology upon the introspective reports furnished by a number of different observers. These reports show, in point of fact, just what we should expect them to show: a fundamental agreement, and a great variety of detail,—the mental differences grouping themselves, as we have seen that physical differences group themselves, about a central type or standard.

If, however, we attribute minds to other human beings, we have no right to deny them to the higher animals. These animals are provided with a nervous system of the same pattern as ours, and their conduct or behaviour, under circumstances that would arouse certain feelings in us, often seems to express, quite definitely, similar feelings in them. Surely we must grant that the highest vertebrates, mammals and birds, have minds. But the lower vertebrates, fishes and reptiles and amphibia, possess a nervous system of the same order, although of simpler construction. And many of the invertebrates, insects and spiders and crustaceans, show a fairly high degree of nervous development. Indeed, it is difficult to limit mind to the animals that possess even a rudimentary nervous system; for the creatures that rank still lower in the scale of life manage to do, without a nervous system, practically everything that their superiors do by its assistance. The range of mind thus appears to be as wide as the range of animal life.

The plants, on the other hand, appear to be mindless. Many of them are endowed with what we may term sense-organs, that is, organs differentiated to receive certain forms of stimulus, pressure, impact, light, etc. These organs are analogous in structure to the sense-organs of the lower animal organisms: thus, plant "eyes" have been found, which closely resemble rudimentary animal eyes, and which—if they belonged to animals—might mediate the perception of light: so that the development of the plant-world has evidently been governed by the same general laws of adaptation to environment that have been at work in the animal kingdom. But we have no evidence of a plant-consciousness.

Just as the scope of psychology extends beyond man to the animals, so does it extend from the individual man to groups of men, to societies. The subject-matter of psychology is human experience considered as dependent upon the individual. But since the individuals of the same race and epoch are organised in much the same way, and since they live together in a society where their conduct affects and is affected by the conduct of others, their view of experience under its dependent aspect naturally becomes, in certain main features, a common or general view; and this common view is embodied in those social institutions to which we have referred above,—in language, religion, law and custom. There is no such thing as a collective mind, or a national mind, or a social mind, if we mean by mind some immaterial being; but there is a collective mind, if we mean by it the sum-total of human experience considered as dependent upon a social group of similar individuals. The study of the collective mind gives us a psychology of language, a psychology of myth, a psychology of custom, etc.; it also gives us a differential psychology of the Latin mind, of the Anglo-Saxon mind, of the Oriental mind, etc.

And this is not all: the scope of psychology extends, still further, from the normal to the abnormal mind. Life, as we know, need not be either complete or completely healthy life. The living organism may show defect, the lack of a limb or of a sense-organ; and it may show disorder and disease, a temporary or a permanent lapse from health. So it is with mind. The consciousnesses of those who are born deaf or blind are defective; they lack certain sensations and images that are normally present. In dreaming and the hypnotic state, during intoxication, after prolonged sleeplessness or severe strain of any kind, we have illustrations of temporary mental derangement. And the various forms of insanity—mania, melancholia, dementia—are forms of permanent mental disorder.

Derangement of the social mind may be studied in the various panics, fads, epidemics of speculation, of false belief, etc., which occur from time to time even in the most highly civilised societies. The mob consciousness stands to a healthy social consciousness very much as dreaming to the waking life. Permanent disorder of the social mind means the downfall of society.

All these various fields of psychology may be cultivated for their own sake, on account of their intrinsic interest and value; they must, indeed, be so cultivated, if psychology is to progress. At the same time, their facts and laws often throw light upon the problems of normal human psychology. Suppose, for instance, that a man, blind from his birth, is rendered able to see by a surgical operation. He must learn to use his eyes, as a child learns to walk. And the gradual perfecting of his vision, the mistakes and confusions to which he is liable, all the details of his visual education, form a storehouse of facts upon which the psychologist can draw when he seeks to illustrate the development of the perception of space in the normal mind,—the manner in which we come to judge of the distance of objects from ourselves and from one another, of their direction, and of their size and shape. Instructive, also, are those forms of mental unsoundness which consist in the derangement of a single group of processes. The various types of morbid fear—agoraphobia, the fear of being alone in open spaces; neophobia, the fear of everything that is new; phobophobia, the nervous dread of being afraid—are only exaggerated forms of experiences that most of us have had. The sanest man will feel lost when he passes, suddenly, from a quiet country life to the bustle of a large town; we are all a little timid when we enter a strange community; we have all been afraid that on such-and-such an occasion we shall show our nervousness. Similarly, the self-importance of paranoia is merely an exaggeration of the pleased self-consciousness, the self-complacency, that we often observe in others and, if we are honest, must often detect in ourselves. In all these instances, the strong lines of the caricature may help us to a more correct picture of the normal consciousness.

NOTES

1 John Locke, *An Essay Concerning Human Understanding,* [1690] Bk. II., Ch. i., §19.
2 Dugald Stewart, *Outlines of Moral Philosophy,* [1793]. Pt. I., Section i., §7.
3 James Mill, *Analysis of the Phenomena of the Human Mind,* [1829] Vol. I., Ch. v. Mill uses the word "feeling" to denote what we have called "mental process."

Did Titchener Commit the Stimulus Error?
The Problem of Meaning in Structural Psychology

Mary Henle

"The observer in a psychological experiment falls into [the stimulus error], as we all know," writes Titchener

> when he exchanges the attitude of descriptive psychology for that of common sense or of natural science; in the typical case, when he attends not to "sensation" but to "stimulus."...The stimulus error is, in fact, the material aspect of what appears, in more formal guise, as the error of logical reflection or of *Kundgabe* (7, p. 488).

Thus the stimulus error in its strict sense, the confusion of sensation with stimulus, is for Titchener an example of a whole class of errors, the confusion of description experience with common sense observation. "Introspection through the glass of meaning...is the besetting sin of the descriptive psychologist," he warns (3, p. 291). Or, expressing it still more broadly, "logical common sense, *c'est l'ennemi*" (6, p. 178). Once more, "we are constantly confusing sensations with their stimuli, with their objects, with their meanings" (4, p. xxvi). It is in this broad sense that the term "stimulus error" will be used here.*

An example will make clear the extent to which this error violates Titchener's conception of psychology. One of his criticisms of the associationists is that they commit an error of this type, for they are dealing with meanings, not with

conscious existences. Take this instance: the word *summer* may suggest the word *winter*. Why? The associationists might invoke the law of association by contrast to account for this sequence. But, as ideas, the two may be exactly alike—both may be carried in the same kind of imagery: perhaps verbal-auditory-motor images, or both may be mental pictures. The contrast is a contrast of meanings, not of mental contents. What we mean by summer contrasts with what we mean by winter, but the *idea* of summer does not contrast with the idea of winter. Or again, explanation by similarity also fails: True, the idea of summer may be exactly like the idea of winter (i.e., as mental contents), but they are also like thousands of other ideas, so this resemblance does not tell us why one suggests the other. Once more, any resemblance that could account for the association is a resemblance of meanings, not of mental constitution. And here we are beyond the scope of psychology (8, p. 149).

Is Titchener himself able to adhere to the strict standards he sets? Can he keep from falling into the forbidden territory of logical analysis, to which he relegates the study of meanings? I will contend that he cannot. I have one instance to display, startling enough to suggest that further scrutiny of Titchener from this point of view is indicated.

My example concerns the psychology of action. One might wonder what place a psychological analysis of action has in a description of the contents of consciousness. Yet Titchener is able to formulate the problem in a way that is perfectly consistent with his idea of the task of psychology. For him the problem is: what kind of consciousness characterizes action? what is the nature of the action consciousness? He takes as his model the reaction experiment:

Henle, M. (1971). Did Titchener commit the stimulus error? The problem of meaning in structural psychology. *Journal of the History of the Behavorial Sciences, 7,* 279–282. Copyright © 1971 by the Clinical Psychology Publishing Company. Reprinted by permission of the publisher.

* Whether this usage is proper, or whether one would do better to speak of "something analogous to the stimulus error" in the case of the confusion of data and their meanings, is unclear. Boring (1, p. 449) points out that the definition of the stimulus error has remained implicit. In any case, the two kinds of confusion are strictly parallel and play the same role in Titchener's thinking.

If...we try to construct a typical action conscious-ness, we get something like this: a preliminary phase, in which the prominent things are kinaesthesis and the idea of end or result; a central phase, in which some object is apprehended in relation to...the idea of end; and a final phase, in which the perception of result is set on a background of kinaesthesis, of the sensations aroused by the actual movement. Each one of these phases may be coloured by feeling.... (5, p. 448).

It is in connection with this idea of end, this perception of result, that my systematic reser-vations arise. What place has an idea of end in a structural psychology? We are told that it may be carried in visual images, in internal speech, etc.; but it is different from other ideas carried in these terms, since it is specific to the action consciousness. "The characteristic feature of the action consciousness, as distinguished from the consciousnesses so far considered, is its prede-termination in the sense of the idea of end" (5, p. 449). I have the sinking feeling that what is spe-cific about the idea of end is a matter of mean-ing, and that Titchener is here committing the much dreaded stimulus error.

A concrete example is to be found in the *Beginner's Psychology:* the author describes his intention to look up a reference:

We begin with a preparatory phase, in which there are two things to notice: the *intention to move* (it occurs to me to look up the reference) and the *idea of the result* of movement (finding the required pas-sage for quotation). Then follows a middle phase, in which the outstanding thing is the *perception of the object* of movement (I see and identify the book on the shelf). The final phase.... (8, pp. 234–235).

Of course this reference to a specific meaningful object, the needed book and the relevant passage in it, is a shorthand description for the beginning student, not an instance of an analytical intro-spection. But what about the idea of end or re-sult itself, apart from this particular content? If it is reduced to elementary terms, does anything

remain that distinguishes it from other ideas? If the essential point concerns not the idea of end as idea, but rather as a source of determining ten-dencies, the whole problem is transferred to physiology; or rather to a physiology of the fu-ture since, with regard to determining tenden-cies, "we know nothing of their intimate nature" (5, p. 449). And, in any case, the problem repeats itself if we ask why certain ideas, and not oth-ers, set up determining tendencies. Once more, if there is anything specific about the idea of end, it seems to be a matter of meaning.

Is this, perhaps, an isolated lapse, of which even so gifted a systematist as Titchener might be capable? I would suggest that the whole prob-lem of meaning is a source of difficulty and em-barrassment for structuralism. Titchener deals with it, we remember, by the famous context the-ory: a perception consists of a sensory core sup-plemented by images which cluster about it; an idea is a core of images, with other images and sensations clustering around this nucleus. The meaning of the perception or idea is carried by these processes that surround the nucleus. Psy-chologically regarded, says Titchener, meaning is always context (5, p. 367). And how is context acquired? It accrues to a sensory or imaginal core through the situation in which the organism finds itself (5, p. 367).

We have still to examine one crucial term in this account—situation. Titchener defines it as the "meaningful experience of a conscious present" (5, p. 369). He is silent on the question of how the situation came to be meaningful *in the first place.* But it is, of course, clear that if some experiences are meaningful without benefit of a context theory, others may equally plausibly be. Even though Titchener is not interested in such genetic questions, we need to ask how meaning is given the first time. Otherwise we assume in advance the meaning to be explained.

Another systematic problem in this connec-tion is one that Titchener himself explicitly rec-ognizes. We have seen that he very emphatically denies that meanings have any place in science. What, then, can be the place of a theory of meaning in a scientific psychology? Titchener's answer seems not entirely convincing:

A science cannot free itself, offhand, from its own history; and, historically, psychology has been much concerned with meaning. Moreover, meaning is of very great practical importance; we communicate meanings, we apprehend meanings, we act upon meanings; and although science is not bound to treat only of what is practically important, yet it can hardly neglect a matter of great practical importance that comes its way. Our question, if we rephrase it a little, merely asks *that a term, familiar to us in our daily life, be translated into the language of science.*...(8, p. 118).

But in other places Titchener does not seem to hold that a science cannot free itself from its own history. Indeed, it must do so. For example: "The man of science...does not chiefly value the things that men ordinarily care for. If he is a Copernicus, he puts away reverence for antiquity...." (9, pp. 30–31). Still clearer is his position that practical importance is of no concern to psychology or to any other science. Thus: "Science deals, not with values, but with facts. There is no good or bad, sick or well, useful or useless, in science" (8, p. 1). Again, "These practical results may be immensely important for everyday life; but science, in its impersonal and disinterested search for facts, makes no difference between one fact and another" (8, p. 5). And as for translating the terms of daily life into scientific ones, Titchener never lets us forget that "common-sense, *c'est l'ennemi.*"

Any student of Titchener will recognize in these latter statements—not in his defense of a theory of meaning—the true intent of his psychology. The context theory remains a problem: Titchener, despite himself, seems to be tempted by the prospect of a psychology relevant to life. A besetting sin would not be besetting if it were not tempting. He quiets his scientific conscience by attempting to reduce meaning to processes that are not in themselves meaningful, i.e., to sensory and imaginal context. But it has been suggested above that this can be accomplished only by assuming in advance the meaning that is to be explained.

Boring once attempted an explanation of Titchener's apparent lack of productivity in his later years—that, having received all the honors too early, he later lacked external incentives to work (2, pp. 502–503). It seems to me that to imply that Titchener needed such incentives in order to complete his systematic work is to do him an injustice. One might equally well offer the guess that inconsistencies such as the ones I have mentioned were beginning to arise out of the inadequacies of his approach. The problem was *not* that Titchener was not a good enough systematist to deal with such difficulties. More likely, he was *too good* a systematic thinker to overlook the indications that, given his approach, such inconsistencies were inevitable.

REFERENCES

1 Boring, E. G. The stimulus-error. *American Journal of Psychology,* 1921, *32,* 449–471.
2 Boring, E. G. Edward Bradford Titchener: 1867–1927. *American Journal of Psychology,* 1927, *38,* 489–506.
3 Titchener, E. B. Structural and functional psychology. *Philosophical Review,* 1899, *8,* 290–299.
4 Titchener, E. B. *Experimental psychology.* Vol. II, Part I. New York: Macmillan, 1905.
5 Titchener, E. B. *A text-book of psychology.* New York: Macmillan, 1909.
6 Titchener, E. B. Description vs. statement of meaning. *American Journal of Psychology,* 1912, *23,* 165–182.
7 Titchener, E. B. The schema of introspection. *American Journal of Psychology,* 1912, *23,* 485–508.
8 Titchener, E. B. *A beginner's psychology.* New York: Macmillan, 1915.
9 Titchener, E. B. *Systematic psychology: prolegomena.* New York: Macmillan, 1929.

E. B. Titchener and His Lost System

Rand B. Evans

When E. B. Titchener died in 1927, the work completed toward his long projected series of books on systematic psychology consisted of only three chapters, and those dealt with general and introductory considerations. The important chapter on method, which was to be the final chapter of the first volume, the *Prolegomena,* was never written and no trace of notes on the other volumes has been found.[1]

There were hints in those last years that a change was in the wind at Cornell[2] and that the new books would unfold a system very different from that published in 1910.[3] We shall never know exactly what Titchener's thinking was on systematic matters at the end, but there is sufficient evidence to give an idea of the direction of that thought.

It may seem surprising to suggest a major change in the systematic thinking on Titchener's part during that last decade. Those last years of Titchener's life have often been represented as unproductive.[4] Even Boring commented that he thought Titchener had "gone to seed."[5] Perusal of the number of pages of Titchener's printed work during that period might give support to such a contention, but it is somewhat dangerous to judge Titchener or his tactics in present-day terms. To understand Titchener, it is necessary to understand the attitudes and privileges of the 19th-Century German *Gelehrter* and Wundt in particular, for it is in that image that Titchener patterned his professional life. Titchener's personal publications, some 50 notes and articles during that last decade, represent only a minor aspect of his thinking and activity.

It is tempting to use a military analogy to represent Titchener and his relation to his school. Titchener served much as a commander-in-chief and tactician. It was he who held the total battle-plan against 'the enemy' and it was he who set the direction and timing of attack. The Cornell faculty served as field generals in charge of implementing directives, sending reports to headquarters and seeing to the training and activities of the graduate students who were, of course, the troops. With doctoral theses and minor studies as their weapons, these troops would assault one adversary, perhaps Würzburg, and then another, perhaps Act psychology. Titchener's notes and articles were used to tie the theaters of conflict together, to demonstrate the significance of a given battle and to present the manifesto for a new assault.

Looking at Titchener and his school in this way, the production of those last ten years comprises some 110 papers.[6] The notes of graduate students as well as correspondence between Titchener and his students show rather clearly how much of the writings of students was Titchener's own expression.[7]

What about the system, then? The system commonly represented as structuralism or Titchenerism is that of Titchener's *A Textbook of Psychology,* published in 1910, although Titchener specifically objected to professional criticism of his system based on a general textbook because "a text-book...is written for the student and not for the professional psychologist...."[8] At any rate, the description of psychology found in the *Textbook* stuck and not that of the many articles written for professional consumption. Unfortunately, most authors seem to have assumed that Titchener's systematic thought solidified in 1910 and that the system remained the same over the next 17 years. Scientific systems, if they are at all viable, are in a con-

Evans, R. B. (1972). E. B. Titchener and his lost system. *Journal of the History of the Behavioral Sciences, 8,* 168–180. Copyright © 1972 by the Clinical Psychology Publishing Company. Reprinted by permission of the publisher.

stant state of flux, although the changes may be barely observable to the casual observer. Titchener's system presents no exception.

A study of the total output of Titchener's school shows not a sudden change, but a gradual development of thought over a number of years.[9] As a reference-point, we might do well to begin with that system of 1910. Titchener described psychology then as the study of experience in terms of the experiencing individual. "We are concerned in psychology with the whole world of human experience; but we are concerned with it solely under its dependent aspect, as conditioned by a nervous system...."[10] It was, in short, an elementistic system with the problems of analysis, synthesis, and explanation in terms of the nervous system. Titchener was dealing with the facts of experience, not the values or meanings commonly attached to those facts. Values and meanings were in the domain of common-sense man and technology, not for scientific psychology. He was devoted to understanding the IS of experience, not the IS FOR, and he held fast to the faith that experience could be stripped of meaning and left as bare facts, sheer existences.

The elementary processes of the system were three: sensations, images, and affections.

> Sensations are, of course, the characteristic elements of perceptions....Images are, in just the same way, the characteristic elements of ideas.... Lastly, affections are the characteristic elements of emotions.[11]

The perception, the idea, and the emotion were the 'given' of experience. They were reduced to their characteristic elements by means of analysis, just as the chemist breaks down complex substances into further unanalyzable substances.[12] Titchener carried out this analysis by an elaborate system of introspection, far more elaborate than that of Wundt.[13] These elements, these products of analysis, were not static, however, but were considered processes capable of being observed in vari-

ous aspects or attributes.[14] "A mental element," according to Titchener, "can be identified only by the enumeration of its attributes."[15] Attributes of sensation were listed as quality, intensity, duration, and clearness (extent was included, but not for every sensation). Image carried the same attributes as sensation, although Perky's thesis had already cast doubt as to the existence of image as something separate from sensation. Image had been virtually relegated to a subclass of sensation in 1910 or at least, along with sensation, to subclasses of some more basic elements.[16] Edward's thesis would resolve the matter, leaving the system with two elements, sensation and affection.[17] Affection was accompanied by the attributes of quality, intensity, and duration, but neither clearness nor extent.

Titchener accepted Külpe's doctrine of inseparability and independent variability of attributes, but only to a point. Inseparability he held to be generally true.

> The attributes of any sensation are always given when the sensation itself is given, and the annihilation of any attribute carries with it the annihilation, the disappearance, of the sensation itself.... A sensation that has no quality, no intensity, no duration, etc., is not a sensation; it is nothing.[18]

As to the matter of independent variability, however, Titchener had his reservations.

> ...We are told...that the attributes of sensation are independently variable; quality may be changed while intensity remains constant, intensity changed while quality remains constant, and so on throughout the list. Is this statement true? Relatively, yes: true for certain cases and under certain conditions.... Absolutely true, however, the statement is not. In certain cases and beyond certain limits the variation of one attribute implies the concomitant variation of another.... What I wish to emphasize is the fact that there are bound attributes as well as free, and that the test of independent variability, useful enough for a preliminary survey, must be applied with caution when we demand accuracy of detail.[19]

These sensory processes with their concomitant attributes were synthesized at the next level to simple perceptions (those with a single attributive basis) and complex perceptions (those with the multi-attributive basis). The structure then progressed by further integrations to more and more complex mental states.

This is only a crude representation of some aspects of Titchener's system, but perhaps it will suffice to show something of the development that would take place over the following 17 years. Two trends will be considered in particular—the structure of the system (at least first-level structure) and the methodology of observation.

The first apparent shift away from the systematic stance of the *Textbook* concerned the elemental structure of the system. In 1913 Carl Rahn in his doctoral thesis for J. R. Angell attacked the logic behind the concepts of sensation as process and attributes in Titchener's system.[20] The criticism touched on several points, but the most important had to do with the relation of elements to attributes.

> What is the method by which these attributes of the element are determined? Titchener tells us that the element is not further analysable by introspection. On the other hand we are told that the element presents different aspects or sides, called attributes, that can be separately attended to. Thus attended to they are discriminated, and what is this other than further analysis? Is it other in kind than that which yielded the elements? And are the precipitants of this further analysis of another sort?[21]

Rahn attacked Titchener's views on sensation and attribute in a round-about way, first identifying Titchener's views with those put forward by E. B. Talbot in an article printed in the 1890's and then turning Calkins' criticism of Talbot on Titchener. Calkins had said:

> Either the sensation has attributes, but then it is complex, no element and has lost its excuse for psychological being; or the sensation is an irreducible and unanalysable element, but then its simplicity

is absolute, not to be trifled with, and not to be explained away by reference to any second process of analysis into elements, which yet are not elements, but only "attributes," "aspects" or something equally vague and meaningless.[22]

Titchener responded to Rahn's use of this criticism and others in his "Sensation and System."[23] As well constructed as was Rahn's criticism, Titchener was still able to get around it with the Wundtian device of burying the opposition in a multitude of references to past publications. In escaping Rahn's criticism, however, Titchener seemed to shift ground, or at least several men in the Cornell laboratory and elsewhere thought so, although Titchener never admitted a shift. He seemed to shift sensation from an observable entity to a classificatory term.[24]

> Sensation is a classificatory term.... We get our systematic notion of it... as the outcome of abstractive analyses performed under various psychological determinations; in other words,—while the common-sense notion, colored very likely by biology or physiology, is always with us,—we build up the notion of sensation, in a strict procedure, from observations of its empirical aspects or attributes.... In point of fact...all experimental investigations of sensation deal with attributes: with qualities, intensities, durations, what not. Even the sensation of Wundt's system, which is constituted solely of quality and intensity, is to be observed under its two attributes in separate experiments. But be that as it may, I should certainly maintain in my own case that a sensation, taken in this way as a psychological object of the first order, must ordinarily, by the number and heterogeneity of its attributes, exceed what is called the "range of attention".... All observation of psychological objects of the first order is, I conceive, observation of attributes.[25]

Just when Titchener made the transition in his own mind between the directly observable 'sensation' to the classificatory concept of sensation is not clear. It was certainly possible in the days of the *Outline* and there is no definite statement to the contrary in the *Textbook*.[26] One may only speculate here, but more than likely, Rahn caught Titchener in an insufficiently explicit description of position. Titchener may not have even realized he had made the transition until Rahn's criticism. Whatever the cause, Titchener would use sensation as an observational term less frequently after 1915.[27]

Mental elements were dropped from Titchener's course in Systematic Psychology as early as 1918 and the system started out from "the ultimate 'dimensions' of psychological subject-matter: quality, intensity, protensity, extensity and attensity."[28] Four years later, in 1923, Titchener announced to an enquiring Boring that he was ready to shelve the concept of elements "for something still more fluid and still more pregnant,"— attributive dimensions.[29] Even earlier in a letter to Ruckmick, Titchener made the change in his systematic thought clear.

What I am concerned with in my own thinking is the number and nature of the dimensions of the psychological world, just precisely as the physicist is concerned with mass and time and space as the dimensions of his physical world.[30]

Dimensions in the form of qualitative or intensive series had been in the system from the days of the *Outline,* but F. L. Dimmick's work on the black-grey-white series seems to have revived interest in the matter.[31] Dimmick's little note is important because it seems to have led Titchener to reorganize his thinking about the color pyramid and to begin questioning intensity as an independent attribute although, as has been shown, Titchener had not held to independent variability as a rule for attributes for some years. The idea of quality and intensity as interactive dimensions seems to have gained ground somewhat later.[32] Relating this to the black-grey-white series, grey becomes not the mid-point of an intensive series running from black to white, but an endpoint on many qualitative-intensive dimensions. The final result was a recasting of the color pyramid.[33]

This work on the pyramid sparked similar work in models of the other modalities.

Our first step in grappling with this dimension is, of course, to secure the intramodal arrangements, such as we already have in the color pyramid, the taste and smell figures, and possibly in my own touch pyramid.[34]

This concern with series led to a search for a general theory of quality. This matter of quality was important to Titchener as he seems to have seen in it a major distinction between the world of the physicist and that of the psychologist.[35]

I have sometimes dallied with the idea that quality too must have a generalized psychological theory, identical in principle for all the modalities. I think we have at some time in the past discussed the possibility of bringing all the modal qualities together; at any rate I have long thought that even if all the psychological qualities do not form a continuum, they may form a sort of hinged or interconnected total,—so that to put it crudely, the color pyramid somewhere hooks on to the smell prism, and that to the taste pyramid, and so forth.[36]

If Titchener was serious in his statement that he was dealing with psychological dimensions "*just precisely*" as is the physicist with mass, time and space in the physical world, this sort of interrelated dimensional arrangement would be just the sort of thing he would be after. By Titchener's own definition, the physicist uses interrelated dimensional explanations, defining one dimension in terms of the other.[37]

One sticky problem with all this talk of dimensions of experience rather than elements and attributes is what happens to affection. If sensation is invalid as an observable entity, then what of affection? If affection is nothing more than dimensional experience, how do those dimensions fit into the rest of the system? There seems to have been thought given at one time to making affection a sensory attribute.[38] The problem was solved with J. P. Nafe's doctoral thesis. His results were simple and surprising:

The affective qualities, pleasantness and unpleasantness turn out, under direct observation, to be modes of pressure: *Pleasantness is a bright pressure, and unpleasantness is a dull pressure.*[39]

This removed any question of affection as a separate element, just as Perky and Edwards had done with image. What was created, then, was another qualitative or at most a protensive dimension. The bright and dull pressures of simple feelings became then,

> ... qualities within the continuum of pressure qualities (what we call the touch pyramid), this continuum contains all the pressures there are, whether sensory or anything else; and no quality is intrinsically sensory.[40]

Sensation and affect had vanished, removing any need for the discrimination between sensory and affective dimensions, although the term was used now and again in a purely systematic way. In 1926, Titchener would chastise a graduate student:

> You must give up thinking in terms of sensations and affections. That was all right ten years ago; but now, as I have told you, it is wholly out of date.... You must learn to think in terms of dimensions rather than in terms of systematic constructs like sensation.[41]

So the first level of Titchener's old system reduced to the five dimensions of quality, intensity, protensity, extensity, and attensity, with quality taking precedence over the others. In this form, protensity and extensity became somewhat more primitive than in the system of the *Textbook,* protensity changing from time to a 'pre-temporal welling-forth' and extensity, from space to a 'pre-spatial spread', as in Katz's film color.[42] Even intensity as a separate dimension from quality was being questioned.[43] By 1927 research was underway on simple combinations of attributive dimensions with particular emphasis on Katz's modes of appearance of colors and on extensions the dimensions previously known as

affect.[44] Titchener's untimely death and the quick disintegration of his school never allowed systematic organization of this later work.

This development of systematic thinking was not the only change going on in that last decade. Sometime in the early 1920's, or perhaps even earlier, Titchener began to question the rigid system of introspection that had been the hallmark of his work since the turn of the century. He seems to have come to the belief that there were at least two possible ways to proceed in the study of qualitative dimensions. In a long letter on the topic in 1924, Titchener wrote:

> One may work by way of unequivocally determined observation; that is, one may set one's observers to observe under a specific rubric, such as pitch (which one borrows from music), or brightness (which one borrows from visual analogy), having got one's rubric, one naturally takes advantage of the standardized procedures, so that the results take the form of judgments of comparison, which can be mathematically treated. Under either of the rubrics mentioned, one gets pretty results—results that seem to indicate that the rubrics themselves are psychologically identical. One gets no assurance, however, that one is dealing with straight quality.
>
> One may also use a generally determined observation, in which one directs the observers to observe quality simply and the judgments of comparison are given in terms of like and unlike. Here the guiding thread for the experimenter must be the qualitative series. I suppose Henning worked on odours in this sort of way. If one can't have recourse to qualitative series one must try some other methodological trick as Nafe did in his study of the affective qualities. The former method, with specification, is logically posterior to the other, but in practice is a good deal simpler. It has the advantage that one may employ observers who are only moderately trained. The second or general method is magnificent if one can take time to live with the experience for a term of years, and if during this period one can strip ones self of all biases and prepossessions....[45]

This "magnificient" method of generally determined observation with its requirements of great familiarity with the experience and absence of systematic constriction seems to have been the method adopted as an alternative to the rigid introspective method in the later years of Titchener's systematic and experimental work. Some evidence of this trend is shown in the theses of Bixby, Kreezer, and Hazzard.[46] In practice, the time interval for familiarity with the experience was somewhat less than years, but the attempt to free observers from systematic bias seems to have been seriously attempted. The systematic bias of greatest importance to the matter at hand was, of course, the pre-supposition of discontinuous elements and attributes as well as the accompanying special vocabulary.

The phrase "to strip ones self of all biases and prepossessions" is an important one in understanding Titchener's thinking at this time. It is very near Titchener's definition of the method of phenomenology which he stated as:

Phenomenology demands that you dispense with theory, that you face the world impartially and describe as faithfully as you can.[47]

It may seem a contradiction in terms to refer to 'Titchener's phenomenology,' but in terms of method, this seems to have been the way Titchener was moving. Students used the term at the time in their correspondence and Titchener used it himself, as we shall see.[48] This is not to say that the more traditional approach of controlled introspection was abandoned, just that a less constricted approach was allowed into the Cornell laboratory. As early as 1912, Titchener had discriminated between the phenomenological and descriptive approaches.

I would warn the reader against confusing descriptive psychology with a 'phenomenological' account of mind. . . . I mean by a phenomenological account of mind, an account which purports to take mental phenomena at their face value, which records them as they are 'given' in everyday experience; the account furnished by a naive, common-sense, non-scientific observer, who has not yet adopted the special attitude of the psychologist, but who from his neutral standpoint aims to be as full and as accurate as the psychologist himself.[49]

Titchener was not particularly confident that such an analysis was possible, at least not in 1912. But even though his terms were generally negative at that time, he did not completely reject some role for phenomenology.

. . . A roughly phenomenological account, a description of consciousness as it shows itself to common sense, may be useful or even necessary as the starting point of a truly psychological description. . . . The psychologist may also have recourse to phenomenology after the event, after he has completed his own first analysis, as an additional check upon the singly motivated and more technical description. Or again, the elaborate phenomenology that issues from a foregone epistemology may be of service as indicating possible lacunae in psychological description.[50]

This sounds encouraging, but Titchener in 1912 hastened to add that "phenomenology . . . is not psychology."[51] The phenomenology Titchener was referring to was that of Husserl, however, and he specifically differentiated between Husserl's phenomenology and that of Stumpf and Brentano.[52] But even here Titchener was emphatic, ". . . no form of phenomenology— phenomenology of mind, *Gegenstandstheorie,* science of selves—can be truly scientific, for the reason that the implied attitude to experience is multiply motivated and fluctuating, while the minimum requirement of science is a fixed and constant point of view."[53] Titchener, so far as the record shows, would always reject Husserl's phenomenology as being the study of the "extracted and essential meanings and the application of applied logic."[54] However, somewhere along the line—just where and when is hard to say—Titchener saw the need for a form of the phenomenological method, perhaps to correct for the "lacunae" of the strict Titchenerian introspective terminology.

It should be clearly understood that Titchener was not suggesting the content of Husserl's phenomenology, nor the Akt of Brentano, nor the Funktion of Stumpf. It was phenomenology as method he was introducing to the Cornell laboratory—"meticulous, minute description, i.e., description in the most pregnant sense."[55] It was this type of observation that was urged on experimenters and observers in Titchener's letters between 1925 and 1927:

> As regards the plan of experiment, you have to remember what you are after is not a determination of conditions but a straight phenomenology. What you then want to get is a straight descriptive account of what the observers see; the reports will at first, in all probability, be rough, . . . but as the observations are repeated you ought to get a full and detailed account of the phenomena.[56]

It would seem that somewhere along the line, descriptive psychology and phenomenological method became compatible.

> If you take a perfectly casual phenomenological attitude, you see what they tell you to see; but if you vary your attitude a hair's breadth in the direction of critical observation, you get all sorts of other things under your eyes.[57]

A very simple visual vocabulary will see you through if you will only keep it mobile, and use it freely in face of the phenomena without letting yourself be biased by preconception.[58]

The last thesis actually edited by Titchener for publication was F. L. Bixby's "A Phenomenological Study of Lustre" and the method employed was phenomenological. Kreezer's thesis, though completed under H. P. Weld, was carried out to a large part during Titchener's lifetime and it bears the definite mark of Titchener's phenomenological method.[59]

It is important to note that phenomenology was the method employed, and that there was no basic change from the object of study being existential contents, that is, the facts of experience separated from the values and meanings of experience. The word 'existential' seems to have been the source of concern in some quarters when it was published, but Titchener merely introduced it in his lectures and *Prolegomena* to stand in opposition to the term 'intentional' used in the discussion of Act psychology.[60] Titchener gave no evidence of swinging toward intentionalism, neither toward Brentano nor Gestalt.[61] The organization of the system had changed and a new attitude had been added to the observational repertoire—that of meticulous, unbiased observation, but the basic study of the contents of experience remained the same.

These developments only scrape the surface of Titchener's final system. We shall never know the implications for all these changes to the overall system Titchener was preparing. Even the chapter on Method for the *Prolegomena* would have been enough to gain a better understanding of what the system would have become. We shall never know where he might have gone with a lifespan like that of Wundt. His faith in the study of the contents of experience remained firm and probably would have continued so. Some writers have suggested a shift towards behaviorism or physicalism, but no evidence of such changes of a compelling sort has been presented, and there is a goodly bit of evidence to the contrary.[62] In his last major psychological paper that remains extant, a talk given before the Experimentalists at Princeton in 1925, Titchener gave his view of psychology's progress and future as follows:

> We have, I think without question, passed from infancy to childhood. Our independence of physiology is a guarantee of that: we no longer feel any necessity of consulting physiology when we lay out our investigations; we do not necessarily borrow physiological apparatus and procedures; it does not occur to us to imitate physiology in the presentation of results; in a word, we are out of our physiological leading-strings. It is pleasant and reassuring, certainly, if while an enquiry is in course or

after it has been brought to completion we can make a cross-correlation with physiology; but we feel ourselves, none the less, to be independent; we do not lean upon physiology. That sign, then, seems unequivocal; and there is another, which a bold spirit might interpret to the effect that we are approaching adolescence—I mean the radical change that has been wrought over the whole field of the science since it turned to phenomenology. We can trace the impulse to this change directly to Hering; and if Hering has had to wait a long time before coming to his own that is partly because he was himself otherwise entangled in a rather crude form of empirical psychology.[63] Phenomenology is not yet, is not of itself, experimental psychology; but it provides today a safe and sure mode of approach to the analysis of our psychological subject matter; and our recourse to it, our realization of its promise may perhaps be taken as a sign of adolescence. If, then, Godfrey Thompson is right, and the intellect is most alert and most capable at the age of sixteen, we may congratulate ourselves that experimental psychology is nearing that critical point, and we may expect far better things from it in the near future than have been accomplished in the past.[64]

So the system of 1925–1927 was very different from that of 1910, both in organization and method, although it is possible to see the later Titchener by careful analysis of the earlier. Existential experience had become completely sensory, or perhaps more accurately, dimensional. A new approach had been added to the acceptable methods of experimental psychology—that of phenomenological observation.[65]

We come, then, full circle back to the *Prolegomena*. To what kind of systematic work was it to be the prolegomena? Would it have been a great catalogue of the facts of psychology like Wundt's *Grundzüge?* Some of his students thought so, and Titchener seems to have intended a work on those lines in his earlier years.[66] At some time in the post-*Textbook* period, however, Titchener's position changed as had Wundt's before him.[67] Just when this happened and why there is not yet enough evidence to say. In 1924 Titchener wrote:

I think I must have told you, when you were here, that I thought it was impossible in our generation to write a system of psychology. That position I still adhere to. I have, however, never denied that we are now in a position to write at psychology systematically; and this is all that I myself have in mind to do. A system of psychology, full rounded out and complete, could hardly nowadays be more than philosophical,—at any rate that is my judgment still. But I think we have a large enough body of data to be able to present the subject in a systematic schema so that future generations may see that we had not been altogether dependent upon philosophy for our conceptual scaffolding.[68]

Why these important developments, which were well known by members of the Cornell department and by several important researchers outside of Cornell, should have become lost in the post-Titchener systemization and ignored in books on psychological systems is an important question. The answer is complex, having to do with changes in psychology in the late 1920's with Titchener's relations with his own department and ex-students in other departments, and with the thinking and development of Titchener, himself. All that, however, is another story.

NOTES

1 Published posthumously as *Systematic Psychology: Prolegomena,* Macmillan: New York, 1929, under the editorship of H. P. Weld.

2 W. B. Pillsbury, The psychology of Edward Bradford Titchener, *Philos. Rev., 37,* 1928, 105.

3 E. B. Titchener, *A Textbook of Psychology,* Macmillan: New York, 1910.

4 Julian Jaynes, Edwin Garrigues Boring: 1886–1968, *J. Hist. Behav. Sci., 5,* 1969, 102.

5 E. G. Boring, Letter to R. M. Ogden, Aug. 18, 1928, Cornell University Archives.

6 W. S. Foster, A bibliography of the published writings of Edward Bradford Titchener 1889–1917, in

Studies in Psychology: Titchener Commemorative Volume, Louis N. Wilson: Worchester, Mass., 1917, 323–337; Karl M. Dallenbach, Bibliography of the writings of Edward Bradford Titchener, *Amer. J. Psychol., 40,* 1928, 121–125.

7 Notes of conversations with E. B. Titchener by Cora Friedline, Archives of American Psychology.

8 Titchener, Sensation and system, *Amer. J. Psychol., 26,* 1915, 258. Titchener would have preferred criticisms be leveled on the basis of his *The Psychology of Feeling and Attention,* Macmillan: New York, 1908; *Lectures on the Experimental Psychology of the Thought Processes,* Macmillan: New York, 1909; as well as articles such as Prolegomena to a study of introspection, *Amer. J. Psychol., 23,* 1912, 427–448; The schema of introspection, *Amer. J. Psychol., 23,* 1912, 485–508; and Description vs. statement of meaning, *Amer. J. Psychol., 23,* 1912, 165–182. This material as well as the *Textbook* will be covered by the phrase 'system of 1910'.

9 Some of this ground has been covered before by E. G. Boring in his article Titchener and the existential, *Amer. J. Psychol., 50,* 1937, 470–483, and is repeated here for the sake of continuity.

10 Titchener, *Textbook,* 25.

11 *Ibid.,* 48.

12 *Ibid.,* 37 f.

13 At least one of Titchener's early students was repulsed by this elaboration of Wundt's introspective method. M. F. Washburn, Some recollections, in Carl Murchison (ed.), *History of Psychology in Autobiography,* Vol. 2, 1930, 343.

14 Titchener, *Textbook,* 50.

15 Titchener, *Lectures on the Experimental Psychology of the Thought Processes,* 214.

16 Titchener, *Textbook,* 52–55, 198 f.; C. W. Perky, An experimental study of imagination, *Amer. J. Psychol., 21,* 1910, 422–452.

17 A. S. Edwards, An experimental study of sensory suggestion, *Amer. J. Psychol., 26,* 1915, 99–129.

18 Titchener, *The Psychology of Feeling and Attention,* 8 f.

19 *Ibid.,* 9 ff.

20 Carl Rahn, The relation of sensation to other categories in contemporary psychology: A study in the psychology of thinking, *Psychol. Rev. Monog.* 67, 1913. See particularly, 19–25, 39–41.

21 *Ibid.,* 22.

22 *Ibid.,* 23 f.; E. B. Talbot's article was The doctrine of conscious elements, *Phil. Rev., 4,* 1895, 154. Calkins' retort is found in her Attributes of sensation, *Psychol. Rev., 6,* 1899, 506. M. F. Washburn attempted to mediate between these views in her Some examples of the use of psychological analysis in system making, *Phil. Rev., 11,* 1902, 445. Titchener was well aware of Calkins' position since he included the reference to her article as well as Talbot's and Washburn's in his *Textbook,* 57, as well as in the notes to his *Feeling and Attention,* 325. One can only speculate as to why Titchener waited for Rahn's use of these criticisms to respond. Perhaps Titchener thought the Washburn distinction between Calkins' and Titchener's elements was sufficient reply, although Washburn tells us that Titchener objected to the paper when she delivered it at one of his seminars. M. F. Washburn, *op. cit.,* Some recollections, 344.

23 Titchener, Sensation and system, 258–267.

24 W. S. Hunter, James Rowland Angell: 1869–1949, *Amer. J. Psychol., 62,* 1949, 445; E. G. Boring, Titchener and the existential, *Amer. J. Psychol., 50,* 1937, 472 f.

25 Titchener, Sensation and system, 259.

26 Titchener, *An Outline of Psychology,* Macmillan: New York, 1899, 2nd edition, 37 f. Titchener wrote once to Boring, "For Wundt, of course, a sensation was observable precisely *as* its two attributes, because two fall within the 'range of attention.' So he could call a simultaneous observation of quality-intensity the observations of 'a sensation,' though what he and his men observed (and said so) was just the intensity-quality.... For me, whose systematic sensation has been steadily growing more complex, a complete observation of a sensation (as sum of attributes), has long been impossible; the range of (observational) attention forbids. My memory is that in the old *Outline* I made 4 attributes simultaneously observable (6 units being at that time the 'range of attention') as a sensation. The object in observation of sensation has always been attributive, by definition and by practice. So long as the attributes were two (or under 6....), one could still talk of observation of sensation. As attributes increased, one could not, and so one naturally spoke more and more discriminitively of ob-

servation of attributes.'' (Letter, E. B. Titchener to E. G. Boring, Sept. 24, 1923, Cornell University Archives.)

27 Titchener, Lectures on elementary psychology, Cornell University, 1916–1925. Notes by Karl M. Dallenbach, in the author's collection.

28 Titchener, The term 'attensity', *Amer. J. Psychol., 35,* 1924, 156; Titchener, Lectures on systematic psychology, 1918–1919, Notes by L. B. Hoisington, copy in the author's collection.

29 Titchener, Letter to E. G. Boring, Oct. 10, 1923, Cornell University Archives and Harvard University Archives.

30 Titchener, Letter to Christian Ruckmick, Oct. 26, 1922, Cornell University Archives.

31 F. L. Dimmick, A note on the series of black, grey, and white, *Amer. J. Psychol., 31,* 1920, 301 f. One source has it that it was Titchener who wrote the note under Dimmick's name. There is little doubt that the reorganization was due to Titchener and Dimmick's conversations, although the idea seems to have been the product of the atmosphere of the whole Cornell laboratory. (K. M. Dallenbach, Letter to E. G. Boring, Oct. 3, 1951, Cornell University Archives.)

32 Titchener, Visual intensity, *Amer. J. Psychol., 34,* 1923, 310 f.

33 *Ibid.,* 310.

34 Titchener, Letter to Christian Ruckmick, Oct. 26, 1922, Cornell University Archives; See also Titchener's Models for the demonstration of sensory qualities in Notes from the psychological laboratory of Cornell University, *Amer. J. Psychol., 31,* 1920, 212 f.

35 *Ibid.,* Letter to Ruckmick, Oct. 26, 1922.

36 Titchener, Letter to E. G. Boring, Nov. 19, 1924, Cornell University Archives. Also quoted in Boring's Titchener and the existential, *Amer. J. Psychol., 50,* 1937, 478.

37 Titchener, *Systematic Psychology: Prolegomena,* Macmillan: New York, 1929, 141.

38 Titchener, Letter to Junichiro Horiguchi, Dec. 9, 1925, Cornell University Archives.

39 J. P. Nafe, An experimental study of the affective qualities, *Amer. J. Psychol., 35,* 1924, 508.

40 Titchener, Letter to Horiguchi.

41 *Ibid.*

42 Titchener, The term 'attensity,' 156.

43 *Ibid.,* See also, Letter from E. B. Titchener to E. G. Boring, Nov. 19, 1924, Cornell University Archives, also quoted in Boring's Titchener and the existential, 478.

44 Dallenbach, Bibliography of the writings of Edward Bradford Titchener, 125; E. Frances Wells, An experimental study of affective experience, Thesis, Cornell University, 1928.

45 Titchener, Letter to E. G. Boring, Nov. 11, 1924, Cornell University Archives. Also quoted in Boring, Titchener and the existential, 477.

46 F. L. Bixby, A phenomenological study of luster, *J. Gen. Psychol., 1,* 1928, 136–174. This was the last thesis edited by Titchener for publication. George Kreezer, Luminous appearances, *J. Gen. Psychol., 4,* 1930, 247–281; F. W. Hazzard, A descriptive account of odors, *J. Exper. Psychol., 13,* 1930, 297–331. This work was completed under the direction of L. B. Hoisington, Titchener's righthand man. It was well underway before Titchener's death.

47 Titchener, Lectures on perception, Cornell University, Lecture 17, July 27, 1920. Notes by K. M. Dallenbach, in the author's collection.

48 F. L. Bixby, Personal communications, 1969.

49 Titchener, The scheme of introspection, *Amer. J. Psychol., 23,* 1912, 489 f.

50 *Ibid.,* 490.

51 *Ibid.,* 490.

52 *Ibid.,* 490.

53 *Ibid.,* 490.

54 Titchener, Lectures on perception, Cornell University, Lecture 4 Summer, 1920. Notes by K. M. Dallenbach, in the author's collection. After studying Husserl's writings for a year Titchener's evaluation is said to have been, ''There is nothing in him.'' (E. G. Boring, Review of Titchener's *Systematic Psychology: Prolegomena, Psych. Bull., 27,* 1930, 127.)

55 Titchener, Lectures on perception, Cornell University, Lecture 4.

56 Titchener, Letter to Max Meenes, March 10, 1925, Cornell University Archives.

57 Titchener, Letter to E. G. Boring, Feb. 8, 1926, Cornell University Archives.

58 Titchener, Letter to J. P. Guilford, Jan. 4, 1926, Cornell University Archives. Guilford was an observer in Bixby's dissertation at the time.

59 The exact dates when Kreezer's experiment was carried out are not given, but the times at which the various observers left Cornell indicate the experimental work must have been completed before Titchener's death. George Kreezer, Luminous appearances, *J. Gen. Psychol., 4,* 1930, 247–281.

60 Titchener, Lectures on elementary psychology, Cornell University, Lecture, 2, Oct. 7, 1919. Notes by K. M. Dallenbach, in the author's collection. See also, Titchener's *Systematic Psychology: Prolegomena,* 256.

61 Had Titchener experienced a softening of heart regarding Act psychology, he would surely have considered a revision of his criticisms in the *Prolegomena.* Letters to C. S. Meyers (Feb. 19, 1925) and to C. A. Ruckmick (Oct. 1, 1925) show clearly that there was no intention of the slightest change in the *Prolegomena* manuscript. As to Titchener's view of Gestalt psychology, we find him referring to it as a fad and adding that, "There is really no remedy for all these eccentric movements except time and the general logic involved in the progress of the science all round." (Letter to G. Tschelpanow, Oct. 25, 1924.) One finds, however, in reviewing Titchener's letters, a decidedly softer tone toward Gestalt psychology after Koffka's stay at Cornell than before. In 1925 he would say to Otto Klemm: "I heartily agree that the Gestalt investigations will bring in a good psychological harvest, my one fundamental criticism is that the Gestalt psychology is not identical with psychology as science." (Letter to Otto Klemm, Oct. 27, 1925.) In 1926 he wrote to President Lowell of Harvard: "[Köhler] and the other configurationists have done much good work, and some brilliant work, the results of which can be taken up fairly easily into the main body of experimental psychology. It is clear, however, that the school must enlarge its space; it is impossible to rear a complete science on the foundation of a single concept." Letter to A. L. Lowell, April 19, 1926. All letters from Cornell University Archives.

62 Boring, Titchener, meaning and behaviorism, in *Schools of Psychology: A Symposium,* David Krantz, (ed.), Appleton-Century-Crofts: New York, 1969; Boring, Titchener on meaning, *Psychol. Rev., 45,* 1938, 94. Titchener's attitude toward Behaviorism in the late years is clearly shown in his letters. "Behaviorism has spread over the country in a great wave, more or less as Freudianism did a few years ago. The actual experimental work that the behaviorists turn out is good enough; but the general logic of their position is ridiculously crude.... I don't think that the movement will continue very long." Letter to G. Tschelpanow, Oct. 25, 1924. "...The more freely the behaviorists write, the more obviously do they expose themselves to criticism." Letter to C. Ladd-Franklin, Oct. 5, 1923. Both letters from Cornell University Archives.

63 Here is another jab at Act psychology. Empirical psychology and the Act psychologies of the Brentano stripe were used as equivalents in much of Titchener's writing. Titchener, Brentano and Wundt: empirical and experimental psychology, *Amer. J. Psychol., 32,* 1921, 108–120; Empirical and experimental psychology, *J. Gen. Psychol., 1,* 1927, 176 f.

64 Titchener, Experimental psychology: a retrospect, *Amer. J. Psychol., 36,* 1925, 322 f.

65 It should be clearly understood that Titchener was not saying that phenomenological observation had replaced the traditional introspective method. Titchener seems always to have discriminated between the phenomenological and psychological attitude. The effect of these attitudes was one task given to George M. Scheck for his doctoral thesis in 1924. Titchener, Letter to L. B. Hoisington, Mar. 11, 1924. Cornell University Archives.

66 W. B. Pillsbury, The psychology of Edward Bradford Titchener, *Phil. Rev., 37,* 1928, 104 f.; Boring, Review of Titchener's *Systematic Psychology: Prolegomena, Psychol. Bull., 27,* 1930, 121 f.

67 Titchener, Wilhelm Wundt, *Amer. J. Psychol., 32,* 1921, 173.

68 Titchener, Letter to G. Tschelpanow, Oct. 25, 1924, Cornell University Archives.

CHAPTER 9

DARWINIAN INFLUENCES: ADAPTATION AND INDIVIDUAL DIFFERENCES

In November of 1859, Charles Darwin's book, *On the Origin of Species,* appeared in the bookshops of London. At the end of the first day, all 1250 copies of the first printing had been sold. It was an appropriate beginning for the book that would be judged by many scholars to be the most influential work published in the last four hundred years. Its influence has been enormous in many fields of inquiry, and psychology is no exception.

At the age of 22, Charles Darwin (1809–1882) signed on as a naturalist aboard *H.M.S. Beagle,* a small British ship scheduled for a scientific voyage around the world. That voyage of five years would change Darwin and the world. In the last year of that voyage, he began to organize his many notes toward eventual publication. He began his writing immediately after his return to England, completing first the five volumes of his *Zoology of the Voyage of H.M.S. Beagle* and then, in 1839, his journal entitled *The Voyage of the Beagle.* Early in the course of this writing, Darwin began to think about the transformation of species, an idea that had been part of scientific conjecture for many years. His own data from the *Beagle* voyage, and the impetus of reading Thomas Malthus's essay on population, provided the basis for his revolutionary book on the theory of evolution by natural selection. Darwin began his writing on that theory around 1840 and by 1844 had produced a manuscript of approximately two hundred pages. Yet he did not publish those ideas until nearly twenty years after he first began work on them. The reasons for this twenty-year delay and the interesting story surrounding the writing of the *Origin* are discussed in one of the selections in this chapter.

The idea of evolution was not original with Darwin. In a 1794 book, *Zoonomia,* his grandfather, Erasmus Darwin (1731–1802), a physician and biologist, had written about attempts at adaptation producing evolution of animal species. These ideas anticipated the evolutionary theory of Jean Baptiste Lamarck (1744–1829), whose *Philosophie Zoologique,* published in 1809, argued for a behavioral theory of evolution. In other words, learned behaviors that proved adaptive were passed to subsequent generations. (Lamarck's ideas remained influential through most of the nineteenth century but fell into disrepute at the beginning of the twentieth century. However, some recent work in the field of evolutionary theory has revived them.) Evolutionary ideas existed outside of biology as well. Charles Darwin's good friend, Charles Lyell (1797–1875), an eminent geologist, had published an evolutionary account of the transformations in the geology of the earth.

These intellectual forces set the stage for a theory that could explain the growing fossil, botanical, and zoological evidence that was inconsistent with a Genesis account of the origin of species, and Darwin was to generate that theory (see Gruber, 1981). His extensive and meticulous work as the *Beagle* naturalist led Darwin to propose natural selection as the mechanism for evolution. Changes in species occurred through random variations. Certain of those variations would be better suited to changing demands in the environment, and those animals and plants would be more likely to survive. Darwin's theory gave new importance to the notion of variation and individual differences and provided an understanding of their role in species adaptation to the environment.

These ideas were influential in Freud's psychoanalytic theory (see Chapter 15), but nowhere were they more important than in American functional psychology, a psychology built on an emphasis on individual differences and their importance for adaptation (see Chapters 10 and 11). Further, Darwin's work significantly strengthened the field of comparative psychology by linking humans with the rest of the animal kingdom (see Chapter 12). Of particular importance in that respect was his 1872 book entitled *The Expression of the Emotions in Man and Animals,* which described the similarity in form and function of emotional expressions in humans and other animals.

Darwin's theory also had a great impact on his cousin, Francis Galton (Erasmus Darwin was Galton's grandfather as well). Galton (1822–1911) was an explorer, statistician, inventor, and scientist, who made significant contributions to many fields, including psychology. His interests were incredibly diverse. For example, he studied fingerprints, the geographic distribution of beauty, the efficacy of prayer, word associations, twins, paranoia, cuckoos, animal hearing, correlation, and intelligence. He even taught himself to perform arithmetical calculations using odors substituted for numbers (see Galton, 1894).

Galton is probably best remembered for his founding of *eugenics,* an ideology that proposed improvement of the human race by selectively mating those individuals who possessed the most desirable characteristics. Needless to say, such ideas produced considerable controversy in and out of the scientific community.

Within a few days of the publication of Darwin's *Origin,* Galton wrote to his cousin:

> Pray let me add a word of congratulations on the completion of your wonderful volume.... I have laid it down in the full enjoyment of a feeling that one rarely experiences after boyhood days, of having been initiated into an entirely new province of knowledge which, nevertheless, connects itself with other things in a thousand ways. (as cited in Fancher, 1979, pp. 261–262)

The social implications of Darwin's book were especially important to Galton as he began his studies of eminent individuals and the reasons for their eminence. He concluded, through statistical studies, that eminence occurred among the members of certain families too frequently to be explained by the influence of the environment. He published his findings in his most famous book, *Hereditary Genius,* which appeared in 1869. Returning the compliment he had received, Darwin wrote to Galton:

> I have only read about 50 pages of your book...but I must exhale myself, else something will go wrong in my inside. I do not think I have ever in my life read anything more interesting and original....You have made a convert of an opponent in one sense, for I have always maintained that, excepting fools, men do not differ in intellect, only in zeal and hard work. (as cited in Fancher, 1979, p. 268)

Galton argued in his book that, like physical traits, natural abilities (i.e., psychological traits such as judgment, intelligence, sociability) were inherited. The next logical step was the improvement of the human race by a eugenics program that ensured the "best kind" of people. In 1884 he established a laboratory in the Natural History Museum in the South Kensington district of London, where for six years he collected anthropometric measurements (visual acuity, strength of grip, color vision, hearing acuity, hand preference, span of arms, etc.) to support his views on the distribution of abilities and physical characteristics. Solomon Diamond (1977) has argued that all of Galton's work in psychology arose from one concern: "how we might best manipulate the forces of evolution to mankind's advantage" (p. 52). Eugenics was thus a practical program to accelerate the progress of evolution.

As noted earlier, the legacy of Darwin and Galton is an important one for psychology, especially for the American school of psychology known as *functionalism.* Consciousness was viewed by this school as having evolutionary significance; obviously it aided an organism's ability to adapt to the environment. Deriving from the concept of evolutionary adaptation was an emphasis on the processes of psychological adjustment, a belief that selection of behavioral acts was determined by the consequences of those actions and a focus on the value of studying individual differences (Kendler, 1987). Those emphases would characterize the work of many American psychologists, such as William James, G. Stanley Hall, James McKeen Cattell, and Edward L. Thorndike (all of whom are discussed in the next three chapters).

In this chapter there are two primary source selections, one from Darwin and the other from Galton. The two secondary source articles also treat the work and influence of those two scientists. The first selection, from Darwin's *Origin of Species,* includes the introduction to the book as well as the third chapter dealing with the struggle for existence. Pay special attention to the hesitancy and caution of Darwin's language in the introduction to the *Origin.* The second selection, from Galton's *Hereditary Genius,* includes the preface and introductory chapter of the book as well as an excerpt from the end of the book treating the "comparative worth of different races."

One of the long-standing questions in the history of science is why Darwin delayed so long in publishing his theory (see Gould, 1977). Not surprisingly, many explanations have been offered. In the third selection, the historian of science Robert J. Richards attempts a definitive answer and, in doing so, discusses what makes for an interesting question in science and what historiographical models can be best used to answer those questions.

The final selection is by Solomon Diamond, a distinguished psychologist who has written much in the field of intellectual history. In this article, Diamond looks at the influence of Galton's ideas in American psychology, focusing especially on James McKeen Cattell and Joseph Jastrow. The influence of both Darwin and Galton on American psychology will become even more evident in the following three chapters of this book.

REFERENCES

Diamond, S. (1977). Francis Galton and American psychology. *Annals of the New York Academy of Sciences, 291,* 47–55.

Fancher, R. E. (1979). *Pioneers of psychology.* New York: W. W. Norton & Co.

Galton, F. (1894). Arithmetic by smell. *Psychological Review, 1,* 61–62.

Gould, S. J. (1977). *Ever since Darwin.* New York: W. W. Norton & Co.

Gruber, H. (1981). *Darwin on man: A psychological study of scientific creativity* (2d ed.). Chicago: University of Chicago Press.

Kendler, H. H. (1987). *Historical foundations of modern psychology.* Chicago: Dorsey Press.

Natural Selection and the Struggle for Existence

Charles Darwin

INTRODUCTION

When on board H.M.S. 'Beagle,' as naturalist, I was much struck with certain facts in the distribution of the organic beings inhabiting South America, and in the geological relations of the present to the past inhabitants of that continent. These facts, as will be seen in the latter chapters of this volume, seemed to throw some light on the origin of species—that mystery of mysteries, as it has been called by one of our greatest philosophers. On my return home, it occurred to me, in 1837, that something might perhaps be made out on this question by patiently accumulating and reflecting on all sorts of facts which could possibly have any bearing on it. After five years' work I allowed myself to speculate on the subject, and drew up some short notes; these I enlarged in 1844 into a sketch of the conclusions, which then seemed to me probable: from that period to the present day I have steadily pursued the same object. I hope that I may be excused for entering on these personal details, as I give them to show that I have not been hasty in coming to a decision.

My work is now (1859) nearly finished; but as it will take me many more years to complete it, and as my health is far from strong, I have been urged to publish this Abstract. I have more especially been induced to do this, as Mr. Wallace, who is now studying the natural history of the Malay archipelago, has arrived at almost exactly the same general conclusions that I have on the origin of species. In 1858 he sent me a memoir on this subject, with a request that I would forward it to Sir Charles Lyell, who sent it to the Linnean Society, and it is published in the third volume of the Journal of that Society. Sir C.

Lyell and Dr. Hooker, who both knew of my work—the latter having read my sketch of 1844—honoured me by thinking it advisable to publish, with Mr. Wallace's excellent memoir, some brief extracts from my manuscripts.

This Abstract, which I now publish, must necessarily be imperfect. I cannot here give references and authorities for my several statements; and I must trust to the reader reposing some confidence in my accuracy. No doubt errors will have crept in, though I hope I have always been cautious in trusting to good authorities alone. I can here give only the general conclusions at which I have arrived, with a few facts in illustration, but which, I hope, in most cases will suffice. No one can feel more sensible than I do of the necessity of hereafter publishing in detail all the facts, with references, on which my conclusions have been grounded; and I hope in a future work to do this. For I am well aware that scarcely a single point is discussed in this volume on which facts cannot be adduced, often apparently leading to conclusions directly opposite to those at which I have arrived. A fair result can be obtained only by fully stating and balancing the facts and arguments on both sides of each question; and this is here impossible.

I much regret that want of space prevents my having the satisfaction of acknowledging the generous assistance which I have received from very many naturalists, some of them personally unknown to me. I cannot, however, let this opportunity pass without expressing my deep obligations to Dr. Hooker, who, for the last fifteen years, has aided me in every possible way by his large stores of knowledge and his excellent judgment.

In considering the Origin of Species, it is quite conceivable that a naturalist, reflecting on the mutual affinities of organic beings, on their embryological relations, their geographical distribu-

From Darwin, C. (1859). *On the origin of species by means of natural selection*. New York: D. Appleton, 1892, pp. 1–4, 48–61.

tion, geological succession, and other such facts, might come to the conclusion that species had not been independently created, but had descended, like varieties, from other species. Nevertheless, such a conclusion, even if well founded, would be unsatisfactory, until it could be shown how the innumerable species inhabiting this world have been modified, so as to acquire that perfection of structure and coadaptation which justly excites our admiration. Naturalists continually refer to external conditions, such as climate, food, &c., as the only possible cause of variation. In one limited sense, as we shall hereafter see, this may be true; but it is preposterous to attribute to mere external conditions, the structure, for instance, of the woodpecker, with its feet, tail, beak, and tongue, so admirably adapted to catch insects under the bark of trees. In the case of the mistletoe, which draws its nourishment from certain trees, which has seeds that must be transported by certain birds, and which has flowers with separate sexes absolutely requiring the agency of certain insects to bring pollen from one flower to the other, it is equally preposterous to account for the structure of this parasite, with its relations to several distinct organic beings, by the effects of external conditions, or of habit, or of the volition of the plant itself.

It is, therefore, of the highest importance to gain a clear insight into the means of modification and coadaptation. At the commencement of my observations it seemed to me probable that a careful study of domesticated animals and of cultivated plants would offer the best chance of making out this obscure problem. Nor have I been disappointed; in this and in all other perplexing cases I have invariably found that our knowledge, imperfect though it be, of variation under domestication, afforded the best and safest clue. I may venture to express my conviction of the high value of such studies, although they have been very commonly neglected by naturalists.

From these considerations, I shall devote the first chapter of this Abstract to Variation under Domestication. We shall thus see that a large amount

of hereditary modification is at least possible; and, what is equally or more important, we shall see how great is the power of man in accumulating by his Selection successive slight variations. I will then pass on to the variability of species in a state of nature; but I shall, unfortunately, be compelled to treat this subject far too briefly, as it can be treated properly only by giving long catalogues of facts. We shall, however, be enabled to discuss what circumstances are most favourable to variation. In the next chapter the Struggle for Existence amongst all organic beings throughout the world, which inevitably follows from the high geometrical ratio of their increase, will be considered. This is the doctrine of Malthus, applied to the whole animal and vegetable kingdoms. As many more individuals of each species are born than can possibly survive; and as, consequently, there is a frequently recurring struggle for existence, it follows that any being, if it vary however slightly in any manner profitable to itself, under the complex and sometimes varying conditions of life, will have a better chance of surviving, and thus be *naturally selected*. From the strong principle of inheritance, any selected variety will tend to propagate its new and modified form.

This fundamental subject of Natural Selection will be treated at some length in the fourth chapter; and we shall then see how Natural Selection almost inevitably causes much Extinction of the less improved forms of life, and leads to what I have called Divergence of Character. In the next chapter I shall discuss the complex and little known laws of variation. In the five succeeding chapters, the most apparent and gravest difficulties in accepting the theory will be given: namely, first, the difficulties of transitions, or how a simple being or a simple organ can be changed and perfected into a highly developed being or into an elaborately constructed organ; secondly, the subject of Instinct, or the mental powers of animals; thirdly, Hybridism, or the infertility of species and the fertility of varieties when intercrossed; and fourthly, the imperfection of the Geological Record. In the next chapter I shall consider the geological succession of organic beings throughout time; in the twelfth and thirteenth; their geographical distribution throughout space; in the fourteenth, their classification or mutual affinities, both when mature and in an embryonic condition. In the last chapter I shall give a brief recapitulation of the whole work, and a few concluding remarks.

No one ought to feel surprise at much remaining as yet unexplained in regard to the origin of species and varieties, if he make due allowance for our profound ignorance in regard to the mutual relations of the many beings which live around us. Who can explain why one species ranges widely and is very numerous, and why another allied species has a narrow range and is rare? Yet these relations are of the highest importance, for they determine the present welfare, and, as I believe, the future success and modification of every inhabitant of this world. Still less do we know of the mutual relations of the innumerable inhabitants of the world during the many past geological epochs in its history. Although much remains obscure, and will long remain obscure, I can entertain no doubt, after the most deliberate study and dispassionate judgment of which I am capable, that the view which most naturalists until recently entertained, and which I formerly entertained—namely, that each species has been independently created—is erroneous. I am fully convinced that species are not immutable; but that those belonging to what are called the same genera are lineal descendants of some other and generally extinct species, in the same manner as the acknowledged varieties of any one species are the descendants of that species. Furthermore, I am convinced that Natural Selection has been the most important, but not the exclusive, means of modification....

STRUGGLE FOR EXISTENCE

Before entering on the subject of this chapter, I must make a few preliminary remarks, to show how the struggle for existence bears on Natural Selection. It has been seen in the last chapter that amongst organic beings in a state of nature there is some individual variability: indeed I am not aware that this has ever been disputed. It is immaterial for us whether a multitude of doubtful forms be called species or sub-species or varieties; what rank, for instance, the two or three hundred doubtful forms of British plants are entitled to hold, if the existence of any well-marked varieties be admitted. But the mere existence of individual variability and of some few well-marked varieties, though necessary as the foundation for the work, helps us but little in understanding how species arise in nature. How have all those exquisite adaptations of one part of the organisation to another part, and to the conditions of life, and of one organic being to another being, been perfected? We see these beautiful co-adaptations most plainly in the woodpecker and the misletoe; and only a little less plainly in the humblest parasite which clings to the hairs of a quadruped or feathers of a bird; in the structure of the beetle which dives through the water: in the plumed seed which is wafted by the gentlest breeze; in short, we see beautiful adaptations everywhere and in every part of the organic world.

Again, it may be asked, how is it that varieties, which I have called incipient species, become ultimately converted into good and distinct species, which in most cases obviously differ from each other far more than do the varieties of the same species? How do those groups of species, which constitute what are called distinct genera, and which differ from each other more than do the species of the same genus, arise? All these results, as we shall more fully see in the next chapter, follow from the struggle for life. Owing to this struggle, variations, however slight, and from whatever cause proceeding, if they be in any degree profitable to the individuals of a species, in their infinitely complex relations to other organic beings and to their physical conditions of life, will tend to the preservation of such individuals, and will generally be inherited by the offspring. The offspring, also, will thus have a better chance of surviving, for, of the many individuals of any species which are periodically born, but a small number can survive. I have called this principle, by which each slight variation, if useful, is preserved, by the term Natural Selection, in order to mark its relation to man's power of selection. But the expression often used by Mr. Herbert Spencer of the Survival of the Fittest is more accurate, and is sometimes equally convenient. We have seen that man by selection can certainly produce great results, and can adapt organic beings to his own uses, through the accumulation of slight but useful variations, given to him by the hand of Nature. But Natural Selection, as we shall hereafter see, is a power incessantly ready for action, and is as immeasurably superior to man's feeble efforts, as the works of Nature are to those of Art.

We will now discuss in a little more detail the struggle for existence. In my future work this subject will be treated, as it well deserves, at greater length. The elder De Candolle and Lyell have largely and philosophically shown that all organic beings are exposed to severe competition. In regard to plants, no one has treated this subject with more spirit and ability than W. Herbert, Dean of Manchester, evidently the result of his great horticultural knowledge. Nothing is easier than to admit in words the truth of the universal struggle for life, or more difficult—at least I have found it so—than constantly to bear this conclusion in mind. Yet unless it be thoroughly engrained in the mind, the whole economy of nature, with every fact on distribution, rarity, abundance, extinction, and variation, will be dimly seen or quite misunderstood. We behold the face of nature bright with gladness, we often see superabundance of food; we do not see or we forget, that the birds which are idly singing round us mostly live on insects or seeds, and are thus constantly destroying life; or we forget how largely these songsters, or their eggs, or their nestlings, are destroyed by birds and beasts of prey; we do not always bear in mind, that, though food may be now superabundant, it is not so at all seasons of each recurring year.

The Term, Struggle for Existence, Used in a Large Sense

I should premise that I use this term in a large and metaphorical sense including dependence of one being on another, and including (which is more important) not only the life of the individual, but success in leaving progeny. Two canine animals, in a time of dearth, may be truly said to struggle with each other which shall get food and live. But a plant on the edge of a desert is said to struggle for life against the drought, though more properly it should be said to be dependent on the moisture. A plant which annually produces a thousand seeds, of which only one on an average comes to maturity, may be more truly said to struggle with the plants of the same and other kinds which already clothe the ground. The misletoe is dependent on the apple and a few other trees, but can only in a far-fetched sense be said to struggle with these trees, for, if too many of these parasites grow on the same tree, it languishes and dies. But several seedling misletoes, growing close together on the same branch, may more truly be said to struggle with each other. As the misletoe is disseminated by birds, its existence depends on them; and it may metaphorically be said to struggle with other fruit-bearing plants, in tempting the birds to devour and thus disseminate its seeds. In these several senses, which pass into each other, I use for convenience' sake the general term of Struggle for Existence.

Geometrical Ratio of Increase

A struggle for existence inevitably follows from the high rate at which all organic beings tend to increase. Every being, which during its natural lifetime produces several eggs or seeds, must suffer destruction during some period of its life, and during some season or occasional year, otherwise, on the principle of geometrical increase, its numbers would quickly become so inordinately great that no country could support the product. Hence, as more individuals are produced than can possibly survive, there must in every case be a struggle for existence, either one individual with another of the same species, or with the individuals of distinct species, or with the physical conditions of life. It is the doctrine of Malthus applied with manifold force to the whole animal and vegetable kingdoms; for in this case there can be no artificial increase of food, and no prudential restraint from marriage. Although some species may be now increasing, more or less rapidly, in numbers, all cannot do so, for the world would not hold them.

There is no exception to the rule that every organic being naturally increases at so high a rate, that, if not destroyed, the earth would soon be covered by the progeny of a single pair. Even slow-breeding man has doubled in twenty-five years, and at this rate, in less than a thousand years, there would literally not be standing-room for his progeny. Linnaeus has calculated that if an annual plant produced only two seeds—and there is no plant so unproductive as this—and their seedlings next year produced two, and so on, then in twenty years there would be a million plants. The elephant is reckoned the slowest breeder of all known animals, and I have taken some pains to estimate its probable minimum rate of natural increase; it will be safest to assume that it begins breeding when thirty years old, and goes on breeding till ninety years old, bringing forth six young in the interval, and surviving till one hundred years old; if this be so, after a period of from 740 to 750 years there would be nearly nineteen million elephants alive, descended from the first pair.

But we have better evidence on this subject than mere theoretical calculations, namely, the numerous recorded cases of the astonishingly rapid increase of various animals in a state of nature, when circumstances have been favourable to them during two or three following seasons. Still more striking is the evidence from our domestic animals of many kinds which have run wild in several parts of the world; if the statements of the rate of increase of slow-breeding cattle and horses in South America, and latterly in Australia, had not been well authenticated, they would have been incredible. So it is with plants; cases could be given of introduced plants which have become common throughout whole islands in a period of less than ten years. Several of the plants, such as the cardoon and a tall thistle, which are now the commonest over the wide plains of La Plata, clothing square leagues of surface almost to the exclusion of every other plant, have been introduced from Europe and there are plants which now range in India, as I hear from Dr. Falconer, from Cape Comorin to the Himalaya, which have been imported from America since its discovery. In such cases, and endless others could be given, no one supposes, that the fertility of the animals or plants has been suddenly and temporarily increased in any sensible degree. The obvious explanation is that the conditions of life have been highly favourable, and that there has consequently been less destruction of the old and young, and that nearly all the young have been enabled to breed. Their geometrical ratio of increase, the result of which never fails to be surprising, simply explains their extraordinarily rapid increase and wide diffusion in their new homes.

In a state of nature almost every full-grown plant annually produces seed, and amongst animals there are very few which do not annually pair. Hence we may confidently assert, that all plants and animals are tending to increase at a geometrical ratio,—that all would rapidly stock every station in which they could any how exist,—and that this geometrical tendency to increase must be checked by destruction at some period of life. Our familiarity with the larger domestic animals tends, I think, to mislead us: we see no great destruction falling on them, but we do not keep in mind that thousands are annually slaughtered for food, and that in a state of nature an equal number would have somehow to be disposed of.

The only difference between organisms which annually produce eggs or seeds by the thousand, and those which produce extremely few, is, that the slow-breeders would require a few more years to people, under favourable conditions, a whole district, let it be ever so large. The condor lays a couple of eggs and the ostrich a score, and yet in the same country the condor may be the more numerous of the two; the Fulmar petrel lays but one egg, yet it is believed to be the most numerous bird in the world. One fly deposits hundreds of eggs, and another, like the hippobosca, a single one; but this difference does not determine how many individuals of the two species can be supported in a district. A large number of eggs is of some importance to those species which depend on a fluctuating amount of food, for it allows them rapidly to increase in number. But the real importance of a large number of eggs or seeds is to make up for much destruction at some period of life; and this period in the great majority of cases is an early one. If an animal can in any way protect its own eggs or young, a small number may be produced, and yet the average stock be fully kept up; but if many eggs or young are destroyed, many must be produced, or the species will become extinct. It would suffice to keep up the full number of a tree, which lived on an average for a thousand years, if a single seed were produced once in a thousand years, supposing that this seed were never destroyed, and could be ensured to germinate in a fitting place. So that, in all cases, the average number of any animal or plant depends only indirectly on the number of its eggs or seeds.

In looking at Nature, it is most necessary to keep the foregoing considerations always in mind—never to forget that every single organic being may be said to be striving to the utmost to increase in numbers; that each lives by a struggle at some period of its life; that heavy destruction inevitably falls either on the young or old, during each generation or at recurrent intervals. Lighten any check, mitigate the destruction ever so little, and the number of the species will almost instantaneously increase to any amount.

Nature of the Checks to Increase

The causes which check the natural tendency of each species to increase are most obscure. Look at the most vigorous species; by as much as it swarms in numbers, by so much will it tend to increase still further. We know not exactly what the checks are even in a single instance. Nor will this surprise any one who reflects how ignorant we are on this head, even in regard to mankind, although so incomparably better known than any other animal. This subject of the checks to increase has been ably treated by several authors, and I hope in a future work to discuss it at considerable length, more especially in regard to the feral animals of South America. Here I will make only a few remarks, just to recall to the reader's mind some of the chief points. Eggs or very young animals seem generally to suffer most, but this is not invariably the case. With plants there is a vast destruction of seeds, but, from some observations which I have made it appears that the seedlings suffer most from germinating in ground already thickly stocked with other plants. Seedlings, also, are destroyed in vast numbers by various enemies; for instance, on a piece of ground three feet long and two wide, dug and cleared, and where there could be no choking from other plants, I marked all the seedlings of our native weeds as they came up, and out of 357 no less than 295, were destroyed, chiefly by slugs and insects. If turf which has long been mown, and the case would be the same with turf closely browsed by quadrupeds, be let to grow, the more vigorous plants gradually kill the less vigorous, though fully grown plants; thus out of twenty species growing on a little plot of mown turf (three feet by four) nine species perished, from the other species being allowed to grow up freely.

The amount of food for each species of course gives the extreme limit to which each can increase; but very frequently it is not the obtaining food, but the serving as prey to other animals, which determines the average numbers of a species. Thus, there seems to be little doubt that the stock of partridges, grouse, and hares on any large estate depends chiefly on the destruction of vermin. If not one head of game were shot during the next twenty years in England, and, at the same time, if no vermin were destroyed, there would, in all probability, be less game than at present, although hundreds of thousands of game animals are now annually shot. On the other hand, in some cases, as with the elephant, none are destroyed by beasts of prey; for even the tiger in India most rarely dares to attack a young elephant protected by its dam.

Climate plays an important part in determining the average numbers of a species, and periodical seasons of extreme cold or drought seem to be the most effective of all checks. I estimated (chiefly from the greatly reduced numbers of nests in the spring) that the winter of 1854–5 destroyed four-fifths of the birds in my own grounds; and this is a tremendous destruction, when we remember that ten per cent, is an extraordinarily severe mortality from epidemics with man. The action of climate seems at first sight to be quite independent of the struggle for existence; but in so far as climate chiefly acts in reducing food, it brings on the most severe struggle between the individuals, whether of the same or of distinct species, which subsist on the same kind of food. Even when climate, for instance extreme cold, acts directly, it will be the least vigorous individuals, or those which have got least food through the advancing winter, which will suffer most. When we travel from south to north, or from a damp region to a dry, we invariably see some species gradually getting rarer and rarer, and finally disappearing; and the change of climate being conspicuous, we are tempted to attribute the whole effect to its direct action. But this is a false view; we forget that each species, even where it most abounds, is constantly suffering enormous destruction at some period of its life, from enemies or from competitors for the same place and food; and if these enemies or

competitors be in the least degree favoured by any slight change of climate, they will increase in numbers; and as each area is already fully stocked with inhabitants, the other species must decrease. When we travel southward and see a species decreasing in numbers, we may feel sure that the cause lies quite as much in other species being favoured, as in this one being hurt. So it is when we travel northward, but in a somewhat lesser degree, for the number of species of all kinds, and therefore of competitors, decreases northwards; hence in going northwards, or in ascending a mountain, we far oftener meet with stunted forms, due to the *directly* injurious action of climate, than we do in proceeding southwards or in descending a mountain. When we reach the Arctic regions, or snow-capped summits, or absolute deserts, the struggle for life is almost exclusively with the elements.

That climate acts in main part indirectly by favouring other species, we clearly see in the prodigious number of plants which in our gardens can perfectly well endure our climate, but which never become naturalised, for they cannot compete with our native plants nor resist destruction by our native animals.

When a species, owing to highly favourable circumstances, increases inordinately in numbers in a small tract, epidemics—at least, this seems generally to occur with our game animals—often ensue; and here we have a limiting check independent of the struggle for life. But even some of these so-called epidemics appear to be due to parasitic worms, which have from some cause, possibly in part through facility of diffusion amongst the crowded animals, been disproportionally favoured: and here comes in a sort of struggle between the parasite and its prey.

On the other hand, in many cases, a large stock of individuals of the same species, relatively to the numbers of its enemies, is absolutely necessary for its preservation. Thus we can easily raise plenty of corn and rape-seed, &c., in our fields, because the seeds are in great excess compared with the number of birds which feed on them; nor can the birds, though having a super-abundance of food at this one season, increase in number proportionally to the supply of seed, as their numbers are checked during winter; but any one who has tried, knows how troublesome it is to get seed from a few wheat or other such plants in a garden: I have in this case lost every single seed. This view of the necessity of a large stock of the same species for its preservation, explains, I believe, some singular facts in nature such as that of very rare plants being sometimes extremely abundant, in the few spots where they do exist; and that of some social plants being social, that is abounding in individuals, even on the extreme verge of their range. For in such cases, we may believe, that a plant could exist only where the conditions of its life were so favourable that many could exist together, and thus save the species from utter destruction. I should add that the good effects of intercrossing, and the ill effects of close interbreeding, no doubt come into play in many of these cases; but I will not here enlarge on this subject.

Complex Relations of All Animals and Plants to Each Other in the Struggle for Existence

Many cases are on record showing how complex and unexpected are the checks and relations between organic beings, which have to struggle together in the same country. I will give only a single instance, which, though a simple one, interested me. In Staffordshire, on the estate of a relation, where I had ample means of investigation, there was a large and extremely barren heath, which had never been touched by the hand of man; but several hundred acres of exactly the same nature had been enclosed twenty-five years previously and planted with Scotch fir. The change in the native vegetation of the planted part of the heath was most remarkable, more than is generally seen in passing from one quite different soil to another; not only the proportional numbers of the heath-plants were wholly changed, but twelve species of plants (not count-

ing grasses and carices) flourished in the plantations, which could not be found on the heath. The effect on the insects must have been still greater, for six insectivorous birds were very common in the plantations, which were not to be seen on the heath; and the heath was frequented by two or three distinct insectivorous birds. Here we see how potent has been the effect of the introduction of a single tree, nothing whatever else having been done, with the exception of the land having been enclosed, so that cattle could not enter. But how important an element enclosure is, I plainly saw near Farnham, in Surrey. Here there are extensive heaths, with a few clumps of old Scotch firs on the distant hilltops: within the last ten years large spaces have been enclosed, and self-sown firs are now springing up in multitudes, so close together that all cannot live. When I ascertained that these young trees had not been sown or planted, I was so much surprised at their numbers that I went to several points of view, whence I could examine hundreds of acres of the unenclosed heath, and literally I could not see a single Scotch fir, except the old planted clumps. But on looking closely between the stems of the heath, I found a multitude of seedlings and little trees which had been perpetually browsed down by the cattle. In one square yard, at a point some hundred yards distant from one of the old clumps, I counted thirty-two little trees; and one of them, with twenty-six rings of growth, had, during many years tried to raise its head above the stems of the heath, and had failed. No wonder that, as soon as the land was enclosed, it became thickly clothed with vigorously growing young firs. Yet the heath was so extremely barren and so extensive that no one would ever have imagined that cattle would have so closely and effectually searched it for food.

Here we see that cattle absolutely determine the existence of the Scotch fir; but in several parts of the world insects determine the existence of cattle. Perhaps Paraguay offers the most curious instance of this; for here neither cattle nor horses nor dogs have ever run wild, though they swarm southward and northward in a feral state; and Azara and Rengger have shown that this is caused by the greater number in Paraguay of a certain fly, which lays its eggs in the navels of these animals when first born. The increase of these flies, numerous as they are, must be habitually checked by some means, probably by other parasitic insects. Hence, if certain insectivorous birds were to decrease in Paraguay, the parasitic insects would probably increase; and this would lessen the number of the navel-frequenting flies—then cattle and horses would become feral, and this would certainly greatly alter (as indeed I have observed in parts of South America) the vegetation: this again would largely affect the insects; and this, as we have just seen in Staffordshire, the insectivorous birds, and so onwards in ever-increasing circles of complexity. Not that under nature the relations will ever be as simple as this. Battle within battle must be continually recurring with varying success; and yet in the long-run the forces are so nicely balanced, that the face of nature remains for long periods of time uniform, though assuredly the merest trifle would give the victory to one organic being over another. Nevertheless, so profound is our ignorance, and so high our presumption, that we marvel when we hear of the extinction of an organic being; and as we do not see the cause, we invoke cataclysms to desolate the world, or invent laws on the duration of the forms of life!

I am tempted to give one more instance showing how plants and animals, remote in the scale of nature, are bound together by a web of complex relations. I shall hereafter have occasion to show that the exotic Lobelia fulgens is never visited in my garden by insects, and consequently, from its peculiar structure, never sets a seed. Nearly all our orchidaceous plants absolutely require the visits of insects to remove their pollen-masses and thus to fertilise them. I find from experiments that humble-bees are almost indispensable to the fertilisation of the heartsease (Viola tricol-

or), for other bees do not visit this flower. I have also found that the visits of bees are necessary for the fertilisation of some kinds of clover: for instance, 20 heads of Dutch clover (Trifolium repens) yielded 2,290 seeds, but 20 other heads protected from bees produced not one. Again, 100 heads of red clover (T. pratense) produced 2,700 seeds, but the same number of protected heads produced not a single seed. Humble-bees alone visit red clover, as other bees cannot reach the nectar. It has been suggested that moths may fertilise the clovers; but I doubt whether they could do so in the case of the red clover, from their weight not being sufficient to depress the wing-petals. Hence we may infer as highly probable that, if the whole genus of humble-bees became extinct or very rare in England, the heartsease and red clover would become very rare, or wholly disappear. The number of humble-bees in any district depends in a great measure on the number of field-mice, which destroy their combs and nests; and Col. Newman, who has long attended to the habits of humble-bees, believes that "more than two-thirds of them are thus destroyed all over England." Now the number of mice is largely dependent, as every one knows, on the number of cats; and Col. Newman says, "Near villages and small towns I have found the nests of humble-bees more numerous than elsewhere, which I attribute to the number of cats that destroy the mice." Hence it is quite credible that the presence of a feline animal in large numbers in a district might determine, through the intervention first of mice and then of bees, the frequency of certain flowers in that district!

In the case of every species, many different checks, acting at different periods of life, and during different seasons or years, probably come into play; some one check or some few being generally the most potent; but all will concur in determining the average number or even the existence of the species. In some cases it can be shown that widely-different checks act on the same species in different districts. When we look at the plants and bushes clothing an entangled bank, we are tempted to attribute their proportional numbers and kinds to what we call chance. But how false a view is this! Every one has heard that when an American forest is cut down, a very different vegetation springs up; but it has been observed that ancient Indian ruins in the Southern United States, which must formerly have been cleared of trees, now display the same beautiful diversity and proportion of kinds as in the surrounding virgin forest. What a struggle must have gone on during long centuries between the several kinds of trees, each annually scattering its seeds by the thousand; what war between insect and insect—between insects, snails, and other animals with birds and beasts of prey—all striving to increase, all feeding on each other, or on the trees, their seeds and seedlings, or on the other plants which first clothed the ground and thus checked the growth of the trees! Throw up a handful of feathers, and all fall to the ground according to definite laws; but how simple is the problem where each shall fall compared to that of the action and reaction of the innumerable plants and animals which have determined, in the course of centuries, the proportional numbers and kinds of trees now growing on the old Indian ruins!

The dependency of one organic being on another, as of a parasite on its prey, lies generally between beings remote in the scale of nature. This is likewise sometimes the case with those which may be strictly said to struggle with each other for existence, as in the case of locusts and grass-feeding quadrupeds. But the struggle will almost invariably be most severe between the individuals of the same species, for they frequent the same districts, require the same food, and are exposed to the same dangers. In the case of varieties of the same species, the struggle will generally be almost equally severe, and we sometimes see the contest soon decided: for instance, if several varieties of wheat be sown together, and the mixed seed be resown, some of the varieties which best suit the soil or climate, or are naturally the most fertile, will beat the others and

so yield more seed, and will consequently in a few years supplant the other varieties. To keep up a mixed stock of even such extremely close varieties as the variously-coloured sweet-peas, they must be each year harvested separately, and the seed then mixed in due proportion, otherwise the weaker kinds will steadily decrease in number and disappear. So again with the varieties of sheep: it has been asserted that certain mountain-varieties will starve out other mountain-varieties, so that they cannot be kept together. The same result has followed from keeping together different varieties of the medicinal leech. It may even be doubted whether the varieties of any of our domestic plants or animals have so exactly the same strength, habits, and constitution, that the original proportions of a mixed stock (crossing being prevented) could be kept up for half-a-dozen generations, if they were allowed to struggle together, in the same manner as beings in a state of nature, and if the seed or young were not annually preserved in due proportion.

Struggle for Life Most Severe between Individuals and Varieties of the Same Species

As the species of the same genus usually have, though by no means invariably, much similarity in habits and constitution, and always in structure, the struggle will generally be more severe between them, if they come into competition with each other, than between the species of distinct genera. We see this in the recent extension over parts of the United States of one species of swallow having caused the decrease of another species. The recent increase of the missel-thrush in parts of Scotland has caused the decrease of the song-thrush. How frequently we hear of one species of rat taking the place of another species under the most different climates! In Russia the small Asiatic cockroach has everywhere driven before it its great congener. In Australia the imported hive-bee is rapidly exterminating the small, stingless native bee. One species of charlock has been known to supplant another species; and so in other cases. We can dimly see why the competition should be most severe between allied forms, which fill nearly the same place in the economy of nature; but probably in no one case could we precisely say why one species has been victorious over another in the great battle of life.

A corollary of the highest importance may be deduced from the foregoing remarks, namely, that the structure of every organic being is related, in the most essential yet often hidden manner, to that of all the other organic beings, with which it comes into competition for food or residence, or from which it has to escape, or on which it preys. This is obvious in the structure of the teeth and talons of the tiger; and in that of the legs and claws of the parasite which clings to the hair on the tiger's body. But in the beautifully plumed seed of the dandelion, and in the flattened and fringed legs of the water-beetle, the relation seems at first confined to the elements of air and water. Yet the advantage of plumed seeds no doubt stands in the closest relation to the land being already thickly clothed with other plants; so that the seeds may be widely distributed and fall on unoccupied ground. In the water-beetle, the structure of its legs, so well adapted for diving, allows it to compete with other aquatic insects, to hunt for its own prey, and to escape serving as prey to other animals.

The store of nutriment laid up within the seeds of many plants seems at first sight to have no sort of relation to other plants. But from the strong growth of young plants produced from such seeds, as peas and beans, when sown in the midst of long grass, it may be suspected that the chief use of the nutriment in the seed is to favour the growth of the seedlings, whilst struggling with other plants growing vigorously all around.

Look at a plant in the midst of its range, why does it not double or quadruple its numbers? We know that it can perfectly well withstand a little more heat or cold, dampness or dryness, for elsewhere it ranges into slightly hotter or colder, damper or drier districts. In this case we can clearly see that if we wish in imagination to give

the plant the power of increasing in number, we should have to give it some advantage over its competitors, or over the animals which prey on it. On the confines of its geographical range, a change of constitution with respect to climate would clearly be an advantage to our plant; but we have reason to believe that only a few plants or animals range so far, that they are destroyed exclusively by the rigour of the climate. Not until we reach the extreme confines of life, in the Arctic regions or on the borders of an utter desert, will competition cease. The land may be extremely cold or dry, yet there will be competition between some few species, or between the individuals of the same species, for the warmest or dampest spots.

Hence we can see that when a plant or animal is placed in a new country amongst new competitors, the conditions of its life will generally be changed in an essential manner, although the climate may be exactly the same as in its former home. If its average numbers are to increase in its new home, we should have to modify it in a different way to what we should have had to do in its native country; for we should have to give it some advantage over a different set of competitors or enemies.

It is good thus to try in imagination to give to any one species an advantage over another. Probably in no single instance should we know what to do. This ought to convince us of our ignorance on the mutual relations of all organic beings; a conviction as necessary, as it is difficult to acquire. All that we can do, is to keep steadily in mind that each organic being is striving to increase in a geometrical ratio; that each at some period of its life, during some season of the year, during each generation or at intervals, has to struggle for life and to suffer great destruction. When we reflect on this struggle, we may console ourselves with the full belief, that the war of nature is not incessant, that no fear is felt, that death is generally prompt, and that the vigorous, the healthy, and the happy survive and multiply.

Natural Abilities and the Comparative Worth of Races

Francis Galton

INTRODUCTORY

I propose to show in this book that a man's natural abilities are derived by inheritance, under exactly the same limitations as are the form and physical features of the whole organic world. Consequently, as it is easy, notwithstanding those limitations, to obtain by careful selection a permanent breed of dogs or horses gifted with peculiar powers of running, or of doing anything else, so it would be quite practicable to produce a highly-gifted race of men by judicious marriages during several consecutive generations. I shall show that social agencies of an ordinary character, whose influences are little suspected, are at this moment working towards the degradation of human nature, and that others are working towards its improvement. I conclude that each generation has enormous power over the natural gifts of those that follow, and maintain that it is a duty we owe to humanity to investigate the range of that power, and to exercise it in a way that, without being unwise towards ourselves, shall be most advantageous to future inhabitants of the earth.

I am aware that my views, which were first published four years ago in *Macmillan's Magazine* (in June and August 1865), are in contradiction to general opinion; but the arguments I then used have been since accepted, to my great gratification, by many of the highest authorities on heredity. In reproducing them, as I now do, in a much more elaborate form, and on a greatly enlarged basis of induction, I feel assured that, inasmuch as what I then wrote was sufficient to earn the acceptance of Mr. Darwin ("Variation under Domestication," ii. 7), the increased amount of evidence submitted in the present volume is not likely to be gainsaid.

The general plan of my argument is to show

that high reputation is a pretty accurate test of high ability; next to discuss the relationships of a large body of fairly eminent men—namely, the Judges of England from 1660 to 1868, the Statesmen of the time of George III., and the Premiers during the last 100 years—and to obtain from these a general survey of the laws of heredity in respect to genius. Then I shall examine, in order, the kindred of the most illustrious Commanders, men of Literature and of Science, Poets, Painters, and Musicians, of whom history speaks. I shall also discuss the kindred of a certain selection of Divines and of modern Scholars. Then will follow a short chapter, by way of comparison, on the hereditary transmission of physical gifts, as deduced from the relationships of certain classes of Oarsmen and Wrestlers. Lastly, I shall collate my results, and draw conclusions.

It will be observed that I deal with more than one grade of ability. Those upon whom the greater part of my volume is occupied, and on whose kinships my argument is most securely based, have been generally reputed as endowed by nature with extraordinary genius. There are so few of these men that, although they are scattered throughout the whole historical period of human existence, their number does not amount to more than 400, and yet a considerable proportion of them will be found to be interrelated.

Another grade of ability with which I deal is that which includes numerous highly eminent, and all the illustrious names of modern English history, whose immediate descendants are living among us, whose histories are popularly known, and whose relationships may readily be traced by the help of biographical dictionaries, peerages, and similar books of reference.

A third and lower grade is that of the English Judges, massed together as a whole, for the purpose of the prefatory statistical inquiry of which I have already spoken. No one doubts that many

From Galton, F. (1869). *Hereditary genius*. New York: D. Appleton, 1891, pp. 1–5, 343–350.

of the ablest intellects of our race are to be found among the Judges; nevertheless the *average* ability of a Judge cannot be rated as equal to that of the lower of the two grades I have described.

I trust the reader will make allowance for a large and somewhat important class of omissions I have felt myself compelled to make when treating of the eminent men of modern days. I am prevented by a sense of decorum from quoting names of their relations in contemporary life who are not recognised as public characters, although their abilities may be highly appreciated in private life. Still less consistent with decorum would it have been, to introduce the names of female relatives that stand in the same category. My case is so overpoweringly strong, that I am perfectly able to prove my point without having recourse to this class of evidence. Nevertheless, the reader should bear in mind that it exists; and I beg he will do me the justice of allowing that I have not overlooked the whole of the evidence that does not appear in my pages. I am deeply conscious of the imperfection of my work, but my sins are those of omission, not of commission. Such errors as I may and must have made, which give a fictitious support to my arguments, are, I am confident, out of all proportion fewer than such omissions of facts as would have helped to establish them.

I have taken little notice in this book of modern men of eminence who are not English, or at least well known to Englishmen. I feared, if I included large classes of foreigners, that I should make glaring errors. It requires a very great deal of labour to hunt out relationships, even with the facilities afforded to a countryman having access to persons acquainted with the various families; much more would it have been difficult to hunt out the kindred of foreigners. I should have especially liked to investigate the biographies of Italians and Jews, both of whom appear to be rich in families of high intellectual breeds. Germany and America are also full of interest. It is a little less so with respect to France, where the Revolution and the guillotine made sad havoc among the progeny of her abler races.

There is one advantage to a candid critic in my having left so large a field untouched; it enables me to propose a test that any well-informed reader may easily adopt who doubts the fairness of my examples. He may most reasonably suspect that I have been unconsciously influenced by my theories to select men whose kindred were most favourable to their support. If so, I beg he will test my impartiality as follows:—Let him take a dozen names of his own selection, as the most eminent in whatever profession and in whatever country he knows most about, and let him trace out for himself their relations. It is necessary, as I find by experience, to take some pains to be sure that none, even of the immediate relatives, on either the male or female side, have been overlooked. If he does what I propose, I am confident he will be astonished at the completeness with which the results will confirm my theory. I venture to speak with assurance, because it has often occurred to me to propose this very test to incredulous friends, and invariably, so far as my memory serves me, as large a proportion of the men who were named were discovered to have eminent relations, as the nature of my views on heredity would have led me to expect....

THE COMPARATIVE WORTH OF DIFFERENT RACES

If we could raise the average standard of our race only one grade, what vast changes would be produced! The number of men of natural gifts equal to those of the eminent men of the present day, would be necessarily increased more than tenfold,... because there would be 2,423 of them in each million instead of only 233; but far more important to the progress of civilization would be the increase in the yet higher orders of intellect. We know how intimately the course of events is dependent on the thoughts of a few illustrious men. If the first-rate men in the different groups had never been born, even if those among them who have a place in my appendices on account of their hereditary gifts, had never existed, the world would be very different to what it is.…

It seems to me most essential to the well-being of future generations, that the average standard of ability of the present time should be raised. Civilization is a new condition imposed upon man by the course of events, just as in the history of geological changes new conditions have continually been imposed on different races of animals. They have had the effect either of modifying the nature of the races through the process of natural selection, whenever the changes were sufficiently slow and the race sufficiently pliant, or of destroying them altogether, when the changes were too abrupt or the race unyielding. The number of the races of mankind that have been entirely destroyed under the pressure of the requirements of an incoming civilization, reads us a terrible lesson. Probably in no former period of the world has the destruction of the races of any animal whatever, been effected over such wide areas and with such startling rapidity as in the case of savage man. In the North American Continent, in the West Indian Islands, in the Cape of Good Hope, in Australia, New Zealand, and Van Diemen's Land, the human denizens of vast regions have been entirely swept away in the short space of three centuries, less by the pressure of a stronger race than through the influence of a civilization they were incapable of supporting. And we too, the foremost labourers in creating this civilization, are beginning to show ourselves incapable of keeping pace with our own work. The needs of centralization, communication, and culture, call for more brains and mental stamina than the average of our race possess. We are in crying want for a greater fund of ability in all stations of life; for neither the classes of statesmen, philosophers, artisans, nor labourers are up to the modern complexity of their several professions. An extended civilization like ours comprises more interests than the ordinary statesmen or philosophers of our present race are capable of dealing with, and it exacts more intelligent work than our ordinary artisans and labourers are capable of performing.

Our race is overweighted, and appears likely to be drudged into degeneracy by demands that exceed its powers. If its average ability were raised a grade or two, our new classes… would conduct the complex affairs of the state at home and abroad as easily as our present [classes]… when in the position of country squires, are able to manage the affairs of their establishments and tenantry. All other classes of the community would be similarly promoted to the level of the work required by the nineteenth century, if the average standard of the race were raised.

When the severity of the struggle for existence is not too great for the powers of the race, its action is healthy and conservative, otherwise it is deadly, just as we may see exemplified in the scanty, wretched vegetation that leads a precarious existence near the summer snow line of the Alps, and disappears altogether a little higher up. We want as much backbone as we can get, to bear the racket to which we are henceforth to be exposed, and as good brains as possible to contrive machinery, for modern life to work more smoothly than at present. We can, in some degree, raise the nature of man to a level with the new conditions imposed upon his existence, and we can also, in some degree, modify the conditions to suit his nature. It is clearly right that both these powers should be exerted, with the view of bringing his nature and the conditions of his existence into as close harmony as possible.

In proportion as the world becomes filled with mankind, the relations of society necessarily increase in complexity, and the nomadic disposition found in most barbarians becomes unsuitable to the novel conditions. There is a most unusual unanimity in respect to the causes of incapacity of savages for civilization, among writers on those hunting and migratory nations who are brought into contact with advancing colonization, and perish, as they invariably do, by the contact. They tell us that the labour of such men is neither constant nor steady; that the love of a wandering, independent life prevents their settling anywhere to work, except for a short time, when urged by want and encouraged by kind treatment. Meadows says that the Chinese call the barbarous races on their borders by a phrase which means "hither and thither, not fixed." And any amount of evidence might be adduced to show how deeply Bohemian habits of one kind or another, were ingrained in the nature of the men who inhabited most parts of the earth now overspread by the Anglo-Saxon and other civilized races. Luckily there is still room for adventure, and a man who feels the cravings of a roving, adventurous spirit to be too strong for resistance, may yet find a legitimate outlet for it in the colonies, in the army, or on board ship. But such a spirit is, on the whole an heirloom that brings more impatient restlessness and beating of the wings against cage-bars, than persons of more civilized characters can readily comprehend, and it is directly at war with the more modern portion of our moral natures. If a man be purely a nomad, he has only to be nomadic, and his instinct is satisfied; but no Englishmen of the nineteenth century are purely nomadic. The most so among them have also inherited many civilized cravings that are necessarily starved when they become wanderers, in the same way as the wandering instincts are starved when they are settled at home. Consequently their nature has opposite wants, which can never be satisfied except by chance, through some very exceptional turn of circumstances. This is a serious calamity, and as the Bohemianism in the nature of our race is destined to perish, the sooner it goes, the happier for mankind. The social requirements of English life are steadily destroying it. No man who only works by fits and starts is able to obtain his living nowadays; for he has not a chance of thriving in competition with steady workmen. If his nature revolts against the monotony of daily labour, he is tempted to the public-house, to intemperance, and, it may be, to poaching, and to much more serious crime: otherwise he banishes himself from our shores. In the first case, he is unlikely to leave as many children as men of more domestic and marrying habits, and, in

the second case, his breed is wholly lost to England. By this steady riddance of the Bohemian spirit of our race, the artisan part of our population is slowly becoming bred to its duties, and the primary qualities of the typical modern British workman are already the very opposite of those of the nomad. What they are now, was well described by Mr. Chadwick, as consisting of "great bodily strength, applied under the command of a steady, persevering will, mental self-contentedness, impassibility to external irrelevant impressions, which carries them through the continued repetition of toilsome labour, 'steady as time.'"

It is curious to remark how unimportant to modern civilization has become the once famous and thoroughbred looking Norman. The type of his features, which is, probably, in some degree correlated with his peculiar form of adventurous disposition, is no longer characteristic of our rulers, and is rarely found among celebrities of the present day; it is more often met with among the undistinguished members of highly-born families, and especially among the less conspicuous officers of the army. Modern leading men in all paths of eminence, as may easily be seen in a collection of photographs, are of a coarser and more robust breed; less excitable and dashing, but endowed with far more ruggedness and real vigour. Such also is the case, as regards the German portion of the Austrian nation; they are far more high-caste in appearance than the Prussians, who are so plain that it is disagreeable to travel northwards from Vienna, and watch the change; yet the Prussians appear possessed of the greater moral and physical stamina.

Much more alien to the genius of an enlightened civilization than the nomadic habit, is the impulsive and uncontrolled nature of the savage. A civilized man must bear and forbear, he must keep before his mind the claims of the morrow as clearly as those of the passing minute; of the absent, as well as of the present. This is the most trying of the new conditions imposed on man by civilization, and the one that makes it hopeless for any but exceptional natures among savages, to live under them. The instinct of a savage is admirably consonant with the needs of savage life; every day he is in danger through transient causes; he lives from hand to mouth, in the hour and for the hour, without care for the past or forethought for the future: but such an instinct is utterly at fault in civilized life. The half-reclaimed savage, being unable to deal with more subjects of consideration than are directly before him, is continually doing acts through mere maladroitness and incapacity, at which he is afterwards deeply grieved and annoyed. The nearer inducements always seem to him, through his uncorrected sense of moral perspective, to be incomparably larger than others of the same actual size, but more remote; consequently, when the temptation of the moment has been yielded to and passed away, and its bitter result comes in its turn before the man, he is amazed and remorseful at his past weakness. It seems incredible that he should have done that yesterday which to-day seems so silly, so unjust, and so unkindly. The newly-reclaimed barbarian, with the impulsive, unstable nature of the savage, when he also chances to be gifted with a peculiarly generous and affectionate disposition, is of all others the man most oppressed with the sense of sin.

Now it is a just assertion, and a common theme of moralists of many creeds, that man, such as we find him, is born with an imperfect nature. He has lofty aspirations, but there is a weakness in his disposition, which incapacitates him from carrying his nobler purposes into effect. He sees that some particular course of action is his duty, and should be his delight; but his inclinations are fickle and base, and do not conform to his better judgment. The whole moral nature of man is tainted with sin, which prevents him from doing the things he knows to be right.

The explanation I offer of this apparent anomaly, seems perfectly satisfactory from a scientific point of view. It is neither more nor less than that the development of our nature, whether under Darwin's law of natural selection, or through the effects of changed ancestral habits, has not yet overtaken the development of our moral civilization. Man was barbarous but yesterday, and therefore it is not to be expected that the natural aptitudes of his race should already have become moulded into accordance with his very recent advance. We, men of the present centuries, are like animals suddenly transplanted among new conditions of climate and of food: our instincts fail us under the altered circumstances.

My theory is confirmed by the fact that the members of old civilizations are far less sensible than recent converts from barbarism, of their nature being inadequate to their moral needs. The conscience of a negro is aghast at his own wild, impulsive nature, and is easily stirred by a preacher, but it is scarcely possible to ruffle the self-complacency of a steady-going Chinaman.

The sense of original sin would show, according to my theory, not that man was fallen from a high estate, but that he was rising in moral culture with more rapidity than the nature of his race could follow. My view is corroborated by the conclusion reached at the end of each of the many independent lines of ethnological research—that the human race were utter savages in the beginning; and that, after myriads of years of barbarism, man has but very recently found his way into the paths of morality and civilization.

Why Darwin Delayed, or Interesting Problems and Models in the History of Science

Robert J. Richards

In October of 1836, Charles Darwin returned from his five-year voyage on the *Beagle*. During his travel around the world, he appears not to have given serious thought to the possibility that species were mutable, that they slowly changed over time. But in the summer and spring of 1837, he began to reflect precisely on this possibility, as his journal indicates: "In July opened first notebook on 'Transformation of Species'—Had been greatly struck from about Month of previous March on character of S. American fossils—& species on Galapagos Archipelago. These facts [are the] origin (especially latter) of all my views."[1] Darwin's views on evolution really only began to congeal some six months after his voyage. In the summer of 1837, he started a series of notebooks in which he worked on the theory that species were transformed over generations. In his first, second, and most of his third transmutation notebooks, he constructed several mechanisms, most of a Lamarckian variety, to account for the evolutionary process.[2] In September of 1838, a bit over a year and a half after he first began to reflect on the meaning of his South American findings, he chanced to read Thomas Malthus's *Essay on Population;* and this, as he related in his *Autobiography,* gave him "a theory by which to work."[3] Darwin credited Malthus with having furnished him the key to his formulation of the principle of natural selection—the principle that not only transformed species but also our very understanding of life. But here a problem arises for the historian of science, and it is this problem that I would like to consider.

Richards, R. J. (1983). Why Darwin delayed, or interesting problems and models in the history of science. *Journal of the History of the Behavioral Sciences, 19,* 45–53. Copyright © 1983 by the Clinical Psychology Publishing Company. Reprinted by permission of the publisher and the author.

THE PROBLEM OF DARWIN'S DELAY

Darwin read Malthus in late September of 1838, and his notebooks show that immediately thereafter he had the essence of what has become known as the theory of evolution by natural selection.[4] Yet he did not publish his discovery in complete form until the *Origin of Species* appeared in 1859, over twenty years later. Certainly he was not slow to recognize the importance of his conception. In 1844 he wrote out a large essay sketching his theory, and had a fair copy made.[5] (Part of this essay was read, along with a paper by Alfred Wallace, before the Linnean Society in 1858 as the first public announcement of the discovery.) When he had finished the 1844 essay, he made arrangements with his wife for its posthumous publication, in case he should die before revealing his great idea.[6] Darwin thus harbored few doubts about the significance of his discovery. What, then, caused him to delay publication of a theory that is perhaps the most intellectually and socially important theory of the nineteenth century, and arguably among the most important scientific conceptions of all time?

In discussing this problem I would like principally to do two things: first, to mention the several kinds of explanation that have been given for Darwin's delay, spending some time on one in particular; and second, to consider the reasons an historian of science might tackle a problem such as this—in general to offer a few reflections on the nature of the history of science, its problems, and its methods.

Explanations of Darwin's Delay

Darwin's delay may not seem like an important or historically significant problem. To see why it is, however, suggests that our first inquiry ought to be historiographic: what makes a problem in history of science interesting in the first place? But before touching on this, I would like to outline the various explanations that have been given for Darwin's delay. This will provide some concrete examples for discussing the larger problem of interesting problems.

The first sort of explanation derives from the conventional interpretation of the hypothetical-deductive method in science: it holds that Darwin formulated his hypothesis in 1838 and then set out collecting facts to support it, which took him twenty years. Charles Coulston Gillispie adopts this account in his *Edge of Objectivity:*

> [Darwin] was held back from publication, and even from giving himself joyfully to his conclusions, by a fear of seeming premature. This went beyond scientific caution in Darwin. It is, perhaps, a disease of modern scholarship to hold back the great work until it can be counted on to overwhelm by sheer factual mass.[7]

Another explanatory strategy is a variant on the first. It contends that Darwin required the services of several correspondents and associates—among whom were Charles Lyell, Joseph Hooker, and Thomas Huxley—to gather facts for him, since he was ill a good deal of the time after his return to England and, really, was a bit lazy. To coordinate others to do one's bidding while one is indisposed would, of course, take time. Gertrude Himmelfarb, in her *Darwin and the Darwinian Revolution,* adds that Darwin was concomitantly attempting to convince his friends of the truth of his theory, but with little success. She implies that he failed for good reasons, since his theory lacked cogency and his arguments were crude.[8]

A third kind of explanation supposes that Darwin was hardly indolent or lazy. Rather, it was because of his work agenda that he was not able to get to his species book more quickly. Indeed, during the twenty years in question, he brought out: *Journal of Researches of the Voyage of H. M. S. Beagle* (1839 and revised in 1845); five volumes of *Zoology of the Voyage of H. M. S. Beagle* (1840–1843), which he edited; three volumes of the *Geology of the Voyage of the Beagle* (1842–1846); and almost thirty papers and reviews.

In 1846 he began an eight-year study of barnacles, resulting in four volumes completed in 1854.[9] The barnacle project seduced Darwin. He initially planned merely to do a little study of one species and ended up investigating the whole group of Cirripedia. His work on barnacles has been singled out as both a necessary stage in preparation for the *Origin of Species* and a significant cause of its delay. Thomas Huxley, in looking back on his friend's accomplishment, wrote to Darwin's son Francis: "Like the rest of us, he had no proper training in biological science, and it has always struck me as a remarkable instance of his scientific insight, that he saw the necessity of giving himself such training, and of his courage, that he did not shirk the labour of obtaining it."[10] Thus, so the explanation goes, he had to fit himself out as a real biologist before he felt confident to tackle the species theory.

A fourth explanation points out that at the time Darwin finished the sketch of his theory in 1844, Robert Chambers published, anonymously, his *Vestiges of the Natural History of Creation.* This book advanced an evolutionary hypothesis, but was extremely speculative and often silly—neither trait slipping past the attention of Darwin's scientific community. J. W. Burrow argues that Chambers's book would have cooled any enthusiasm Darwin might have had for quickly publishing his ideas: "Darwin regarded *The Vestiges* as rubbish, and Huxley reviewed it devastatingly, but the fear of being taken for simply another evolutionary speculator haunted Darwin and enjoined caution in announcing his views and patience in marshalling his evidence."[11]

A fifth explanation looks to the impact Darwin presumably anticipated his theory as having. It was, after all, materialistic; it assumed the rise of human reason and morality out of animal intelligence and instinct. Howard Gruber, in his *Darwin on Man,* divines that "Darwin sensed that some would object to seeing rudiments of human mentality in animals, while others would recoil at the idea of remnants of animality in man."[12] Darwin closed the link between humankind and animals, and thus chained himself to the dread doctrine of materialism. Stephen Gould, supporting Gruber's argument, finds evidence for this reconstruction in Darwin's early notebooks, which

> include many statements showing that he espoused but feared to expose something he perceived as far more heretical than evolution itself: philosophical materialism—the postulate that matter is the stuff of all existence and that all mental and spiritual phenomena are its by-products. No notion could be more upsetting to the deepest traditions of Western thought than the statement that mind—however complex and powerful—is simply a product of brain.[13]

The proffered hypothesis suggests, then, that Darwin was acutely sensitive to the social consequences of equating human beings with animals and therefore mind with brain, and that he thus shied from publicly revealing his views until the intellectual climate became more tolerable.[14]

The social-psychological approach, of which this last explanation discreetly makes use, is more overtly appealed to in another kind of explanation, the psychoanalytic. Some psychoanalysts emphasize that Darwin suffered from a variety of illnesses during his later adulthood—he was always taking the waters and different kinds of faddish cures for his nervousness, palpitations, exhaustion, headaches, and gastrointestinal eruptions.[15] Anyone examining the letters written to Darwin, from about 1840 till his death in 1882, is struck by what seems their invariable salutation: "Dear Darwin, sorry to hear you've been ill." The analyst Rankine Good interprets Darwin's maladies as neurotic symptoms, expressing an unconscious hate for his father:

> His illness was compounded of depressive, obsessional anxiety, and hysterical symptoms which, for the most part, co-existed, though he appears to have gone through phases when one or other group of symptoms predominated for a time. Further, there is a wealth of evidence that unmistakably points to these symptoms as a distorted expression of the aggression, hate, and resentment felt at an unconscious level, by Darwin towards his tyrannical father.... The symptoms represent in part, the punishment Darwin suffered for harboring such thoughts about his father. For Darwin did revolt against his father. He did so in a typical obsessional way (and like most revolutionaries) by transposing the unconscious emotional conflict to a conscious intellectual one—concerning evolution. Thus if Darwin did not slay his father in the flesh, then in his *Origin of Species* and *Descent of Man,* he certainly slew the Heavenly Father in the realm of natural history.[16]

Hamlet-like, then, Darwin hesitated to commit the symbolic murder of his despised father; he could not quite bring himself to plunge in the knife that the *Origin* represented.

A somewhat less dramatic explanation looks to Darwin's social and professional, rather than filial, relationships. Michael Ruse, in his recent book *The Darwinian Revolution,* sets some previous accounts within a sociological framework. He argues:

> The true answer [for his delay] has to be sought in Darwin's professionalism.... Darwin was not an amateur outsider like Chambers. He was part of the scientific network, a product of Cambridge and a close friend of Lyell, and he knew well the dread and the hatred most of the network had for evolutionism.... When telling Hooker of his evolutionism, Darwin confessed that it was like admitting to a murder. It was a murder—the purported murder of Christianity, and Darwin was not keen to be cast in this role. Hence the Essay of 1844 went unpublished.[17]

In order to protect his status as a professional, a status that presumably included defending the faith, Darwin laid down his pen.

INTERESTING PROBLEMS AND MODELS IN THE HISTORY OF SCIENCE

The Context of Interesting Problems

I have mentioned some seven different explanations for Darwin's delay, but not yet the one I wish to propose. Before considering that, let me suggest why a question such as Darwin's delay is historically interesting in the first place. Historians of science, as well as philosophers of science, scientists, and other scholars want to work on interesting problems—not just interesting because of personal idiosyncracies, but problems that are in some sense objectively interesting, interesting in terms of their disciplines.

What, then, makes for an interesting problem in history of science? There are at least three contexts in which a problem can become historically interesting. The first is that of normal expectations. Initially those expectations derive from present circumstances. The historian might note, for instance, that in the contemporary period scientists rush to publish important discoveries, a feature of the modern temper vividly illustrated by James Watson's *Double Helix*. In this light, Darwin's delay becomes puzzling. But most historians do not regard the present context as the controlling one. The question is, what would be the expectation for a mid-nineteenth-century scientist? If it is presumed that Victorian intellectual life ambled at a more leisurely pace or that the social convention for scientists of the period was to publish their big books as the summation of a career's work—the usual practice during the Renaissance—then a solution is had for what turns out to be not a very interesting problem after all. But in Darwin's case, we know that neither of these explanations rings true. He published fairly rapidly and often throughout his career. And consider the keen anguish he felt when he got the letter from Alfred Wallace in 1858 announcing the discovery of virtually the same theory that he had been toiling over some twenty years—this feeling of intellectual emasculation clearly demonstrates that Darwin feared being anticipated as much as any present-day scientist. The problem of his delay again becomes interesting—in terms both of our general expectations for scientific practice and expectations for the professional situation of the nineteenth-century scientist.

A second context determining interest is that of scholarship: if other historians have treated a problem as interesting, ipso facto it becomes so—for the moment at least. In the case of Darwin's delay, scholars have, simply by dint of their explanatory attempts, made it a problem of interest. Anyone undertaking a comprehensive analysis of Darwin's accomplishment must therefore contend with the problem, if only to show that it is historically intractable or actually not very interesting—interesting, that is, in either the first or the third sense I have in mind.

The third context that determines the interest invested in a problem is provided by a particular scientific theory or a nexus of theories constituting a scientific movement. In this context, interest becomes a function both of the importance of the theory, or theories, and of the proximity of the problem to such a reference base. Thus a problem even at the heart, say, of the major theory of an obscure physiologist should hold little interest for the historian of science—unless the theory and problem are representative of some larger and more significant movements in science. Nor should it be of interest to the historian of science *as such* to discover whether Darwin was really neurotic—except that the question bears on the origin and development of his theory of evolution.

This last contextual control implies that the present-day state of science ultimately fixes those problems of interest for the historian. Some scholars would find this suggestion destructive of the historical ideal, which, they believe, requires the reconstruction of the past only on its own terms, without use of present conceptual resources. To aim for less would be to indulge in Whig history, the unwarranted reading of contemporary ideas, motives, social conditions, and interests into the past.[18] But the historicist ideal can be realized in neither practice nor theory. The historian is ineluctably a product of his or her time and therefore must bring to the study of the past the conceptual equipment of the present. Any historical analysis, explicitly or implicitly, steps off from the present. Every historian of science initially learns, for instance, the contemporary meaning of the concept of science itself, and in its light regressively traces the evolutionary descent of its past embodiments. Of course, the sensitive historian seeks continually to enrich the concept of science, recognizing that though ancient practices and notions evolved into those of the present, they may appear structurally very different—just as eohippus seems worlds apart from the modern horse.

In terms of this third context, Darwin's delay is certainly interesting. For the very fact of delay suggests either something not finished, something left undone for the theory to be logically acceptable, or something about the theory that made it unacceptable in the scientific and social climate of Victorian England. In either case, the problem beckons because it hints that there is something about Darwin's theory that we have not yet considered; and to understand its origins, development, structure, and impact, this something needs to be recovered.

Models in History of Science

Assuming that the historian has an interesting problem—and perhaps now it will be granted that Darwin's delay is interesting—what approach should be taken in attempting to resolve it? Initially, there seem to be two options.

Historians of science seem innately disposed to one of two basic approaches, internalism or externalism. Internalists focus on the development of scientific ideas and theories, tracing their internal logic and conceptual linkages. In extreme form, internalists treat the historical movement from one set of ideas to another much as Platonic philosophers, weaving together the logical forms of ideas while ignoring their physical and social embodi-

ments. Externalists, by contrast, embed scientific ideas and theories in the human world, in the minds of scientists who move in a variety of interlocking societies. In the extreme, externalists cloak themselves in Durkheim or Freud; they suppose that ideas reflect only social relationships or psychological complexes. Of the several approaches to the problem of Darwin's delay, Gillispie clearly represents the internalist perspective, while Good represents the externalists; the others cluster more or less closely to one of these poles.

Historians disposed toward internalism or externalism specify their tendencies by adopting— usually unreflectively—an historiographic model, in light of which they articulate their subject. In this respect they function much like scientists. For historians, after all, do formulate theories, construct hypotheses, gather evidence, and, of necessity, employ models. Historiographic models comprise sets of assumptions concerning the nature of science, its developmental character, and the modes of scientific knowing. That historians *must* use models can be argued a priori: without antecedent conceptions about the character of science, they would have no idea where to look for their subject matter, nor could they define its limits or determine what evidence would be relevant. That models have in fact been used can be established easily by an empirical survey of histories of science since the Renaissance.[19] So, for instance, a model familiar to most is Thomas Kuhn's paradigm model of science. Gillispie, more traditionally, employs a revolutionary model (not to be confused with Kuhn's conception of scientific revolutions). This model, introduced by historians in the eighteenth century, assumes that a discipline must undergo a fundamental upheaval to put it on the road to modern science—before the revolution (for example, that produced in physics by Galileo) there was not science; afterward scientists gradually laid a path of scientific truth leading right up to the modern age. A more recently formulated model, which has considerable advantage over the others available, is a natural selection model of scientific evolution. It treats conceptual systems as comparable to biological species, and regards this evolution as ultimately determined by a natural selection of scientific ideas against a variety of intellectual environments.

I will not rehearse here the whole litany of models available to the historian of science, but simply point out that some are more congenial to those of internalist temper, others to those of externalist, while a few will appeal to historians whose attitudes about the issue are a healthy mix. It is the latter class of models, the ones suitable to those of hybrid sentiment, that, I believe, will generally be the most successful. This is not merely because extreme positions—that of the hard-headed internalist or the soft-minded externalist—are generally to be avoided. Barry Goldwater once admonished, with some justice, that extremism in the cause of truth is no vice. These starkly restrictive approaches should be avoided because they lead historians down some very dark byways.

The internalists forget that ideas alone are causally impotent—one idea cannot, of itself, generate another. Moreover, the connections among sets of historically developed scientific ideas are not usually logical, at least not in any deductive sense. It is breathing human beings who produce ideas. Ideas become historically linked only by passing through embodied minds, which respond to logical implication and evidentiary support, of course, but also to emotion, prejudice, class attitudes, and, sometimes perhaps, oedipal anxieties. Hence, to deal with their subject—the growth of scientific ideas—historians of science cannot neglect the explanatory strategies of social, political, and cultural historians.

Extreme externalists, say of the Durkheimian or Marxian variety, those who interpret scientific ideas as totally determined by social structures (and who seem to ply their trade these days mostly in Edinburgh)[20] can be terminally infected, and, if gentlemen, will succumb to a simple *reductio* argument: their thesis of social determinism must also be determined; but why should we listen to those who take a position from extrinsic compulsion instead of relevant good reason? Even the less extreme sorts often forget that the most intimate society to which the scientist belongs and whose attitudes he or she most readily adopts is that of other scientists. Externalists thus usually ignore something that their own assumptions imply: that scientists are enculturated to respond to the logical and objective character of theories and evidence. Demonstrations of logical consistency and empirical confirmation usually bear the most weight, even for the natural philosophers of ages past. This suggests, incidentally, that well-trained historians of science will also know the more detailed workings of the science they profess to chronicle, as well as be apprised of what contemporary philosophers have had to say about the logical character of theories and explanations in science.

Hybrids between the internalists and the externalists enjoy advantage over both. They can adjust their considerations to the structure of the problem with which they are concerned. That is, they will be ready to construe the problem in terms of the internal structure of the science, which should logically be their first step, or in terms of external influences, if the evidence warrants. Usually they will find both approaches, in different measures, necessary. And this for a simple reason, which I will briefly mention and which will return us to the problem at hand, Darwin's delay.

DARWIN'S DELAY AGAIN

In arriving at a possible solution to the perplexity of Darwin's delay, one must recognize a critical difficulty which always faces the historian: scientific theories and the activities of scientists are overdetermined. A multitude of factors impinge on the scientist, and the historian must apportion different conceptual and causal weightings to these factors. It is conceivable, and I think likely, that most of the explanations mentioned earlier for Darwin's delay have some merit. The factors they isolate did bear on his delay.

The mistake usually made, however, is to assume that one explanation is *the* explanation. Having offered this caveat, let me suggest which inhibiting factor did cause Darwin no end of difficulty and which, therefore, must be accorded considerable conceptual weight.

In reading several natural theological discussions of animal instinct in the early 1840s, Darwin came upon one particular example that the natural theologians made much of—the "wonderful" instincts of worker bees and slave-making ants. Only God, they argued, could have endowed the hive bee with a geometer's knowledge of how to construct perfect hexagonal cells, or *Formica rufescens* with the gentleman's unerring sense of what other species would make the best domestic servants.[21] What struck Darwin about these instincts—actually whole sets of related innate behaviors—was that they were exhibited by sterile castes of insects. The account of instinctive behavior on which he had been working in the early 1840s—which likened the fixed patterns of instinct to anatomical structures and argued that both could be explained by natural selection—seemed precluded for neuter insects, since they left no progeny that could inherit profitable variations.

That this quickly loomed as a critical difficulty for the validity of his theory of evolution by natural selection can be fairly estimated from the annotations Darwin left in the margins of those natural theological treatises he was reading in the 1840s.[22] Moreover, in the *Origin of Species,* he stated flatly that he initially thought the problem of instincts of neuter insects "fatal to my whole theory."[23] This was precisely the kind of stumbling block—a conceptual failure at the heart of his theory—that would cause him to hesitate in publishing his views.

Manuscript evidence indicates that Darwin discovered this difficulty in 1843.[24] Shortly thereafter he attempted to construct several possible explanations compatible with the theory of natural selection. But these were weak, and he knew it. In his 1844 essay Darwin sketched several potential objections to his theory, and then, with a soft note of triumph, proceeded to answer them. Conspicuously absent, however, was any mention of that difficulty he thought fatal to his theory—he had no explanation for it. Further evidence shows that the problem of neuter insects continued to plague him. In 1848 he composed a four-page manuscript detailing the problem of the instincts of neuter insects, and concluded that it was "the greatest *special* difficulty I have met with."[25]

Even after Darwin sat down, in 1856, to begin work on a manuscript that would be, he hoped, the definitive description and justification of his theory of evolution by natural selection, he still had not settled on one explanation of the wonderful instincts of social insects. In fact, he proposed several, only one of which contained elements of what we now accept as the correct explanation—kin selection: the idea that selection does not work on the individual, but on the whole hive or nest in competition with other communal groups of the same species. Darwin came to recognize the solution to his difficulty and to flesh it out only in late December of 1857, as he wrote what would become the chapter on instinct in the *Origin of Species.*[26] In the very act of writing the chapter, he resolved the difficulty he regarded as threatening the existence of his theory. In the explanation of Darwin's delay, much conceptual weight must thus be given to his struggles with the wonderful instincts of neuter insects. And this, I believe, is a good part of the solution to an interesting problem in the history of science.

NOTES

1 Charles Darwin, "Journal," ed. Gavin de Beer, in *Bulletin of the British Museum (Natural History),* Historical Series 2 (1959): 7.

2 Gavin de Beer edited and transcribed "Darwin's Notebooks on Transmutation of Species" and "Pages Excised by Darwin," in *Bulletin of the British Museum (Natural History),* Historical Series 2 and 3 (1960, 1967). For an account of Darwin's

early theories about evolution, see Sandra Herbert, "The Place of Man in the Development of Darwin's Theory of Transmutation," *Journal of History of Biology* 7 (1974): 217–258; 10 (1977): 243–273; David Kohn, "Theories to Work By: Rejected Theories, Reproduction and Darwin's Path to Natural Selection," *Studies in History of Biology* 4 (1980): 67–170; Camille Limoges, *La Selection Naturelle* (Paris: Presses Universitaires de France, 1970); and Robert Richards, "Influence of Sensationalist Tradition on Early Theories of the Evolution of Behavior," *Journal of History of Ideas* 40 (1979): 85–105.

3 Charles Darwin, *Autobiography,* ed. Nora Barlow (New York: Norton, 1969), p. 120.

4 Darwin, "Third Notebook on Transmutation," MS pp. 134–135 (de Beer, "Excised Pages," pp. 162–163).

5 The essay is transcribed in *The Foundations of the Origin of Species,* ed. Francis Darwin (Cambridge: Cambridge University Press, 1909).

6 Charles Darwin, *The Life and Letters of Charles Darwin,* ed. Francis Darwin, 2 vols. (New York: D. Appleton, 1891), 1: 377–379.

7 Charles Coulston Gillispie, *The Edge of Objectivity* (Princeton, N.J.: Princeton University Press, 1960), p. 312.

8 Gertrude Himmelfarb, *Darwin and the Darwinian Revolution* (New York: Norton, 1968), pp. 126–146, 203–215, 312–352.

9 Charles Darwin, *A Monograph of the Sub-Class Cirripedia,* 4 vols. (London: Ray Society, 1851–1854).

10 Thomas Huxley to Francis Darwin, quoted in *Life and Letters of Charles Darwin,* 1:315.

11 J. W. Burrow, "Editor's Introduction," in Charles Darwin, *The Origin of Species* (Baltimore: Penguin Books, 1968), p. 32.

12 Howard Gruber, *Darwin on Man* (New York: Dutton, 1974), p. 202.

13 Stephen Gould, "Darwin's Delay," in his *Ever Since Darwin* (New York: Norton, 1977), p. 24. Silvan Schweber, in "The Origin of the *Origin* Revisited," *Journal of History of Biology* 10 (1977): 310–315, concurs with Gruber and Gould that fear of materialism was a considerable restraining influence on Darwin.

14 In "Instinct and Intelligence in British Natural Theology: Some Contributions to Darwin's Theory of the Evolution of Behavior," *Journal of History of*

Biology 14 (1981): 193–230, I have taken specific exception to this explanation of Darwin's delay.

15 Ralph Colp, Jr., gives an extensive account of Darwin's illness in *To Be an Invalid* (Chicago: University of Chicago Press, 1977).

16 Rankine Good, "The Life of the Shawl," *Lancet* (9 January 1953): 106.

17 Michael Ruse, *The Darwinian Revolution* (Chicago: University of Chicago Press, 1979), p. 185.

18 Whiggish history was carefully diagnosed in Herbert Butterfield's *The Whig Interpretation of History* (New York: Norton, 1965; originally published, 1931). There he described it as "the tendency in many historians to write on the side of Protestants and Whigs, to praise revolutions provided they have been successful, to emphasise certain principles of progress in the past and to produce a story which is the ratification if not the glorification of the present."

19 I have offered such a survey in "Natural Selection and Other Models in the Historiography of Science," in *Scientific Inquiry and the Social Sciences: A Volume in Honor of Donald T. Campbell,* ed. Marilynn B. Brewer and Barry E. Collins (San Francisco: Jossey-Bass, 1981), pp. 37–76.

20 See, for example, the work of the Edinburgh sociologists of science David Bloor, *Knowledge and Social Imagery* (London: Routledge and Kegan Paul, 1976), and Barry Barnes, *Interests and the Growth of Knowledge* (London: Routledge and Kegan Paul, 1977).

21 Darwin's authority for the habits of social insects was the work of two natural theologians and premier entomologists, William Kirby and William Spence, in their *Introduction to Entomology,* 2nd ed., 4 vols. (London: Longman, Hurst, Rees, Orme, and Brown, 1818); see especially vol. 2.

22 I have discussed these annotations in "Instinct and Intelligence."

23 Charles Darwin, *On the Origin of Species* (London: Murray, 1859), p. 236.

24 From Darwin's reading notebooks, we know that he read Kirby and Spence's *Introduction to Entomology* in 1843 (see the transcription of these notebooks by Peter Vorzimmer, "The Darwin Reading Notebooks [1838–1860]," *Journal of History of Biology* 10 [1977]: 130). On p. 55 of vol. 2 of the work, where Kirby and Spence describe some of the wonderful instincts of worker bees, Darwin scribbled his frustration in the margin: "Neuters

do not breed! How instinct acquired.'' Darwin's books are held in the Manuscript Room of Cambridge University Library.

25 Darwin's four-page manuscript is in container-book #73, held in the Manuscript Room of Cambridge University Library.

26 The manuscript version of what Darwin abridged into the *Origin of Species* has been published by R. C. Stauffer as *Charles Darwin's Natural Selection: Being the Second Part of His Big Species Book Written from 1856 to 1858* (Cambridge: Cambridge University Press, 1975).

Francis Galton and American Psychology

Solomon Diamond

Karl Pearson has told us that Galton's motto was *Whenever you can, count.*[40] He followed it with extraordinary persistence. For example, having had his portrait painted at 60 and again at 81, he could report that each artist had touched the brush to canvas about 20,000 times, although the first used slow, methodical strokes, and the second (in the impressionist era) made flurries of quick dabs.[29] The habit of counting repetitive acts is also a conspicuous behavior of many American psychologists. I have been told that at a round table of distinguished persons, one of our present conferees skilfully increased the rate of finger-wagging by a long-winded participant, by reinforcing each such gesture with a nod of his head. This is not in itself proof of Galton's enduring influence, but it does illustrate the fact that American psychology is largely imbued with the essence of Galtonism: the conviction that any significant problem can be stated in terms which make it accessible to quantitative study. That conviction was the foundation for each of Galton's many important contributions. Some that have had very wide application in the work of other psychologists are these:

(1) The method of word association,[19] which first opened the way to quantitative analysis of the higher thought processes and individual dynamics.

Diamond, S. (1977). Francis Galton and American psychology. *Annals of the New York Academy of Sciences, 291,* 47–55. Copyright © 1977 by the New York Academy of Sciences. Reprinted by permission of the publisher and the author.

(2) The introduction of test batteries,[24] to arrive at a many-sided assessment of abilities for a given person.

(3) Systematic use of the questionnaire,[20] out of which all inventory-type tests were developed.

(4) Use of the normal distribution for purposes of classification,[15] which has been a boon to the sophisticated, as well as devising the system of scoring by percentile ranks,[25] which has made it possible for us to communicate with the unsophisticated.

(5) The method of twin comparison,[18] which, aside from its special application to the problem of nature vs. nurture, is notable as the first use of a control group in psychological research, since Galton compared results based on pairs of identical twins with those based on fraternal twins.

(6) Finally, and most important in this abbreviated list, the concepts of regression[26] and correlation,[27] which opened up new possibilities for the analysis of complex phenomena which, like heredity, are dependent on multiple influences.

In early textbooks and manuals of experimental psychology Galton's name is cited most often in connection with Galton's whistle, Galton's bar, or Galton's weights. These products of his anthropometric research were to be found in almost every laboratory in which students were trained in the psychophysical methods. His more important innovations in experimental design and statistical analysis of data were assimilated more slowly, but without them it would have been a far more difficult task to give psychology its new direction, that is, to change it from a normative science, which had been conceived as the propaedeutic basis for philosophy, into a functional science of behavior, independent of philosophy.

Cattell was the most important conduit of Galton's influence on American psychology. His fellow psychologists ranked him second in importance only to William James.[8] When Galton died, only five months after the passing of James, Cattell wrote that these were the two greatest men he had known.[10] In later years he said flatly that Galton was the greatest man he ever knew.[12,13] Rating scientists for distinction was a serious matter to Cattell, and he would not have made such a judgment without due deliberation.

Since Cattell had both G. Stanley Hall and Wundt as his formal teachers, we cannot assess his relationship to Galton without reviewing the full course of his university studies. In 1880 Cattell, not yet 20, heard Lotze at Göttingen.[45] After an interlude of study at Paris and Geneva, he spent a semester at Leipzig, where he heard both Wundt and Heinze. After this double exposure to the new psychology, he planned to continue his work under Lotze,[44] but this plan was upset by Lotze's unexpected death. In 1882, Cattell enrolled at Johns Hopkins University, Baltimore, Md., and won a scholarship with an essay on Lotze's philosophy. There were no psychology courses during the first semester, and his principal interests then were team sports and personal experimentation with drugs. Then Hall was brought in, and Cattell enrolled in his laboratory course along with John Dewey, Joseph Jastrow, and E. M. Hartwell. Except for Cattell, they were all to complete doctorates at Johns Hopkins. In Hall's laboratory, Cattell performed the pioneer experiment on the time required to recognize letters. The next year Cattell left Johns Hopkins because of what he perceived, probably correctly, as double-dealing on Hall's part.[43] He returned to Leipzig and Wundt, *faute de mieux.*

The results of the experiment performed at Johns Hopkins are included in Cattell's first article in the *Philosophische Studien.*[5] The clue to the fact that it was not performed at Leipzig is in the initials of the observers who participated. They include J.D. for Dewey, E.H. for Hartwell, and G.H. for Hall. One can only speculate as to what extent Cattell's resentment toward Hall, to what extent Wundt's jealousy of other laboratories, contributed to the failure to mention where the experiment had been performed.

Cattell was justly proud of this experiment, but he is not strictly accurate in the claim that it was the first to be concerned with individual differences, and to make no appeal to introspection. This point is not trivial, because it is so often said that interest in individual differences was an autocthonous development of American soil. In 1879 Obersteiner, a collaborator of Exner at Vienna, published an account of reaction-time experiments in which he emphasized the importance of differences between individuals.[39] He found no difference between the sexes, said that members of the serving class are less consistent in performance, and that extremely long times are an indication of mental derangement. Since this article appeared in English, it might well have been known to Cattell, and was almost certainly known to Hall, before Cattell did his experiment. Furthermore, in 1883 Galton's friend Romanes reported an experiment in which the subjects were allowed 20 seconds to read a short printed paragraph and were then required to write down all they could remember.[42] Although all the subjects were "accustomed to much reading," they showed "a positively astonishing difference... with respect to the rate at which they were able to read." Romanes also remarked that the swifter readers generally retained more of the content than the slow readers. Even at this early date, therefore, Cattell and America had no monopoly on psychological research in individual differences, or on using objective criteria of performance.

At Leipzig, Cattell broke precedent by rejecting the introspective problem which Wundt assigned to him, and he was permitted to continue work on his own problem. This time he used far more elegant apparatus of his own design—the gravity tachistoscope and the voice-key—and the work was carried on in his own rooms "in part because Wundt would not allow the testing in his laboratory of individuals who could not profit from introspection."[40]

After Leipzig, Cattell spent the greater part of two years in England. He participated in a still-born effort to establish a psychological laboratory at Cambridge,[46] but worked chiefly at Galton's laboratory, which had originally been established at the International Health Exhibition. Cattell states that he helped set it up in its new quarters at the South Kensington Museum of Science and that he and Galton "began in co-operation the preparation of a book of instructions for a laboratory course in psychology."[12] It was an ideal learning situation. The famous article "Mental Tests and Measurements" was the outgrowth of this experience, and the recommendation in it that all students should take a battery of anthropometric tests followed a line of thought which Galton had initiated much earlier.[16] The battery of tests described was an amplified version of the Galton program, which had been fitted to a level of public tolerance. But the most important outcome was the fact that Walker points out, that Cattell's psychology courses were the first "to make consistent and systematic use of statistical methods."[51] It was a sharp turn from the Leipzig orientation, for, as Walker also states, "It does not appear that Wundt himself was committed to a belief in the statistical treatment of the results of experimentation." It was from Galton that Cattell acquired that faith which caused it to be said, supposedly first by Titchener, that "Cattell's god is Probable Error."[52]

Galton was a figure with whom Cattell could readily identify. Both men had a flair for mechanical invention, and they also shared an obvious pride of membership in that natural aristocracy of talent which even Thomas Jefferson[37] recog-

nized as deserving of recognition. By calling Galton the greatest man he ever knew, Cattell, who was probably conscious of the many points of resemblance, was not lowering his own stature. His career might have been quite different had it not happened that, as Lyman Wells put it, his "formative years brought him into contact with another exceptional man through whom his interests were fixed upon the quantitative properties of the human mind."[52] It is clear that Cattell profited from his contact with Galton immeasurably more than from his contact with Wundt, and American psychology profited as a result.

Joseph Jastrow was another conduit of Galton's influence.[36] He inherited no silver spoon, and had no opportunity to study abroad. While still a student he began earning money by writing papers of a popular scientific character. Thus he was launched on his career as a popularizer of scientific psychology, whose own contributions were of secondary importance. The titles of some of his early papers show the Galton influence already at work: Some peculiarities in the age statistics of the United States;[30] Composite portraiture;[31] The longevity of great men;[32] The dreams of the blind;[33] Eye-mindedness and ear-mindedness.[34]

In 1888, Cattell returned from England to a chair at the University of Pennsylvania, Jastrow received an appointment at Wisconsin, and Hall and Sanford went from Johns Hopkins to newly founded Clark University. Almost overnight America had four active psychology laboratories in place of one.

With a means of livelihood at last assured, Jastrow took leave the following spring for his first trip abroad. Characteristically, on his return he published a series of articles on "Aspects of Modern Psychology."[35] He said of Galton's work that it "could not readily be classified in the psychological activity of any country," but formed "a unique chapter of science, interesting no one more deeply than the students of scientific psychology." He described American psychology as characterized by "a readiness to introduce innovations whenever circumstances will allow, and...utilizing the freedom...of intellectual and educational youthfulness." With hindsight we may read these statements to mean that Galton was laying down new lines for psychology, and only the Americans were free enough from the restraints of traditional university disciplines to follow in the path he indicated.

Jastrow was active in the AAAS, and he was asked to organize the psychology exhibit for the World's Columbian Exposition, which opened in Chicago in 1893. Galton's influence was dominant in shaping the result, which Jastrow later described as "the first attempt to introduce tests to the American public."[37] The Official Directory[54] informed all visitors that "any one who wishes can have, by the payment of a small fee, various tests applied and can be measured and recorded upon cards which are given to the person, while the record is made upon the charts and tables hanging on the walls of the laboratory." It was as if Galton's anthropometric laboratory had been transported to Chicago. Popplestone[41] points out that the lack of any historical record of the public response compels us to wonder if the affair may not have been a dud, perhaps because it was located in a remote corner of the vast Exposition grounds. Whatever the public response may have been, this mobilization of all the current techniques of testing surely stimulated additional interest among psychologists themselves.

Even before the Exposition opened, Titchener[49] deplored the manner in which the exhibit confused anthropometrics with psychology, using the very argument which had driven Cattell to experiment in his own rooms: that a psychological experiment presupposes introspectively practiced observers. "It is one of the commonest errors," he wrote, "that since we are all using our minds, in some way or another, everyone is qualified to take part in psychological experimentation. As well maintain, that because we eat bread, we are all qualified to bake it." His

protest was futile. Soon most of the new psychology laboratories, though they might be headed by Wundt's former students, were busy with anthropometrics. Titchener[50] in desperation wrote to Galton to solicit aid to repulse the invasion. "You would speak with authority," he wrote, "as you could not be suspected of wanting to undervalue Anthropometry. Unless some sort of protest is made, the American laboratories will all run over into anthropometrical statistics: which are, of course, valuable—but not psychology." The appeal is testimony to the high prestige that Galton enjoyed, but he must have been amused to be thus solicited to assist in throttling his own creation to defend the purity of experimental psychology.

Madison Bentley, then a student at Cornell, later said of this period that among the "adventitious" factors that shaped the careers of young psychologists might be the "worship of a Wundt or a Galton."[1] Among the partisans of Galton we must count Terman and Thorndike. Terman wrote in his autobiography: "Of the founders of modern psychology, my greatest admiration is for Galton."[47] Thorndike wrote: "Excellent work can surely be done by men with widely different notions of what psychology should be, the best work of all perhaps being done by men like Galton, who gave little or no thought to what it is or should be."[48]

The case of Woodworth is most interesting.[53] If we say, with Boring,[4] that "it is almost true that American psychology was personified in the person of Cattell," we may add that it is equally true that his student Woodworth personified the shift of orientation without which such a statement could not approach validity. Woodworth's undergraduate teacher in philosophy directed him to study science, as a preparation for philosophy; when later he abandoned philosophy in favor of a career in psychology, he spent more than five years of apprenticeship as a physiologist, to complete the preparation; yet he found in Cattell, whose attention went to the probable error and not to the brain, "the chief of all (his) teachers in giving shape to (his) psychological thought and work." This epitomizes the development of American psychology during the last quarter of the nineteenth century. Having begun the study of psychology as a propaedeutic to philosophy, it was soon caught up in the fascination of research on the physiology of brain, nerves, sense organs, and muscle, but then transferred its principal energies to the study of behavior, including especially the quantitative study of competence in all its manifestations. Psychology was able to pass through the two earlier phases because of the fluidity of the new universities, one consequence of which was that instruction in "mental science" passed from the hands of the college presidents, who almost invariably had theological training, into the hands of specialists. If we wish to claim the third phase as distinctively American, we shall have to give Galton a posthumous grant of American citizenship. We must ask whether the swift progress of individual psychology in the United States is not to be explained by the absence of the restraints on such development which were imposed by the more rigid university structure in Europe, at least as much as by the presence of stronger motivating forces in that direction.

In 1904, when the world met at St. Louis, psychology had another chance to speak to the nation. On that occasion Cattell not only rejected mentalism, in his statement that "it is no more necessary for the subject to be a psychologist than it is for the vivisected frog to be a physiologist," but he also rejected all limiting definitions for the new science, declaring that psychology consists of what psychologists wish to do "*qua* psychologists."[9] It was the first time that psychology had been defined broadly enough to include Cattell's true mentor, Galton.

By the time of the entry of the United States into World War I, the study of individual differences accounted for well over half of all work reported at meetings of the APA,[11] if we omit papers of historical and philosophical nature, which had by then declined from the largest to the small-

est category. American psychologists had developed the skills which they put to work in the war effort.

In 1929, Cattell presided over the International Congress at New Haven, Conn. It was neither in his nature nor in the American character to acknowledge the full extent of our indebtedness to foreign mentors. "Wundt and Galton," he said, "are the foreign psychologists whom we most honor, but it may be that if neither of them had lived psychology in America would be much what it is."[13] Boring[2] concurred in part, writing that "it is an open question as to how much [Galton] influenced Cattell and the American tradition of individual psychology and the mental tests." In the revised edition of his history[3] this passage is omitted, and we read instead: "Perhaps it is true that America, while giving homage to Wundt, has overlooked Galton, to whom it owes a greater debt." Let us consider some of the reasons why we have been so much more ready to give homage to one than to the other.

The rise of American psychology was linked with the reform of American higher education, which was signaled in 1869 by the election of a chemist, Charles Eliot, as president of Harvard University. The theological domination of the colleges was to give way to an industrial-scientific orientation. The German universities were taken as models. Their great strength was in their laboratories, which had originated with Liebig's chemical laboratory at Giessen in 1824, and had subsequently provided the basis for Germany's world leadership in physiology. For a young man seeking a job in the expanding system of American universities, experience in a German laboratory was like money in the bank. Students of chemistry and physiology flocked to Germany. Psychologists were a miniscule group, but when they heard of a psychology laboratory at Leipzig, it became their Mecca. Even those who disliked what they found there were victims of the cognitive dissonance effect. After a young man spends several years of effort to earn a degree in a foreign country, all the while yearning for a sweetheart back home, and then returns triumphantly to a prestigious job and chances of advancement, he is unlikely to say that another course of study might have been more satisfying. Wundt was more than a prophet: he really led his American students into the promised land. Galton, on the other hand, was a man who lacked university status in a country which lacked a psychology laboratory, and where the leading universities were still primarily devoted to educating country divines who might make a hobby of science. Americans might read his books and articles with excitement, but there was no economic inducement to acclaim him as a leader.

It is universally agreed that all Galton's work in psychology radiated from one dominant concern: to learn how we might best manipulate the forces of evolution to mankind's advantage. While philosophers battled over the ethical implications of natural selection, or attempted to subordinate it to a cosmic drive toward higher forms of existence, Galton the pragmatist turned his attention to the phenomenon of variation, as providing the means by which we might accelerate the process. The anthropometric laboratory he set up at great personal expense was a device to tease the public into providing the data he needed for his research. His interest in individual differences was therefore derivative, not primary, but the resulting anthropometric work attracted the interest of psychologists. His ideas about evolution were more correct than Spencer's, and his ideas on the mechanism of heredity were more correct than Darwin's, but they had little following. It was Spencer who was almost universally regarded as the grand theorist of evolution. The American historian Fiske[14] had ranked Spencer's achievement with that of Newton, and the British zoologist Mitchell[38] compared him to Descartes and declared that his writings "may be regarded as the *Principes de la Philosophie* of the 19th century."

Galton's influence derived wholly from his genius in quantitative investigation. He arrived at the concepts of regression and correlation because they were peculiarly appropriate to the study of heredity, and thus also to the study of any complex phenomenon that is influenced in its quantitative manifestation by a large number of causal factors. Indeed, it has proved even more valuable for econometrics than for anthropometrics. No rival claims of priority, no record of independent discovery by others, dims the brilliance of this discovery. For Cattell to have said that American psychology might have been much the same without Galton is an understandable expression of vanity, but it is difficult to see how a historian can concur in that judgment. As we have seen, Boring did retreat from it.

The principal focus of this paper has been on Galton's positive contributions. There was also a negative aspect, of which we are all aware. Galton's advocacy of eugenics provided racists with a rationale for genocide which has been extensively exploited in the United States. When, however, we assess the degree of his culpability on this issue, we should not attribute to him opinions that were not his own. His views, as he himself remarked,[28] were often misrepresented. I shall discuss briefly some aspects of his thinking which are usually overlooked.

(1) It was not in Galton's manner of thinking to condemn a whole race as inferior. Once, after hearing a paper about the "dealings of colonists with aborigines," he said in discussion (which was reported in the third person) that "ethnologists were apt to look upon race as something more definite than it really was. He presumed it meant no more than the average of the characteristics of all the persons who were supposed to belong to the race, and this average was continually varying."[21] He went on to indicate regret that Englishmen did not, like the ancient Romans, live more closely with the populations of the subject colonies, and make them more welcome in England. The notion of racial "purity" had no place in Galton's scheme of eugenics.

(2) Galton was always more interested (as Pearson[40] points out with obvious regret) in raising high intelligence rather than in eliminating low intelligence, which he was much more willing to leave to the slow processes of natural selection. He never subscribed to the theory of degeneration, which was so popular late in the nineteenth century, and which was the basis of the direction which the eugenic movement took after Galton's death.

(3) He always insisted that the great need was for research, to acquire a knowledge of heredity which would be a sufficient basis for wise eugenic practices (or, as we would now say, for informed genetic counseling). He fully recognized the danger of even well-intentioned programs based on inadequate knowledge. He said, for example, in 1884: "Our present ignorance of the conditions by which the level of humanity may be raised is so gross, that I believe if we had some dictator of the Spartan type, who exercised absolute power over marriages...and who acted with the best intentions, he might perhaps do even more harm than good to the race."[23]

(4) Finally, Galton was fully aware of the need for attention to environmental influences, both in research on heredity and in efforts to improve society. The conclusion of his study of twins, in which he defined the nature-nurture issue, was stated thus: "Nature prevails enormously over nurture when the differences in nurture do not exceed what is commonly to be found among persons of the same rank of society and in the same country."[18] He perfectly appreciated the statistical fact that more genetic gold can be mined from the great masses of the disadvantaged than from the thin layer of those who have risen to distinction.[26] That is why he could claim that "the sterling values of nurture, including all kinds of sanitary improvements," were "powerful auxiliaries" to his cause.[17] He also emphasized that "it cannot be too strongly hammered into popular recognition that a well-developed human being, capable in mind and body, is an expensive animal to rear."[28] To rear, be it noted, not to breed.

On the occasion of the conference on which this volume is based, it is especially fitting to recall one more expression of Galton's recognition of the power of environment: "The most likely nest...for self-reliant natures is to be found in States founded and maintained by emigrants."[22] Surely this is one reason why American psychology displayed what Jastrow called "a readiness to introduce innovations." Galton's innovative methods for the study of human capacities were accepted as a part of psychology, and they helped to give American psychology its distinctive character. It seems quite unlikely that the same development could have taken place in anything like the same time span without Galton's influence.

REFERENCES

1 Bentley, M. 1936. In *History of Psychology in Autobiography*. C. Murchison, Ed. Vol. **3**: 53–67. Clark University Press. Worcester, Mass.

2 Boring, E. G. 1929. *A History of Experimental Psychology*. D. Appleton-Century Co. New York, N.Y.

3 Boring, E. G. 1950. *A History of Experimental Psychology*. 2nd edit. Appleton-Century-Crofts. New York, N.Y.

4 Boring, E. G. 1950. The influence of evolutionary theory upon American psychological thought. In *Evolutionary Thought in America*. S. Persons, Ed.: 267–298.

5 Cattell, J. McK. 1885. Ueber die Zeit der Erkennung und Bennenung von Schriftzeichen, Bildern und Farben. *Philosophische Studien* 2:635–650.

6 Cattell, J. McK. 1886. Psychometrische Untersuchungen. **I.** Apparate und Methoden. *Philosophische Studien* **3**: 305–335.

7 Cattell, J. McK. 1890. Mental tests and measurements. *Mind* **15**: 373–380.

8 Cattell, J. McK. 1903. Statistics of American psychologists. *Amer. J. Psychol.* **14**: 310–328.

9 Cattell, J. McK. 1904. The conceptions and methods of psychology. *Popular Science Monthly* **66**: 176–186.

10 Cattell, J. McK. 1911. Francis Galton. *Popular Science Monthly* **78**: 309–311.

11 Cattell, J. McK. 1917. Our psychological association and research. *Science* **45**: 275–284.

12 Cattell, J. McK. 1928. Early psychological labo-

ratories. In *Feelings and Emotions,* the Wittenberg Symposium. M.L. Reymert, Ed.: 427–433. Clark University Press. Worcester, Mass.

13 Cattell, J. McK. 1929. *Psychology in America.* Address of the president of the Ninth Int. Congr. of Psychology. Science Press. New York, N.Y.

14 Fiske, J. 1874. *Outlines of Cosmic Philosophy.* 2 vols. Macmillan & Co. London, England.

15 Galton, F. 1869. *Hereditary Genius.* Macmillan & Co. London, England.

16 Galton, F. 1874. Proposal to apply for anthropological statistics from schools. *J. Anthropol. Inst.* 3: 308–311.

17 Galton, F. 1873. Hereditary improvement. *Fraser's Mag.* NS 7: 116–130.

18 Galton, F. 1876. The history of twins, as a criterion of the relative powers of nature and nurture. *J. Anthropol. Inst.* 5: 391–406.

19 Galton, F. 1879. Psychometric experiments. *Brain* 2: 149–162.

20 Galton, F. 1880. Statistics of mental imagery. *Mind* 5: 301–318.

21 Galton, F. 1882. *J. Anthropol. Inst.* 11: 352–353.

22 Galton, F. 1883. *Inquiries into Human Faculty and Its Development:* 82 Macmillan & Co. New York. N.Y.

23 Galton, F. 1884. *Record of Family Faculties.* Macmillan & Co. London, England.

24 Galton, F. 1885. On the anthropometric laboratory of the late International Health Exhibition. *J. Anthropol. Inst.* 14: 205–219.

25 Galton, F. 1885. Some results of the anthropometric laboratory. *J. Anthropol. Inst.* 14: 275–287.

26 Galton, F. 1885. Types and their inheritance. *Science* 6: 268–274.

27 Galton, F. 1888. Co-relations and their measurement, chiefly from anthropometric data. *Proc. Roy. Soc.* 45: 135–145.

28 Galton, F. 1903. The Daily Chronicle (London). July 29. Excerpts in K. Pearson. 1930. *The Life, Letters and Labours of Francis Galton.* The University Press. Cambridge, England. Vol. IIIA: 252–253.

29 Galton, F. 1905. Number of strokes of the brush in a picture. *Nature* 72: 198.

30 Jastrow, J. 1885. *Science* 5: 461–464.

31 Jastrow, J. 1885. *Science* 6: 165–168.

32 Jastrow, J. 1886. *Science* 8: 294–296.

33 Jastrow, J. 1888. *New Princeton Rev.* 5: 18–24.

34 Jastrow, J. 1888. *Popular Science Monthly* 33: 597–608.

35 Jastrow, J. 1890. Aspects of modern psychology. In *Epitomes of Three Sciences.* H. Oldenberg, J. Jastrow and C.H. Cornill. :59–100. The Open Court Publishing Co. Chicago, Ill.

36 Jastrow, J. 1930. In *History of Psychology in Autobiography.* C. Murchison. Ed.: 2: 297–331. Clark University Press. Worcester, Mass.

37 Jefferson, T. 1925. Letter dated Oct. 28, 1818. In *Correspondence of John Adams and Thomas Jefferson.* P. Wilstach, Ed. The Bobbs-Merrill Co. Indianapolis, Ind.

38 Mitchell, P. C. 1910. Evolution. In *Encyclopedia Brittanica.* 11th edit. 10: 22–37. The University Press. Cambridge, England.

39 Obersteiner, H. 1879. Experimental researches on attention. *Brain* 1: 439–453.

40 Pearson, K. 1914–1930. *The Life, Letters and Labours of Francis Galton.* 3 vols. in 4. The University Press. Cambridge, England.

41 Popplestone, J. A. 1976. The psychological exhibit at the Chicago World's Fair of 1893. Paper presented at the meeting of the Western Psychol. Assoc. Los Angeles, Calif. April, 1976.

42 Romanes, G. J. 1883. *Mental Evolution in Animals.* Kegan Paul & Co. London, England.

43 Ross, D. 1972. G. Stanley Hall: *The Psychologist as Prophet.* Chicago University Press. Chicago, Ill.

44 Sokal, M. M. 1969. Influences on a young psychologist: James McKeen Cattell, 1880–1890. Paper presented at mtg. of the History of Science Society. Washington, D.C., December, 1969.

45 Sokal, M. M. 1971. The unpublished autobiography of James McKeen Cattell. *Amer. Psychol.* 26: 626–635.

46 Sokal, M. M. 1972. Psychology at Victorian Cambridge—the unofficial laboratory of 1887–1888. *Proc. Amer. Phil. Soc.* 116: 145–147.

47 Terman, L. M. 1932. In *History of Psychology in Autobiography.* C. Murchison, Ed.: 2: 297–331. Clark University Press, Worcester, Mass.

48 Thorndike, E. L. 1936. In *History of Psychology in Autobiography.* C. Murchison, Ed.: 3: 263–270. Clark University Press. Worcester, Mass.

49 Titchener, E. B. 1893. Anthropometry and experimental psychology. *Phil. Rev.* 2: 187–192.

50 Titchener, E. B. 1898. Letter to Francis Galton, dated 18 IV 1898. Copy in Archives of the History of American Psychology, The University of Akron. Akron, Ohio.

51 Walker, H. M. 1929. *Studies in the History of Statistical Method.* Williams & Wilkins Co. Baltimore, Md.

52 Wells, F. L. 1944. James McKeen Cattell: 1860–1944. *Amer. J. Psychol.* 57 270–275.

53 Woodworth, R. S. 1932. In *History of Psychology in Autobiography.* C. Murchison, Ed.: 2: 359–380. Clark University Press. Worcester, Mass.

54 World's Columbian Exposition. 1893. Official Directory. Chicago, Ill.

CHAPTER 10

AMERICAN ANTECEDENTS TO FUNCTIONALISM

The first three psychology laboratories in the United States were founded by William James, G. Stanley Hall, and James McKeen Cattell. On both conceptual and methodological grounds, the psychology of each of those men contributed greatly to the founding of functionalism.

William James (1842–1910) earned his medical degree from Harvard in 1869. Although he had no course work in scientific psychology, he had spent some time in 1867–68 in Europe, visiting the laboratories of Fechner, Helmholtz, and Wundt. In 1875 James established a demonstrational laboratory at Harvard to accompany a course he was teaching on the relations between psychology and physiology (see Harper, 1949; Perry, 1935). Because it was not a laboratory used for original research, many historians discount its priority among American psychology laboratories.

That honor is often given to G. Stanley Hall (1844–1924), a student of James's at Harvard, where he earned in 1878 what is often labeled the first psychology doctorate in the United States. Following his graduation, Hall went to Leipzig, where he studied briefly with Wundt and more extensively with the physiologist Karl Ludwig. Hall also studied for a time with Helmholtz in Berlin. His first full-time position was at Johns Hopkins University, where he founded a psychology laboratory in 1883. One of his graduate students at Johns Hopkins was James McKeen Cattell (1860–1944).

Cattell and Hall did not get along (see Sokal, 1982), so Cattell went to Leipzig, where he earned his doctorate with Wundt in 1886. A year later he established the psychology laboratory at the University of Pennsylvania. He took a leave of absence the next year and went to England where for a while he worked in

Francis Galton's laboratory (recall Diamond's article in the previous chapter regarding Galton's substantial influence on Cattell).

The content of James's, Hall's, and Cattell's scientific work all reflected, in one way or another, Darwinian concerns for function, development, adaptation, and individual differences, and many later psychologists—especially those who called themselves functionalists, partly in response to Titchener's attempt to limit psychology's scope—followed their lead. But their contributions to the emergence of a science of psychology went beyond the intellectual. Each proved to be a major spokesperson for psychology, explaining—sometimes selling—psychology to students, educators, businesses, and the general public. Word about the *new psychology,* this laboratory science that had seemingly evolved so suddenly from the merger of philosophy and physiology, needed to reach those in the university community as well as those in the world outside of academe (see Benjamin, 1986). James's principal contribution in this regard was through a book that he took twelve years to write.

In 1890, Henry Holt Company published James's two-volume work, *The Principles of Psychology.* It was James's assemblage of the world's psychological knowledge as only James could write it. Many historians consider it the best-written book in the history of psychology, and indeed James's prose is masterful (in comparison with his famous author-brother, Henry, it was said that William was a psychologist who wrote like a novelist, whereas Henry was a novelist who wrote like a psychologist). James's *Principles* became popular reading in colleges at the end of the nineteenth century, and later many eminent psychologists, for example, Edward L. Thorndike, would say that they were drawn into a career in psychology after reading it. The opening line of the book is "Psychology is the Science of Mental Life," and in the nearly 1400 pages that followed, James explained what was known about the mind *and* lauded the great potential for human understanding that was promised by a scientific approach to psychology. It was that promise of psychology as a natural science that was so enormously influential in recruiting many of the next generation of psychologists.

The success of the *Principles* encouraged Holt to produce a version of the book that was more appropriate in size for classroom use. So in 1892, Holt published James's *Psychology: Briefer Course,* which was only slightly more than a third the length of the *Principles* (people referred to the large work as "James" and the briefer version as "Jimmy").

The Darwinian influences are clear in James's writing. He argued that the content of consciousness was not as important as what consciousness does for the organism, and, according to James, what it does is to enhance the organism's capability of adapting to the environment. It accomplishes that by its role in choice; that is, it enables the organism to decide among choices and motivates the organism toward making a particular choice—one that has survival value. In short, consciousness has evolved because it has survival value.

Hall and Cattell played roles very different from that of James in the beginnings of the new psychology in the United States. Both published a great deal, but neither produced any written work that would shape psychology in the way James did with the *Principles*. Instead, their role was more of organization, founding, promotion, application, and even entrepreneurship. Hall founded the first psychology journal in the United States in 1887 (the *American Journal of Psychology*) and the American Psychological Association in 1892. He founded three other journals as well: *Pedagogical Seminary* (now published as the *Journal of Genetic Psychology*), the *Journal of Religious Psychology,* and the *Journal of Applied Psychology*. He is remembered for bringing Sigmund Freud to the United States for his only visit; Freud lectured at Clark University (where Hall was president) on the occasion of its twentieth anniversary in 1909.

Although Hall had diverse interests in psychology and related fields, he might best be characterized as a developmental psychologist. For much of his career he wrote about developmental topics—his two-volume magnum opus on adolescence (1904); his many publications on child study; and his 1922 book on the psychology of aging, written when he was 78. The ideas of Darwin and Galton figured prominently in Hall's research and writing. In one of his two autobiographies, Hall (1923) recalled that when as a young boy he heard about Darwin's theory, he greeted it as music to his ears.

Hall's *recapitulation theory* was a direct outgrowth of Darwinian evolution. It stated that in the course of development, from embryo to old age, every human repeated all the stages of development that had existed in the course of human evolution. Thus an evolutionary account of the human race was available by a detailed study of the life course of humans. An understanding of these developmental stages was particularly important for schoolteachers and reflected Hall's interest in child study.

Hall was one of the first to promote the application of psychology outside the university. In describing the new psychology he wrote, "The one chief and immediate field of application for all this work is its application to education" (Hall, 1894, p. 718). Using new experimental methods, psychology could learn all there was to know about the child—about sensory capabilities, physical characteristics, sense of humor, religious ideas, memory, play, attention span, and so forth. With this new knowledge, education would be no longer guesswork but a science. Pedagogical techniques could be planned and used in such a way as to be maximally effective for all kinds of students. Not all of Hall's colleagues agreed with his claims about the applicability of psychology to education, but he persisted in his efforts for two decades as part of the child study movement, a national movement he initiated (see Davidson & Benjamin, 1987). One of the by-products of Hall's work in child study was that he gave American psychology a new research method—the questionnaire. Hall did not invent the questionnaire, but his extensive use of the technique greatly popularized it, making it part of the methodological arsenal of the functionalists.

Cattell began his psychology research as a graduate student at Johns Hopkins, where he used reaction time tasks to measure the speed of mental operations. He completed those studies in Leipzig. His greatest influence, by his own acknowledgment, was not Hall or Wundt but Galton. From Wundt he acquired a set of research methods, whereas Galton provided him with his scientific goal: "The measurement of the psychological differences between people" (Sokal, 1982, p. 327). (The influence of Galton was evident even in Cattell's offer to pay $1000 each to his seven children if they would marry the sons or daughters of college professors.)

Cattell coined the term *mental test* and for more than a decade worked on a program of anthropometric mental testing designed to predict mental abilities from physical and sensory characteristics. It was a failure that essentially signaled the end of his research career. Instead he turned to his editing duties, mostly to the weekly journal *Science,* which he had purchased from Alexander Graham Bell in 1894. As editor of this prestigious publication, Cattell became one of the most visible persons in science and the first psychologist to be admitted to the National Academy of Sciences. He used his position to promote psychology among the natural sciences, and he promoted it well. There is no denying that psychology made far greater strides in the scientific community in the first quarter of the twentieth century than would have been possible without Cattell's influence.

Although Cattell had abandoned his own testing research, he did not leave the field altogether. His students at Columbia were involved with mental testing, most notably Edward L. Thorndike. Further, in the 1920s Cattell founded the Psychological Corporation, then and now one of the principal publishers of psychological tests.

There are six selections in this chapter. The first is the initial chapter from James's *Principles*. In it he defines the scope of psychology in some of the elegant prose described earlier.

The second selection, by G. Stanley Hall, was published in 1894 in a popular magazine of the day. It describes child study as a program of research that will make education a science. It is an excellent example of the combination of science and zeal that were characteristic of the child study movement.

The third selection, from Cattell, was published in 1893 in an education journal. In it Cattell reviews the new psychology and the work on mental testing, extolling the virtues of this work for the teacher.

The remaining three articles are secondary sources related to the three figures emphasized in this chapter. The first of these articles, by Lewis R. Rambo, discusses James's views on ethics and evolution as they relate to the writing of his *Principles of Psychology*.

The next selection, by Lesley A. Diehl, describes G. Stanley Hall's views on women as related to his recapitulation theory of development and the influence of his work on the beginnings of psychology's interest in sex differences. Diehl's analysis of Hall takes the form of an investigation of the paradox of his opposition to coeducation and his education of women graduate students at Clark University.

The final article is authored by Michael M. Sokal, a historian of science at Worcester Polytechnic Institute. He is the acknowledged authority on James McKeen Cattell and an expert, as well, on the history of mental testing (see

Sokal, 1987). This article describes Cattell's anthropometric mental testing program and Galton's influence on that work.

Together, these six articles provide substantial information about the beginnings of the new psychology in America and the influences borrowed from England in the writings of Darwin and Galton.

REFERENCES

Benjamin, L. T. (1986). Why don't they understand us? A history of psychology's public image. *American Psychologist, 41,* 941–946.

Davidson, E. S., & Benjamin, L. T. (1987). A history of the child study movement in America. In J. Glover & R. Ronning (Eds.), *Historical foundations of educational psychology.* New York: Plenum Press, pp. 41–60.

Hall, G. S. (1894, August). The new psychology as a basis of education. *Forum,* pp. 688–702.

Hall, G. S. (1923). *The life and confessions of a psychologist.* New York: D. Appleton.

Harper, R. S. (1949). The laboratory of William James. *Harvard Alumni Bulletin, 52,* 169–173.

Perry, R. B. (1935). *The thought and character of William James* (2 vols.). Boston: Little Brown.

Sokal, M. M. (1982). James McKeen Cattell and the failure of anthropometric mental testing, 1890–1901. In W. R. Woodward & M. G. Ash (Eds.), *The problematic science: Psychology in nineteenth-century thought.* New York: Praeger, pp. 322–345.

Sokal, M. M. (Ed.) (1987). *Psychological testing and American society, 1890–1930.* New Brunswick, NJ: Rutgers University Press.

The Scope of Psychology

William James

Psychology is the Science of Mental Life, both of its phenomena and of their conditions. The phenomena are such things as we call feelings, desires, cognitions, reasonings, decisions, and the like; and, superficially considered, their variety and complexity is such as to leave a chaotic impression on the observer. The most natural and consequently the earliest way of unifying the material was, first, to classify it as well as might be, and, secondly, to affiliate the diverse mental modes thus found, upon a simple entity, the personal Soul, of which they are taken to be so many facultative manifestations. Now, for instance, the Soul manifests its faculty of Memory, now of Reasoning, now of Volition, or again its Imagination or its Appetite. This is the orthodox 'spiritualistic' theory of scholasticism and of common-sense. Another and a less obvious way of unifying the chaos is to seek common elements *in* the diverse mental facts rather than a common agent behind them, and to explain them constructively by the various forms of arrangement of these elements, as one explains houses by stones and bricks. The 'associationist' schools of Herbart in Germany, and of Hume the Mills and Bain in Britain have thus constructed a *psychology without a soul* by taking discrete 'ideas,' faint or vivid, and showing how, by their cohesions, repulsions, and forms of succession, such things as reminiscences, perceptions, emotions, volitions, passions, theories, and all the other furnishings of an individual's mind may be engendered. The very Self or *ego* of the individual comes in this way to be viewed no longer as the pre-existing source of the representations, but rather as their last and most complicated fruit.

Now, if we strive rigorously to simplify the phenomena in either of these ways, we soon become aware of inadequacies in our method. Any partic-

ular cognition, for example, or recollection, is accounted for on the soul-theory by being referred to the spiritual faculties of Cognition or of Memory. These faculties themselves are thought of as absolute properties of the soul; that is, to take the case of memory, no reason is given why we should remember a fact as it happened, except that so to remember it constitutes the essence of our Recollective Power. We may, as spiritualists, try to explain our memory's failures and blunders by secondary causes. But its *successes* can invoke no factors save the existence of certain objective things to be remembered on the one hand, and of our faculty of memory on the other. When, for instance, I recall my graduation-day, and drag all its incidents and emotions up from death's dateless night, no mechanical cause can explain this process, nor can any analysis reduce it to lower terms or make its nature seem other than an ultimate *datum,* which, whether we rebel or not at its mysteriousness, must simply be taken for granted if we are to psychologize at all. However the associationist may represent the present ideas as thronging and arranging themselves, still, the spiritualist insists, he has in the end to admit that *something,* be it brain, be it 'ideas,' be it 'association,' *knows* past time *as* past, and fills it out with this or that event. And when the spiritualist calls memory an 'irreducible faculty,' he says no more than this admission of the associationist already grants.

And yet the admission is far from being a satisfactory simplification of the concrete facts. For why should this absolute god-given Faculty retain so much better the events of yesterday than those of last year, and, best of all, those of an hour ago? Why, again, in old age should its grasp of childhood's events seem firmest? Why should illness and exhaustion enfeeble it? Why should repeating an experience strengthen our recollection of it? Why should drugs, fevers, asphyxia,

Adapted from James, W. (1890). *The principles of psychology*. New York: Henry Holt, pp. 1–11.

and excitement resuscitate things long since forgotten? If we content ourselves with merely affirming that the faculty of memory is so peculiarly constituted by nature as to exhibit just these oddities, we seem little the better for having invoked it, for our explanation becomes as complicated as that of the crude facts with which we started. Moreover there is something grotesque and irrational in the supposition that the soul is equipped with elementary powers of such an ingeniously intricate sort. Why *should* our memory cling more easily to the near than the remote? Why should it lose its grasp of proper sooner than of abstract names? Such peculiarities seem quite fantastic; and might, for aught we can see *a priori,* be the precise opposites of what they are. Evidently, then, *the faculty does not exist absolutely, but works under conditions;* and *the quest of the conditions* becomes the psychologist's most interesting task.

However firmly he may hold to the soul and her remembering faculty, he must acknowledge that she never exerts the latter without a *cue,* and that something must always precede and *remind* us of whatever we are to recollect "An *idea!*" says the associationist, "an idea associated with the remembered thing; and this explains also why things repeatedly met with are more easily recollected, for their associates on the various occasions furnish so many distinct avenues of recall." But this does not explain the effects of fever, exhaustion, hypnotism, old age, and the like. And in general, the pure associationist's account of our mental life is almost as bewildering as that of the pure spiritualist. This multitude of ideas, existing absolutely, yet clinging together, and weaving an endless carpet of themselves, like dominoes in ceaseless change, or the bits of glass in a kaleidoscope,—whence do they get their fantastic laws of clinging, and why do they cling in just the shapes they do?

For this the associationist must introduce the order of experience in the outer world. The dance of the ideas is a copy, somewhat mutilated and altered, of the order of phenomena. But the slight-est reflection shows that phenomena have absolutely no power to influence our ideas until they have first impressed our senses and our brain. The bare existence of a past fact is no ground for our remembering it. Unless we have seen it, or somehow *undergone* it, we shall never know of its having been. The experiences of the body are thus one of the conditions of the faculty of memory being what it is. And a very small amount of reflection on facts shows that one part of the body, namely, the brain, is the part whose experiences are directly concerned. If the nervous communication be cut off between the brain and other parts, the experiences of those other parts are non-existent for the mind. The eye is blind, the ear deaf, the hand insensible and motionless. And conversely, if the brain be injured, consciousness is abolished or altered, even although every other organ in the body be ready to play its normal part. A blow on the head, a sudden subtraction of blood, the pressure of an apoplectic hemorrhage, may have the first effect; whilst a very few ounces of alcohol or grains of opium or hasheesh, or a whiff of chloroform or nitrous oxide gas, are sure to have the second. The delirium of fever, the altered self of insanity, are all due to foreign matters circulating through the brain, or to pathological changes in that organ's substance. The fact that the brain is the one immediate bodily condition of the mental operations is indeed so universally admitted nowadays that I need spend no more time in illustrating it, but will simply postulate it and pass on. The whole remainder of the book will be more or less of a proof that the postulate was correct.

Bodily experiences, therefore, and more particularly brain-experiences, must take a place amongst those conditions of the mental life of which Psychology need take account. *The spiritualist and the associationist must both be 'cerebralists,'* to the extent at least of admitting that certain peculiarities in the way of working of their own favorite principles are explicable only by the fact that the brain laws are a codeterminant of the result.

Our first conclusion, then, is that a certain

amount of brain-physiology must be presupposed or included in Psychology.

In still another way the pyschologist is forced to be something of a nerve-physiologist. Mental phenomena are not only conditioned *a parte ante* by bodily processes; but they lead to them *a parte post*. That they lead to *acts* is of course the most familiar of truths, but I do not merely mean acts in the sense of voluntary and deliberate muscular performances. Mental states occasion also changes in the calibre of blood-vessels, or alteration in the heart-beats, or processes more subtle still, in glands and viscera. If these are taken into account, as well as acts which follow at some *remote period* because the mental state was once there, it will be safe to lay down the general law that *no mental modification ever occurs which is not accompanied or followed by a bodily change*. The ideas and feelings, *e.g.*, which these present printed characters excite in the reader's mind not only occasion movements of his eyes and nascent movements of articulation in him, but will some day make him speak, or take sides in a discussion, or give advice, or choose a book to read, differently from what would have been the case had they never impressed his retina. Our psychology must therefore take account not only of the conditions antecedent to mental states, but of their resultant consequences as well.

But actions originally prompted by conscious intelligence may grow so automatic by dint of habit as to be apparently unconsciously performed. Standing, walking, buttoning and unbuttoning, piano-playing, talking, even saying one's prayers, may be done when the mind is absorbed in other things. The performances of animal *instinct* seem semi-automatic, and the *reflex acts* of self-preservation certainly are so. Yet they resemble intelligent acts in bringing about the *same ends* at which the animals' consciousness, on other occasions, deliberately aims. Shall the study of such machine-like yet purposive acts as these be included in Psychology?

The boundary-line of the mental is certainly vague. It is better not to be pedantic, but to let the science be as vague as its subject, and include such phenomena as these if by so doing we can throw any light on the main business in hand. It will ere long be seen, I trust, that we can; and that we gain much more by a broad than by a narrow conception of our subject. At a certain stage in the development of every science a degree of vagueness is what best consists with fertility. On the whole, few recent formulas have done more real service of a rough sort in psychology than the Spencerian one that the essence of mental life and of bodily life are one, namely, 'the adjustment of inner to outer relations.' Such a formula is vagueness incarnate; but because it takes into account the fact that minds inhabit environments which act on them and on which they in turn react; because, in short, it takes mind in the midst of all its concrete relations, it is immensely more fertile than the old-fashioned 'rational psychology,' which treated the soul as a detached existent, sufficient unto itself, and assumed to consider only its nature and properties. I shall therefore feel free to make any sallies into zoology or into pure nerve-physiology which may seem instructive for our purposes, but otherwise shall leave those sciences to the physiologists.

Can we state more distinctly still the manner in which the mental life seems to intervene between impressions made from without upon the body, and reactions of the body upon the outer world again? Let us look at a few facts.

If some iron filings be sprinkled on a table and a magnet brought near them, they will fly through the air for a certain distance and stick to its surface. A savage seeing the phenomenon explains it as the result of an attraction or love between the magnet and the filings. But let a card cover the poles of the magnet, and the filings will press forever against its surface without its ever occurring to them to pass around its sides and thus come into more direct contact with the object of their love. Blow bubbles through a tube into the bottom of a pail of water, they will rise to the surface and mingle with the air. Their action may again be poetically interpreted as due to a longing to recombine with the mother-atmosphere above the surface. But if you invert a jar full of water over the pail, they will rise and remain lodged beneath its bottom, shut in from the outer air, although a slight deflection from their course at the outset, or a re-descent towards the rim of the jar when they found their upward course impeded, would easily have set them free.

If now we pass from such actions as these to those of living things, we notice a striking difference. Romeo wants Juliet as the filings want the magnet; and if no obstacles intervene he moves towards her by as straight a line as they. But Romeo and Juliet, if a wall be built between them, do not remain idiotically pressing their faces against its opposite sides like the magnet and the filings with the card. Romeo soon finds a circuitous way, by scaling the wall or otherwise, of touching Juliet's lips directly. With the filings the path is fixed; whether it reaches the end depends on accidents. With the lover it is the end which is fixed, the path may be modified indefinitely.

Suppose a living frog in the position in which we placed our bubbles of air, namely, at the bottom of a jar of water. The want of breath will soon make him also long to rejoin the mother-atmosphere, and he will take the shortest path to his end by swimming straight upwards. But if a jar full of water be inverted over him, he will not, like the bubbles, perpetually press his nose against its unyielding roof, but will restlessly explore the neighborhood until by re-descending again he has discovered a path round its brim to the goal of his desires. Again the fixed end, the varying means!

Such contrasts between living and inanimate performances end by leading men to deny that in the physical world final purposes exist at all. Loves and desires are to-day no longer imputed to particles of iron or of air. No one supposes now that the end of any activity which they may

display is an ideal purpose presiding over the activity from its outset and soliciting or drawing it into being by a sort of *vis a fronte*. The end, on the contrary, is deemed a mere passive result, pushed into being a *tergo,* having had, so to speak, no voice in its own production. Alter the pre-existing conditions, and with inorganic materials you bring forth each time a different apparent end. But with intelligent agents, altering the conditions changes the activity displayed, but not the end reached; for here the idea of the yet unrealized end co-operates with the conditions to determine what the activities shall be.

The pursuance of future ends and the choice of means for their attainment are thus the mark and criterion of the presence of mentality in a phenomenon. We all use this test to discriminate between an intelligent and a mechanical performance. We impute no mentality to sticks and stones, because they never seem to move for *the sake of* anything, but always when pushed, and then indifferently and with no sign of choice. So we unhesitatingly call them senseless.

Just so we form our decision upon the deepest of all philosophic problems: Is the Kosmos an expression of intelligence rational in its inward nature, or a brute external fact pure and simple? If we find ourselves, in contemplating it, unable to banish the impression that it is a realm of final purposes, that it exists for the sake of something, we place intelligence at the heart of it and have a religion. If, on the contrary, in surveying its irremediable flux, we can think of the present only as so much mere mechanical sprouting from the past, occurring with no reference to the future, we are atheists and materialists.

In the lengthy discussions which psychologists have carried on about the amount of intelligence displayed by lower mammals, or the amount of consciousness involved in the functions of the nerve-centres of reptiles, the same test has always been applied: Is the character of the actions such that we must believe them to be performed *for the sake* of their result? The result in question, as we shall hereafter abundantly see, is as a rule a useful one,—the animal is, on the whole, safer under the circumstances for bringing it forth. So far the action has a teleological character; but such mere outward teleology as this might still be the blind result of *vis a tergo*. The growth and movements of plants, the processes of development, digestion, secretion, etc., in animals, supply innumerable instances of performances useful to the individual which may nevertheless be, and by most of us are supposed to be, produced by automatic mechanism. The physiologist does not confidently assert conscious intelligence in the frog's spinal cord until he has shown that the useful result which the nervous machinery brings forth under a given irritation *remains the same when the machinery is altered*. If, to take the stock instance, the right knee of a headless frog be irritated with acid, the right foot will wipe it off. When, however, this foot is amputated, the animal will often raise the *left* foot to the spot and wipe the offending material away.

Pflüger and Lewes reason from such facts in the following way: If the first reaction were the result of mere machinery, they say; if that irritated portion of the skin discharged the right leg as a trigger discharges its own barrel of a shotgun; then amputating the right foot would indeed frustrate the wiping, but would not make the *left* leg move. It would simply result in the right stump moving through the empty air (which is in fact the phenomenon sometimes observed). The right trigger makes no effort to discharge the left barrel if the right one be unloaded; nor does an electrical machine ever get restless because it can only emit sparks, and not hem pillow-cases like a sewing-machine.

If, on the contrary, the right leg originally moved for the *purpose* of wiping the acid, then nothing is more natural than that, when the easiest means of effecting that purpose prove fruitless, other means should be tried. Every failure must keep the animal in a state of disappointment which will lead to all sorts of new trials and devices; and tranquillity will not ensure till one of these, by a happy stroke, achieves the wished-for end.

In a similar way Goltz ascribes intelligence to the frog's optic lobes and cerebellum. We alluded above to the manner in which a sound frog imprisoned in water will discover an outlet to the atmosphere. Goltz found that frogs deprived of their cerebral hemispheres would often exhibit a like ingenuity. Such a frog, after rising from the bottom and finding his farther upward progress checked by the glass bell which has been inverted over him, will not persist in butting his nose against the obstacle until dead of suffocation, but will often re-descend and emerge from under its rim as if, not a definite mechanical propulsion upwards, but rather a conscious desire to reach the air by hook or crook were the mainspring of his activity. Goltz concluded from this that the hemispheres are not the sole seat of intellect in frogs. He made the same inference from observing that a brainless frog will turn over from his back to his belly when one of his legs is sewed up, although the movements required are then very different from those excited under normal circumstances by the same annoying position. They seem determined, consequently, not merely by the antecedent irritant, but by the final end,—though the irritant of course is what makes the end desired.

Another brilliant German author, Liebmann, argues against the brain's mechanism accounting for mental action, by very similar considerations. A machine as such, he says, will bring forth right results when it is in good order, and wrong results if out of repair. But both kinds of result flow with equally fatal necessity from their conditions. We cannot suppose the clock-work whose structure fatally determines it to a certain rate of speed, noticing that this speed is too slow or too fast and vainly trying to correct it. Its conscience, if it have any, should be as good as that of the best chronometer, for both alike obey equally well the same eternal mechanical laws— laws from behind. But if the *brain* be out of order and the man says "Twice four are two," instead of "Twice four are eight," or else "I must go to the coal to buy the wharf," instead of "I must go to the wharf to buy the coal," instantly there arises a consciousness of error. The wrong performance, though it obey the same mechanical law as the right, is nevertheless condemned, —condemned as contradicting the inner law— the law from in front, the purpose or ideal for which the brain *should* act, whether it do so or not.

We need not discuss here whether these writers in drawing their conclusion have done justice to all the premises involved in the cases they treat of. We quote their arguments only to show how they appeal to the principle that *no actions but such as are done for an end, and show a choice of means, can be called indubitable expressions of Mind.*

I shall then adopt this as the criterion by which to circumscribe the subject-matter of this work

so far as action enters into it. Many nervous performances will therefore be unmentioned, as being purely physiological. Nor will the anatomy of the nervous system and organs of sense be described anew. The reader will find in H. N. Martin's 'Human Body,' in G. T. Ladd's 'Physiological Psychology,' and in all the other standard Anatomies and Physiologies, a mass of information which we must regard as preliminary and take for granted in the present work.* Of the functions of the cerebral hemispheres, however, since they directly subserve consciousness, it will be well to give some little account.

* Nothing is easier than to familiarize one's self with the mammalian brain. Get a sheep's head, a small saw, chisel, scalpel and forceps (all three can best be had from a surgical-instrument maker), and unravel its parts either by the aid of a human dissecting book, such as Holden's 'Manual of Anatomy,' or by the specific directions *ad hoc* given in such books as Foster and Langley's 'Practical Physiology' (Macmillan) or Morrell's 'Comparative Anatomy and Dissection of Mammalia' (Longmans).

Child-Study: The Basis of Exact Education

G. Stanley Hall

The study of children is now attempted by very different methods, for purposes quite diverse, and with all degrees of scientific exactness. The points of view here taken, and the literature, now numbering many hundred titles, are so new that I can find nowhere any attempt at a general survey of the various lines of work now under way to aid me in presenting such an outline as the editor of "The Forum" has requested; while new material is accumulating so fast and the future promises so much that any attempt to map out the field even by a text-book could have only temporary value.

That so considerable a part of the work has been done in this country, which, if it has not had

a large share in the development of the physical sciences, now shows signs of making up its arrears by advancing several branches of the great science of man, is a fact well befitting a republic, new and without tradition, which most needs to take a fresh, free look at every aspect of human nature, which alone is true and to which school, as well as church, state and family, must conform to be true, good or stable. The future of the movement depends largely upon long, hard work yet to be done and requires the coöperative effort of many people—teachers, parents and men of science, whose efforts may now be coördinated in a national society, the organization of which was projected last July in Chicago.

Most of this vast and growing material has been wrought out by investigators who made little attempt to coördinate their work with what others

From Hall, G. S. (1893). Child-study: The basis of exact education. *Forum, 16,* 429–441.

had done. The doctors, the anthropologists, the psychologists, parents and teachers, have each given little attention to each other's work.

The first study on the contents of children's minds was made in Berlin in 1869 and showed an astonishing ignorance of things every child ought and was supposed to know. By the liberality of Mrs. Quincy Shaw I was enabled to make comprehensive studies in 1880 of a large number of Boston children just after they had entered the lowest grade of the primary school. The tactful and experienced questioners were convinced that fourteen per cent of these six-year old children had never seen the stars and had no idea about them; that thirty-five per cent had never been into the country; that twenty per cent did not know that milk came from cows; fifty-five per cent did not know that wooden things came from trees; that from thirteen to fifteen per cent did not know the colors, green, blue and yellow, by name; that forty-seven per cent had never seen a pig; sixty per cent had never seen a robin; from thirteen to eighteen per cent did not know where their cheek, forehead or throat was, and fewer yet knew elbow, wrist, ribs, etc. More than three-fourths of all the children had never seen to know them any of the common cereals, trees, or vegetables growing. These subjects were chosen because most of them constitute the material of school primers or elementary instruction which this new science of ignorance shows must make mere verbal cram of much matter of instruction. What idea can the eighteen per cent of children who thought a cow no larger than its picture get from all instruction about hide, horns, milk, etc.? Country children excel in this kind of knowledge, and, while they know less, know it better and have greater power of concentration. In Annaberg, Germany, careful and repeated studies of such general and local items, about one hundred in all, like the Boston tests, are now made the natural basis of the school-work of the first year or two. Color tests have been made by H. K. Wolfe, Professor Barnes, Mrs. Hicks, and others. Wolfe examined many children between five and seventeen years of age as to power of

discriminating and naming colors, and found the order of knowledge to be white, black, red, blue, yellow, green, pink, orange, violet.

Here, too, might be mentioned the interesting studies on colored hearing and number forms by Miss Calkins and others, on the individuality of numerals by Miss Whiting, which not only explain anomalies more common than was thought but tell how to meet them; and the statistical study of six species of lies children are prone to. T. L. Bolton tested memory-span for numbers up to nine places and found that memory-span increased with age rather than intelligence, that it was better in girls than boys, that it measures power of prolonged and concentrated attention, that the first stage of forgetfulness is loss of order, that if the number of ideas is too great it is overestimated and that they are forgotten inversely as they are removed from the beginning of the series.

The theological and religious life of children has been investigated in large numbers of children. These studies show that the sky is the chief field for religious ideas, that God, angels, heaven, are very distinctly imagined, connected with stars, clouds and thunder in the most material way. For example, God is a big blue man who pours rain out of big buckets, thumps clouds to make thunder, puts the sun and moon to bed, takes dead people, birds and even broken dolls up there, distributes babies, and is closely related to Santa Claus. This infant philosophy although intimidated and broken through at every point and on the ebb at the beginning of school life, is very persistent, though as hard for an adult to get at as for an electric light to study shadows. Barnes found that from seven to ten years of age there began to be occasional vague questionings and doubts about early conceptions which had hitherto been accepted without question or comment, that doubt grew with age and culminated at the age of thirteen or fourteen when criticism was more severe than later. Barnes has studied also the delicate subject of feelings and ideas of sex in children. Miss A. E. Wyckoff has studied constitutionally bad spellers.

This entire class of studies shows how easily

school-work may miscarry, how supremely important the imagination is for this stage of child life, how large a part imitation and the struggle to be and do like older people play. The work of Mr. Russell, which is described above, belongs here and promises to be of great value. We want also minute objective studies, such as any intelligent mother or teacher could make if they would focus their attention on one subject, such as fear, shame, anger, pity, the phenomena of crying, unusual manifestations of will, traits made worse or better by school, effects of defect and physical malformation, of wise or unwise religious teaching, or any of the remarkable periodicities so common and described by Siegert, who thinks every kind of growth is zig-zag toward its goal, and that bright children have periods of muddle. We cannot here speak of exceptional children or pedagogical pathology, as it has been called by Strumpel, and worked out by Nicolay, Siegert, and others, nor of the studies made upon blind, deaf, idiot, criminal children; these last would make a chapter by themselves. Human nature at this stage is so vastly complex that only those of unusual attainments and genius can study it as a whole. It is clear that boys and girls are now being understood in a new light which may lead to much reconstruction of school methods and matter.

Passing now to the ephebic stage of youth we find that adolescence is a physiological second-birth; new traits and diseases, organs, and cells are developed; boys and girls become independent, must devote themselves to others and to causes; the life of the individual terminates and that of the race begins; the religious sense is deepened, and almost every religious cult has marked this period by its most solemn ceremonials. Dr. Burnham has well stated the great increase of vitality and energy at this period when nature gives man his capital of life force, and Dr. Daniels has now shown both by statistics and psychology how closely it is related to regeneration, in a religious sense. The great danger is that the lower elements will be developed in excess or disproportion. But nothing is so educable as love. It can attach itself, as recent morbid

studies show, to almost any act or object; it can suck up all that is vile in the environment, or it can climb Godward up the stages of a heavenly ladder, as Plato describes in the "Symposium." Excitement young men must have, which like a breeze swelling new sails brings the new nerve tissue and faculties into activity without which they atrophy. If there is no enthusiasm, deep and strong interests in intellectual and moral fields, passion is stronger. The two are in a sense physiological or kinetic equivalents, and if the young man vents this erethic tendency during the adolescent decade in drink or vice, he will really be, as so many youth absurdly affect, apathetic, stoical, indifferent, and ashamed of enthusiasm. Alas for our academic youth if they lose freshness, and *naiveté,* and college freshmen become poised men of the world instead of being a little green and awkward. It is to be hoped that those who think that there is an increase of vice among boys in our high and preparatory schools in recent years, are mistaken.

Very few systematic studies have been made of collegians in this country, except the systematic weighing and measuring connected with gymnastics. Mr. Drew collected 356 love poems in student papers and published interesting figures of the features and traits of the beloved most often referred to. Eleven professors in larger Eastern colleges asked their seniors to answer four questions concerning their philosophical electives, points of interest therein, etc.; the returns are full of interest but cannot be presented in any composite-portrait way. College sentiment and opinion seem to be more and more influential; college teams and captains can keep order where faculties fail; student ideals are the best material for prophecy. The student chooses for himself not only what to study but whether to study or not. Inside academic administration is a kind of psychological engineering applied to the sentiments and ideals of later adolescence. A body of select young men taught by select professors, exempt from all practical life, brought in contact with the choicest minds of all time, ought to exhibit in the spontaneous drift of their disinterested ideals the dominant drift of the *volks-soul*; with a peculiar fascination, all their own, they are perhaps most of all things in the world interesting and worthy of study. Student life has its own laws quite apart from a curriculum and is for many more important than it. If its tone deteriorates, as it does in occasional periods and institutions, the whole *morale* of the place may decay.

This paper closes with a practical suggestion for farther work here—that one or two of the largest colleges cause a well trained and tactful man to devote his time to the study and improvement of college life, calling freely upon others to coöperate. Abundant material for a study of the natural history of students is afforded by the more than 200 college periodicals now published in this country. Sentiment and custom might be acted on by occasional lectures on the history of student life from the Middle Ages down. The corps, codes of honor, fraternities, sports, occupations, etc.; the tabulation of choices of study with reasons therefor; essays, and now the daily themes as at Harvard, the religious life and needs of students—a new problem lately forced upon many college preachers; and, above all, habitual intimacy with students and personal acquaintance on the ball ground and in the study;—these suggest a new field and method which might be called the higher anthropology.

Tests of the Senses and Faculties

James McKeen Cattell

Tests of the senses and faculties concern the teacher from three points of view. In the first place, those who wish to contribute to the advancement of psychology will find here a convenient opening. In the second place, such tests give a useful indication of the progress, condition, and aptitudes of the pupil. In the third place, the carrying out of the tests might serve as a means of training and education.

The senses and faculties have been studied hitherto by men of science, who have mostly made the determinations upon themselves. This is a necessary beginning, but now that methods have been elaborated, it is very desirable that the measurements should be extended so as to include different classes of persons. There are no individuals better suited for such experiments than the pupils in our schools. They are classified according to age, acquirements, and sex, and the teacher has considerable knowledge of their ability, character, and heredity. A careful investigation of the variation in the senses and faculties under such conditions would at the present time be an important contribution to science. In so far as experiment can be used in the study of mind, scientific progress is assured. The traditional psychology is vague and inexact, and cannot rank as co-ordinate with physical science. But when we regard the history of the several physical sciences, we see that they too at one time consisted of inexact descriptions, artificial classifications, dubious anecdotes, and verbal explanations. With the introduction of experiment and measurement astrology has become astronomy, alchemy has become chemistry, and natural history has become natural science. Physical sciences, such as astronomy, in which measurements could be readily undertaken were the first to be developed, while those, such as electricity, in which it is difficult to make measurements, are still backward. Matter in motion is more readily subject to experiment when passive than when organic and living. Physics has consequently preceded biology in its development. But the progress of biology has recently been rapid,

From Cattell, J. McK. (1893). Tests of the senses and faculties. *Educational Review, 5,* 257–265.

and it will be found that nearly all advances have been due to the application of experiment and measurement. As the living organism is more complex and changeable than inert matter, so the mind is more complicated, protean, and inaccessible than the body. It is natural, therefore, that psychology should be the last science to be weaned by philosophy and to begin an independent growth. Those who have followed the recent development of psychology know that this has been the result of experiment and measurement. Each new application of experimental methods subserves the advancement of psychology, and the very backwardness of the science gives the teacher an opportunity to contribute to its progress.

When our knowledge of the normal variation of mental processes has been somewhat further increased, its determination will give useful indications of individual condition, progress, and ability. In conjunction with the ordinary school examination such tests would show whether the course of study is improving or blunting the fundamental processes of perception and mental life. Tests made at the beginning and end of the day, week, and session would show whether the student is exhausted by the required curriculum. They could be used in comparing different systems of education, different schools, the advantages of city and country, etc. They would show whether girls are able, without injury to health, to follow the same courses of study as boys. Careful tests must almost of necessity be introduced into the public schools. If attendance be made compulsory, the state is undoubtedly responsible for any bad consequences which could be avoided. Thus if the eyesight of a student be injured, so as to involve a loss of ability to earn a living, the state would, under our present laws, probably be liable for damages. In many cases tests which could readily be made would indicate disease, especially of the nervous system, long before it becomes apparent to common observation. The tendency to certain diseases counterindicate certain employments. Thus a very large

percentage of women teachers become insane; consequently those having neuropathic tendencies should not enter on this profession. One boy in twenty is color blind, and this defect, which is never discovered by the individual himself, but may be determined by the teacher in one minute, unfits him for work so far separated as that of the railway signal man or of the artist. As our knowledge increases we shall, on the one hand, be able to indicate very early in the life of the child tendencies to insanity and other diseases, to dipsomania and other vices, and to crime, and precautions may be taken which will limit the range of these abnormal tendencies in the individual, and prevent their spreading in the race. On the other hand, valuable qualities may be early discovered and developed. Special aptitudes will not be lost through unsuitable surroundings and uncongenial work, but the child may be led to the course of life in which he will be most happy and most useful. Many tendencies are likely to be eliminated or increased in offspring according to the marriage of the parents. While instinct is probably a better guide to suitable marriage than scientific principles, it cannot be denied that parents and the conventions of society have much to do with the conditions under which choice is made. Somewhat of the backwardness of the dark ages may be due to the fact that many of the best men were celibates. If a code of honor (such as obtains in some aristocracies, and prevents its members from marrying below their rank) could be developed, and directed toward eliminating degenerative tendencies, and developing valuable traits, the race would be greatly strengthened and perfected.

Such experiments on the senses and faculties would not only advance our knowledge of the mind, and serve as a useful criterion in many ways, but they would also be a valuable training for the pupil. The senses and faculties would be developed as well as measured. In the child and savage every sensation from without is apt to distract the attention and lead to some movement. In the language of physiology, afferent impulses are immediately converted into efferent, and nothing is stored up within. Education seeks to prevent such dispersion, and the importance of manual training and laboratory work for this purpose is now universally admitted. The senses and faculties are trained wherever the student makes special movements and independent observations, but the direction in which these should be undertaken remains an open question. It should be remembered that a laboratory course, as in chemistry, is intended rather for training the pupil than for learning about the combinations of elements, etc. It is, in fact, a course in experimental psychology as much as a course in experimental physics. It can only be decided after practical trial whether a laboratory course expressly directed to studying the senses and faculties would serve better or worse than a physical or biological science as a means of training. Such tests certainly require the most complete abstraction and concentration, and every wandering of the attention is at once betrayed by the experiments themselves. The stimulus of competition and of the effort to improve will certainly secure the interest of the student. It may be found that the experiments will become too much of a "game." But they require a steady hand, undimmed senses, and a clear mind, and any effort to secure these cannot but benefit the student. Those who have marked the improvement in health of students in the English universities as they train for a boat race must wish that some such healthy competition could be more widespread in schools and colleges.

In this paper suitable tests can be indicated only; the teacher who wishes to study methods and results must work over special books and papers.* Experiments can be made in an hour which would

* We are fortunate in having the recent psychologies of Professor James and Professor Ladd. Those who know German should also read Professor Wundt's *Physiologische Psychologie*. Mr. Galton's *Inquiries into Human Faculty* and other writings are of special interest. Professor Jastrow has given in the *Educational Review* (II:442) an excellent example of tests on memory and association.

leave a record of permanent value both to science and to the individual student. If the experiments be regarded as a means of training and made part of the school curriculum, and an hour a week throughout the year be devoted to them, much more can be accomplished. In this case the senses may be taken up in order, beginning, say, with vision. The sharpness of sight may be easily measured by determining the distance at which a printed page can be read. If the sharpness be defective an oculist should be consulted, as the difficulty is usually mechanical and may be readily corrected. Each eye should be tested separately, as one eye is often defective, and an excess of strain is needlessly thrown on the better eye. Color blindness may be detected by letting the student select all the green shades from a heap of colored wools, and more exactly determined by matching colors on revolving wheels. The size of the field of vision may be mapped out by letting the observer look at a fixed point and determining how far in every direction letters can be read and colors seen.

The error in perceiving size may be tested by drawing a line as nearly as possible the length of a standard line, and in perceiving intensity by matching shadows or revolving wheels. The perception of size, distance, and solidity with one and with two eyes may be studied, and its exactness measured. If time permit contrast and after-images may be observed, and the individual variation determined. Useful training in subjective observation may be obtained by noticing that things not looked at directly are seen double, and by observing entoptic phenomena. These are various images due to the structure of the eye. They are often discovered by the individual, and lead him to think that his eyes are failing.

The sharpness of hearing may be tested by determining the distance at which the ticking of a watch can be heard. The test should be made for each ear separately. The range of pitch which can be heard varies considerably with different individuals, and this may be determined. The accuracy with which small differences in pitch can be distinguished and with which intervals can be adjusted should be measured. Time is often mis-spent by girls who learn to play the piano me-chanically with no ear for music. The exactness with which distance and direction can be recog-nized with the ear may be measured. Learning to distinguish the simple tones in a complex sound is a useful training.

Touch may be tested and trained by determin-ing how far apart two points must be in order that they may be recognized as two when they touch the skin. This distance differs greatly in differ-ent parts of the body. Taste and smell are ne-glected senses, and ones peculiarly open to ed-ucation. Considering its importance to comfort and health, cooking is a backward art, and our housewives should be trained to distinguish and value small differences. If good water could be distinguished from bad by the average individ-ual as well as it is by the horse, many cases of typhoid fever and diphtheria would be avoided. The same holds for smells, which are invaluable criteria of unhygienic surroundings. The sense of temperature could also be trained so that one may know when a room becomes overheated, and may distinguish subjective from objective causes. The organic changes within the body are obscure and not easy to observe and study, but they are of enormous importance. To recognize correctly the need for fresh air, food, sleep, rest, and exercise would be an acquirement whose value cannot be overstated. If the causes lead-ing to *malaise* and *bien être,* tedium and com-fort, could be learned and the mode of living ad-justed accordingly, the value of life and all the institutions of society would be affected.

Movement and its perception offer a valuable series of tests. The strength of the grasp of the hand and the rate at which a blow can be struck should be measured. These are convenient tests of bodily condition, and a difference between two hands is often characteristic. The tremor of the hand and the sway of the body give early and important in-dications of overstrain. The way we judge move-ments by their extent, their force, and their time

should be studied, and the accuracy of discrimina-tion measured. It is easy to find how much differ-ence there must be between two weights, in order that their difference may be noticed.

Feelings of pleasure and pain may be tested in such a course, and possibly elementary aes-thetic perceptions trained. It would be a great gain if students could learn to appreciate simplic-ity and taste in dress and surroundings. The col-ors and their combinations liked best and least may be determined, as also shapes, relative siz-es, etc. A corresponding experiment may be made for the combinations of tones used in speech and music. The pressure or temperature which just hurts may be determined.

Leaving the senses and turning to the facul-ties we find that imagination, memory, and the association of ideas may be tested. Thus a series of questions can be framed the answers to which will throw light on the mental imagery of the pu-pil. The thoughts of some are accompanied by vivid pictures, others think more in sounds or movements. Some can call up a scene so as to see all the details before them, others only re-member the relations. Such differences are highly characteristic, and indicate special apti-tudes which should not be disregarded. The ac-curacy of ordinary observation may be tested by requiring the student to draw the plan of the hall of the schoolhouse, or to give an account of some event, say something that happened in the school the day before. Casual observation will be found very defective, and the student will learn that but little reliance can be placed on stories of extraor-dinary events, or even on the testimony in a court of justice. He may also learn to distinguish clearly what he in fact knows, and what he sur-mises and invents. If so he will have acquired nothing more valuable in his whole school course. Memory may be tested by reading a pas-sage aloud, and requiring the student to write down afterward as much as he can remember. It can be measured more exactly by reading a se-ries of numerals, and determining how many can be remembered. The experiment may be varied by choosing a series of numerals greater than can be remembered on hearing once and determining how often it must be repeated in order that it may be learned. The same series may be used a day or a week afterward; the greater rapidity with which it is learned indicates unconscious memory, and the experiment may be arranged to measure the rate of forgetting. The rate at which a simple sensation fades from the memory may also be determined. The range of consciousness may be measured by uncovering objects for a very short time and determining how much the student can perceive simultaneously. The association of ideas may be studied by giving a word to the class, and letting them write down what idea or other word is suggested by it. The train of ideas for twenty seconds may be recorded. Questions may also be arranged in such a manner that the answers will throw light on the acquirements and interests of the student.

The time of mental processes is a useful test. The accuracy with which an interval of time can be judged is a somewhat different matter; it may be tested readily by giving the student an interval, say one minute, and letting him note when an equal period has elapsed. The time passing before a movement can be made in answer to a stimulus may be measured, but it is so short that delicate apparatus is required. The time needed to see and name series of colors, letters, and words should be found. An educated man can read words making sentences in about half the time that he can read disconnected words. The absolute and relative times are consequently a good test of progress in learning to read. The rate of reading foreign languages measures familiarity with the language. The time of mental processes, such as translating words from one language to another, adding or multiplying digits, remembering the country in which a city is situated, or the author of a book, may be measured readily by letting the student make ten trials in succession. The time in coming to a decision or

in making a judgment may also be measured. In normal mental life the attention waxes and wanes and the duration of this rhythm may be measured.

In conjunction with these mental tests certain anthropometric data should be secured. Such are the height, weight, breathing capacity, the color of eyes and hair, etc. Age and sex and the nationality and position of the parents should always be noted. If possible it will be well to record what diseases the student has suffered, as also the age, state of health, etc., of his brothers and sisters, his parents, and other near relatives.

This series of tests of the senses and faculties by no means exhausts such as may be made to advantage. Those wishing to undertake more advanced work will seek to study and measure mental time, intensity and extensity, and the correlation of these magnitudes. But all the tests enumerated here may be made by an intelligent teacher on even the youngest school children, and without expensive or complicated apparatus. It may seem surprising that, with the exception of a few isolated tests, this has not as yet been attempted anywhere; but it must be remembered that experimental psychology is a recent study even in our universities. The first laboratory for research work was established by Professor Wundt at Leipzig in 1879, and the second by Dr. G. Stanley Hall at Baltimore in 1882. The first course in which students carried out a series of experiments in the laboratory was given by the writer in 1888. Now, however, the teacher can prepare himself for such work in most of the leading universities—at Harvard, Yale, Columbia, Pennsylvania, Cornell, Clark, Brown, Washington, Chicago, Wisconsin, Michigan, Indiana, Nebraska, Stanford, and Toronto. The rapid extension of the study of experimental psychology in American universities leads to the expectation that tests of the senses and faculties will soon be undertaken in many schools, and will perhaps be made part of the regular curriculum.

Ethics, Evolution, and the Psychology of William James

Lewis R. Rambo

William James's life and thought continues to elicit appreciation, analysis, and controversy. Scholars in diverse fields continue to find James's writings illuminating and relevant to contemporary issues. Indeed, within the last decade there have been numerous studies which have argued for James's importance to psychology, phenomenology, psychology of religion, ethics, and religious thought.[1] Generally neglected in this spate of writing has been an examination of the historical context of James's philosophy of human nature and normative ethics. It should be emphasized that James's concern for ethics was not merely descriptive or technical in the sense of the philosophical analysis of ethical discourse. His interest was in *normative* ethics—what people *should* or *ought* to be. These concerns pervade James's thought and offer an illuminating perspective from which to view the continuities of his writings and to correct some misinterpretations of his work.[2]

The core of James's normative vision was his notion of the strenuous life, the contours of which were explicitly articulated in a series of essays written between 1879 and 1896. James began his monumental *The Principles of Psychology* in 1878, and it was published in 1890. The chronology of these writing efforts is important because it demonstrates that James was concerned simultaneously with normative ethics and with a scientific psychology. Hence, the thesis of this paper is that James's vision of human possibility was manifested in *The Principles of Psychology* in two ways: first, the ethical concerns of James's psychology were continuous with his

more explicit and fully developed normative ethics contained in *The Will to Believe* (a compilation of the major essays produced between 1879 and 1896); second, James's view of the psychological constitution and the attendant capacities of the human being was the foundation for his concept of the strenuous life. There seems to have been a constant process of cross-fertilization during these years. James's ethical concerns are articulated with vigor and certainty, and one is given the impression that the psychological works are explorations into a psychology which will confirm his position on the ethical capacities of human beings.

James published "Great Men, Great Thoughts, and the Environment" in 1880.[3] This essay provided the evolutionary context in which James elaborated his normative vision of the human being. James is sometimes criticized for being too concerned with the individual, but such an interpretation does not take into account James's pervasive interest in evolution and his explicit articulation of a theory of social evolution. In "Great Men, Great Thoughts, and the Environment," he discussed the reasons why communities change from generation to generation and attacked the position advocated by Herbert Spencer and his disciples that the human being is merely the product of his environment. Individuals, according to Spencer's evolutionary schema, cannot effect change by their actions because their actions are all *reactions* to external stimuli. The core of James's critique of the Spencerian view of social evolution was that it failed to take Darwin's theories in a radical form. Spencer focused his views on the Darwinian notion of environmental selection to the neglect of spontaneous variation. Spencer thought that social change was determined strictly by the environment, whereas James argued that one must consider the role of spontaneous

Rambo, L. R. (1980). Ethics, evolution, and the psychology of William James. *Journal of the History of the Behavioral Sciences, 16,* 50–57. Copyright © 1980 by the Clinical Psychology Publishing Company. Reprinted by permission of the publisher and the author.

variation in the development of the genius. The genius is that individual with remarkable or unique abilities who inserts something novel into the social environment. Having accepted the genius as a social fact, James then argued for the selection and interaction of the genius with the environment. James was not critical of evolutionary theory qua evolutionary theory; rather, he felt that Spencer and others distorted Darwin's contribution by overemphasizing environmental elements of the theory. James explained the ways in which the great man influences his environment in the following:

> The mutations of societies, then, from generation to generation, are in the main due directly or indirectly to the acts or the example of individuals whose genius was so adapted to the receptivities of the moment, or whose accidental position of authority was so critical that they became fermenters, initiators of movement, setters of precedent or fashion, centers of corruption, or destroyers of other persons, whose gifts, had they had free play, would have led society in another direction.[4]

James was not, of course, advocating a position that only individual actions mold society; rather, he saw the process as reciprocal:

> Social evolution is a resultant of the interaction of two wholly distinct factors,—the individual deriving his peculiar gifts from the play of physiological and infra-social forces, but bearing all the power of initiative and origination in his hands; and, second, the social environment, with its power of adopting or rejecting both him and his gifts. Both factors are essential to change. The community stagnates without the impulse of the individual. The impulse dies away without the sympathy of the community.[5]

The moral agency of individuals was important for James because there are, in his words, "ambiguous potentialities of development." Decisions are crucial because each choice means a real bifurcation of the future. Once a decision is made, there is a restriction of future development.

Another essay written very soon after "Great Men, Great Thoughts, and the Environment," but not published until 1890, was "The Importance of Individuals."[6] This article was written in response to several rebuttals of "Great Men." James did not mean to imply that he was concerned only with "great men." Indeed, the style of life and the decisions of every individual are vitally important. He selected the "great man" because his actions are most dramatically efficacious in making a difference in the social context. Individual moral agency in decision making is so fundamentally important because it is a "zone of insecurity" and the "formative zone." James used the analogy of a growing tree to make the point. The soft layer just below the bark is where the growth takes place. It is the zone of individual decisions where social evolution transpires.

In the "formative zone" or "moving present," the passions, interests, desires, and preferences of individuals are of great relevance. Because the mind is not, in James's view, a passive reflector of the environment, but an active agent, he appealed to the strenuous life and seriousness, maintaining that a different result can be achieved by ethical striving than by merely capitulating to what he called "the most pernicious and immoral of fatalisms"—a sense that everything is determined by prior events and the individual can thus effect no change. The following is a good summary of James's position:

> The evolutionary view of history, when it denies the vital importance of individual initiative, is, then, an utterly vague and unscientific conception, a lapse from modern scientific determinism into the most ancient oriental fatalism. The lessons of the analysis that we have made...forms an appeal of the most stimulating sort to the energy of the individual.[7]

"Great Men and Their Environment" and "The Importance of Individuals" demonstrate James's passionate concern for the overall social situation and the active role of the individual in the broader, evolutionary context. While it is true that James did not develop a sophisticated sociological theory and study the nature of institutional growth and development, it is nevertheless important to emphasize, especially because it is so often neglected in discussions of James, that he was concerned with the individual because of his/her role in social evolution. It is also important to stress that James self-consciously and explicitly related evolution and ethics. Although he rarely made explicit reference to the connection, as he did in "Great Men, Great Thoughts, and the Environment" and "The Importance of Individuals," the relationship was an undercurrent throughout many of James's books and essays.

"The Moral Philosopher and the Moral Life" was originally an address which James delivered to the Yale Philosophical Club in 1891. In it he dealt with the nature of moral obligation or the foundation of ethical values and also gave an extensive description of the strenuous life. James asserted:

> The deepest difference, practically, in the moral life of man is the difference between the easy-going and strenuous mood. When in the easy-going mood the shrinking from present ill is our ruling consideration. The strenuous mood, on the contrary, makes us quite indifferent to present ill, if only the greater ideal be attained. The capacity for the strenuous mood probably lies slumbering in every man, but it has more difficulty in some than in others in waking up. It needs the wilder passions to arouse it, the big fears, loves, and indignations; or else the deeply penetrating appeal of some of the higher fidelities, like justice, truth, or freedom.[8]

Furthermore,

> The capacity of the strenuous mood lies so deep down among our natural human possibilities that even if there were no metaphysical or traditional grounds for believing in a God, men would postulate one simply as a pretext for living hard, and getting out of the game of existence its keenest pos-

sibilities of zest. Our attitude towards concrete evils is entirely different in a world where we believe there are none but finite demanders, from what it is in one where we joyously face tragedy for an infinite demander's sake. Every sort of energy and endurance, of courage and capacity for handling life's evils, is set free in those who have religious faith. For this reason the strenuous type of character will on the battlefield of human history always outwear the easy-going type, and religion will drive irreligion to the wall.[9]

The strenuous life was a central concern of the ethical essays which James wrote during the same time period as *The Principles of Psychology*. His belief in a way of life which is characterized by risk, courage, and selflessness for the purpose of the melioration and evolution of the human community is clearly evident. James developed other facets of the strenuous life in essays such as "Is Life Worth Living?" "The Dilemma of Determinism," and "The Sentiment of Rationality," which are contained in *The Will to Believe*. In James's later books, *The Varieties of Religious Experience* (1902), *Pragmatism* (1907), and *A Pluralistic Universe* (1909), and in the essay "The Energies of Men" (1907), he developed the notion of the strenuous life in terms of religion and philosophy. Indeed, it may be argued that a major concern of James's entire enterprise dealt with the multifarious implications of his normative vision and philosophy of the person. According to James, religion is an experience of the transcendent which empowers people to embody the strenuous life, and saints are paradigms for self-sacrifice, community concern, courage, and living for a purpose larger than personal pleasure. James's cosmology consisted of the belief that the future is undetermined and full of risk and possibility; hence, it is pluralistic and requires that humans respond with the strenuous life. Philosophy, from James's point of view, is not mere speculation, but a vital human endeavor which focuses on ethical issues. The remainder of this discussion will examine James's psychology in order to show that his normative vision was important to psychology and that man's psychological capacities enable him to actualize the strenuous life.

In *The Principles of Psychology* James discussed the selective quality of the stream of consciousness, the social and spiritual self, will, and attention as capacities which make possible the strenuous life. Chapter 9 of *The Principles of Psychology* is entitled "The Stream of Thought," and it is probably one of the best known of all the chapters. James enumerated five characteristics of the stream of consciousness (in the 1892 edition of the *Principles,* he uses the word "consciousness" instead of "thought" in the chapter title): personal, changing, sensible continuous, and *of* objects. The fifth, and, for the purposes of this paper, the most important characteristic of the stream of thought is that it is selective. Out of what James calls a "teeming multiplicity of objects and relations" consciousness must, by emphasis and accentuation, select those objects in which it is interested. Through one's attention objects are eliminated or selected according to one's interests. Interests may be of several different varieties; for instance, there can be practical interests, scientific interests, religious interests. On religious interests James writes:

> An act has no ethical quality whatever unless it be chosen out of several all equally possible. To sustain the arguments for the good course and keep them ever before us, to stifle out longing for more flowery ways, to keep the foot unflinchingly on the arduous path, these are characteristic ethical energies. But more than these; for these but deal with the means of compassing interests already felt by the man to be supreme. The ethical energy par excellence has to go farther and choose which interest out of several, equally coercive, shall become supreme. The issue here is of the utmost pregnancy, for it decides a man's entire career... his choice really lies between one of several equally possible future Characters. What he shall become is fixed by the conduct of this moment.... The problem with the man is less what act he shall

now choose to do, than what being he shall now resolve to become.[10]

"The Consciousness of Self," chapter 10 of *The Principles of Psychology,* begins with a broad definition of the self: "A man's Self is the sum total of all that he can call his." The constituents of this self are the following: the material self, the social self, the spiritual self, and the pure Ego. The material self includes a person's body, clothes, family, home, and the products of one's labor. The social self develops from man's "innate propensity to get ourselves noticed, and noticed favorably, by our kind." The spiritual self is those "psychic faculties or dispositions, taken concretely... which are the most enduring and intimate part of the self...." James rejected the theories of the transcendental ego or the soul, but he did admit there is a feeling of "something more" which is accessible to introspection. However, he did not feel that the transcendental ego or soul was necessary as an explanation for the unity of the stream of consciousness.

There is, according to James, a hierarchical scale on which we order the various dimensions of the self. The spiritual self is at the top of the scale; the social self and then the bodily self follow. For James, the spiritual and social self could merge when considered from the perspective of a possible potential self. For instance, he wrote, "I am always strengthened in my course and steeled against the loss of my actual social self by the thought of other and better *possible* social judges than those whose verdict goes against me now."[11] The material, social, and spiritual selves are sustained and guided by interests. On the material level, interests are those things which appeal to primitive and instinctive impulses in one's nature. Selfishness can be transcended when one is more concerned with the interests of other selves. Such transcendence of the biological is essential for the cultivation of the social self.

Chapter 11 of *The Principles of Psychology* focuses on attention. Attention, like the self and stream of consciousness, is seminal to the present discussion. Attention was important to James's psychology for it directly challenged the empirical school of psychology (Locke, Hume, Mills, and Spencer) which propounded the theory that the mind is merely the passive reflection of external stimuli. James firmly rejected that position when he wrote:

> Millions of items of the outward order are present to my senses which never properly enter into my experience. Why? Because they have no *interest* for me. *My experience is what I agree to attend to.* Only those items which I *notice* shape my mind— without selective interest, experience is an utter chaos. Interest alone gives accent and emphasis, light and shade, background and foreground—intelligible perspective, in a word.[12]

Another key element in the capacity for attention is the concept of effort. Effort is crucial in voluntary or active attention. James recognized, of course, that one's attention is often the result of a simple reaction to outside stimuli. For his purposes, however, the crucial issue and the one that distinguishes his psychology from his contemporaries' and points to the strenuous life was that of voluntary attention; in fact, James asserted that "the faculty of voluntarily bringing back a wandering attention, over and over again, is the very root of judgment, character, and will."[13] Moreover, "The practical and theoretical life of whole species, as well as of individual beings, results from the selection which the habitual direction of their attention involves . . . each of us literally *chooses,* by his ways of attending to things, what sort of universe he shall appear to himself to inhabit."[14] James realized that he was unable to verify his position philosophically or scientifically, but he vigorously argued for the centrality of the experience of effort. He said in one impassioned passage:

> The whole feeling of reality, the whole sting and excitement of our voluntary life, depends on our sense that in it things are *really being decided* from one moment to another, and that it is not the dull

rattling off of a chain that was forged innumerable ages ago. This appearance, which makes life and history tingle with such a tragic zest, *may* not be an illusion.[15]

Whatever the psychological or philosophical explanation may be, James emphasized that the experience of effort and attention is faithful to the discernment of experience as it appears to one who examines it carefully. Inextricably related to James's concern for effort and attention is his concept of will.

Chapter 26 of *The Principles of Psychology* focuses on the nature and purpose of will. Fundamental to James's understanding of the will was the assumption that ideas lead directly to their discharge in movements, a notion James called "ideo-motor action." According to James there is nothing between the conception and the execution of the idea. Most voluntary action is of the simple variety of merely having the idea and then fulfilling it in action. However, there is a more complex type of voluntary action which involves the holding of two conflicting ideas which prevents their immediate discharge. When there is such an inhibition of action by conflicting ideas, deliberation or decision making is necessary.

While recognizing that most decisions are relatively simple, James was especially interested in those in which one experiences the "feeling of effort" and conflict. His concern was with the specific sphere of effort in which there are no instinctive motives or which are not predetermined by habit. It is important to note that James distinguished between the healthy and unhealthy will. The unhealthy will is either explosive or obstructed: the explosive will has no inhibitions to the immediate gratification of an impulse; and the obstructed, as the name implies, is apathetic and lacks the ability to focus on a particular idea or goal. The healthy will, in contrast, consists of the capacity of envisioning what is right and the action necessary to fulfill it. Effort enters the picture when there is a need to expend energy in order to focus upon and enact that which is perceived to be right and which tends to receive the least intrinsic reward. For example, effort is necessary to reinforce a more ideal motive in the face of instinctive habitual motives or when explosive or obstructive tendencies must be overcome.

James stressed that because ideas stimulate action, the most important phase of decision making or the volitional process is mental. In order to sustain a decision, or in other words, will something, one must maintain the idea firmly in the mind: "The essential achievement of the will, in short, when it is most 'voluntary,' is to *attend* to a difficult object and hold it fast before the mind."[16] Moreover,

> The strong-willed man...is the man who hears the still small voice unflinchingly, and who, when the death-bringing consideration comes, looks at its face, consents to its presence, clings to it, affirms it, and holds it fast, in spite of the host of exciting mental images which rise in revolt against it and would expel it from the mind. Sustained in this way by a resolute effort of attention, the difficult object erelong begins to call up its own congeries and associates and ends by changing the disposition of the man's consciousness altogether. And with his consciousness, his action changes, for the new object, once stably in possession of the field of his thoughts, infallibly produces its own motor effects. The difficulty lies in the gaining possession of that field. Though the spontaneous drift of thought is all the other way, the attention must be kept strained on that one object until at last it *grows,* so as to maintain itself before the mind with ease. This strain of the attention is the fundamental act of will.[17]

In the context of the chapter on the will James discussed the issue of free will, although he was quick to point out that this complex problem cannot be resolved as a psychological issue. He did not, however, fail to indicate his reasons for his personal belief in the freedom of the will. The first and most important evidence is the experi-

ence of effort itself. We sense that real effort is expended in the process of attending to an idea and thus willing something. Second, he believed in free will for ethical reasons. In other words, "It is a *moral* postulate about the Universe, the postulate that *what ought to be can be, and that bad acts cannot be fated, but that good ones must be possible in their place....*"[18]

This paper has focused on the descriptive or phenomenological sections of *The Principles of Psychology,* but it should be remembered that James was attempting to write a textbook on scientific psychology, a psychology concerned with finite minds, their feelings, cognitions, and conations and an understanding of their physiological correlates. Much of human behavior can be understood as reflective action or response to various stimuli in the environment. Such a scientific psychology, however, did not restrict James's view of human nature because he could at once affirm biological rootedness and the capacity for behavior which transcends biological and environmental determination. Through human consciousness and sense of self, people are capable of dealing with the world in novel and creative ways. These capacities do not free humans from a struggle with nature, the environment, and other people; indeed, James characterized the whole of life as a struggle and as "living on the perilous edge." Human psychological makeup is such that people can effectively live for the betterment of the community through the capacities for attention, will, selective consciousness, social self, and spiritual self.

James rarely mentioned the strenuous life explicitly in *The Principles of Psychology*. Nevertheless, it is evident from this discussion that ethical considerations permeate James's textbook on psychology. It has also been noted that James inserted ethical issues into the discussion of many psychological topics. Thus, not only is James's psychology continuous with the explicit vision of the strenuous life articulated in the ethical essays written concurrently with *The Principles of Psychology,* but the psychological capacities of human beings as outlined by James make the strenuous life possible and necessary for the evolution of the human community.

NOTES

1 See Ignas K. Skrupskelis, *William James: A Reference Guide* (Boston: G. K. Hall, 1977) for a comprehensive bibliography of the books and articles about James.

2 A typical misunderstanding is to see James's career as broken into discrete phases during which he was a physiologist, a psychologist, a religious thinker, and a philosopher. A result of such an approach has been for psychologists to ignore the later work of James as merely philosophical speculation and for philosophers to relegate the psychology to a period before James's full maturity. In fact, James combined all these interests even when one may have been professionally dominant. The author's dissertation demonstrated that James's ethical concerns were central throughout his life. See Lewis R. Rambo, "The Strenuous Life: William James' Normative Vision of the Human" (Ph. D. diss., University of Chicago, 1975). See also Don S. Browning, "William James' Philosophy of the Person: The Concept of the Strenuous Life," *Zygon* 10 (1975): 162–174. Ethical striving was also important in James's own life. See Gay Wilson Allen, *William James* (New York: Viking, 1967), pp. 162–170. The role of ethics is also stressed in two excellent books on James published within the last decade. See John Wild, *The Radical Empiricism of William James* (Garden City, New York: Doubleday, 1969) and P. K. Dooley, *Pragmatism as Humanism: The Philosophy of William James* (Chicago: Nelson-Hall, 1974). Wild and Dooley discuss the strenuous life, but subsume the topic to other issues. It is my opinion that the role of the strenuous life was James's dominant and central concern, not merely one of many topics which fascinated him.

3 William James, "Great Men, Great Thoughts and the Environment," *Atlantic Monthly* 46 (October 1880): 441–459.

4 William James, *The Will to Believe* (New York: Longmans, Green, 1897), p. 227. James's argument for the importance of the individual's moral striving is in stark contrast to many of the thinkers of his time. R. Jackson Wilson's *In Quest of Community: Social Philosophy in the United States,* 1860–1920 (New York: Oxford University Press, 1968) makes a convincing case for the view that most major thinkers after 1860 believed that individuals are merely the by-products of the evolutionary process, in other words, that people are only passive residue of evolution. From the perspective of Wilson, one may say that James was mediating between a view of mankind as transcendental individuals (as seen by Ralph Waldo Emerson, for example) and the new view of Herbert Spencer, among others, who saw humans as passive products of the evolutionary scheme. James did not reject evolutionary theory as such, but denied the extrapolations from that theory to a view of people which would relegate ethical capacities to being epiphenomena.

5 James, *Will to Believe,* p. 232.

6 "The Importance of Individuals" was originally published in *Open Court* 4 (1890): 2437–2440. It should be noted that James's first published essay adumbrates many of the themes which were developed later. See "Remarks on Spencer's Definition of Mind as Correspondence," *Journal of Speculative Philosophy* 12 (1878): 1–18. Also see "Quelques considerations sur la methode subjective," *Critique Philosophique* 2 (24 January 1878): 407–413. Both early articles demonstrate James's interest in ethics and its evolutionary context.

7 James, *Will to Believe,* p. 245.

8 Ibid., p. 211.

9 Ibid., p. 213.

10 William James, *The Principles of Psychology,* 2 vols. (New York: Holt, 1890), 1: 287–288.

11 Ibid., p. 315.

12 Ibid., p. 402.

13 Ibid., p. 424.

14 Ibid.

15 Ibid., p. 453.

16 Ibid., p. 561.

17 Ibid., pp. 563–564.

18 Ibid., p. 573.

The Paradox of G. Stanley Hall:
Foe of Coeducation and Educator of Women

Lesley A. Diehl

Recent feminist scholarship in the area of sex differences (e.g., Rosenberg, 1982; Shields, 1975) has established that the origin of the question of feminine character within psychology predated psychoanalytic theory and can be found in the late 19th- and early 20th-century functionalist movement. Such scholarship, acknowledging the impact of an intellectual climate dominated by Darwinism on the formation of psychological theory, also asserts the significance of Victorian social attitudes in shaping the profession's attitudes toward women. In addition, these analyses along with those provided earlier by Schwendinger and Schwendinger (1971), Smith-Rosenberg and Rosenberg (1973), and Trecker (1974) imply a causal link between the genesis of scientific thought within such a social milieu and contemporary social sciences' biases about women's nature, calling attention to "the tenacity of the 'scientific' arguments, not their eventual defeat" (Trecker, 1974, p. 365).

Among the functionalists discussed by both Rosenberg and Shields, G. Stanley Hall emerges as significant in the study of woman's psychological makeup. In light of Hall's prolific writings in psychology and education and in popular magazines about woman's nature, it is surprising that he has not received more consideration among feminist scholars interested in the origin and development of the topic of sex differences.

Most accounts of Hall's contributions to functionalist psychology treat him as one of the many functionalists interested in shaping the emergence of the new American psychology (e.g.,

Boring, 1929/1950; Watson, 1978). Not surprisingly, these accounts portray Hall as well as his contemporaries as being concerned with the major themes of functionalism, that is, mental functions and adaptive processes. Even the most complete biographical study of Hall, provided by Ross in 1972, omits mention of his interest in sex differences and woman's nature, topics of significance to his theory of development, and provides no information on his role as leader of the early 20th-century movement against coeducation. Though these accounts accurately portray Hall's relationship to the emergence and development of American psychology, they provide little insight into Hall's significance in shaping psychology's perspectives on women. Furthermore, mainstreaming Hall into functionalist psychology ignores the significance that Hall himself accorded to the issue of women's nature, evidenced in the considerable time he devoted to the topic in his writings.

The present article discusses the significance of Hall to the development of psychology's perspective on sex differences and woman's nature by exploring the paradox of Hall as both opponent of coeducation and educator of women graduate students. The evolution of this paradox and its resolution by Hall can be understood by examining the three areas of Hall's professional eminence—as psychologist, educational theorist, and president of Clark University.

RECAPITULATION AND THE NATURE OF WOMAN

Hall's recapitulation theory was the direct outcome of the impact of Darwinian evolutionary principles on Hall's attempts to understand mental development. That Darwin provided the basis for all of

Hall's research and theorizing in psychology is apparent in Hall's (1923) confession, "As soon as I first heard it in my youth I think I must have been almost hypnotized by the word "evolution," which was music to my ear and seemed to fit my mouth better than any other" (p. 357).

So important was evolution to Hall that he argued that it, rather than physics, should form the basis for science and be understood as the genesis of democracy and government (Hall, 1923). He saw in evolution a great organizing principle uniting the phylogenetic emergence of the species with the ontogenetic development of a single individual. Evolutionary recapitulation in Hall's theory assumed that "every child, from the moment of conception to maturity, recapitulates, very rapidly at first, and then more slowly, every stage of development through which the human race from its lowest animal beginnings has passed" (Hall, 1923, p. 380).

Prenatally, recapitulation called for rapid fetal change from a single-celled organism to a newborn parallel in maturity to mammals lower than humans on the phylogenetic scale. In childhood, Hall saw evidence of the expression of savage impulses, cruelty, and immorality representative of earlier, less civilized stages of human development, or of contemporary temperament produced in primitive societies (Hall, 1904b). Not only was recapitulation viewed as a necessary outcome of the evolution of humans, but the expression of primitive impulses was deemed cathartic by Hall. Thus, Hall's view of education for the child was pedocentric, that is, encouraged the schools and teachers to construct an atmosphere that encouraged the expression of these impulses in order that they would not be carried into adulthood (Hall, 1904b).

Hall did not create a unique theory of psychological nature, however. Before him, Galton (1907) had used evolutionary doctrine to argue for psychological sex differences. Few 19th-century functionalists argued with the use of Darwinism to account for the contention that men and women possessed inherently different natures and were, therefore, suited for vastly different roles—man as

competitive and creative genius, and woman as mother of the species. As an extension of Geddes and Thomson's (1890) view of the sexes, many functionalists asserted that men were more active (katabolic) and variable than women, who were more passive (anabolic) and generic. Not only were men believed to differ more among themselves than were women, they were viewed as the agents introducing variability into offspring. Brain weight and brain size differences between men and women were employed as concrete expressions of the relationship between evolutionary structural and mental functional change (Ellis, 1894; Gould, 1981; Hall 1904a; Shields, 1975). Therefore, Hall drew little criticism from his colleagues for the manner in which he incorporated evolution into his theory of psychological development. Although 19th-century functionalists believed that human mental abilities were the product of evolution, few had articulated as clearly as did Hall evolution's impact on ontogenetic development and, therefore, its significance in creating and sustaining differentiation between the sexes.

Although Hall had written extensively about sex differences in the late 1800s, his concentration on recapitulation in infants and children and his interest in developing data to support his theory had directed most of his energy into child study and the use of his questionnaire method. Although his child-centered education found some favor with educators, psychologists became critical of his methodology and of his inability to tie collected data to his theory. The publication of *Adolescence: Its Psychology and Its Relations to Physiology, Anthropology, Sociology, Sex, Crime, Religion and Education* in 1904 focused Hall's interest on the critical period of puberty and specifically on the significance of sex differentiation for psychological development. This two-volume work was widely read and reviewed, although not favorably by some leading psychologists (e.g., Thorndike, 1904). Other functionalists were directing their research toward principles of learning and the development of testing materials while Hall continued to elaborate on a general developmental theory for which he had little supporting data (Siegel & White, 1982). However, because Hall had in the past attended to education for the young, *Adolescence* received some acceptance among educators and, because of its chapter topics (e.g., "Diseases of Body and Mind," "Juvenile Faults, Immorality, and Crimes," "Social Instincts and Institutions"), among those who were working with adolescents in institutions and clinics.

In his chapter entitled "Adolescent Girls and Their Education," Hall applied recapitulation theory to adolescent development, presenting a view of female development derived from evolutionary doctrine. The adolescent girl, according to Hall, could be looked upon as the springboard for the future evolution of the species, for she was "at the top of the human curve from which the higher super-man of the future is to evolve, while man is phylogenetically by comparison a trifle senile, if not decadent" (Hall, 1904a, p. 561). Thus, Hall asserted the importance of adolescence, age 14 or 15 through age 25 (Hall, 1905), as a critical period in the progression of civilization. As such, the biological differentiation of the sexes at puberty seemed to necessitate educational and role separation beginning in adolescence. Hall was well aware that the 19th-century battle against coeducation had been lost. Therefore, he focused on the need for separation of the sexes in adolescence only, a period during which he felt women were highly susceptible to reproductive organ damage. Puberty prepared a woman for her natural function of motherhood, to which, Hall felt, she should single-mindedly devote herself. That some women did not understand this need was not surprising to Hall, for the "hidden" but "all-pervasive" nature of the female reproductive organs could conceal their functioning from the individual woman as well as from science (Hall, 1904a, p. 562).

Woman's place within Hall's theory, as in the theories of many other functionalists, was that of mother of the species. She alone could determine by her reproductive abilities whether the race would grow, flourish, and progress or whether it would cease to exist. Her interest in motherhood assured the production of men of genius and of more daughters to bear more children. In contemporary terms, she was a baby factory; in Hall's eyes she was "by nature more typical and a better representative of the race and less prone to specialization" (Hall, 1904a, p. 562). Woman was closer in psychological nature to the child than was man, and she was at all stages of development a perennial adolescent, possessing larger lower brain centers presumably to more adequately govern the maternal functions of milk production, fertility, natality, and general nurturing (Hall, 1904a). Did Hall see her as inferior to man? Hall would quickly have answered "no" to such a question, asserting that if the two sexes could be compared, woman was superior, at least in a moral sense: "The glorified madonna ideal shows us how much more whole and holy it is to be a woman than to be an artist, orator, professor, or expert" (Hall, 1904a, p. 646).

Despite Hall's attempts to couch his views of women in positive and often religious terms, some feminists took issue with his theory (e.g., Thomas, 1901), not because, as Hall believed, all feminists viewed the sexes as identical, but because Hall's insistence that woman's biological nature fitted her only for motherhood denied her access to the same social, economic, and political considerations given to men. Hall often misrepresented feminist positions on the nature of women and often used his interpretation of their views to argue his own position. For example, Hall (1908) charged feminists with viewing the menstrual function as "immodest" and suggested that they denied young girls the right to complain of monthly pain (p. 10240). Because Hall was extremely well read, his interpretation of feminist ideology was probably a misrepresentation of their views. Hall (1904a) revealed some awareness that feminists differed among themselves by referring to "the cranky and extreme left wing of this movement, which strives to theoretically ignore and practically escape the monthly function" (p. 609). Unlike most of his conservative and like-minded colleagues, Hall was more than willing to label feminism his enemy and to label those psychologists who did not share his perspective on women as feminists. When Helen Bradford Thompson Woolley chose to interpret her research findings on the mental traits of the sexes in terms of early environmental influences, Hall (1904a) labeled her thinking "feminist" and dismissed her interpretation as absurd in the light of evolutionary doctrine (p. 565).

Not only did some feminists find Hall's theory an impediment to social change for women, but feminist concerns over women's rights had, by the end of the 19th century, found their way into psychological theorizing. Some functionalists, particularly those at Chicago and Columbia, as the result of their exposure to and sympathy with reform movements such as urban and social reform and the women's rights movement, began to focus their understanding of the development of adult sex differences on the role played by social institutions in creating and sustaining sex differentiation (Rosenberg, 1982). Thus, psychologists such as Dewey, Angell, and later Thorndike were willing to entertain interpretations of sex differences in terms of social construction. In turn, they produced women graduate students such as Helen Bradford Thompson Woolley and Hollingworth, whose research on sex differences pointed to the significance of social and educational variables in shaping adult sex differences.

The desire on the part of younger functionalists at Chicago and Columbia to experiment with possible social reconstructions of woman's role was particularly offensive to Hall, not because his recapitulation theory denied modifiability of the organism by environmental factors, but because Hall questioned the desirability of alterations that might interfere with woman's primary role as mother of the race. The view of woman as mother was for Hall almost a religious as well as a scientific principle, and one he chose to translate into political, social, and educational terms:

> As the foliage of delicate plants first shows the early warmth of spring, and the earliest frost of autumn,

so the impressible, susceptible organization of woman appreciates and exhibits far sooner than that of man the manifestation of national progress or decay. (Hall, 1904a, p. 571)

The most serious challenge to the role of woman as mother was perceived by Hall to be found in the turn-of-the-century movement toward coeducation for women. Whereas social reformers, feminists, and some of Hall's functionalist colleagues applauded the higher education of women, Hall felt education was one social modification that had far-reaching detrimental implications for the nature of men and women, and especially for family life. Much of Hall's writing and many of his speeches before professional and lay audiences alike in the early 1900s discussed the application of recapitulation theory in the home and the school. The focus of many of these discussions was the significance of proper education for motherhood as well as education for adolescent boys and girls.

COEDUCATION AND WOMEN

By 1900, 98 percent of public high schools were coeducational and the question of mixed-sex classrooms was viewed by many as a dead issue in all areas of the country but the South (Woody, 1929/1974). However, arguments about the education of boys and girls, particularly during adolescence, continued well into the 20th century, for although coeducation was a practical reality in most grade schools and high schools, the presence of women in colleges and universities had had a relatively short history by the turn of the century. Some observers viewed their presence as due less to a resolution of the coeducational controversy in terms of educational wisdom or sexual equality and more to the financial crises that plagued many institutions during the 1870s, resulting in the opening of college doors to women students (MacMechan, 1903; Woody, 1929/1974).

By virtue of undergraduate degrees obtained from coeducational institutions, women's colleges, or coordinate colleges, women presented credentials for graduate study, and numerous institutions during the 1890s allowed women into postgraduate work. The fate of these women was far from equal to that of their male counterparts. For example, although Mary Calkins completed all necessary requirements for her doctorate at Harvard, the school refused to confer the degree upon her (Stevens & Gardner, 1982). Women who were granted graduate degrees, for example, at Chicago, Columbia, Cornell, and Clark, found traditional advanced degree positions in teaching, administration, and research closed to them (Bryan & Boring, 1944; Woody, 1929/1974). Instead, women were encouraged to take positions in two areas deemed appropriate for the career-minded professional woman: social welfare work and teaching in women's colleges. Because these positions denied women professionals access to the usual means of recognition in professional fields, research publication, and recognition by professional organizations or the university, these well-trained and capable young women fell into professional oblivion. Recent efforts (e.g., Stevens & Gardner, 1982) to document their impact on psychology suggest that, because they occupied peripheral positions in academe, their contributions to theory and research often went unrecognized.

The presence of women in colleges and universities, rather than settling the issue of higher education for women as was hoped by advocates of women's education (e.g., Thomas, 1901, 1908), seemed to rekindle the fires of controversy over the issue of coeducation. For example, after 10 years as a coeducational institution, Chicago in 1902 proposed segregation in order to improve its reputation and establish itself as a research center (Rosenberg, 1982; Woody, 1929/1974). Concerned about the "feminizing" effect of women on men students, institutions such as Chicago were more comfortable with presenting the issue of segregation as a matter of educational philosophy rather than as a matter of political expediency or public image.

Regardless of whether the question of the presence of women in colleges was a matter of educational philosophy or merely financial necessity, the rationale against coeducation in the early 20th century often took the form of arguments "reheated" from their original 19th-century serving. Not surprisingly, in light of Hall's recapitulation theory of development, Hall became the spokesperson for the anticoeducational movement as revived in the early 1900s. Derived from and united by recapitulation theory, Hall's arguments had the appearance of being more scientific than those of his predecessors. In actuality, Hall simply rehashed what had gone before, adding the appeal of his position as an educational and psychological authority and extending his influence by selecting parents' groups as his audience and writing in popular magazines as well as educational journals. Although some people viewed Hall as being 20 years behind the times (e.g., "Notes and News," 1902), both the *Educational Review* and the *Proceedings of the National Education Association,* from 1903 through 1906, published numerous letters, essays, and reports discussing the issue of coeducation. In 1903 and again in 1904, Hall addressed the issue of coeducation at the annual meetings of the National Education Association, receiving both favorable and unfavorable responses to his remarks.

If some of the educational establishment chose to see Hall's views as antiquated, his appeal to parents afforded him a more sympathetic audience, for it was during the early 1900s Hall aired his stance on coeducation in various popular magazines, such as *Harper's* and the *Ladies Home Journal.* Some of the articles provided advice to parents on how to handle problems with adolescents (e.g., Hall, 1900, 1907a). Others extolled the virtues of motherhood (e.g., Hall, 1909d). All of them connected coeducation with problems of decay in relationships, in the family and nationally. In all of his writings as well as his speeches on education, Hall affected an expression (probably successfully) of sympathetic understanding of what it is to feel the responsibilities and joys of motherhood. His professed sympathy with womanhood was the basis of his persuasive arguments that coeducation undermined woman's role and thereby destroyed the future of the race. Before the National Congress of Mothers in 1905, Hall concluded his remarks in the following manner:

> I do not know, and I do not suppose any one knows, whether the Holy Mother knew Chaldee or Greek, or whether she even knew how to read, but the whole world has united in reverence of her because she illustrates the complete glory of motherhood. (p. 27)

The premises of Hall's argument against coeducation were derived from three concerns of recapitulation: (a) that adolescence was a critical period in the development of the reproductive organs in women, (b) that the adolescent male needed freedom to engage in cathartic expression of his savage impulses, and (c) that natural sexual differentiation during adolescence was the basis for later attraction between the sexes.

Concern over the development of women's reproductive organs had received the most attention in the 19th-century coeducational movement. Edward Clarke (1873) had argued that the development of women's reproductive organs during adolescence left little power for the tasks of schooling and that education for women could result in arrested development of the reproductive system. Like Clarke, Hall appealed to medical authorities to testify to the damage done to women's reproductive organs by too much mental activity, especially in competition with men. The net result of overexposure in the classroom would be loss of mammary function, followed by lack of interest in motherhood, decreased fertility, and the production, of few and sickly children, if any (Hall, 1904a).

Because many of the proponents of coeducation were not persuaded by the medical testimony, which consisted mostly of opinion and not fact, they discounted it. Hall, too, felt the need to support his arguments about the physical damage caused by coeducation with empirical data. Therefore, he employed his questionnaire approach to assess the health of college women. The results,

admitted Hall, were disappointing. Undaunted by the evidence provided using his own instrument, Hall rejected the questionnaire method as a legitimate way of assessing the effects of coeducation, saying that women would often lie about health matters in order to not "bias their education" and, he concluded, the effects of coeducation on health were not really measurable although they were, in his opinion, "probably great and common" (Hall, 1904a, p. 586).

According to Hall, the truest measures of the effects of education on the development of the reproductive organs were the reduced number of marriages among female college graduates and the smaller number of children produced. In order to keep up the species, Hall (1904a) contended, each woman would need to produce at least six children, and the college woman produced far fewer than this. Therefore, the real victim of coeducation was the bachelor woman who had "overdrawn her account with heredity" (Hall, 1904a, p. 633). Although Hall described her as fine in body and mind, he felt that she, having fallen "a conscious prey to the gospel of the feminists" (Hall, 1904a, p. 611), would eventually become bitter when she discovered that she could not keep up with the intellectual capabilities of her male counterparts. Hall (1904a) warned that a bachelor woman was really neither male nor female, neither masculine nor feminine, but "agamic," a third sex produced by the removal of sex from the female (p. 622). Thus, Hall saw her as a sterile accident of evolution, doomed not to reproduce more of her kind.

Hall's position on the abnormality of the unmarried female hints at concerns of female sexuality being expressed by sexologists such as Ellis and Westphal in the late 19th century (Faderman, 1981). Whether or not Hall entertained any notion of female sexuality outside the realm of heterosexual expression, he chose not to mention such a possibility. However, Hall clearly perceived the avoidance of heterosexuality on the part of women as a threat to the continuation of the species and, therefore, as aberrant. In addition, Hall laid the cause for such avoidance at the feet of education.

According to Hall, if women were to be educated at all, they should be educated to motherhood. He suggested (1904a) that the mothers of most great men were of "strong mind" though not highly educated (p. 573). In arguing against the co-education of girls, Hall (1908) insisted that he was not taking a step backward in the "great movement of emancipation and the higher education of women" (p. 10243), but rather that he had begun to examine the kind of education fully suited to women. Ironically, though Hall often found himself at odds with social feminists on the issue of the professionalization of the domestic sphere in the form of home economics and social welfare work, he and some feminists shared the view that women in these areas of professional concern could positively influence family and societal matters (M. P. Ryan, 1979). Thus, Hall considered appropriate training for women to include both education that taught about motherhood and education leading to a professionalization of nurturing qualities, such as social work, home economics, and elementary school teaching, as long as such professions did not replace motherhood.

Recapitulation would also be adversely affected in the male if he were exposed to an educational environment that discouraged the development of his masculine nature. In an attempt to recapture the path of evolutionary development for the male, Hall argued that nature also decreed the separation of adolescent boys from feminine influence. Hall supported the Boy Scouts and the reading of masculinizing books such as the Tarzan series as ways of allowing expression of adolescent male savage impulses. To encourage boys to become gentlemanly through exposure to girls was anathema to Hall, for it denied recapitulatory catharsis and would result in a wild or feminized adult male. Hall held female teachers responsible for the wildness in adult men, even suggesting that no man would beat his wife if he had "been flogged early," a task easily undertaken by a male teacher (Hall, 1908, p.

10239). In general Hall (1903) felt that women teachers did not belong in the high school, for it was during adolescence that boys needed the firm hand of a man and a model to emulate.

Some educators were in close agreement with Hall on this issue (e.g., Barnes, 1912), as his ideas represented an extension of growing social concern over perceived declining masculinity in the American male (Filene, 1975). The issue of women teachers in the high school had wide ramifications for the teaching profession. In 1904, the Male Teachers' Association of New York City filed with the *Educational Review* a report arguing for male teachers in the high schools. The report suggested that boys could not grow into manhood without the firm and forceful presence of a male and without a masculine ideal ("Report of the Male Teachers' Association," 1902). Female teachers were under attack in many school systems, and school officials and parents alike applauded when they married or had children and left the schools (Sohen, 1972).

Hall's case against coeducation included the assertion that recapitulation called for separation of the sexes in adolescence (adolescence lasted for 10 to 15 years) also because segregation of the sexes was responsible for sexual attraction. Overexposure of the sexes in adolescence often resulted in "contempt or disillusionment in both men and women" (Hall, 1908, p. 10243) and was responsible for slovenly appearance in women and a disgust for women and sex in men (Hall, 1904a, 1911). Women clearly were responsible for the lack of attraction between the sexes because women's competitiveness with men and failure to hold motherhood as the basis for sexual relations, both the outcome of education, resulted in the early 20th-century American males finding their female counterparts unattractive.

WOMEN AT CLARK

The question of the position of women at Clark arose often during Hall's years there, and his handling of the issue through his position as president appears to be a clear expression of his antico-educational policy as well as his theoretical bias about the nature of women. An examination of Hall's policies and his treatment of women graduate students at Clark shows that apparent departures from a firmly established policy against coeducation during adolescence, which included college and graduate years, were not failures of his theory nor did they represent a change of mind on Hall's part, but rather they may be interpreted as political and economic moves enacted in such a way as to leave his original biases about the nature and education of women wholly intact.

As at other universities and colleges, Clark's entertainment of the question of allowing women to enroll in graduate programs was representative of a general movement following the Civil War toward higher education for women. As already discussed, the financial crises of the 1870s encouraged increasing enrollments, and many institutions found that economic necessity dictated the development of coeducational policy. In addition, proponents of higher education for women and of coeducation found voice through the establishment of women's colleges and through the opening of coeducational institutions such as Chicago and Michigan. Thus, it was merely a matter of time before women would present respectable baccalaureate degrees for entrance into graduate programs.

In the 1890s institutions such as Yale, Brown, Harvard, Chicago, and Johns Hopkins allowed graduate admission to women (Woody, 1929/1974). In the case of Harvard, however, female students became candidates for Radcliffe degrees, an indication that coeducation was not yet firmly established. From the academic year 1892–1893 to the year 1919–1920, the number of women students enrolled in graduate programs in public and private institutions increased from 484 to 5,775 (Woody, 1929/1974). As pointed out by Woody, however, the prevailing opinion of women in graduate programs was that they were intellectually inferior to their male counterparts in creative work areas.

Although the large increase in three decades is impressive, it appears that the "prevailing opin-

ion" about women dictated their career opportunities and development more than did the women's credentials. In psychology, for example, Stevens and Gardner (1982) found that early 20th-century women psychologists found work primarily in small colleges and universities, and especially in women's colleges. Stevens and Gardner concluded that these career moves isolated women from the "old boy" networks so useful in furthering careers and in attaining a student following. Furthermore, commensurate with their traditional socialization, women psychologists gravitated toward social issues areas and applied psychology areas sometimes trivialized by historians of psychology (Rosenberg, 1982; Stevens & Gardner, 1982).

Thus, although the decade beginning the 20th century can be viewed as representing a freeing up of anti-coeducational policies in both undergraduate and graduate programs, two matters continued to plague the woman PhD. First, there remained serious educational policy questions about the appropriate education for women. Second, the professional woman found few opportunities in which she could exercise her newly obtained graduate degree. Thus, it is not Clark's policy on women graduate students that is worthy of attention here, but rather the process, under the direction of Hall, by which Clark University changed its stance on women that provides insight into how Hall, an avowed enemy of coeducation, headed a university that graduated a substantial number of women PhDs.

The question of the presence of undergraduate women in the college (as differentiated from the university) did not arise in Clark's early years because, as Hall (undated) suggested, it was the founder's (Jonas Clark's) intention to exclude women as students. Hall acknowledged that Clark fully intended to establish a university department for women, but only when money could be made available to establish it in a building of its own. Furthermore, Jonas Clark wanted this money to come from private endowments and not from the Clark estate. On September 26, 1889, the Board of Trustees, with Hall as secretary, voted that, in accordance with Clark's original plans for a separate university department for women, "the subject of the admission of women be postponed until the University shall receive such endowment as will enable the corporation to make suitable provision for that purpose" (Hall, undated, p. 2).

Hall served as chief administrative officer of the university from its founding in 1888 until 1920 and during those years often served as interpreter of Jonas Clark's intentions to the Board of Trustees. There is little question that Hall attempted to govern the institution in an autocratic manner. This manner coupled with the financial problems at Clark and the "raid" on Clark faculty by the University of Chicago resulted in the resignation of many faculty and students early in Clark's history (Rosenberg, 1982; Ross, 1972). It is clear, too, that Hall successfully bent the will of the Board of Trustees in accordance with his own desires and perspectives on higher education. An examination of documents and letters to and from the president's office during Hall's tenure reveal him to have been a clever politician, intensely aware of the temper of the times and the position of Clark, a fledgling institution plagued by major financial difficulties (*G. Stanley Hall Papers,* 1888–1920).

However, exceptional women (as determined by Hall) were admitted to special courses in the university, such policy having been enacted by the board in 1896. In the years following, not only did women enter special courses, but graduate degrees were also conferred upon women. In 1908, $500 was granted for a "retiring room" for women (Hall, undated).

In 1909 Hall felt it necessary to deal more specifically with university policy on women. The issue arose primarily because the college and the university had been called by the Boston Chamber of Commerce to answer questions as to what Clark was accomplishing for the "public weal" that would exempt the university from taxation (Hall, undated). In addition, according to Hall (undated), Carnegie and Rockefeller money could be made available to Clark depending on Clark's record as a pioneer in educational policy.

Ever in touch with public sentiment and recognizing the university's need for tax exemption as well as for financial backing from the private sector, Hall (undated) drafted a memorandum to the board outlining the past status of women at Clark and proposing future educational policy on women. The policy, proposed by Hall and adopted by the board, recommended that women, as in the past, not be admitted to take the bachelor's nor any other undergraduate degree at Clark, but that those women already in individual classes in the college be allowed to remain so as to "call less attention" (p. 6). Furthermore, an Educational Department was to be established. This department was to be formed from the Child Bureau and the Saturday classes that had been established to serve teachers. The Educational Department would be allowed to grant master's degrees to women, but women were to be excluded from other master's programs. The founding of such a department would, according to the memorandum, "exclude them too from the Main Building and the Chemical Building and segregate them after this year to one floor in the new building and to the Educational Department" (p. 7). This move by Hall was a recognition of the role the university might play in establishing good relations with public schools in teacher training. His intention was that this department would be interpreted as providing service to education and to the public, thereby assuring Clark of tax exemption. In addition, Hall (undated) asserted, "On general principles too, it seems undesirable, especially in view of the present state of public sentiment on the woman question, to take steps that are liable to result in calling public attention to any discrimination against women" (p. 7).

That Hall was making some concessions to public opinion was clear, for in a letter in 1909 to a friend and board member, Col. George Bullock, he wrote

I am strongly opposed to giving women the slightest foothold in the College....On the other hand, as to the Doctor's degree, of which we have given an average of one in ten years, I am inclined to think that, if we still continue to leave that open, it would save us a good deal of pounding by feminists; and by depriving it we would needlessly shut off possible bequests from women sho [*sic*] have bourne a pretty large part in the endowment of Universities. (Hall, 1909a)

Hall was willing to alter his educational policy on women to meet the exigencies of public opinion and financial need.

Not only would the establishment of the Educational Department ensure tax exemption, but Hall (undated) felt that Clark's record on education would warrent endowments "from several wealthy women who are deeply interested in this work" (p. 9). Finally, the door was left open to admitting women to the PhD program, but not without personal reservation on Hall's part:

> My own hope is that we may find some way to dispense with the presence of all women in the University proper (outside the Educational Department) except a few very exceptional ones of rare promise and efficiency for science. (Hall, 1909b)

From 1896, when exceptional women were admitted to graduate study, until Hall stepped down as president in 1920, approximately 150 women students enrolled in courses of study at Clark. The first graduate degrees to women were granted in 1907 to Louise Ellison, Edith Dixon, and Caroline Osborne; Osborne was the first woman to be granted a PhD from Clark in 1908 (File on Hall's Students, 1888–1920). During Hall's years as president, almost 50% of the women scholars in graduate study at Clark received graduate degrees. In keeping with Hall's policy, many of the master's degrees were in education, but many were in such fields as psychology, biology, physics, history, foreign relations, and chemistry (File on Hall's Students, 1888–1920). Although Clark drew to it such eminent scholars as Mary Calkins and Phyllis Blanchard, most of the women from Clark were no more successful in obtaining positions in universities or in research institutions than were their sisters who obtained advanced degrees from other institutions. Like other women with graduate degrees, the Clark women obtained positions in teaching and in social welfare work, positions Hall had advocated as the natural lot for scholarly women.

Ironically, however, Hall's attempts to isolate women within the Educational Department were obviously unsuccessful, not because he was overruled by the board or by the faculty at Clark, for Hall himself was responsible for admissions to Clark. Requests for admission to graduate study were submitted to the president's office. There is little evidence from the records of that office that Hall treated the inquiries about graduate study from women any differently than those from men (Presidential Papers). None of the letters to women who had requested entrance to the university used board policy as a way of excluding them from graduate study.

Individuals within the profession who were critical of Hall's psychology were willing to admit that Hall created an atmosphere of learning at Clark that allowed for open and flexible intellectual development for its students. The financial and organizational crisis in the early years of Clark forced Hall back into the classroom, and he set up Monday evening seminars, which, according to both W. C. Ryan (1939) and Tanner (1908), were significant in creating an atmosphere of learning that encouraged the best from each student. Although these seminars were not required and the number and composition of students varied from week to week, students approached them with great enthusiasm. Hall allowed exchange of ideas from the participating students; his major function was to summarize what had been said during the evening.

Hall appeared to place few restrictions on topics for investigation, and it appears that this freedom extended even into research concerning women. For example, the *Topical Syllabi* developed by women students through the Child Study Institute included questionnaires entitled "The Developmental Value of Women's Special

Work" (Boggs, 1909a) and "The Monthly Period" (Brown, 1899). Theses and dissertations also revealed interest in women: "Wages of Women Workers in Department and Retail Stores" (Waite, 1913), "An Introduction to the Modern History of the Education of Women" (Wood, 1911), and "The Adolescent Girl" (Blanchard, 1919). That these studies incorporated Hall's biases is unquestionable. Blanchard's (1919) dissertation on adolescent girls, later published in book form, was an extension and elaboration of Hall's work on adolescence with additional incorporation of psychoanalytic theory. However, it would be incorrect to assume that Hall was insistent that psychological study at Clark use only his theoretical orientation. The graduate research in psychology included work in human and animal learning, physiological psychology, introspection, and psychoanalysis. Although Hall was criticized for looseness in his psychological theorizing (Thorndike, 1904), this characteristic may have been of benefit to his students' intellectual freedom and development.

Additionally surprising in light of his stance on women was Hall's support of and personal interest in a number of women students and a woman staff member, Amy Tanner. Tanner, who obtained her PhD from the University of Chicago and who had worked with John Dewey, was granted a fellowship at Clark in 1907. She wrote to Hall to ask his advice as to whether she should continue in teaching and come to Clark or go into social work, having been offered a position in the South (Tanner, 1907). Hall's reply to her, if there was one, has been lost or was not issued out of the president's office. The latter would seem to have been the case because Tanner's request was personal. She did come to Clark, but her interest in social work and her indecision about her career choice continued to plague her throughout her years there.

For all but her last two years at Clark, Tanner was on annual appointment as an honorary fellow or as a research assistant to Hall. In May of 1916 she requested that she be put on staff, having completed her ninth year of service at Clark

(Tanner, 1916). Hall supported her request, and she was placed on the continued list; half her salary came from the university, where she was his assistant, and the other half came from the Children's Institute, where she was lecturer. In the latter position Tanner came as close as any woman to being a university colleague of Hall.

Hall's support of Tanner extended beyond her position and duties at Clark and included his numerous attempts to get her poetry and translations of French fairy tales published. Although his efforts were unsuccessful, he was instrumental in the publication and promotion of a second edition of her book, *The Child* (1904), written prior to her arrival at Clark.

The relationship between Hall and Tanner had its difficult moments, however. After granting her authority to order equipment for the Children's Institute, Hall submitted her order to Sanford, chair of psychology, for review, a move that Tanner resented. She expressed her disapproval in a letter to Hall suggesting that if her judgment were not deemed "trustworthy enough to be taken as final . . . it was best not to have me doing the ordering at all" (Tanner, 1909). She further recommended that all future agreements and arrangements as to her position be put in writing. In his reply Hall (1909c) assured her that he had utmost confidence in her, but had wanted to make certain that there would be no laboratory duplication with psychology; his reply was given, as she had requested, in writing.

Tanner left Clark in 1918 to go into settlement house work in the Italian (Shrewsbury Street) district of Worcester. Her reason for leaving Clark, according to Hall (1918), was "solely because she was (with too much ground, alas) dissatisfied that women were not recognized in the university, and that she was the only one who has ever done any teaching here." It is probable that Hall correctly expressed Tanner's reasons for leaving, but his professed sympathy with her position on women at Clark can be viewed only as openly hypocritical in the light of his role in establishing the university's policies. Although he extended to Tanner a colleaguelike status, her position as a Saturday lecturer within the Child Study Institute was commensurate with Hall's perspective on women in education. In correspondence between himself and Tanner (e.g., Hall, 1907b), Hall often expressed sympathy for the difficulty women had in obtaining positions in universities, yet this sympathy must be considered somewhat superficial; Hall's pronouncements on women's education and womanly career pursuits expressed the kinds of sentiments that kept the doors to male-dominated professions closed to women.

Despite the duplicity in his relationship with Tanner, his support for her was strong. Perhaps he did not view this support as a violation of his philosophy on women; he had often stated that child study was to be a science undertaken by women because he believed them to be the best observers of children, and Tanner's position was primarily within the Children's Institute.

Hall appeared to be generally supportive of the women students at Clark and was as unreserved in his praise for them as he was for the men students. His favorite student was Phyllis Blanchard, to whom he often referred as his best research assistant in his 32 years at Clark. Hall clearly saw Blanchard as a case of the apple not falling far from the tree, as her work on adolescence reinforced his earlier interest in the area. Other women students asked for and obtained support from Hall even after they had left Clark. Lucinda Pearl Boggs, who attended Clark for only one summer, frequently wrote to Hall and obtained his endorsement of her extension course in home life offered through the University of Illinois in 1909 ("Lecture and Correspondence," undated). Boggs's respect for Hall and his for her were apparently the result of Hall's having converted her from feminist philosophy (Boggs, 1909b). This "conversion" stimulated her interest in a social psychology of the home and resulted in the home life courses, which were similar to others offered around the country and were the forerunners of the professionalization

of the domestic sphere by way of the discipline of home economics.

Although Hall's educational policies at Clark were consistent with his psychological theory and educational doctrine on sex differences, his treatment of women graduate students appeared to contain little that was connected with his educational and psychological position on women. Indeed, it is somewhat surprising that Hall provided higher education for women in an institution over which he clearly maintained considerable control.

RESOLUTION

In view of Hall's theoretical perspective on women that led to an orientation against coeducation, his enrollment of women into graduate programs at Clark is particularly confusing. But there is little to suggest that it was a problem for Hall. Nowhere in his correspondence with potential women students nor in his treatment of women at Clark is there any evidence that Hall considered their presence a violation of his presidential pronouncements on graduate study for women. Scholars examining the Clark experience have remarked on the excellence of training obtained at Clark (W. C. Ryan, 1939), and some contemporary feminist scholars have suggested that at the beginning of the 20th century the two schools most open to women were Clark and Cornell (Rosenberg, 1982). Thus, unlike President Harper at Chicago, Hall apparently saw no damage to Clark's reputation or public image resulting from admitting women to the graduate programs. In fact, so highly did Hall laud the Clark education that visitors from Europe were led to the erroneous conclusion that the only real graduate education in the United States was at Clark (Ross, 1972).

The resolution of the paradox of Hall as an enemy of coeducation and a teacher of women may be found, in part, in Hall's perspective on the women at Clark. Many of the women graduate students were single women and thus might be considered in that category of bachelor women to which Hall referred in *Adolescence*. Such women were for Hall "individuals," that is, not representative of most women. In terms of variability, Hall must have perceived them as abnormal, as women who would not produce children and, thus, who were terminal products of evolution (Hall, 1904a; Trecker, 1974). Thus, it is possible to resolve the paradox by referring to Hall's perception that the women at Clark had an unusual aptitude for scholarship. (It should be noted, however, that although the majority of the women who studied at Clark were unmarried, about 40% were not.) Although alumni information on these women does not indicate how many of them produced children, few had families when they were enrolled at Clark (File on Hall's Students, 1888–1920; Clark University Library, 1930, 1940, 1951).

Another explanation, not necessarily contradictory to that just offered, is based on Hall's perspective on the kinds of careers appropriate to women. An examination of the careers of the women graduates of Clark suggests that they fared as poorly as did graduates from other institutions in obtaining positions in university teaching and research. Many of the Clark women graduates found positions in teaching, mostly in public and private schools in the elementary grades (Clark University Library, 1930, 1940, 1951). Women who obtained university or college positions were located in women's colleges and not in coeducational institutions. Equally likely as employment for Clark graduates were private or public social and welfare agencies. Within the area of psychology, the best-known graduate of Clark is probably Phyllis Blanchard, who remained until her retirement at the Child Guidance Clinic in Philadelphia. Many Clark women graduates found employment in private practice in psychology or in consulting work with hospitals and other agencies (Clark University Library, 1930, 1940, 1951). Although there is no evidence to suggest that Hall directed women into these areas, he would not have had to do so because there were few positions open to profes-

sionally trained women in traditional male academe (Woody, 1929/1974). Thus, Hall educated his women students for careers considered to be appropriate for females, so this education did not violate his perspective on women's nature.

Finally, the possible attitudes of the women themselves must be considered. It is clear that women like Bradford Thompson Woolley at Chicago and Hollingworth at Columbia entered their institutions with questions about women's psychological makeup, questions stimulated by their sympathy with social reform movements (Rosenberg, 1982). In addition, these women entered institutions where they found instructors who shared their perspectives on sex differences. Most likely there was a similar correspondence between the views of the women entering Clark and those of G. Stanley Hall. Surely these students would not have been unaware of Hall's well-known views on women. Thus, if the women of Clark questioned the traditional status of women, perhaps such questioning began after the Clark years, for the atmosphere at Clark would not have been particularly sympathetic to feminist positions on women's education or legal status.

In short, the significance of such a suggestion for the resolution of Hall's apparent paradox is that Hall would not have been exposed to women with feminist sympathies, unlike the men at Chicago and Columbia (Rosenberg, 1982). Therefore, he would have been able to maintain correspondence between an educational policy that dictated education for motherhood and womanly careers, such as education and social work, and his position as an educator engaged in providing just such an education to women who behaved according to his theoretical notions of womanhood. The only evidence to suggest that Hall was ever directly challenged by a woman graduate student on feminist issues is found in L. P. Boggs's letter (1909b) to him, and in this case Hall converted her to his perspective, meriting him her gratitude; he later assumed the role of her mentor in establishing her career in the social psychology of the home. If any of the Clark women were feminists, their sympathies with women's issues in the early 20th century have remained undiscovered for more than a half century.

Conversely, there is no evidence to suggest that Hall's exposure to women graduate students at Clark changed his view of women or that he ever viewed these women as other than exceptions. In 1922, Hall published *Senescence* (Hall, 1922b), a work dedicated to the later years of development. In it, he reasserted his view of sex differences, suggesting again the eternal adolescence of the female and her generic nature. In a final work before his death in 1924, Hall commented on the newest woman, the flapper. The freedom of the flapper was not viewed by Hall as a departure from his theory on woman's nature, but rather as the "bud of a new and better womanhood" (Hall, 1922a, p. 780), one that would assert anew the distinction between the sexes.

In conclusion, the paradox under investigation in this article can be resolved by the underlying consistency that emerges from an examination of the many ways Hall chose to understand the nature of women. Hall's developmental theory clearly necessitated an educational stance against coeducation, a stance he was willing to take by proposing and enacting educational policy that encouraged the professional development of women in accordance with traditional womanly virtues. In this effort, he was helped by a social-educational system that barred women from the usual areas of male professional advancement. Thus, Hall emerges as unique only in that he may be viewed as the 19th-century bridge to the development of 20th-century social sciences' perspectives on women's nature. Until recently these perspectives have remained grounded within the 19th-century patriarchal structures of womanhood often found as unconscious biases within the theoretical perspectives on sex differences proposed by Hall and other early functionalists. A more complete understanding of the enduring nature of these perspec-

tives on women is necessary and could be accomplished through an examination of the early Clark women graduates within their chosen professions.

REFERENCES

Barnes, E. (1912). The feminizing of culture. *Atlantic Monthly, 109,* 770–776.

Blanchard, P. (1919). *The adolescent girl.* Unpublished doctoral dissertation, Clark University, Worcester, MA.

Boggs, L. P. (1909a). The development value of women's special work. Topical syllabi. In *G. Stanley Hall papers.* (Available from Clark University Archives, Goddard Library, Clark University, Worcester, MA)

Boggs, L. P. (1909b, September 27). [Letter to Hall]. In *G. Stanley Hall papers.* (Available from Clark University Archives, Goddard Library, Clark University, Worcester, MA)

Boring, E. G. (1950). *A history of experimental psychology.* New York: Appleton-Century-Crofts. (Original work published 1929)

Brown, A. (1899). The monthly period. Topical syllabi. In *G. Stanley Hall papers.* (Available from Clark University Archives, Goddard Library, Clark University, Worcester, MA)

Bryan, A. I., & Boring, E. G. (1944). Women in American psychology: Prolegomenon. *Psychological Bulletin, 41,* 447–454.

Clark University Library. (1930, May). *Alumni directory* (No. 76). Worcester, MA: Author.

Clark University Library. (1940, June). *Alumni directory* (Vol. 9, No. 1). Worcester, MA: Author.

Clark University Library. (1951, April). *Alumni directory* (No. 201). Worcester, MA: Author.

Clarke, E. (1873). *Sex in education: Or, a fair chance for the girls.* Boston: Osgood.

Ellis, H. (1894). *Man and woman: A study of human secondary sexual characteristics.* New York: Scribner's.

Faderman, L. (1981). *Surpassing the love of men.* New York: Morrow. [File on Hall's students]. (1888–1920). (Available from Clark University Archives, Goddard Library, Clark University, Worcester, MA)

Filene, P. G. (1975). *Him/her self: Sex roles in modern America*. New York: Mentor Books.

G. Stanley Hall Papers. (1888–1920). (Available from Clark University Archives, Goddard Library, Clark University, Worcester, MA)

Galton, F. (1907). *Inquiries into the human faculty and its development*. London: Dent.

Geddes, P., & Thomson, J. A. (1890). *The evolution of sex*. New York: Scribner & Welford.

Gould, S. J. (1981). *The mismeasure of man*. New York: Norton.

Hall, G. S. (1900, August). The awkward age. *Appleton's Magazine*, pp. 149–156.

Hall, G. S. (1903). Coeducation in the high school. *Addresses and Proceedings of the National Education Association, 446–460*.

Hall, G. S. (1904a). *Adolescence: Its psychology and its relations to physiology, anthropology, sociology, sex, crime, religion and education* (Vols. 1 & 2). New York: Appleton.

Hall, G. S. (1904b, June 27–July 1). Coeducation. *Addresses and Proceedings of the National Education Association, 538–542*.

Hall, G. S. (1905). New ideals of motherhood suggested by child study. *Report of the National Congress of Mothers, 14–27*.

Hall, G. S. (1907a, September). How and when to be frank with boys. *Ladies' Home Journal*.

Hall, G. S. (1907b, February 3). [Letter to Tanner]. In *G. Stanley Hall papers*. (Available from Clark University Archives, Goddard Library, Clark University, Worcester, MA)

Hall, G. S. (1908). Feminization in school and home. *World's Work, 16*, 10237–10244.

Hall, G. S. (1909a, November 20). [Letter to Bullock]. In *G. Stanley Hall papers*. (Available from Clark University Archives, Goddard Library, Clark University, Worcester, MA)

Hall, G. S. (1909b, November 27). [Letter to Bullock]. In *G. Stanley Hall papers*. (Available from Clark University Archives, Goddard Library, Clark University, Worcester, MA)

Hall, G. S. (1909c, December 20). [Letter to Tanner]. In *G. Stanley Hall papers*. (Available from Clark University Archives, Goddard Library, Clark University, Worcester, MA)

Hall, G. S. (1909d, June). A man's adventure in domestic industry. *Appleton's Magazine*, pp. 677–683.

Hall, G. S. (1911). *Educational problems* (Vol. 2). New York: Appleton.

Hall, G. S. (1918, August 8). [Letter to Ellis]. In *G. Stanley Hall papers*. (Available from Clark University Archives, Goddard Library, Clark University, Worcester, MA)

Hall, G. S. (1922a, June). Flapper americana novissima. *Harper's*, pp. 771–780.

Hall, G. S. (1922b). *Senescence*. New York: Appleton.

Hall, G. S. (1923). *Life and confessions of a psychologist*. New York: Appleton.

Hall, G. S. (undated). [Memorandum in re women students at Clark]. In *G. Stanley Hall papers*. (Available from Clark University Archives, Goddard Library, Clark University, Worcester, MA)

Lecture and correspondence courses on home life [Brochure on course offered by L. P. Boggs at Urbana, IL]. (undated). In *G. Stanley Hall papers*. (Available from Clark University Archives, Goddard Library, Clark University, Worcester, MA)

MacMechan, A. (1903). Of girls in a Canadian college. *Atlantic Monthly, 92*, 402–406.

Notes and News: Dr. Hall on high school conditions. (1902). *Educational Review, 28*, 323–324.

Presidential papers. In *G. Stanley Hall papers*. (Available from Clark University Archives, Goddard Library, Clark University, Worcester, MA)

Report of the Male Teachers' Association of New York City. (1902). *Educational Review, 23*, 323–324.

Rosenberg, R. (1982). *Beyond separate spheres: Intellectual roots of modern feminism*. New Haven, CT: Yale University Press.

Ross, D. (1972). *G. Stanley Hall: The psychologist as prophet*. Chicago: University of Chicago Press.

Ryan, M. P. (1979). *Womanhood in America: From colonial times to the present* (2nd ed.). New York: New Viewpoints.

Ryan, W. C. (1939). *Studies in early graduate education*. New York: The Carnegie Foundation, Merrymount Press.

Schwendinger, J., & Schwendinger, H. (1971). Sociology's founding fathers: Sexists to a man. *Journal of Marriage and the Family, 33*, 783–799.

Shields, S. (1975). Functionalism, Darwinism, and the psychology of women. *American Psychologist, 30*, 739–754.

Siegel, A. W., & White, S. H. (1982). The child study movement: Early growth and development of the symbolized child. In H. W. Reese (Ed.), *Advances in child development and behavior* (Vol. 17, pp. 233–285). New York: Academic Press.

Smith-Rosenberg, C., & Rosenberg, C. (1973). The female animal: Medical and biological views of woman and her roles in nineteenth century America. *Journal of American History, 60,* 350–352.

Sohen, J. (1972). *The new woman in Greenwich Village.* New York: Quadrangle.

Stevens, G., & Gardner, S. (1982). *The women of psychology: Vol. I. Pioneers and innovators.* Cambridge, MA: Schenkman.

Tanner, A. (1904). *The child: His thinking, feeling, and doing.* Chicago: Rand McNally.

Tanner, A. (1907, July 17). [Letter to Hall]. In *G. Stanley Hall papers.* (Available from Clark University Archives, Goddard Library, Clark University, Worcester, MA)

Tanner, A. (1908). *History of Clark University through the interpretation of the will of the founder.* Unpublished manuscript. (Available from Clark University Archives, Goddard Library, Clark University, Worcester, MA)

Tanner, A. (1909, December 16). [Letter to Hall]. In *G. Stanley Hall papers.* (Available from Clark Uni-

versity Archives, Goddard Library, Clark University, Worcester, MA)

Tanner, A. (1916, May 22). [Letter to Hall]. In *G. Stanley Hall papers.* (Available from Clark University Archives, Goddard Library, Clark University, Worcester, MA)

Thomas, M. C. (1901). Should the higher education of women differ from that of men? *Educational Review, 21,* 1–10.

Thomas, M. C. (1908). Present tendencies in women's college and university education. *Educational Review, 35,* 64–85.

Thorndike, E. (1904). The newest psychology. *Educational Review, 28,* 217–227.

Trecker, J. L. (1974). Sex, science, and education. *American Quarterly, 26,* 352–366.

Waite, M. A. (1913). *Wages of women workers in department and retail stores.* Unpublished master's thesis, Clark University, Worcester, MA.

Watson, R. I. (1978). *The great psychologists* (4th ed.). New York: Lippincott.

Wood, I. (1911). *An introduction to the modern history of the education of women.* Unpublished master's thesis, Clark University, Worcester, MA.

Woody, T. A. (1974). *A history of women's education in the U.S.* New York: Octagon Books. (Original work published 1929)

James McKeen Cattell and the Failure of Anthropometric Mental Testing, 1890–1901

Michael M. Sokal

CATTELL'S PROGRAM FOR ANTHROPOMETRIC MENTAL TESTING

On January 1, 1889, Cattell was appointed to a professorship of psychology at the University of Pennsylvania that he later claimed (erroneously) to be

Adapted from Sokal, M. M. (1982). James McKeen Cattell and the failure of anthropometric mental testing, 1890–1901. In W. R. Woodward & M. G. Ash (Eds.), *The problematic science: Psychology in nineteenth-century thought.* New York: Praeger, pp. 322–345. Copyright © 1982 by Praeger Publishers. Adapted and reprinted by permission of the publisher.

the world's first. His father's advocacy and his European scientific pedigree played a part in this high honor to a twenty-nine-year-old youth. Within a year, he had established a laboratory, begun to train students, and sketched out a research program on "mental tests and measurements," which coined the term now in common use.[1] He explicitly ignored the simple measurements of bodily dimensions that had been so much a part of Galton's program; instead, he concentrated on procedures to examine both physiological and psychological characteristics. These tests, carried out sporadically on his students at the University, were dynamometer pressure, rate of movement, sensation areas, pressure causing pain, least noticeable difference in weight, reaction time to sound, time for naming colors, bisection of a 50 cm line, judgment of 10 seconds' time, and number of letters remembered on one hearing.

Cattell was clearly skillful in parlaying this simple program into a major institutional and eventually public commitment. He effectively alluded to Helmholtzian science with the term "mental energy," flimsily applied to the tasks measuring strength of squeeze and rate of arm movement in the first two tests above. The ideology of evolution was also invoked by his claim that the tests "would be of considerable value in discovering the constancy of mental processes, their interdependence, and their variation under different circumstances." Galton himself amplified this point in a series of comments, comparing Cattell's testing to "sinking shafts... at a few critical points." He admitted that one goal of Cattell's procedures was exploratory, to determine "which of the measures are the most instructive."[2] Cattell also hinted at a public need when he commented that the tests might "perhaps [be] useful in regard to training, mode of life or indication of disease."

Cattell was not the only American to sense a public need to be tapped by mental testing in the 1890s. By that decade, scientists working in physical anthropometry began to claim that they could measure "The Physical Basis of Precocity and Dullness," and though their claim was disputed,[3] their studies continued throughout the decade. Within the discipline just beginning to identify itself as psychology, testing boomed. At Clark University, for example, Edmund C. Sanford extended his colleague Franz Boas's anthropometric studies of school children.[4] At the University of Nebraska, Harry K. Wolfe, the second American doctoral student of Wundt in experimental psychology, urged the adoption of mental tests in the local public schools. Like Cattell, he admitted that he was not sure what he was studying, and he reminded teachers "not [to] be uneasy because the meaning of any peculiarities is obscure."[5] At Yale, another of Wundt's students, Edward Wheeler Scripture, tried out various mental testing procedures and even published a paper on fencing as an indication of mental ability.[6]

Most important from the viewpoint of legitimating the new discipline in the public eye was the work of Joseph Jastrow. He had earned a Ph.D. with G. Stanley Hall at Johns Hopkins in 1886. He began corresponding with Francis Galton about his anthropometric interest in 1887, and he became professor of psychology at the University of Wisconsin in 1888. By 1890, his concern with mental testing paralleled Cattell's; early in 1892 he published a proposal for "Some Anthropological and Psychological Tests on College Students" based almost completely on Galton's program.[7] He also used tests to investigate sex differences and clashed with Mary Whiton Calkins, the distinguished Wellesley psychologist, as to the meaning of the differences his tests revealed.[8]

Under Jastrow's direction in 1893, the two streams of interest in anthropometric mental testing converged at the World's Columbian Exposition in Chicago. At this World's Fair, Frederic Ward Putnam, Curator of the Peabody Museum of American Archaeology and Ethnology at Harvard University, planned a Department of Ethnology to include a Section on Physical Anthropology under the direction of Franz Boas. Part of Boas's plan was to carry out a program of anthropometric measurements on the visitors to the Fair, including as many foreign visitors as possible, and the members of the Indian tribes brought to Chicago for the occasion. Jastrow, Boas, and Putnam saw no reason why the program should be limited to physical anthropometry and extended it to include mental tests.[9] The result was to be an outgrowth of Galton's Anthropometric Laboratory, and Jastrow wrote to Galton in 1892, asking for suggestions as to procedures and apparatus. He even went before the preliminary meeting of the American Psychological Association and "asked the cooperation of all members for the Section of Psychology at the World's Fair and invited correspondence on the matter."[10] Using a schedule of tests that resembled Galton's and Cattell's, Jastrow tested thousands of individuals with the help of the army of graduate student volunteers he had assembled for the occasion.

Despite this flurry of interest in testing that he had in large part set off, Cattell was unable to devote much time to this work between 1891 and 1894. About the time he published his "Mental Tests and Measurements" paper, he began to commute to New York from Philadelphia to lecture a day or so a week at Columbia College. In 1891, Cattell moved to Columbia and so had to give up his program of testing at Pennsylvania. He devoted the next three years to establishing the psychological laboratory at Columbia, completing two major experimental studies[11] and planning the *Psychological Review*. He did find time to review books on anthropometry of interest to psychologists and to prepare a popular article on mental testing at the invitation of the editor of the *Educational Review*.[12]

In January 1893, Cattell wrote to the President of Columbia "concerning the possibility of using tests of the senses and faculties in order to determine the condition and progress of students, the relative value of different courses of study, etc." Beneath his rationale for educational efficiency, he had to admit that he did not have specific tests designed for specific purposes; he compared his program of testing with the work of researchers in electricity 50 years earlier: "they believed that practical applications would be made, but knew that their first duty was to obtain more exact knowledge." He carried this argument to its Baconian conclusion: "The best way to obtain the knowledge we need is to make the tests, and determine from the results what value they have."[13]

It was not, however, until September 1894 that Cattell finally received authorization for the test-

ing program he wanted. He was granted permission to examine every student on entering Columbia College and the Columbia School of Mines for the next four years, and in fact he tested students throughout the 1890s and into the twentieth century. Cattell, his junior colleague Livingston Farrand, and all their graduate students were deeply involved in the testing program, which soon began to attract national attention. The scope of their reputation may be appreciated from the diversity of their audiences. Cattell and Farrand described their work in papers presented at meetings of the New York Schoolmasters' Association, The New York Academy of Sciences, the American Psychological Association, and the American Association for the Advancement of Science.[14] The day had yet to come when errors in the Scholastic Aptitude Test were front-page news, but the clipping service to which Cattell subscribed certainly kept busy.

The schedule of tests that Cattell prepared at Columbia was explicitly concerned with both physical and mental measurements. Cattell stressed again that he did not "wish to draw any definite conclusions from the results of the tests made so far" because they were "mere facts." However, like the positivist he was, he noted that "they are quantitative facts and the basis of science." He concluded with the pragmatic resolution that "there is no scientific problem more important than the study of the development of man, and no practical problem more urgent than the application of our knowledge to guide this development." The questions he hoped to answer were:

> To what extent are the several traits of body, of the senses and of mind interdependent? How far can we predict one thing from our knowledge of another? What can we learn from the tests of elementary traits regarding the higher intellectual and emotional life?[15]

Within a few years, Cattell's testing program provided answers to at least the last two of these questions, but these were to be extremely disappointing to him.

Perhaps the weakness of his testing program stemmed from the ad hoc manner in which Cattell adapted Wundt's reaction-time experiment into a testing instrument. The technical details are of interest in appreciating just what he was offering to society. The experimenter, now called a tester, sits at the left in front of a Hipp chronoscope, which measures time intervals accurately to milliseconds.... The subject or person being tested sits...in front of a Cattell gravity chronograph, with a Cattell lip key in his mouth. The experiment or test begins when the experimenter, or tester, pulls the string... to start the mechanism of the chronoscope and then closes the switch.... The closing of the switch completes an electric circuit that starts the hands of the chronoscope revolving and allows the screen of the chronograph to fall, thus revealing a card to the subject, on which is printed a stimulus. He then responds verbally in a previously agreed-upon way, thus opening the lip key and breaking the electric circuit, which stops the hands of the chronoscope. The experimenter, or tester, then reads the reaction time directly from the chronoscope dials.[16]

The transformation of an experimental situation into a testing one brought with it several major innovations. Wundt required that his subjects introspect while carrying out the reaction, while Cattell arranged his tests so that those being tested did not have to introspect at all. To be sure, Wundt's use of this technique did not resemble the systematic introspection developed by Edward B. Titchener, and both he and Cattell were concerned primarily with the reaction time itself as a self-contained datum, rather than as an adjunct to a subject's mental observations. Titchener, in fact, complained in print when Jastrow adopted Cattell's approach to the reaction-time experiment at the Chicago World's Fair.[17] In any event, by adopting only the mechanics of Wundt's procedures while ignoring his broader concerns, Cattell was acting no differently with respect to his German teacher than did the American historians who studied with Ranke or the American chemists who studied with

Liebig.[18] Paradoxically, what they lost by oversimplifying their European models the Americans gained back in social usefulness.

PROFESSIONAL JUDGMENTS ABOUT MENTAL TESTING

Interest in mental testing in the United States reached a peak in December 1895, when the American Psychological Association, meeting under Cattell's presidency, appointed a committee "to consider the feasibility of cooperation among the various psychological laboratories in the collection of mental and physical characteristics." The committee took upon itself the task to "draw up a series of physical and mental tests which are regarded as especially appropriate for college students."[19] It consisted of Cattell, Jastrow, Sanford, and two other psychologists: James Mark Baldwin of Princeton University and Lightner Witmer of the University of Pennsylvania. Witmer had been Cattell's student at Pennsylvania and had earned a Ph.D. with Wundt, at Cattell's insistence. He then succeeded Cattell to the chair of psychology at Pennsylvania, and in many ways his approach to psychology was similar to Cattell's.[20] Baldwin, by contrast, was broadly educated in philosophy and, though he had experimented, was not convinced that the laboratory provided the best approach to an understanding of individuals. Instead, he worked on broader questions and in 1895 had published his *Mental Development in the Child and the Race*.[21] As such, he was the only member of the committee to come to the problem of testing without a commitment to an anthropometric approach to the study of human differences.

The committee presented a preliminary report in December 1896 and a detailed report in December 1897, and both accounts stressed mental anthropometry as a preferred method. Sanford, for example, wrote that he "approved the Columbia schedule as it stands." Jastrow did recognize that at least three categories of tests could be developed, namely, those of "(a) the senses,

(b) the motor capacities, and (c) the more complex mental processes." But he argued that the last category should be ignored and that "it is better to select, even if in part arbitrarily, on part of a certain sense capacity" than a broader aspect of mental life.[22]

But the report of the committee was not unanimous. Baldwin presented a minority report in which he agreed that tests of the senses and motor abilities were important, but he argued that such essentially physiological tests had received too great a place in a schedule developed by a committee of the American Psychological Association. He asked for additional tests of the higher mental processes and discussed several possible approaches that could be used in testing memory. He concluded by arguing for "giving the tests as psychological a character as possible."[23]

Baldwin's criticisms of the anthropometric tests were the first, but not the last. Some of the critiques took the form of attacks on the assumptions made by the testers. Hugo Münsterberg, for example, director of the psychological laboratory at Harvard, wrote about the "danger" of believing that psychology could never help educators. More directly, he attacked Scripture's work and the scientific assumptions that underlay much of the test, claiming that "I have never measured a psychical fact, I have never heard that anyone has measured a psychical fact, I do not believe that in centuries to come a psychical fact will ever be measured."[24] To be sure, there were other reasons for Münsterberg's attack,[25] and it went beyond the criticisms that most psychologists would make of what the testers were doing. Furthermore, it was not directed at Scripture solely as a tester and, if Baldwin's criticisms were taken seriously, it was not clear that the testers were trying to measure psychological quantities. But to deny that psychological processes were in principle measureable was to undercut the positivistic assumption of Cattell that quantifiable data was the only type worthy of scientific attention.

Other critics were to compare Cattell's tests then being developed in France by Alfred Binet and his collaborators, which were explicitly concerned with the higher mental processes.[26] Cattell knew of Binet—who was a cooperating editor of the *Psychological Review*—and of his work. He even cited Binet's work in his major paper on anthropometric tests. There he noted that he and his coauthor "fully appreciate the arguments urged by...M M. Binet and Henri in favor of making tests of a strictly psychological character," but he stressed that "measurements of the body and of the senses come as completely within our scope as the higher mental processes." They went even further, noting that "if we undertake to study attention or suggestibility we find it difficult to measure definitely a definite thing."[27] In other words, Cattell's stress on quantification led him to avoid investigating that which was difficult to quantify and to concentrate on what he could measure. His positivistic Baconianism therefore had him avoid what he knew was more important, or at least what his colleagues told him was more important, to focus on that which he could work with easily. He was like a man who lost a quarter one night in the middle of the block, but who looked for it at the corner, because that was where the light was better.

One psychologist who compared Cattell's work with Binet's was Stella Emily Sharp, a graduate student of Edward Bradford Titchener at Cornell. In 1898, she published her doctoral dissertation in which she compared the theories of "individual psychology"—the phrase is Binet's—of the American and French testers. In it, she stressed that "the American view is founded upon no explicit theory," a conclusion with which Cattell would have agreed entirely, and presented Binet's view as the belief that "the complex mental processes...are those the variations of which give most important information in regard to those mental characteristics whereby individuals are commonly classed." She did not describe her classification scheme but informally tried out some of Binet's suggested procedures on several of her graduate student classmates.

For example, she asked them to remember sentences (rather than Cattell's series of letters) and to describe a picture that they had seen sometime before (rather than reproduce the length of a line seen earlier). Her results for some tests seemed to form "a basis of a general classification of the individuals," but she also found that "a lack of correspondences in the individual differences observed in the various tests was quite as noticeable as their presence." She therefore concluded that she had demonstrated the "relative independence of the particular mental activities under investigation" and hence the uselessness of Binet's procedures. But she went further. If Binet's tests did not give a good picture of the variations among individuals, she argued, then "mental anthropometry," which lacked any theoretical superstructure, could not yield results of any value either.[28]

Sharp's results are still quoted today,[29] but other events of the late 1890s had more to do with the failure of anthropometric mental testing. At least two were personal. At Yale, Scripture's personality had led him into conflicts with most of his colleagues and in the last years of the decade he was too busy fighting for his academic life to continue testing. Jastrow, meanwhile, had given up his struggle to publish the results of his testing program; this effort had led to conflicts with the officials at the Exposition and contributed to his nervous breakdown in the mid-1890s.[30] Scripture's and Jastrow's abandonment of anthropometric mental testing left Cattell and Witmer the only prominent psychologists working in the area, and Witmer's attention was soon focused on narrow applications of tests in his clinical psychology. Cattell was therefore left alone with his tests, which he continued throughout the decade, and by the late 1890s he was able to subject the data he collected to a new form of analysis. And this analysis, carried out by one of his graduate students, led most directly to the failure of his testing program.

Clark Wissler was an 1897 graduate of Indiana University who had come to Columbia as a graduate student primarily to work with Cattell on his anthropometric testing program. At Columbia, he was especially impressed by Franz Boas, the distinguished anthropologist whom Cattell had brought to the University, and soon grew interested in the anthropological implications of Cattell's work. He later had an important career as an anthropologist, but his studies with Boas in the late 1890s had a more immediate effect. Cattell was mathematically illiterate—his addition and subtraction were often inaccurate—but Boas, with a Ph.D. in physics, was mathematically sophisticated. Cattell knew that Galton had developed mathematical techniques to measure how closely two sets of data were related, or were correlated, and he made sure that Wissler learned these procedures from Boas. He then had Wissler apply these techniques to the data collected during his decade-long testing program at Columbia.[31]

Wissler calculated the correlation between the results of any one of Cattell's tests and the grades the students tested earned in their classes; and between the grades earned in any class and those earned in any other. His results showed that there was almost no correlation among the results of the various tests. For example, in calculating the correlation between the results of the reaction-time test and the marking-out-A's test,[32] Wissler found that 252 students took both tests, and he measured the correlation between the results of the two tests as −0.05. Consequently, despite the fact that the two tests might appear to be closely related "an individual with a quick reaction-time [was] no more likely to be quick in marking out the A's than one with a slow reaction-time." Furthermore, Wissler's analysis showed that there was no correlation between the results of any of Cattell's tests and the academic standing of any of the students tested. In contrast, Wissler found that academic performance in most subjects correlated very well with that in other subjects. Even "the gymnasium grade, which [was] based chiefly on faithfulness in attendance, correlated with the average class standing to about the same degree as one course with another."[33] In all, Wissler's analysis struck most psychologists as definitive and, with it, anthropometric mental testing, as a movement, died.

Cattell, of course, abandoned his career as an experimental psychologist, but he continued his activity within the American psychological community. For example, in the 1920s he founded The Psychological Corporation. From about 1900 on, he was better known as an editor and as an entrepreneur of science than he was as a psychologist. In many ways, his later career is more interesting than his earlier one, though as his experience with The Psychological Corporation shows, it may not have been any more successful.[34]

THE INFLUENCE OF THE MENTAL TESTING MOVEMENT

But despite the death of the anthropometric movement as such, anthropometric testing itself—in many ways a product of nineteenth-century philosophy of science—continued into the first years of the twentieth century. America at that time was engaged in what has been called "The Search for Order."[35] Millions of new immigrants—most with cultural backgrounds totally different from those of the early nineteenth century—were flocking to the New World. The rapid industrialization of the period and the rise of the new professions placed a heavy premium on a standardized work style and on the development of formalized criteria for judging applicants for universities and jobs. Many citizens looked to education as an ordering, and Americanizing, process, and compulsory education laws were enacted by 1900. The rising concern for the welfare, and evil influence, of the delinquent, dependent, and defective classes led to the rapid growth of institutions to serve their needs and to protect the public from them.[36]

In such an atmosphere of social concern, mental testing was seen to be too valuable a tool to be completely abandoned, even if anthropometric mental testing was shown to have extreme limitations. On one level, specialized anthropometric tests, designed for specialized uses, were found to be useful. Even one of Titchener's students, who was studying the sense of hearing and techniques for evaluating it, had to admit that they served "practical purposes" when designed carefully. In many ways, the clinical psychology developed by Witmer in the late 1890s illustrates the point perfectly. After all, in diagnosing what are today called sensory disorders and learning disabilities, Witmer applied the tests developed by Cattell and others in particularly appropriate ways. Similarly, Scripture's best-known student—Carl E. Seashore—merely developed a set of specialized tests relating to the sense of hearing when he constructed his widely used tests of musical talent.[37] In these ways anthropometric mental tests, especially designed to focus on specific sensory problems, played (and continue to play) a major role in bringing order to American society and, especially to American education.

On another level, however, the continued use of anthropometric tests in the early twentieth century was much less successful. Though testing worked when applied narrowly, it yielded essentially useless results when the testers set larger goals. One can readily see eugenical implications in Cattell's goals for his early tests. Similarly, Jastrow believed that his tests demonstrated the proper spheres of activity for each of the sexes. Others used anthropometric tests to justify, and argue for, their own ideas as to the proper relations between the races.[38] More prosaically, though still on a large scale, Frank Parsons in the early 1900s established a vocational guidance bureau in Boston with a goal of helping young men find the profession for which they were best suited. Here he used tests of the "delicacy of touch, nerve, sight and hearing reactions, association time, etc." And as late as 1908, Parsons argued that reaction-time tests had a great value for judging an "individual's probable aptitudes and capacities."[39]

More important for psychology was the work of Henry H. Goddard, a Clark Ph.D. and student of G. Stanley Hall. In 1906, after several years of teaching psychology at a small state college, he became director of the psychological laboratory at the Vineland, New Jersey, Training School for the Feeble-Minded. There he worked with children who would today be called retarded or developmentally disabled. To obtain some estimate of the children's abilities, he used various anthropometric techniques—more than five years after Wissler's analysis was published. Although he did not find this approach very helpful, he continued to employ it for lack of another. Finally, in the last years of the decade, he traveled to France and there discovered in detail the full range of the work of Binet and his colleagues. When he brought this knowledge back to America, his English version of Binet's tests finally supplanted anthropometric mental testing, at least outside its narrower applications.[40] Thereby, Goddard introduced a new testing movement, which has done much to shape modern America. But that is another story...

NOTES

(1) James McKeen Cattell, "Mental Tests and Measurements," *Mind* 15 (1890):373–81.

(2) Ibid., pp. 373, 379–81.

(3) William T. Porter, "The Physical Basis of Precocity and Dullness," *Transactions of the Academy of Science of St. Louis* 6 (1893):161–81; Franz Boas, "On Dr. William Townsend Porter's Investigation of the Growth of School Children of St. Louis," *Science* 1 (1895):225–30.

(4) For example, Arthur MacDonald, "Mental Ability in Relation to Head Circumference, Cephalic Index, Sociological Conditions, Sex, Age, and Nationality," unpublished paper, Arthur MacDonald files, U.S. Office of Education papers, U.S. National Archives, Washington, D.C. See also Michael M. Sokal, "Anthropometric Mental Testing in Nineteenth-Century America," James Allen Young, "Height, Weight, and Health: Anthropometric Study of Human Growth in Nineteenth-Century American Medicine," *Bulletin of the History of Medicine* 53 (1979):214–43; Elizabeth Lomax, "Late Nineteenth-Century American Growth Studies: Objectives, Methods and Outcomes," unpublished paper, Fifteenth International Congress of the History of Science, Edinburgh, Scotland, August 1977.

(5) Sokal, M.M., "Anthropometric Mental Testing in Nineteenth-Century America," unpublished Sigma Xi national, Lecture, 1979–81; Harry K. Wolfe, "Simple Observations and Experiments: Mental Tests and Their Purposes," *North-Western Journal of Education* 7 (1896):36–37.

(6) Edward W. Scripture, "Tests of Mental Ability as Exhibited in Fencing," *Studies from the Yale Psychological Laboratory* 2 (1894):114–19; Michael M. Sokal, "The Psychological Career of Edward Wheeler Scripture," *Historiography of Modern Psychology: Arms, Resources, Approaches*, ed. Josef Brožek and Ludwig J. Pongratz (Toronto: C.J. Hogrefe, 1980), pp. 255–78.

(7) For example, Joseph Jastrow to Galton, August 19, 1887, Galton papers; Joseph Jastrow, "Some Anthropometric and Psychologic Tests on College Students; A Preliminary Survey," *American Journal of Psychology* 4 (1892):420–28.

(8) Joseph Jastrow, "A Study in Mental Statistics," *New Review* 5 (1891):559–68; Mary Whiton Calkins, "Community of Ideas of Men and Women," *Psychological Review* 3 (1896):426–30. Cf. Laurel Furumoto, "Mary Whiton Calkins (1863–1930)," *Psychology of Women Quarterly* 5 (1980):55–68.

(9) World's Columbian Exposition, *Official Catalogue, Department M Ethnology: Archaeology, Physical Anthropology, History, Natural History, Isolated and Collective Exhibits* (Chicago: W. B. Conkey, 1893).

(10) Jastrow to Galton, July 17, 1892, Galton papers; Michael M. Sokal (ed.), "APA's First Publication: Proceedings of the American Psychological Association, 1892–1893," *American Psychologist* 28 (1973):277–92.

(11) James McKeen Cattell and George S. Fullerton, *On the Perception of Small Differences, with Special Reference to the Extent, Force and Time of*

Movement, Publications of the University of Pennsylvania, Philosophical Series, no. 2 (Philadelphia: University of Pennsylvania, 1892): James McKeen Cattell and Charles S. Dolley, "On Reaction-Times and the Velocity of the Nervous Impulse," *Proceedings of the National Academy of Sciences* 7 (1896):393–415.

(12) James McKeen Cattell, "Psychological Literature: Anthropometry," *Psychological Review* 2 (1895):510–11; James McKeen Cattell, "Tests of the Senses and Faculties," *Education Review* 5 (1893):257–65.

(13) Cattell to Seth Low, January 30, 1893, James McKeen Cattell collection, Columbia University Archives, New York, N.Y.

(14) Sokal, "Anthropometric Mental Testing."

(15) James McKeen Cattell and Livingston Farrand, "Physical and Mental Measurements of the Students of Columbia University," *Psychological Review* 3 (1896):618–48.

(16) Michael M. Sokal, Audrey B. Davis, and Uta C. Merzbach, "Laboratory Instruments in the History of Psychology," *Journal of the History of the Behavioral Sciences* 12 (1976):59–64.

(17) Edward B. Titchener, "Anthropometry and Experimental Psychology," *Philosophical Review* 2 (1893):187–92.

(18) George G. Iggers, "The Image of Ranke in American and German Historical Thought," *History and Theory* 2 (1962):17–33; Margaret W. Rossiter, *The Emergence of Agricultural Science: Justus Liebig and the Americans, 1840–1880* (New Haven, Conn.: Yale University Press, 1975). Cf. Sokal, "Foreign Study before Fulbright: American Students at European Universities in the Nineteenth Century," unpublished Sigma Xi National Lecture, 1979–81.

(19) Edmund C. Sanford, "The Philadelphia Meeting of the American Psychological Association" *Science* 3 (1896):119–21.

(20) John O'Donnell, "The Clinical Psychology of Lightner Witmer: A Case Study of Institutional Innovation and Intellectual Change," *Journal of the History of the Behavioral Sciences* 15 (1979): 3–17.

(21) James Mark Baldwin, *Mental Development in the Child and the Race: Methods and Processes* (New York: Macmillan, 1895).

(22) Sanford to Baldwin, December 7, 1896, Cattell papers; James Mark Baldwin, James McKeen Cattell, and Joseph Jastrow, "Physical and Mental Tests," *Psychological Review* 5 (1898): 172–79.

(23) Baldwin et al., "Physical and Mental Tests."

(24) Hugo Münsterberg, "The Danger from Experimental Psychology," *Atlantic Monthly* 81 (1898): 159–67.

(25) Matthew Hale, Jr., *Human Science and Social Order: Hugo Münsterberg and the Origins of Applied Psychology* (Philadelphia: Temple University Press, 1980); Sokal, "The Psychological Career of Edward Wheeler Scripture."

(26) Alfred Binet and Victor Henri, "La psychologie individuelle," *L'Annee psychologique* 2 (1895): 411–15.

(27) Cattell and Farrand, "Physical and Mental Measurements."

(28) Stella Emily Sharp, "Individual Psychology: A Study in Psychological Method," *American Journal of Psychology* 10 (1898):329–91.

(29) See Richard J. Herrnstein and Edwin G. Boring (ed.), *A Source Book in the History of Psychology* (Cambridge: Harvard University Press, 1965), pp. 438–42.

(30) Sokal, "The Psychological Career of Edward Wheeler Scripture," Joseph Jastrow, autobiography, *A History of Psychology in Autobiography,* vol. 1, edited by Carl Murchison (Worcester: Clark University Press, 1930), pp. 135–62. Cf. Jastrow, correspondence with Frederic Ward Putnam, 1891–1900, Frederic Ward Putnam papers, Harvard University Archives, Cambridge, Massachusetts.

(31) Clark Wissler, "The Contribution of James McKeen Cattell to American Anthropology," *Science* 99 (1944):232–33; James McKeen Cattell, "Memorandum for Miss Helen M. Walker," undated note, Cattell papers.

(32) Individuals were presented with a ten-by-ten array of one hundred letters in which were scattered ten A's. The time required to strike out all A's was measured.

(33) Clark Wissler, "The Correlation of Mental and Physical Tests," *Psychological Review Monograph Supplements* 3, no. 6 (1901).

(34) Sokal, M.M. "The Origins of the Psychological

Corporation." *Journal of the History of the Behaviorial Science* 17 (1981):54–67.

(35) Robert H. Wiebe, *The Search for Order, 1877–1920* (New York: Hill and Wang, 1967).

(36) This paragraph summarizes many years of scholarship in the social history of American ideas. See Wiebe, *The Search for Order;* Henrika Kuklick, "The Organization of Social Science in the United States," *American Quarterly* 28 (1976): 124–41; Burton J. Bledstein, *The Culture of Professionalism: The Middle Class and the Development of Higher Education in America* (New York: Norton, 1978).

(37) Benjamin Richard Andrews, "Auditory Tests," *American Journal of Psychology* 15 (1904):14–56; O'Donnell, "The Clinical Psychology of Lightner Witmer;" Audrey B. Davis and Uta C. Merzbach, *Early Auditory Studies: Activities in the Psychology Laboratories of American Universities,* Smithsonian Studies in History and Technology, no. 31 (Washington: Smithsonian Institute Press, 1975).

(38) R. Meade Bache, "Reaction Time with Reference to Race," *Psychological Review* 2 (1895): 475–86; Anna Tolman Smith, "A Study of Race Psychology," *Popular Science Monthly* 50 (1896): 354–60; Arthur MacDonald, "Colored Children—A Psycho-Physical Study," *Journal of the American Medical Association* 32 (1899): 1140–44. Cf. Charles S. Johnson and Horace M. Bond, "The Investigation of Racial Difference Prior to 1910," *Journal of Negro History* 3 (1934): 328–39.

(39) Frank Parson, "The Vocation Bureau: First Report to Executive Committee and Trustees, May 1st, 1908," as reprinted in John M. Brewer, *History of Vocational Guidance: Origins and Early Development* (New York: Harper and Brothers, 1942), pp. 303–8.

(40) Henry H. Goddard, *The Research Department: What It Is, What It Is Doing, What It Hopes to Do* (Vineland, New Jersey: The Training School 1914).

CHAPTER 11

FUNCTIONALISM

Previous chapters made freqent references to functionalism, first concerning its opposition to Titchener's structuralism, second with regard to its debt to the writings of Darwin and Galton, and third in terms of the conceptual and methodological base provided by early American psychologists—James, Hall, and Cattell. This chapter will describe this school of psychology as it became identified with the University of Chicago.

In her classic book, *Seven Psychologies,* Edna Heidbreder (1933) wrote, "In functionalism, American psychology made its first definite and organized stand against domination by the Titchenerian, or Wundtian, school" (p. 201). A similar point is made by D.P. Schultz and S. E. Schultz (1987), who state that "functionalism was the first uniquely American system of psychology" (p. 107). To call it "uniquely American" is not to deny the influence from England but to say that, as a system of psychology, it took root in American soil. In truth, functionalism was never a "school," at least not in the sense that that label could be applied to a much more systematized position like structuralism (see Krantz, 1969; O'Donnell, 1985). There was no single leader, as Titchener was for his school, nor was there a common conceptual and methodological base that defined functionalism (Hilgard, 1987). Nevertheless, functionalism, or more accurately, several functionalisms, characterized much of American psychology in the early part of the twentieth century. Although it lacked the focus of structuralism, its impact was much more substantial.

As noted in Chapter 8, functionalism arose in opposition to Titchener's structuralism. Indeed, Titchener (1898) gave the school its name in an article he wrote that contrasted his approach to psychology with what he saw as an emerging approach that emphasized the functions of consciousness. Titchener did not deny the importance of the questions the functionalists were asking, but he did believe they were premature. For Titchener, function could not be understood without a complete understanding of structure. Drawing on an analogy with the field of biology, Titchener argued that the work on anatomy had to precede physiology. The initial step was to dissect the organism (consciousness), identifying the various structures (mental elements); then, once the structures were known, the next appropriate step was to investigate their functions (the mental operations of consciousness). Titchener warned his psychological colleagues that they must guard against being seduced by the attractiveness of functional questions and adhere to what was, for him, the natural order of science and the only proper way for scientific psychology to proceed.

It was against those restrictions and absolute certainty that the functionalists rebelled. James Rowland Angell (1869–1949), one of the most influential of the functionalists, used his presidential address before the annual meeting of the American Psychological Association to deal with that issue. According to Angell (1907), functionalism "gains its vitality primarily perhaps as a protest against the exclusive excellence of another starting point for the study of the mind." (p. 61). Angell was not denying the validity of the structural approach, only objecting to its claim for exclusivity.

The functionalists were happy to coexist with their structural colleagues, although the reverse cannot be said to be true. The controversy fueled many psychological conversations around the turn of the century, but by 1905 functionalism had become the dominant view in American psychology (Leahey, 1987). Its formal beginning is often traced to a decade earlier, when John Dewey (1859–1952) published his classic article on the *reflex arc concept* (Dewey, 1896). Dewey had studied with G. Stanley Hall at Johns Hopkins, where he earned his doctoral degree in 1884. Two years later he published a textbook on psychology, but it was not a treatise on functionalist psychology—those ideas were yet to materialize in Dewey's thought. By the time he arrived at the University of Chicago in 1894, however, he was convinced of the artificiality of the atomistic approach to the study of consciousness. Studies of reflexive behavior involved analysis of the reflex into its component elements, namely *stimulus* (sensation) and *response* (movement). Dewey opposed such reductionism, arguing that the *reflex arc* was a continuous whole that must be studied in that form. Using the example of a child seeing a candle flame and then reaching for it, he noted that the structuralist approach was to view the sensation (seeing) as the initial part of the act and the movement (reaching) as the second part of the act. Dewey argued that the act was not divisible and, indeed, that it was not clear that the second part followed from the first. For example, head movements and eye movements are an integral part of the looking process. Further, the interplay between sensory functioning and motor processes is critical to the reaching response so that coordinated movements can be made using visual and kinesthetic feedback. So the two interact, rather than one following from the other. In this way they form a conscious event that must be studied as the entity (whole) that it is. Acts, such as the child reaching for a flame, occur in a functional context and must be studied in that framework.

The reflex arc paper was Dewey's last important contribution to psychology; thereafter he turned most of his energies to his involvement in what became known as the progressive education movement. His successor in psychology at the University of Chicago was James Rowland Angell, who had been his student as an undergraduate. Angell did graduate work with William James and went to Germany for his doctorate in psychology. Although he completed all of his course work, the degree was never awarded because he never finished rewriting his dissertation into better German, as his doctoral committee had requested.

Under Angell's administration of psychology at Chicago, functionalism became a more formalized position. The laboratory there was the site of an active research program whose studies defined functional psychology. Much of this research appeared in Angell's textbook, *Psychology,* (1904) the first textbook written from a functionalist perspective, although it was not a statement of the functionalist position. He made that philosophical statement in his APA presidential address, mentioned earlier.

The functionalist research at Chicago was much more directed to learning as an area of investigation, in contrast to the work on sensation-perception that was characteristic of the structuralists. The functional psychologists certainly researched perceptual questions (e.g., Harvey Carr's 1935 book on space perception), but the learning investigations were more prominent in their laboratories. Physiological studies were more prevalent, an emphasis that had come from Angell himself, and animal studies at Chicago became commonplace (for example, the work of Carr, John B. Watson, and Walter Hunter), because of the methodological eclecticism.

The functionalists used the method of introspection, but not in the microanalytic way it was employed by the structuralists. In addition to that method and the physiological techniques, they used mental tests, questionnaires, and experimental techniques in which stimulus-response relationships were studied. Thus, they broadened the goals of psychology, added greatly to the list of accepted methodologies, and significantly expanded the domain of psychological inquiry to include animal studies, studies on children, and even studies on the mentally ill.

The first selection in this chapter is the APA presidential address that Angell delivered in 1906 (published in 1907). It is considered to have spelled out the philosophical base for functional psychology in the way that Titchener's (1898) article had done for structuralism. In his article, Angell states that at the time of that writing, functional psychology was "little more than a point of view, a program, an ambition" (p. 61). But he was being much too modest. The program begun by Dewey at Chicago, and continued by Angell, had already made functionalism into the dominant theme of American psychology.

The second selection is by Alfred C. Raphelson, a historian of psychology at the University of Michigan at Flint. It is an intellectual history of John Dewey that traces the evolution of Dewey's ideas in the influence of George S. Morris, Charles S. Peirce, and G. Stanley Hall. It also presents an interesting case for why the functionalist movement came to fruition at the University of Chicago.

The third selection, by the social psychologist Stephanie A. Shields, deals with the historical roots of the psychology of women in the ideas of Darwin and those psychologists involved in functionalism. With it and the article by Lesley A. Diehl in the previous chapter, the reader should get a detailed view of the history of psychology's concern with sex differences, a topic typically omitted from most history of psychology textbooks.

In summary, the three selections in this chapter trace the intellectual development of Dewey that gave rise to the founding of the functionalist school at the University of Chicago; show how Angell, at the height of functionalism, described the functional approach; and illustrate psychology's views on women as rooted in Darwinian and functionalist thought.

REFERENCES

Angell, J. R. (1904). *Psychology*. New York: Henry Holt.

Angell, J. R. (1907). The province of functional psychology. *Psychological Review, 14,* 61–91.

Carr, H. A. (1935). *An introduction to space perception*. New York: Longmans, Green.

Dewey, J. (1896). The reflex arc concept in psychology. *Psychological Review, 3,* 357–370.

Heidbreder, E. (1933). *Seven psychologies*. New York: Appleton-Century-Crofts.

Hilgard, E. R. (1987). *Psychology in America: A historical survey*. San Diego: Harcourt, Brace, Jovanovich.

Krantz, D. L. (Ed.) (1969). *Schools of psychology: A symposium*. New York: Appleton-Century-Crofts.

Leahey, T. H. (1987). *A history of psychology: Main currents in psychological thought* (2d ed.). Englewood Cliffs, NJ: Prentice-Hall.

O'Donnell, J. M. (1985). *The origins of behaviorism: American psychology, 1870–1920*. New York: New York University Press.

Schultz, D. P., & Schultz, S. E. (1987). *A history of modern psychology* (4th ed.). San Diego: Harcourt, Brace, Jovanovich.

Titchener, E. B. (1898). The postulates of a structural psychology. *Philosophical Review, 7,* 449–465.

The Province of Functional Psychology

James Rowland Angell

Functional psychology is at the present moment little more than a point of view, a program, an ambition. It gains its vitality primarily perhaps as a protest against the exclusive excellence of another starting point for the study of the mind, and it enjoys for the time being at least the peculiar vigor which commonly attaches to Protestantism of any sort in its early stages before it has become respectable and orthodox. The time seems ripe to attempt a somewhat more precise characterization of the field of functional psychology than has as yet been offered. What we seek is not the arid and merely verbal definition which to many of us is so justly anathema, but rather an informing appreciation of the motives and ideals which animate the psychologist who pursues this path. His status in the eye of the psychological public is unnecessarily precarious. The conceptions of his purposes prevalent in non-functionalist circles range from positive and dogmatic misapprehension, through frank mystification and suspicion up to moderate comprehension. Nor is this fact an expression of anything peculiarly abstruse and recondite in his intentions. It is due in part to his own ill-defined plans, in part to his failure to explain lucidly exactly what he is about. Moreover, he is fairly numerous and it is not certain that in all important particulars he and his confrères are at one in their beliefs. The considerations which are herewith offered suffer inevitably from this personal limitation. No psychological council of Trent has as yet pronounced upon the true faith. But in spite of probable failure it seems worth while to hazard an attempt at delineating the scope of functionalist principles. I formally renounce any intention to strike out new plans; I am engaged in

what is meant as a dispassionate summary of actual conditions.

Whatever else it may be, functional psychology is nothing wholly new. In certain of its phases it is plainly discernible in the psychology of Aristotle and in its more modern garb it has been increasingly in evidence since Spencer wrote his *Psychology* and Darwin his *Origin of Species*. Indeed, as we shall soon see, its crucial problems are inevitably incidental to any serious attempt at understanding mental life. All that is peculiar to its present circumstances is a higher degree of self-consciousness than it possessed before, a more articulate and persistent purpose to organize its vague intentions into tangible methods and principles.

A survey of contemporary psychological writing indicates, as was intimated in the preceding paragraph, that the task of functional psychology is interpreted in several different ways. Moreover, it seems to be possible to advocate one or more of these conceptions while cherishing abhorrence for the others. I distinguish three principal forms of the functional problem with sundry subordinate variants. It will contribute to the clarification of the general situation to dwell upon these for a moment, after which I propose to maintain that they are substantially but modifications of a single problem.

I

There is to be mentioned first the notion which derives most immediately from contrast with the ideals and purposes of structural psychology so-called. This involves the identification of functional psychology with the effort to discern and portray the typical *operations* of consciousness under actual life conditions, as over against the attempt to analyze and describe its elementary and complex *contents*. The structural psychology of sensation, *e.g.*, undertakes to determine the number and character of the various unanalyzable sensory materials, such as the varieties of color, tone, taste, etc. The functional psychology of sensation would on the other hand find its appropriate sphere of interest in the determination of the character of the various sense activities as differing in their *modus operandi* from one another and from other mental processes such as judging, conceiving, willing and the like.

In this its older and more pervasive form functional psychology has until very recent times had no independent existence. No more has structural psychology for that matter. It is only lately that any motive for the differentiation of the two has existed and structural psychology—granting its claims and pretensions of which more anon— is the first, be it said, to isolate itself. But in so far as functional psychology is synonymous with descriptions and theories of mental action as distinct from the materials of mental constitution, so far it is everywhere conspicuous in psychological literature from the earliest times down.

When the structural psychologists define their field as that of mental *process,* they really preëmpt under a fictitious name the field of function, so that I should be disposed to allege fearlessly and with a clear conscience that a large part of the doctrine of psychologists of nominally structural proclivities is in point of fact precisely what I mean by one essential part of functional psychology, *i.e.,* an account of psychical operations. Certain of the official exponents of structuralism explicitly lay claim to this as their field and do so with a flourish of scientific rectitude. There is therefore after all a small but nutritious core of agreement in the structure-function apple of discord. For this reason, as well as because I consider extremely useful the analysis of mental life into its elementary forms, I regard much of the actual work of my structuralist friends with highest respect and confidence. I feel, however, that when they use the term structural as opposed to

the term functional to designate their scientific creed they often come perilously near to using the enemy's colors.

Substantially identical with this first conception of functional psychology, but phrasing itself somewhat differently, is the view which regards the functional problem as concerned with discovering how and why conscious processes are what they are, instead of dwelling as the structuralist is supposed to do upon the problem of determining the irreducible elements of consciousness and their characteristic modes of combination. I have elsewhere defended the view that however it may be in other sciences dealing with life phenomena, in psychology at least the answer to the question 'what' implicates the answer to the questions 'how' and 'why.'

Stated briefly the ground on which this position rests is as follows: In so far as you attempt to analyze any particular state of consciousness you find that the mental elements presented to your notice are dependent upon the particular exigencies and conditions which call them forth. Not only does the affective coloring of such a psychical moment depend upon one's temporary condition, mood and aims, but the very sensations themselves are determined in their qualitative texture by the totality of circumstances subjective and objective within which they arise. You cannot get a fixed and definite color sensation for example, without keeping perfectly constant the external and internal conditions in which it appears. The particular sense quality is in short functionally determined by the necessities of the existing situation which it emerges to meet. If you inquire then deeply enough what particular sensation you have in a given case, you always find it necessary to take account of the manner in which, and the reasons why, it was experienced at all. You may of course, if you will, abstract from these considerations, but in so far as you do so, your analysis and description is manifestly partial and incomplete. Moreover, even when you do so abstract and attempt to describe certain isolable sense qualities, your descriptions are of necessity couched in terms not of the experienced quality itself, but in terms of the conditions which produced it, in terms of some other quality with which it is compared, or in terms of some more overt act to which the sense stimulation led. That is to say, the very description itself is functionalistic and must be so. The truth of this assertion can be illustrated and tested by appeal to any situation in which one is trying to reduce sensory complexes, *e.g.,* colors or sounds, to their rudimentary components.

II

A broader outlook and one more frequently characteristic of contemporary writers meets us in the next conception of the task of functional psychology. This conception is in part a reflex of the prevailing interest in the larger formulae of biology and particularly the evolutionary hypotheses within whose majestic sweep is nowadays included the history of the whole stellar universe; in part it echoes the same philosophical call to new life which has been heard as pragmatism, as humanism, even as functionalism itself. I should not wish to commit either party by asserting that functional psychology and pragmatism are ultimately one. Indeed, as a psychologist I should hesitate to bring down on myself the avalanche of metaphysical invective which has been loosened by pragmatic writers. To be sure pragmatism has slain its thousands, but I should cherish scepticism as to whether functional psychology would the more speedily slay its tens of thousands by announcing an offensive and defensive alliance with pragmatism. In any case I only hold that the two movements spring from similar logical motivation and rely for their vitality and propagation upon forces closely germane to one another.

The functional psychologist then in his modern attire is interested not alone in the operations of mental process considered merely of and by and for itself, but also and more vigorously in mental activity as part of a larger stream of biological forces which are daily and hourly at work before our eyes and which are constitutive of the most important and most absorbing part of our world. The psychologist of this stripe is wont to take his cue from the basal conception of the evolutionary movement, *i.e.,* that for the most part organic structures and functions possess their present characteristics by virtue of the efficiency with which they fit into the extant conditions of life broadly designated the environment. With this conception in mind he proceeds to attempt some understanding of the manner in which the psychical contributes to the furtherance of the sum total of organic activities, not alone the psychical in its entirety, but especially the psychical in its particularities—mind as judging, mind as feeling, etc.

This is the point of view which instantly brings the psychologist cheek by jowl with the general biologist. It is the presupposition of every philosophy save that of outright ontological materialism that mind plays the stellar rôle in all the environmental adaptations of animals which possess it. But this persuasion has generally occupied the position of an innocuous truism or at best a jejune postulate, rather than that of a problem requiring, or permitting, serious scientific treatment. At all events, this was formerly true.

It is not unnatural perhaps that the frequent disposition of the functional psychologist to sigh after the flesh-pots of biology should kindle the fire of those consecrated to the cause of a pure psychology and philosophy freed from the contaminating influence of natural science. As a matter of fact, alarms have been repeatedly sounded and the faithful called to subdue mutiny. But the purpose of the functional psychologist has never been, so far as I am aware, to scuttle the psychological craft for the benefit of biology. Quite the contrary. Psychology is still for a time at least to steer her own untroubled course. She is at most borrowing a well-tested compass which biology is willing to lend and she hopes by its aid to make her ports more speedily and more surely. If in use it prove treacherous and unreliable, it will of course go overboard.

This broad biological ideal of functional psychology of which we have been speaking may be phrased with a slight shift of emphasis by connecting it with the problem of discovering the fundamental utilities of consciousness. If mental process is of real value to its possessor in the life and world which we know, it must perforce be by virtue of something which it does that otherwise is not accomplished. Now life and world are complex and it seems altogether improbable that consciousness should express its utility in one and only one way. As a matter of fact, every surface indication points in the other direction. It may be possible merely as a matter of expression to speak of mind as in general contributing to organic adjustment to environment. But the actual contributions will take place in many ways and by multitudinous varieties of conscious process. The functionalist's problem then is to determine if possible the great types of these processes in so far as the utilities which they present lend themselves to classification.

The search after the various utilitarian aspects of mental process is at once suggestive and disappointing. It is on the one hand illuminating by virtue of the strong relief into which it throws the fundamental resemblances of processes often unduly severed in psychological analysis. Memory and imagination, for example, are often treated in a way designed to emphasize their divergences almost to the exclusion of their functional similarities. They are of course functionally but variants on a single and basal type of control. An austere structuralism in particular is inevitably disposed to magnify differences and in consequence under its hands mental life tends to fall apart; and when put together again it generally seems to have lost something of its verve and vivacity. It appears stiff and rigid and corpse-like. It lacks the vital spark. Functionalism tends just as inevitably to bring mental phenomena together, to show them focalized in actual vital service. The professional psychologist, calloused by long apprenticeship, may not feel this distinction to be scientifically important. But to the young student the functionalistic stress upon community of service is of immense value in clarifying the intricacies of mental organization. On the other hand the search of which we were speaking is disappointing perhaps in the paucity of the basic modes in which these conscious utilities are realized.

III

The third conception which I distinguish is often in practice merged with the second, but it involves stress upon a problem logically prior perhaps to the problem raised there and so warrants separate mention. Functional psychology, it is often alleged, is in reality a form of psychophysics. To be sure, its aims and ideals are not explicitly quantitative in the manner characteristic of that science as commonly understood. But it finds its major interest in determining the relations to one another of the physical and mental portions of the organism.

It is undoubtedly true that many of those who write under functional prepossessions are wont to introduce frequent references to the physiological processes which accompany or condition mental life. Moreover, certain followers of this faith are prone to declare forthwith that psychology is simply a branch of biology and that we are in consequence entitled, if not indeed obliged, to make use where possible of biological materials. But without committing ourselves to so extreme a position as this, a mere glance at one familiar region of psychological procedure will disclose the leanings of psychology in this direction.

The psychology of volition affords an excellent illustration of the necessity with which descriptions of mental process eventuate in physiological or biological considerations. If one take the conventional analysis of a voluntary act drawn from some one or other of the experiences of adult life, the descriptions offered generally portray ideational activities of an anticipatory and deliberative character which serve to initiate immediately or remotely certain relevant expressive movements. Without the execution of the movements the ideational performances would be as futile as the tinkling cymbals of Scripture. To be sure, many of our psychologists protest themselves wholly unable to suggest why or how such muscular movements are brought to pass. But the fact of their occurrence or of their fundamental import for any theory of mental life in which consciousness is other than an epiphenomenon, is not questioned.

Moreover, if one considers the usual accounts of the ontogenesis of human volitional acts one is again confronted with intrinsically physiological data in which reflexes, automatic and instinctive acts, are much in evidence. Whatever the possibilities, then, of an expurgated edition of the psychology of volition from which should be blotted out all reference to contaminating physiological factors, the actual practice of our representative psychologists is quite otherwise, and upon their showing volition cannot be understood either as regards its origin or its outcome without constant and overt reference to these factors. It would be a labor of supererogation to go on and make clear the same doctrine as it applies to the psychology of the more recondite of the cognitive processes; so intimate is the relation between cognition and volition in modern psychological theory that we may well stand excused from carrying out in detail the obvious inferences from the situation we have just described.

Now if someone could but devise a method for handling the mind-body relationships which would not when published immediately create cyclonic disturbances in the philosophical atmosphere, it seems improbable that this disposition of the functional psychologist to inject physiology into his cosmos would cause comment and much less criticism. But even parallelism, that most insipid, pale and passionless of all the inventions begotten by the mind of man to accomplish this end, has largely failed of its pacific purpose. It is no wonder, therefore, that the more rugged creeds with positive programs to offer and a stock of red corpuscles to invest in their propagation should also have failed of universal favor.

This disposition to go over into the physiological for certain portions of psychological doctrine is represented in an interesting way by the frequent tendency of structural psychologists to find explanation in psychology substantially equivalent to physiological explanation. Professor Titchener's recent work on *Quantitative Psychology* represents this position very frankly. It is cited here with no intent to comment disparagingly upon the consistency of the structuralist position, but simply to indicate the wide-spread feeling of necessity at certain stages of psychological development for resort to physiological considerations.

Such a functional psychology as I have been presenting would be entirely reconcilable with Miss Calkins' 'psychology of selves' (so ably set forth by her in her presidential address last year) were it not for her extreme scientific conservatism in refusing to allow the self to have a body, save as a kind of conventional biological ornament. The real psychological self, as I understand her, is pure disembodied spirit—an admirable thing of good religious and philosophic ancestry, but surely not the thing with which we actually get through this vale of tears and not a thing, before which psychology is under any obligation to kowtow.

It is not clear that the functional psychologist because of his disposition to magnify the significance in practice of the mind-body relationships is thereby committed to any special theory of the character of these relationships, save as was said a moment since, that negatively he must seemingly of necessity set his face against any epiphenomenalist view. He might conceivably be an interactionist, or a parallelist or even an advocate of some wholly outworn creed. As a matter of fact certain of our most ardent functionalists not only cherish highly definite articles of faith as regards this issue, they would even go so far as to test functional orthodoxy by the acceptance of these tenets. This is to them the most momentous part of their functionalism, their holy of holies. It would display needless temerity to attempt within the limitations of this occasion a formulation of doctrine wholly acceptable to all concerned. But I shall venture a brief reference to such doctrine in the effort to bring out certain of its essentials.

The position to which I refer regards the mind-body relation as capable of treatment in psychology as a methodological distinction rather than a metaphysically existential one. Certain of its expounders arrive at their view by means of an analysis of the genetic conditions under which the mind-body differentiation first makes itself felt in the experience of the individual. This procedure clearly involves a direct frontal attack on the problem.

Others attain the position by flank movement, emphasizing to begin with the insoluble contradictions with which one is met when the distinction is treated as resting on existential differences in the primordial elements of the cosmos. Both methods of approach lead to the same goal, however, *i.e.,* the conviction that the distinction has no existence on the genetically lower and more naif stages of experience. It only comes to light on a relatively reflective level and it must then be treated as instrumental if one would avoid paralogisms, antinomies and a host of other metaphysical nightmares. Moreover, in dealing with psychological problems this view entitles one to reject as at least temporarily irrelevant the question whether mind *causes* changes in neural action and conversely. The previous question is raised by defenders of this type of doctrine if one insists on having such a query answered. They invite you to trace the lineage of your idea of causality, insisting that such a searching of one's intellectual reins will always disclose the inappropriateness of the inquiry as formulated above. They urge further that the profitable and signif-

icant thing is to seek for a more exact appreciation of the precise conditions under which consciousness is in evidence and the conditions under which it retires in favor of the more exclusively physiological. Such knowledge so far as it can be obtained is on a level with all scientific and practical information. It states the circumstances under which certain sorts of results will appear.

One's view of this functionalistic metaphysics is almost inevitably colored by current philosophical discussion as to the essential nature of consciousness. David Hume has been accused of destroying the reality of mind chiefly because he exorcised from it relationships of various kinds. If it be urged, as has so often been done, that Hume was guilty of pouring out the baby with the bath, the modern philosopher makes good the disaster not only by pouring in again both baby and bath, but by maintaining that baby and bath, mind and relations, are substantially one. Nor is this unity secured after the manner prescribed by the good Bishop Berkeley. At all events the metaphysicians to whom I refer are not fond of being called idealists. But the psychological functionalist who emphasizes the instrumental nature of the mind-body distinction and the metaphysician who regards mind as a relation are following roads which are at least parallel to one another if not actually convergent.

Whether or not one sympathizes with the views of that wing of the functionalist party to which our attention has just been directed it certainly seems a trifle unfair to cast up the mind-body difficulty in the teeth of the functionalist as such when on logical grounds he is no more guilty than any of his psychological neighbors. No courageous psychology of volition is possible which does not squarely face the mind-body problem, and in point of fact every important description of mental life contains doctrine of one kind or another upon this matter. A literally pure psychology of volition would be a sort of hanging-garden of Babylon, marvelous but inaccessible to psychologists of terrestrial habit. The functionalist is a greater sinner than others only in so far as he finds necessary and profitable a more constant insistence upon the translation of mental process into physiological process and conversely.

IV

If we now bring together the several conceptions of which mention has been made it will be easy to show them converging upon a common point. We have to consider (1) functionalism conceived as the psychology of mental operations in contrast to the psychology of mental elements; or, expressed otherwise, the psychology of the how and why of consciousness as distinguished from the psychology of the what of consciousness. We have (2) the functionalism which deals with the problem of mind conceived as primarily engaged in mediating between the environment and the needs of the organism. This is the psychology of the fundamental utilities of consciousness; (3) and lastly we have functionalism described as psychophysical psychology, that is the psychology which constantly recognizes and insists upon the essential significance of the mind-body relationship for any just and comprehensive appreciation of mental life itself.

The second and third delineations of functional psychology are rather obviously correlated with each other. No description of the actual circumstances attending the participation of mind in the accommodatory activities of the organism could be other than a mere empty schematism without making reference to the manner in which mental processes eventuate in motor phenomena of the physiological organism. The overt accommodatory act is, I take it, always sooner or later a muscular movement. But this fact being admitted, there is nothing for it, if one will describe accommodatory processes, but to recognize the mind-body relations and in some way give expression to their practical significance. It is only in this regard, as was indicated a few lines above, that the functionalist departs a trifle in his practice and a trifle more in his theory from the rank and file of his colleagues.

The effort to follow the lead of the natural sciences and delimit somewhat rigorously—albeit artificially—a field of inquiry, in this case consciousness conceived as an independent realm, has led in psychology to a deal of excellent work and to the uncovering of much hidden truth. So far as this procedure has resulted in a focusing of scientific attention and endeavor on a relatively narrow range of problems the result has more than justified the means. And the functionalist by no means holds that the limit of profitable research has been reached along these lines. But he is disposed to urge in season and out that we must not forget the arbitrary and self-imposed nature of the boundaries within which we toil when we try to eschew all explicit reference to the physical and physiological. To overlook this fact is to substitute a psychology under injunction for a psychology under free jurisdiction. He also urges with vigor and enthusiasm that a new illumination of this preëmpted field can be gained by envisaging it more broadly, looking at it as it appears when taken in perspective with its neighboring territory. And if it be objected that such an inquiry however interesting and advantageous is at least not psychology, he can only reply; psychology is what we make it, and if the correct understanding of mental phenomena involves our delving in regions which are not at first glance properly mental, what recks it, provided only that we are nowhere guilty of untrustworthy and unverifiable procedure, and that we return loaded with the booty for which we set out, and by means of which we can the better solve our problem?

In its more basal philosophy this last conception is of course intimately allied to those appraisals of mind which emphasize its dominantly social characteristics, its rise out of social circumstances and the pervasively social nature of its constitutive principles. In our previous intimations of this standpoint we have not distinguished sharply between the physical and the social aspect of environment. The adaptive activities of mind are very largely of the distinctly social type. But this does not in any way jeopardize the genuineness of the connection upon which we have been insisting between the psychophysical aspects of a functional psychology and its environmental adaptive aspects.

It remains then to point out in what manner the conception of functionalism as concerned with the basal operations of mind is to be correlated with the other two conceptions just under discussion. The simplest view to take of the relations involved would apparently be such as would regard the first as an essential propaedeutic to the other two. Certainly if we are intent upon discerning the exact manner in which mental process contributes to accommodatory efficiency, it is natural to begin our undertaking by determining what are the primordial forms of expression peculiar to mind. However plausible in theory this conception of the intrinsic logical relations of these several forms of functional psychology, in practice it is extremely difficult wholly to sever them from one another.

Again like the biological accommodatory view the psychophysical view of functional psychology involves as a rational presupposition some acquaintance with mental processes as these appear to reflective consciousness. The intelligent correlation in a practical way of physiological and mental operations evidently involves a preliminary knowledge of the conspicuous differentiations both on the side of conscious function and on the side of physiological function.

In view of the considerations of the last few paragraphs it does not seem fanciful nor forced to urge that these various theories of the problem of functional psychology really converge upon one another, however divergent may be the introductory investigations peculiar to each of the several ideals. Possibly the conception that the fundamental problem of the functionalist is one of determining just how mind participates in accommodatory reactions, is more nearly inclusive than either of the others, and so may be chosen to stand for the group. But if this vicarious duty is assigned to it, it must be on clear terms of remembrance that the other phases of the problem are equally real and equally necessary.

Indeed the three things hang together as integral parts of a common program.

The functionalist's most intimate persuasion leads him to regard consciousness as primarily and intrinsically a control phenomenon. Just as behavior may be regarded as the most distinctly basic category of general biology in its functional phase so control would perhaps serve as the most fundamental category in functional psychology, the special forms and differentiations of consciousness simply constituting particular phases of the general process of control. At this point the omnipresent captious critic will perhaps arise to urge that the knowledge process is no more truly to be explained in terms of control than is control to be explained in terms of knowledge. Unquestionably there is from the point of view of the critic a measure of truth in this contention. The mechanism of control undoubtedly depends on the cognitive processes, to say nothing of other factors. But if one assumes the vitalistic point of view for one's more final interpretations, if one regards the furtherance of life in breadth and depth and permanence as an end in itself, and if one derives his scale of values from a contemplation of the several contributions toward this end represented by the great types of vital phenomena, with their apex in the moral, scientific and aesthetic realms, one must certainly find control a category more fundamental than the others offered by psychology. Moreover, it may be urged against the critic's attitude that even knowledge itself is built up under the control mechanism represented by selective attention and apperception. The basic character of control seems therefore hardly open to challenge.

One incidental merit of the functionalist program deserves a passing mention. This is the one method of approach to the problem with which I am acquainted that offers a reasonable and cogent account of the rise of reflective consciousness and its significance as manifested in the various philosophical disciplines. From the vantage point of the functionalist position logic and ethics, for instance, are no longer mere disconnected items in the world of mind. They take their place with all the inevitableness of organic organization in the general system of control, which requires for the expression of its immanent meaning *as psychic* a theoretical vindication of its own inner principles, its modes of procedure and their results. From any other point of view, so far as I am aware, the several divisions of philosophical inquiry sustain to one another relations which are almost purely external and accidental. To the functionalist on the other hand they are and must be in the nature of the case consanguineous and vitally connected. It is at the point, for example, where the good, the beautiful and the true have bearing on the efficacy of accommodatory activity that the issues of the normative philosophical sciences become relevant. If good action has no significance for the enriching and enlarging of life, the contention I urge is futile, and similarly as regards beauty and truth. But it is not at present usually maintained that such is the fact.

These and other similar tendencies of functionalism may serve to reassure those who fear that in lending itself to biological influences psychology may lose contact with philosophy and so sacrifice the poise and balance and sanity of outlook which philosophy undertakes to furnish. The particular brand of philosophy which is predestined to functionalist favor cannot of course be confidently predicted in advance. But anything approaching a complete and permanent divorce of psychology from philosophy is surely improbable so long as one cultivates the functionalist faith. Philosophy cannot dictate scientific method here any more than elsewhere, nor foreordain the special facts to be discovered. But as an interpreter of the psychologist's achievements she will always stand higher in the functionalist's favor than in that of his colleagues of other persuasions, for she is a more integral and significant part of his scheme of the cosmos. She may even outgrow under his tutelage that 'valiant inconclusiveness' of which the last of her long line of lay critics has just accused her.

A sketch of the kind we have offered is un-happily likely to leave on the mind an impression of functional psychology as a name for a group of genial but vaguer ambitions and good intentions. This, however, is a fault which must be charged to the artist and to the limitations of time and space under which he is here working. There is nothing vaguer in the program of the functionalist when he goes to his work than there is in the purposes of the psychologist wearing any other livery. He goes to his laboratory, for example, with just the same resolute interest to discover new facts and new relationships, with just the same determination to verify and confirm his previous observations, as does his colleague who calls himself perhaps a structuralist. But he looks out upon the surroundings of his science with a possibly greater sensitiveness to its continuity with other ranges of human interest and with certainly a more articulate purpose to see the mind which he analyzes as it actually is when engaged in the discharge of its vital functions. If his method tempts him now and then to sacrifice something of petty exactitude, he is under no obligation to yield, and in any case he has for his compensation the power which comes from breadth and sweep of outlook.

So far as he may be expected to develop methods peculiar to himself—so far, indeed, as in genetic and comparative psychology, for example, he has already developed such—they will not necessarily be iconoclastic and revolutionary, nor such as flout the methods already devised and established on a slightly different foundation. They will be distinctly complementary to all that is solid in these. Nor is it in any way essential that the term functionalism should cling to this new-old movement. It seems at present a convenient term, but there is nothing sacrosanct about it, and the moment it takes unto itself the pretense of scientific finality its doom will be sealed. It means to-day a broad and flexible and organic point of view in psychology. The moment it becomes dogmatic and narrow its spirit will have passed and undoubtedly some worthier successor will fill its place.

The Pre-Chicago Association of the Early Functionalists

Alfred C. Raphelson

It is generally agreed among those who write of its history, that American psychology made its first distinctive stand against European psychology in the form of functionalism. There may, indeed, have been individuals who differed on matters of concepts, methods or goals, but before 1900, no distinctly "American" school had emerged.

The historians often emphasize that it was no mere coincidence that this new viewpoint first appeared at the University of Chicago. They argue that the time was ripe for the emergence of a "native" psychology, and, as Roback, for example put it:

> ...It was only fit that such should spring up in a region of comparatively recent settlement and far inland.... About half way from each coast and therefore relatively free from foreign influences... the University of Chicago... was a brand new university, founded only the same year Titchener... arrived in America. To this day, this University represents American initiative and enterprise rather than tradition and dignity.... If the location is typically American, with its bustling packing houses, political machines, etc., the particular brand of psychology which would issue, therefore, would be expected to correspond to the American genius which is characterized by action, utility and practicality?...[1]

The story is then detailed how John Dewey (1859–1952) was invited to come to Chicago in 1894 as the Chairman of the Department of Philosophy, how he found James H. Tufts (1862–1942) already there and interested in psychological topics. Within a year George H. Mead (1863–1931) and James R. Angell (1867–1949) arrived, the latter to take charge of the psycholog-

Raphelson, A. C. (1973). The pre-Chicago association of the early functionalists. *Journal of the History of the Behavioral Sciences, 9,* 115–122. Copyright © 1973 by the Clinical Psychology Publishing Company. Reprinted by permission of the publisher

ical laboratory. These men brought to Chicago backgrounds in philosophy, the new psychology of Germany as well as interests in ethics, education, sociology and political science. Furthermore, they were unusually effective teachers. Largely because of their combined effect, the University of Chicago emerged as a flourishing center of psychological activity that in a few years appeared to take a form that justifiably could be called a "school of thought."

One need not quarrel with the above facts to point out, however, that though functional psychology did develop at Chicago as a set of ideas, it was not mere "fate" that determined that its originators happened to appear on the staff of that new university. Another way of looking at the history of any set of ideas is to consider, in addition to the immediate circumstance of its creation, how it happened that at a certain place and point in time, a particular group of men with particular interests and experiences happened to become joined in a fertile intellectual enterprise.[2] This social-psychological approach is often neglected in detailing the history of new ideas and their innovators. In the case of these early functionalists, their association clearly preceded their meeting at Chicago and reflected the influences of the specific character of philosophy and psychology as it was taught at Johns Hopkins University and the University of Michigan.

In the late 1870's the newly-organized Johns Hopkins University was seeking someone to add to its philosophy staff. The Trustees, after looking in vain toward Europe, invited three Americans to lecture in Baltimore in alternative semesters. The invitations went to Charles S. Peirce (1839–1914), G. Stanley Hall (1844–1924) and George S. Morris (1840–1889). Three more diverse thinkers and personalities could hardly have been found.[3]

The backgrounds of Peirce and Hall are well

known. It will be useful, however, to briefly consider their diversity to set in perspective the intellectual environment created at Johns Hopkins by their overlapping presence with Morris. Peirce had been recommended by William James who had been first offered the position but had turned it down after considering it favorably for some time. Peirce had lectured on several occasions at Harvard and had had, of course, a great influence on James. He was well inclined toward mathematics and the natural sciences. However, Peirce's personality showed a strong trend toward emotional instability which was expressed in a quarrelsomeness that had precluded his receiving a permanent academic post. As a matter of fact, he had been employed since 1859 by the United States Coast Survey and kept that position during his part-time lectureship at Johns Hopkins.

G. Stanley Hall had been educated at Williams College and the Union Theological Seminary but had discovered he was not made to be a minister. He then became interested in the "new" psychology being offered by Wundt and was about to leave for Leipzig when he was offered a part-time position teaching English at Harvard. While there he was able to carry out graduate work with James and earned what is usually considered the first American doctorate in psychology in 1878. Hall then went to Germany where he absorbed the new work going on in physiology as well as in Wundt's laboratory in Leipzig. After returning to America, he received the call from Johns Hopkins to offer a series of lectures on the new experimental psychology.

Morris had also studied at the Union Theological Seminary but had decided upon a career in philosophy rather than the ministry. He studied further in Germany for several years becoming greatly influenced by German Idealism—especially Hegel, Kant, and Schilling. Although he did not earn a doctoral degree, his articles and translations earned him a good reputation as a philosopher. In 1870 Morris accepted a position as head of the Department of Modern Languages and Literature at the University of Michigan... this despite his reputation as a philosopher.[4]

Morris was the first of the three to arrive on the Hopkins scene. During the spring term of 1878, he gave twenty lectures on the history of philosophy. The next spring he returned to give ten lectures on historical and practical ethics. In 1881, he was then offered a three year appointment as a lecturer on the condition that he would remain at Johns Hopkins at least one semester a year. He was to alternate with Peirce who would lecture on logic and Hall who would offer work in the new German physiological psychology.

The Johns Hopkins University, in the 1880's, was an institute offering only advanced study, so the three lecturers were guaranteed a good group of students. As a matter of fact, the particular group they were to meet in the philosophy courses included a number who would become quite successful members of the American academic scene. Among them were Joseph Jastrow, James McKeen Cattell, H. H. Donaldson, E. C. Sanford, Fred M. Taylor, and John Dewey.

Morris, although perceived by the Hopkins community as being intelligent, accessible and cooperative, was not comfortable with the philosophical climate that was being created there. Being a Hegelian idealist with a strong religious interest, Morris did not fit in with "the exaggerated scientism" he found. The students were well-informed about the physiological and experimental side of psychology Hall presented and were impressed with this orientation. Hall had also set up a small laboratory which enabled the students to experience first hand the new methods. Peirce's lectures strongly reinforced Hall's presentations. Morris, on the other hand, saw philosophy's function in the curriculum as acting as a "liberalizing agency...preventing the... narrowing tendencies of extreme specialism... and to serve the public aim of the University by producing leaders capable of recognizing the true ideals and intelligently directing the nation's energies to their accomplishment."[5] He was not convinced that an empirical psychology had a claim to be called philosophy. But Morris' views, perhaps due to his less forceful style and personality, could not hold their own in face of the combined empirical and pragmatic orientations of Hall and Peirce.

In 1884, the Johns Hopkins trustees ended the part-time lecturer arrangement by appointing Hall professor of Psychology and Pedagogy. At Michigan, the chairmanship of the Department of Philosophy had become vacant and it was offered to Morris. Morris accepted it and immediately wrote to one of his most brilliant students at Hopkins to offer him an instructorship at a salary of $900. John Dewey accepted the position and together they proceeded to change the orientation and scope of the instruction of both philosophy and psychology at Michigan.[6]

It was not altogether surprising that Dewey accepted Morris' offer. He had been greatly influenced by his work with Morris. The experience had led the young man into German Idealism, and despite his later deviation, had left a very definite mark on his thought. Dewey himself once remarked that regardless of their differences, he would be happy to believe that Morris' teaching had an enduring influence on him.[7]

But Dewey was also greatly impressed with Hall's arguments that while psychology and philosophy were closely related, psychology had to be worked out on the basis of the new experimental approach that he had observed at Leipzig and Berlin. Experiment would replace the older idealistic and rational approaches to the questions raised by the mental philosophers. At Michigan Dewey devoted his full energies to developing this new approach.[8]

During his first term (1884–1885) Dewey offered a course in Empirical Psychology using Sully's *Outline of Psychology* (1884), Special Topics (Physiological, Comparative, and Morbid Psychology), and a third course covering special topics in psychology and philosophy with reference to the history of philosophy in Great Britain. In subsequent terms he introduced courses in experimental, speculative and historical psy-

chology. Sully's text was soon replaced with a printed syllabus which was his own digest of the new field. This work, published in 1887 under the title, *Psychology,* was Dewey's first book and became the standard text at Michigan for the next ten years.[9]

It is, in many ways, a curious book which attempts to integrate the older idealistic epistemology with the new empirical development in psychological research. The twenty-six year old Dewey was groping and in this book is discovered straddling the two positions. Introspection is the preferred method. The works of Helmholtz, Hering, Wundt, Volkmann and Stumpf are all cited. Sensation is stressed, reaction patterns are described and the concept of habit is extensively employed. There are discussions of other adaptive mechanisms (e.g. will, feeling, intuition) which became important features of the functional psychology that was still a dozen years away. For these reasons perhaps Brett was correct when he described the text as "the first grey dawn of that tomorrow for which the psychology of the American colleges was waiting."[10]

It was only a "first" dawn, however, for the text fell back on an older metaphysics to support the new science. This strange mixture gave the book an uncomfortably disorganized appearance. Mind, for example, is denied existence as an entity but is mentioned as "causing attention." The units of mental life had to be accounted for and Dewey saw no other way except to evoke the activity of the self defined somewhat vaguely as "the activity of synthesis upon sensation." Sensation itself is the "elementary consciousness which arises from the reaction of the soul upon a nervous impulse conducted to the brain from the affection of some sensory nerve-ending by a physical stimulus." Every "concrete act of knowledge involves an intuition of God for it involves a unity of the real and the ideal, of the objective and the subjective."[11]

It was not until Dewey read James' *Principles of Psychology* (1890) that he was helped from the fence on which he perched with his text. So certain was James in his endorsement of the empirically-oriented new psychology, that Dewey felt encouraged to abandon the idealistic psychology completely in favor of a more empirical and objective functionalism. This was, of course, more clearly expressed in 1896, in his landmark paper, "The Reflex Arc Concept in Psychology."[12]

In 1888 Dewey accepted a position at the University of Minnesota. His association with Michigan, however, was only interrupted by this appointment. During a spring vacation in 1889, Morris, who had gone camping, caught pneumonia and died. Dewey was immediately recalled and made head of the department of philosophy. He remained at Michigan for five years and began to devote more of his attention to philosophy and his growing interest in education.[13]

At Michigan Dewey found ample stimulation for his new interest in education. It had one of the earliest chairs in education in this country. A regular program of statewide high school visitations by faculty members had been established and Dewey made many trips to determine the preparation given college-bound students. As an early member of the Schoolmaster Club, he cooperated in bringing secondary and higher educational practices together. These experiences led him to study the educative process from the standpoint of psychology. He frequently spoke throughout the state at teachers' meetings on such topics as attention, memory, imagination, habit and thinking and their relation to teaching and learning. In his *Applied Psychology* (1889), written with J. A. McLellan of the University of Toronto, he presented these concepts in a practical manner that appeared appropriate to the problems of education.[14]

Dewey, as head of the department, did not neglect the psychological tradition he had begun. Though no longer interested in teaching these subjects, he did bring in competent people to handle their instruction. He immediately engaged James H. Tufts (1862–1942) to offer the psychology courses. Tufts was not specifically trained in psychology and was, as a matter of fact, to

make his reputation in philosophy through his translation of Windleband's influential *History of Philosophy* (1893). Originally a New Englander, Tufts completed his undergraduate work at Amherst (A.B. 1884) and Yale (B.D. 1889) and later (1892) took a doctorate at Freiberg. During the two years he was in Ann Arbor, Tufts formed a deep personal and intellectual friendship with Dewey that lasted throughout their lives.[15]

During the academic years 1889–90 and 1890–91 Tufts offered the courses in general and physiological psychology. At that time there were only eight psychology laboratories established in America. In 1890 Dewey encouraged Tufts to establish one at Michigan. He managed to collect some pieces of equipment and set them up on the top floor of the old medical building. Three hours a week were devoted to elementary studies of reaction time, color, Weber's Law, and physiological exercises. One of the students enrolled in this laboratory course was James R. Angell, son of the University's president.[16]

Angell received his undergraduate and masters training at Michigan, electing most of his work in the philosophy department. His first psychology was gained from reading Dewey's text. He also took ethics, aesthetics, metaphysics and Hegel's logic under Dewey and history of philosophy under Tufts. In his autobiographical sketch, Angell writes

> ...most rewarding of all in the year following my graduation, which I spent as a graduate student at Michigan, a seminar with Dewey in William James' freshly published *Principles of Psychology*. The book unquestionably affected my thinking for the next 20 years more profoundly than any other.... During this period, I greatly increased my obligations to Dewey and to Tufts, both later my colleagues for many years at the University of Chicago. For my intellectual awakening, for many basic elements in my subsequent habits of thought, and for endless kind and helpful acts in later years, I am under the deepest obligation to John Dewey, whose simplicity of character, originality, and virility of mind, brought him the unqualified affection, admiration, and devotion of thousands of students....[17]

On Dewey's recommendation, Angell left Michigan in 1891 to study at the Harvard Graduate School under William James, Josiah Royce, and George Herbert Palmer. He also undertook more intense laboratory work in the one that James had set up but had turned over to Hugo Münsterberg.[18]

In 1891 Tufts left Michigan for a position as assistant professor of philosophy at the newly established University of Chicago. It was necessary for Dewey to replace him with two instructors in order to handle the increasing number of students enrolled in philosophy and psychology. One instructor was engaged to handle the psychology offerings and the other to handle the philosophy courses. George H. Mead (1863–1931) was brought in for the psychology part.[19]

Mead had been reared in the orthodox tradition of his minister father who had himself descended from a long line of Puritan clergymen. As a young man, however, Mead had been sufficiently influenced by contemporary naturalistic thought to have succeeded in refuting the dogma of the church to his own satisfaction. After completing his undergraduate work he matriculated at Harvard, where he studied under James and Royce and also served as tutor for the James children for over a year. In the fall of 1888 he went to Germany to study at Leipzig and Berlin. While at Leipzig Mead met G. Stanley Hall, who convinced the young man (as he had Dewey and others at John Hopkins) that physiological psychology was the direction in which he should move. Mead soon came to see that he should make a specialty of this area,

> ...because in America...poor, bated, unhappy Christianity, trembling for its life, claps the gag into the mouth of Free Thought and says, "Hush, hush, not a word or nobody will believe in me any more. He (Mead) thinks it will be hard for him to get a chance to utter any ultimate philosophical opinions savouring of independence. In physiological psychology, on the other hand, he has a harmless territory in which he can work quietly without drawing down upon himself the anathema and excommunication of all-patent Evangelicanism...."[20]

Mead was ready and willing, therefore, to accept Dewey's offer to give the work in physiological psychology. A single-unit room was obtained where Mead carried out laboratory instruction for three years. Dewey was quite enthusiastic about this work and informed the students that all introspective psychology had come to an end. The "new psychology" was what Mead was offering. One student, recalling the experience years later, remembered only the tedious routine of dissecting frogs. Tradition has associated only one "empirical" outcome with Mead's laboratory. While preparing and shellacking a brain, Mead allowed it to catch fire, which in turn, spread to the laboratory walls before being brought under control.[21]

In 1894, the University of Chicago, at the urging of Tufts, approached Dewey with an offer of the chairmanship of the Department of Philosophy. One of the main reasons that Dewey accepted the offer was that work in pedagogy and psychology were included in the department. Thus, the assignment was compatible with all three of the major interests he had developed at Michigan. In addition, he would be able to renew his relationship with Tufts. Mead agreed to move to Chicago with Dewey.[22]

The next year Dewey called Angell to Chicago to direct the psychology laboratory. After leaving Harvard, Angell had gone to Europe intending to study with Wundt at Leipzig. Wundt's laboratory, however, was filled so he went to Berlin to work with Paulsen, Ebbinghaus and Helmholtz and later to Halle to work with Erdmann in psychology and Vaihinger in philosophy. Before completing his doctorate, he accepted a position at the University of Minnesota, where he taught the elementary psychology courses and set up a modest laboratory. Angell was at Minnesota when he received the offer from Dewey at Chicago. Though the officials at Minnesota urged him to stay, he could not resist the opportunity to have as colleagues men like Dewey, Tufts and Mead, the men who had inspired him so at Michigan. It was a decision that he never had cause to regret.[23]

In this manner, then, the four men who formed the main nucleus of the Chicago school of functionalism came to be together. Dewey's article, "The Reflex Arc Concept in Psychology," that first stated the main thesis of functionalism was published two years (1896) after the four were joined as a group at Chicago.

Ben-David and Collins, in their study of social factors in the origins of a new science, have argued that "ideas are not self-generating, and even if potentially fertile, have to be carried from person to person and implanted in some special way in order to give rise to new generation."[24] The necessary ideas for the development of a new scientific prescription or paradigm are usually available over a relatively prolonged time period and in several places. Since only a few of these potential beginnings eventually lead to further growth, it can be argued that fruition occurs only where and when individuals become involved with a new idea not only as intellectual content but as a means of establishing a new intellectual identity that redefines an entire problem area.[25]

The point of view, then, that developed at Chicago can be better understood if one takes into account the intellectual experiences Dewey had at Johns Hopkins and their subsequent development at Michigan. The empiricism of Hall and the pragmatism of Pierce were worked through to supplant the idealism of Morris that initially attracted him. His involvement in questions of statewide education reinforced Dewey's growing sense of the importance of the role played by mental processes in adaptation. At Michigan he found the vital support he needed from a group of young and stimulating colleagues and students. A new intellectual context began to form and the group gave it the social reinforcement it needed to take on a new identity.

Chicago provided the fertile intellectual climate that was needed to bring to fruition this new thought. A new institution, it was founded upon enthusiasm for, as well as a vision of, a new kind of American intellectual environment. This spirit encouraged the innovative thinking of this group of men who had a past association of proven mutual stimulation and commonality of ideas. They looked to Chicago as an opportunity to continue their association in hopes that it would be satisfying to them and fruitful for American scholarship. Chicago did not fail them nor they Chicago. The results of their association, which drew heavily upon their past collaboration, gave very quickly that university an illustrious beginning as it also gave American psychology a history of its own.

NOTES

1 Roback, A. A., *History of American Psychology,* rev. ed (New York: Collier Books, 1964) p. 238.
2 See for example, Ben-David, Joseph and Collins, Randall, "Social Factors in the Origins of a New Science: The Case of Psychology," *Amer. Sociol. Rev.,* 1966, 51, 451–464.
3 Hawkins, Hugh, *Pioneer: A History of the Johns Hopkins University, 1874–1889* (Ithaca, New York: Cornell University Press, 1960) pp. 187–210. All references to the Johns Hopkins University experiences of Morris, Hall and Peirce are taken from these pages.
4 Hinsdale, Burke A., *History of the University of Michigan,* Isaac N. Demmon (ed.) (Ann Arbor, Mich.: 1906) p. 245.
5 Hawkins, op. cit., p. 199.
6 Parker, Dewitt H. and Vibbert, Charles B., "The Department of Philosophy," in *The University of Michigan: An Encyclopedic Survey,* v. II, W. B. Shaw (ed.) (Ann Arbor: University of Michigan Press, 1944) pp. 672–73; Dewey, Jane, "Biography of John Dewey," in Paul A. Schlipp (ed.) *The Philosophy of John Dewey,* (New York: Tudor Publishing Co., 1951) p. 19.
7 Dewey, Jane, op. cit., pp. 18–19; Hawkins, op. cit., pp. 269–270.
8 Ibid.
9 Parker and Vibbert, op. cit., p. 673.
10 Roback, op. cit., pp. 115–118; Allport, Gordon W., "Dewey's Individual and Social Psychology," in P. A. Schlipp (ed.) *Philosophy of John Dewey,* op. cit., pp. 266–267.
11 Pillsbury, Walter B., "John Dewey, 1859–1952," *Nat. Acad. Sci. Bio. Mem.,* 1957, 30, 113.

12 Allport, op. cit., p. 267.
13 Parker and Vibbert, op. cit., pp. 673–674.
14 Ibid; Dewey, Jane, op. cit., pp. 26–27.
15 Dewey, Jane, op. cit., p. 24; *Calendar, University of Michigan,* Ann Arbor, Michigan, 1884–1892.
16 Pillsbury, Walter B., "The Department of Psychology" in *The University of Michigan: An Encyclopedic Survey,* v. II, W. B. Shaw (ed.) (Ann Arbor: University of Michigan Press, 1940) p. 709; Morris, Amos R., "Machines Aid in the Teaching of English," *Mich. Alum.,* 1929, 35, 322.
17 Angell, James R., "Autobiographical Sketch" in *A History of Psychology in Autobiography,* C. Murchinson (ed.) (New York: Russell and Russell, 1961) pp. 5–6.
18 Ibid., pp. 6–7.
19 Pillsbury, W. B., "The Department of Psycholo-

gy," op. cit., p. 709; Parker and Vibbert, op. cit., p. 674; Dewey, Jane, op. cit., p. 25.
20 Letter from Henry Northrup Castle, dated February, 1889, Leipzig, Germany, quoted in Wallace, David, "Reflections on the Education of George Herbert Mead," *Amer. Jour. Sociol.,* 1967, 72, 406.
21 Lamont, Corliss (ed.) *Dialogue on John Dewey* (New York: Horizon Press, 1954) pp. 19–20; Pillsbury, "The Department of Psychology," op. cit., pp. 709–710.
22 Dewey, Jane, op. cit., p. 27; Pillsbury, "The Department of Psychology," op. cit., p. 710.
23 Angell, op. cit., pp. 10–12; Pillsbury, "The Department of Psychology," op. cit., p. 710.
24 Ben-David and Collins, op. cit., p. 452.
25 Ibid.

Functionalism, Darwinism, and the Psychology of Women: A Study in Social Myth

Stephanie A. Shields

The psychology of women is acquiring the character of an academic entity as witnessed by the proliferation of research on sex differences, the appearance of textbooks devoted to the psychology of women, and the formation of a separate APA division, Psychology of Women. Nevertheless, there is almost universal ignorance of the psychology of women as it existed prior to its incorporation into psychoanalytic theory. If the maxim "A nation without a history is like a man without a memory" can be applied, then it would behoove the amnesiacs interested in female psychology to investigate its pre-Freudian past.

This article focuses on one period of that past (from the latter half of the 19th century to the first third of the 20th) in order to clarify the important issues of the time and trace their development to the position they occupy in current psy-

Adapted from Shields, S. A. (1975). Functionalism, Darwinism, and the psychology of women: A study in social myth. *American Psychologist, 30,* 739–754. Copyright © 1975 by the American Psychological Association. Adapted and reprinted by permission of the publisher and the author.

chological theory. Even a limited overview leads the reader to appreciate Helen Thompson Woolley's (1910) early appraisal of the quality of the research on sex differences:

> There is perhaps no field aspiring to be scientific where flagrant personal bias, logic martyred in the cause of supporting a prejudice, unfounded assertions, and even sentimental rot and drivel, have run riot to such an extent as here. (p. 340)

THE FUNCTIONALIST MILIEU

Although the nature of woman had been an academic and social concern of philosopher psychologists throughout the ages, formal psychology (its inception usually dated 1879) was relatively slow to take up the topic of female psychology. The "woman question" was a social one, and social problems did not fall within the sharply defined limits of Wundt's "new" psychology. The business of psychology was the description of the "generalized adult mind," and it is not at all clear whether "adult" was meant to include both sexes. When the students of German psychology did venture outside of the laboratory, however, there is no evidence that they were sympathetic to those defending the equality of male and female ability (cf. Wundt, 1901).

It was the functionalist movement in the United States that fostered academic psychology's study of sex differences and, by extension, a prototypic psychology of women. The incorporation of evolutionary theory into the practice of psychology made the study of the female legitimate, if not imperative. It would be incorrect to assume that the psychology of women existed as a separate specialty within the discipline. The female was discussed only in relation to the male, and the function of the female was thought to be distinctly different from and complementary to the function of the male. The leitmotiv of evolutionary theory as it came to be applied to the social sciences was the evolutionary supremacy of the Caucasian male. The notion of the supplementary, subordinate role of the female was ancillary to the development of that theme.

The influence of evolutionary theory on the psychology of women can be traced along two major conceptual lines: (a) by emphasizing the biological foundations of temperament, evolutionary theory led to serious academic discussion of maternal instinct (as one facet of the general topic of instinct); and (b) by providing a theoretical justification of the study of individual differences, evolutionary theory opened the door to the study of sex differences in sensory, motor, and intellectual abilities. As a whole, the concept of evolution with its concomitant emphasis on biological determinism provided ample "scientific" reason for cataloging the "innate" differences in male and female nature.

This article examines three topics that were of special significance to the psychology of women during the functionalist era: (a) structural differences in the brains of males and females and the implications of these differences for intelli-

gence and temperament, (b) the hypothesis of greater male variability and its relation to social and educational issues, and (c) maternal instinct and its meaning for a psychology of female "nature." As the functionalist paradigm gave way to behaviorism and psychoanalytic theory, the definition and "meaning" of each of these issues changed to fit the times. When issues faded in importance, it was not because they were resolved but because they ceased to serve as viable scientific "myths" in the changing social and scientific milieu. As the times change, so must the myths change.

THE FEMALE BRAIN

The topic of female intelligence came to 19th-century psychology via phrenology and the neuroanatomists. Philosophers of the time (e.g., Hegel, Kant, Schopenhauer) had demonstrated, to their satisfaction, the justice of woman's subordinate social position, and it was left to the men of science to discover the particular physiological determinants of female inadequacy. In earlier periods, woman's inferiority had been defined as a general "state" intimately related to the absence of qualities that would have rendered her a male and to the presence of reproductive equipment that destined her to be female. For centuries the mode of Eve's creation and her greater guilt for the fall from grace had been credited as the cause of woman's imperfect nature, but this was not an adequate explanation in a scientific age. Thus, science sought explanations for female inferiority that were more in keeping with contemporary scientific philosophy.

Although it had long been believed that the brain was the chief organ of the mind, the comparison of male and female mental powers traditionally included only allusions to vague "imperfections" of the female brain. More precise definition of the sites of these imperfections awaited the advancement of the concept of cortical localization of function. Then, as finer distinctions of functional areas were noted, there was a parallel recognition of the differences between those sites as they appeared in each sex.

At the beginning of the 19th century, the slowly increasing interest in the cerebral gyri rapidly gathered momentum with the popularization of phrenology. Introduced by Franz Joseph Gall, "cranioscopy," as he preferred to call it, postulated that the seat of various mental and moral faculties was located in specific areas of the brain's surface such that a surfeit or deficiency could be detected by an external examination of the cranium. Phrenology provided the first objective method for determining the neurological foundation of sex differences in intelligence and temperament that had long been promulgated. Once investigation of brain structure had begun, it was fully anticipated that visible sex differences would be found: Did not the difference between the sexes pervade every other aspect of physique and physiological function? Because physical differences were so obvious in every other organ of the body, it was unthinkable that the brain could have escaped the stamp of sex.

Gall was convinced that he could, from gross anatomical observation, discriminate between male and female brains, claiming that "if there had been presented to him in water, the fresh brains of two adult animals of any species, one male and the other female, he could have distinguished the two sexes" (Walker, 1850, p. 317). Gall's student and colleague, Johann Spurzheim, elaborated on this basic distinction by noting that the frontal lobes were less developed in females, "the organs of the perceptive faculties being commonly larger than those of the reflective powers." Gall also observed sex differences in the nervous tissue itself, "confirming" Malebranche's belief that the female "cerebral fibre" is softer than that of the male, and that it is also "slender and long rather than thick" (Walker, 1850, p. 318). Spurzheim also listed the cerebral "organs" whose appearance differed commonly in males and females: females tended to have the areas devoted to philoprogenetiveness and other "tender" traits most prominent, while in males,

areas of aggressiveness and constructiveness dominated. Even though cranioscopy did not survive as a valid system of describing cortical function, the practice of comparing the appearance of all or part of the brain for anatomical evidence of quality of function remained one of the most popular means of providing proof of female mental inferiority. Most comparisons used adult human brains, but with the rise of evolutionary theory, increasing emphasis was placed on the value of developmental and cross-species comparisons. The argument for female mental inferiority took two forms: some argued that quality of intellect was proportional to absolute or relative brain size; others, more in the tradition of cortical localization, contended that the presence of certain mental qualities was dependent upon the development of corresponding brain centers.

The measurement of cranial capacity had long been in vogue as one method of determining intellectual ability. That women had smaller heads than men was taken by some as clear proof of a real disparity between male and female intelligence. The consistently smaller brain size of the female was cited as another anatomical indicator of its functional inferiority. More brain necessarily meant better brain; the exception only proved this rule. Alexander Bain (1875) was among those who believed that the smaller absolute brain size of females accounted for a lesser mental ability. George Romanes (1887) enumerated the "secondary sex characteristics" of mental abilities attributable to brain size. The smaller brain of women was directly responsible for their mental inferiority, which "displays itself most conspiciously in a comparative absence of originality, and this more especially in the higher levels of intellectual work" (p. 655). He, like many, allowed that women were to some degree compensated for intellectual inferiority by a superiority of instinct and perceptual ability. These advantages carried with them the germ of female failure, however, by making women more subject to emotionality.

Proof of the male's absolute brain-size superiority was not enough to secure his position of intellectual superiority, since greater height and weight tended to offset the brain-size advantage. Reams of paper were, therefore, dedicated to the search for the most "appropriate" relative measures, but results were equivocal: if the ratio of brain weight to body weight is considered, it is found that women possess a proportionately larger brain than men; if the ratio of brain surface to body surface is computed, it is found to favor men. That some of the ratios "favored" males while others "favored" females led some canny souls to conclude that there was no legitimate solution to the problem. That they had ever hoped for a solution seems remarkable; estimates of brain size from cranial capacity involve a large margin of error because brains differing as much as 15 percent have been found in heads of the same size (Elliott, 1969, p. 316).

Hughlings Jackson has been credited as the first to regard the frontal cortex as the repository of the highest mental capacities, but the notion must have held popular credence as early as the 1850s because that period saw sporadic references to the comparative development of the frontal lobes in men and women. Once the function of the frontal lobes had been established, many researchers reported finding that the male possessed noticeably larger and more well-developed frontal lobes than females. The neuroanatomist Hischke came to the conclusion in 1854 that woman is *homo parietalis* while man is *homo frontalis* (Ellis, 1934). Likewise, Rudinger in 1877 found the frontal lobes of man in every way more extensive than those of women, and reported that these sex differences were evident even in the unborn fetus (Mobius, 1901).

At the turn of the century, the parietal lobes (rather than the frontal lobes) came to be regarded by some as the seat of intellect, and the necessary sex difference in parietal development was duly corroborated by the neuroanatomists. The change in cerebral hierarchy involved a bit of revisionism:

the frontal region is not, as has been supposed smaller in woman, but rather larger relatively.... But the parietal lobe is somewhat smaller, [furthermore,] a preponderance of the frontal region does not imply intellectual superiority...the parietal region is really the more important. (Patrick, 1895, p. 212)

Once beliefs regarding the relative importance of the frontal and parietal lobes had shifted, it became critical to reestablish congruence between neuroanatomical findings and accepted sex differences. Among those finding parietal predominance in men were Paul Broca, Theodore Meynert, and the German Rudinger (see Ellis, 1934, p. 217).

Other neuroanatomical "deficiencies" of the female were found in (a) the area of the corpus callosum, (b) the complexity of the gyri and sulci, (c) the conformation of gyri and sulci, and (d) the rate of development of the cortex of the fetus (Woolley, 1910, p. 335). Franklin Mall (1909) objected to the use of faulty research methods that gave spurious differences the appearance of being real. Among the most serious errors he noted was the practice of making observations with a knowledge of the sex of the brain under consideration.

The debate concerning the importance of brain size and anatomy as indicators of intelligence diminished somewhat with the development of mental tests; nevertheless, the brain-size difference was a phenomenon that many felt obligated to interpret. Max Meyer (1921) attempted to settle the matter by examining the various measures of relative difference that had been employed. After finding these methods far too equivocal, he concluded, in the best behavioristic terms, that sex differences in intelligence were simply "accidents of habits acquired."

Characteristics of the female brain were thought not simply to render women less intelligent but also to allow more "primitive" parts of human nature to be expressed in her personality. Instinct was thought to dominate woman, as did her emotions, and the resulting "affectability" was considered woman's greatest weakness, the reason for her inevitable failure. Affectability was typically defined as a general state, the manifestation of instinctive and emotional predispositions that in men were kept in check by a superior intellect.

One of the most virulent critics of woman was the German physiologist Paul Mobius (1901), who argued that her mental incapacity was a necessary condition for the survival of the race. Instinct rendered her easily led and easily pleased, so much the better for her to give her all to bearing and rearing children. The dependence of woman also extracted a high price from man:

> All progress is due to man. Therefore the woman is like a dead weight on him, she prevents much restlessness and meddlesome inquisitiveness, but she also restrains him from noble actions, for she is unable to distinguish good from evil. (p. 629)

Mobius observed that woman was essentially unable to think independently, had strong inclinations to be mean and untrustworthy, and spent a good deal of her time in an emotionally unbalanced state. From this he was forced to conclude that: "If woman was not physically and mentally weak, if she was not as a rule rendered harmless by circumstances, she would be extremely dangerous" (Mobius, 1901, p. 630). Diatribes of this nature were relatively common German importations; woman's severest critics in this country seldom achieved a similar level of acerbity. Mobius and his ilk (e.g., Weininger, 1906) were highly publicized and widely read in the United States, and not a little of their vituperation crept into serious scientific discussions of woman's nature. For example, Porteus and Babcock (1926) resurrected the brain-size issue, discounting the importance of size to intelligence and instead associating it with the "maturing of other powers." Males, because of their larger brains, would be more highly endowed with these "other powers," and so more competent and achieving. Proposals such as these, which were less obviously biased than those of Mobius, Weininger, and others, fit more easily into the current social value system and so were more easily assimilated as "good science" (cf. Allen, 1927, p. 294).

THE VARIABILITY HYPOTHESIS

The first systematic treatment of individual differences in intelligence appeared in 1575. Juan Huarte attributed sex differences in intelligence to the different humoral qualities that characterized each sex, a notion that had been popular in Western thought since ancient Greece. Heat and dryness were characteristic of the male principle, while moisture and coolness were female attributes. Because dryness of spirit was necessary for intelligence, males naturally possessed greater "wit." The maintenance of dryness and heat was the function of the testicles, and Huarte (1959) noted that if a man were castrated the effects were the same "as if he had received some notable dammage in his very braine" (p. 279). Because the principles necessary for cleverness were only possessed by males, it behooved parents to conduct their life-style, diet, and sexual intercourse in such a manner as to insure the conception of a male. The humoral theory of sex differences was widely accepted through the 17th century, but with the advent of more sophisticated notions of anatomy and physiology, it was replaced by other, more specific, theories of female mental defect: the lesser size and hypothesized simpleness of the female brain, affectability as the source of inferiority, and complementarity of abilities in male and female. It was the developing evolutionary theory that provided an overall explanation for why these sex differences existed and why they were necessary for the survival of the race.

The theory of evolution as proposed by Darwin had little to say regarding the intellectual capacity of either sex. It was in Francis Galton's (Charles Darwin's cousin) anthropometric laboratory that the investigation of intellectual differences took an empirical form (Galton, 1907). The major conclusion to come from Galton's research was that women tend in all their capacities to be inferior to men. He looked to common experience for confirmation, reasoning that:

> If the sensitivity of women were superior to that of men, the self interest of merchants would lead to their being always employed; but as the reverse is the case, the opposite supposition is likely to be the true one. (pp. 20–21)

This form of logic—women have not excelled, therefore they cannot excel—was often used to support arguments denigrating female intellectual ability. The fact of the comparative rarity of female social achievement was also used as "evidence" in what was later to become a widely debated issue concerning the range of female ability.

Prior to the formulation of evolutionary theory, there had been little concern with whether deviation from the average or "normal" occurred more frequently in either sex. One of the first serious discussions of the topic appeared in the early 19th century when the anatomist Meckel concluded on pathological grounds that the human female showed greater variability than the human male. He reasoned that because man is the superior animal and variability a sign of inferiority, this conclusion was justified (in Ellis, 1903, p. 237). The matter was left at that until 1871. At that time Darwin took up the question of variability in *The Descent of Man* while attempting to explain how it could be that in many species males had developed greatly modified secondary sexual characteristics while females of the same species had not. He determined that this was originally caused by the males' greater activity and "stronger passions" that were in turn more likely (he believed) to be transmitted to male offspring. Because the females would prefer to mate with the strong and passionate, sexual selection would insure the survival of those traits. A tendency toward greater variation per se was not thought to be responsible for the

appearance of unusual characteristics, but "development of such characters would be much aided, if the males were more liable to vary than the females" (Darwin, 1922, p. 344). To support this hypothesis of greater male variability, he cited recent data obtained by anatomists and biologists that seemed to confirm the relatively more frequent occurrence of physical anomaly among males.

Because variation from the norm was already accepted as the mechanism of evolutionary progress (survival and transmission of adaptive variations) and because it seemed that the male was the more variable sex, it soon was universally concluded that the male is the progressive element in the species. Variation for its own sake took on a positive value because greatness, whether of an individual or a society, could not be achieved without variation. Once deviation from the norm became legitimized by evolutionary theory, the hypothesis of greater male variability became a convenient explanation for a number of observed sex differences, among them the greater frequency with which men achieved "eminence." By the 1890s it was popularly believed that greater male variability was a principle that held true, not only for physical traits but for mental abilities as well:

> That men should have greater cerebral variability and therefore more originality, while women have greater stability and therefore more "common sense," are facts both consistent with the general theory of sex and verifiable in common experience. (Geddes & Thomson, 1890, p. 271)

Havelock Ellis (1894), an influential sexologist and social philosopher, brought the variability hypothesis to the attention of psychologists in the first edition of *Man and Woman*. After examining anatomical and pathological data that indicated a greater male *variational tendency* (Ellis felt this term was less ambiguous than *variability*), he examined the evidence germane to a discussion of range of intellectual ability. After noting that there were more men than women in homes for the mentally deficient, which indicated a higher incidence of retardation among males, and that there were more men than women on the roles of the eminent, which indicated a higher incidence of genius among males, he concluded that greater male variability probably held for all qualities of character and ability. Ellis (1903) particularly emphasized the wide social and educational significance of the phenomenon, claiming that greater male variability was "a fact which has affected the whole of our human civilization" (p. 238), particularly through the production of men of genius. Ellis (1934) was also adamant that the female's tendency toward the average did not necessarily imply inferiority of talent; rather, it simply limited her expertise to "the sphere of concrete practical life" (p. 436).

The variability hypothesis was almost immediately challenged as a "pseudo-scientific superstition" by the statistician Karl Pearson (1897). Though not a feminist, Pearson firmly believed that the "woman question" deserved impartial, scientific study. He challenged the idea of greater male variability primarily because he thought it contrary to the fact and theory of evolution and natural selection. According to evolutionary theory (Pearson, 1897), "the more intense the struggle the less is the variability, the more nearly are individuals forced to approach the type fittest to their surroundings, if they are to survive" (p. 258). In a "civilized" community one would expect that because men have a "harder battle for life," any difference in variation should favor women. He took Ellis to task by arguing it was (a) meaningless to consider secondary sex characteristics (as Ellis had done) and, likewise, (b) foolish to contrast the sexes on the basis of abnormalities (as Ellis had done). By redefining the problem and the means for its solution, he was able to dismiss the entire corpus of data that had been amassed: "the whole trend of investigations concerning the relative variability of men and women up to the present seems to be erroneous" (Pearson, 1897, p. 261). Confining his measurements to "normal variations in organs

or characteristics not of a secondary sexual character," he assembled anthropometric data on various races, from Neolithic skeletons to modern French peasants. He also challenged the adequacy of statistical comparison of only the extremes of the distribution, preferring to base his contrasts on the dispersion of measures around the mean. Finding a slight tendency toward greater female variability, he concluded that the variability hypothesis as stated remained a "quite unproven principle."

Ellis countered Pearson in a lengthy article, one more vicious than that ordinarily due an intellectual affront. Pearson's greatest sins (according to Ellis) were his failure to define "variability" and his measurement of characteristics that were highly subject to environmental influence. Ellis, of course, overlooked his own failure to define variability and his inclusion of environmentally altered evidence.

In the United States the variability hypothesis naturally found expression in the new testing movement, its proponents borrowing liberally from the theory of Ellis and the statistical technique of Pearson. The favor that was typically afforded the hypothesis did not stem from intellectual commitment to the scientific validity of the proposal as much as it did from personal commitment to the social desirability of its acceptance. The variability hypothesis was most often thought of in terms of its several corollaries: (a) genius (seldom, and then poorly, defined) is a peculiarly male trait; (b) men of genius naturally gravitate to positions of power and prestige (i.e., achieve eminence) by virtue of their talent; (c) an equally high ability level should not be expected of females; and (d) the education of women should, therefore, be consonant with their special talents and special place in society as wives and mothers.

Woman's Education

The "appropriate" education for women had been at issue since the Renaissance, and the implications of the variability hypothesis favored those who had been arguing for a separate female education. Late in the 18th century, Mary Wollstonecraft Godwin (1759–1797) questioned the "natural" roles of each sex, contending that for both the ultimate goal was the same: "the first object of laudable ambition is to obtain a character as a human being, regardless of the distinction of sex" (Wollstonecraft, 1955, p. 5). Without education, she felt, women could not contribute to social progress as mature individuals, and this would be a tragic loss to the community. Though not the first to recognize the social restrictions arbitrarily placed on women, she was the first to hold those restrictions as directly responsible for the purported "defective nature" of women. She emphasized that women had never truly been given an equal chance to prove or disprove their merits. Seventy years later, John Stuart Mill (1955) also took up the cause of women's education, seeing it as one positive action to be taken in the direction of correcting the unjust social subordination of women. He felt that what appeared as woman's intellectual inferiority was actually no more than the effort to maintain the passive-dependent role relationship with man, her means of support:

> When we put together three things—first, the natural attraction between the sexes; secondly, the wife's entire dependence on the husband...and lastly, that the principal object of human pursuit, consideration, and all objects of social ambition, can in general be sought or obtained by her only through him, it would be a miracle if the object of being attractive to men had not become the polar star of feminine education and formation of character. (pp. 232–233)

Although Mill objected to fostering passivity and dependency in girls, other educators felt that this was precisely their duty. One of the more influential of the 19th century, Hannah More, rejected outright the proposal that women should share the same type of education as men, because "the chief end to be proposed in cultivating the understanding of women" was "to qualify them for the practical purposes of life" (see Smith, 1970, p. 101). To set one's sights on other than harmonious domesticity was to defy the natural order. Her readers were advised to be excellent women rather than indifferent men; to follow the "plain path which Providence has obviously marked out to the sex...rather than... stray awkwardly, unbecomingly, and unsuccessfully, in a forbidden road" (Smith, 1970, pp. 100–101). Her values were consonant with those held by most of the middle class, and so her *Strictures on the Modern System of Female Education* (More, 1800) enjoyed widespread popularity for some time.

By the latter part of the century, the question had turned from whether girls should be educated like boys to how much they should be educated like boys. With the shift in emphasis came the question of coeducation. One of the strongest objections to coeducation in adolescence was the threat it posed to the "normalization" of the menstrual period. G. Stanley Hall (1906) waxed poetic on the issue:

> At a time when her whole future life depends upon normalizing the lunar month, is there not something not only unnatural and unhygienic, but a little monstrous, in daily school associations with boys, where she must suppress and conceal her instincts and feelings, at those times when her own promptings suggest withdrawal or stepping a little aside to let Lord Nature do his magnificent work of efflorescence. (p. 590)

Edward Clarke (see Sinclair, 1965, p. 123) had earlier elucidated the physiological reason for the restraint of girls from exertion in their studies: by forcing their brains to do work at puberty, they would use up blood later needed for menstruation.

Hall proposed an educational system for girls that would not only take into consideration their delicate physical nature but would also be tailored to prepare them for their special role in society. He feared that women's competition with men "in the world" would cause them to neglect their instinctive maternal urges and so bring about "race suicide." Because the glory of the female lay in motherhood, Hall believed that all educational and social institutions should be structured with that end in mind. Domestic arts would therefore be emphasized in special schools for adolescent girls, and disciplines such as philosophy, chemistry, and mathematics would be treated only superficially. If a girl had a notion to stay in the "male" system, she should be able to, but, Hall warned, such a woman selfishly interested in self-fulfillment would also be less likely to bear children and so be confined to an "agamic" life, thus failing to reproduce those very qualities that made her strong (Hall, 1918).

Throughout Hall's panegyric upon the beauties of female domestic education, there runs an undercurrent of the *real* threat that he perceived in coeducation, and that was the "feminization" of the American male. David Starr Jordan (1902) shared this objection but felt that coeducation would nevertheless make young men more "civilized" and young women less frivolous, tempering their natural pubescent inclinations. He was no champion of female ability though, stressing that women "on the whole, lack originality" (p. 100). The educated woman, he said, "is likely to master technic rather than art; method, rather than substance. She may know a good deal, but she can do nothing" (p. 101). In spite of this, he did assert that their training is just as serious and important as that of men. His position strongly favored the notion that the smaller range of female ability was the cause of lackluster female academic performance.

The issue of coeducation was not easily settled, and even as late as 1935, one finds debates over its relative merits (*Encyclopedia of the Social Sciences,* 1935, pp. 614–617).

The Biological Bases of Sex Differences

The variability hypothesis was compatible not only with prevailing attitudes concerning the appropriate form of female education but also with a highly popular theory of the biological complementarity of the sexes. The main tenet of Geddes and Thomson's (1890) theory was that males are primarily "catabolic," females "anabolic." From this difference in metabolism, all other sex differences in physical, intellectual, and emotional makeup were derived. The male was more agile, creative, and variable: the female was truer to the species type and therefore, in all respects, less variable. The conservatism of the female insured the continuity of the species. The author stressed the metabolic antecedents of female conservatism and male differentiation rather than variational tendency per se, and also put emphasis on the complementarity of the two natures:

> The feminine passivity is expressed in greater patience, more open-mindedness, greater appreciation of subtle details, and consequently what we call more rapid intuition. The masculine activity lends a greater power of maximum effort, of scientific insight, or cerebral experiment with impressions, and is associated with an unobservant or impatient disregard of minute details, but with a more stronger grasp of generalities. (p. 271)

The presentation of evolutionary theory anchored in yin-yang concepts of function represents the most positive evaluation of the female sex offered by 19th-century science. Whatever woman's shortcomings, they were necessary to complete her nature, which itself was necessary to complete man's: "Man thinks more, woman feels more. He discovers more, but remembers less; she is more receptive, and less forgetful" (Geddes & Thomson, 1890, p. 271).

Variability and the Testing Movement

Helen Thompson (later Woolley) put Geddes and Thompson's and other theories of sex differences in ability to what she felt was a crucial experimental test (see Thompson, 1903). Twenty-five men and 25 women participated in nearly 20 hours of individual testing of their intellectual, motor, and sensory abilities. Of more importance than her experimental results (whether men or women can tap a telegraph key more times per minute has lost its significance to psychology) was her discussion of the implications of the resulting negligible differences for current theories of sex differences. She was especially critical of the mass of inconsistencies inherent in contemporary biological theories:

> Women are said to represent concentration, patience, and stability in emotional life. One might logically conclude that prolonged concentration of attention and unbiased generalization would be their intellectual characteristics, but these are the very characteristics assigned to men. (p. 173)

In the face of such contradictions, she was forced to conclude that 'if the author's views as to the mental differences of sex had been different, they might as easily have derived a very different set of characteristics" (pp. 173–174). Thompson singled out the variability hypothesis for special criticism, objecting not only to the use of physical variation as evidence for intellectual variation but also to the tendency to minimize environmental influences. She held that training was responsible for sex differences in variation, and to those who countered that it is really a fundamental difference of instincts and characteristics that determines the differences in training, she replied that if this were true, "it would not be necessary to spend so much time and effort in making boys and girls follow the lines of conduct proper to their sex" (p. 181).

Thompson's recommendation to look at environmental factors went unheeded, as more and more evidence of woman's incapability of attaining eminence was amassed. In the surveys of eminent persons that were popular at the turn of the century, more credence was given to nature (à la Hall) than nurture (à la Thompson) for the near absence of eminent women (Cattell, 1903; Ellis, 1904). Cattell (1903) found a ready-made explanation in the variability hypothesis: "Women depart less from the normal than man," ergo "the distribution of women is represented by a narrower bell-shaped curve" (p. 375). Cora Castle's (1913) survey of eminent women was no less crit-

ical of woman's failure to achieve at the top levels of power and prestige.

One of the most influential individuals to take up the cause of the variability hypothesis was Edward Thorndike. Much of the early work in the testing movement was done at Columbia University, which provided the perfect milieu for Thorndike's forays into the variability problem as applied to mental testing and educational philosophy. Thorndike based his case for the acceptance of the variability hypothesis on the reevaluation of the results of two studies (Thompson, 1903; Wissler, 1901) that had not themselves been directed toward the issue. Thorndike insisted that greater male variability only became meaningful when one examined the distribution of ability at the highest levels of giftedness. Measurement of more general sex differences could only "prove that the sexes are closely alike and that sex can account for only a very small fraction of human mental differences in the abilities listed" (Thorndike, 1910, p. 185). Since the range of female ability was narrower, he reasoned, the talents of women should be channeled into fields in which they would be most needed and most successful because "this one fundamental difference in variability is more important than all the difference between the average male and female capacities" (Thorndike, 1906):

> Not only the probability and the desirability of marriage and the training of children as an essential feature of woman's career, but also the restriction of women to the mediocre grades of ability and achievement should be reckoned with by our educational systems. The education of women for... professions... where a very few gifted individuals are what society requires, is far less needed than for such professions as nursing, teaching, medicine, or architecture, where the average level is the essential. (p. 213)

He felt perfectly justified in this recommendation because of "the patent fact that in the great achievements of the world in science, as, invention, and management, women have been far excelled by men'' (Thorndike, 1910, p. 35). In Thorndike's view, environmental factors scarcely mattered.

Others, like Joseph Jastrow (1915), seemed to recognize the tremendous influence that societal pressure had upon achievement. He noted that even when women had been admitted to employment from which they had previously been excluded, new prejudices arose: ''allowances and considerations for sex intrude, favorably or unfavorably; the avenues of preferment, though ostensibly open are really barred by invisible barriers of social prejudice'' (pp. 567–568). This was little more than lip service because he was even more committed to the importance of variational tendency and its predominance over any possible extenuating factors: the effects of the variability of the male and the biological conservatism of the female ''radiates to every distinctive aspect of their contrasted natures and expressions'' (p. 568).

A small but persistent minority challenged the validity of the variability hypothesis, and it is not surprising that this minority was composed mainly of women. Although the ''woman question'' was, to some degree, at issue, the larger dispute was between those who stressed ''nature'' as the major determinant of ability (and therefore success) and those who rejected nature and its corollary, instead emphasizing the importance of environmental factors. Helen Thompson Woolley, while remaining firmly committed to the investigation of the differential effects of social factors of each sex, did not directly involve herself in the variability controversy. Leta Stetter Hollingworth, first a student and then a colleague of Thorndike's at Teachers College of Columbia University, actively investigated the validity of the hypothesis and presented sound objections to it. She argued that there was no real basis for assuming that the distribution of ''mental traits'' in the population conforms without exception to the Gaussian distribution. The assumption of normality was extremely important to the validity of the variability hypothesis, be-

cause only in a normal distribution would a difference in variability indicate a difference in range. It was the greater range of male ability that was used to ''prove'' the ultimate superiority of male ability. Greater range of male ability was usually verified by citing lists of eminent persons (dominated by men) and the numbers and sex of those in institutions for the feebleminded (also dominated by men). Hollingworth (1914) saw no reason to resort to biological theory for an explanation of the phenomenon when a more parsimonious one was available in social fact. Statistics reporting a larger number of males among the feebleminded could be explained by the fact that the supporting data had been gathered in institutions, where men were more likely to be admitted than women of an equal degree of retardation. That better ability of feebleminded women to survive outside the institutional setting was simply a function of female social role:

> Women have been made and are a dependent and non-competitive class, and when defective can more easily survive outside of institutions, since they do not have to compete *mentally* with normal individuals, as men do, to maintain themselves in the social *milieu*. (Hollingworth, 1914, p. 515)

Women would therefore be more likely to be institutionalized at an older age than men, after they had become too old to be ''useful'' or self-supporting. A survey of age and sex ratios in New York institutions supported her hypothesis: the ratio of females to males increased with the age of the inmates (Hollingworth, 1913). As for the rarity of eminence among women, Hollingworth (1914) argued that because the social role of women was defined in terms of housekeeping and child-rearing functions, ''a field where eminence is not possible,'' and because of concomitant constraints placed on the education and employment of women by law, custom, and the demands of the role, one could not possibly validly compare the achievements of women with those of men who ''have followed the greatest possible range of occupations, and have at the same time procreated unhindered'' (p. 528). She repeatedly emphasized (Hollingworth, 1914, 1916) that the true potential of woman could only be known when she began to receive social acceptance of her right to choose career, maternity, or both.

Hollingworth's argument that unrecognized differences in social training had misdirected the search for *inherent* sex differences had earlier been voiced by Mary Calkins (1896). Just as Hollingworth directed her response particularly at Thorndike's formulation of the variability hypothesis, Calkins objected to Jastrow's (1896) intimations that one finds ''greater uniformity amongst women than amongst men'' (p. 431).

Hollingworth's work was instrumental in bringing the variability issue to a crisis point, not only because she presented persuasive empirical data to support her contentions but also because this was simply the first major opposition that the variability hypothesis had encountered. Real resolution of this crisis had to await the development of more sophisticated testing and statistical techniques. With the United States' involvement in World War I, most testing efforts were redirected to wartime uses. This redirection effectively terminated the variability debate, and although it resumed during the postwar years, the renewed controversy never attained the force of conviction that had characterized the earlier period. ''Variational tendency'' became a statistical issue, and the pedagogic implications that had earlier colored the debate were either minimized or disguised in more egalitarian terms.

After its revival in the mid-1920s, investigation of the variability hypothesis was often undertaken as part of larger intelligence testing projects. Evidence in its favor began to look more convincing than it ever had. The use of larger samples, standardized tests, and newer methods of computing variation gave an appearance of increased accuracy, but conclusions were still based on insubstantial evidence of questionable character. Most discussions of the topic concluded that there were not enough valid data to resolve the issue and that even if those data were available, variation within each sex is so much greater than the difference in variation between sexes that the ''meaning'' of the variability hypothesis was trival (Shields, Note 1).

MATERNAL INSTINCT

The concept of maternal instinct was firmly entrenched in American psychology before American psychology itself existed as an entity. The first book to appear in the United States with ''psychology'' in its title outlined the psychological sex differences arising from the physical differences between men and women. Differences in structure were assumed to imply differences in function, and therefore differences in abilities, temperament, and intelligence. In each sex a different set of physical systems was thought to predominate: ''In man the arterial and cerebral system prevail, and with them irritability; in woman the venous and ganglion systems and with them plasticity and sensibility'' (Rausch, 1841, p. 81). The systems dominant in woman caused her greatest attributes to lie in the moral sphere in the form of love, patience, and chastity. In the intellectual sphere, she was not equally blessed, ''and this is not accidental, not because no opportunity has offered itself to their productive genius...but because it is their highest happiness to be mothers'' (Rausch, 1841, p. 83).

Although there was popular acceptance of a maternal instinct in this country, the primary impetus for its incorporation into psychology came by way of British discussion of social evolution. While the variability hypothesis gained attention because of an argument, the concept of maternal instinct evolved without conflict. There was consistent agreement as to its existence, if not its precise nature or form. Typical of the evolutionary point of view was the notion that woman's emotional nature (including her tendency to nurturance) was a direct consequence of her reproductive physiology. As Herbert Spencer (1891) explained it, the female's energies were directed toward preparation for pregnancy and lactation, reducing the energy available for the development of other qualities. This resulted in a "rather earlier cessation of individual evolution" in the female. Woman was, in essence, a stunted man. Her lower stage of devolpment was evident not only in her inferior mental and emotional powers but also in the resulting expression of the parental instinct. Whereas the objectivity of the male caused his concern to be extended "to all the relatively weak who are dependent upon him" (p. 375), the female's propensity to "dwell on the concrete and proximate rather than on the abstract and remote" made her incapable of the generalized protective attitude assumed by the male. Instead, she was primarily responsive to "infantile helplessness."

Alexander Sutherland (1898) also described a parental instinct whose major characteristic (concern for the weak) was "the basis of all other sympathy," which is itself "the ultimate basis of all moral feeling" (p. 156). Like his contemporaries (e.g., McDougall, 1913, 1923; Shand, 1920; Spencer, 1891), Sutherland revered maternal sentiment but thought the expression of parental instinct in the male, that is, a protective attitude, was a much more significant factor in social evolution, an attitude of benevolent paternalism more in keeping with Victorian social ethic than biological reality. The expression of the parental instinct in men, Sutherland thought, must necessarily lead to deference toward women out of "sympathetic regard for women's weakness." He noted that male protectiveness had indeed wrought a change in the relations between the sexes, evident in a trend away from sexual motivations and toward a general improvement in moral tone, witness the "large number of men who lead perfectly chaste lives for ten or twenty years after puberty before they marry," which demonstrated that the "sensuous side of man's nature is slowly passing under the control of sympathetic sentiments" (p. 288).

Whatever facet of the activity that was emphasized, there was common agreement that the maternal (or parental) instinct was truly an instinct.

A. F. Shand (1920) argued that the maternal instinct is actually composed of an ordered "system" of instincts and characterized by a number of emotions. Despite its complexity, "maternal love" was considered to be a hereditary trait "in respect not only of its instincts, but also of the bond connecting its primary emotions, and of the end which the whole system pursues, namely, the preservation of the offspring" (p. 42). The sociologist L. T. Hobhouse (1916) agreed that maternal instinct was a "true" instinct, "not only in the drive but in some of the detail." He doubted the existence of a corresponding paternal instinct, however, since he had observed that few men have a natural aptitude with babies.

The unquestioning acceptance of the maternal instinct concept was just as prevalent in this country as it was in Britain. William James (1950) listed parental love among the instincts of humans and emphasized the strength with which it was expressed in women. He was particularly impressed with the mother-infant relationship and quoted at length from a German psychologist concerning the changes wrought in a woman at the birth of her child: "She has, in one word, transferred her entire egoism to the child, and lives only in it" (p. 439). Even among those who employed a much narrower definition of instinct than James, maternal behavior was thought to be mediated by inherent neural connections. R. P. Halleck (1895) argued that comparatively few instincts are fully developed in humans, because reason intervenes and modifies their expression to fit the circumstances. Maternal instinct qualified as a clear exception, and its expression seemed as primitive and unrefined as that of infants' reflexive behavior.

Others (e.g., Jastrow, 1915; Thorndike, 1914a, 1914b) treated instinct more as a quality of character than of biology. Edward Thorndike (1911) considered the instincts peculiar to each sex to be the primary source of sex differences: "it appears that if the primary sex characters—the instincts directly related to courtship, love, childbearing, and nursing—are left out of account, the average man differs from the average woman far less than many men differ from one another" (p. 30). Thorndike taught that the tendency to display maternal concern was universal among women, although social pressures could "complicate or deform" it. He conceded that males share in an instinctive "good will toward children," but other instincts, such as the "hunting instinct," predominated (Thorndike, 1914b). He was so sure of the innate instinctual differences between men and women that it was his contention (Thorndike, 1914b) that even "if we should keep the environment of boys and girls absolutely similar these instincts would produce sure and important differences between the mental and moral activities of boys and girls" (p. 203). The expression of instincts therefore was thought to have far-reaching effects on seemingly unrelated areas of ability and conduct. For example, woman's "nursing instinct," which was most often exhibited in "unreasoning tendencies to pet, coddle, and 'do for' others," was also "the chief source of woman's superiorities in the moral life" (Thorndike, 1914a, p. 203). Another of the female's instinctive tendencies was described as "submission to mastery":

> Women in general are thus by original nature submissive to men in general. Submissive behavior is apparently not annoying when assumed as the instinctive response to its natural stimulus. Indeed, it is perhaps a common satisfier. (Thorndike, 1914b, p. 34)

The existence of such an "instinct" would, of course, validate the social norm of female subservience and dependence. An assertive woman would be acting contrary to instinct and therefore contrary to *nature*. There is a striking similarity between Thorndike's description of female nature and that of the Freudians with their mutual emphasis on woman's passivity, dependency, and masochism. For Thorndike, however, the *cause* of such a female attitude was thought to be something quite different from mutilation fears and penis envy.

The most vocal proponent of instinct, first in England and later in this country, was William McDougall (1923). Unlike Shand, he regarded "parental sentiment" as a primary instinct and did not hesitate to be highly critical of those who disagreed with him. When his position was maligned by the behaviorists, his counterattack was especially strong:

> And, when we notice how in so many ways the behavior of the human mother most closely resembles that of the animal-mother, can we doubt that... if the animal-mother is moved by the impulse of a maternal instinct, so also is the woman? To repudiate this view as baseless would seem to me the height of blindness and folly, yet it is the folly of a number of psychologists who pride themselves on being strictly "scientific." (p. 136)

In McDougall's system of instincts, each of the primary instincts in humans was accompanied by a particular emotional quality. The parental instinct had as its primary emotional quality the "tender emotion" vaguely defined as love, tenderness, and tender feeling. Another of the primary instincts was that of "pairing," its primary emotional quality that of sexual emotion or excitement, "sometimes called love—an unfortunate and confusing usage" (p. 234). Highly critical of what he called the "Freudian dogma that all love is sexual," McDougall proposed that it was the interaction of the parental and pairing instincts that was the basis of heterosexual "love." "Female coyness," which initiated the courtship ritual, was simply the reproductively oriented manifestation of the instincts of self-display and self-abasement. The appearance of a suitable male would elicit coyness from the female, and at that point the male's parental instinct would come into play:

> A certain physical weakness and delicacy (probably moral also) about the normal young woman or girl constitute in her a resemblance to a child. This resemblance...throws the man habitually into the protective attitude, evokes the impulse and emotion of the parental instinct. He feels that he

wants to protect and shield and help her in every way. (p. 425)

Once the "sexual impulse" had added its energy to the relationship, the young man was surely trapped, and the survival of the species was insured. McDougall, while firmly committed to the importance of instinct all the way up the evolutionary ladder, never lost his sense of Victorian delicacy: while pairing simply meant reproduction in lower animals, in humans it was accorded a tone of gallantry and concern.

The fate of instinct at the hands of the radical behaviorists is a well-known tale. Perhaps the most adamant, as well as notorious, critic of the instinct concept was J. B. Watson (1926). Like those before him who had relied upon observation to prove the existence of maternal instinct, he used observation to confirm its nonexistence:

> We have observed the nursing, handling, bathing, etc. of the first baby of a good many mothers. Certainly there are no new ready-made activities appearing except nursing. The mother is usually as awkward about that as she can well be. The instinctive factors are practically nil. (p. 54)

Watson attributed the appearance of instinctive behavior to the mother's effort to conform to societal expectations of her successful role performance. He, like the 19th-century British associationist Alexander Bain, speculated that not a little of the mother's pleasure in nursing and caring for the infant was due to the sexually stimulating effect of those activities.

Even the most dedicated behaviorists hedged a bit when it came to discarding the idea of instinct altogether. Although the teleology and redundancy of the concept of instinct were sharply criticized, some belief in "instinctive activity" was typically retained (cf. Dunlap, 1919–1920). W. B. Pillsbury (1926), for example, believed that the parental instinct was a "secondary" instinct. Physical attraction to the infant guided the mother's first positive movements toward the in-

fant, but trial and error guided her subsequent care. Instinct was thought of as that quality which set the entire pattern of maternal behavior in motion.

In time instinct was translated into *drive* and *motivation,* refined concepts more in keeping with behavioristic theory. Concomitantly, interest in the maternal instinct of human females gave way to the study of mothering behavior in rodents. The concept of maternal instinct did find a place in psychoanalytic theory, but its definition bore little resemblance to that previously popular. Not only did maternal instinct lose the connotation of protectiveness and gentility that an earlier generation of psychologists had ascribed to it, but it was regarded as basically sexual, masochistic, and even destructive in nature (cf. Rheingold, 1964).

THE ASCENDANCY OF PSYCHOANALYTIC THEORY

The functionalists, because of their emphasis on "nature," were predictably indifferent to the study of social sex roles and cultural concepts of masculine and feminine. The behaviorists, despite their emphasis on "nurture," were slow to recognize those same social forces. During the early 1930s, there was little meaningful ongoing research in female psychology: the point of view taken by the functionalists was no longer a viable one, and the behaviorists with their emphasis on nonsocial topics (i.e., learning and motivation) had no time for serious consideration of sex differences. While the functionalists had defined laws of behavior that mirrored the society of the times, behaviorists concentrated their efforts on defining universal laws that operated in any time, place, or organism. Individual differences in nature were expected during the functionalist era because they were the sine qua non of a Darwinian view of the world and of science. The same individual differences were anathema to early learning-centered psychology because, no longer necessary or expedient, they were a threat to the formulation of universal laws of behavior.

In the hiatus created by the capitulation of functionalism to behaviorism, the study of sex differences and female nature fell within the domain of psychoanalytic theory—the theory purported to have all the answers. Freudian theory (or some form of it) had for some years already served as the basis for a psychology of female physiological function (cf. Benedek & Rubenstein, 1939). The application of principles popular in psychiatry and medicine (and their inescapable identification with pathology) to academic psychology was easily accomplished. Psychoanalytic theory provided psychology with the first comprehensive theoretical explanation of sex differences. Its novelty in that respect aided its assimilation.

Psychology proper, as well as the general public, had been well-prepared for a biological, and frankly sexual, theory of male and female nature. Havelock Ellis, although himself ambivalent and even hostile toward Freudian teachings, had done much through his writing to encourage openness in the discussion of sexuality. He brought a number of hitherto unmentionable issues to open discussion, couching them in the commonly accepted notion of the complementarity of the sexes, thus insuring their popular acceptance. Emphasis on masculinity and femininity as real dimensions of personality appeared in the mid-1930s in the form of the Terman Masculinity-Femininity Scale (Terman & Miles, 1968). Although Lewis Terman himself avoided discussion of whether masculinity and femininity were products of nature or nurture, social determinants of masculinity and femininity were commonly deemphasized in favor of the notion that they were a type of psychological secondary sexual characteristic. Acceptance of social sex role soon came to be perceived as an indicator of one's mental health.

The traps inherent in a purely psychoanalytic concept of female nature were seldom recognized. John Dewey's (1957) observation, made in 1922, merits attention, not only for its accuracy but because its substance can be found in present-day refutations of the adequacy of psychoanalytic theory as an explanation of woman's behavior and "nature":

> The treatment of sex by psycho-analysts is most instructive, for it flagrantly exhibits both the consequences of artificial simplification and the transformation of social results into psychic causes. Writers, usually male, hold forth on the psychology of women, as if they were dealing with a Platonic universal entity, although they habitually treat men as individuals, varying with structure and environment. They treat phenomena which are peculiarly symptoms of civilization of the West at the present time as if they were the necessary effects of fixed nature impulses of human nature. (pp. 143–144)

The identification of the psychology of women with psychoanalytic theory was nearly complete by the mid-1930s and was so successful that many psychologists today, even those most deeply involved in the current movement for a psychology of women, are not aware that there was a psychology of women long before there was a Sigmund Freud. This article has dealt only with a brief period in that history, and then only with the most significant topics of that period. Lesser issues were often just as hotly debated, for example, whether there is an innate difference in the style of handwriting of men and women (cf. Allen, 1927; Downey, 1910).

And what has happened to the issues of brain size, variability, and maternal instinct since the 1930s? Where they are politically and socially useful, they have an uncanny knack of reappearing, albeit in an altered form. For example, the search for central nervous system differences between males and females has continued. Perhaps the most popular form this search has taken is the theory of prenatal hormonal "organization" of the hypothalamus into exclusively male or female patterns of function (Harris & Levine, 1965). The proponents of this theory maintain an Aristotelian view of woman as an incomplete man:

> In the development of the embryo, nature's first choice or primal impulse is to differentiate a female.... The principle of differentiation is always that to obtain a male, something must be added. Subtract that something, and the result will be a female. (Money, 1970, p. 428)

The concept of maternal instinct, on the other hand, has recently been taken up and refashioned by a segment of the woman's movement. Pregnancy and childbirth are acclaimed as important expressions of womanliness whose satisfactions cannot be truly appreciated by males. The idea that women are burdened with "unreasoning tendencies to pet, coddle, and 'do for' others" has been disposed of by others and replaced by the semiserious proposal that if any "instinctive" component of parental concern exists, it is a peculiarly male attribute (Stannard, 1970). The variability hypothesis is all but absent from contemporary psychological work, but if it ever again promises a viable justification for existing social values, it will be back as strongly as ever. Conditions which would favor its revival include the renaissance of rugged individualism or the "need" to suppress some segment of society, for example, women's aspirations to positions of power. In the first case the hypothesis would serve to reaffirm that there are those "born to lead," and in the latter that there are those "destined to follow."

Of more importance than the issues themselves or their fate in contemporary psychology is the recognition of the role that they have played historically in the psychology of women: the role of social myth. Graves (1968, p. v) included among the functions of mythologizing that of justification of existing social systems. This function was clearly operative throughout the evolutionist-functionalist treatment of the psychology of women: the "discovery" of sex differences in brain structure to correspond to "appropriate" sex differences in brain function; the biological justification (via the variability hypothesis) for the enforcement of woman's subordinate social status; the Victorian weakness and gentility associated with maternity; and pervading each of these themes, the assumption of an innate emotional, sexless, unimaginative female character that played the perfect foil to the Darwinian male. That science played handmaiden to social values cannot be denied. Whether a parallel situation exists in today's study of sex differences is open to question.

REFERENCE NOTE

1 Shields, S. A. *The variability hypothesis and sex differences in intelligence.* Unpublished manuscript, 1974. (Available from Department of Psychology, Pennsylvania State University.)

REFERENCES

Allen, C. N. Studies in sex differences. *Psychological Bulletin,* 1927, *24,* 294–304.

Bain, A. *Mental science.* New York: Appleton, 1875.

Benedek, T., & Rubenstein, B. B. The correlations between ovarian activity and psychodynamic processes. II. The menstrual phase. *Psychosomatic Medicine,* 1939, *1,* 461–485.

Calkins, M. W. Community of ideas of men and women. *Psychological Review,* 1896, *3,* 426–430.

Castle, C. A. A statistical study of eminent women. *Columbia Contributions to Philosophy and Psychology,* 1913, *22*(27).

Cattell, J. McK. A statistical study of eminent men. *Popular Science Monthly,* 1903, *62,* 359–377.

Darwin, C. *The descent of man* (2nd ed.). London: John Murray, 1922. (Originally published, 1871; 2nd edition originally published, 1874.)

Dewey, J. *Human nature and conduct.* New York: Random House, 1957.

Downey, J. E. Judgment on the sex of handwriting. *Psychological Review,* 1910, *17,* 205–216.

Dunlap, J. Are there any instincts? *Journal of Abnormal and Social Psychology,* 1919–1920, *14,* 307–311.

Elliott, H. C. *Textbook of neuroanatomy* (2nd ed.). Philadelphia: Lippincott, 1969.

Ellis, H. *Man and woman: A study of human secondary sexual characters.* London: Walter Scott; New York: Scribner's, 1894.

Ellis, H. Variation in man and woman. *Popular Science Monthly,* 1903, *62,* 237–253.

Ellis, H. *A study of British genius.* London: Hurst & Blackett, 1904.

Ellis, H. *Man and woman, a study of secondary and tertiary sexual characteristics* (8th rev. ed.). London: Heinemann, 1934.

Encyclopedia of the Social Sciences. New York: Macmillan, 1935.

Galton, F. *Inquiries into the human faculty and its development.* London: Dent, 1907.

Geddes, P., & Thomson, J. A. *The evolution of sex.* New York: Scribner & Welford, 1890.

Graves, R. Introduction. In *New Larousse encyclopedia of mythology* (Rev. ed.). London: Paul Hamlyn, 1968.

Hall, G. S. The question of coeducation. *Munsey's Magazine,* 1906, *34,* 588–592.

Hall, G. S. *Youth, its education, regimen and hygiene.* New York: Appleton, 1918.

Halleck, R. *Psychology and psychic culture.* New York: American Book, 1895.

Harris, G. W., & Levine, S. Sexual differentiation of the brain and its experimental control. *Journal of Physiology,* 1965, *181,* 379–400.

Hobhouse, L. *Morals in evolution.* New York: Holt, 1916.

Hollingworth, L. S. The frequency of amentia as related to sex. *Medical Record,* 1913, *84,* 753–756.

Hollingworth, L. S. Variability as related to sex differences in achievement. *American Journal of Sociology,* 1914, *19,* 510–530.

Hollingworth, L. S. Social devices for impelling women to bear and rear children. *American Journal of Sociology,* 1916, *22,* 19–29.

Huarte, J. *The examination of mens wits* (trans. from Spanish to Italian by M. Camilli; trans. from Italian to English by R. Carew). Gainesville, Fla.: Scholars' Facsimiles and Reprints, 1959.

James, W. *The principles of psychology.* New York: Dover, 1950.

Jastrow, J. Note on Calkins' "Community of ideas of men and women." *Psychological Review,* 1896, *3,* 430–431.

Jastrow, J. *Character and temperament.* New York: Appleton, 1915.

Jordan, D. S. The higher education of women. *Popular Science Monthly,* 1902, *62,* 97–107.

Mall, F. P. On several anatomical characters of the human brain, said to vary according to race and sex, with especial reference to the weight of the frontal lobe. *American Journal of Anatomy,* 1909, *9,* 1–32.

McDougall, W. *An introduction to social psychology* (7th ed.). London: Methuen, 1913.

McDougall, W. *Outline of psychology.* New York: Scribner's, 1923.

Meyer, M. *Psychology of the other-one.* Columbia: Missouri Book, 1921.

Mill, J. S. *The subjection of women.* London: Dent, 1955.

Mobius, P. J. The physiological mental weakness of woman (A. McCorn, Trans.). *Alienist and Neurologist, 1901, 22,* 624–642.

Money, J. Sexual dimorphism and homosexual gender identity. *Psychological Bulletin,* 1970, *74,* 425–440.

More, H. *Strictures on the modern system of female education. With a view of the principles and conduct prevalent among women of rank and fortune.* Philadelphia, Pa.: Printed by Budd and Bertram for Thomas Dobson, 1800.

Patrick, G. T. W. The psychology of women. *Popular Science Monthly,* 1895, *47,* 209–225.

Pearson, K. Variation in man and woman. In *The chances of death* (Vol. 1). London: Edward Arnold, 1897.

Pillsbury, W. B. *Education as the psychologist sees it.* New York: Macmillan, 1926.

Porteus, S., & Babcock, M. E. *Temperament and race.* Boston: Gorham Press, 1926.

Rausch, F. A. *Psychology; Or, a view of the human soul including anthropology* (2nd rev. ed.). New York: Dodd, 1841.

Rheingold, J. *The fear of being a woman.* New York: Grune & Stratton, 1964.

Romanes, G. J. Mental differences between men and women. *Nineteenth Century,* 1887, *21,* 654–672.

Shand, A. F. *The foundations of character.* London: Macmillan, 1920.

Sinclair, A. *The better half: The emancipation of the American woman*. New York: Harper & Row, 1965.

Smith, P. *Daughters of the promised land*. Boston: Little, Brown, 1970.

Spencer, H. *The study of sociology*. New York: Appleton, 1891.

Stannard, U. Adam's rib, or the woman within. *Trans-Action*, 1970, *8*, 24–35.

Sutherland, A. *The origin and growth of the moral instinct* (Vol. 1). London: Longmans, Green, 1898.

Terman, L., & Miles, C. C. *Sex and personality*. New York: Russell and Russell, 1968.

Thompson, H. B. *The mental traits of sex*. Chicago: University of Chicago Press, 1903.

Thorndike, E. L. Sex in education. *The Bookman*, 1906, *23*, 211–214.

Thorndike, E. L. *Educational psychology* (2nd ed.). New York: Teachers College, Columbia University, 1910.

Thorndike, E. L. *Individuality*. Boston: Houghton Mifflin, 1911.

Thorndike, E. L. *Educational psychology* (Vol. 3). New York: Teachers College, Columbia University, 1914. (a)

Thorndike, E. L. *Educational psychology briefer course*. New York: Teachers College, Columbia University, 1914. (b)

Walker, A. *Woman physiologically considered*. New York: J. & H. G. Langley, 1850.

Watson, J. B. Studies on the growth of the emotions. In *Psychologies of 1925*. Worcester, Mass.: Clark University Press, 1926.

Weininger, O. *Sex and character* (trans.). London: Heinemann, 1906.

Wissler, C. The correlation of mental and physical tests. *Psychological Review Monograph Supplements*, 1899–1901, *3*(6, Whole No. 16).

Wollstonecraft, M. *A vindication of the rights of woman*. New York: Dutton, 1955.

Woolley, H. T. Psychological literature: A review of the recent literature on the psychology of sex. *Psychological Bulletin*, 1910, *7*, 335–342.

Wundt, W. *Ethics*. Vol. 3: *The principles of morality, and the departments of the moral life* (M. F. Washburn, Trans.). London: Sonnenschein, 1901.

CHAPTER 12

ANIMAL EXPERIMENTAL PSYCHOLOGY

The next chapter considers behaviorism, probably the most important school of thought in the history of American psychology. In starting its conceptual revolution, behaviorism borrowed from functionalism. But of equal importance was the legacy from animal psychology. This chapter focuses on animal work, not in the sense of providing a history of animal psychology but for providing the context necessary to understand its contributions to behaviorism.

Once Darwin had removed humans from their lofty perch and placed them with the rest of the animal kingdom, the study of animal behavior took on a new meaning. In 1882, the year of Darwin's death, George Romanes (1848–1894), an English biologist, published his *Animal Intelligence,* a book that is considered by many historians as the first textbook on comparative psychology. Romanes studied both vertebrates and invertebrates, attempting to compare their mental processes, which he investigated by his technique of *introspection by analogy*. That means that in observing animals he would try to understand their behavior by asking himself what he would do in a similar situation. Not surprisingly, his book was considerably anthropomorphic.

C. Lloyd Morgan (1852–1936), another of the English biologists influenced by Darwin, objected to the practice of Romanes and others of attributing human faculties, such as reason, to animals lower in the phylogenetic scale, when in fact such attributions might not be warranted. In his 1894 book, *Introduction to Comparative Psychology,* Morgan stated what has become known as Morgan's Canon: that in explaining animal behavior, a higher mental process should not be invoked if the behavior can be adequately explained by a lower mental process. Although Morgan insisted on parsimonious explanations for animal behavior, he did not object to introspection by analogy and used the method himself. However, he also performed experiments with animals in their natural settings, an important step forward for animal psychology.

Whereas Romanes, Morgan, and others sought to explain the mental processes of animals, the German biologist Jacques Loeb (1859–1924), who did much of his research in the United States, was arguing that much animal behavior occurred without regard to any mental activity. He introduced his concept of *tropism,* meaning a response that occurred involuntarily to a stimulus. He noted that plants turned their leaves toward the sun in an automatic response (heliotropism) and argued that much animal behavior could be explained in a similar fashion. For the behaviorists, Loeb's ideas had special appeal: "If the actions of lower organisms can be explained without reference to mental events, why cannot human behavior be explained in the same way?" (Kendler, 1987, p. 153).

In opposition to Loeb, an American psychologist, Edward L. Thorndike (1874–1949), sought to show the relationship between mental processes in lower animals and those in humans. Thorndike, whose interests in animal behavior were attributed to C. Lloyd Morgan, began his animal research career testing baby chicks in mazes set up in the basement of William James's home. He later moved from Harvard University to Columbia University, where he continued his animal research in Cattell's laboratories, taking his doctorate in psychology there in 1898. His dissertation, entitled "Animal Intelligence," described his maze studies with chicks and his now-classic puzzle-box experiments with cats and dogs. Thorndike constructed fifteen puzzle boxes in which the animals were placed (see Burnham, 1972). Each box required a different response for escape. Once the animal had made the correct response and had escaped from the box, it was rewarded with food. Thorndike found that his animal subjects learned to escape the boxes in a trial-and-error fashion (which he took as evidence against the operation of mental processes); the correct responses were gradually learned, whereas those responses that did not lead to escape were gradually eliminated from the animal's behavior in the box. From this he formulated his *law of effect,* which is today recognized as the forerunner of the *law of reinforcement:*

> Any act which in a given situation produces satisfaction becomes associated with that situation, so that when the situation recurs the act is more likely than before to recur also. Conversely, any act which in a given situation produces discomfort becomes disassociated from the situation, so that when the situation recurs the act is less likely than before to recur. (Thorndike, 1905, p. 203)

The first part of that law describes the effects of what has come to be called reinforcement, and the second part the effects of punishment. Much later, Thorndike eliminated the second part when research showed that punishment suppressed stimulus-response connections but did not necessarily weaken them (this subsequent version is called the *truncated law of effect*).

Thorndike was a busy researcher and a prolific writer throughout his career, publishing more than five hundred works, a number of those books. But his animal research was confined to the early years of his career, and was largely abandoned by 1911 as he pursued his interests in educational psychology and mental testing (see O'Donnell, 1985). Nevertheless, his animal work ranks among his most important work, both methodologically and theoretically. It would play a very influential role in the rise of learning research and the dominance of learning theory throughout the reign of behaviorism (see Chapters 13 and 14). Further, Thorndike was among the first scientists (some historians say the first) to conduct research with animals in a laboratory setting. His procedures served as models for much of the early animal psychology in the United States (Gottlieb, 1979).

Some histories of psychology label Thorndike a functionalist, others see him as a behaviorist. He denied membership in either. His placement in this chapter is meant to show his work as intermediate between the two.

While Thorndike was watching his animals escape from the puzzle boxes, a Russian physiologist was beginning to explore what he termed a *psychic reflex*—the salivation that could be elicited in an animal upon ringing a bell, when the bell had been previously paired with food. Ivan Pavlov (1849–1936) spent the last thirty-four years of his life working out the various facets of what we call *classical conditioning* (or Pavlovian conditioning). Independent of Thorndike, he discovered the principle of reinforcement and many other learning phenomena such as extinction, spontaneous recovery, generalization, discrimination, conditioned inhibition, conditioned emotional reactions, and higher-order conditioning. Once his work became known to American psychologists, around 1909, it proved to be an important influence for those looking to move psychology away from mentalism to a more objective study of observable behavior.

Unlike Romanes, who had attributed much consciousness to animals, Thorndike found little evidence for animal consciousness in his puzzle-box studies. Consistent with that view was Loeb's emphasis on animal tropisms, which discarded any need for assuming animal consciousness. Pavlov's work added weight to this view as well. He rejected the mentalism of psychology (indeed, he rejected all of psychology until the last few years of his life) and called for a total explanation of the higher mental processes in terms of physiological processes. Perhaps, as the behaviorists would soon assert, psychology could discard the mind and provide a wholly scientific account based on observable behavior and physiology.

The first selection in this chapter is on the psychology of learning, written by Edward L. Thorndike. In it he discusses his laws of effect, exercise, and readiness in the context of his animal studies. It is an elegant statement of this classic early work in learning.

The second selection is on Pavlov's work, but it was not written by Pavlov. Instead, it is the article published in the *Psychological Bulletin* in 1909 that first introduced American psychologists to the work of Pavlov. The authors are Robert M. Yerkes (1876–1956), a pioneer researcher in animal behavior, and a Russian student, Sergius Morgulis. In spite of Pavlov's negative views toward psychology, it was a paper that would generate considerable interest, particularly for behaviorist John B. Watson (whose use of it is described in the next chapter).

The third selection is by Philip J. Pauly, a historian of science, and concerns a debate on animal tropisms between Jacques Loeb and another American biologist, Herbert Spencer Jennings (1868–1947). The paper discusses the significance of the debate for the science of animal behavior and concludes with a brief section considering the influence of Loeb and Jennings on the work of John B. Watson.

The last selection, by another historian of science, Deborah J. Coon, focuses on the dissertation research on the knee-jerk reflex by the University of Pennsylvania psychologist Edwin B. Twitmyer (1873–1943). In his research, Twitmyer rang a bell to signal to the subject that the patellar tendon was about to be struck with a rubber hammer. He discovered that eventually the ringing of the bell alone would produce a knee-jerk response. He reported those results at a 1904 meeting of the American Psychological Association and published them in *Psychological Bulletin* the following year, a year before Pavlov's initial publication on the subject. Was Twitmyer the discoverer of the conditioned response as some historians claim, or did the conditioned response discover him (see Misceo & Samelson, 1983)? Coon discusses the various hypotheses that have been offered to explain why Twitmyer's work was not recognized and provides her own interpretation in the social and intellectual contexts of both Pavlov and Twitmyer. Perhaps this controversy is best settled in the context of a distinction between anticipation and foundation as described by Sarup in the first chapter of this book. Whatever the verdict, the Coon article provides an interesting look at a little-known episode in the history of the conditioned reflex.

REFERENCES

Burnham, J. C. (1972). Thorndike's puzzle boxes. *Journal of the History of the Behavioral Sciences, 8,* 159–167.

Gottlieb, G. (1979). Comparative psychology and ethology. In E. Hearst (Ed.), *The first century of experimental psychology*. Hillsdale, NJ: Lawrence Erlbaum, pp. 147–173.

Kendler, H. H. (1987). *Historical foundations of modern psychology*. Chicago: Dorsey Press.

Misceo, G., & Samelson, F. (1983). History of psychology: XXXIII. On textbook lessons from history, or how the conditioned reflex discovered Twitmyer. *Psychological Reports, 52,* 447–454.

Morgan, C. L. (1894). *An introduction to comparative psychology*. London: Walter Scott.

O'Donnell, J. M. (1985). *The origins of behaviorism: American psychology, 1870–1920*. New York: New York University Press.

Thorndike, E. L. (1905). *The elements of psychology*. New York: A. G. Seiler.

The Laws of Learning in Animals

Edward L. Thorndike

SAMPLES OF ANIMAL LEARNING

The complexities of human learning will in the end be best understood if at first we avoid them, examining rather the behavior of the lower animals as they learn to meet certain situations in changed, and more remunerative, ways.

Let a number of chicks, say six to twelve days old, be kept in a yard (YY of Figure 1) adjoining which is a pen or maze (A B C D E of Figure 1). A chick is taken from the group and put in alone at A. It is confronted by a situation which is, in essence, *Confining walls and the absence of the other chicks, food and familiar surroundings.* It reacts to the situation by running around, making loud sounds, and jumping at the walls. When it jumps at the walls, it has the discomforts of thwarted effort, and when it runs to B, or C, or D, it has a continuation of the situation just described; when it runs to E, it gets out and has the satisfaction of being with the other chicks, of eating, and of being in its usual habitat. If it is repeatedly put in again at A, one finds that it jumps and runs to B or C less and less often, until finally its only act is to run to D, E, and out. It has formed an association, or connection, or bond, between the situation due to its removal to A and the response of going to E. In common language, it has learned to go to E when put at A—has learned the way out. The decrease in the useless running and jumping and standing still finds a representative in the decreasing amount of time taken by the chick to escape. The two chicks that formed this particular association, for example, averaged three and a half minutes (one about three and the other about four) for their

Adapted from Thorndike, E. L. (1913). *Educational psychology: The psychology of learning,* Volume 2. New York: Teachers College Press, pp. 6–16. Copyright © 1913 by Teachers College Press. Adapted and reprinted by permission of the publisher.

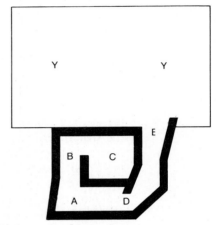

FIGURE 1

first five trials, but came finally to escape invariably within five or six seconds.

The following schemes represent the animal's behavior (1) during an early trial and (2) after the association has been fully formed—after it has learned the way out perfectly. A graphic representation of the progress from an early trial to a

1
BEHAVIOR IN AN EARLY TRIAL

Situation	Responses	Resulting States of Affairs
As described above, in the text	To chirp, etc.	Annoying continuation of the situation and thwarting of the inner tendencies.
	To jump at various places.	" " "
	To run to B.	" " "
	To run to C.	" " "
	To run to D.	" " "
	To run to E.	Satisfying company, food and surroundings.

2
BEHAVIOR IN A TRIAL AFTER LEARNING

Situation	Responses	Resulting States of Affairs
Same as in (1).	To run to E.	Satisfying as above.

trial after the association has been fully formed is given in the following figures, in which the dotted lines represent the path taken by a turtle in his fifth (Figure 2) and fiftieth (Figure 3) experiences in learning the way from the point A to his nest. The straight lines represent walls of boards. Besides the useless movements, there were, in the fifth trial, useless stoppings. The time taken to reach the nest in the fifth trial was seven minutes; in the fiftieth, thirty-five seconds. The figures represent typical early and late trials, chosen from a number of experiments on different individuals in different situations, by Dr. R. M. Yerkes, to whom I am indebted for permission to use these figures.

Let us next examine a somewhat more ambitious performance than the mere discovery of the proper path by a chick or turtle. If we take a box twenty by fifteen by twelve inches, replace its cover and front side by bars an inch apart, and make in this front side a door arranged so as to fall open when a wooden button inside is turned from a vertical to a horizontal position, we shall have means to observe such. A kitten, three to six months old, if put in this box when hungry, a bit of fish being left outside, reacts as follows: It tries to squeeze through between the bars, claws at the bars and at loose things in and out of the box, stretches its paws out between the bars, and bites at its confining walls. Some one of all these promiscuous clawings, squeezings, and bitings turns round the wooden button, and the kitten gains freedom and food. By repeating the experience again and again, the animal gradually comes to omit all the useless clawings, and the like, and to manifest only the particular impulse (e.g., to claw hard at the top of the button with the paw, or to push against one side of it with the nose) which has resulted successfully. It turns the button around without delay whenever put in the box. It has formed an association between the situation, *confinement in a box of a certain appearance,* and the response of *clawing at a certain part of that box in a certain definite way.* Popularly speaking, it has learned to open a door by turning a button. To the uninitiated observer the behavior of the six kittens that

FIGURE 2
The path taken by a turtle in finding his way from A to his nest, in his 5th trial.

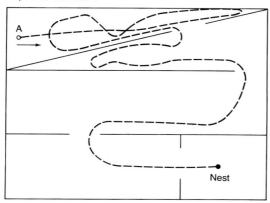

FIGURE 3
The path taken by a turtle in finding his way from A to his nest, in his 50th trial.

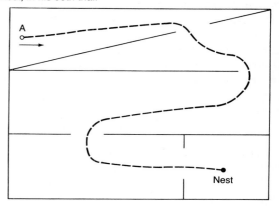

thus freed themselves from such a box would seem wonderful and quite unlike their ordinary accomplishments of finding their way to their food or beds, but the reader will realize that the activity is of just the same sort as that displayed by the chick in the pen. A certain situation arouses, by virtue of accident or, more often, instinctive equipment, certain responses. One of these happens to be an act appropriate to secure freedom. It is stamped in connection with that situation. Here the act is clawing at a certain spot instead of running to E, and is selected from a far greater number of useless acts.

In the examples so far given there is a certain congruity between the 'set' associated with the situation and the learning. The act which lets the cat out is hit upon by the cat while, as we say, trying to get out, and is, so to speak, a likely means of release. But there need be no such congruity between the 'set' and the learning. If we confine a cat, opening the door and letting it out to get food only when it scratches itself, we shall, after enough trials, find the cat scratching itself the moment it is put into the box. Yet in the first trials it did not scratch itself in order to get out, or indeed until after it had given up the unavailing clawings and squeezings, and stopped to rest. The association is formed with such an 'unlikely' or 'incongruous' response as that of scratching, or licking, or (in the case of chicks) pecking at the wing to dress it, as truly as with a response which original nature or previous habit has put in connection with the set of the organism toward release, food, and company.

The examples chosen so far show the animal forming a single association, but such may be combined into series. For instance, a chick learns to get out of a pen by climbing up an inclined plane. A second pen is then so arranged that the chick can, say by walking up a slat and through a hole in the wall, get from it into pen No. 1. After a number of trials the chick will, when put in pen No. 2, go at once to pen No. 1, and thence out. A third pen is then so arranged that the

chick, by forming another association, can get from it to pen No. 2, and so on. In such a series of associations the response of one brings the animal into the *situation* of the next, thus arousing its response, and so on to the end. Three chicks thus learned to go through a sort of long labyrinth without mistakes, the 'learning' representing twenty-three associations.

The learning of the chick, turtle, and kitten in the cases quoted is characterized negatively by the absence of inferential, ratiocinative thinking; and indeed by the absence of effective use of 'ideas' of any sort. Were the reader confined in a maze or cage, or left at some distance from home, his responses to these situations would almost certainly include many ideas, judgments, or thoughts about the situation; and his acts would probably in large measure be led up to or 'mediated' by such sequences of ideas as are commonly called reasoning. Between the annoying situation and the response which relieves the annoyance there might for the reader well intervene an hour of inner consideration, thought, planning, and the like. But there is no evidence that any ideas about the maze, the cage, the food, or anything else, were present to determine the acts of the chicks or kittens in question. Their responses were made directly to the situation as sensed, not *via* ideas suggested by it. The three cases of learning quoted are adequately accounted for as the strengthening and weakening of bonds between a situation present to sense and responses in the nervous system which issue then and there in movement. The lower animals do occasionally show signs of ideas and of their influence on behavior, but the great bulk of their learning has been found explainable by such direct binding of acts to situations, unmediated by ideas.

CHARACTERISTICS OF ANIMAL LEARNING

These cases, and the hundreds of which they are typical, show the laws of readiness, exercise, and effect, uncomplicated by any pseudo-aid from imitation, ideo-motor action, or superior faculties of inference. There are certain states of affairs which the animal welcomes and does nothing to avoid—its satisfiers. There are others which it is intolerant of and rejects, doing one thing or another until relieved from them. Of the bonds which the animal's behavior makes between a situation and responses those grow stronger which are accompanied by satisfying states of affairs, while those accompanied by annoyance weaken and disappear. Exercise strengthens and disuse weakens bonds. Such is the sum and substance of the bulk of animal learning.

These cases exemplify also five characteristics of learning which are secondary in scope and importance only to the laws of readiness, exercise, and effect.

The first is the fact of *multiple response to the same external situation*. The animal reacts to being confined in the pen in several ways, and so has the possibility of selecting for future connection with that situation one or another of these ways. Its own inner state changes when jumping at the wall at B produces a drop back into the pen, so that it then is less likely to jump again— more likely to chirp and run. Running to C and being still confronted with the confining walls may arouse an inner state which impels it to turn and run back. So one after another of the responses which, by original nature or previous learning, are produced by the confining walls *plus* the failure of the useless chirpings, jumpings, and runnings, are made.

This principle of *Multiple Response* or *Varied Reaction* will be found to pervade at least nine-tenths of animal and human learning. As ordinarily interpreted, it is not universal, since, even if only one response is made, the animal may change its behavior—that is, learn—either by strengthening the connection so as to make that response more surely, more quickly, and after a longer interval of disuse; or by weakening

the connection so as to be more likely to do nothing at all in that situation, inactivity being a variety of response which is always a possible alternative. If we interpret variety of reaction so as to include the cases where an animal either makes one active response or is inactive—that is, either alters what it was doing when the situation began to act, or does not alter what it was doing—the principle of varied response is universal in learning.

The second of the five subsidiary principles is what we may call the law of the learner's *Set* or *Attitude* or *Adjustment* or *Determination*. The learning cannot be described adequately in a simple equation involving the pen and a chick taken abstractly. The chick, according to his age, hunger, vitality, sleepiness and the like, may be in one or another attitude toward the external situation. A sleepier and less hungry chick will, as a rule, be 'set' less toward escape-movements when confined; its neurones involved in roaming, perceiving companions and feeding will be less ready to act; it will not, in popular language, 'try so hard to' get out or 'care so much about' being out. As Woodworth says in commenting upon similar cases of animal learning:

> In the first place we must assume in the animal an adjustment or determination of the psychophysical mechanism toward a certain end. The animal desires, as we like to say, to get out and to reach the food. Whatever be his consciousness, his behavior shows that he is, as an organism, set in that direction. This adjustment persists till the motor reaction is consummated; it is the driving force in the unremitting efforts of the animal to attain the desired end. His reactions are, therefore, the joint result of the adjustment and of stimuli from various features of the cage. Each single reaction tends to become associated with the adjustment. [Ladd and Woodworth, 1911, p. 551.]

The principle that in any external situation, the responses made are the product of the 'set' or 'attitude' of the animal, that the satisfyingness or annoyingness produced by a response is conditioned by that attitude, and that the 'successful' response is by the law of effect connected with that attitude as well as with the external situation *per se*—is general. Any process of learning is conditioned by the mind's 'set' at the time.

Animal learning shows also the fact, which becomes of tremendous moment in human learning, that one or another element of the situation may be prepotent in determining the response. For example, the cats with which I experimented, would, after a time, be determined by my behavior more than by other features of the general situations of which that behavior was a part; so that they could then learn, as they could not have done earlier, to form habits of response to signals which I gave. Similarly, a cat that has learned to get out of a dozen boxes—in each case by pulling some loop, turning some bar, depressing a platform, or the like—will, in a new box, be, as we say, 'more attentive to' small objects on the sides of the box than it was before. The connections made may then be, not absolutely with the gross situation as a total, but predominantly with some element or elements of it. Thus, it makes little or no difference whether the box from which a cat has learned to escape by turning a button, is faced North, South, East, or West; and not much difference if it is painted ten per cent blacker or enlarged by a fifth. The cat will operate the mechanism substantially as well as it did before. It is, of course, the case that the animals do not, as a thoughtful man might do, connect the response with perfect strictness just to the one essential element of the situation. They can be much more easily confused by variations in the element's concomitants; and in certain cases many of the irrelevant concomitants have to be supplied to enable them to give the right response. Nevertheless they clearly make connections with certain parts or elements or features of gross total situations. Even in the lower animals, that is, we find that the action of a situation is more or less separable into the action of the elements that compose it—that even they illustrate the general *Law of Partial Activity*—that a part or element or as-

pect of a situation may be prepotent in causing response, and may have responses bound more or less exclusively to it regardless of some or all of its accompaniments.

If a cat which has never been confined in a box or cage of any sort is put into a box like that described a few pages back, it responds chiefly by trying to squeeze through the openings, clawing at the bars and at loose objects within the box, reaching out between the bars, and pulling at anything then within its grasp. In short, it responds to this artificial situation as it would by original nature to confinement, as in a thicket. If a cat which has learned to escape from a number of such boxes by manipulating various mechanical contrivances, is confined in a new box, it responds to it by a mixture of the responses originally bound to confining obstacles and of those which it has learned to make to boxes like the new one.

In both cases it illustrates the *Law of Assimilation* or *Analogy* that to any situations, which have no special original or acquired response of their own, the response made will be that which by original or acquired nature is connected with some situation which they resemble. For S_2 to resemble S_1 means for it to arouse more or less of the sensory neurones which S_1 would arouse, and in more or less the same fashion.

The last important principle which stands out clearly in the learning of the lower animals is that which I shall call *Associative Shifting*. The ordinary animal 'tricks' in response to verbal signals are convenient illustrations. One, for example, holds up before a cat a bit of fish, saying, ''Stand up.'' The cat, if hungry enough, and not of fixed contrary habit, will stand up in response to the fish. The response, however, contracts bonds also with the total situation, and hence to the human being in that position giving that signal as well as to the fish. After enough trials, by proper arrangement, the fish can be omitted, the other elements of the situation serving to evoke the response. Association may later be further shifted to the oral signal alone. With certain limitations due to the necessity of getting an element of a situation attended to, a response to the total situation A B C D E may thus be shifted to B C D E to C D E, to D E, to E. Moreover, by adding to the situation new elements F, G, H, etc., we may, subject to similar limitations, get *any response of which a learner is capable* associated with *any situation to which he is sensitive*. Thus, what was at the start utterly without power to evoke a certain response may come to do so to perfection. Indeed, the situation may be one which at the start would have aroused an exactly opposite response. So a monkey can be taught to go to the top of his cage whenever you hold a piece of banana at the bottom of it.

These simple, semi-mechanical phenomena—multiple response, the coöperation of the animal's set or attitude with the external situation, the predominant activity of parts or elements of a situation, the response to new situations as to the situations most like them, and the shifting of a response from one situation to another by gradually changing a situation without disturbing the response to it—which animal learning discloses, are the fundamentals of human learning also. They are, of course, much complicated in the more advanced stages of human learning, such as the acquisition of skill with the violin, or of knowledge of the calculus, or of inventiveness in engineering. But it is impossible to understand the subtler and more planful learning of cultivated men without clear ideas of the forces which make learning possible in its first form of directly connecting some gross bodily response with a situation immediately present to the senses. Moreover, no matter how subtle, complicated, and advanced a form of learning one has to explain, these simple facts—the selection of connections by use and satisfaction and their elimination by disuse and annoyance, multiple reaction, the mind's set as a condition, piecemeal activity of a situation, with prepotency of certain elements in determining the response, response by analogy, and shifting of bonds—will, as a matter of fact, still be the main, and perhaps the only, facts needed to explain it.

The Method of Pavlov in Animal Psychology

Robert M. Yerkes and Sergius Morgulis

About eight years ago Professor J. P. Pawlow,[*] Director of the physiological department of the Institute of Experimental Medicine in St. Petersburg, devised and introduced into his great research laboratory an ingenious and valuable new method of investigating the physiology of the nervous system in its relations to the so-called psychic reactions of organisms. This method—now widely known as the Pawlow salivary reflex method—has been extensively employed by Pawlow and his students in St. Petersburg. Recently it has been introduced into the Physiological Institute of Berlin by Nicolai, a former student of Pawlow. It consists in the quantitative study of those modifications of the salivary reflex which are conditioned by complex receptive and elaborative processes (psychic reactions) in the central nervous system.

Inasmuch as practically all of the results of the method have been published in Russia, it has seemed to us important that a general descrip-

Adapted from Yerkes, R. M., & Morgulis, S. (1909). The method of Pawlow in animal psychology. *Psychological Bulletin, 6,* 257–273. Copyright © 1909 by the American Psychological Association. Adapted and reprinted by permission of the publisher.

[*] J. P. Pawlow is, of course, Ivan P. Pavlov. The spelling is due to the differences between the Russian and English alphabets. (Ed. note)

tion of the technique of the method, together with a statement of certain of the important results which it has yielded, should be published at this time in English. Our purposes in preparing this article were two: first, to present a body of facts which is of great importance to both physiologists and animal psychologists; and second, to familiarize American investigators with the salivary reflex method and hasten the time when it shall be as advantageously used in this country as it now is in Russia.

The materials for this discussion we have obtained chiefly from six papers. Of these the first four are, in the main, general accounts of the method and its results from the strikingly different points of view and interests of Pawlow and Nicolai. The papers of Selionyi and Orbeli are admirable reports of facts.... We are indebted to Professor Pawlow for a number of the titles included in this list and also for a thorough revision and correction of the bibliography.

Our discussion naturally falls into four parts: (1) A general description of the method of its application, from the standpoints of Pawlow, Nicolai, and Selionyi; (2) an expository summary of the study of the auditory reactions of the dog as reported by Selionyi; (3) a similar summary of Orbeli's study of the visual reactions of the dog; and (4) a general summary of the results of the method.* To give a complete account of the investigations of the St. Petersburg laboratory—for already more than forty papers have been published— would be possible only if each paper were dismissed with a sentence or two. We have preferred to consider two representative papers in some detail instead of mentioning several casually.

DESCRIPTION OF THE SALIVARY REFLEX METHOD

The salivary reflex (secretion of saliva) occurs under two strikingly different conditions: (*a*) when the mouth is stimulated by certain chemi-

cal processes (the specific stimuli for secretion); and (*b*) when the animal is stimulated by sights, sounds, odors, temperatures, touches which have been present previously in connection with stimuli of the first class. The environment of the dog may be said to consist of two sets of properties, the essential and non-essential. Essential, for a given reaction, are those stimulating properties of an object which regularly and definitely determine that reaction of the organism; non-essential, for the reaction in point, are those properties of an object which only in a highly variable and inconstant manner condition the reaction. The chemical property of food, whereby it acts upon the receptors of the mouth of the dog, is an 'essential' property, for it invariably causes a salivary reflex. The appearance of the same food—its lightness, color, etc.—is a 'non-essential,' for it may or may not cause the reflex. Pawlow has termed reflexes in response to 'essential' properties 'unconditioned,' and those in response to 'non-essential' properties 'conditioned.'

It was Pawlow's idea that the perfectly constant and dependable 'unconditioned' salivary reflex might be used to advantage as a basis for the investigation of those complex nervous processes one of whose expressions is a 'conditioned' reflex of the same glands. Since many, if not all, changes in the nervous system gain expression in one way or another, through the salivary reflex, why not, Pawlow asks, investigate these processes by observing their relation to this particular reflex? That there was nothing novel in this idea is evident when we recollect that numerous reflexes have been used, by other investigators, for the study of psychic reactions. Respiration, heartbeat, and certain secretory changes have been studied, in this connection, with varying success. But what Pawlow may claim, apparently, is the discovery of that particular reflex which seems to be best adapted for the investigation of complex nervous processes.

The technique of the method we shall describe, with the help of two figures which have been re-drawn from Nicolai. The first of these

* The section on Orbeli's study of visual reactions has been omitted. (Ed. note)

figures represents a dog prepared for experiments in accordance with the method used in St. Petersburg. The second of the figures represents the modification of experimental technique which has been devised by Nicolai in Berlin.

The experimental procedure is as follows. A normally active and healthy dog of vigorous salivary reaction having been selected, the duct of one of the salivary glands—the parotid for example—is exposed on the outer surface of the cheek and a salivary fistula is formed. The wound heals completely within a few days and the dog exhibits no signs of discomfort or inconvenience. Those who have used the method insist, indeed, that their animals are perfectly normal in all respects. In further preparation for the study of the salivary reflex a small glass funnel is fastened over the opening to the duct with Mendelejeff cement. To this funnel is attached a tube which conducts the saliva to a graduate.

Three methods of measuring the quantity of saliva secreted are in use. (1) As the secretion flows from the tube into a graduate the drops are counted, and if the experimenter so desires, an additional measurement may subsequently be obtained by readings from the scale of the graduate. (2) The saliva is permitted, as Figure 1 shows, to flow through a short tube into a graduate bottle and the amount of the secretion is then determined by reading the scale on the bottle. This method necessitates the replacing of the

FIGURE 1

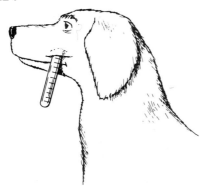

partially filled bottle by a clean one and the careful cleaning of the funnel between experiments. (3) A small metal canula, inserted in the duct of the gland, is connected by a heavy walled rubber tube with a small glass tube. The saliva drops from this tube upon the lever of a Marey tambour, as is shown in Figure 2. As it falls drop by drop upon this lever a record is made upon a smoked drum. From this record the experimenter may read the quantity of the secretion in drops and the rate of flow, *i.e.,* how many drops fell in a given interval. This graphic method of recording the salivary reaction is Nicolai's improvement on the Pawlow method as used in Russia. In addition to enabling the experimenter to obtain more detailed and accurate data concerning the reaction, it has the important advantage of permitting him to withdraw from the experiment room during the experiments. This is desirable because his presence is likely to influence the dog in unexpected and undesirable ways.

The Pawlow method lends itself readily to the investigation of many psychic reactions. In order to get clearly in mind the remaining essential points of experimental procedure we may consider its application to the study of visual discrimination of colors. A dog, which has been selected for observation and in which a salivary fistula has been created, is subjected to a course of training to establish a 'conditioned' reflex on the basis of visual stimulation. This is accomplished by showing the animal a particular color—say green—at intervals and at the same time giving it food. After numerous repetitions of this procedure the visual stimulus becomes the sign of food and induces the salivary reflex in the absence of the food. An animal so trained is ready for experiments on the discrimination of colors. If it appears that no color except green produces the 'conditioned' reflex, there is reason to believe that the dog perceives green as distinct from the other colors.

Pawlow devised and employs this method not for the study of psychic phenomena, as Nicolai proposes to do, but simply as a means of ap-

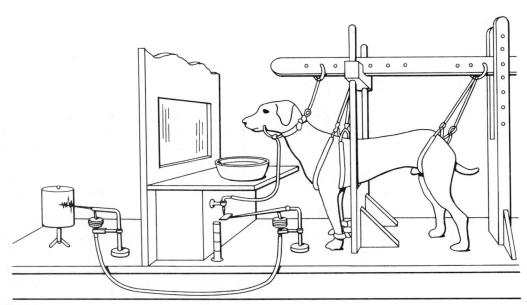

FIGURE 2

proach to the physiology of the nervous system. Of his insistence upon the objective point of view the following quotation from his Huxley lecture is excellent proof. "Up to the present time the physiology of the eye, the ear, and other superficial organs which are of importance as recipients of impressions has been regarded almost exclusively in its subjective aspect; this presented some advantages, but at the same time, of course, limited the range of inquiry. In the investigation of the conditioned stimuli in the higher animals, this limitation is got rid of and a number of important questions in this field of research can be at once examined with the aid of all the immense resources which experiments on animals place in the hands of the physiologist.... The investigation of the conditioned reflexes is of very great importance for the physiology of the higher parts of the central nervous system. Hitherto this department of physiology has throughout most of its extent availed itself of ideas not its own, ideas borrowed from psychology, but now there is a possibility of its being liberated from such evil influences. The condi-

tioned reflexes lead us to the consideration of the position of animals in nature: this is a subject of immense extent and one that must be treated objectively."

Although psychology—or rather psychologists—deserves all of the criticisms which the physiologists have made, students of animal behavior and comparative psychology should not allow Pawlow's attitude to discourage them. Nor should they be slow to appreciate the immediate importance, and promise for the advancement of their science, of the Pawlow method and its results. That it can be used to advantage by animal psychologists, as well as by those physiologists for whom the psychic phenomenon is merely an unescapable nuisance, is obvious.

Already Nicholai has ably discussed the relations of the method to psychological problems. He contends, with reason, that the salivary reflex method possesses the four essential characteristics of a scientific method in psychology: (*a*) it is general, in its applicability to the study of psychic processes; (*b*) it is constant; (*c*) it permits accurate measurement; and (*d*) it is specific.

Undoubtedly the method may be applied to the study of various aspects of sensation and the mutual relations of sensations, to memory and ideation, to the formation of judgments and will acts. Its obvious limitation appears in the number of organisms with which it may be employed. Evidently it can not be used for the study of animals which lack salivary glands, and even among those animals which do possess these glands there are many which surely would not lend themselves satisfactorily to the method. It seems, therefore, as if Pawlow's method were especially important in animal psychology as a means to the intensive study of the mental life of a limited number of mammals. The dog evidently is especially well suited to the experiments.

SELIONYI'S STUDY OF AUDITORY REACTIONS

With this brief general sketch of the method and its purposes in mind we may turn to the investigation reported by Selionyi. In order, we shall state the problem, the principal points of method, and the results of his study of the auditory reactions of the dog.

The initial purpose of the work was to determine, by means of one form of the Pawlow method, how great must be the difference in the quality or the intensity of two auditory stimuli in order that they shall produce perceivably different effects upon the auditory apparatus of the dog. The problem as it presented itself to the investigator was primarily one of the physiology of the nervous system, and secondarily one of animal psychology.

Starting with the familiar fact that sounds which have been associated with food may under certain conditions stimulate the salivary reflex, Selionyi first of all, as a necessary preliminary to his research, attempted to ascertain whether certain unusual or unfamiliar sounds, as well as those which have become familiar through their association with food, cause the secretion of saliva. He

discovered that only 'familiar' sounds—those which the dog has learned to recognize as significant—have this effect as a rule.

No dogs were used for the investigation whose salivary reaction was not vigorous. An animal after having been tested for its normal reaction and prepared for the experiments by the creation of a salivary fistula, was trained until a definite 'conditioned' reflex appeared in connection with some particular sound. Repeatedly, in the training experiments, this sound was produced near the dog at the instant food was given. Sometimes the two stimuli were presented simultaneously; sometimes the sound preceded the food by five to thirty seconds. The combined action of the stimuli was permitted to continue for thirty to sixty seconds. This procedure was repeated at intervals of ten to thirty minutes, on a number of different days, until the sound, when given alone, would rapidly bring about the secretion of saliva. This usually occurred after twenty to forty repetitions. A particular sound—of definitely determined pitch, intensity, and quality—was thus rendered significant and 'familiar.' It now differed from other distinguishably different sounds in that it had its specific salivary reflex, whereas they caused no reaction.

During these training tests it is extremely important, Selionyi points out, that the experimenter make no unusual movements or otherwise produce conditions which may regularly and markedly stimulate the dog, else these irrelevant stimuli may become associated with food and spoil the result of the training experiment. In all of the experiments the experimenter has to guard against irregularities of condition. If he moves too quickly or if he holds himself too rigidly quiet, as the inexperienced worker is likely to do, the dog is disturbed and the salivary reaction modified.

The sounds whose influence was carefully observed by Selionyi were produced by an organ, by organ pipes, and by two whistles one of which (a tuning pipe) gave a number of tones of different pitch and the other a rattling sound.

A dog whose normal salivary reaction had been carefully observed and in which the habit of responding to a certain sound had been developed was placed in an apparatus similar to that of Figure 2. The 'familiar' sound was then produced and the reaction noted. The experimenter took account of both the quantity and the quality of the saliva. A quantitative expression for the former was obtained either by counting the drops as they left the fistula or by measuring the secretion in a graduate. The quality (viscidity) was determined by a measurement of the rate of flow through a capillary tube. Some ten minutes after the 'familiar' sound, an 'unfamiliar' sound whose influence upon the reaction the experimenter wished to discover, was given in the same way, and the reaction was again observed. After another interval, the 'familiar' sound was repeated. Thus, for the purpose of comparison, the observer obtained reactions to both kinds of stimuli in rapid succession. The experimenter noted the interval (latent period) between application of a stimulus and the appearance of the first drop of saliva, and he collected and measured the saliva which was secreted between stimulations as well as immediately after the application of each stimulus.

The sample record reproduced herewith will serve to illustrate the results obtained by this procedure.

TABLE
EXPERIMENT 54: 'MARGARET'

Familiar sound, A, of Tuning Pipe.
Unfamiliar sound, A, of Tuning Pipe and
'Rattling' Whistle.

Time	Sound	Duration of Stim.	Quantity of Saliva in Drops
4:25	Unfamiliar	1'40"	0
4:55	Familiar	30"	15
5:05	Familiar	20"	5
5:19	Unfamiliar	2'15"	0
5:29	Familiar	30"	9

In order to render a translation of Selionyi's summary of results intelligible it will be necessary to define a number of the terms which he employs.

A 'conditioned reflex' is a reaction (salivary in this case) to a stimulus which is only secondarily and indirectly a condition of the reflex. (For example, the sight of meat may produce a 'conditioned' salivary reflex.)

An 'unconditioned reflex' is a reaction to a stimulus which regularly and constantly conditions the reflex. (For example, food placed in the mouth causes an 'unconditioned' salivary reflex.)

A 'familiar' stimulus (sound, in this investigation) is one which experience has taught the animal to respond to as if it were the precursor of food. It is in fact a sound which produces a 'conditioned reflex' ordinarily.

An 'unfamiliar' stimulus is one which the animal has not been trained to respond to.

A 'fundamental reflex' is one which is caused by a 'familiar' sound.

An 'additional reflex' is one which is caused by an 'unfamiliar' sound which differs from the 'familiar' sound only in pitch.

A 'partial reflex' is one which is caused by some part of a complex 'familiar' sound. As, for example, when one tone of a 'familiar' chord causes a reflex.

In reading the summary of Selionyi's results it is important that the reader remember (1) that conditioned reflexes die out with repetition. (2) That edible substances, when used as stimuli repeatedly, produce a constantly diminishing secretion of saliva, whereas inedible substances, when used repeatedly, produce a constantly increasing secretion. (3) That the secretion in response to edible substances increases as the interval between stimuli is lengthened, whereas the secretion to inedible substances diminishes as the interval is lengthened. Selionyi states that he made use mostly of edible substances. He did, however, at times make use of weak acid solutions as a substitute for food.

1 Separate sounds are received by the auditory apparatus of the dog as distinct stimuli even when they differ from one another by only a quarter of a tone.

2 Sounds which differ from one another only very slightly in quality are received as distinct stimuli.

3 A conditioned reflex of definite intensity is specific of (results from) a sound ('familiar') of a given pitch which has become its stimulus.

4 'Unfamiliar' sounds which differ from the 'familiar' sound by a slight variation in pitch, produce in some dogs 'additional' reflexes which are much less intense than the reflex to the 'familiar' sound.

5 Even comparatively slight changes in the quality of 'familiar' sounds result in a diminution and disappearance of the fundamental salivary reflex.

6 Sounds which differ from one another very little in pitch (the quality and intensity remaining constant) may become the stimuli for the secretion of saliva of different degrees of viscidity: some cause the flow of liquid saliva; others, of viscid saliva.

7 The specificity of conditioned reflexes for the sounds which induce them may persist for two months.

8 Diminishing the strength of the 'familiar' sound causes the weakening or even the complete disappearance of its conditioned reflex.

9 A 'familiar' sound, which very gradually reaches such an intensity that a conditioned reflex would ordinarily result from it, fails to call forth its reflex if it was too weak at the beginning.

10 Separate components of a complex sound which conditions a 'fundamental' reflex, will produce reflexes (the so-called partial reflexes) at a certain relative intensity.

11 The intensity of partial reflexes depends upon the relative intensity of the sounds by which they are induced. The more intense the partial sound, the stronger is the partial reflex. A single tone of a familiar chord of three tones, of the same quality and intensity, produces a less intense partial reflex than do two tones of the same chord.

12 Each partial sound has its specific partial reflex just as each 'familiar' tone has its fundamental reflex.

13 The substitution of an irrelevant tone for one element of a 'familiar' chord tends to inhibit the reflex.

14 The addition of an irrelevant sound to the 'familiar' sound tends to inhibit the conditioned reflex.

15 The degree of inhibition is directly related to the intensity of the new or inhibiting sound.

16 Simultaneous stimulation by two sounds, each of which produces, when alone, the conditioned reflex (in connection with a non-conditioned reflex which is induced by the same food substance) brings about different results according to the character of the sound. In some cases the reflex which is thus produced is equal in intensity to the reflex caused by one of the two sounds; in other cases it is of considerably less intensity.

17 Under certain conditions of excitability or permanency, a conditioned reflex which has been worn out by repetitions may spontaneously reappear at the end of the interval which separated the previous repetitions.

18 The statement that a worn-out conditioned reflex may be restored by any unconditioned stimulus must be recognized as false.

19 The wearing out, by repetitions, of a fundamental reflex to a particular sound tends also to weaken the reflex to a second sound, which occurs in connection with the same non-conditioned reflex as the first sound.

20 The wearing out of an 'additional' reflex causes a slight weakening—in an acute experiment—of the fundamental reflex with which it is associated.

21 The wearing out of a fundamental reflex—in an acute experiment—causes a complete loss of the additional reflex which is associated with it.

22 The wearing out of a partial reflex—in an acute experiment—causes some weakening of the fundamental reflex.

23 The wearing out of one partial reflex causes the wearing out of another of the same intensity as the first. This phenomenon is observable in an acute as well as in a chronic experiment (at least in those cases in which the partial sounds are of the same quality).

24 By subjecting additional and partial reflexes to wear by repetition in a chronic experiment, and by simultaneously reinforcing the fundamental conditioned reflex by means of a non-conditioned reflex, it is possible to destroy completely the additional and partial reflexes while retaining the fundamental reflex in its full original intensity.

25 The independent restoration of two partial reflexes which have disappeared in a chronic experiment by reason of the repetition of one of them comes about differently. At the time when the partial reflex which was subjected to the influence of repetition has not yet reappeared the other partial reflex is fully expressed.

26 'Unfamiliar' sounds which differ from a 'familiar' sound only very slightly in pitch, when given before the 'familiar' sound tend to inhibit its reflex.

27 A 'familiar' sound, the conditioned reflex of which has been worn out, produces an inhibitory effect upon the unworn reflex of another 'familiar' sound, when it is given simultaneously with the latter sound....

LAWS OF CONDITIONED REFLEXES AND CONCLUSIONS CONCERNING THE RELATIVE IMPORTANCE OF THE SENSES OF THE DOG

The work in Pawlow's laboratory has rendered it possible to formulate a number of laws concerning the conditioned reflex. We shall mention only three of the most important of these, as examples.

Law I. A conditioned reflex can be worn out or destroyed by repetition of its conditioning stimulus or stimulus complex. Whereas at first a particular sound, sight, or odor which is indicative of food causes the secretion of several drops of saliva, after a few repetitions at short intervals and without the presentation of food to the dog it causes no secretion. This wearing out of the conditioned reflex serves to distinguish it from the unconditioned reflex.

Law II. The destruction of a conditioned reflex by repetition does not influence other conditioned reflexes. For example, the wearing out of the conditioned reflex to the sight of a particular kind of food leaves unmodified the reflex to the odor of the food.

Law III. Irrelevant stimuli (a sudden noise, a new object in the environment, etc.) produce a depressing effect upon conditioned reflexes. In regard to the nature of their influence, they may be conveniently classed in two groups: (1) those that temporarily diminish or even suspend the activity of the conditioned reflex, but lose this retarding effect after a few repetitions; (2) those which at first tend to reduce the intensity of the reflex and finally inhibit it completely....

Finally we may be permitted to quote from Nicolai his conclusions concerning the relation of the Pawlow method to animal psychology.

> The Pawlow salivary reflex is a relatively complicated process which is connected only indirectly with the exciting stimulus and for the occurrence of which the idea of eating is always necessary.
>
> Pawlow's salivary reflex method gives us a better explanation of the manner in which a dog learns spontaneously [than do most other methods], but it remains to be shown how far the learning can be carried. In the solving of related questions, the method does not seem to be superior to Kalischer's training method, and the latter is much the more convenient.
>
> One can show experimentally that a dog learns by subsuming certain new ideas under general ideas which he has already acquired in the course of the experiment.

The Loeb-Jennings Debate and the Science of Animal Behavior

Philip J. Pauly

In the early years of the twentieth century two major figures in American biology engaged in a debate regarding animal behavior. The controversy, which extended from 1900 to 1910, involved the German-American physiologist Jacques Loeb (1859–1924), professor at the Universities of Chicago and California, and the protozoologist Herbert Spencer Jennings (1868–1947), who worked at the Universities of Michigan and Pennsylvania and at Johns Hopkins University. The specific subject of the debate was the nature of tropisms in invertebrates, but general issues were raised that influenced psychology in general and behaviorism in particular.[1]

Loeb and Jennings were members of the first generation of American "experimental biologists." These biologists, associated with graduate institutions such as Johns Hopkins, Harvard, Chicago, Columbia, and Bryn Mawr, and directly linked through the Woods Hole Marine Biological Laboratory, self-consciously set themselves against the older tradition of systematizers and "speculative" naturalists. They were confident of their ability to move toward solutions of longstanding problems through more rigorous observation and more stringent standards of scientific explanation.[2] While their central activities were in embryology and cytology, they also devoted substantial effort to what would now be considered behavioral questions. In considering this subject, Loeb and Jennings were seeking to determine the categories, methods, and aims that would make the study of behavior biologically respectable.

Some historians who have looked at Loeb and Jennings have described them both as objectivists and neuromechanists whose differences were relatively minor.[3] Others have considered their debate, but have viewed it from a one-sided perspective. Loeb is described as a mechanistic reductionist dedicated to an outdated metaphysics of crude materialism. While valuable as an advocate of experimentation, he was justifiably—and even, it is assumed, correctly—criticized and countered by the more balanced empirical approach of Jennings.[4]

These analyses are too simple, for it is just as possible to present Jennings as a speculative theoretician and Loeb as a narrow empiricist. It is more productive to view their conflict as the initial explication of a polarity in the study of behavior that was to divide American scientists for decades to come. The simplest adequate distinction is between Loeb's commitment to Machian positivism and Jennings's equally fervid interest in Spencerian or Deweyite evolutionism. Loeb's interest was rapid and efficient control of behavior; Jenning's basic concern was the exploration of the mechanisms whereby various organisms adapted to their surroundings. The outcome of their debate was more complex than victory or defeat. Study of their disagreements can indicate the range of aims perceived in the biological analysis of behavior at the beginnings of this century. In addition, it may be possible to illuminate a more narrowly focused historical question—the development of behaviorism by Loeb's student and Jennings's junior colleague, John B. Watson.

LOEB'S CONCEPT OF ANIMAL TROPISMS

In the 1880s the study of invertebrate behavior proceeded along four different paths, each with its own possibilities and attendant difficulties. Physiologists analyzed reflexes and sensory capabilities, but they faced major problems in relating their information regarding isolated systems

Pauly, P. J. (1981). The Loeb-Jennings debate and the science of animal behavior. *Journal of the History of the Behavioral Sciences, 17,* 504–515. Copyright © 1981 by the Clinical Psychology Publishing Company. Reprinted by permission of the publisher and the author.

to the activities of the organism as a whole. Natural history description of instincts, primarily those of insects, was a field with a long tradition and one that was expanding as a result of Darwinism. But it dealt with such varied phenomena that it lacked a guiding thread, apart from the recognition that instincts were generally adaptive. More speculative evolutionists such as Ernst Haeckel and Max Verworn sought to identify the evolutionary units of behavior through the study of protozoa but soon became caught up in speculation regarding the psychic properties of matter. And a few psychologists, such as Alfred Binet, sought to analyze behavior of microorganisms with the categories of faculty psychology, a venture of limited promise. The most sophisticated combination of all these approaches was in the work of George J. Romanes, whose studies of jellyfish integrated the physiological and evolutionary approaches prevalent at the time.[5] Scientists interested in behavior turned to the study of invertebrates partly for practical reasons such as ease of handling and opportunities for controlled observation. They also felt that fundamental knowledge could come from work on simple forms. But there was no clear sense of the immediate significance of an extensive research program. As a result, no well-defined schools or intellectual polarities arose.[6]

Jacques Loeb's theory of animal tropisms, developed in the years 1888–1891, provided the foundation for a research program whose aims were quite different from those then prevalent. Its significance lay not so much in its experimentalism or its rejection of "anthropomorphism"— these themes were already common—but rather, in its single-minded emphasis on controlling the motions of animals.

Loeb's earliest work was quite similar to that of Romanes. As a student of the brain physiologist Friedrich L. Goltz at the German University of Strassburg in the early 1880s, he sought to integrate the results of cerebral ablation experiments with an antimechanistic emphasis on the purposefulness of behavior. His interest shifted to the experimental control of behavior only as the result of contact with two other scientists in the latter 1880s, Ernst Mach and Julius Sachs.[7]

Ernst Mach's *Analysis of Sensations* significantly altered Loeb's conception of the nature and purpose of science. Soon after reading the book Loeb wrote to Mach that "your ideas are scientifically and ethically the basis on which I stand, and on which, in my opinion, the scientist must stand." Loeb took from Mach the idea that the purpose of science was economy of thought and improved ability to deal with the practical needs of life, and not the development of a causal-analytical "picture" of external reality. He applied to the study of behavior the Machian conviction that scientific knowledge was a technical tool. The tropism concept was important to Loeb because it was a means "to control the 'voluntary' movements of a living animal just as securely and unequivocally as the engineer has been able to control the movements in inanimate nature."[8]

The Machian aim of subordinating analytical explanation to technical control meant little, however, without a concrete research program by which it could be realized. Loeb found a framework suited to his purposes in the work of the botanist Julius Sachs, his senior colleague at Würzburg in 1886–1888. Sachs, a largely self-taught scientist who began his career in a school of forestry, was unusual among botanists in his emphasis on physiological questions. This self-limitation, a concern for applications, the relatively simple anatomy and physiology of plants (in particular the absence of a nervous system), and the more obvious dependence of plant motions on the environment led Sachs to concentrate on determining how external forces controlled the direction of motion and the growth of parts of organisms. Directed motions such as growth of a plant towards the light were the result of undirected growth plus a tropism—the reorientation of leaf surfaces so that the light rays would strike symmetrically. By altering the forces it was possible to control growth and movement of the plant as a whole; and this problem could be separated from the need for detailed knowledge of the internal processes underlying the observed tropisms.[9]

Loeb's theory of "the heliotropism of animals and its identity with the heliotropism of plants," first presented in 1888, was a direct extension of Sachs's approach. The orientations of plant surfaces, of motile algae, and of animals were all tropistic, identically dependent upon the action of light on physicochemically irritable protoplasm. When light shone unequally on the two sides of a bilaterally symmetric animal, the animal would reorient so that the illumination was equalized. If the animal were then to move (as it generally did) the motion would be either toward or away from the light.[10]

Heliotropism was only the beginning. His own experiments and those of others soon provided Loeb evidence for geotropism (orientation with respect to gravity), stereotropism or contact irritability (orientation with respect to friction-producing surfaces), galvanotropism (electric currents), chemotropism (a diffusing substance), and possibly others. In addition to tropistic reactions, he argued for the existence of *Unterschiedsempfindlichkeit* (differential sensibility), a change in motion due not to a constant impinging force but to change in the level of that force. Loeb also showed how changes in level of illumination, temperature, the strengths of ions in solution, and other manipulable, quantifiable factors could induce, eliminate, or change the direction of reactions.[11]

Loeb's intellectual position was in sharp contrast to the approaches then dominant. He strongly attacked the notion that it was necessary to explain actions such as tropisms in terms of sensorimotor physiology. Tropisms were processes that were mediated—in animals as in plants—through the whole organism. The central nervous system did not necessarily play an indispensable role, and in any case neurological research would only lead to a dead end in the brain—what Loeb called "the mysticism of the ganglion cells."[12] Natural history accounts were

even more misguided, since overconcern for the peculiarities of the reaction mechanisms of each species would mire the study of behavior in masses of confused detail. It was necessary to concentrate on those aspects of behavior common to many different types of organisms, and not individual adaptations to particular circumstances. Galvanotropism was an important phenomenon because it was a pure laboratory artifact whose mode of action was not obscured by the peculiar adaptive mechanisms of various individual species. Similarly, explanations of the evolution of tropisms were trivial. As the discovery of galvanotropism seemed to show, only a small fraction of potential phenomena were currently being manifested by organisms; explanation of the origins of present combinations was insignificant compared to the potential for transformation that a science of behavior control could provide. As for psychological explanations, they depended upon factors that no "engineer has been able to control."[13]

The framework within which Loeb conceptualized the problem of animal behavior was that of general physiology.[14] This science, as promoted by men such as Claude Bernard, Eduard Pflüger, and Wilhelm Engelmann, sought to determine the basic properties of life, the functions of living matter underlying the variety of visible biological phenomena. General physiology, however, was primarily cellular physiology: the attempt to localize and identify the chemical conditions of life, and to define the submicroscopic structures whose physical properties could account for important vital functions. General physiology was reductionist in its search to explain biological manifestations in terms of theories involving simpler, more fundamental entities.

The relevance of such an analytic aim to the study of complex molar phenomena of behavior was unclear. Loeb accepted only the science's overall goal—to understand the properties of life—and redefined it positivistically, rejecting the aim of reducing biology to analytical chemistry and subcellular mechanics. While often appealing to "physical and chemical conditions which are outside the realm of histology," he showed little interest in the actual task of reducing changes to all their physical and chemical determinants. For Loeb, causal analysis need only extend to identification of "the most notable condition of a change."[15] His appeals to reduction were continually to *physical* chemistry, understood in the broad sense of the search for mathematical regularities in molar processes. Physical chemistry merely provided a set of phenomenal laws that might apply to various aspects of behavior, independent of detailed questions concerning its *material* basis. Loeb showed no more interest in complete physicochemical analysis than he did in physiological analysis. He sought laws that could be used to engineer behavior.[16]

JENNINGS AND THE BEHAVIOR OF PROTOZOA

Jacques Loeb came to America in 1891 for a combination of personal and political reasons. After a year at Bryn Mawr he joined the University of Chicago at the invitation of its chief biologist, C. O. Whitman. While gradually shifting his own interests to study of development and reproduction, Loeb promoted study of tropisms among biologists at both Chicago and at the Marine Biological Laboratory of Woods Hole, Massachusetts. C. B. Davenport was also influential in spreading interest in tropisms among his advanced students, first at Harvard and after 1899 at Chicago. By 1901 notable papers on the subject had been written by Davenport, E. B. Wilson, G. H. Parker, Walter B. Cannon, Edwin B. Holt, F. T. Lewis, F. S. Lee, and Robert M. Yerkes.[17]

A typical example of the use made of Loeb's ideas was a paper written by Davenport and Cannon in 1897. "On the Determination of the Direction and Rate of Movement of Organisms by Light" tested whether *Daphnia* moved toward light due to an "attempt to place the head in a brighter region than the tail," as Verworn had argued, or due to "different (chemical?) effects produced upon the differentiated body"—the opinion of Loeb. By using an appropriate apparatus to separate the intensity gradient from the direction of the light source, they showed that Loeb's view was correct. The authors also found that speed of response was a function of the intensity of the source. This paper unequivocally determined the factor controlling behavior in a given case, while it ignored the problem of identifying the nature of the "different (chemical?) effects." As such, it represented the work that Loeb's program deemed necessary.[18]

Herbert Spencer Jennings studied with Davenport at Harvard, but he was much less impressed with Loeb's work than his teacher was. Jennings was the son of an itinerant Midwestern doctor-farmer and "village infidel" (his brother was named Darwin). He was raised on evolutionism, but the character of his beliefs changed when he entered the University of Michigan in 1890. There "Professor Dewey's attacks on Herbert Spencer's Philosophy and on Materialism showed that they had no monopoly on rigid logical thinking and partially at least set one free from my heretofore compelled adherence to such doctrines, a change which, though the process was painful, as all upheavals of established principles must be, was very welcome."[19]

Jennings's early exposure to Spencerian evolutionism and his desire to get beyond its cruder aspects shaped his approach to biology. His Harvard dissertation, on the processes of early embryological development, concluded that gastrulation must be seen as a fundamentally adaptive interaction between internal protoplasmic processes and "influences determining and preserving the form of the egg as a whole." He viewed the purpose of embryology to be the closer analysis of developmental mechanisms and appreciation of their adaptiveness.[20]

Jennings chose to do his postdoctoral research at the University of Jena with Max Verworn. A follower of Ernst Haeckel, Verworn was at this time trying to develop a Haeckelian physiology. He believed that all matter was in some sense "ensouled," and that individual development and evolutionary development were parallel in all important respects. Investigation of the psychological properties of primitive life forms would provide a foundation for understanding the ontogenetic and phylogenetic processes whereby cells united and specialized in forming complex cell states. As he concluded from a study of the reactions of protozoa to stimuli:

> ...the psychological processes in the realm of the protista are the bridge which connects the chemical processes of inorganic nature with the mental life of the highest animals....the development of the human psyche begins with those very psychological processes found in the protista, since the human egg has essentially the same status as a single unicellular organism.[21]

Jennings went to Jena hoping to examine the similarities between movements of protozoa and the movements of cells in morphogenesis. Verworn, however, interested him in behavior as a problem in itself, and when Jennings returned from Germany he began to publish on the reactions of protozoa to external stimuli. Protozoan behavior was important to Jennings because it provided "important points of support for the general theory of the origin and development of psychic powers." In particular Jennings sought to show that protozoan behavior could be cast in terms of sensorimotor physiology on the assumption that each species possessed a few structurally determined "motor reactions." Study of these reactions could provide a basis for understanding the nature and development of complex behavior in more highly evolved species.[22]

Conflict between Jennings and Loeb began in 1900 when Loeb's student W. E. Garrey criticized Jennings for not resolving his species-specific "motor reaction" into tropisms and differential sensibilities.[23] Jennings replied that Garrey began with a "preconceived view that chemotropism must take place according to Professor Loeb's generalization," a generalization

that did not apply to the peculiar motions of asymmetrical *Paramecia*. In the next years Jennings developed a full scale attack on Loeb's ideas on tropisms, giving it final expression in his extensive study, *Behavior of the Lower Organisms* (1906).[24]

In this work Jennings argued that there were two different ways to think of tropisms and differential sensibility. As purely descriptive terms they were acceptable but not very useful. The word "tropism" could only have real significance if it could be shown that it represented a class of orientations due to *totally independent* physiological processes occurring in the two halves of a bilaterally symmetric animal—what Jennings called "the local action tropism theory."[25] It was necessary to explain how the mechanics of the reaction resulted from the particular structure of each species. Galvanotropism was such a "local action," but this proved nothing, because galvanotropism was unnatural, a *mere* laboratory artifact. "Local action" tropisms certainly played no role in the behavior of the asymmetrical protozoa, from an evolutionary viewpoint the simplest, most fundamental organisms. Differential sensibility was merely a name for many different physiological reaction mechanisms; as such it was of little explanatory value.[26]

Jennings was concerned with describing the natural activities—the adaptations—of his animals as accurately as possible. Stimuli to which these simple organisms reacted appeared only as the result of previous "spontaneous" movements; motion was caused by specific internal physiological processes. Jennings argued that the behavior of a paramecium depended upon the totality of its changing physiological state. While very little was known about these states, some things could be stated about them through observation of behavior itself. Noxious stimuli tended to produce negative reactions, and through a process of trial and error those conditions most conducive to life were selected. In fact, repeated encounters with gradually arising harmful situations would lead to the "readier resolution of physiological states," whereby the animal responded not to the noxious stimulus but to other stimuli, neutral in themselves, which generally led to the noxious stimulus.[27]

Such a conception depended upon the intimate linkage of experience, physiology, heredity, and evolution. Since Jennings erroneously believed that conjugation played an insignificant role in the life cycle of protozoa, he thought that successful trial and error reactions to a new situation would gradually (through their readier resolution) move to deeper physiological levels, would be maintained in the continuity of the fission chain, and could thus cause variation in instincts and evolutionary adaptation. A chain of generations of protozoa was essentially a single organism. It accumulated knowledge with repeated trial and error experiences and as a result gradually improved its adaptation to the environment.

Jennings allied himself most explicitly with the ideas of C. Lloyd Morgan, J. Mark Baldwin, and L. T. Hobhouse. His linkage of trial and error learning to evolution was an exemplification of and foundation for Baldwin's view—adopted from Herbert Spencer and Alexander Bain—that the ability to learn arose in the early history of life from selection of random movements by "the organic analogue of the hedonic consciousness." Jennings shared with Baldwin and Morgan the desire to show that individual learning was a major force in evolutionary progress even if, as seemed increasingly likely, the neo-Lamarckian belief in the direct inheritance of acquired habits were untrue.[28]

Jennings's book prompted responses from Loeb (then at Berkeley), H. B. Torrey (an assistant professor there), and G. H. Parker of Harvard. Loeb restricted himself to pointing out that the inapplicability of the tropism concept to asymmetrical paramecia was irrelevant to its use in other cases.[29] Parker's objections were similar. He felt that Jennings had raised a straw man with the demand that tropistic responses be traced to independent physiological processes in the two body halves. It was a fact that there were many orientations to stimuli which were the direct result of different levels of stimulation of receptor organs of the two body halves. Even if it did not account for all behavior, the tropism concept was a useful start in these cases.[30]

The more extensive criticism was provided by Torrey.[31] He began by noting how Jennings's theory of the transformation of behavior through trial and error into instinct depended upon Baldwin and Morgan's evolutionary speculations. Basing an account of behavior on the adaptiveness of "natural" reactions would have to include "the selection hypothesis and the mass of unestablished inferences which it has gathered to itself."[32] The idea that "trial and error" was a basic physiological process required an appeal to either the inherent progressiveness of evolution or to animals' primitive consciousness of pleasure or pain; both were unwarranted assumptions. Galvanotropism, because it was a "pure" reaction, had a greater claim to being the fundamental unit of analysis. If one reaction could be established on a secure basis without appeal to evolutionary hypotheses, could not the rest? Explanation in terms of trial and error might seem appealing in some cases, but it was evident "that it not only does not simplify the general problem which these facts present; but that it actually tends to divert inquiry from a line of investigation which has been shown by recent achievements to be not only promising but fertile."[33] The hypothetical "physiological states" to which Jennings referred were too vague to provide guidance in determining the causes of behavior; they would inevitably lead to a nebulous vitalism.

In replying to his critics Jennings made his scale of scientific values explicit. He argued that a general deterministic program was very different from completed detailed descriptions of the physiology of motion. His investigations had uncovered great variability in different tropistic reactions. The only way to encompass this variability was through "a topographic survey of behavior in the lowest organisms'' and explanations in terms of trial and error—activity determined internally by processes of adaptation.[34] He admitted, however, that acceptance of his ideas would change the general significance of research in animal behavior:

> ...to demonstrate the complexity and difficulty of a field of work is not an achievement to be compared in value with the demonstration that this field is simple and easily explicable on a few known principles. I am under no illusion in regard to this. The clear-cut, narrow tropism theory would be of infinitely greater value for predicting and controlling the behavior of animals than anything I have offered, if only it were true.[35]

In place of Loeb's assertions that with each experiment he was laying the foundations for a predictive science, Jennings could only say that ''my conclusions are of the same character as are drawn from a large mass of statistical data.... My conclusion, like all statistical conclusions, is nothing that will enable one to predict for a given individual case; if it were, it would of course be of much greater value than it is. No single observation whatever is inconsistent with my general conclusions.''[36]

SIGNIFICANCE OF THE LOEB-JENNINGS DEBATE

From one point of view Jennings won the debate. He was able to write to Davenport after meeting with Loeb in January 1900:

> I couldn't help but feel that he suffers a little from his lack of acquaintance with the animals—their structure, etc.—just as some zoologists suffer from lack of chemistry and physics. His theory of tropisms depends on the symmetry of animals and when I incidentally mentioned that the Infusoria were as a rule unsymmetrical it seemed to strike him very suddenly that there was a difficulty somewhere.[37]

Jennings, as a zoologist, was much better acquainted with the details of the structure and be-

havior of infusoria than was Loeb. He was able to point to Loeb's many oversimplifications and unsubstantiated generalizations about different types of animals. And Loeb was unwilling to argue on this level. By 1900 his interest had shifted to what he considered the more important problem of artificial parthenogenesis, and his views on tropisms and behavior had become quite rigid. He wrote to T. H. Morgan some years later:

> ...the truth of the matter is I have never been able to read Jennings through; his whole criticism of the tropism theory seemed so strange to me that I always lost patience whenever I began to read, and turned the pages aside; and when finally Mast began to write I stopped reading them altogether.[38]

As his position rigidified Loeb's use of the term ''tropism'' became less precise. He began to confuse orientations to specific forces and reactions to more general situations, a problem Jennings often noted. This ambiguity was evident in both ''The Mechanistic Conception of Life'' and in his 1918 book reviewing the subject one last time.[39] The major English work published between the wars on movements of invertebrates, Fraenkel and Gunn's *Orientation of Animals,* repeated Jennings's criticisms of Loeb in an historical introduction, and this evaluation then made its way into the historical literature.[40]

Assessment of the debate's results, however, involves more than a judgment regarding who provided a better description of the behavior of lower organisms. As Torrey argued, ''promise'' and ''fertility'' were as important as immediate appeal. In place of Loeb's search for control Jennings was calling for a ''topographic survey.'' While it was hard to question the truth of a survey's results, such Baconian science was dry, dull, and poorly rewarded. In fact, American interest in behavior of the lower organisms virtually disappeared soon after the publication of Jennings's book. Jennings himself abandoned the field in favor of genetics. The research basis for Fraenkel and Gunn's book was almost completely European, and primarily German. The only American to continue to work on these problems was Mast, whom Jennings had given a position at Hopkins.

The deeper argument between Loeb and Jennings, regarding the nature and purpose of the biological study of behavior, remained unsettled. Studies of invertebrate behavior provided models for what could be done with vertebrates and humans from an objectivist and deterministic standpoint. Loeb and Jennings set forth the two main paths to be taken from such assumptions.

Jennings looked for causes internal to the organism (its overall physiological state), while Loeb emphasized factors in the animal's surroundings. Jennings pointed to the complexity of an animal's responses and the diversity among species; Loeb saw simplicity of reaction and the characteristics common to many types. Jennings sought to analyze the mechanics of reactions, hypothesizing and searching for the details of action of different subcellular structures. Loeb described reactions as wholes without concern for the intricacies of internal processes. The goal set for behavior analysis by Jennings was to understand as exactly as possible how the animal worked and how it maintained itself in a changing environment. This was quite different from Loeb's aim of establishing widespread control over many aspects of behavior as soon as possible.

These contrasts all derived from a fundamental disagreement regarding the basic purpose of their science. Jennings wanted to demonstrate the existence of and to understand the nature of evolutionary progress as described by his namesake Herbert Spencer in the Synthetic Philosophy a half century before. For Jennings, as for Spencer, behavior was the mutual adjustment between organism and environment, a process of automatic self-regulation.[41] Scientific inquiry was an evolving appreciation of the workings of this intricate mechanism. Loeb's goal, on the other hand, was engineering: control of existing and production of new forms of behavior. The present mechanism needed to be understood only to the extent necessary to change it.

WATSON AND BEHAVIORISM AS SCIENCE

One of the attentive readers of the works of Loeb and Jennings was John B. Watson. He studied physiology with Loeb in 1900–1901, and had to be dissuaded by J. R. Angell and H. H. Donaldson from writing his dissertation under Loeb. He reviewed Jennings's publications as they appeared, and in 1908 became Jennings's colleague at Johns Hopkins University.[42] To what extent and in what way were these contacts important to the origins of behaviorism? As John C. Burnham and John M. O'Donnell have argued, behaviorism's importance depended crucially upon the intellectual and professional dynamics of the discipline of psychology in America, and upon Watson's position in that discipline.[43] Yet insofar as Watson's aim was the application to humans of methods used to study animal behavior, the earlier biological work of Loeb and Jennings was significant.

Those who have looked at Loeb's and Jennings's influence on Watson have not discussed the differences between the two biologists. When Watson's work is viewed in terms of the polarity outlined above, one can see that on every issue Watson sided with Loeb. Watson emphasized external and peripheral factors at the expense of internal and central ones; he sought broad generalizations across individuals and species; his approach was holistic and dynamic, not structural-mechanical; and, above all, his goals were experimental control and engineering, quite independent of evolutionary concerns. He differed from Loeb on two points. The latter confessed an inability to apply his experimental approach to problems of associative memory (although he recognized as early as 1909 that Pavlov had found a possible solution with the conditioned reflex concept); Watson's important achievement was to extend the science of behavior control to the higher "mental" processes. And Watson disapproved of Loeb's tendency when attacked to appeal to models from physical chemistry; he saw no need to go further than Pavlov's conditioning experiments.[44]

Emphasis on Watson as a synthesizer and professional leader obscures the status of behaviorism as an approach to scientific investigation. Many psychologists saw the potential applications of their discipline to social control; even Hugo Münsterberg, deeply concerned with metaphysical questions, saw no contradiction in using his science to manipulate behavior.[45] But almost all psychologists distinguished basic studies from applied topics. Watson's innovation was to place the control of behavior at the foundation of psychology as a science. By arguing that control was fundamental knowledge, he broke down the barriers between the aims of pure psychology and those of behavioral technology. In this sense behaviorism was an exemplar of the program Loeb had enunciated from the beginning of the 1890s, that the purpose of the biological sciences was "to get the life phenomena under our control."[46]

NOTES

1 While Loeb and Jennings provided the occasion for an extended session at the 1909 International Psychological Congress, the debate remained within the academic community. A reporter at the 1907 International Zoological Congress in Boston was merely bemused by Jennings's interest in learning and coordination in starfish. *Rapports et Comptes Rendus, VIme Congrès International de Psychologie* (Geneva: Librairie Kündig, 1910), pp. 283–358; "Our Scientific 'Nature Fakers': When It Comes to the Matter of Starfish Intelligence, the Amateur Is Lost—The Zöological Congress," *New York Evening Post,* 24 August 1907, 3:5.

2 Hamilton Cravens, *The Triumph of Evolution: American Scientists and the Heredity-Environment Controversy,* 1900–1941 (Philadelphia: University of Pennsylvania Press, 1978), pp. 15–55; Garland E. Allen, "The Transformation of a Science: T. H. Morgan and the Emergence of a New American Biology," in *The Organization of Knowledge in Modern America, 1860–1920,* ed. Alexandra Oleson and John Voss (Baltimore: Johns Hopkins University Press, 1979), pp. 173–210.

3 Donald Jensen, "Foreword to the 1962 Edition," in Herbert Spencer Jennings, *Behavior of the*

Lower Organisms (Bloomington, Ind.: Indiana University Press, 1962), pp. xi–xiv; John C. Burnham, "On the Origins of Behaviorism," *Journal of the History of the Behavioral Sciences* 4 (1968): 151.

4 A. E. S. Gussin, "Jacques Loeb: The Man and His Tropism Theory of Animal Conduct," *Journal of the History of Medicine and Allied Sciences* 18 (1963): 326–327; Donald Fleming, "Introduction," in Jacques Loeb, *The Mechanistic Conception of Life* (Cambridge: Harvard University Press, 1964), pp. xxxvi–xxxix.

5 Vitus Graber, *Grundlinien zur Erforschung des Helligkeits- und Farbensinnes der Tiere* (Leipzig: 1884); Charles Darwin, *The Formation of Vegetable Mould, Through the Action of Worms, with Observations on Their Habits* (New York: D. Appleton, 1882), pp. 8–128; John Lubbock, *Ants, Bees, and Wasps: A Record of Observations on the Habits of the Social Hymenoptera* (New York: D. Appleton, 1882); Max Verworn, *Psychophysiologische Protisten-Studien* (Jena: 1889); Alfred Binet, *The Psychic Life of Micro-Organisms,* trans. T. J. McCormack (Chicago: Open Court, 1889); George J. Romanes, *Jelly-Fish, Star-Fish and Sea-Urchins, Being a Research on Primitive Nervous Systems* (London: Kegan Paul, and Trench, 1885).

6 The entomologist J. H. Fabre, isolated geographically, intellectually, and professionally, was the exception that proved the rule. See William Morton Wheeler, "Jean-Henri Fabre," *Journal of Animal Behavior* 6 (1916): 74–80. Julian Jaynes, "The Historical Origins of 'Ethology' and 'Comparative Psychology,' " *Animal Behavior* 17 (1969): 601–606, emphasizing studies on vertebrates, argues that naturalists and experimentalists were split throughout the nineteenth century; I feel, however, that the distinction is made artificially sharp through explicit reference to present-day issues.

7 A detailed discussion of Loeb's intellectual development can be found in Philip J. Pauly, "Jacques Loeb and the Control of Life: An Experimental Biologist in Germany and America, 1859–1924" (Ph.D. diss., Johns Hopkins University, 1980), pp. 50–118.

8 John T. Blackmore, *Ernst Mach: His Work, Life, and Influence* (Berkeley: University of California Press, 1972); Jacques Loeb to Ernst Mach, 21 July

1887, Ernst Mach Papers, Ernst-Mach-Institut, Freiburg-im-Breisgau, West Germany; Loeb, "On Instinct and Will in Animals" (1890), in Loeb, *Studies in General Physiology* (Chicago: University of Chicago Press, 1905), p. 107.

9 E. G. Pringsheim, *Julius Sachs der Begründer der neuen Pflanzenphysiologie,* 1832–1897 (Jena: G. Fischer, 1932); Martin Bopp, "Julius von Sachs," *Dictionary of Scientific Biography,* 12: 58–60; Julius Sachs, *Lectures on the Physiology of Plants,* trans. H. Marshall (Oxford: Clarendon Press, 1887), pp. 587–602, 677–697.

10 Loeb, "Die Orientierung der Tiere gegen das Licht (tierischer Heliotropismus)," *Sitzungsberichte der physikalisch-medicinische Gesellschaft zu Würzburg,* 1888, pp. 1–5; idem, "The Heliotropism of Animals and Its Identity with the Heliotropism of Plants" (1890), *Studies,* pp. 1–88.

11 Loeb, "Heliotropism," pp. 20–23, 66–67; idem, "Die Orientierung der Tiere gegen die Schwerkraft der Erde (tierischer Geotropismus)," *Sitzungsberichte der physikalisch-medicinische Gesellschaft zu Würzburg,* 1888, pp. 5–10; idem, "The Artificial Transformation of Positively Heliotropic Animals into Negatively Heliotropic and *Vice Versa*" (1893), *Studies,* pp. 265–294; idem, "Contributions to the Brain Physiology of Worms" (1894), *Studies,* pp. 345–369; Jacques Loeb and S. S. Maxwell, "Zur Theorie des Galvanotropismus," *Archiv für die gesamte Physiologie des Menschen und der Tiere* 63 (1896): 121–144.

12 Loeb, "Instinct and Will," p. 114.

13 Pauly, "Loeb," pp. 79–93; 212–216.

14 On "general physiology" in the nineteenth century see Everett Mendelsohn, "Cell Theory and the Development of General Physiology," *Archives Internationales d'Histoire des Sciences* 16 (1963): 419–429; Thomas S. Hall, *Ideas of Life and Matter,* 2 vols. (Chicago: University of Chicago Press, 1969), 2: 307–364; William Coleman, *Biology in the Nineteenth Century* (New York: Wiley, 1971), pp. 130–166.

15 Loeb, *Comparative Physiology of the Brain and Comparative Psychology* (New York: Putnam, 1900), p. 167; Loeb to Ernst Mach, 6 August 1891, Mach Papers.

16 Use of the word "reductionism" often obscures as much as it clarifies. Many historians have assumed that the primary goal of a substantial group of biologists in the latter nineteenth century, including Loeb, was reductionism—the demonstration that all biological phenomena were nothing but "physico-chemical" phenomena, and that physical and chemical theories could explain all aspects of biology. Philosophers of science have argued that scientific practice has been more complex. They point out that it is necessary to specify the nature of the phenomena to be reduced, the nature of the reducing theory, and the relation of such explanations to the other aims of a given scientist. Given these requirements, a coherent reductionism in late nineteenth-century biology is rather difficult to locate. See Everett Mendelsohn, "Physical Models and Physiological Concepts: Explanations in Nineteenth Century Biology," *British Journal for the History of Science* 2 (1964): 203–219; Garland E. Allen, *Life Science in the Twentieth Century* (New York: Wiley, 1975), pp. 73–111; Kenneth F. Schaffner, "The Peripherality of Reductionism in the Development of Molecular Biology," *Journal of the History of Biology* 7 (1974): 111–139; David Hull, *Philosophy of Biological Science* (Englewood Cliffs, N.J.: Prentice-Hall, 1974).

17 E. B. Wilson, "The Heliotropism of Hydra," *American Naturalist* 25 (1891): 413–433: E. B. Holt and F. S. Lee, "The Theory of Phototactic Response," *American Journal of Physiology* 4 (1901): 460–481; W. E. Garrey, "The Effects of Ions upon the Aggregation of Ciliated Infusoria," *ibid.* 3 (1900): 291–315; S. J. Holmes, "Phototaxis in the Amphipoda," *ibid.* 5 (1901): 211–234; G. H. Parker and F. L. Burnett, "The Reactions of Planarians, with and without Eyes, to Light," *ibid.* 4 (1901): 373–385; C. B. Davenport, *Experimental Morphology* (New York: Macmillan, 1896–1898); Davenport and Walter B. Cannon, "On the Determination of the Direction and Rate of Movement of Organisms by Light," *Journal of Physiology* 21 (1897): 22–32; Davenport and Helen Perkins, "A Contribution to the Study of Geotaxis in the Higher Animals," *ibid.* 22 (1897): 99–110; Robert M. Yerkes, "Reaction of Entomostraca to Stimulation by Light. I," *American Journal of Physiology* 3 (1899): 157–182. A substantial bibliography of this work is in Loeb, *Forced Movements, Tropisms, and Animal Conduct* (Philadelphia: Lippincott, 1918), pp. 173–205. "Heliotropism" and "phototaxis" were used interchangeably.

18 Davenport and Cannon, "Determination," p. 22.
19 Herbert Spencer Jennings, "Autobiography," quoted in Tracy Sonneborn, "Herbert Spencer Jennings," *National Academy of Sciences, Biographical Memoirs* 47 (1975): 152.
20 Jennings, "The Early Development of *Asplanchna Herrickii de Guerne:* A Contribution to Developmental Mechanics," *Bulletin of the Museum of Comparative Zoology* 30 (1896): 1–117; esp. pp. 62, 86, 110.
21 Verworn, *Protisten-Studien,* pp. 211–212; idem, "Modern Physiology," *Monist* 4 (1894): 370–372.
22 Jennings, "The Behavior of Unicellular Organisms," *Biological Lectures from the Marine Biological Laboratory of Woods Hole,* 1899 (Boston: Ginn, 1900), p. 112; see also idem, "The Psychology of a Protozoa," *American Journal of Psychology* 10 (1899): 503–515; idem, "Studies on the Reactions to Stimuli in Unicellular Organisms. II. The Mechanism of the Motor Reaction in *Paramecium,*" *American Journal of Physiology* 2 (1899): 311–341.
23 Garrey, "Effects of Ions," p. 291. "Differential sensibility" was Loeb's term for reaction to a change in the level of stimulation.
24 Jennings, "Reactions of Infusoria to Chemicals: A Criticism," *American Naturalist* 34 (1900): 259–265; idem, "The Theory of Tropisms," *Contributions to the Study of the Behavior of the Lower Organisms* (Washington, D.C.: Carnegie Institution, 1904), pp. 91–107; idem, *Behavior of the Lower Organisms,* foreword Donald Jensen (Bloomington, Ind.: Indiana University Press, 1962; first published 1906).
25 Jennings, *Behavior,* pp. 265–276.
26 Ibid., pp. 270–271.
27 Ibid., pp. 324–327. For Jennings the adaptiveness of behavior was a fact. Whether the animals were "conscious" of errors and of resulting "pain" was a separate question. There might be practical value in assuming consciousness in amoeba. "If it were as large as a whale, it is quite conceivable that occasions might arise when the attribution to it of the elemental states of consciousness might save the unsophisticated human being from the destruction that would result from the lack of such attribution." But the question of consciousness was irrelevant to the objective investigator's accounts of behavior. The use of psychically connotative language was merely a shorthand for the objective phenomena—the animal's physiological state. Ibid., pp. 336–337.
28 Ibid., pp. 314–327; J. Mark Baldwin, *Mental Development in the Child and the Race: Methods and Processes* (New York: Macmillan, 1894), pp. 170–220, quotation p. 177; idem, *Development and Evolution* (New York: Macmillan, 1902), pp. vii–x, 91–120; C. Lloyd Morgan, *Habit and Instinct* (London: Edward Arnold, 1896), pp. 140–162. Jennings's use of the term "trial and error" was also probably taken from Baldwin and Morgan, and not from E. L. Thorndike. Both Jennings and Thorndike were graduate students at Harvard (though in different departments) in 1896 when Morgan delivered the Lowell Lectures that were published as *Habit and Instinct,* but Jennings left for Germany before Thorndike began research work. Thorndike's movement away from evolutionary aspects of learning theory toward more atheoretic empiricism was antithetical to Jenning's concern with behavior as an aspect of biology. See Geraldine Joncich, *The Sane Positivist: A Biography of Edward L. Thorndike* (Middletown, Conn.: Wesleyan University Press, 1968), pp. 87–148. I have benefited here from study of parts of *From Darwinism to Behaviourism: Psychologists and Animals,* a forthcoming book by R. A. Boakes, University of Sussex.
29 Loeb, "Concerning the Theory of Tropisms," *Journal of Experimental Zoology* 4 (1907): 151–165.
30 G. H. P.[arker], "Behavior of the Lower Organisms," *Science* 26 (1907): 548–549.
31 H. B. Torrey, "The Method of Trial and the Tropism Hypothesis," *Science* 26 (1907): 313–323.
32 Ibid., p. 313.
33 Ibid., p. 319.
34 Jennings, "The Interpretation of the Behavior of the Lower Organisms," *Science* 27 (1907): 698–710.
35 Ibid., p. 710.
36 Ibid., p. 703. While Jennings argued that his use of psychological terms was merely a convenience, and that even if a physiological state were not determinable it was determinate, others were unable to maintain such a balance. His protegé S. O. Mast argued that since physiological states were almost impossible to determine completely, "subjective factors, entelechies, or psychoids, factors foreign to inorganics, may have a hand in controlling phys-

iological changes and consequently the reactions." S. O. Mast, *Light and the Behavior of Organisms* (New York: Wiley, 1911), p. 375; on Loeb see pp. 23–38, 369–372. Hans Driesch saw Jennings's work as one of the bases for his fully developed theory of vitalism; see Driesch, *The Science and Philosophy of the Organism,* 2 vols. (London: A. & C. Black, 1908), 2: 16–26.

37 Jennings to Davenport, 5 January 1900, Charles Benedict Davenport Papers, American Philosophical Society Library, Philadelphia, Pennsylvania. Their personal relations remained polite, although others did not always assume this was so. Jennings wrote in his diary about meeting Loeb at a reception in Berkeley soon after the appearance of *Behavior of the Lower Organisms:* "Prof. Loeb was very cordial and agreeable, although we have had some difficulties on matters of scientific views, etc., that I had feared might not leave him feeling pleasantly toward me. As he and I stood talking, a Mr. Williamson[?] (elderly gentleman in charge of deaf and dumb institution) comes up and made a very *tactful* speech about how surprised he was not to find Prof. Loeb and I clawing each other's hair, instead of talking pleasantly." "Italian Year Notebook," final leaf, Herbert Spencer Jennings Papers, American Philosophical Society Library.

38 Loeb to T. H. Morgan, 26 January 1918, Jacques Loeb Papers, Manuscript Division, Library of Congress, Washington, D.C. On Mast see note 36 above.

39 Loeb, *Mechanistic Conception,* pp. 28–32; idem, *Forced Movements, Tropisms, and Animal Conduct,* intro. Jerry Hirsch (New York: Dover, 1973; first published 1918).

40 Gottfried Fraenkel and Donald L. Gunn, *The Orientation of Animals: Kineses, Taxes, and Compass Reactions* (London: Oxford University Press, 1940), pp. 6–9; see note 4 above. Jerry Hirsch, "Introduction to the Dover Edition," in Loeb, *Forced Movements,* pp. v–xxvi, provides a dissenting view.

41 Jennings, *Behavior,* p. 327.

42 John B. Watson, (Autobiography), in *History of Psychology in Autobiography,* vol. 3, ed. Carl Murchison (Worchester, Mass.: Clark University Press, 1936), pp. 273–275; David Cohen, *J. B. Watson: The Founder of Behaviourism* (London: Routledge and Kegan Paul, 1979), pp. 24–54.

43 Burnham, "Origins," p. 151; John M. O'Donnell, "The Origins of Behaviorism: American Psychology, 1870–1920" (Ph.D. diss., University of Pennsylvania, 1979), pp. 531–535, 610–617.

44 Loeb, *Mechanistic Conception,* p. 63; J. B. W.[atson], "The Dynamics of Living Matter," *Psychological Bulletin* 4 (1907): 292; Watson to Loeb, 2 January 1914, Loeb Papers.

45 Matthew Hale, *Human Science and Social Order: Hugo Münsterberg and the Origins of Applied Psychology* (Philadelphia: Temple University Press, 1979). E. B. Titchener's well-known critique of Watson's manifesto depended upon the premise that a sharp line could be drawn between science ("a transcription of the world from a particular standpoint") and technology ("the control of behavior"). Once this distinction had been made, Titchener could accept applied psychology while rejecting the *science* of behaviorism. His grounds for rejection were the same as those used by Jennings against Loeb—that in order to reach its true goal of analytic description of activity, behaviorism required inclusion of internal (primarily neurological) processes. Such inclusion could only be expected in the far future, if at all. See Titchener, "On 'Psychology as the Behaviorist Views It,' " *Proceedings of the American Philosophical Society* 53 (1914): 14–16.

46 Loeb, "Introduction," *Studies,* p. ix. Franz Samelson, "Reactions to Watson's Behaviorism, Part 2: Some Puzzles and Some Answers," (unpublished paper, 1979), p. 15, comes to similar conclusions regarding Loeb's influence on Watson from study of the latter.

Eponymy, Obscurity, Twitmyer, and Pavlov

Deborah J. Coon

The idea of the evolutionary nature of thought and discoveries is now almost a commonplace. That the same discovery is made independently at two different places simultaneously argues for the influence of a prevailing Zeitgeist[1] which sets the stage for that discovery. Simply stated, when the intellectual climate is ripe for study of a certain sort of problem, interesting aspects of that problem are much more apt to become salient than if research into that problem were not favored.

Once the discovery occurs, however, what happens with it depends on a variety of factors involving the individual investigator and his or her entire context, social, economic, psychological, and intellectual. This article is an attempt to explore some of the factors involved in the eponymy and obscurity, respectively, of two independent discoverers of the "conditioned response," Ivan P. Pavlov and Edwin B. Twitmyer.[2]

Both discoveries were of an accidental nature. Pavlov, while investigating the activity of the digestive glands of dogs, fortuitously observed that his subjects began to salivate at the sound of a metronome which had preceded and accompanied food on previous occasions. Thus, "...a stimulus which was neutral of itself...had acquired the property of stimulating salivary secretion and of evoking the motor reactions characteristic of the alimentary reflex."[3]

Upon accepting the Nobel Prize in 1904 for his work on the digestive system, he stated that the new direction of his research lay in this conditioning of alimentary processes to psychical stimuli.[4] A decade later, his work had captured the interest of John B. Watson,[5] and eventually it contributed substantially to the development of American behavioristic psychology.

Concurrent with Pavlov's observations of the digestive secretions of dogs, Edwin B. Twitmyer investigated the patellar tendon reflex (the knee jerk) for his doctoral dissertation at the University of Pennsylvania. He also noticed that subjects began to respond to stimuli other than the original stimulus (the tap of a hammer below the knee). He devoted nearly half of his dissertation to description and tentative explanation of the discovery.[6] He stated that "Here...we have a new and unusual reflex arc"[7] and that "the phenomenon occurs with sufficient frequency and regularity to demand an inquiry as to its nature."[8] In 1904, he spoke at the Thirteenth Annual Meeting of the American Psychological Association (APA), at a session chaired by William James, before an audience of America's distinguished psychologists.[9] In his talk, he clearly stated that "knee jerks without taps on the tendons were obtained from all the subjects after a large number of preliminary experiments had been performed in which a bell was struck 150° [.5 seconds] before the blow fell on the tendons."[10] Yet his finding elicited no discussion at the meeting[11] and was virtually ignored by his contemporaries. Pavlov's reputation grew and his name became synonymous with the "conditioned reflex"; for years, "classical conditioning" has been identified with "Pavlovian conditioning." But Twitmyer's name fell into relative obscurity.[12]

The case of Twitmyer is, as mentioned previously, another manifestation of the evolutionary nature of thought and discoveries. Twitmyer's case is intriguing for several reasons. Having made an important discovery and having realized its significance, he apparently dropped pursuit of the phenomenon after encountering uncomfortable silence at his APA presentation and receiving no encouragement thereafter. Certainly social, motivational, and personality factors influence whether or not an idea eventually becomes associated with a given person's name.

Coon, D. J. (1982). Eponymy, obscurity, Twitmyer, and Pavlov. *Journal of the History of the Behavioral Sciences, 18*, 255–262. Copyright © 1982 by the Clinical Psychology Publishing Company. Reprinted by permission of the publisher and the author.

The extent of the influence of these factors is frequently overlooked yet seems particularly worth exploring in Twitmyer's case.

Twitmyer's dissertation, entitled "A Study of the Knee Jerk," was printed privately in 1902. It was not readily accessible to the public until published posthumously in 1974 in the *Journal of Experimental Psychology*.[13] While the private publication of the work could account, in part, for its lack of impact,[14] Twitmyer's presentation before the APA should have brought his discovery to the attention of the best academicians of his day.

The patellar tendon reflex was a reasonable and unstartling object of study for Twitmyer as a graduate student at the University of Pennsylvania. Reflexes in general had been legitimate objects of study since Descartes described them in the seventeenth century. (While Descartes is generally credited as being the "discoverer" of the reflex, it should be noted that Galen had described the pupillary reflex in the second century.[15]) Richard Müller-Freienfels pointed out that from Johannes Müller's time (1801–1858) on, "psychology occupied itself more and more with the problem of the reflex, and evolved the theory of the reflex arc."[16]

Certainly psychologists considered the knee jerk a worthy candidate for study. In his *Principles of Psychology*, William James noted that:

> Everyone is familiar with the *patellar reflex,* or jerk upwards of the foot, which is produced by smartly tapping the tendon below the knee-pan when the leg hangs over the other knee. Drs. Mitchell and Lombard have found that when other sensations come in simultaneously with the tap, the jerk is increased. Heat, cold, pricking, itching, or faradic stimulation of the skin, sometimes strong optical impressions, music, all have this dynamogenic effect, which also results whenever voluntary movements are set up in other parts of the body simultaneously with the tap.[17]

Warren P. Lombard published his classic paper, "The Variations of the Normal Knee-jerk,

and Their Relation to the Central Nervous System," in 1887,[18] only a decade before Twitmyer became a graduate student at the University of Pennsylvania.

The only official professor of psychology at the University at the time of Twitmyer's arrival was Lightner Witmer.[19] Witmer studied the knee jerk in the early to mid-1890s and delivered a paper on the topic at the APA meeting of 1895.[20] Thus, as a student of psychology in general, American psychology in particular, and Lightner Witmer's specifically, it was not surprising that Twitmyer undertook to study the knee jerk.

Twitmyer based his work primarily on Lombard's demonstration that "the extent of the knee-jerk varies greatly on different days, at different parts of the same day, and even in experiments which rapidly succeed each other."[21] Because of this variability in the reflex, Twitmyer initially attempted simply to determine "the extent of the unaugmented or normal knee jerk for normal subjects,"[22] and to observe its changes over time. He intended his experiments essentially as replications of Lombard's, using a greater number of subjects (Lombard had studied only himself). In a second series of experiments designed to study the augmented knee jerk, Twitmyer again used Lombard's basic procedure. There was a crucial difference in methodology: Twitmyer preceded his hammer taps with a signal bell. In the experiments attempting to augment the knee jerk, subjects were to clench their fists, say "ah," or simply think about clenching their fists at the sound of the bell.

Twitmyer did not replicate Lombard's finding of diurnal variation in the reflex, but he did find augmentation by reenforcing stimuli. More importantly, however, "During the adjustment of the apparatus for an earlier group of experiments with one subject...a decided kick of both legs was observed to follow a tap of the signal bell occurring without the usual blow of the hammers on the tendons."[23] The subject denied having voluntarily kicked out his legs. Twitmyer suggested that either the subject had been wrong in his introspective judgment, or that "the true knee jerk (or a movement resembling it in appearance) had been produced by a stimulus other than the usual one."[24] When he repeated the extensive series of experiments with five other subjects, he found that all of them eventually came to respond to the bell, though they ranged from requiring 125 to 230 experiments (bell-tap-kick pairings) prior to exhibiting the kick at the sound of the bell alone. Twitmyer also found that after repeated pairings of a mild electric shock with the hammer tap, or of a mildly painful prick on the thigh with the tap, subjects frequently (though not regularly) responded to the new stimulus (shock or pinprick) as if it were the hammer tap. He ruled out the idea of incorrect introspections and concluded that in fact the tap on the patellar tendon had been replaced by new and unusual stimuli.

Twitmyer's explanation of how this phenomenon might occur is a clear one, based on the existing notion of pathways in the nervous system which become worn with use.[25]

> After a certain number of such trials [bell-tap-kick], the number varying for different subjects, the association of the sound of the bell and the kick becomes so fixed that the bell itself is capable of serving as a stimulus to the movement. Physiologically the repeated association of the functioning of the motor cells in the lumbar segment of the cord, upon which the kick immediately depends, with the excitation of centers in the nuclei of the medulla connected with the auditory conduction path, has resulted in developing a fixed relationship between them. The impulse entering the latter therefore finds an accustomed channel to the former.... The results of the experiments herein reported, however, would seem to indicate that it is only after a habit of interaction between the two involved centers has been developed by repetition, i.e., when the connecting pathway of discharge has become well worn, that the sound of the bell alone is an adequate stimulus to the movement.[26]

In his conclusion, Twitmyer acknowledged that he considered his experiments, designed as they were to study matters other than psychical

stimulation of reflex responses, only as preliminary, and that he would undertake further investigation in the near future.

Especially considering this explicit expression of intent, why did he drop pursuit of what he believed to be a significant discovery? In his work Twitmyer touched upon many of the principles which we now associate with classical (Pavlovian) conditioning: the necessity for temporal priority of the to-be-associated stimulus, the variety of stimuli possible (including mildly aversive ones), the necessity for numerous pairings, and of course, the association of a previously neutral stimulus with a reflex response. Why, then, did we hear little more of Edwin Twitmyer? Why was his presentation at the APA in 1904 so poorly received that Twitmyer recalled the experience "with feelings of disappointment at the failure of his auditors to express interest in his results, of which he recalled no discussion whatever?"[27]

Several possibilities for Twitmyer's obscurity suggest themselves. One possibility is that the main body of his work might have been so uninteresting to psychologists that they obscured the exciting aspects. A second possibility is one proposed by Karl M. Dallenbach, which emphasized Twitmyer's lack of salesmanship and inability to persevere. The third possibility, advanced by Francis W. Irwin in Twitmyer's 1943 obituary, is that Twitmyer and American psychology were not ready in 1904 to grasp the full implications of his observations. Finally, I should mention Twitmyer's own suggestion, that the failure of his APA presentation "was due to William James's becoming bored or hungry at noontime and adjourning the meeting without allowing for discussion of the paper."[28] The first three suggestions will form the substance of the remainder of this paper; the last is left for the reader to ponder.

The first possibility for the failure of American psychologists to take note of Twitmyer's work is that the body of his work may have been so uninteresting as to obscure the important findings expressed within it. This is not implausible since the thesis began as a simple replication of Lombard's experiments, the results of which seem already to have been accepted by psychologists when Twitmyer undertook his work.[29] This explanation cannot, though, account for his talk's silent reception at the APA meeting. The talk was explicitly entitled "Knee Jerks without Stimulation of the Patellar Tendon," at least providing some hint of unusual findings. Further, his presentation concentrated not on the partial replication of Lombard, but on the discovery of the new and unusual reflex arc. Nevertheless, the news was poorly received. Thus, a more adequate explanation is needed.[30]

Dallenbach's hypothesis places responsibility on Twitmyer for having remained obscure. Dallenbach's main point is that Twitmyer failed to promote his "product." "Twitmyer, and he alone, is accountable for that" obscurity.[31] The title of his dissertation "was not particularly exciting nor attention-compelling,"[32] and the thesis itself was privately printed and therefore not readily accessible to most psychologists. "He 'missed the boat,' . . . because he was a young, inexperienced scholar, not a promoter. He did not know how to promote his discovery and he could not withstand discouragement."[33] Pavlov, on the other hand, did promote his discovery and continued his research despite the fact that when he first announced it in his Nobel Prize speech, "it did not fare much better than Twitmyer's" announcement.[34]

Dallenbach's argument concerning Twitmyer's obscurity points out the fairly obvious importance of personal qualities such as persistence in the face of adversity. It also suggests the necessity for scientists to be promoters as well. Yet the argument ultimately proves unfair to both Twitmyer and Pavlov because it considers them apart from their respective contexts. Neither Twitmyer nor Pavlov operated in a social or intellectual vacuum. As Dallenbach suggests, the majority of Pavlov's colleagues did not immediately seize upon his work on psychical reflexes as important.[35] It is therefore of some interest to

note several factors which may have contributed to Pavlov's ability to withstand discouragement.

In 1904, Pavlov was not a newcomer to the science of physiology. He had received his medical degree in 1883 and had taken a position as lecturer in physiology at the Military-Medical Academy in St. Petersburg. In 1890, he was offered the chair of pharmacology at the University of Tomsk in Siberia. He accepted but was shortly offered an even better position, the chair of pharmacology at the Military-Medical Academy. Within a year, Pavlov was appointed director of the physiological department of the Institute of Experimental Medicine which had opened in St. Petersburg in 1890. Thus, well before his work on psychical secretions, Pavlov had received recognition and respect from fellow scientists. His colleagues regarded his long record of experimentation as impeccable, and Pavlov's friends included some of the most influential scientists of his day.[36]

Further, Pavlov's laboratory was equipped with a full complement of doctors, medical students, and paid research assistants. Even when Pavlov turned his complete attention to his somewhat unorthodox study of the central nervous system through conditioned reflexes, part of his laboratory was still devoted to the less controversial work on the digestive system for which he had first received acclaim. His laboratory was handsomely funded by the government and found additional financial support through the private sale of gastric juice for medicinal purposes.[37]

Finally, while the majority of physiologists did not applaud his notion of conditioned reflexes, a core of scientists, including Drs. Vladimir Bekhterev, Anton T. Snarsky, Ivan F. Tolochinov, and S. G. Wolfson, quickly and enthusiastically embraced the discovery and its implications for the study of the central nervous system.[38]

Pavlov was securely established as a prominent scientist and was encouraged tremendously when he became the recipient of the Nobel Prize in 1904. Surely all of these personal, economic, and social factors provided Pavlov with a substantial support system, the importance of which should not be overlooked.

In contrast, consider Twitmyer's circumstances in 1904. Twitmyer was a young Lecturer at the University of Pennsylvania, striving for promotion to Assistant Professor, when he announced his discovery to the American Psychological Association. He had only recently received his doctorate and was at the beginning of his career. Presumably there were enormous pressures on him to undertake interesting work which would make him a valuable member of the academic community. He had none of the manpower or economic resources available to Pavlov, nor the renown or respect accorded Pavlov. Twitmyer had yet to carve his niche in the academic community; Pavlov was well-settled in his. Finally, we can find no evidence of even a small core of scientists who supported Twitmyer's work. His announcement before the APA was met with silence, and apparently no one spoke to him about it subsequently.

In sum, comparison between the two men's personal qualities (of which we can only conjecture after the fact) seems inappropriate when so many social and institutional factors were also operative. Dallenbach's explanation falls short by failing to consider these individuals as part of their immediate contexts.

The third possibility is a somewhat more satisfying one. Irwin suggests that the intellectual climate in American psychology was such that psychologists (perhaps including Twitmyer himself) were not ready to grasp the import of Twitmyer's observation. American psychology at the turn of the century was inherently dualistic. It concerned itself with the contents of mind —and mind for psychologists was distinct from the physical, mechanical world of reflexes. While it was recognized that states of consciousness are dependent upon activity in the cerebral hemispheres, to have suggested that richly complex mental phenomena in man could be understood solely in terms of primitive, mechanical reflexes

would have been untenable for the dualistic American psychologist. As James clearly stated, "Although we affirm that the *coming to pass* of thought is a consequence of mechanical laws... we do not in the least explain the *nature* of thought by affirming this dependence...."[39] It was also commonly accepted that mental states are necessarily followed by bodily activity. Thus, Twitmyer's finding that an idea causes a physical reaction was, superficially, barely interesting, and certainly noncontroversial. It did nothing to reveal the nature of thought.

Pavlov, however, was a physiologist, not a psychologist. Since his experimental subjects were animals, he was able to set aside any dualistic tendencies he may have had[40] and approach the conditioned reflex as a materialist, viewing the operations of the central nervous system in animals as fundamentally physical or mechanical. His method and theory were consistently physicalistic, and the community of scientists he addressed were also physicalists.[41]

Thus, for Pavlov, the discovery of psychical stimulation of digestive gland secretion provided an objective means of studying activity in the central nervous system,[42] thereby suggesting an avenue of study which turned out to be extremely fruitful. Americans viewed Twitmyer's discovery of psychically elicited reflexes as a curious extension of associationistic principles, but not terribly important in elucidating the nature of the contents of mind.

Perhaps, then, their different foci led the two men to different ends. Pavlov, as a physiologist, continued studying psychically caused reflexes and gradually developed an extensive body of research concerning them. Twitmyer, as a psychologist, dropped pursuit of psychically caused reflexes as interesting, but not very significant to the science of psychology, and took up work of a kind more acceptable to the psychological community.[43]

Thus, we are provided with some answers concerning why psychologists did not readily embrace Twitmyer's discovery, and why he did not continue to pursue it. In sum, American psychologists at the turn of the century only had three chances to confront Twitmyer's work: in his dissertation, which was privately printed and therefore relatively inaccessible, at his talk before the APA, or in the abstract of the talk in the *Psychological Bulletin*.[44] Even if they had come across his work, they probably would not have been prepared to understand its significance: psychologists at the time were concerned with knowledge of the contents of mind, and it was not immediately obvious how a "primitive" mechanism such as the reflex might account for those contents. (It took Watson years of work, a complete redefinition of the science of psychology, and the overcoming of much resistance to get his message across). Finally, Twitmyer did not receive the support of his psychologist colleagues for his work, nor was he in a position of job security in which he could afford to risk that approval. All of these factors undoubtedly contributed to the fact of Twitmyer's obscurity and Pavlov's eponymy.

NOTES

1 Edwin G. Boring, *A History of Experimental Psychology* (New York: Appleton-Century-Crofts, 1950).

2 Mark R. Rosenzweig, in "Salivary Conditioning before Pavlov," *American Journal of Psychology* 72 (1959): 628–633, points out (p. 630) that "psychical stimulation of salivation had indeed been long known and extensively commented upon before Pavlov's work." However, Pavlov was the first to discover and explicitly create associations between food and stimuli not normally associated with food.

3 Ivan P. Pavlov, *Conditioned Reflexes: An Investigation of the Physiological Activity of the Cerebral Cortex,* trans. Gleb Vasilievitch Anrep (New York: Dover, 1927), p. 26.

4 Boris P. Babkin, *Pavlov: A Biography* (Chicago: University of Chicago Press, 1949).

5 Mark R. Rosenzweig, "Pavlov, Bekhterev, and Twitmyer on Conditioning," *American Journal of Psychology* 73 (1960): 312–316, points out that Vladimir Bekhterev is actually responsible for Watson's introduction to Pavlov's work. Bekhterev's *La Psychologie Objective,* traduit du Russe par Nicolas Kostyleff (Paris: F. Alcan, 1913), was apparently Watson's first exposure to the Russian work on conditioned reflexes.

6 Edwin B. Twitmyer, "A Study of the Knee Jerk," *Journal of Experimental Psychology* 103 (1974): 1047–1066. This is a posthumous publication of Twitmyer's 1902 doctoral dissertation. It should be noted that the posthumous publication of Twitmyer's dissertation after seventy years and the accompanying editorial note by then-Editor David A. Grant (see Twitmyer, "Study," pp. 1048–1049) were an unusual contribution to the journal. Grant clearly believed in the importance of the paper and felt it valuable to bring it to the attention of a wider readership.

7 Ibid., p. 1064.

8 Ibid., p. 1061.

9 See "Proceedings of the Thirteenth Annual Meeting of the American Psychological Association, University of Pennsylvania, Philadelphia, December 28, 29, and 30, 1904," *Psychological Bulletin* 2 (1905): 37–63.

10 Edwin B. Twitmyer, "Knee Jerks without Stimulation of the Patellar Tendon," in "Proceedings," ibid.: 43–44.

11 Francis W. Irwin, "Edwin Burket Twitmyer: 1873–1943," *American Journal of Psychology* 56 (1943): 451–453.

12 It would be inaccurate to suggest that no credit was given to Twitmyer's work prior to the time of his obituary by Irwin (ibid.). He was briefly mentioned in Ernest R. Hilgard and Donald G. Marquis's 1940 text, *Conditioning and Learning* (New York: Appleton-Century) as being an independent discoverer of conditioning in America. His research was also discussed in Robert S. Woodworth's *Experimental Psychology* (New York: Henry Holt, 1938). Additionally, both Harold Schlosberg ("A Study of the Conditioned Patellar Reflex," *Journal of Experimental Psychology* 11 [1928]: 468–494) and Franklin Fearing ("The History of the Experimental Study of the Knee-Jerk," *American Journal of Psychology* 40 [1928]: 92–111) discussed Twitmyer's dissertation extensively. However, all

of these citations were made at least twenty-six years after Twitmyer's work and well after conditioning principles had been embraced by Watson for use in the burgeoning science of behaviorism. The question still remains why Twitmyer's contemporaries were unimpressed with the significance of his work at the time of his APA talk, and why he abandoned research he considered important.

13 See note 6.

14 Karl M. Dallenbach, "Twitmyer and the Conditioned Response," *American Journal of Psychology* 72 (1959): 628–633.

15 Richard Müller-Freienfels, *The Evolution of Modern Psychology,* trans. W. Beran Wolfe (New Haven: Yale University Press, 1935).

16 Ibid., p. 229.

17 William James, *The Principles of Psychology,* 2 vols. (New York: Henry Holt, 1890), 2: 380.

18 Warren P. Lombard, "The Variations of the Normal Knee-jerk, and Their Relation to the Central Nervous System," *American Journal of Psychology* 1 (1887): 1–71.

19 Information provided by the University of Pennsylvania Archives, Philadelphia, Pennsylvania. Specifically, see *Catalogue of the University of Pennsylvania,* 1897–1898.

20 See "Proceedings of the Fourth Annual Meeting of the American Psychological Association, 1895," *Psychological Review* 3 (1896): 121–133. Professor Witmer's abstract (p. 131) unfortunately includes only the title of his talk: "Variations in the Patellar Reflex as an Aid to the Mental Analysis."

21 Lombard, "Variations," p. 2.

22 Twitmyer, "Study," p. 1050.

23 Ibid., p. 1059.

24 Ibid.

25 See James, *Principles.*

26 Twitmyer, "Study," p. 1065.

27 Irwin, "Twitmyer," p. 452.

28 Irwin to Coon, 9 March 1979.

29 See James, *Principles.*

30 Twitmyer's findings also may have been obscured by a controversy in the late-nineteenth century concerning whether or not the knee jerk was a "true" reflex, since the "time between the stroke on the tendon and the beginning of the muscular contraction is too brief to allow for conduction to and from the spinal cord" (Fearing, "History," p.

93). The refinement of experimental techniques eventually led to evidence that the knee jerk was a true reflex (ibid., p. 97), but at the time of Twitmyer's talk, it was still in question. Thus, it may be that the uncertain status of the knee jerk as a reflex effectively masked Twitmyer's more important findings.

31 Dallenbach, "Twitmyer," p. 637.

32 Ibid., p. 635.

33 Ibid., p. 637.

34 Ibid.

35 See Babkin, *Pavlov.*

36 See ibid.

37 See ibid. The author is tempted to speculate on the economic advantages afforded by psychically induced production of gastric juice but will refrain from doing so.

38 See ibid.

39 William James, *Psychology: Briefer Course* (New York: Henry Holt, 1892), p. 6.

40 See Babkin, *Pavlov.*

41 Perhaps the initial suggestion that "mind" could be studied as a physical object is one which not accidentally came from a physiologist and not a psychologist. Psychology at the turn of the century was a science of the mind and its contents. As such, psychology was the propaedeutic science, for without knowledge of the mind, through which all else is known, we really could not know what we know. To assert that the mind is nothing more than a complex of primitive reflexes which can be studied through physiological methods and explained in the language of physiology denies psychology its role as the fundamental science. If mind can be explained strictly in physical terms, then physiology is the ground of understanding and psychology is superfluous. This view is heretical to the psychology of the early twentieth century. Consider the manner in which Watson introduced the Russian work on physiology to American psychology. He adopted the methodology, the objective, rigorous techniques, and some of the explanations, but did not allow psychology to be reduced to physiology. Psychology would study function; physiology would study structure (see John B. Watson, "Psychology as the Behaviorist Views It," *Psychological Review* 20 [1913]: 158–177). Later, he revised this somewhat—physiology would study

function of parts, psychology would study function of the whole organism (see John B. Watson, *Behaviorism* [New York: Norton, 1925]). For our purposes, the thrust was still the same—psychology and physiology were to be companion sciences, neither one reducible to the other. The overthrow (temporarily) of dualistic psychology was difficult in itself, but perhaps maintaining some semblance of psychology's place of importance was crucial in order for it to occur at all.

42 Irwin, "Twitmyer."

43 Specifically, he became involved in, and eventually headed, a program in speech therapy at the psychological clinic which Witmer had founded in 1896 (the first in the nation).

44 Twitmyer, "Knee Jerks without Stimulation."

CHAPTER 13

BEHAVIORISM

By the beginning of the twentieth century, the new psychology had a firm foothold in American universities. After the founding of Hall's laboratory at Johns Hopkins University in 1883, nearly forty more universities followed suit by 1900. James's *Principles,* having been in print for ten years, had led many new converts to psychology's promised land. That book played an important role in functionalism's establishment as a viable alternative to the more restrictive brand of structural psychology espoused by Titchener.

Although only a decade old in 1900, the University of Chicago was a university on the move, largely due to the efforts of the founding president, William Rainey Harper, who raided the established universities (especially G. Stanley Hall's Clark University) in search of their best faculty talent. Chicago was an exciting place to be at the turn of the century. The biology department included Jacques Loeb (see Chapter 12) and Henry H. Donaldson (1857–1938), an internationally known authority on the human brain who had studied with G. S. Hall at Johns Hopkins. John Dewey and James Rowland Angell were members of the Philosophy Department.

In 1900, John Broadus Watson (1878–1958) arrived at the University of Chicago from his home in Traveler's Rest, South Carolina, having completed his baccalaureate and master's degrees at a southern Baptist college, Furman University. Watson had planned to pursue his doctorate in philosophy but lost interest in Dewey's classes. In Angell, though, he found the new psychology more to his liking. He took classes from Loeb and Donaldson as well, with Angell and Donaldson eventually directing his doctoral dissertation research. Watson's research was a comparative psychological investigation using infant rats of varying ages to study the relationship between neurological development and behavioral complexity. By 1903 the university granted authority for a degree in psychology, separate from philosophy, and the first psychology doctorate was awarded to Watson in that year. His dissertation was entitled, "Animal Education: The Psychical Development of the White Rat." Watson had several job offers upon graduation but elected to stay at Chicago when Angell offered him a position in psychology. There he continued his animal research until he was offered a professorship and head of the department of psychology at Johns Hopkins in 1908. The offer was too good to refuse.

According to his autobiography, Watson's dissatisfaction with the prevailing psychology of his day began in 1904 when he was at Chicago (Watson, 1936). Influenced by his physiological training, he searched for a way to make his own science more objective. More and more he was troubled by the mentalism of a psychology defined as the study of consciousness. He greatly doubted the validity of the introspective method, preferring the more controlled stimulus-response conditions of his laboratory studies with rats. For Watson, those ideas were expressed in some detail in an address he delivered at Columbia University in 1913 entitled "Psychology as the Behaviorist Views It." A few months later that address was published under the same title in the *Psychological Review,* a journal founded by Cattell and James Mark Baldwin, and edited by Watson since his arrival at Johns Hopkins. The paper became known as the "Behaviorist Manifesto" and marked the beginning of a revolution in psychology (although not an immediate rebellion—see the Samelson article in this chapter).

Watson's manifesto began:

> Psychology as the behaviorist views it is a purely objective experimental branch of natural science. Its theoretical goal is the prediction and control of behavior. Introspection forms no essential part of its methods, nor is the scientific value of its data dependent upon the readiness with which they lend themselves to interpretation in terms of consciousness. (Watson, 1913, p. 158)

He rebuked not only the structuralists but also the functionalists among whom he had trained. He claimed that he could not distinguish between them, that both were mired in a mentalism that thwarted objective science. In continuing his attack he wrote:

> I do not wish unduly to criticize psychology. It has failed signally, I believe, during the fifty-odd years of its existence as an experimental discipline to make its place in the world as an undisputed natural science....The time seems to have come when psychology must discard all reference to consciousness; when it need no longer delude itself into thinking that it is making mental states the object of observation. (Watson, 1913, p. 163)

Needless to say, those were harsh words from this brash young man who had received his doctorate in psychology only ten years earlier. Regarding Watson's admonition against consciousness and other mentalistic terms, some psychologists have referred to it as "the time when psychology lost its mind."

Watson was not alone in his dissatisfaction with the subjectivism of psychology, and his 1913 paper was by no means the initial appearance of such ideas. The unmistakable rumblings of behaviorism were all too apparent in the earliest days of the twentieth century. Behavioral ideas, in one form or another, were espoused by William McDougall (a British psychologist), Herbert S. Jennings, Adolf Meyer (a psychiatrist), Knight Dunlap, and others. Jennings, Meyer, and Dunlap were Watson's colleagues at Johns Hopkins University and all exerted identifiable influences on Watson's thinking. Indeed, in his autobiography, Dunlap (1932) lamented the fact that Watson had received the credit for behavioristic ideas that were largely Dunlap's. Interestingly, in his own autobiography Watson (1936) acknowledged Dunlap's priority.

Other early behaviorists included Max F. Meyer (1873–1967), a psychologist at the University of Missouri, whose 1911 book, *The Fundamental Laws of Human Behavior,* attacked introspection and a psychology of subjective states, especially the notion of consciousness. Historian John O'Donnell (1985) has said of Meyer: "Had he been an American working in a more prominent eastern institution and capable of communicating his notions in the evangelical language of a southern Baptist, the name John B. Watson might be less prominent today" (p. 216).

The intellectual roots of behaviorism obviously predate Watson and they extend beyond the boundaries of psychology into the allied fields of physiology, medicine, and sociology (see Parmelee, 1912). But behaviorism as a movement in psychology belongs to Watson. Some historians, for example John Burnham (1968), have argued against labeling Watson as the *founder* of behaviorism. Burnham prefers to view Watson's role in behaviorism as that of "charismatic leader." Yet that label does not seem to do justice to Watson's role, if it implies that in 1913 the philosophical tenets of behaviorism were already in place in any centralized formulation. Watson's contribution was that he crystallized those scattered ideas into a systematic formulation that was *new*. In Burnham's (1968) words, "Watson combined these elements into a synthesis, the whole of which was greater than its parts" (p. 145). If anyone deserves the label of founder of behavioral psychology, it is John B. Watson. The impact of his words, while not immediate, has been profound in the history of modern psychology.

For Watson, psychology was to be the science of behavior, not mental states. Processes that were not directly observable would have no place in a behavioral psychology. Not only was the subject matter of psychology to be changed, but so were its methods. Introspection was rejected; it was a method that only pretended to produce accurate observations. Watson did recognize the possible value of verbal report from subjects, but only in conjunction with other corroborating observations. Instead Watson called for more objective forms of observation, with and without the use of scientific instruments. He approved of the reaction time studies and the experimental research of Hermann Ebbinghaus on learning and memory. Further, he approved of some psychological tests, so long as they were not mental tests. Somewhat later, Watson called for extended use of the conditioned reflex method of Pavlov. He noted how it could be used to answer questions that heretofore seemed answerable only by the method of introspection, for example in determining the range of the visible spectrum to which the human eye is sensitive.

> We start with any intermediate wave length and by the use of the electric shock establish a conditioned reflex. Each time the light appears the reflex occurs. We then increase the length of the wave rather sharply and if the reflex appears we again increase the wave length. We finally reach a point where the reflex breaks down, even when punishment is used to restore it—approximately 760 millimicrons. This wave length represents the human being's spectral range at the red end. We then follow the same procedure with respect to the violet end (397 millimicrons). In this way we determine the individual's range just as surely as if we had stimulated the subject with monochromatic lights varying in wave lengths and asked him if he saw them. (Watson, 1919, pp. 35–36)

Watson followed the publication of his manifesto with his first book, *Behavior: An Introduction to Comparative Psychology* (1914), in which he lauded the value of animal research in psychology and expressed his views about a wholly behavioral psychology. By the time his next book appeared, *Psychology from the Standpoint of a Behaviorist* (1919), he had shifted his work to human infants. In 1919 he was engaged in the most famous research study of his career. Indeed, it is one of the most famous studies in the history of American psychology. With the assistance of a graduate student, Rosalie Rayner (whom he would later marry), Watson sought to demonstrate that fear could be acquired in humans as the result of conditioning, an idea he had proposed in an earlier article (Watson & Morgan, 1917). Using an 11-month-old infant, Albert B., they presented first a white rat (which the infant did not fear) and then a loud noise (which the infant did fear). After repeated pairings, Watson and Rayner (1920) reported that fear had been conditioned to the rat. It was an important claim for Watson because it supported his largely environmentalistic theory of emotion in humans. The success of the conditioning and the generalization of the fear demonstrated that conditioning was a fact, not just in the lives of laboratory dogs but in humans as well.

That classic study was Watson's last as an academic psychologist. Scandal over his affair with Rayner forced him to leave Johns Hopkins at the age of 42. He went to New York City, where he pursued a successful career in advertising and wrote a number of books and articles on psychology for the popular press.

Watson's impact on psychology was substantial, perhaps more so than any other figure in the history of American psychology. Yet the value of his legacy is debated today. In arguing for an objective science of behavior he eliminated a number of topics that have only begun to reappear in American psychology in the last twenty years, for example, consciousness, thinking, dreaming, and emotion. Some psychologists believe that Watson's philosophy was too radical, that in throwing out what he saw as bad, he also contributed to the elimination of much that was good. They would argue that in the long run he inhibited psychology's progress.

Others would argue that psychology's progress as a science was largely because of Watson, that he was the one figure who demanded a complete break with philosophy and the mentalistic baggage attached to it. Watsonian behaviorism strengthened the role of physiological processes in psychological explanations, expanded psychological methods, and made apparent the ties between animal and human psychology.

Whatever the value of the legacy, Watson's ideas dominated American psychology for more than fifty years through many varieties of behaviorism (see the next chapter). Although the cognitive psychology movement has weakened the stronghold of the behaviorists, they continue to be a major force in contemporary psychology.

The first selection in this chapter is Watson's famous 1913 paper that started the behaviorist revolution. Histories of psychology have generally reported that the rebellion was immediate, that psychologists were instantly upon Watson's bandwagon, waving the banners of objectivism. But recent historical research (see the second selection in this chapter) suggests that the acceptance of Watson's ideas was much slower in coming. This second selection, by the historian of psychology Franz Samelson, an authority on behaviorism, represents extensive research in the published and unpublished sources of psychology in search of the impact of Watson's ideas and the timetable for their acceptance.

The final selection is by another historian of psychology, Ben Harris. Its subject matter is the famous infant conditioning study of Watson and Rayner, a study that has perhaps been more misquoted and misunderstood than any other in the history of psychology. Harris discusses the famous experiment and its numerous misrepresentations in contemporary psychology. He concludes (as does Samelson, 1980) that the study is interesting but so poorly designed and controlled that its data are uninterpretable. Both the Harris and the Samelson papers in this chapter are good examples of the reevaluation of the "truths" in the history of psychology, in what is being called *critical history*. They challenge some of the many legends built up around the figure of John Watson and behaviorism and give us new ways to think about these subjects.

REFERENCES

Burnham, J. C. (1968). On the origins of behaviorism. *Journal of the History of the Behavioral Sciences, 4,* 143–151.

Dunlap, K. (1932). Autobiography. In C. Murchison (Ed.), *A history of psychology in autobiography* (Volume 2). Worcester, MA: Clark University Press, pp. 35–61.

Meyer, M. F. (1911). *The fundamental laws of human behavior.* Boston: Badger.

O'Donnell, J. M. (1985). *The origins of behaviorism: American psychology, 1870–1920.* New York: New York University Press.

Parmelee, M. (1912). *The science of human behavior: Biological and psychological foundations.* New York: Macmillan.

Samelson, F. (1980). J. B. Watson's Little Albert, Cyril Burt's twins, and the need for a critical science. *American Psychologist, 35,* 619–625.

Watson, J. B. (1913). Psychology as the behaviorist views it. *Psychological Review, 20,* 158–177.

Watson, J. B. (1914). *Behavior: An introduction to comparative psychology.* New York: Henry Holt.

Watson, J. B. (1919). *Psychology from the standpoint of a behaviorist.* Philadelphia: J. B. Lippincott.

Watson, J. B. (1936). Autobiography. In C. Murchison (Ed.), *A history of psychology in autobiography* (Volume 3). Worcester, MA: Clark University Press, pp. 271–281.

Watson, J. B., & Morgan, J. J. B. (1917). Emotional reactions and psychological experimentation. *American Journal of Psychology, 28,* 163–174.

Watson, J. B., & Rayner, R. (1920). Conditioned emotional reactions. *Journal of Experimental Psychology, 3,* 1–14.

Psychology as the Behaviorist Views It

John B. Watson

Psychology as the behaviorist views it is a purely objective experimental branch of natural science. Its theoretical goal is the prediction and control of behavior. Introspection forms no essential part of its methods, nor is the scientific value of its data dependent upon the readiness with which they lend themselves to interpretation in terms of consciousness. The behaviorist, in his efforts to get a unitary scheme of animal response, recognizes no dividing line between man and brute. The behavior of man, with all of its refinement and complexity, forms only a part of the behaviorist's total scheme of investigation.

It has been maintained by its followers generally that psychology is a study of the science of the phenomena of consciousness. It has taken as its problem, on the one hand, the analysis of complex mental states (or processes) into simple elementary constituents, and on the other the construction of complex states when the elementary constituents are given. The world of physical objects (stimuli, including here anything which may excite activity in a receptor), which forms the total phenomena of the natural scientist, is looked upon merely as means to an end. That end is the production of mental states that may be 'inspected' or 'observed.' The psychological object of observation in the case of an emotion, for example, is the mental state itself. The problem in emotion is the determination of the number and kind of elementary constituents present, their loci, intensity, order of appearance, etc. It is agreed that introspection is the method *par excellence* by means of which mental states may be manipulated for purposes of psychology. On this assumption, behavior data (including under this term everything which goes under the name of comparative psychology) have no value *per se*. They possess significance only in so far as they may throw light upon conscious states. Such data must have at least an analogical or indirect reference to belong to the realm of psychology.

Indeed, at times, one finds psychologists who are sceptical of even this analogical reference. Such scepticism is often shown by the question which is put to the student of behavior, "what is the bearing of animal work upon human psychology?" I used to have to study over this question. Indeed it always embarrassed me somewhat. I was interested in my own work and felt that it was important, and yet I could not trace any close connection between it and psychology as my questioner understood psychology. I hope that such a confession will clear the atmosphere to such an extent that we will no longer have to work under false pretences. We must frankly admit that the facts so important to us which we have been able to glean from extended work upon the senses of animals by the behavior method have contributed only in a fragmentary way to the general theory of human sense organ processes, nor have they suggested new points of experimental attack. The enormous number of experiments which we have carried out upon learning have likewise contributed little to human psychology. It seems reasonably clear that some kind of compromise must be effected: either psychology must change its viewpoint so as to take in facts of behavior, whether or not they have bearings upon the problems of 'consciousness'; or else behavior must stand alone as a wholly separate and independent science. Should human psychologists fail to look with favor upon our overtures and refuse to modify their position, the behaviorists will be driven to using human beings as subjects and to employ methods of investigation which are exactly comparable to those now employed in the animal work.

Any other hypothesis than that which admits the independent value of behavior material, regardless of any bearing such material may have upon consciousness, will inevitably force us to the absurd position of attempting to *construct* the conscious content of the animal whose behavior we have been studying. On this view, after having determined our animal's ability to learn, the simplicity or complexity of its methods of learning, the effect of past habit upon present response, the range of stimuli to which it ordinarily responds, the widened range to which it can respond under experimental conditions,—in more general terms, its various problems and its various ways of solving them,—we should still feel that the task is unfinished and that the results are worthless, until we can interpret them by analogy in the light of consciousness. Although we have solved our problem we feel uneasy and unrestful because of our definition of psychology: we feel forced to say something about the possible mental processes of our animal. We say that, having no eyes, its stream of consciousness cannot contain brightness and color sensations as we know them,—having no taste buds this stream can contain no sensations of sweet, sour, salt and bitter. But on the other hand, since it does respond to thermal, tactual and organic stimuli, its conscious content must be made up largely of these sensations; and we usually add, to protect ourselves against the reproach of being anthropomorphic, "if it has any consciousness." Surely this doctrine which calls for an analogical interpretation of all behavior data may be shown to be false: the position that the standing of an observation upon behavior is determined by its fruitfulness in yielding results which are interpretable only in the narrow realm of (really human) consciousness.

This emphasis upon analogy in psychology has led the behaviorist somewhat afield. Not being willing to throw off the yoke of consciousness he feels impelled to make a place in the scheme of behavior where the rise of consciousness can be determined. This point has been a

shifting one. A few years ago certain animals were supposed to possess 'associative memory,' while certain others were supposed to lack it. One meets this search for the origin of consciousness under a good many disguises. Some of our texts state that consciousness arises at the moment when reflex and instinctive activities fail properly to conserve the organism. A perfectly adjusted organism would be lacking in consciousness. On the other hand whenever we find the presence of diffuse activity which results in habit formation, we are justified in assuming consciousness. I must confess that these arguments had weight with me when I began the study of behavior. I fear that a good many of us are still viewing behavior problems with something like this in mind. More than one student in behavior has attempted to frame criteria of the psychic—to devise a set of objective, structural and functional criteria which, when applied in the particular instance, will enable us to decide whether such and such responses are positively conscious, merely indicative of consciousness, or whether they are purely 'physiological.' Such problems as these can no longer satisfy behavior men. It would be better to give up the province altogether and admit frankly that the study of the behavior of animals has no justification, than to admit that our search is of such a 'will o' the wisp' character. One can assume either the presence or the absence of consciousness anywhere in the phylogenetic scale without affecting the problems of behavior by one jot or one tittle; and without influencing in any way the mode of experimental attack upon them. On the other hand, I cannot for one moment assume that the paramecium responds to light; that the rat learns a problem more quickly by working at the task five times a day than once a day, or that the human child exhibits plateaux in his learning curves. These are questions which vitally concern behavior and which must be decided by direct observation under experimental conditions.

This attempt to reason by analogy from human conscious processes to the conscious processes in animals, and *vice versa:* to make consciousness, as the human being knows it, the center of reference of all behavior, forces us into a situation similar to that which existed in biology in Darwin's time. The whole Darwinian movement was judged by the bearing it had upon the origin and development of the human race. Expeditions were undertaken to collect material which would establish the position that the rise of the human race was a perfectly natural phenomenon and not an act of special creation. Variations were carefully sought along with the evidence for the heaping up effect and the weeding out effect of selection; for in these and the other Darwinian mechanisms were to be found factors sufficiently complex to account for the origin and race differentiation of man. The wealth of material collected at this time was considered valuable largely in so far as it tended to develop the concept of evolution in man. It is strange that this situation should have remained the dominant one in biology for so many years. The moment Zoölogy undertook the experimental study of evolution and descent, the situation immediately changed. Man ceased to be the center of reference. I doubt if any experimental biologist today, unless actually engaged in the problem of race differentiation in man, tries to interpret his findings in terms of human evolution, or ever refers to it in his thinking. He gathers his data from the study of many species of plants and animals and tries to work out the laws of inheritance in the particular type upon which he is conducting experiments. Naturally, he follows, the progress of the work upon race differentiation in man and in the descent of man, but he looks upon these as special topics, equal in importance with his own yet ones in which his interests will never be vitally engaged. It is not fair to say that all of his work is directed toward human evolution or that it must be interpreted in terms of human evolution. He does not have to dismiss certain of his facts on the inheritance of coat color in mice because, forsooth, they have little bearing upon the differentiation of the *genus homo* into separate races, or upon the descent of the *genus homo* from some more primitive stock.

In psychology we are still in that stage of development where we feel that we must select our material. We have a general place of discard for processes, which we anathematize so far as their value for psychology is concerned by saying, "this is a reflex"; "that is a purely physiological fact which has nothing to do with psychology." We are not interested (as psychologists) in getting all of the processes of adjustment which the animal as a whole employs, and in finding how these various responses are associated, and how they fall apart, thus working out a systematic scheme for the prediction and control of response in general. Unless our observed facts are indicative of consciousness, we have no use for them, and unless our apparatus and method are designed to throw such facts into relief, they are thought of in just as disparaging a way. I shall always remember the remark one distinguished psychologist made as he looked over the color apparatus designed for testing the responses of animals to monochromatic light in the attic at Johns Hopkins. It was this: "And they call this psychology!"

I do not wish unduly to criticize psychology. It has failed signally, I believe, during the fifty-odd years of its existence as an experimental discipline to make its place in the world as an undisputed natural science. Psychology, as it is generally thought of, has something esoteric in its methods. If you fail to reproduce my findings, it is not due to some fault in your apparatus or in the control of your stimulus, but it is due to the fact that your introspection is untrained. The attack is made upon the observer and not upon the experimental setting. In physics and in chemistry the attack is made upon the experimental conditions. The apparatus was not sensitive enough, impure chemicals were used, etc. In these sciences a better technique will give reproducible results. Psychology is otherwise. If you can't observe 3–9 states of clearness in attention, your introspection is poor. If, on the other hand, a feeling seems reasonably clear to you, your introspection is again faulty. You are seeing too much. Feelings are never clear.

The time seems to have come when psychology must discard all reference to consciousness; when it need no longer delude itself into thinking that it is making mental states the object of observation. We have become so enmeshed in speculative questions concerning the elements of mind, the nature of conscious content (for example, imageless thought, attitudes, and Bewusseinslage, etc.) that I, as an experimental student, feel that something is wrong with our premises and the types of problems which develop from them. There is no longer any guarantee that we all mean the same thing when we use the terms now current in psychology. Take the case of sensation. A sensation is defined in terms of its attributes. One psychologist will state with readiness that the attributes of a visual sensation are *quality, extension, duration,* and *intensity.* Another will add *clearness.* Still another that of *order.* I doubt if any one psychologist can draw up a set of statements describing what he means by sensation which will be agreed to by three other psychologists of different training. Turn for a moment to the question of the number of isolable sensations. Is there an extremely large number of color sensations—or only four, red, green, yellow and blue? Again, yellow, while psychologically simple, can be obtained by superimposing red and green spectral rays upon the same diffusing surface! If, on the other hand, we say that every just noticeable difference in the spectrum is a simple sensation, and that every just noticeable increase in the white value of a given color gives simple sensations, we are forced to admit that the number is so large and the conditions for obtaining them so complex that the concept of sensation is unusable, either for the purpose of analysis or that of synthesis. Titchener, who has fought the most valiant fight in this country for a psychology based upon introspection, feels that these differences of opinion as to the number of sensations and their attributes, as to whether there are

relations (in the sense of elements) and on the many others which seem to be fundamental in every attempt at analysis, are perfectly natural in the present undeveloped state of psychology. While it is admitted that every growing science is full of unanswered questions, surely only those who are wedded to the system as we now have it, who have fought and suffered for it, can confidently believe that there will ever be any greater uniformity than there is now in the answers we have to such questions. I firmly believe that two hundred years from now, unless the introspective method is discarded, psychology will still be divided on the question as to whether auditory sensations have the quality of 'extension,' whether intensity is an attribute which can be applied to color, whether there is a difference in 'texture' between image and sensation and upon many hundreds of others of like character.

The condition in regard to other mental processes is just as chaotic. Can image type be experimentally tested and verified? Are recondite thought processes dependent mechanically upon imagery at all? Are psychologists agreed upon what feeling is? One states that feelings are attitudes. Another finds them to be groups of organic sensations possessing a certain solidarity. Still another and larger group finds them to be new elements correlative with and ranking equally with sensations.

My psychological quarrel is not with the systematic and structural psychologist alone. The last fifteen years have seen the growth of what is called functional psychology. This type of psychology decries the use of elements in the static sense of the structuralists. It throws emphasis upon the biological significance of conscious processes instead of upon the analysis of conscious states into introspectively isolable elements. I have done my best to understand the difference between functional psychology and structural psychology. Instead of clarity, confusion grows upon me. The terms sensation, perception, affection, emotion, volition are used as much by the functionalist as by the structuralist. The addition of the word 'process' ('mental act as a whole,' and like terms are frequently met) after each serves in some way to remove the corpse of 'content' and to leave 'function' in its stead. Surely if these concepts are elusive when looked at from a content standpoint, they are still more deceptive when viewed from the angle of function, and especially so when function is obtained by the introspection method. It is rather interesting that no functional psychologist has carefully distinguished between 'perception' (and this is true of the other psychological terms as well) as employed by the systematist, and 'perceptual process' as used in functional psychology. It seems illogical and hardly fair to criticize the psychology which the systematist gives us, and then to utilize his terms without carefully showing the changes in meaning which are to be attached to them. I was greatly surprised some time ago when I opened Pillsbury's book and saw psychology defined as the 'science of behavior.' A still more recent text states that psychology is the 'science of mental behavior.' When I saw these promising statements I thought, now surely we will have texts based upon different lines. After a few pages the science of behavior is dropped and one finds the conventional treatment of sensation, perception, imagery, etc., along with certain shifts in emphasis and additional facts which serve to give the author's personal imprint.

One of the difficulties in the way of a consistent functional psychology is the parallelistic hypothesis. If the functionalist attempts to express his formulations in terms which make mental states really appear to function, to play some active rôle in the world of adjustment, he almost inevitably lapses into terms which are connotative of interaction. When taxed with this he replies that it is more convenient to do so and that he does it to avoid the circumlocution and clumsiness which are inherent in any thoroughgoing parallelism. As a matter of fact I believe the functionalist actually thinks in terms of interaction and resorts to parallelism only when forced to give expression to his views. I feel that *behav-iorism* is the only consistent and logical functionalism. In it one avoids both the Scylla of parallelism and the Charybdis of interaction. Those time-honored relics of philosophical speculation need trouble the student of behavior as little as they trouble the student of physics. The consideration of the mind-body problem affects neither the type of problem selected nor the formulation of the solution of that problems. I can state my position here no better than by saying that I should like to bring my students up in the same ignorance of such hypotheses as one finds among the students of other branches of science.

This leads me to the point where I should like to make the argument constructive. I believe we can write a psychology, define it as Pillsbury, and never go back upon our definition: never use the terms consciousness, mental states, mind, content, introspectively verifiable, imagery, and the like. I believe that we can do it in a few years without running into the absurd terminology of Beer, Bethe, Von Uexküll, Nuel, and that of the so-called objective schools generally. It can be done in terms of stimulus and response, in terms of habit formation, habit integrations and the like. Furthermore, I believe that it is really worth while to make this attempt now.

The psychology which I should attempt to build up would take as a starting point, first, the observable fact that organisms, man and animal alike, do adjust themselves to their environment by means of hereditary and habit equipments. These adjustments may be very adequate or they may be so inadequate that the organism barely maintains its existence; secondly, that certain stimuli lead the organisms to make the responses. In a system of psychology completely worked out, given the response the stimuli can be predicted; given the stimuli the response can be predicted. Such a set of statements is crass and raw in the extreme, as all such generalizations must be. Yet they are hardly more raw and less realizable than the ones which appear in the psychology texts of the day. I possibly might illustrate my point better by choosing an everyday problem which anyone is likely to meet in the course of his work. Some time ago I was called upon to make a study of certain species of birds. Until I went to Tortugas I had never seen these birds alive. When I reached there I found the animals doing certain things: some of the acts seemed to work peculiarly well in such an environment, while others seemed to be unsuited to their type of life. I first studied the responses of the group as a whole and later those of individuals. In order to understand more thoroughly the relation between what was habit and what was hereditary in these responses, I took the young birds and reared them. In this way I was able to study the order of appearance of hereditary adjustments and their complexity, and later the beginnings of habit formation. My efforts in determining the stimuli which called forth such adjustments were crude indeed. Consequently my attempts to control behavior and to produce responses at will did not meet with much success. Their food and water, sex and other social relations, light and temperature conditions were all beyond control in a field study. I did find it possible to control their reactions in a measure by using the nest and egg (or young) as stimuli. It is not necessary in this paper to develop further how such a study should be carried out and how work of this kind must be supplemented by carefully controlled laboratory experiments. Had I been called upon to examine the natives of some of the Australian tribes, I should have gone about my task in the same way. I should have found the problem more difficult: the types of responses called forth by physical stimuli would have been more varied, and the number of effective stimuli larger. I should have had to determine the social setting of their lives in a far more careful way. These savages would be more influenced by the responses of each other than was the case with the birds. Furthermore, habits would have been more complex and the influences of past habits upon the present responses would have appeared more clearly. Finally, if I had been called upon to work out the psychology of the educated European, my problem would have required several lifetimes. But in the

one I have at my disposal I should have followed the same general line of attack. In the main, my desire in all such work is to gain an accurate knowledge of adjustments and the stimuli calling them forth. My final reason for this is to learn general and particular methods by which I may control behavior. My goal is not "the description and explanation of states of consciousness as such," nor that of obtaining such proficiency in mental gymnastics that I can immediately lay hold of a state of consciousness and say, "this, as a whole, consists of gray sensation number 350, of such and such extent, occurring in conjunction with the sensation of cold of a certain intensity; one of pressure of a certain intensity and extent," and so on *ad infinitum*. If psychology would follow the plan I suggest, the educator, the physician, the jurist and the business man could utilize our data in a practical way, as soon as we are able, experimentally, to obtain them. Those who have occasion to apply psychological principles practically would find no need to complain as they do at the present time. Ask any physician or jurist today whether scientific psychology plays a practical part in his daily routine and you will hear him deny that the psychology of the laboratories finds a place in his scheme of work. I think the criticism is extremely just....

In concluding, I suppose I must confess to a deep bias on these questions. I have devoted nearly twelve years to experimentation on animals. It is natural that such a one should drift into a theoretical position which is in harmony with his experimental work. Possibly I have put up a straw man and have been fighting that. There may be no absolute lack of harmony between the position outlined here and that of functional psychology. I am inclined to think, however, that the two positions cannot be easily harmonized. Certainly the position I advocate is weak enough at present and can be attacked from many standpoints. Yet when all this is admitted I still feel that the considerations which I have urged should have a wide influence upon the type of psychology which is to be developed in the future. What we need to do is to start work upon psychology, making *behavior,* not *consciousness,* the objective point of our attack. Certainly there are enough problems in the control of behavior to keep us all working many lifetimes without ever allowing us time to think of consciousness *an sich.* Once launched in the undertaking, we will find ourselves in a short time as far divorced from an introspective psychology as the psychology of the present time is divorced from faculty psychology.

Struggle for Scientific Authority:
The Reception of Watson's Behaviorism, 1913–1920

Franz Samelson

If retrospectively the appearance of Watson's manifesto was a major historical event, primary sources do not quite reflect it as such. Except for Howard C. Warren's reference to the fact that he had repeatedly urged Watson to publish his position paper, none of the autobiographies of prominent psychologists of the period have marked it as a red letter day. In fact, the dean of psychology's historians, E. G. Boring, in an extended reminiscence of his professional life history, did not find it necessary to recall any encounter with Watson or Watson's ideas, even though his own orientation changed from Titchnerian structuralism to a (behavioral) "physicalism."[1]

INITIAL RESPONSES: THREE THEMES AND SOME HOSTILITY

To be sure, the contemporary literature did not ignore Watson's paper completely; neither did it give his challenge singular prominence. A summary of the events of 1913 in psychology, written by Langfeld for the *American Year Book,* started out by dealing with two other "important discussions" before mentioning the "behaviorist movement"; even then it cited Maurice Parmelee's new book *The Science of Human Be-*

Adapted from Samelson, F. (1981). Struggle for scientific authority: The reception of Watson's behaviorism, 1913–1920. *Journal of the History of the Behavioral Sciences, 17,* 399–425. Copyright © 1981 by the Clinical Psychology Publishing Company. Adapted and reprinted by permission of the publisher and the author.

havior rather than Watson's work. The discussion of Watson's paper came only in the second section, entitled "Psychological Method," and treated it mainly as another attack on introspection. A second overview of the preceding year, the summary on "General Problems: Mind and Body" in the January 1914 *Psychological Bulletin* did open with the question whether psychology was purely a study of behavior, or of mental states and processes, or both; commenting that the behaviorists especially were attracting attention in the debate, it then quoted half a page from Watson's paper before going on, noncommittally, to other views on the issue.[2]

Beyond such summaries we find that, in an address on the "Study of Human Behavior" for a June 1913 Eugenics Conference, Robert M. Yerkes had begun to use the term "behaviorist" (apparently coined in late 1912 independently by both Watson and James R. Angell);[3] but his references were to three recent books: Parmelee's work mentioned above, Max Meyer's book on *The Fundamental Laws of Human Behavior,* and William McDougall's *Introduction to Social Psychology,* not to Watson's paper (with which he was familiar).[4] Apart from some footnote references added on to papers written before the appearance of Watson's article, the first direct response in print came in a short article by Mary W. Calkins, entitled "Psychology and the Behaviorist."[5] Critical of Watson's "vigorous" paper, she expressed her "radical disagreement with [its] main thesis" of the uselessness of introspection, questioned his supporting arguments, and insisted that certain kinds of psychological processes could be studied only by introspection. However, she also expressed much sympathy with the "important truth embedded" in Watson's criticism of the "undue abstractness" of the present psychology as the "study of mental state." Instead, psychology needed to be concerned with "problems of life." The study of behavior by objective methods was indeed important, as long as "behavior" was understood not merely as "mechanical," but meant the study of "self related to environment."[6]

Here we have the emergence of three themes which in one form or another came to predominate in the published reactions to Watson for some time: (1) although Calkins conceded some problems with the method of introspection and granted the legitimacy of objective procedures, she nevertheless maintained the usefulness of introspection as one of the methods of psychology (what we might call the "don't throw out the baby with the bath" argument); (2) she expressed a strong desire to expand the subject matter of psychological study to a concern with real people in the real world (the "relevance" argument, as we might call it today); and (3) accepting the notion of behavior, but questioning Watson's narrow definition of the term, she attempted to redirect Watson's thrust toward her own goal, a special "self psychology" version of a functionalist approach (the "cooptation" theme). It is tempting to argue, by the way, that, taking psychology as a whole, Mary Calkins's view was more nearly prophetic of what psychology would become half a century later than was Watson's narrower position, even though his slogan of the "study of behavior" eventually carried the day.

The other direct, and quite enthusiastic, response to Watson came from Fred L. Wells, perhaps best described as a hybrid experimentalist-clinician working at McLean Hospital for the Insane. Once in the context of a review of Parmelee's book, and again in a summary review of "Dynamic Psychology" for the *Psychological Bulletin,* he put himself into Watson's corner, lauding Watson's "well-aimed blow at the autistic method in psychology...."[7] and quoting with obvious relish some of his attacks on the "pure" psychologists and their lack of concern with human life. "Experimental psychology...dodges... the more actual and vital questions...[and retreats] into a burrow of trivial inquiries...," Wells complained.[8] Yet he, like Calkins (and Angell before them, in an APA address on "Behavior as a Psychological Category," delivered about the time Watson was preparing his paper for publication), argued that at least for practical purposes some use of introspection was unavoidable. Furthermore, the crucial issue to be settled was the meaning of "behavior"; in order to be useful it could not be restricted to activities describable in physical or physiological terms, but had to include "*mental* [!] behavior."[9]

A very brief comment in a review of "Criminology and Delinquency" by Jean Weidensall (who as a student had known Watson at Chicago and was, like Wells, working in a nonacademic setting) concludes the list of references to Watson in the *Psychological Bulletin* of 1913: Though Watson's paper seemed a bit radical, she felt that "in truth [it was outlining] the psychology we shall find most useful."[10]

There were also three brief items in the *Journal of Philosophy, Psychology, and Scientific Method.* In the last paragraph of a short paper on the definition of Comparative Psychology, Yerkes protested strongly against Watson's attempt to "throw overboard...the method of self-observation" and to usurp the science of psychology for the study of behavior, although he supported wholeheartedly the integration of behavior methods into psychology. Angell put in a brief demurrer against Watson's claim, that Angell's research on imagery had justified the dismissal of the image from psychology. And finally philosopher Henry R. Marshall, in a paper asking, "Is Psychology Evaporating?," briefly referred to Thorndike, Watson, and the objective science of behavior which was, in his view, legitimate; but it was not psychology.[11]

In late December 1913 the American Psychological Association held its annual convention at Yale University (which hosted the American Philosophical Association at the same time). APA president H. C. Warren gave an address on "The Mental and the Physical." Rejecting any solution of the metaphysical mind-body problem as premature, he went on to argue for the adoption of a double-aspect view as a working hypothesis. This position required a redefinition of psychology to embrace both inner and outer aspects of experience and made it the "science of the relations between the individual and his environment, [to] be studied either objectively as behavior, or introspectively as events of consciousness."[12]

A page-long summary of Warren's address in the proceedings did not refer to Watson at all. The paper itself contained a number of references to Watson and his position; yet it was clearly not a response to him, but to a problematic which had been debated by psychologists for some time. Warren agreed with Watson that the hope for the future might lie in the study of behavior, since it revealed "dynamic aspects" more than did introspection. But he could not accept an autocratic decree prohibiting introspective study; introspection had produced many results of scientific worth; Watson's critique was too "destructive."[13] In summary, Warren's argument, while different in the specifics, was basically the same as Calkins's: don't throw out the baby of introspection, but accept behavior for the sake of "dynamics," and fashion a "double-aspect" compromise instead of splitting psychology into two different disciplines.

At the same convention, a joint session with the philosophers on the "standpoint of psychology" heard, among others, John Dewey and Hugo Münsterberg refer favorably but briefly to behaviorism. Wishing behaviorism well, Dewey expressed both fear and hope—fear, if "behavior" meant just the mechanics of the nervous system; hope, if it included the "attitudes and responses towards others which cannot be located under the skin...." Münsterberg, in an exposition of his scheme of two psychologies,

one "causal" and the other "teleological," expressed the opinion that behaviorism might be successful in an applied psychology derived from the causal approach. In the discussion, Knight Dunlap raised some questions about "delimiting the behaviorist's field...." Earlier that year, Dunlap had presented a talk at Johns Hopkins, in which he distanced himself sharply from Watson and protested against the latter's "extreme doctrine" likely to produce opposition to more moderate innovations.[14]

The earliest recorded reference to Watson's manifesto apparently occurred in a discussion of "four recent tendencies" in psychology, presented by G. Stanley Hall at a Mental Hygiene Conference in April 1913. After introspection and psychoanalysis, "a rich, rank, seething mass of new facts and new ideas, sure to revolutionize..." psychology, Hall mentioned behaviorism briefly and in rather neutral fashion, obviously quoting or paraphrasing Watson's major thesis. From there he proceeded to an extended discussion of the last tendency, Pavlov's "amazing" work on salivary conditioning, which had barely touched American psychology as yet.[15] The seventy-year old Hall still had his ear to the ground.

The only indication of a "violent reaction" and "furor"[16] caused by Watson's polemic is found in a short notice reporting on the meeting of the Experimental Psychologists (largely the inner, Titchenerian circle of the academic discipline), held at Wesleyan University in April 1913. It appears that a "lively discussion" on introspection and behaviorism developed in one of the sessions. Introspection had been hotly debated—without Watson—at a meeting two years earlier, with Titchener on one side and Dodge and Holt on the other.[17] This time, "the hostility to an identification of psychology with 'behaviorism' was surprisingly unanimous...."[18] That is unfortunately all we know about the meeting.

Concerning the other meeting, the year-end APA convention, Melvin E. Haggerty's report remarked that "in spirit [it] had a decidedly behavioristic tendency. More than half the papers either championed the behavioristic point of view in one or another form or [used] behavioristic methods [in their experiments]. A considerable part of the time the word itself was in the air."[19] Here at last is an indication of an apparently broad-based and positive response to Watson. Yet when we look for specifics (beyond the comments by Dewey, Münsterberg, and Warren), we cannot find, either in the titles or in the texts of the paper abstracts for the convention, any mention of Watson or behaviorism; at least for the modern reader, it turns out to be rather difficult to see which of these papers (with one or two exceptions) were supposed by Haggerty to champion the behaviorist point of view. (Judged by subsequent comments, Haggerty himself sympathized with behaviorism, but he also called Watson's refusal to consider introspective knowledge "the merest folly."")[20] And a different report on the convention, by APA secretary Walter V. Bingham, failed to notice any wave of behaviorism. It only remarked, with some relief, that in spite of the presence of the philosophers at the convention the paper sessions had not produced an inordinate number of philosophical or theoretical papers; instead, it had been a well-balanced program (and, we might add, apparently without major surprises).[21] We shall meet this problem again: after discovering a tantalizing reference to the popularity of behaviorism among a certain group of persons, if we ask just who was involved and how it was expressed, we find the concrete evidence to be very elusive.

A BEHAVIORISTIC UNDERGROUND?

On this note ends our account of the recorded responses to Watson in the first year.[22] They were not overwhelming either in their frequency or their intensity, and furthermore came mainly from authors already in favor of some changes before Watson's appeal. Criticism of introspection was not new; neither was the use of objective methods or the advocacy of the study of behavior, as references to other authors like Meyer,

Parmelee, and Thorndike indicate. (As Wells had expressed it, Watson had produced an "unusually concrete statement of a central idea that has always claimed certain adherents among us...."[23])

Was there a behaviorist revolution in the year 1913? The terms "behaviorist" and "behaviorism" had been accepted into professional language; there certainly was some awareness and, on occasion, lively discussion of Watson's contribution to the ongoing debate about the methods and objects of the science. In print, a few direct but mixed reactions agreed with some aspects of Watson's challenge with some enthusiasm while firmly rejecting others. But no reminiscence has described memories of a dramatic encounter with the manifesto; we have not found any contemporary evidence for the conversion of a single individual to Watson's position. While he may have issued a call to revolution, as yet we have seen no clear signs of a mass uprising. But scientific revolutions may take a bit more time. Or perhaps there was a behaviorist "movement," though it was underground, below the printed surface.[24]

Unfortunately, a laborious search of various archival collections has failed to be of much help. Indeed, I have not yet turned up a single letter from the year 1913 containing reactions to Watson's Columbia presentation or its printed version. The only contemporary references came from Watson himself. Sending some reprints of his paper to Yerkes, Watson commented: "I understand that [Yale's Roswell P.] Angier thinks I am crazy. I should not be surprised if this was the general consensus of opinion." (This estimate seems not far off the mark at least in terms of the consensus among the experimentalists, meeting at Wesleyan the following month.) While unfortunately Yerkes's reply is not preserved, Watson's next letter referred to some differences of opinion. At a later date, when the rift between Watson and Yerkes was widening, Yerkes implied that he had held back sharp criticism of the manifesto at the time.[25] And in another place,

Watson indicated that James M. Cattell had scolded him for being "too radical."[26]

I have located very few additional pre-war comments (there are more later on) related to behaviorism in various archives: a very positive though brief one by Gilbert V. Hamilton, and two years later a rather solemn declaration by Margaret F. Washburn that she thought "JBW an enemy to psychology." In addition, there is the exchange of critical comments between Titchener, Angell, and Yerkes, reported earlier by Cedric A. Larson and John J. Sullivan.[27]

There are probably three reasons for this disappointing outcome of an extensive archival search. The most obvious one is that the relevant source material may be lost. Still, some of the surviving collections might have been expected to contain references to the allegedly revolutionary events. Thus a second reason, I would suggest, is that—at least by that time—the function of academic correspondence had shifted. It was no longer a scholarly discussion and sharing of views between colleagues about the substantive issues of their field (assuming gratuitously that it had been so in earlier times); it was rather (with some exceptions) a somewhat hurried bureaucratic exchange, dealing mainly with concrete administrative-political problems: jobs, students, technical details of research and publishing activities, arrangements for meetings, etc., topped off by a bit of gossip and brief personal news. The typewriter had come to the office, but not yet the secretary; letters were usually typed, but mostly by their authors (and therefore without copies). In short, writing letters had become a chore. The discussion of substantive psychological issues may have been displaced to oral exchanges at formal meetings and informal visits; major statements on psychological issues were put into print.

And yet, I believe there is a third reason for this lack of references to behaviorism. Watson had said some strongly provocative and offensive things; but criticism of important aspects of the discipline and/or proposals for new directions

had appeared before and after 1913, as they have on and off throughout the history of psychology. Usually, they are taken notice of, if coming from authors with some visibility, and may even produce a bit of a stir; some new terms may become fashionable; but then business goes on as usual for the vast majority of psychologists. Their activities are determined by other forces than verbal appeals—as any good behaviorist would know. After all, Watson's initial statement had not contained many concrete suggestions, except for the prohibition on introspective procedures. His main point had been a call for reconceptualization. We shall return to this issue later.

Two additional events occurring at year's end must be mentioned. Watson was elected president of the Southern Society for Philosophy and Psychology; he also became editor of the new *Journal of Experimental Psychology*, started by Warren upon Watson's suggestion.[28] But whether these honors were bestowed on him because of his call to arms or in spite of it (i.e. were based on his reputation as an outstanding young scientist acquired before 1913) is impossible to tell. We can only note that any hostility felt by the establishment was either not intense or not powerful enough to prevent these nominations....

If, on the assumption that publication lag or other reasons delayed the response to Watson's historic paper, we search the psychology journals for the following year in order to find evidence of the full impact, we are in for another disappointment. Apart from registering some of the events and talks of 1913 already described, the *Psychological Bulletin* mentioned Watson or behaviorism hardly at all.... Langfeld's survey of the year 1914 in the *American Year Book* noticed no major changes; he reported a continued discussion of the fundamental problem of psychology: the relation of the mental and the physical world, with references to Warren, Holt, Münsterberg, and Prince. Mention of behaviorism remained relegated to the Methods section, according to which "discussion still center[ed] about the question of introspection *versus* behaviorism...''; although Watson was still maintaining his radical view, ''many psychologists believe in the combination of these two methods....''[29]

By 1915, Watson's first book, *Behavior: An Introduction to Comparative Psychology,* had been published. The introductory chapter had reprinted his 1913 papers with only minor changes; the main text had fleshed out Watson's behaviorist program a bit more in a discussion of instincts, reflexes, and habit development in animal psychology. A short description of the book's content by Langfeld and three special reviews by Carr, Thorndike and Herrick, and Haggerty were quite favorable overall; the longer ones criticized some details and all rejected Watson's more extreme theoretical statements, especially the ban on introspection.[30] In a 1910 APA paper and in the introduction to the 1911 edition of *Animal Intelligence,* Thorndike had argued strongly for the importance of objective studies of behavior. Now he expressed his regret that Watson had not added a chapter on *human* psychology to show that recognized psychologists had, for thirty years, carried out behavioral studies of humans. Watson should have corrected the impression that human psychology had been exclusively an introspective affair. But even Thorndike found it unwise to ignore the special form of observation of themselves humans were capable of; it might ''well play some part in science.''[31]

Apart from the reviews, few references to Watson or his book can be found in the 1915 *Psychological Bulletin*. In the *Psychological Review* of 1915, Watson's name does not seem to have appeared even once (except on the masthead, as the journal's editor). Only one passing reference to the ''behaviorist standpoint'' could be located,[32] while five of the six issues of the journal contained at least one article dealing with imageless thought, images, or imagery of one sort or another. The 1915 volume of the *Journal of Philosophy, Psychology, and Scientific Method* included a protest by Walter Hunter against

Watson's misinterpretation of Hunter's delayed reaction experiment, and a few articles on the issues of consciousness and behavior, with both positive and critical references to Watson.[33] ...

At year's end of 1916, the twenty-fifth anniversary of the APA and of the *Philosophical Review* elicited a number of papers by renowned psychologists discussing the past, present, and future of their science. In general, these papers treated behaviorism as only one trend among many and dealt with it briefly. Margaret Washburn defended introspection against Watson's attacks. Joseph Jastrow mentioned behaviorism in passing. Pillsbury pointed to the disagreement between Watson and Yerkes regarding animal consciousness. Cattell, while strongly urging the replacement of introspective studies of the mind by experiments on ''behavior and conduct,'' was more concerned with other issues, especially the economics of research support. Dewey's address on the future of social psychology applauded behaviorism as a promising trend, which could—in a twist surprising to modern readers—in combination with McDougall's work on instincts lead to an understanding of the social emergence of mind— not strictly a Watsonian position. Finally G. Stanley Hall, little concerned with theoretical quibbles, speculated in the grand manner about the role of psychology in the cataclysm looming on the horizon: the war, which was soon to disrupt the lives of many psychologists.[34]

The events of the war years did not silence the behaviorism debate completely. And even before that time Watson had expanded his position in his presidential address on the conditioned reflex, begun his observational studies of human infants, and written an early version of the first chapter for his new book on behaviorism.[35] However, the narration of events will conclude with three more indications of Watson's influence, or lack thereof. In 1915, Dunlap's efforts had initiated the formation of an APA Committee on Terminology, charged with producing some agreed-upon definitions of crucial psychological terms. The first installment of this work was published in the 1918 *Psychological Bulletin*. But Watson's position was not represented in these definitions. With the exception of one subcategory, which accepted "behavior" as the "reaction of an organism to the environment" but expressly restricted it to biological usage, all relevant definitions, e.g., of "psychobiological," led back to others containing the words "mental" or "conscious."[36]

This omission of behavioristic views was apparently no accident. The papers of Mary Calkins, one of the committee members, contain a preprint of the committee report, dated September 1917, and bearing some handwritten corrections. Instead of the twenty-eight definitions published in the *Psychological Bulletin,* this document listed twenty-nine items. Number 29 was: "Behaviorism. Identification of *psychology* with the science of *behavior*." But this definition had been crossed out in ink.[37] The subsequently published version did not include the term behaviorism.

Unfortunately, no correspondence is attached to this preprint. Thus it remains uncertain whether the elimination of Watson's slogan was a bit of skullduggery on the part of one or more committee members, or whether it reflected the result of a mail survey of sixty psychologists in the fall of 1917. Still, in either case this "smoking gun" supports the argument that, five years after his manifesto, any inroads Watson had made in psychology did not lead very far into its center. Even an updated version of the committee's work published in 1922, defining eight varieties of psychology, did not include behaviorism among them. The one closest to it, "Objective Psychology," described in an added note as a "synonym for *Behavior Psychology*," was defined as "concerned with *mental* [!] *phenomena* expressed in the *behavior* of the organism to the exclusion of *introspective data*."[38] ...

This rather detailed (though not exhaustive) account of recorded reactions to Watson stands in definite contrast to some retrospective histories which claim or at least imply that Watson's behaviorism, supported by an anonymous Zeitgeist, quickly swept the field. ...

IN SEARCH OF EXPLANATIONS

Obviously, this is not the whole story. For instance, although the Terminology Committee of the APA had failed to print a definition of Behaviorism in 1918, the *Encyclopedia Americana* carried a two-page article on "Behavior and Behaviorism" in the same year.[39] Although Watson's 1914 book was never reviewed by *Science,* in spite of Watson's anxious inquiries, Edwin B. Holt had recommended it to his readers as a "valiant and clear-headed volume."[40] And though it turned out to be difficult to identify many pro-behaviorists in the contemporary records, later sources do indicate that behaviorism had, in the teens, an impact on a number of mainly younger people besides Weiss and Hunter: Karl S. Lashley, Harold C. Bingham, Melvin E. Haggerty, John F. Dashiell, and a group of Harvard students, among them Floyd H. and Gordon W. Allport, Richard M. Elliott, and Edward C. Tolman. (However, at Harvard the influence had come less from Watson than from Holt, who was teaching a "red-hot behaviorism" at the time,[41] and from Ralph B. Perry.)

Neither is this the end of the story of the behaviorist revolution, only of its first phase. But it is high time to ask what all the details reported so far add up to. Perhaps the general drift of this account has not really come as a surprise to the reader. Though I had initially expected a rather different course of events, once I started to think about it I found the emerging story not too surprising either. Nevertheless, it may present difficulties for some traditional explanations: If there was a Zeitgeist, it seems that so far he (or she) communicated mainly like God to Moses, on a one-to-one basis. If the fact that Watson's program was a strictly American product had any influence on its acceptance, so far we have not seen any direct or even indirect reference to it. Fred Wells, Watson's first vocal supporter, was anything but parochial; his writings were sprinkled generously with German, French, and Latin quotes.

Another popular explanation has to do with the acceptance of behaviorism because it was so practical. Although this argument touches on what I believe to be a crucial aspect (and though we have found mostly favorable responses to what was called the "relevance" theme), it puts some complex issues too simply. For instance, the (American) *Journal of Applied Psychology* did not begin publication until 1917; the similarly titled German *Zeitschrift für Angewandte Psychologie* had first appeared in 1907. An "*Institut für Angewandte Psychologie*" had been established in Berlin in 1906, almost a decade before the start of an applied psychology program at Carnegie Institute of Technology. (And the *Journal of Educational Psychology,* appearing in 1910, had been preceded by a decade by the *Zeitschrift für Pädagogische Psychologie und Experimentelle Pädagogik*.) When Titchener had warned, in 1909, against the undesirable developments toward applied psychology, his specific references were to five German psychologists (and one Frenchman: Binet).[42] While such a list may in part reflect Titchener's European orientation, it should also help to scuttle the myth that applied psychology was "ganz amerikanisch," and that the impractical German professors were preoccupied with nothing but abstruse and esoteric speculations of a philosophical nature. Applied psychology had its roots at least as much in Europe as in America. Furthermore, as the European example shows clearly, an applied psychology does not have to be behavioristic at all (unless, of course, we view it through behaviorist eyes).

Another myth should also be laid to rest: that behaviorism developed out of animal psychology because the situation there forced the researcher into a behavioristic stance. As others[43] have pointed out before, this does not seem altogether true. At least some of the major figures in the small group of American animal psychologists did not feel at all compelled by their subject matter to adopt this position. Washburn and Yerkes both rejected Watsonian behaviorism (though Yerkes claimed that in his early days around 1900 he had been a pre-Watsonian Watsonian behaviorist).[44] Carr belongs in this category, too. In fact, in the early twenties we find more philosophers than animal psychologists among those taking a behaviorist stance; the psychologists in this group (Holt, Tolman, Edwin R. Guthrie, and a bit later Clark L. Hull) were more likely to turn to animal work after their conversion than to move in the reverse direction.

Abandoning such obviously post hoc explanations as, at the very least, overstatements, we should look at a different version of explanation, which is not new but in our days has been formulated in Kuhnian terms.[45] It goes like this: Around 1912 the "imageless thought" controversy laid bare an "anomaly" which the existing science could not deal with; this produced a "crisis" which led to the abandonment of the old "paradigm" and the acceptance of a better one, which could account for the anomaly. But this version, too, is at least a gross oversimplification; it seems to fit neither the facts nor Kuhn's theory. The imageless thought controversy was indeed a problem, but one among at least several; only retrospective historians and polemicists have made it into a "crisis." In his original paper, Watson referred to it only in one sentence in a footnote, in which he listed other problems of introspective psychology.[46] Robert S. Woodworth, not a bad scientist, was trying to solve the problem two years later; he did not see it as an anomaly creating a crisis.[47] And Titchener, in my view quite properly, replied to Watson's claims about the failure of introspection that in many scientific areas the results of observations did not always agree; it was reasonable to allow some time to work out the apparent contradictions. After all, his kind of introspection had been introduced less than ten years before, and not fifty, as Watson had asserted.[48] (We might add that after a turn to behavioral methods, the results obtained by different experimenters have not always agreed either). And when we look carefully at Kuhn's argument, we find that anomalies are always around in science. Only rarely do they touch off crises and revolutions.

A (Slow) Perceptual Shift and a Missing Paradigm-Exemplar

I am impressed by the applicability of one of Kuhn's ideas: the change in the way of seeing things involved in paradigm change. Such a shift did occur in, I believe, a fundamental way. It is most visible in the manner psychologists described their methods of observation. In the earlier phase we find again and again the statement that the introspective method constitutes direct and immediate contact with the subject matter, while what we now mean by objective observation was then only an indirect or mediate one.[49] After the revolution, the meanings are reversed: objective observation is the direct contact, while information obtained through introspection, if not altogether impossible or irrelevant, is at best indirect, a tenuous base for fragile inferences from questionable verbal reports. I think this is more than a manner of speaking; it reflects a real change in the way psychologists experienced, or had been trained to experience, their reality. For most psychologists, however, this shift did not seem to occur suddenly, as an ''aha'' experience with a reversible figure; it took a long time to develop—even if for us, immersed as we are in post-Watson ''behavior'' language, it is hard to look upon the earlier construction as anything but patently contrived and transparent. But this shift is what Watson, having made it himself, demanded from others. To accept the addition of objective observations and performance measures was not so difficult for many psychologists (as we have heard), because they had said or done so even before Watson.[50] But he rejected such a mixture of methods, such a compromise; he was asking for the reversal in the definition of what was real—this made him

appear so radical, and made it difficult for others to follow him.

Besides the crisis-inducing anomaly, another element of Kuhn's theory seems to be missing: the new paradigm. Many people have, in my view, misread Kuhn (helped along by his ambiguities) and assimilated his concept of paradigm to other, more familiar ideas: theories, conceptual systems, viewpoints. But such an understanding turns Kuhn's argument into an old story. What may be novel in Kuhn was his emphasis on the role of the paradigm-exemplar, the specific case of the successful solution of a (crucial) problem, which becomes a relatively concrete model-example for the solution of other problems.[51] But where was Watson's paradigm-exemplar? It was not there.

Should one not cite the conditioned reflex and Pavlov's salivating dogs? Our textbooks often seem to portray the development of modern psychology as an historical chain, from Darwin to Pavlov to Watson, and on to Hull and Skinner. But this compact story is not entirely true. While eventually coming to play the role of paradigm-exemplar (a count of the textbooks reprinting the original line drawing of Pavlov's dog is overdue), the conditioned reflex entered only slowly and in stages into Watson's thinking and did not gain its dominant role until the mid-twenties. Even then, a close look shows the surprising fact that the actual experimental data underlying the diagram, the concrete observations made, were almost nonexistent, as far as Watson and American psychology in general were concerned. After all, Pavlov's dogs lived in a far-away country. Knowledge of them came only through indirect channels, in translations and third-hand reports; some of these reports were imprecise, obscure, or clearly wrong.[52] Did nobody try to replicate the work?

Watson's APA address describing his own and Lashley's observations on motor conditioning was actually based only on pilot studies, which had raised at least as many questions as they had answered. The literature contains no final report of Lashley's elaborate studies of salivary conditioning; a close reading of his progress reports seems to indicate that he gave up the effort because it had failed. (Hilgard and Marquis's classic on conditioning drew a similar conclusion.) As for Watson, he once mentioned briefly an attempt to develop an experimental analogue to reactions to lightning and thunder, by exposing infants to a strong light followed by a loud sound.[53] Subsequently, Watson never referred to this experiment again—had it been a failure too?

The only concrete observation Watson produced (in 1920) was the famous case of "Albert and the rat." But while this case did come to serve as a powerful exemplar, it was not a very solid data-base which could carry a whole theory. It was, after all, an experiment with a sample of one; it also involved some fairly problematic procedures.[54] Some years later, Elsie O. Bregman tried to replicate Watson's experiment in a more systematic manner. As Hilgard and Marquis summed up: "Later experiments have been unsuccessful in duplicating it.... The process is not as simple as the story of Albert suggests."[55]

But surely, there must have been other American conditioning studies. Not really. The first bona fide American conditioning experiment with humans was not reported until 1922, by Hulsey Cason; and he did not feel compelled to accept a Watsonian interpretation. The mass of conditioning experiments did not appear until after the translation of Pavlov's work had become available to American psychologists in 1927 and 1928. All Watson had was Little Albert. Yet while he presented a beautiful example of an idea, if one had already accepted this idea, he did not provide solid scientific evidence to a skeptical observer. The actual paradigm-exemplar, as a way of doing things, did not produce the paradigm shift at all; the exemplar came after the formula had been developed, and even then it was more like a diagram than a way of actually doing things.[56]

Here we may have put a finger on one of the places where Watson was hurting, on one of the facts at least partly responsible for the slow rate of conversion of his fellow scientists. What was it, after all, that Watson had to offer them? He had used some strong words in attacking their psychology and had exploited some of their troubles; he had proposed some intriguing ideas. But in spite of his insistence on a new, harder science, objective observations, etc., when it came to experimental data he had very few (apart from his animal studies) to justify his attempt to usurp scientific authority.

Watson's 1913 research program, loose as it was, seems to have been plagued by false leads or experimental failures. The two concrete proposals of 1913, the identification of thinking with subvocal movements and his explanation of affection, in good Freudian fashion, in terms of activity of the sex glands, had been proffered without any empirical evidence. (The two major specifics radical behaviorism eventually became identified with, environmentalism and the conditioned response, did not become central to Watson's system until ten years later.)

Apparently, Watson spent some time trying to collect data on laryngeal movements, but eventually gave up.[57] His first attack on conditioning (still within a limited theoretical context) also seems to have ended with an impasse, and with a shift to observational work on infants. By 1920, not one concrete experimental problem of human psychology had been solved convincingly by Watson and had provided him with a Kuhnian paradigm.

Yet he was addressing professionals who had been trained in the use of introspective methods, and were so training others; who had believed all along that what they were doing was indeed real science, since it involved laboratories, observations, measurements, controlled conditions, etc. Watson was asking these professionals to throw their tools overboard as not scientific, to declare all the hard-won generalizations that filled their textbooks and their lectures to be artifacts of bad methods. This was too much to ask, as we heard one psychologist after another assert in their reactions to Watson. Though obviously they had not yet solved all the difficult problems of mental phenomena, nevertheless they were the professional experts on the mind, on the inner experience of man. All of a sudden they should forswear their claim to this expertise, surrender their scientific authority?

In recent years we have heard some calls for radical changes in psychology or in its specialities. Their reception, with responses ranging from hostility to indifference—even though there are at least *some* anomalies around in our science—should let us empathize with the feelings of the established psychologists of Watson's time. What did Watson have to offer them in return for their renunciation? He promoted a different version of science which, so it seemed to them, would make them lose their professional identity and turn them into either biologists or physiologists. Why should they risk such an exchange?

A New Goal for Psychology

After all, Watson's call for a revolution in psychology had been largely programmatic. His main thrust had aimed at a redefinition of scientific standards and a redirection of psychology. Put simply, this redefinition proceeded on three different levels: First was the change in *method:* the call for objective procedures and the elimination of "unscientific" introspection. This argument, having the most direct impact on the workday of psychologists, drew the largest share of public responses. While the emphasis on objective methods, already widely used and advocated, met with a good deal of sympathy, the total proscription of introspection ran into strong resistance, if only for the intolerant tone of its imposition (even from those not using introspection in their own work, like Thorndike and Yerkes).

The second level concerned the *subject matter* of psychology, changing it from mental contents and/or processes to movement and behavior, with its attendant peripheralism, rejection of central processes, and associated metaphysical connotations. This issue, too, met with considerable debate. Its acceptance required a fundamental figure-ground reversal which was not easy to accomplish and took its time in coming about, although the expansion of the field to problems of "real life" had widespread support in the growing discipline.

I would like to propose, however, that the crucial argument occurred at a third level and dealt with the *goal* for psychology. According to Watson, this goal was to be the "prediction and control of behavior." Here Watson proposed something radical and new for psychology. All textbooks before him had defined psychology's aim in a different way, as description and/or explanation of mental phenomena, their understanding (on occasion including self-understanding, even self-improvement), etc.: the traditional goals of academic science.

Where Watson obtained his formula about prediction and control is not quite clear. Initially I assumed that he had taken a cliché from the natural sciences which he was trying to emulate, but a somewhat cursory search complicated this answer. Most sources I found (discussions of philosophy of science and encyclopedia definitions of "science")[58] did not define science in terms of prediction and control, mentioned prediction only in passing, and were more concerned with the problem raised by positivism: the banishment of causes, description versus explanation. However, the biologist Jacques Loeb had on several occasions described the goal of modern biology as the "control of life-phenomena" and in 1912 even referred to two outcomes, control or quantitative prediction. Watson, who had studied with Loeb at Chicago, may well have derived his novel definition of the goal of psychology from Loeb's ideas.[59] Of course some psychologists had, if only in passing, spoken of control before Watson: William James had once talked about "practical prediction and control" as the aim of all sciences, and about the demand on psychologists from all kinds of managers for "practical rules" for the "control of states of mind."[60] Cattell's famous St. Louis address had eagerly anticipated the "application of systematized knowledge to the control of human nature," to the "control of ourselves and our fellow men."[61] Thorndike had mentioned "control [of man's] acts" in a 1911 essay defining psychology as the study of behavior.[62] Yerkes's 1911 textbook contained, as sixth and final part, a rather abstract discussion of foresight and the control of mental events.[63] And finally, in England William McDougall had published a little book, in which he stated as psychology's aim: "to increase our understanding of, and our power of guidance and control over, the behaviour of men and animals."[64] (Watson knew McDougall's earlier books.)

Still I believe that Watson's treatment of the issue constituted a quantum jump. Only with him did control become a fundamental idea, part of the textbook definition; and it came right at the start, appearing in the second sentence of his 1913 paper (and at least four more times in fourteen pages): The "theoretical goal [of psychology] is the prediction and control of behavior." Why did Watson use this phrase? Why "theoretical goal," why not "practical" goal, or just "the" goal? Did theoretical mean hypothetical, ideal—a goal unreachable in practice? I do not think that this is what Watson tried to say.

Before Watson, the aims of psychology had been seen in terms of the category of pure science, as contrasted to either applied science or art. Of course, most psychologists have had their dreams of glory, in which their science would affect the real world and solve some of its problems. Even defenders of an ascetic science, like Titchener, believed that scientific knowledge would eventually produce its practical fruit and thus justify science to the impure, though true scientists ignored the question of application. But James's brief remark concerned the pressures from the *outside* for practical rules, presumably

derived from theoretical knowledge. The quote from Cattell referred to the *application* of systematized knowledge. And Yerkes ended his discussion by saying: "Control is the outcome, albeit not the avowed goal, of scientific research.... Psychology is *not* the science of mental control."[65] It merely would make it possible. In other words, traditionally the issue was seen as involving two steps: first, the acquisition of knowledge as the task of science, and then its application to practical affairs. What was debatable, and debated, was the desirability, the timing, and the division of labor in such application. Watson saw the issue differently. His phrase "theoretical goal" shows him reshuffling the traditional categories[66]; prediction and control were no longer indirect or second-stage outcomes, but had become the direct focus and criterion of theory development. I think this notion was radically new (for psychology) and provided the fulcrum for the reorientation of psychology in subsequent decades, so that today any psychology major will state what is self-evident to him: that the goal of (behavioristic as well as cognitive) psychology is the prediction and control of behavior.

It is interesting, and somewhat puzzling, that the early reactions to Watson, the more intensive debate over behaviorism in the early twenties, and more recent analyses of Watson's contribution were largely silent on this point.[67] Only Titchener's rebuttal focused on the behaviorist's goal, in his accusation that Watson was trying to create a technology rather than a science. Thorndike's and Carr's reviews of Watson's *Comparative* book, which reprinted the 1913 papers, reacted in passing to this point; yet both seem to have misunderstood it. In part, I believe, the Janus-face of the term *control* is responsible for the lack of discussion. Control could mean control of conditions, precision in experimentation, elimination of unwanted influence; but that was a commonplace. Or it could mean what Watson clearly intended, at least much of the time (he also used a more abstract formula about predicting stimuli from responses and responses from stimuli), and spelled out later: *social control,* i.e., manipulation of human beings for the benefit of society.[68] But the experimental psychologists failed to confront this aspect of behaviorism in their theoretical debate and eventually defined the issue away.

Yet others did get the message. The first text in applied psychology—while not strictly Watsonian—opened on a distinctly behavioristic note. It introduced the ideas of prediction and control, and explained that the change in emphasis from consciousness to behavior may have been due in part to theoretical difficulties (as with imageless thought); but it was also due to the demands of practical life.[69] About the same time, John Dewey's address on the need for social psychology linked behaviorism with the development of a social psychology in the service of social control. Reviewing the applications of psychology to industry in 1920, Henry Link cited the Gilbreths, involved in time and motion work in industry, as the "ideal behaviorists" and concluded: "Watson's work is, in fact, the conscious methodology which practically all recent literature in industrial psychology has more or less explicitly *implied.*"[70] Soon after, W. V. Bingham, head of the applied psychology unit at Carnegie Tech, was to complain about this accidental (and to him unfortunate) identification of behaviorism with applied psychology, which made his attempt to separate an applied science from the pure science of psychology more difficult. And Floyd Allport described social psychology as becoming "the study of the social behavior of the individual...[needed] for study and control of the socially significant aspects of individual response." He also wrote in his lecture notes: "Responsibilities incident to human control. Practical psychology is essentially behavioristic in method."[71]

CONCLUSION

Such beginnings are part of a larger and complex pattern of developments in the twenties, which

is discussed elsewhere.[72] So far, it appears that a less than monolithic mainstream of experimental psychology, debating issues of method and concepts, resisted Watson's advances for a long time, assimilating them gradually in the form of the more abstract S-R formula. Yet in the meantime others, inside and outside psychology, more immediately concerned with problems of social control and helped along by the exigencies and opportunities of World War I, were finding Watson's arguments a convenient or inspiring rationale. Even if they may not have accepted all of his theoretical ideas, Watson had given the discipline a strong push in the direction of technological science.

Certainly, Watson had not singlehandedly transformed psychology. Too many of the specifics of his argument had not been original with him—although the common practice of briefly quoting one or another author's use of "behavioral" definitions of psychology before 1913,[73] in order to demolish Watson's claim to priority, misses the mark. It overlooks the fact that Watson had already in 1907 declared that the "science of behavior" was "thoroughly established."[74] It is true enough that at this time he did not yet apply it to all of psychology; nonetheless, the phrase had been abroad long before 1913. What counted were its corollaries.

But while using ideas from others, as well as appealing to their dissatisfactions with the status quo, Watson had sharpened the arguments into a revolutionary weapon. Provoking a good deal of resistance with his rhetoric, he also discovered the price to be paid for his shift, in 1913, from a strategy of succession to, in Pierre Bourdieu's terms, a high-risk strategy of subversion of established scientific authority.[75] When the shift finally paid off, others reaped the benefits. Watson was no longer a part of the professional community, when eventually the reestablished monopoly of scientific authority had accepted prediction and control as the criterion of positive science and declared only outward manifestations, "behavior," to be legitimate scientific data. Anything mental had become unobservable, an at best problematic inference if not a superstition pure and simple.

In a sense, the present research effort turned out to be a failure. Looking for the sources of behaviorism's powerful appeal to American psychologists, we found more often criticisms or partial acceptance. Did we look in the wrong place? What I had not realized at the outset was that the victory of behaviorism took so much longer in coming about. And at least this scientific revolution did not involve simply conceptual transformations and conversions, but something Kuhn has not talked about—a power struggle in a discipline, affected by events without. Like the other social sciences,[76] the young profession of psychology grew up facing a predicament, in its dependence on a larger clientele, on the one hand, and its desire for autonomy and academic status, on the other—as reflected in the rhetorics of relevance and purity. Eventually, psychology adopted Watson's ingenious solution combining the appeals of hardheaded science, pragmatic usefulness, and ideological liberation.

NOTES

(1) Howard C. Warren, (Autobiography), in *A History of Psychology in Autobiography,* vol. 1, ed. Carl Murchison (Worcester, Mass.: Clark University Press, 1930), p. 462. See also John B. Watson "Psychology as the Behaviorist Views It," *Psychological Review* 20 (1913): 158–177. Walter B. Pillsbury recalled, in his autobiography, that he had read Watson's paper while in Germany. However, his only concern was Watson's misinterpretation of a comment Pillsbury had made about Watson's animal lab. See Pillsbury, *A History of Psychology in Autobiography,* vol. 2 (1932), p. 285. Finally, John F. Dashiell's autobiography mentions Watson's "prompt appeal" without giving any specifics (although Dashiell attended Columbia University at the time of Watson's presentation); nor do his early writings show much of a behavioristic influence. Dashiell, (Autobiography), in *A History of Psychology in Autobiography,* vol. 5 (1967), pp. 117–118; and

"Spirit and Matter: A Philosophical Tradition," *Journal of Philosophy, Psychology, and Scientific Method* 14 (1917): 66–74. E. G. Boring, *Psychologist at Large* (New York: Basic Books, 1961).

(2) H. S. Langfeld, "Psychology," in *The American Year Book, 1913,* ed. Francis G. Wickware (New York: Appleton, 1914), p. 704; Maurice Parmelee, *The Science of Human Behavior* (New York: Macmillan, 1913); Walter T. Marvin, "General Problems; Mind and Body," *Psychological Bulletin* 11 (1914): 1–7.

(3) Robert M. Yerkes, "The Study of Human Behavior," *Science* 39 (1914): 625–633; James R. Angell, "Behavior as a Category of Psychology," *Psychological Review* 20 (1913): 225–270, pp. 261, 264; for the origin of the term see also Howard C. Warren, "Terminology," *Psychological Bulletin* 11 (1914): 10–11.

(4) Max F. Meyer, *The Fundamental Laws of Human Behavior* (Boston: Badger, 1911); William McDougall, *An Introduction to Social Psychology* (London: Methuen, 1908).

(5) Angell, "Behavior as a Category"; Fredrick J. E. Woodbridge, "The Belief in Sensations," *Journal of Philosophy, Psychology, and Scientific Method* 10 (1913): 599–608; Mary W. Calkins, "Psychology and the Behaviorist," *Psychological Bulletin* 10 (1913): 288–291.

(6) Calkins, "Psychology," p. 289.

(7) Fredrick L. Wells, "Special Reviews" and "Dynamic Psychology," *Psychological Bulletin* 10 (1913): 280–281 and 434–440, p. 434.

(8) Wells, "Special Reviews," p. 281.

(9) James R. Angell, "Behavior as a Psychological Category" (abstract), *Psychological Bulletin* 10 (1913): 48–49; Wells, "Special Reviews," p. 281.

(10) Jean Weidensall, "Criminology and Delinquency," *Psychological Bulletin* 10 (1913): 229–237, p. 232.

(11) Robert M. Yerkes, "Comparative Psychology: A Question of Definitions," *Journal of Philosophy, Psychology, and Scientific Method* 10 (1913): 580–582, p. 581; James R. Angell, "Professor Watson and the Image," *Journal of Philosophy, Psychology, and Scientific Method* 10 (1913): 609; Henry R. Marshall, "Is Psychology Evaporating?" *Journal of Philosophy, Psychology, and Scientific Method* 10 (1913): 710–716.

(12) Howard C. Warren, "The Mental and the Phys-

ical,'' *Psychological Bulletin* 11 (1914): 35–36 (abstract), and *Psychological Review* 21 (1914): 79–100, p. 100.

(13) Ibid., pp. 97, 95.

(14) John Dewey, ''Psychological Doctrine and Philosophical Teaching,'' *Journal of Philosophy, Psychology, and Scientific Method* 11 (1914): 505–511, p. 511; Harold C. Brown, ''The Thirteenth Annual Meeting of the American Philosophical Association,'' *Journal of Philosophy, Psychology, and Scientific Method* 11 (1914): 57–67, p. 65; Knight Dunlap, ''Images and Ideas,'' *Johns Hopkins University Circular* 33 (1914): 25–41.

(15) G. Stanley Hall, ''Food and Mind,'' Mental Hygiene Conference, Boston, 4 April 1913 (typed ms.), p. 3, Box 29, G. Stanley Hall Papers, Clark University Archives. (I am indebted to David E. Leary for making this item available to me.)

(16) John C. Burnham, ''On the Origins of Behaviorism,'' *Journal of the History of the Behavioral Sciences 4* (1968): 143–151.

(17) E. G. Boring, ''The Society of Experimental Psychologists; 1904–1938,'' *American Journal of Psychology* 51 (1938): 410–423.

(18) ''Notes and News,'' *Psychological Bulletin* 10 (1913): 211–212; see also Samuel W. Fernberger, ''Convention of Experimental Psychologists,'' *American Journal of Psychology* 24 (1913): 445; and for a retrospective account in almost the same words, Boring, ''The Society,'' p. 414.

(19) Melvin E. Haggerty, ''The Twenty-second Annual Meeting of the American Psychological Association,'' *Journal of Philosophy, Psychology, and Scientific Method* 11 (1914): 85–109, p. 86.

(20) Melvin E. Haggerty, ''The Relation of Psychology and Pedagogy,'' *Psychological Bulletin* 13 (1916): 55–56, and ''Reviews and Abstracts of the Literature,'' *Journal of Philosophy, Psychology, and Scientific Method* 13 (1916): 470–472, p. 472.

(21) Walter V. Bingham, ''Proceedings of the Twenty-second Annual Meeting of the American Psychological Association,'' *Psychological Bulletin* 11 (1914): 29–35, p. 29.

(22) This account is not exhaustive. For instance, a summary of Watson's manifesto by J. R. Tuttle appeared in the *Philosophical Review* 22 (1913): 674; ''Notes and News,'' *Journal of Educational Psychology* 4 (1913): 180, reported briefly on Watson's Columbia address.

(23) F. L. Wells, ''Dynamic Psychology,'' p. 434.

(24) Howard C. Warren's autobiography (p. 462) recounted two decades later that, although he could not accept Watson's position, ''the younger psychologists hailed Watson as a second Moses.'' Yet specifics supporting and detailing this dramatic image are hard to find in the contemporary record. In ''The Origins of Behaviorism,'' (1979 Ph.D. dissertation) John O'Donnell discusses at length what he calls Watson's ''silent majority'' which, however, was not a group converted by the manifesto (as Warren had it), but which had been interested in applied psychology, and thus been behavioristic, before 1913. But even if there was such a majority for behaviorism, the very fact that its members are hard to track down in the record (even O'Donnell gives us only a few names) indicates their marginal role in the development of the academic discipline, its publications, and its training of students. Finally, O'Donnell's argument, in which applied interests are equated with behaviorism, seems problematical to me; at the very least it proceeds at a more global level of analysis than does the present paper.

(25) J. B. Watson to R. M. Yerkes, 26 March 1913; R. M. Yerkes to J. B. Watson, 16 May 1916, Robert M. Yerkes Papers, Historical Library, Yale Medical Library, New Haven, Conn.

(26) John B. Watson, ''Image and Affection in Behavior,'' *Journal of Philosophy, Psychology, and Scientific Method 10* (1913): 421–428.

(27) Gilbert V. Hamilton to R. M. Yerkes, 22 December 1914. (Hamilton was a former Yerkes student with an M.D. degree, involved in animal research at the time); Margaret F. Washburn to R. M. Yerkes, 26 May 1916, Yerkes Papers. Cedric A. Larson and John J. Sullivan, ''Watson's Relation to Titchener,'' *Journal of the History of the Behavioral Sciences* 1 (1965): 338–354.

(28) ''Notes and News,'' *Psychological Bulletin* 11 (1914): 28, 79.

(29) H. S. Langfeld, ''Psychology,'' in *American Year Book, 1914* (New York: Appleton, 1915), 674.

(30) John B. Watson, *Behavior: An Introduction to Comparative Psychology* (New York: Holt, 1914); H. S. Langfeld, ''Text-books and General Treatises,'' *Psychological Bulletin* 12 (1915): 30–37; Harvey A. Carr, ''Special Reviews,'' *Psychological Bulletin* 12 (1915): 308–312; Edward L. Thorndike and C. Judson Herrick, ''Watson's

'Behavior'," *Journal of Animal Behavior* 5 (1915): 462–470; M. E. Haggerty, "Reviews and Abstracts of Literature," *Journal of Philosophy, Psychology, and Scientific Method* 13 (1916): 470–472.

(31) E. L. Thorndike, "The Study of Consciousness and the Study of Behavior" (abstract), *Psychological Bulletin* 8 (1911): 39; Thorndike, *Animal Intelligence* (New York: Macmillan, 1911); Thorndike and Herrick, "Watson's 'Behavior'," p. 464.

(32) George A. Coe, "A Proposed Classification of Mental Functions," *Psychological Review* 22 (1915): 87–98, p. 91.

(33) Walter S. Hunter, "A Reply to Some Criticisms of the Delayed Reaction," *Journal of Philosophy, Psychology, and Scientific Method* 12 (1915): 38–41; Edwin B. Holt, "Response and Cognition," *Journal of Philosophy, Psychology, and Scientific Method* 12 (1915): 365–373 and 393–409; C. Judson Herrick, "Introspection as a Biological Method," *Journal of Philosophy, Psychology, and Scientific Method* 12 (1915): 543–551.

(34) Margaret F. Washburn, "Some Thoughts on the Last Quarter Century in Psychology," *Philosophical Review* 26 (1917): 46–55; Joseph Jastrow, "Varieties of Psychological Experience," *Psychological Review* 24 (1917): 249–265; Walter B. Pillsbury, "The New Developments in Psychology in the Past Quarter Century," *Philosophical Review* 26 (1917): 56–59; James M. Cattell, "Our Psychological Association and Research," *Science* 45 (1917): 275–284; John Dewey, "The Need for Social Psychology," *Psychological Review* 24 (1917): 266–277; G. Stanley Hall, "Practical Relations between Psychology and the War," *Journal of Applied Psychology* 1 (1917): 9–16.

(35) John B. Watson, "The Place of the Conditioned-Reflex in Psychology," *Psychological Bulletin* 23 (1916): 89–117. Apparently this address did not produce much of a reaction. See H. S. Langfeld to H. Münsterberg, 1 January 1916, Hugo Münsterberg Papers, Boston Public Library; Watson, "An Attempted Formulation of the Scope of Behavior Psychology," *Psychological Review* 24 (1917): 329–352; Watson and John J. B. Morgan, "Emotional Reactions and Psychological Experimentation," *American Journal of Psychology* 28 (1917): 163–174.

(36) Howard C. Warren, Mary W. Calkins, Knight Dunlap, H. N. Gardiner, and C. A. Ruckmich, "Definitions and Delimitations of Psychological Terms," *Psychological Bulletin* 15 (1918): 89–95, p. 94.

(37) Preprint located in 3P, Mary Whiton Calkins Unprocessed Papers, Wellesley College Archives, Wellesley, Mass.

(38) Warren et al., "Definitions, II," *Psychological Bulletin* 19 (1922): 230–235, p. 231.

(39) Walter B. Pillsbury, "Behavior and Behaviorism," *Encyclopedia Americana* (New York: Encyclopedia Americana Corporation, 1918): 446–448.

(40) See J. B. Watson to J. M. Cattell, 15 January 1915, Cattell Papers, and J. B. Watson to R. M. Yerkes, 27 March 1916, Yerkes Papers; Holt, "Response and Cognition," p. 409n.

(41) Gardner Murphy to Robert S. Woodworth, n.d. (in reply to Woodworth's letter dated 27 October 1932), Robert S. Woodworth Papers, Library of Congress.

(42) E. B. Titchener, "The Past Decade in Experimental Psychology," *American Journal of Psychology* 21 (1910): 404–422.

(43) David Bakan, "Behaviorism and American Urbanization," *Journal of the History of the Behavioral Sciences* 2 (1966): 5–28.

(44) R. M. Yerkes, "Behaviorism and Genetic Psychology," *Journal of Philosophy, Psychology, and Scientific Method* 14 (1917): 154–161, p. 151.

(45) Thomas S. Kuhn, *The Structure of Scientific Revolutions* (Chicago: University of Chicago Press, 1962).

(46) Watson, "Psychology," p. 163n.

(47) Robert S. Woodworth, "A Revision of Imageless Thought," *Psychological Review* 22 (1915): 1–27.

(48) Edward B. Titchener, "On 'Psychology as the Behaviorist Views It,'" *Proceedings of the American Philosophical Society* 53 (1914): 1–17, p. 8. See also Kurt Danziger, "The History of Introspection Reconsidered," *Journal of the History of the Behavioral Sciences* 16 (1980): 241–262.

(49) E.g., James R. Angell, *Psychology*, 3rd ed. (New York: Holt, 1906), p. 4; Harvey A. Carr, *Psychology* (New York: Longmans Green, 1926), p. 7.

(50) See Danziger, "History of Introspection," pp. 257–258.

(51) Franz Samelson, "Paradigms, Labels, and His-

torical Analysis," *American Psychologist* 28 (1973): 1141–1143. See also Brian D. Mackenzie, *Behaviourism and the Limits of Scientific Method* (London: Routledge & Kegan Paul, 1977).

(52) Karl S. Lashley, "Recent Literature of a General Nature on Animal Behavior," *Psychological Bulletin 11* (1914): 269–277, p. 272.

(53) Watson, "The Place of the Conditioned-Reflex"; Karl S. Lashley, "The Human Salivary Reflex and Its Use in Psychology," *Psychological Review* 23 (1916): 445–464; Lashley, "Reflex Secretions of the Human Parotid Gland," *Journal of Experimental Psychology,* 1 (1916): 461–495; Ernest R. Hilgard and Donald G. Marquis, *Conditioning and Learning* (New York: Appleton-Century, 1940), p. 13. Watson and Morgan, "Emotional Reactions," p. 171.

(54) J. B. Watson and Rosalie Rayner, "Conditioned Emotional Reactions," *Journal of Experimental Psychology* 3 (1920): 1–14; J. B. Watson and R. R. Watson, "Studies in Infant Psychology," *Scientific Monthly* 13 (1921): 493–515. For a more detailed discussion, see Franz Samelson, "John B. Watson's Little Albert, Cyril Burt's Twins, and the Need for a Critical Science," *American Psychologist* 35 (1980): 619–625.

(55) Elsie O. Bregman, "An Attempt to Modify the Emotional Attitudes of Infants by the Conditioned Response Technique," *Journal of Genetic Psychology* 45 (1934): 169–198; Hilgard and Marquis, *Conditioning and Learning,* pp. 293, 294.

(56) Hulsey Cason, "The Conditioned Pupillary Reaction," *Journal of Experimental Psychology* 5 (1922): 108–146; Ivan P. Pavlov, *Conditioned Reflexes,* trans. G. V. Anrep (London: Oxford University Press, 1927); Pavlov, *Lectures on Conditioned Reflexes,* trans. W. Horsley Gantt (New York: International Publishers, 1928). Two earlier American conditioning studies do not qualify for inclusion, for different technical reasons: Ignatius A. Hamel, "A Study and Analysis of the Conditioned Reflex," *Psychological Monographs* 27 (1919): No. 1; Florence Mateer, *Child Behavior* (Boston: Badger, 1918). Of course, others had started to *talk* about conditioning (F. L. Wells, "Von Bechterew and Uebertragung," *Journal of Philosophy, Psychology, and Scientific Method* 13 [1916]: 354–356; William H.

Burnham, "Mental Hygiene and the Conditioned Reflex," *Pedagogical Seminary* 24 [1917]: 449–488), but that only proves my point. Cf. Hilgard and Marquis, *Conditioning and Learning,* on this issue, although their emphasis is different.

(57) J. B. Watson to R. M. Yerkes, 22 October 1915 and 17 February 1916, Yerkes Papers.

(58) For instance, Karl Pearson, *The Grammar of Science,* 2nd ed. (London: Black, 1900).

(59) Jacques Loeb, *Comparative Physiology of the Brain and Comparative Psychology* (New York: Putnam, 1907), p. 287; Loeb, *The Mechanistic Conception of Life* (Chicago: University of Chicago Press, 1912), pp. 3, 196. Philip J. Pauly's recent work on Loeb comes independently to similar conclusions; see his "Jacques Loeb and the Control of Life," unpublished Ph.D. dissertation, Johns Hopkins University, 1980. Of course, in at least a loose sense these ideas go back to Auguste Comte and beyond.

(60) William James, "A Plea for Psychology as a 'Natural Science'," *Philosophical Review* 1 (1892): 146–153, p. 148 (I am indebted to John O'Donnell for this reference).

(61) James M. Cattell, "The Concepts and Methods of Psychology," *Popular Science Monthly* 66 (1904): 176–186, pp. 185, 186.

(62) Thorndike, *Animal Intelligence,* p. 15.

(63) Robert M. Yerkes, *Introduction to Psychology* (New York: Holt, 1911).

(64) William McDougall, *Psychology: The Study of Behavior* (London: Butterworth, 1912), p. 21.

(65) Yerkes, *Introduction to Psychology,* p. 416 (italics added). Thorndike had said: "Science seeks to know the world; the arts, to control it." *The Elements of Psychology* (New York: Seiler, 1905), p. 324.

(66) See Watson's argument that "applied psychology" was a misnomer; "Psychology," p. 169.

(67) Gustav Bergman, "The Contribution of John B. Watson," *Psychological Review* 63 (1956): 265–276; Herrnstein, Introduction to Watson's *Behavior;* Mackenzie, *Behaviorism;* not so John C. Burnham, whose repeated references to the "social control" theme helped to direct my attention to this issue. See also Lucille C. Birnbaum, *Behaviorism: John Broadus Watson and American Social Thought,* unpublished Ph.D. dissertation (Berkeley: University of California, 1965).

(68) John B. Watson, "An Attempted Formulation of

the Scope of Behavior Psychology," *Psychological Review 24* (1917): 329–352 and *Psychology from the Standpoint of a Behaviorist* (Philadelphia: Lippincott, 1919), p. 2. See also Paul T. Young to J. B. Watson, 27 May 1917, P. T. Young Papers.

(69) Harry L. Hollingworth and Albert T. Poffenberger, *Applied Psychology* (New York: Appleton, 1917), pp. 5, 6.

(70) Dewey, "The Need for Social Psychology"; Henry C. Link, "The Application of Psychology to Industry," *Psychological Bulletin* 17 (1920): 335–346, pp. 341, 345 (italics added).

(71) Walter V. Bingham, "On the Possibility of an Applied Psychology," *Psychological Review* 30 (1923): 289–305; Floyd H. Allport, "Social Psychology," *Psychological Bulletin* 17 (1920): 85–94, p. 85; F. H. Allport, Lecture Notes, "Psychology 35; Industrial and Vocational Psychology," (typed, 1923?), Box 3, Walter V. Bingham

Papers, University Archives, Carnegie-Mellon University, Pittsburgh, Penn.

(72) Franz Samelson, "Early Behaviorism, Pt. 3. The Stalemate of the Twenties," Paper presented at the 12th annual meeting of Cheiron, Bowdoin College, Brunswick, ME, June 1980; See also F. Samelson, "Putting Psychology on the Map," *Psychology in Social Context,* pp. 101–168.

(73) For instance, O'Donnell, "Origins," p. 537.

(74) John B. Watson, "Comparative Psychology," *Psychological Bulletin* 4 (1907): 208.

(75) Pierre Bourdieu, "The Specificity of the Scientific Field and the Social Conditions of the Progress of Reason," *Social Science Information* 14, no. 6 (1975): 19–47.

(76) Cf. Dorothy Ross, "The Development of the Social Sciences," in *The Organization of Knowledge in Modern America, 1860–1920,* ed. Alexandra Oleson and John Voss (Baltimore: Johns Hopkins University Press, 1979), pp. 107–138.

Whatever Happened to Little Albert?

Ben Harris

Almost 60 years after it was first reported, Watson and Rayner's (1920) attempted conditioning of the infant Albert B. is one of the most widely cited experiments in textbook psychology. Undergraduate textbooks of general, developmental, and abnormal psychology use Albert's conditioning to illustrate the applicability of classical conditioning to the development and modification of human emotional behavior. More specialized books focusing on psychopathology and behavior therapy (e.g., Eysenck, 1960) cite Albert's conditioning as an experimental model of psychopathology (i.e., a rat phobia) and often use Albert to introduce a discussion of systematic desensitization as a treatment of phobic anxiety.

Unfortunately, most accounts of Watson and Rayner's research with Albert feature as much

Adapted from Harris, B. (1979). Whatever happened to little Albert? *American Psychologist, 34,* 151–160. Copyright © 1979 by the American Psychological Association. Adapted and reprinted by permission of the publisher and the author.

fabrication and distortion as they do fact. From information about Albert himself to the basic experimental methods and results, no detail of the original study has escaped misrepresentation in the telling and retelling of this bit of social science folklore.

There has recently been a revival of interest in Watson's conditioning research and theorizing (e.g., MacKenzie, 1972; Seligman, 1971; Weimer & Palermo, 1973; Samelson, Note 1), and in the mythology of little Albert (Cornwell & Hobbs, 1976; Larson, 1978; Prytula, Oster, & Davis, 1977). However, there has yet to be a complete examination of the methodology and results of the Albert study and of the process by which the study's details have been altered over the years. In the spirit of other investigations of classic studies in psychology (e.g., Ellenberger, 1972; Parsons, 1974) it is time to examine Albert's conditioning in light of current theories of learning. It is also time to examine how the Albert study has been portrayed over the years, in the hope of discovering how changes in psychological theory have affected what generations of psychologists have told each other about Albert.

THE EXPERIMENT

As described by Watson and Rayner (1920), an experimental study was undertaken to answer three questions: (1) Can an infant be conditioned to fear an animal that appears simultaneously with a loud, fear-arousing sound? (2) Would such fear transfer to other animals or to inanimate objects? (3) How long would such fears persist? In attempting to answer these questions, Watson and Rayner selected an infant named Albert B., whom they described as "healthy," and "stolid and unemotional" (p. 1). At approximately 9 months of age, Albert was tested and was judged to show no fear when successively observing a number of live animals (e.g., a rat, a rabbit, a dog, and a monkey), and various inanimate objects (e.g., cotton, human masks, a burning newspaper). He was, however, judged to show fear whenever a long steel bar was unexpectedly struck with a claw hammer just behind his back.

Two months after testing Albert's apparently unconditioned reactions to various stimuli, Watson and Rayner attempted to condition him to fear a white rat. This was done by presenting a white rat to Albert, followed by a loud clanging sound (of the hammer and steel bar) whenever Albert touched the animal. After seven pairings of the rat and noise (in two sessions, one week apart), Albert reacted with crying and avoidance when the rat was presented without the loud noise.

In order to test the generalization of Albert's fear response, 5 days later he was presented with the rat, a set of familiar wooden blocks, a rabbit, a short-haired dog, a sealskin coat, a package of white cotton, the heads of Watson and two assistants (inverted so that Albert could touch their hair), and a bearded Santa Claus mask. Albert seemed to show a strong fear response to the rat, the rabbit, the dog, and the sealskin coat; a "neg-

ative" response to the mask and Watson's hair; and a mild response to the cotton. Also, Albert played freely with the wooden blocks and the hair of Watson's assistants.

After an additional 5 days, Watson reconditioned Albert to the rat (one trial, rat paired with noise) and also attempted to condition Albert directly to fear the previously presented rabbit (one trial) and dog (one trial). When the effects of this procedure were tested in a different, larger room, it was found that Albert showed only a slight reaction to the rat, the dog, and the rabbit. Consequently, Watson attempted "to freshen the reaction to the rat" (p. 9) by presenting it with the loud noise. Soon after this, the dog began to bark loudly at Albert, scaring him and the experimenters and further confounding the experiment.

To answer their third question concerning the permanence of conditioned responses over time, Watson and Rayner conducted a final series of tests on Albert after 31 days of neither conditioning nor extinction trials. In these tests, Albert showed fear when touching the Santa Claus mask, the sealskin coat, the rat, the rabbit, and the dog. At the same time, however, he initiated contact with the coat and the rabbit, showing "strife between withdrawal and the tendency to manipulate" (Watson & Rayner, 1920, p. 10). Following these final tests, Albert's mother removed him from the hospital where the experiment had been conducted. (According to their own account, Watson and Rayner knew a month in advance the day that Albert would no longer be available to them.)

THE CONTEXT OF WATSON AND RAYNER'S STUDY

What was the relationship of the Albert experiment to the rest of Watson's work? On a personal level, this work was the final published project of Watson's academic career, although he supervised a subsequent, related study of the deconditioning of young children's fears (M. C. Jones, 1924a, 1924b). From a theoretical perspective, the Albert study provided an empirical test of a theory of behavior and emotional development that Watson had constructed over a number of years.

Although Watson had publicly declared himself a "behaviorist" in early 1913, he apparently did not become interested in the conditioning of motor and autonomic responses until late 1914, when he read a French edition of Bekhterev's *Objective Psychology* (see Hilgard & Marquis, 1940). By 1915, Watson's experience with conditioning research was limited to this reading and his collaboration with his student Karl Lashley in a few simple studies. Nevertheless, Watson's APA Presidential Address of that year made conditioned responses a key aspect of his outline of behaviorism and seems to have been one of the first American references to Bekhterev's work (Hilgard & Marquis, 1940, p. 24; Koch, 1964, p. 9; Watson, 1916b). Less than a year after his APA address, two articles by Watson (1916a, 1916c) were published in which he hypothesized that both normal defense mechanisms and psychiatric disorders (e.g., phobias, tics, hysterical symptoms) could be understood on the basis of conditioning theory.

Six months later, the *American Journal of Psychology* featured a more extensive article by Watson and J. J. B. Morgan (1917) that formulated a theory of emotion, intended to serve both experimentalists and clinicians. Its authors hypothesized that the fundamental (unlearned) human emotions were fear, rage, and love; these emotions were said to be first evoked by simple physical manipulations of infants, such as exposing them to loud sounds (fear) or restricting their movements (rage). Concurrently, they hypothesized that "the method of conditioned reflexes" could explain how these basic three emotions become transformed and transferred to many objects, eventually resulting in the wide range of adult emotions that is evoked by everyday combinations of events, persons, and objects. In support of these theoretical ideas, Watson and Morgan began to test whether infants' fears could be experimentally conditioned, using laboratory analogues of thunder and lightning. In the de-

scription of this work and the related theory, a strong appeal was made for its practical importance, stating that it could lead to a standard experimental procedure for "bringing the human emotions under experimental control" (p. 174).

By the early months of 1919, Watson appears not yet to have found a reliable method for experimentally eliciting and extinguishing new emotional reactions in humans. However, by this time he had developed a program of research with infants to verify the existence of his hypothesized three fundamental emotions. Some early results of this work were described in May 1919, as part of a lengthy treatise on both infant and adult emotions. Anticipating his work with Albert, Watson (1919b) for the first time applied his earlier principles of emotional conditioning to children's fears of animals. Based on a case of a child frightened by a dog that he had observed, Watson hypothesized that although infants do not naturally fear animals, if "one animal succeeds in arousing fear, any moving furry animal thereafter may arouse it" (p. 182). Consistent with this hypothesis, the results of Watson and Rayner's experiments with Albert were reported 9 months later.

Although Watson's departure from Johns Hopkins prematurely ended his own research in 1920, he continued to write about his earlier findings, including his work with Albert. In 1921, he and Rayner (then Rosalie Rayner Watson) summarized the results of their interrupted infant research program, concluding with a summary of their experience with Albert. Although this was a less complete account than their 1920 article, it was the version that was always referenced in Watson's later writings. These writings included dozens of articles in the popular press (e.g., Watson, 1928b, 1928c), the books *Behaviorism* (1924) and *Psychological Care of Infant and Child* (1928a), and a series of articles in *Pedagogical Seminary* (Watson, 1925a, 1925b, 1925c). Many of these articles retold the Albert story, often with photographs and with added comments elaborating on the lessons of this study.

INTRODUCTORY-LEVEL TEXTBOOK VERSIONS OF ALBERT

A selective survey of textbooks used to introduce students to general, developmental, and abnormal psychology revealed that few books fail to refer to Watson and Rayner's (1920) study in some manner. Some of these accounts are completely accurate (e.g., Kennedy, 1975; Page 1975; Whitehurst & Vasta, 1977). However, most textbook versions of Albert's conditioning suffer from inaccuracies of various degrees. Relatively minor details that are misrepresented include Albert's age (Calhoun, 1977; Johnson & Medinnus, 1974), his name (Galanter, 1966), the spelling of Rosalie Rayner's name (e.g., Biehler, 1976; Helms & Turner, 1976; McCandless & Trotter, 1977; Papalia & Olds, 1975), and whether Albert was initially conditioned to fear a rat or a rabbit (CRM Books, 1971; Staats, 1968).

Of more significance are texts' misrepresentations of the range of Albert's postconditioning fears and of the postexperimental fate of Albert. The list of spurious stimuli to which Albert's fear response is claimed to have generalized is rather extensive. It includes a fur pelt (CRM Books, 1971), a man's beard (Helms & Turner, 1976), a cat, a pup, a fur muff (Telford & Sawrey, 1968), a white furry glove (Whittaker, 1965), Albert's aunt, who supposedly wore fur (Bernhardt, 1953), either the fur coat or the fur neckpiece of Albert's mother (Hilgard, Atkinson, & Atkinson, 1975; Kisker, 1977; Weiner, 1977), and even a teddy bear (Boring, Langfeld, & Weld, 1948). In a number of texts, a happy ending has been added to the story by the assertion that Watson removed (or "reconditioned") Albert's fear, with this process sometimes described in detail (Engle & Snellgrove, 1969; Gardiner, 1970; Whittaker, 1965).

What are the causes of these frequent errors by the authors of undergraduate textbooks? Prytula et al. (1977) cataloged similar mistakes but offered little explanation of their source. Cornwell and Hobbs (1976) suggested that such distortions, if not simply due to overreliance on secondary sources, can be generally seen as authors' attempts to paint the Albert study (and Watson) in a more favorable light and to make it believable to undergraduates. Certainly, many of the common errors *are* consistent with a brushed-up image of Watson and his work. For example, not one text mentions that Watson knew when Albert would leave his control—a detail that might make Watson and Rayner's failure to recondition Albert seem callous to some modern readers.

However, there are other reasons for such errors besides textbooks' tendencies to tell ethically pleasing stories that are consistent with students' common sense. One major source of confusion about the Albert story is Watson himself, who altered and deleted important aspects of the study in his many descriptions of it. For example, in the *Scientific Monthly* description of the study (Watson & Watson, 1921), there is no mention of the conditioning of Albert to the dog, the rabbit, and the rat that occurred at 11 months 20 days; thus Albert's subsequent responses to these stimuli can be mistaken for a strong generalization effect (for which there is little evidence). A complementary and equally confusing omission occurs in *Psychological Care of Infant and Child* (Watson, 1928a). There, Watson begins his description of the Albert study with Albert's being conditioned to a rabbit (apparently the session occurring at 11 months 20 days). As a result, the reader is led to believe that Albert's fear of a rat (a month later) was the product of generalization rather than the initial conditioning trials. Besides these omissions, Watson and Rayner (1920) also made frequent editorial comments, such as the assertion that fears such as Albert's were "likely to persist indefinitely, unless an accidental method for removing them is hit upon" (p. 12). Given such comments, it is understandable that one recent text overestimates the duration of the Albert experiment by 300% (Goldenberg, 1977), and another states that Albert's "phobia became resistant to extinction" (Kleinmuntz, 1974, p. 130).

A second reason for textbook authors' errors,

it seems, is the desire of many of us to make experimental evidence consistent with textbook theories of how organisms should act. According to popular versions of learning theory (as described by Herrnstein, 1977), organisms' conditioning should generalize along simple stimulus dimensions; many textbooks list spurious fear-arousing stimuli (for Albert) that correspond to such dimensions. To illustrate the process of stimulus generalization, Albert is often said to have feared every white, furry object—although he actually showed fear mostly of nonwhite objects (the rabbit, the dog, the sealskin coat, Watson's hair), and did not even fear everything with hair (the observers). But to fit a more simplified view of learning, either new stimuli appear in some texts (e.g., a *white* rabbit, a white glove) or it is simply asserted that Albert's conditioning generalized to all white and furry (or hairy) stimuli (see Biehler, 1976; Craig, 1976; Helms & Turner, 1976). Though it might seem as if Albert's fear did generalize to the category of all animate objects with fur (e.g., the rabbit) or short hair (e.g., Watson's head), this is impossible to show conclusively. The only experimental stimuli not fitting this category were the blocks and the observers' hair. Apparently the blocks were a familiar toy (thus not a proper stimulus), and Albert's familiarity with the observers is not known (although we may guess that one might have been his mother). . . .

CONCLUSIONS

What can be deduced from reviewing the many versions of Watson and Rayner's study of Albert? One somewhat obvious conclusion is that we should be extremely wary of secondhand (and more remote) accounts of psychological research. As Cornwell and Hobbs (1976) suggested, this may be most relevant to often-cited studies in psychology, since we may be more likely to overestimate our knowledge of such bulwarks of textbook knowledge.

What about the process by which secondary sources themselves come to err in their description of classic studies? A simple explanation might assume that more recent authors, like any recipients of secondhand information (e.g., gossip), are more likely to present an account of much-cited research that has "drifted well away from the original" (Cornwell & Hobbs, 1976, p. 9). For the Albert study at least, this relatively passive model of communication is an oversimplified view. Not only was Watson quick to *actively* revise his own description of his research (e.g., Watson, 1928a; Watson & Watson, 1921) but it took little time for textbook authors to alter the details of Albert's conditioning. For example, within a year after Watson's original article, one text (Smith & Guthrie, 1921) had already invented spurious stimuli to which Albert's initial fear generalized; such errors were also contained in early texts by H. L. Hollingworth (1928) and J. W. Bridges (1930).

There has undoubtedly been some distortion due to the simple retelling of the Watson and Rayner study, but a more dynamic influence on textbook accounts seems to have been the authors' opinions of behaviorism as a valid theoretical viewpoint. For example, the agreement of Harvey Carr's (1925) text with Watson's overgeneralizations about Albert was consistent with Carr's (1915) relatively favorable review of Watson's early work. Similarly, as behaviorism's influence grew, even relative skeptics seem to have been willing to devote more attention to the Albert study. For example, the fourth edition of Robert S. Woodworth's (1940) text, *Psychology*, mentioned that Albert's "conditioned fear was 'transferred' from the rat to similar objects" (p. 379), though the previous edition of the text (Woodworth, 1934) did not mention this generalization and was more critical of Watson's theory of emotional development. Woodworth's 1934 text also had Albert initially conditioned to a rabbit, while the 1940 one correctly described the conditioned stimulus of a rat. This greater accuracy in Woodworth's later account is an indication of at least one author's ability to resist any general drift toward increasing misinformation.

Any attempted explanation of textbook errors concerning Albert raises the question of the role of classic studies and the nature of historical changes in psychology. As discussed by Samelson (1974) and Baumgardner (1977), modern citations of classic studies can often be seen as attempts by current theorists to build a false sense of continuity into the history of psychology. In social psychology, for example, claiming Auguste Comte as a founder of the field (see Allport, 1968) gives the impression that our contemporary motives (especially the wish for a well-developed behavioral science) have directed the field's progress for almost a century (Samelson, 1974). To cite another classic "origin," the Army's psychological testing program during World War I is taken by some clinical psychologists as an early example of how the profession of psychology has always grown in relation to its increased usefulness. However, it has recently been shown that World War I intelligence testing was of little practical use at the time (Samelson, 1977).

In reviewing these classic studies or *origin myths* in psychology, it should be emphasized that this myth-making process is not anyone's attempt to defraud the public. Instead, it arises "as largely a byproduct of pedagogy: as a means to elucidate the *concepts* of a scientific specialty, to establish its *tradition,* and to attract students" (Samelson, 1974, p. 223). This seems a fair explanation of the Albert case—one that casts the frequent "rediscoverers" of Watson and Rayner (Garrett, 1941; Harlow, 1949; Salter, 1949; Seligman, 1971; Watson, 1928a; Wolpe, 1958) as participants in the process of building historical support for new theoretical perspectives (e.g., preparedness theory).

As Samelson (1974) noted, the major difficulty with such reevaluations of classic studies is that they obscure the actual factors that determine the course of scientific research. In the case of the Albert study, debate still surrounds the question, How did behaviorism become a dominant force in American psychology (MacKenzie, 1972, 1977; Weimer & Palermo, 1973)? The answer is beyond the scope of this study, since it involves much more than an evaluation of the Albert study. However, it is now possible to assert that by itself the Albert study was not very convincing proof of the correctness of Watson's general view of personality and emotions. In addition to the study's reliance on only one subject, the experimental stimuli were insufficient to test for generalization effects, the observers' accounts were too subjective, and the technology did not exist to permit reliable assessment of emotional responses (see Sherman, 1927); there was insufficient follow-up and there was a confounding of instrumental and classical conditioning paradigms. These methodological flaws were also apparent to critical reviewers of the day (e.g., English, 1929; Valentine, 1930) and surely to Watson and Rayner themselves. However, they are worth emphasizing here because of continuing attempts to integrate the study into the early conditioning literature (e.g., Seligman, 1971). It may be useful for modern learning theorists to see how the Albert study prompted subsequent research (i.e., Bregman, 1934), but it seems time, finally, to place the Watson and Rayner data in the category of "interesting but uninterpretable results."

REFERENCE NOTE

1 Samelson, F. *Reactions to Watson's behaviorism: The early years.* Paper presented at the meeting of the Cheiron Society, Wellesley, Massachusetts, June 1978.

REFERENCES

Allport, G. The historical background of modern social psychology. In G. Lindzey & E. Aronson (Eds.), *The handbook of social psychology* (2nd ed., Vol. 1). Reading, Mass.: Addison-Wesley, 1968.

Baumgardner, S. R. Critical studies in the history of social psychology. *Personality and Social Psychology Bulletin,* 1977, *3,* 681–687.

Behaviorist babies. *Review of Reviews,* November 1928, pp. 548–549.

Bernhardt, K. S. *Practical psychology* (2nd ed.). New York: McGraw-Hill, 1953.

Biehler, R. F. *Child development: An introduction.* Boston: Houghton Mifflin, 1976.

Boring, E. G., Langfeld, H. S., & Weld, H. P. (Eds.). *Foundations of psychology.* New York: Wiley, 1948.

Bregman, E. O. An attempt to modify the emotional attitudes of infants by the conditioned response technique. *Journal of Genetic Psychology,* 1934, *45,* 169–198.

Bridges, J. W. *Psychology: Normal and abnormal.* New York: Appleton, 1930.

Calhoun, J. F. *Abnormal psychology* (2nd ed.). New York: CRM Books, 1977.

Can science determine your baby's career before it can talk? *New York American Sunday Magazine,* January 8, 1922.

Carr, H. A. Review of *Behavior, an introduction to comparative psychology* by J. B. Watson. *Psychological Bulletin,* 1915, *12,* 308–312.

Carr, H. A. *Psychology: A study of mental activity.* New York: Longmans, Green, 1925.

Cornwell, D., & Hobbs, S. The strange saga of little Albert. *New Society,* March 18, 1976, pp. 602–604.

Craig, G. J. *Human development.* Englewood Cliffs, N. J.: Prentice-Hall, 1976.

CRM Books. *Developmental psychology today.* Del Mar, Calif.: Author, 1971.

Ellenberger, H. F. The story of "Anna O": A critical review with new data. *Journal of the History of the Behavioral Sciences,* 1972, *8,* 267–279.

Engle, T. L., & Snellgrove, L. *Psychology: Its principles and applications* (5th ed.). New York: Harcourt, Brace & World, 1969.

English, H. B. Three cases of the "conditioned fear response." *Journal of Abnormal and Social Psychology,* 1929, *34,* 221–225.

Eysenck, H. J. Learning theory and behaviour therapy. In H. J. Eysenck (Ed.), *Behaviour therapy and the neuroses: Readings in modern methods of treatment derived from learning theory.* Oxford, England: Pergamon Press, 1960.

Galanter, E. *Textbook of elementary psychology.* San Francisco: Holden-Day, 1966.

Gardiner, W. L. *Psychology: A story of a search.* Belmont, Calif.: Brooks/Cole, 1970.

Garrett, H. E. *Great experiments in psychology.* New York: Appleton-Century-Crofts, 1941.

Goldenberg, H. *Abnormal psychology.* Monterey, Calif.: Brooks/Cole, 1977.

Harlow, H. F. The formation of learning sets. *Psychological Review,* 1949, *56,* 51–65.

Helms, D. B., & Turner, J. S. *Exploring child behavior.* Philadelphia, Pa.: Saunders, 1976.

Herrnstein, R. J. The evolution of behaviorism. *American Psychologist,* 1977, *32,* 593–603.

Hilgard, E. R., Atkinson, R. C., & Atkinson, R. L. *Psychology* (6th ed.). New York: Harcourt Brace Jovanovich, 1975.

Hilgard, E. R., & Marquis, D. G. *Conditioning and learning.* New York: Appleton-Century, 1940.

Hollingworth, H. L. *Mental growth and decline.* New York: Appleton, 1928.

Johnson, R. C., & Medinnus, G. R. *Child psychology: Behavior and development* (3rd ed.). New York: Wiley, 1974.

Jones, M. C. The elimination of children's fears. *Journal of Experimental Psychology,* 1924, *7,* 383–390. (a)

Jones, M. C. A laboratory study of fear: The case of Peter. *Pedagogical Seminary,* 1924, *31,* 308–315. (b)

Jones, M. C. A 1924 pioneer looks at behavior therapy. *Journal of Behavior Therapy and Experimental Psychiatry,* 1975, *6,* 181–187.

Kennedy, W. A. *Child psychology* (2nd ed.). Englewood Cliffs, N.J.: Prentice-Hall, 1975.

Kisker, G. W. *The disorganized personality* (3rd ed.). New York: McGraw-Hill, 1977.

Kleinmuntz, B. *Essentials of abnormal psychology.* New York: Harper & Row, 1974.

Koch, S. Psychology and emerging conceptions of knowledge as unitary. In T. Wann (Ed.), *Behaviorism and phenomenology: Contrasting bases for modern psychology.* Chicago: University of Chicago Press, 1964.

Larson, C. Some further notes on the "rat rabbit" problem and John B. Watson. *Teaching of Psychology,* 1978, *5,* 35.

MacKenzie, B. D. Behaviourism and positivism. *Journal of the History of the Behavioral Sciences,* 1972, *8,* 222–231.

MacKenzie, B. D. *Behaviourism and the limits of scientific method.* Atlantic Highlands, N.J.: Humanities Press, 1977.

McCandless, B. R., & Trotter, R. J. *Children: Behavior and development* (3rd ed.). New York: Holt, Rinehart & Winston, 1977.

Page, J. D. *Psychopathology: The science of understanding deviance* (2nd ed.). Chicago: Aldine, 1975.

Papalia, D. E., & Olds, S. W. *A child's world: Infancy through adolescence.* New York: McGraw-Hill, 1975.

Parsons, H. M. What happened at Hawthorne? *Science,* 1974, *183,* 922–932.

Prytula, R. E., Oster, G. D., & Davis, S. F. The "rat rabbit" problem: What did John B. Watson really do? *Teaching of Psychology,* 1977, *4,* 44–46.

Salter, A. *Conditioned reflex therapy.* New York: Creative Age Press, 1949.

Samelson, F. History, origin myth and ideology: "Discovery" of social psychology. *Journal for the Theory of Social Behaviour,* 1974, *4,* 217–231.

Samelson, F. World War I intelligence testing and the development of psychology. *Journal of the History of the Behavioral Sciences,* 1977, *13,* 274–282.

Seligman, M. E. P. Phobias and preparedness. *Behavior Therapy,* 1971, *2,* 307–320.

Sherman, M. The differentiation of emotional responses in infants: I. Judgments of emotional responses from motion picture views and from actual observation. *Journal of Comparative Psychology,* 1927, *7,* 265–284.

Shettleworth, S. J. Food reinforcement and the organization of behaviour in golden hamsters. In R. A. Hinde & J. Stevenson-Hinde (Eds.), *Constraints on learning.* London: Academic Press, 1973.

Smith, S., & Guthrie, E. R. *General psychology in terms of behavior.* New York: Appleton, 1921.

Staats, A. W. *Learning, language and cognition.* New York: Holt, Rinehart & Winston, 1968.

Telford, C. W., & Sawrey, J. M. *Psychology.* Belmont, Calif.: Brooks/Cole, 1968.

Valentine, C. W. The innate bases of fear. *Journal of Genetic Psychology,* 1930, *37,* 394–420.

Watson, J. B. Behavior and the concept of mental disease. *Journal of Philosophy,* 1916, *13,* 589–597. (a)

Watson, J. B. The place of the conditioned reflex in psychology. *Psychological Review,* 1916, *23,* 89–116. (b)

Watson, J. B. The psychology of wish fulfillment. *Scientific Monthly,* 1916, *3,* 479–487. (c)

Watson, J. B. *Experimental investigation of babies* (Film). Chicago: Stoelting, 1919. (a) (*Psychological Abstracts,* 1937, *11,* No. 6061.)

Watson, J. B. A schematic outline of the emotions. *Psychological Review,* 1919, *26,* 165–196. (b)

Watson, J. B. *Behaviorism.* New York: Norton, 1924.

Watson, J. B. Experimental studies on the growth of the emotions. *Pedagogical Seminary,* 1925, *32,* 328–348. (a)

Watson, J. B. Recent experiments on how we lose and change our emotions. *Pedagogical Seminary,* 1925, *32,* 349–371. (b)

Watson, J. B. What the nursery has to say about instincts. *Pedagogical Seminary,* 1925, *32,* 293–327. (c)

Watson, J. B. *Psychological care of infant and child.* New York: Norton, 1928. (a)

Watson, J. B. The heart or the intellect. *Harper's Magazine,* February 1928, pp. 345–352. (b)

Watson, J. B. What about your child? *Cosmopolitan,* October 1928, pp. 76–77; 108; 110; 112. (c)

Watson, J. B., & Morgan, J. J. B. Emotional reactions and psychological experimentation. *American Journal of Psychology,* 1917, *28,* 163–174.

Watson, J. B., & Rayner, R. Conditioned emotional reactions. *Journal of Experimental Psychology,* 1920, *3,* 1–14.

Watson, J. B., & Watson, R. R. Studies in infant psychology. *Scientific Monthly,* 1921, *13,* 493–515.

Weimer, W. B., & Palermo, D. S. Paradigms and normal science in psychology. *Science Studies,* 1973, *3,* 211–244.

Weiner, B. (Ed.). *Discovering psychology.* Chicago: Science Research Associates, 1977.

Whitehurst, G. J., & Vasta, R. F. *Child behavior.* Boston: Houghton Mifflin, 1977.

Whittaker, J. O. *Introduction to psychology.* Philadelphia, Pa.: Saunders, 1965.

Wolpe, J. *Psychotherapy by reciprocal inhibition.* Stanford, Calif.: Stanford University Press, 1958.

Woodworth, R. S. *Psychology* (3rd ed.). New York: Holt, 1934.

Woodworth, R. S. *Psychology* (4th ed.). New York: Holt, 1940.

CHAPTER 14

NEOBEHAVIORISM

Recall Watson's 1913 claim from the previous chapter that the theoretical goal of psychology is the prediction and control of behavior. That goal would be the focus of American psychology during the period from 1930 through 1960, a period that marked the dominance of a view usually labeled *neobehaviorism*. Although Watson had lost his academic position in 1920, he continued to be the principal spokesperson for behaviorism during the 1920s. He certainly was the chief promoter of behavioral psychology with the general public, largely through his many popular writings. Within the psychology of the 1920s, much of conceptual, and even methodological, behaviorism was accepted as the wave of the future. But there were disciples whose displeasure with Watson's radical views led them to propose alternative behavioral psychologies. These psychologies were characterized by an emphasis on theory, operational definitions, animal studies, and the processes underlying learning.

In addition to Watsonian behaviorism, at least four other sources of influence were important to the development of neobehaviorism. One source was a philosophical view known as *logical positivism,* a view of science largely associated with philosophers in Vienna around the time of World War I (see Smith, 1986). As positivists, their emphasis was on knowledge that is objectively determined, but they went beyond the positivism of Auguste Comte and Ernst Mach in arguing for the inclusion of theoretical concepts grounded in observations. They were adamant in their view of the scientific method as the one proper road to knowledge, eschewing other approaches such as philosophy, poetry, and religion.

Science had proven to be humankind's most powerful means of understanding reality, of producing knowledge, so that the task of epistemology should be to explicate and formalize the scientific method, making it available to new disciplines and improving its practice among working scientists. Thus the logical positivists purported to provide a formal recipe for doing science, offering exactly what psychologists thought they needed. (Leahey, 1987, p. 312)

For the psychologists of the 1920s and 1930s, this view of science as the one valid route to knowledge strengthened their resolve to create a true science of psychology.

Related to logical positivism was the second influence, the concept of *operationism,* the belief that theoretical constructs had reality only with regard to the operations used to observe or measure those constructs. Popularized by a Harvard physicist, Percy Bridgman (1882–1961), and promoted in psychology by the Harvard psychologist S. S. Stevens (1906–1973), operationism became one of the watchwords of American psychology in the 1930s. Definitions of psychological constructs had to be operational definitions, that is, definitions that specified the objective measures underlying those constructs. Thus, hunger was a scientific construct only if it could be specified in objective measures such as hours of food deprivation or the percentage of body weight reduction. If a construct could not be defined operationally, then it was not a scientific construct and should be discarded.

A third influence was the focus on animal studies, a legacy of functionalism, which was also emphasized in the work of Watson, Thorndike, Pavlov, and others. Use of animal subjects, like the laboratory rat, afforded a number of benefits. First, greater precision could be obtained in experiments because it was possible to control the relevant variables in an animal's life experience better. Second, it was believed that processes, such as perception and learning, were less complex in animals than in humans and that studying a conceptually simpler system could give valuable insights into the more complex human systems.

A fourth influence, also a bequest from functionalism, was an emphasis on learning and a belief that adaptation to the environment was the result of learning. Learning capacity was seen as a sign of adjustive capability, which in turn would become psychology's definition of *intelligence,* that is, the ability to adapt to the environment. Animal learning was the topic of principal interest for the neobehaviorists, who viewed these studies as laying the groundwork for the important questions concerning how humans learn (see Jenkins, 1979).

Watson had called for a scientific psychology capable of prediction and control of behavior. The scientific recipe of the logical positivists, the emphasis on operational definitions, and the advantages of animal subjects promised the achievement of Watson's hope for psychology. The new generation of behaviorists pursued Watson's goal, constructing the grand theories of learning that characterized American psychology in the 1930s and 1940s. Although there are a number of psychologists who made contributions as neobehaviorists, this chapter will focus on the work of three whose influence has been especially important: Edward C. Tolman, Clark L. Hull, and B. F. Skinner. These psychologists produced some of their most important work in the 1930s, yet their periods of maximum influence have differed. In the 1930s, the theoretical debates on learning surrounded the competing views of Tolman and Hull, with Skinner's work being largely ignored. By the 1940s, Hull's ideas had gained the upper hand, and his theories dominated research in the 1940s and 1950s. By the late 1960s, Hullian learning theory had been supplanted by the operant psychology of Skinner, partly because of the greater applicability of Skinner's ideas to education and modification of problem behavior. The 1970s, with the growing strength of the cognitive revolution, brought new attention to the purposive behaviorism of Tolman. Thus the ideas of these three men have spanned fifty years of modern psychology and continue to be influential (although not equally so) today.

Edward C. Tolman (1886–1959) published his most important book in 1932, entitled *Purposive Behavior in Animals and Men.* For Tolman, behavior is, in a word, *purposive.* And, the purposiveness of behavior is determined by cognitions. How does a behaviorist justify such obviously mentalistic terms?

> Behavior as behavior, that is, as molar, *is* purposive and *is* cognitive....it must nonetheless be emphasized that purposes and cognitions which are thus immediately, immanently, in behavior are wholly objective as to definition. They are defined by characters and relationships which we observe out there in the behavior. (Tolman, 1932, p. 5)

Tolman argued that with experience, an organism builds up expectancies about the environment, and these expectancies are one of the determinants of responding. In essence, according to Tolman, organisms learn what leads to what. He objected to the molecular approach of Watson, who used a limited stimulus-response framework. Tolman called for a model that recognized the existence of intervening variables—processes within the organism that intervened between stimuli and responses. Cognitions were examples of those intervening variables and were scientifically respectable so long as they could be tied to observable referents.

Tolman also objected to Thorndike's notion of trial-and-error learning and to the idea that reinforcement was an important determinant of learning, a view championed by his theoretical rival Hull. Influenced by the Gestalt psychologists (see Chapter 16) and a group of philosopher-psychologists known as the *neorealists* (see the fourth selection in this chapter), Tolman proposed that learning occurred because of the accumulation of *sign-Gestalts,* which he viewed as cognitive representations of what leads to what. With experience, these sign-Gestalts were combined into a more complex cognitive structure, a kind of *cognitive map* of the organism's environment (more about that later).

Clark L. Hull (1884–1952) published much of his theoretical work in a series of articles in the *Psychological Review* in the 1930s (see Amsel & Rashotte,

1984). The integration and extension of that work appeared in his 1943 book, *Principles of Behavior*. Throughout much of the 1930s and 1940s, Hull and Tolman debated one another, either in the printed literature or at the annual meetings of the American Psychological Association.

Hull made reinforcement his central concept in accounting for learning. His theory contained several intervening variables, but it was largely a strict stimulus-response psychology, often viewed as more rigorous than Watson's behaviorism. Evidence of that rigor is provided in the complex mathematico-deductive theory of behavior so fully described in his 1943 book. Using a number of postulates and corollaries, stated in logical deductive form, Hull created a theory of behavior that has no peer in the history of psychology, including the psychology of the present. Melvin Marx and W. A. Cronan-Hillix (1987) have described it as follows: "Hull deliberately laid out the system as explicitly as he could in order to expedite empirical checking. This explicitness was probably the most important feature of his systematic endeavor" (p. 317).

The empirical checking began almost immediately, as literally thousands of master's and doctoral students tested some prediction of Hull's grand theory, making him the most frequently cited psychologist in the research of the 1950s. Unlike Tolman, whose theory of learning was vague on several critical issues (a fact admitted by Tolman), Hull made painstaking efforts to spell out his theoretical concepts in precise (often mathematical) detail. Some historians have argued that the domination of Hull's ideas was not owing to their appeal but that they lent themselves so readily to empirical testing.

While Tolman and Hull battled over whether learning involved cognitive maps or stimulus-response associations, the third principal neobehaviorist was beginning his important work. B. F. Skinner (1904–) is a radical behaviorist, much in the mold of Watson in his total opposition to mentalism in psychology. Although his early interests were in literature and a career as a writer, he soon abandoned those interests for a devotion to science, which, the reader will remember, the logical positivists had proclaimed was the only valid road to knowledge.

There was no place for intervening variables in Skinner's system of psychology. The inner world of the organism was off limits to the scientist, a view that caused his psychology to be labeled *the psychology of the empty organism*. Skinner saw no need for explanations of behavior that appealed to inner events. Behavior was the result of *consequences,* events that followed particular responses. Psychologists would achieve Watson's goal of prediction and control once they could understand the relationships between responses and the stimulus events that preceded and followed those responses. Environmental events (consequences) alter the probabilities of responses, with some behaviors made more probable and others less probable. Unlike Thorndike in his statement of the law of effect, Skinner made no references to internal states of affairs (satisfaction or annoyance) in his definition of reinforcement. These ideas were spelled out rather clearly in his first book, *The Behavior of Organisms* (1938), which defined the new field of operant conditioning as a model of animal and human learning.

Many of the psychologists of the 1930s and 1940s did not know what to make of Skinner or his work. He criticized the value of theory in a time when theory construction was revered; he tolerated no references to internal states, even in terms of objective behavioral referents; he argued against the necessity of large samples in research and elaborate statistical treatments of data and offered instead studies involving one or two subjects whose data were presented in the form of response rate curves. In 1948, ten years after its publication, his book had sold only approximately five hundred copies, whereas Hull's 1943 book had sold nearly five thousand copies in only five years. All of that would change in the 1960s with the application of Skinner's work to education and clinical psychology.

Obviously only the barest of facts have been provided in this brief overview of what amounts to a thirty-year period in American psychology. The five selections in this chapter are intended to flesh out these comments and, in particular, to give the reader an example of the views of the three neobehaviorists discussed.

The first selection is by Tolman. It is not taken from his famous 1932 book but is instead from what many historians would argue was his most important article, "Cognitive Maps in Rats and Men" (1948). It is an excellent description of years of work in his Berkeley laboratory and of his disagreements with Hull. It also illustrates some of Tolman's social activism as he seeks to apply his rat studies to improvement of the social fabric of the world.

The second selection is an excerpt from Hull's 1943 book, *Principies of Behavior*. The very nature of that book as an elaborate and heavily interconnected theory makes it difficult to extract a section that is easily understood in isolation. The section selected is from the end of the book and deals with learning and the problems of reinforcement.

The last of the primary selections, by Skinner, is an excerpt from the opening chapter of his 1938 book. Entitled "A System of Behavior," the chapter treats Skinner's distinctions between classical and operant conditioning.

The fourth selection is by the historian of psychology Laurence D. Smith, a member of the faculty at the University of Maine. This article looks at the influence of the neorealism of Edwin B. Holt and Ralph Barton Perry of Harvard University on the neobehaviorist views of Tolman, especially on his views on purpose and cognition. Further, the article makes clearer some of the linkages of neorealism to modern cognitive psychology.

In the final selection, Norman Guttman compares the careers and psychologies of Hull and Skinner. In doing so he attempts to answer the question of Skinner's substantially greater popularity in contemporary psychology and looks at the probable influence of both in the centuries that will follow. Although not a citation analysis, such data are used by Guttman in making his assessments and predictions. Collectively, these five selections provide a good overview of the history of learning theory in psychology.

REFERENCES

Amsel, A., & Rashotte, M. E. (1984). *Mechanisms of adaptive behavior: Clark L. Hull's theoretical papers with commentary.* New York: Columbia University Press.

Hull, C. L. (1943). *Principles of behavior.* New York: Appleton-Century-Crofts.

Jenkins, H. M. (1979). Animal learning and behavior theory. In E. Hearst (Ed.), *The first century of experimental psychology.* Hillsdale, NJ: Lawrence Erlbaum, pp. 177–228.

Leahey, T. H. (1987). *A history of psychology: Main currents in psychological thought* (2d. ed.). Englewood Cliffs, NJ: Prentice-Hall.

Marx, M., & Cronan-Hillix, W. A. (1987). *Systems and theories in psychology* (4th ed.). New York: McGraw-Hill.

Skinner, B. F. (1938). *The behavior of organisms.* New York: Appleton-Century-Crofts.

Smith, L. D. (1986). *Behaviorism and logical positivism: A reassessment of the alliance.* Stanford, CA: Stanford University Press.

Tolman, E. C. (1932). *Purposive behavior in animals and men.* New York: Appleton.

Tolman, E. C. (1948). Cognitive maps in rats and men. *Psychological Review, 55,* 189–208.

Cognitive Maps in Rats and Men

Edward C. Tolman

I shall devote the body of this paper to a description of experiments with rats. But I shall also attempt in a few words at the close to indicate the significance of these findings on rats for the clinical behavior of men. Most of the rat investigations, which I shall report, were carried out in the Berkeley laboratory. But I shall also include, occasionally, accounts of the behavior of non-Berkeley rats who obviously have misspent their lives in out-of-State laboratories. Furthermore, in reporting our Berkeley experiments I shall have to omit a very great many. The ones I *shall* talk about were carried out by graduate students (or underpaid research assistants) who, supposedly, got some of their ideas from me. And a few, though a very few, were even carried out by me myself.

Let me begin by presenting diagrams for a couple of typical mazes, an alley maze and an elevated maze. In the typical experiment a hungry rat is put at the entrance of the maze (alley or elevated), and wanders about through the various true path segments and blind alleys until he finally comes to the food box and eats. This is repeated (again in the typical experiment) one trial every 24 hours and the animal tends to make fewer and fewer errors (that is, blind-alley entrances) and to take less and less time between start and goal-box until finally he is entering no blinds at all and running in a very few seconds from start to goal. The results are usually presented in the form of average curves of blind-entrances, or of seconds from start to finish, for groups of rats.

All students agree as to the facts. They disagree, however, on theory and explanation.

(1) First, there is a school of animal psychologists which believes that the maze behavior of rats is a matter of mere simple stimulus-response connections. Learning, according to them, consists in the strengthening of some of these connections and in the weakening of others. According to this 'stimulus-response' school the rat in progressing down the maze is helplessly responding to a succession of external stimuli—sights, sounds, smells, pressures, etc. impinging upon his external sense organs—plus internal stimuli coming from the viscera and from the skeletal muscles. These external and internal stimuli call out the walkings, runnings, turnings, retracings, smellings, rearings, and the like which appear. The rat's central nervous system, according to this view, may be likened to a complicated telephone switchboard. There are the incoming calls from sense-organs and there are the outgoing messages to muscles. Before the learning of a specific maze, the connecting switches (synapses according to the physiologist) are closed in one set of ways and produce the primarily exploratory responses which appear in the early trials. *Learning,* according to this view, consists in the respective strengthening and weakening of various of these connections; those connections which result in the animal's going down the true path become relatively more open to the passage of nervous impulses, whereas those which lead him into the blinds become relatively less open.

It must be noted in addition, however, that this stimulus-response school divides further into two subgroups.

(a) There is a subgroup which holds that the mere mechanics involved in the running of a maze is such that the crucial stimuli from the maze get presented simultaneously with the correct responses more frequently than they do with any of the incorrect responses. Hence, just on a basis of this greater frequency, the neural connections between the crucial stimuli and the correct

Adapted from Tolman, E. C. (1948). Cognitive maps in rats and men. *Psychological Review, 55,* 189–208. Copyright © 1948 by the American Psychological Association. Adapted and reprinted by permission of the publisher.

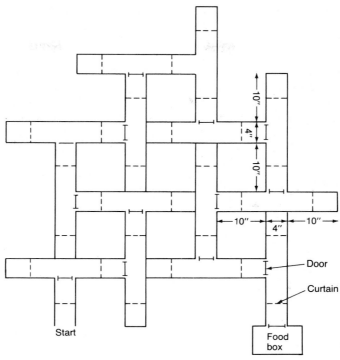

FIGURE 1
Plan of maze: 14-unit T-alley maze.

responses will tend, it is said, to get strengthened at the expense of the incorrect connections.

(b) There is a second subgroup in this stimulus-response school which holds that the reason the appropriate connections get strengthened relatively to the inappropriate ones is, rather, the fact that the responses resulting from the correct connections are followed more closely in time by need-reductions. Thus a hungry rat in a maze tends to get to food and have his hunger reduced *sooner* as a result of the true path responses than as a result of the blind alley responses. And such immediately following need-reductions or, to use another term, such 'positive reinforcements' tend somehow, it is said, to strengthen the connections which have most closely preceded them. Thus it is as if—although this is certainly not the way this subgroup would themselves

state it—the satisfaction-receiving part of the rat telephoned back to Central and said to the girl: ''Hold that connection; it was good; and see to it that you blankety-blank well use it again the next time these same stimuli come in.'' These theorists also assume (at least some of them do some of the time) that, if bad results—'annoyances,' 'negative reinforcements'—follow, then this same satisfaction-and-annoyance-receiving part of the rat will telephone back and say, ''Break that connection and don't you dare use it next time either.''

So much for a brief summary of the two subvarieties of the 'stimulus-response,' or telephone switchboard school.

(2) Let us turn now to the second main school. This group (and I belong to them) may be called the field theorists. We believe that in the course

of learning something like a field map of the environment gets established in the rat's brain. We agree with the other school that the rat in running a maze is exposed to stimuli and is finally led as a result of these stimuli to the responses which actually occur. We feel, however, that the intervening brain processes are more complicated, more patterned and more often, pragmatically speaking, more autonomous than do the stimulus-response psychologists. Although we admit that the rat is bombarded by stimuli, we hold that his nervous system is surprisingly se-

lective as to which of these stimuli it will let in at any given time.

Secondly, we assert that the central office itself is far more like a map control room than it is like an old-fashioned telephone exchange. The stimuli, which are allowed in, are not connected by just simple one-to-one switches to the outgoing responses. Rather, the incoming impulses are usually worked over and elaborated in the central control room into a tentative, cognitive-like map of the environment. And it is this tentative map, indicating routes and paths and environ-

FIGURE 2
14-unit T-elevated mazes.

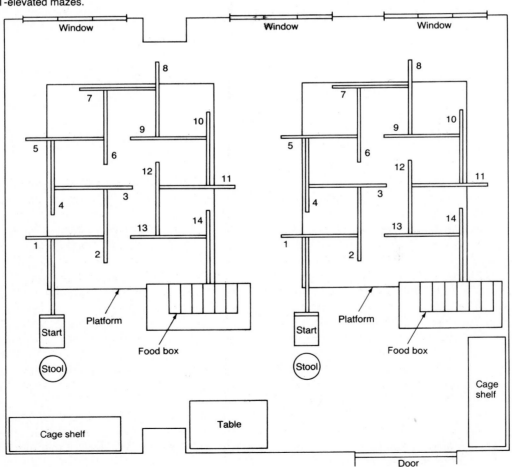

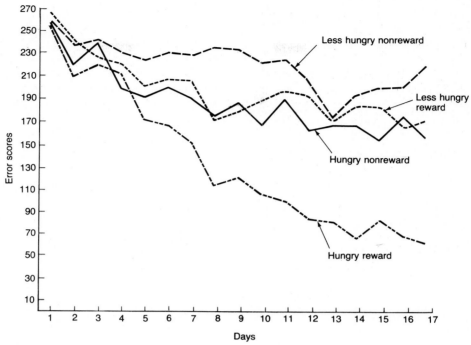

FIGURE 3
Error curves for four groups, 36 rats.

mental relationships, which finally determines what responses, if any, the animal will finally release.

Finally, I, personally, would hold further that it is also important to discover in how far these maps are relatively narrow and strip-like or relatively broad and comprehensive. Both strip-maps and comprehensive-maps may be either correct or incorrect in the sense that they may (or may not), when acted upon, lead successfully to the animal's goal. The differences between such strip maps and such comprehensive maps will appear only when the rat is later presented with some change within the given environment. Then, the narrower and more strip-like the original map, the less will it carry over successfully to the new problem; whereas, the wider and the more comprehensive it was, the more adequately it will serve in the new set-up. In a strip-map the

given position of the animal is connected by only a relatively simple and single path to the position of the goal. In a comprehensive-map a wider arc of the environment is represented, so that, if the starting position of the animal be changed or variations in the specific routes be introduced, this wider map will allow the animal still to behave relatively correctly and to choose the appropriate new route.

But let us turn, now, to the actual experiments. The ones, out of many, which I have selected to report are simply ones which seem especially important in reinforcing the theoretical position I have been presenting. This position, I repeat, contains two assumptions: First, that learning consists not in stimulus-response connections but in the building up in the nervous system of sets which function like cognitive maps, and second, that such cognitive maps may be

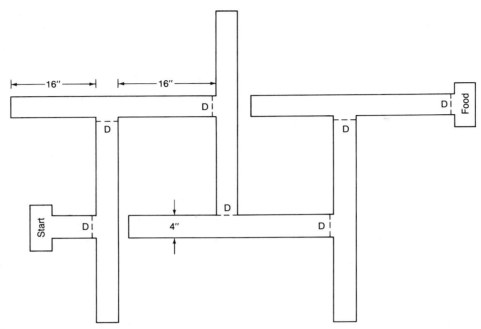

FIGURE 4
6-unit alley T-maze.

usefully characterized as varying from a narrow strip variety to a broader comprehensive variety.

The experiments fall under five heads: (1) "latent learning," (2) "vicarious trial and error" or "VTE," (3) "searching for the stimulus," (4) "hypotheses" and (5) "spatial orientation."*

1 "LATENT LEARNING" EXPERIMENTS

The first of the latent learning experiments was performed at Berkeley by Blodgett. It was published in 1929. Blodgett not only performed the experiments, he also originated the concept. He ran three groups of rats through a six-unit alley maze, shown in Figure 4. He had a control group and two experimental groups. The error curves for these groups appear in Figure 5. The solid line shows the error curve for Group I, the control group. These animals were run in orthodox fash-

---

* The experiments in categories 2, 3, and 4 have been omitted in this adapted version of Tolman's paper. (Ed. note)

ion. That is, they were run one trial a day and found food in the goal-box at the end of each trial. Groups II and III were the experimental groups. The animals of Group II, the dash line, were not fed in the maze for the first six days but only in their home cages some two hours later. On the seventh day (indicated by the small cross) the rats found food at the end of the maze for the first time and continued to find it on subsequent days. The animals of Group III were treated similarly except that they first found food at the end of the maze on the third day and continued to find it there on subsequent days. It will be observed that the experimental groups as long as they were not finding food did not appear to learn much. (Their error curves did not drop.) But on the days immediately succeeding their first finding of the food their error curves did drop astoundingly. It appeared, in short, that during the non-rewarded trials these animals had been learning much more than they had exhibited. This learning, which did not manifest itself until after the food had been introduced, Blodgett called "latent learning." Interpreting these results anthropomorphically, we would say that as long as the animals were not getting any food at the end of the maze they continued to take their time in going through it—they continued to enter many blinds. Once, however, they knew they were to get food, they demonstrated that during these preceding non-rewarded trials they had learned where many of the blinds were. They had been building up a 'map,' and could utilize the latter as soon as they were motivated to do so.

Honzik and myself repeated the experiments (or rather he did and I got some of the credit) with the 14-unit T-mazes shown in Figure 1, and with larger groups of animals, and got similar results. The resulting curves are shown in Figure 6. We used two control groups—one that never found food in the maze (HNR) and one that found it throughout (HR). The experimental group (HNR-R) found food at the end of the maze from the 11th day on and showed the same sort of a sudden drop.

But probably the best experiment demonstrating latent learning was, unfortunately, done not in Berkeley but at the University of Iowa, by Spence and Lippitt. Only an abstract of this experiment has as yet been published. However, Spence has sent a preliminary manuscript from which the following account is summarized. A simple Y-maze (see Figure 7) with two goalboxes was used. Water was at the end of the right arm of the Y and food at the end of the left arm. During the training period the rats were run neither hungry nor thirsty. They were satiated for both food and water before each day's trials. However, they were willing to run because after each run they were taken out of whichever end box they had got to and put into a living cage, with other animals in it. They were given four trials a day in this fashion for seven days, two trials to the right and two to the left.

In the crucial test the animals were divided into two subgroups, one made solely hungry and one solely thirsty. It was then found that on the first trial the hungry group went at once to the left, where the food had been, statisti-

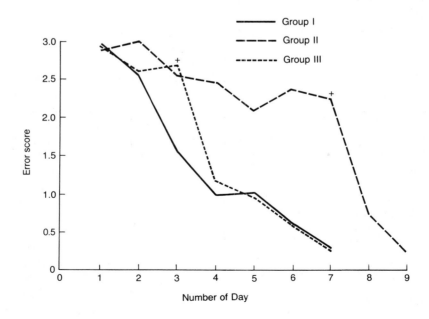

FIGURE 5

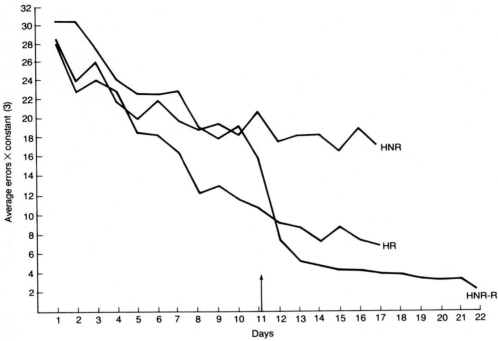

FIGURE 6
Error curves for HR, HNR, and HNR-R.

FIGURE 7
Ground plan of the apparatus.

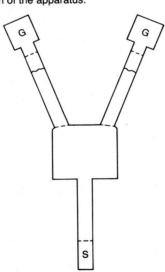

cally more frequently than to the right; and the thirsty group went to the right, where the water had been, statistically more frequently than to the left. These results indicated that under the previous non-differential and very mild rewarding conditions of merely being returned to the home cages the animals had nevertheless been learning where the water was and where the food was. In short, they had acquired a cognitive map to the effect that food was to the left and water to the right, although during the acquisition of this map they had not exhibited any stimulus-response propensities to go more to the side which became later the side of the appropriate goal.

There have been numerous other latent learning experiments done in the Berkeley laboratory and elsewhere. In general, they have for the most part all confirmed the above sort of findings....

5 "SPATIAL ORIENTATION" EXPERIMENTS

As early as 1929, Lashley reported incidentally the case of a couple of his rats who, after having learned an alley maze, pushed back the cover near the starting box, climbed out and ran directly across the top to the goal-box where they climbed down in again and ate. Other investigators have reported related findings. All such observations suggest that rats really develop wider spatial maps which include more than the mere trained-on specific paths. In the experiments now to be reported this possibility has been subjected to further examination.

In the first experiment, Tolman, Ritchie and Kalish (actually Ritchie and Kalish) used the set-up shown in Figure (8).

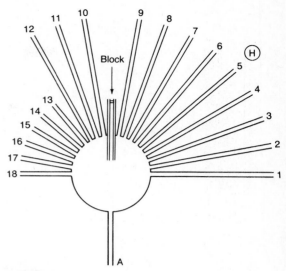

FIGURE (9)
Apparatus used in the test trial.

FIGURE (8)
Apparatus used in preliminary training.

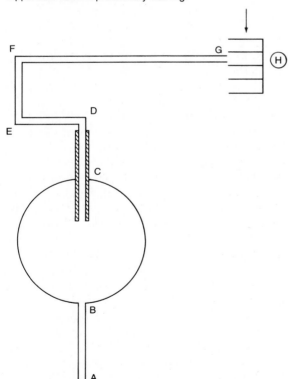

This was an elevated maze. The animals ran from A across the open circular table through CD (which had alley walls) and finally to G, the food box. H was a light which shone directly down the path from G to F. After four nights, three trials per night, in which the rats learned to run directly and without hesitation from A to G, the apparatus was changed to the sun-burst shown in Figure (9). The starting path and the table remained the same but a series of radiating paths was added.

The animals were again started at A and ran across the circular table into the alley and found themselves blocked. They then returned onto the table and began exploring practically all the radiating paths. After going out a few inches only on any one path, each rat finally chose to run all the way out on one. The percentages of rats finally choosing each of the long paths from 1 to 12 are shown in Figure (10). It appears that there was a preponderant tendency to choose path No. 6 which ran to a point some four inches in front of where the entrance to the food box had been. The only other path chosen with any apprecia-

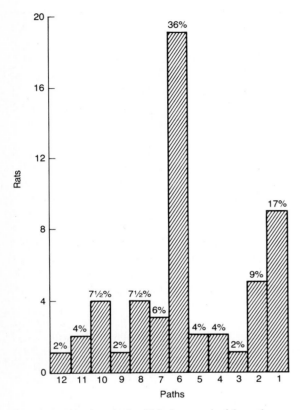

Number of rats which chose each of the paths

FIGURE (10)
Numbers of rats which chose each of the paths. (*From E. C. Tolman, B. F. Ritchie and D. Kalish, Studies in spatial learning. I. Orientation and the short-cut.* J. exp. Psychol., *1946, **36**, p.19.*)

ble frequency was No. 1—that is, the path which pointed perpendicularly to the food-side of the room.

These results seem to indicate that the rats in this experiment had learned not only to run rapidly down the original roundabout route but also, when this was blocked and radiating paths presented, to select one pointing rather directly towards the point where the food had been or else at least to select a path running perpendicularly to the food-side of the room.

As a result of their original training, the rats had, it would seem, acquired not merely a strip-

map to the effect that the original specifically trained-on path led to food but, rather, a wider comprehensive map to the effect that food was located in such and such a direction in the room....

This completes my report of experiments. There were the *latent learning experiments,* the *VTE experiments,* the *searching for the stimulus experiment,* the *hypothesis experiments,* and these last *spatial orientation experiments....*

And now, at last, I come to the humanly significant and exciting problem: namely, what are the conditions which favor narrow strip-maps and what are those which tend to favor broad comprehensive maps not only in rats but also in men?

There is considerable evidence scattered throughout the literature bearing on this question both for rats and for men. Some of this evidence was obtained in Berkeley and some of it elsewhere. I have not time to present it in any detail. I can merely summarize it by saying that narrow strip-maps rather than broad comprehensive maps seem to be induced: (1) by a damaged brain, (2) by an inadequate array of environmentally presented cues, (3) by an overdose of repetitions on the original trained-on path and (4) by the presence of too strongly motivational or of too strongly frustrating conditions.

It is this fourth factor which I wish to elaborate upon briefly in my concluding remarks. For it is going to be my contention that some, at least, of the so-called 'psychological mechanisms' which the clinical psychologists and the other students of personality have uncovered as the devils underlying many of our individual and social maladjustments can be interpreted as narrowings of our cognitive maps due to too strong motivations or to too intense frustration....

Over and over again men are blinded by too violent motivations and too intense frustrations into blind and unintelligent and in the end desperately dangerous hates of outsiders. And the expression of these their displaced hates ranges all the way from discrimination against minorities to world conflagrations.

What in the name of Heaven and Psychology can we do about it? My only answer is to preach again the virtues of reason—of, that is, broad cognitive maps. And to suggest that the child-trainers and the world-planners of the future can only, if at all, bring about the presence of the required rationality (*i.e.,* comprehensive maps) if they see to it that nobody's children are too over-motivated or too frustrated. Only then can these children learn to look before and after, learn to see that there are often round-about and safer paths to their quite proper goals—learn, that is, to realize that the well-beings of White and of Negro, of Catholic and of Protestant, of Christian and of Jew, of American and of Russian (and even of males and females) are mutually interdependent.

We dare not let ourselves or others become so over-emotional, so hungry, so ill-clad, so over-

motivated that only narrow strip-maps will be developed. All of us in Europe as well as in America, in the Orient as well as in the Occident, must be made calm enough and well-fed enough to be able to develop truly comprehensive maps, or, as Freud would have put it, to be able to learn to live according to the Reality Principle rather than according to the too narrow and too immediate Pleasure Principle.

We must, in short, subject our children and ourselves (as the kindly experimenter would his rats) to the optimal conditions of moderate motivation and of an absence of unnecessary frustrations, whenever we put them and ourselves before that great God-given maze which is our human world. I cannot predict whether or not we will be able, or be allowed, to do this; but I *can* say that, only insofar as we *are* able and *are* allowed, have we cause for hope.

Behavior Theory, Learning, and the Problem of Reinforcement

Clark L. Hull

BEHAVIOR THEORY AND SYMBOLIC CONSTRUCTS

Scientific theories are mainly concerned with dynamic situations, i.e., with the consequent events or conditions which, with the passage of time, will follow from a given set of antecedent events or conditions. The concrete activity of theorizing consists in the manipulation of a limited set of symbols according to the rules expressed in the postulates (together with certain additional rules which make up the main substance of logic) in such a way as to span the gap separating the antecedent conditions or states from the subsequent ones. Some of the symbols represent observable and measurable elements or aggregates of the situation, whereas others represent pre-

Adapted from Hull, C. L. (1943). *Principles of behavior.* New York: Appleton-Century-Crofts, pp. 382–389. Copyright © 1943 by Richard H. Hull. Adapted and reprinted by permission of Richard H. Hull.

sumptive intervening processes not directly subject to observation. The latter are theoretical constructs. All well-developed sciences freely employ theoretical constructs wherever they prove useful, sometimes even sequences or chains of them. The scientific utility of logical constructs consists in the mediation of valid deductions; this in turn is absolutely dependent upon every construct, or construct chain, being securely anchored both on the antecedent and on the consequent side to conditions or events which are directly observable. If possible, they should also be measurable.

The theory of behavior seems to require the use of a number of symbolic constructs, arranged for the most part in a single chain. The main links of this chain are represented in Figure (1). In the interest of clarity, the symbolic constructs are accompanied by the more important and relevant symbols representing the objectively anchoring

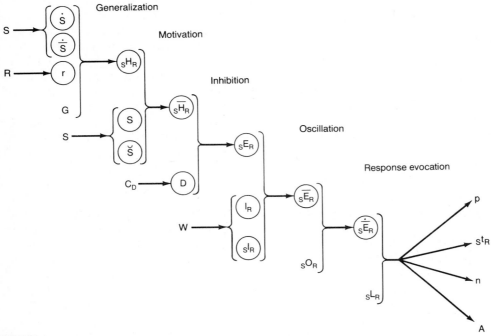

FIGURE (1)

Diagram summarizing the major symbolic constructs (encircled symbols) employed in the present system of behavior theory, together with the symbols of the supporting objectively observable conditions and events. In this diagram $\dot{S}$ represents the physical stimulus energy involved in learning; R, the organism's reaction; s, the neural result of the stimulus; $\dot{s}$, the neural interaction arising from the impact of two or more stimulus components; r, the efferent impulse leading to reaction; G, the occurrence of a reinforcing state of affairs; $_sH_R$, habit strength; S, evocation stimulus on the same stimulus continuum as S; $_s\bar{H}_R$, the generalized habit strength; C_D, the objectively observable phenomena determining the drive; D, the physiological strength of the drive to motivate action; $_sE_R$, the reaction potential; W, work involved in an evoked reaction; I_R, reactive inhibition; $_sI_R$, conditioned inhibition; $_s\bar{E}_R$, effective reaction potential; $_sO_R$, oscillation; $_s\dot{\bar{E}}_R$, momentary effective reaction potential; $_sL_R$, reaction threshold; p, probability of reaction evocation; $_st_R$, latency of reaction evocation; n, number of unreinforced reactions to produce experimental extinction; and A, amplitude of reaction. Above the symbols the lines beneath the words *reinforcement, generalization, motivation, inhibition, oscillation,* and *response evocation* indicate roughly the segments of the chain of symbolic constructs with which each process is especially concerned.

conditions or events. In order that the two types of symbols shall be easily distinguishable, circles have been drawn around the symbolic constructs. It will be noticed that the symbols representing observables, while scattered throughout the sequence, are conspicuously clustered at the beginning and at the end of the chain, where they must be in order to make validation of the constructs possible. Frequent reference will be made to this summarizing diagram throughout

the present chapter, as it reveals at a glance the groundwork of the present approach to the behavior sciences.

ORGANISMS CONCEIVED AS SELF-MAINTAINING MECHANISMS

From the point of view of biological evolution, organisms are more or less successfully self-maintaining mechanisms. In the present context *a mechanism is defined as a physical aggregate whose behavior occurs under ascertainable conditions according to definitely stable rules or laws.* In biology, the nature of these aggregates is such that for individuals and species to survive, certain optimal conditions must be approximated. When conditions deviate from the optimum, equilibrium may as a rule be restored by some sort of action on the part of the organism; such activity is described as "adaptive." The organs effecting the adaptive activity of animals are for the most part glands and muscles.

In higher organisms the number, variety, and complexity of the acts required for protracted survival is exceedingly great. The nature of the act or action sequence necessary to bring about optimal conditions in a given situation depends jointly (1) upon the state of disequilibrium or need of the organism and (2) upon the characteristics of the environment, external and internal. For this reason a prerequisite of truly adaptive action is that both the condition of the organism and that of all relevant portions of the environment must somehow be brought simultaneously to bear on the reactive organs. The first link of this necessary functional *rapport* of the effector organs with organismic needs and environmental conditions is constituted by receptors which convert the biologically more important of the environmental energies (S) into neural impulses (s). For the most part these neural impulses flow to the brain, which acts as a kind of automatic switchboard mediating their efferent flow (r) to the effectors in such a way as to evoke response (R). In this connection there are two important neural principles to be noted.

The first of these principles to be observed is that after the stimulus (S) has ceased to act upon the receptor, the afferent impulse (s) continues its activity for some seconds, or possibly minutes under certain circumstances, though with gradually decreasing intensity. This *perseverative stimulus trace* is biologically important because it brings the effector organ *en rapport* not only with environmental events which are occurring at the time but with events which have oc-

curred in the recent past, a matter frequently critical for survival. Thus is effected a short-range temporal integration. . . .

The second neural principle is that the receptor discharges and their perserverative traces (s) generated on the different occasions of the impact of a given stimulus energy (S) upon the receptor, while usually very similar, are believed almost never to be exactly the same. This lack of uniformity is postulated as due (1) to the fact that many receptors are activated by stimulus energies simultaneously and (2) to "afferent neural interaction." The latter hypothesis states that the receptor discharges interact, while passing through the nervous system to the point where newly acquired receptor-effector connections have their locus, in such a way that each receptor discharge changes all the others to a greater or less extent; i.e., s is changed to $š_1$, $š_2$, or $š_3$, etc., in accordance with the particular combination of other stimulus energies which is acting on the sensorium at the time (see Figure (1)). This type of action is particularly important because the mediation of the responses of organisms to distinctive combinations or patterns of stimuli, rather than to the components of the patterns, is presumably dependent upon it. . . .

The detailed physiological principles whereby the nervous system mediates the behavioral adaptation of the organism are as yet far from completely known. As a result we are forced for the most part to get along as best we can with relatively coarse molar formulations derived from conditioned-reflex and other behavior experiments. From this point of view it appears that the processes of organic evolution have yielded two distinct but closely related means of effective behavioral adaptation. One of these is the laying down of unlearned receptor-effector connections ($_sU_R$) within the neural tissue which will directly mediate at least approximate behavioral adjustments to urgent situations which are of frequent occurrence but which require relatively simple responses. . . . The second means of effecting behavioral adjustment is probably evolution's most impressive achievement; this is the capacity of organisms themselves to acquire automatically adaptive receptor-effector connections. Such acquisition is *learning*.

LEARNING AND THE PROBLEM OF REINFORCEMENT

The substance of the elementary learning process as revealed by much experimentation seems to be this: A condition of need exists in a more or less complex setting of receptor discharges initiated by the action of environmental stimulus energies. This combination of circumstances activates numerous vaguely adaptive reaction potentials mediated by the unlearned receptor-effector organization ($_sU_R$) laid down by organic evolution. The relative strengths of these various reaction potentials are varied from instant to instant by the oscillation factor($_sO_R$). The resulting spontaneous variability of the momentary unlearned reaction potential ($_sU_R$) produces the randomness and variability of the unlearned behavior evoked under given conditions. In case one of these random responses, or a sequence of them, results in the reduction of a need dominant at the time, there follows as an indirect effect what is known as reinforcement (*G,* of Figure (1)). This consists in (1) a strengthening of the particular receptor-effector connections which originally mediated the reaction and (2) a tendency for all receptor discharges (*s*) occurring at about the same time to acquire new connections with the effectors mediating the response in question. The first effect is known as primitive trial-and-error learning; the second is known as conditioned-reflex learning. In most adaptive situations both processes occur concurrently; indeed, *very likely they are at bottom the same process, differing only in the accidental circumstance that the first begins with an appreciable strength, whereas the second sets out from zero.* As a result, when the same need again arises in this or a similar situation, the stimuli will activate the same effectors more certainly, more promptly, and more vigorously than on the first occasion. Such action, while by no means

adaptively infallible, in the long run will reduce the need more surely than would a chance sampling of the unlearned response tendencies ($_sU_R$) at the command of other need and stimulating situations, and more quickly and completely than did that particular need and stimulating situation on the first occasion. Thus the acquisition of such receptor-effector connections will, as a rule, make for survival; i.e., it will be adaptive.

Careful observation and experiment reveal, particularly with the higher organisms, large numbers of situations in which learning occurs with no associated primary need reduction. When these cases are carefully studied it is found that the reinforcing agent is a situation or event involving a stimulus aggregate or compound which has been closely and consistently associated with the need reduction. Such a situation is called a secondary reinforcing agent, and the strengthening of the receptor-effector connections which results from its action is known as secondary reinforcement. This principle is of immense importance in the behavior of the higher species.

The organization within the nervous system brought about by a particular reinforcement is known as a habit; since it is not directly observable, habit has the status of a symbolic construct. Strictly speaking, habit is a functional connection between *s* and *r;* it is accordingly represented by the symbol $_sH_r$. Owing, however, to the close functional relationship between *S* and *s* on the one hand, and between *r* and *R* on the other, the symbol $_sH_R$ will serve for most expository purposes; the latter symbol has the advantage that *S* and *R* both refer to conditions or events normally open to public observation. The position of $_sH_R$ in the chain of constructs of the present system is shown in Figure (1).

While it is difficult to determine the quantitative value of an unobservable, various indirect considerations combine to indicate as a first approximation that habit strength is a simple increasing growth function of the number of reinforcements. The unit chosen for the expression of habit strength is called the *hab,* a shortened form of the word "habit"; a hab is 1 per cent of the physiological limit of habit strength under completely optimal conditions.

CONDITIONS WHICH INFLUENCE THE MAGNITUDE OF HABIT INCREMENT PER REINFORCEMENT

A more careful scrutiny of the conditions of reinforcement reveals a number which are subject to variation, and experiments have shown that the magnitude of the habit increment ($\Delta_S H_R$) per reinforcement is dependent in one way or another upon the quantitative variation of these conditions. One such factor concerns the primary reinforcing agent. It has been found that, quality remaining constant, the magnitude of the increment of habit strength per reinforcement is a negatively accelerated increasing function of the quantity of the reinforcing agent employed per reinforcement.

A second factor of considerable importance in determining the magnitude of $\Delta_S H_R$ is the degree of asynchronism between the onset of the stimulus and of the response to which it is being conditioned. This situation is complicated by whether or not the stimulus terminates its action on the receptor before the response occurs. In general the experimental evidence indicates that in case both the stimulus and the response are of very brief duration, the increment of habit strength per reinforcement is maximal when the reaction (and the reinforcement) occurs a short half second after the stimulus, and that it is a negatively accelerated decreasing function of the extent to which asynchronisms in either direction depart from this optimum. In case the reaction synchronizes with the continued action of the stimulus on the receptor, the increment of habit strength per reinforcement is a simple negative growth function of the length of time that the stimulus has acted on the receptor when the reaction occurs.

A third important factor in the reinforcing situation is the length of time elapsing between the occurrence of the reaction and of the reinforcing state of affairs (G, Figure (1)). Experiments indicate that this "gradient of reinforcement" is a negatively accelerated decreasing growth function of the length of time that reinforcement follows the reaction. The principle of secondary reinforcement, combined with that of the gradient of reinforcement, explains the extremely numerous cases of learning in which the primary reinforcement is indefinitely remote from the act reinforced. A considerable mass of experimental evidence indicates that a kind of blending of the action of these two principles generates a secondary phenomenon called the "goal gradient." Upon empirical investigation this turns out to be a decreasing exponential or negative growth function of the time (t) separating the reaction from the primary reinforcement for delays ranging from ten seconds to five or six minutes; delays greater than six minutes have not yet been sufficiently explored to make possible a quantitative statement concerning them.

There are doubtless other conditions which influence the magnitude of the increment of habit strength resulting from each reinforcement. Those listed above certainly are typical and probably comprise the more important of them. An adequate statement of the primary law or laws of learning would accordingly take the form of an equation in which $_S H_R$ would be expressed as a joint function not only of N but of the quantity and quality of the reinforcing agent, and of the temporal relationships of S to R and of R to G. A formula which purports to be a first approximation to such a general quantitative expression of the primary laws of learning is given as equations 16 and 17.

---

* Equations 16 and 17 are presented earlier in Hull's book but are not included in this excerpt. (Ed. note)

A System of Behavior

B. F. Skinner

A DEFINITION OF BEHAVIOR

It is necessary to begin with a definition. Behavior is only part of the total activity of an organism, and some formal delimitation is called for. The field might be defined historically by appeal to an established interest. As distinct from the other activities of the organism, the phenomena of behavior are held together by a common conspicuousness. Behavior is what an organism is *doing*—or more accurately what it is observed by another organism to be doing. But to say that a given sample of activity falls within the field of behavior simply because it normally comes under observation would misrepresent the significance of this property. It is more to the point to say that behavior is that part of the functioning of an organism which is engaged in acting upon or having commerce with the outside world. The peculiar properties which make behavior a unitary and unique subject matter follow from this definition. It is only because the receptors of other organisms are the most sensitive parts of the outside world that the appeal to an established interest in what an organism is doing is successful.

By behavior, then, I mean simply the movement of an organism or of its parts in a frame of reference provided by the organism itself or by various external objects or fields of force. It is convenient to speak of this as the action of the organism upon the outside world, and it is often desirable to deal with an effect rather than with the movement itself, as in the case of the production of sounds....

TYPE S AND TYPE R CONDITIONING

In the course of this book I shall attempt to show that a large body of material not usually consid-

ered in this light may be expressed with dynamic laws which differ from the classical examples only in the nature of the operations. The most important instances are conditioning and extinction (with their subsidiary processes of discrimination), drive, and emotion, which I propose to formulate in terms of changes in reflex strength. One type of conditioning and its corresponding extinction may be described here.

The Law of Conditioning of Type S. The approximately simultaneous presentation of two stimuli, one of which (the 'reinforcing' stimulus) belongs to a reflex existing at the moment at some strength, may produce an increase in the strength of a third reflex composed of the response of the reinforcing reflex and the other stimulus.

The Law of Extinction of Type S. If the reflex strengthened through conditioning of Type S is elicited without presentation of the reinforcing stimulus, its strength decreases.

These laws refer to the Pavlovian type of conditioned reflex....I wish to point out here simply that the observed data are merely changes in the strength of a reflex. As such they have no dimensions which distinguish them from changes in strength taking place during fatigue, facilitation, inhibition, or, as I shall show later, changes in drive, emotion, and so on. The process of conditioning is distinguished by what is done to the organism to induce the change; in other words, it is defined by the operation of the simultaneous presentation of the reinforcing stimulus and another stimulus. The type is called Type S to distinguish it from conditioning of Type R (see below) in which the reinforcing stimulus is contingent upon a response.

Before indicating how other divisions of the field of behavior may be formulated in terms of reflex strength, it will be necessary to consider another kind of behavior, which I have not yet mentioned. The remaining dynamic laws will then be taken up in connection with both kinds at once.

OPERANT BEHAVIOR

With the discovery of the stimulus and the collection of a large number of specific relationships of stimulus and response, it came to be assumed by many writers that all behavior would be accounted for in this way as soon as the appropriate stimuli could be identified. Many elaborate attempts have been made to establish the plausibility of this assumption, but they have not, I believe, proved convincing. There is a large body of behavior that does not seem to be *elicited,* in the sense in which a cinder in the eye elicits closure of the lid, although it may eventually stand in a different kind of relation to external stimuli. The original 'spontaneous' activity of the organism is chiefly of this sort, as is the greater part of the conditioned behavior of the adult organism, as I hope to show later. Merely to assert that there *must* be eliciting stimuli is an unsatisfactory appeal to ignorance. The brightest hope of establishing the generality of the eliciting stimulus was provided by Pavlov's demonstration that part of the behavior of the adult organism could be shown to be under the control of stimuli which had *acquired* their power to elicit. But a formulation of this process will show that in every case the response to the conditioned stimulus must first be elicited by an unconditioned stimulus. I do not believe that the 'stimulus' leading to the elaborate responses of singing a song or of painting a picture can be regarded as the mere substitute for a stimulus or a group of stimuli which originally elicited these responses or their component parts.

Most of the pressure behind the search for eliciting stimuli has been derived from a fear of 'spontaneity' and its implication of freedom. When spontaneity cannot be avoided, the attempt is made to define it in terms of unknown stimuli. Thus, Bethe says that the term 'has long been used to describe behavior for which the stimuli are not known and I see no reason why the word should be stricken from a scientific vocabulary.' But an event may occur without any observed antecedent event and still be dealt with adequately in a descriptive science. I do not mean that there are no originating forces in spontaneous behavior but simply that they are not located in the environment. We are not in a position to see them, and we have no need to. This kind of behavior might be said to be *emitted* by the organism, and there are appropriate techniques for dealing with it in that form. One important independent variable is time. In making use of it I am simply recognizing that the observed datum is the appearance of a given identifiable sample of behavior at some more or less orderly rate. The use of a rate is perhaps the outstanding characteristic of the general method to be outlined in the following pages, where we shall be concerned very largely with behavior of this sort.

The attempt to force behavior into the simple stimulus-response formula has delayed the adequate treatment of that large part of behavior which cannot be shown to be under the control of eliciting stimuli. It will be highly important to recognize the existence of this separate field in the present work. Differences between the two kinds of behavior will accumulate throughout the book, and I shall not argue the distinction here at any length. The kind of behavior that is correlated with specific eliciting stimuli may be called *respondent* behavior and a given correlation *a respondent*. The term is intended to carry the sense of a relation to a prior event. Such behavior as is not under this kind of control I shall call *operant* and any specific example *an operant*. The term refers to a posterior event, to be noted shortly. The term reflex will be used to include both respondent and operant even though in its original meaning it applied to respondents only. A single term for both is convenient because both are topographical units of behavior and because an operant may and usually does acquire a relation to prior stimulation. In general, the notion of a reflex is to be emptied of any connotation of the active 'push' of the stimulus. The terms refer here to correlated entities, and to nothing more. All implications of dynamism and all metaphorical and figurative definitions should be avoided as far as possible.

An operant is an identifiable part of behavior of which it may be said, not that no stimulus can be found that will elicit it (there may be a respondent the response of which has the same topography), but that no correlated stimulus can be detected upon occasions when it is observed to occur. It is studied as an event appearing spontaneously with a given frequency. It has no static laws comparable with those of a respondent since in the absence of a stimulus the concepts of threshold, latency, after-discharge, and the R/S ratio are meaningless. Instead, appeal must be made to frequency of occurrence in order to establish the notion of strength. The strength of an operant is proportional to its frequency of occurrence, and the dynamic laws describe the changes in the rate of occurrence that are brought about by various operations performed upon the organism.

OTHER DYNAMIC LAWS

Three of the operations already described in relation to respondent behavior involve the elicitation of the reflex and hence are inapplicable to operants. They are the refractory phase, fatigue, and conditioning of Type S. The refractory phase has a curious parallel in the rate itself, as I shall note later, and a phenomenon comparable with fatigue may also appear in an operant. The conditioning of an operant differs from that of a respondent by involving the correlation of a reinforcing stimulus with a *response*. For this reason the process may be referred to as of Type R. Its two laws are as follows.

The Law of Conditioning of Type R. If the occurrence of an operant is followed by presentation of a reinforcing stimulus, the strength is increased.

The Law of Extinction of Type R. If the occurrence of an operant already strengthened through conditioning is not followed by the reinforcing stimulus, the strength is decreased.

The conditioning is here again a matter of a change in strength. The strength cannot begin at zero since at least one unconditioned response must occur to permit establishment of the relation with a reinforcing stimulus. Unlike conditioning of Type S the process has the effect of determining the form of the response, which is provided for in advance by the conditions of the correlation with a reinforcing stimulus or by the way in which the response must operate upon the environment to produce a reinforcement....

It is only rarely possible to define an operant topographically (so that successive instances may be counted) without the sharper delineation of properties that is given by the act of conditioning. This dependence upon the posterior reinforcing stimulus gives the term operant its significance. In a respondent the response is the result of something previously done to the organism. This is true even for conditioned respondents because the operation of the simultaneous presentation of two stimuli precedes, or at least is independent of, the occurrence of the response. The operant, on the other hand, becomes significant for behavior and takes on an identifiable form when it acts upon the environment in such a way that a reinforcing stimulus is produced. The operant-respondent distinction goes beyond that between Types S and R because it applies to unconditioned behavior as well; but where both apply, they coincide exactly. Conditioning of Type R is impossible in a respondent because the correlation of the reinforcing stimulus with a response implies a correlation with its eliciting stimulus. It has already been noted that conditioning of Type S is impossible in operant behavior because of the absence of an eliciting stimulus.

An operant may come to have a relation to a stimulus which seems to resemble the relation between the stimulus and response in a respondent. The case arises when prior stimulation is correlated with the reinforcement of the operant. The stimulus may be said to set the occasion upon which a response will be reinforced, and therefore (through establishment of a discrimination) upon which it will occur; but it does not elicit the response. The distinction will be emphasized later.

One kind of operation that affects the strength of reflexes (both operant and respondent) falls within the traditional field of drive or motivation. It would be pointless to review here the various ways in which the field has been formulated. In a description of behavior in terms of the present system the subject presents itself simply as a class of dynamic changes in strength. For example, suppose that we are observing an organism in the presence of a bit of food. A certain sequence of progressive, manipulative, and ingestive reflexes will be evoked. The early stages of this sequence are operants, the later stages are respondents. At any given time the strengths may be measured either by observing the rate of occurrence in the case of the former or by exploring the static properties in the case of the latter. The problem of drive arises because the values so obtained vary between wide extremes. At one time the chain may be repeatedly evoked at a high rate, while at another no response may be forthcoming during a considerable period of time. In the vernacular we should say that the organism eats only when it is hungry. What we observe is that the strengths of these reflexes vary, and we must set about finding the operations of which they are a function. This is not difficult. Most important of all are the operations of feeding and fasting. By allowing a hungry organism, such as

a rat, to eat bits of food placed before it, it is possible to show an orderly decline in the strength of this group of reflexes. Eventually a very low strength is reached and eating ceases. By allowing a certain time to elapse before food is again available it may be shown that the strength has risen to a value at which responses will occur. The same may be said of the later members of the chain, the strengths of which (as respondents) must be measured in terms of the static properties. Thus, the amount of saliva secreted in response to a gustatory stimulus may be a similar function of feeding and fasting. A complete account of the strengths of this particular group of reflexes may be given in terms of this operation, other factors being held constant. There are other operations to be taken into account, however, which affect the same group, such as deprivation of water, illness, and so on.

In another important group of changes in reflex strength the chief operation with which the changes are correlated is the presentation of what may be called 'emotional' stimuli—stimuli which typically elicit changes of this sort. They may be either unconditioned (for example, an electric shock) or conditioned according to Type S where the reinforcing stimulus has been emotional (for example, a tone which has preceded a shock). Other operations which induce an emotional change in strength are the restraint of a response, the interruption of a chain of reflexes through the removal of a reinforcing stimulus (see later), the administration of certain drugs, and so on. The resulting change in behavior is again in the strength of reflexes....

The operations characterizing drive and emotion differ from the others listed in that they effect concurrent changes in *groups* of reflexes. The operation of feeding, for example, brings about changes in all the operants that have been reinforced with food and in all the conditioned and unconditioned respondents concerned with ingestion. Moreover, a single operation is not unique in its effect. There is more than one way of changing the strength of the group of reflexes varying with ingestion or with an emotional stimulus. In addition to the formulation of the effect upon a single reflex, we must deal also with *the* drive or *the* emotion as the 'state' of a group of reflexes. This is done by introducing a hypothetical middle term between the operation and the resulting observed change. 'Hunger,' 'fear,' and so on, are terms of this sort. The operation of feeding is said to affect the hunger and the hunger in turn the strength of the reflex. The notion of an intermediate state is valuable when (a) more than one reflex is affected by the operation, and (b) when several operations have the same effect. Its utility may perhaps be made clear with the following schemes. When an operation is unique in its effect and applies to a single reflex, it may be represented as follows:

Operation I ——— (   ) ———Strength of Reflex I,

where no middle term is needed. When there are several operations having the same effect and affecting several reflexes, the relation may be represented as follows:

Operation I ⟍   ⟋ Strength of Reflex I
Operation II —— 'State' —— Strength of Reflex II
Operation III ⟋   ⟍Strength of Reflex III

In the present system hypothetical middle terms ('states') will be used in the cases of drive and emotion, but no other properties will be assigned to them. A dynamic law always refers to the change in strength of a single reflex as a function of a single operation, and the intermediate term is actually unnecessary in its expression.

An observation of the state of a reflex at any given time is limited to its strength. Since the data are changes in strength and therefore the same in all dynamic laws, the system emphasizes the great importance of defining and classifying operations. The mere strength of the reflex itself is an ambiguous fact. It is impossible to tell from a momentary observation of strength whether its value is due especially to an operation of drive, conditioning, or emotion. Suppose, for example, that we have been working with an operant that has been reinforced with food and that at a given time we observe that the organism does not respond (*i.e.,* that the strength is low). *From the state of the reflex itself,* it is impossible to distinguish between the following cases. (1) The organism is hungry and unafraid, but the response has been extinguished. (2) The response is conditioned and the organism is hungry but afraid. (3) The response is conditioned, and the organism is unafraid but not hungry. (4) The response is conditioned, but the organism is both not hungry and afraid. (5) The organism is hungry, but it is afraid, and the response has been extinguished. (6) The organism is not afraid, but it is not hungry and the response has been extinguished. (7) The response has been extinguished, and the organism is afraid but not hungry. We can decide among these possibilities by referring to other behavior. If we present the stimulus of an *unconditioned* reflex varying with hunger and fear (say, if we present food), the question of conditioning is eliminated. If the organism eats, the first case listed above is proved. If it does not eat, the possibilities are then as follows. (1) The organism is hungry but afraid. (2) It is unafraid but not hungry. (3) It is both not hungry and afraid. If we then test another reflex, the strength of which decreases in a state of fear but which does not vary with hunger, and find it strong, the organism is not afraid and must therefore not be hungry.

The strength of a reflex at any given time is a function of all the operations that affect it. The principal task of a science of behavior is to isolate their separate effects and to establish their functional relationships with the strength.

The development of dynamic laws enables us to consider behavior which does not invariably occur under a given set of circumstances as, nevertheless, reflex (*i.e.*, as lawful). The early classical examples of the reflex were those of which the lawfulness was obvious. It was obvious because the number of variables involved was limited. A flexion reflex could be described very early because it was controlled by a stimulus and was not to any considerable extent a function of the operations of drive, emotion, or conditioning, which cause the greatest variability in strength. The discovery of conditioning of Type S brought under the principle of the reflex a number of ac-

tivities the lawfulness of which was not evident until the conditioning operation was controlled. Operants, as predictable entities, are naturally isolated last of all because they are not controlled through stimuli and are subject to many operations. They are not *obviously* lawful. But with a rigorous control of all relevant operations the kind of necessity that naturally characterizes simple reflexes is seen to apply to behavior generally. I offer the experimental material described later in this book in support of this statement.

Purpose and Cognition: The Limits of Neorealist Influence on Tolman's Psychology

Laurence D. Smith

Since the earliest days of behaviorism, John B. Watson's prohibitions against the use of such concepts as "mind," "consciousness," and "purpose" have drawn widespread attention and criticism. Watsonian behaviorism presented organisms, human and infrahuman alike, as exhibiting movements and glandular activities but not as engaging in the purposeful acquisition and use of knowledge. Because of Watson's prominence in the behaviorist movement and his outright rejection of cognitive concepts, psychologists and philosophers have tended to perceive a deep rift between the cognitive and behaviorist approaches to psychology. In some respects, there has been genuine antagonism between these approaches, but the perception of any sharp division between them fails to acknowledge the diversity and evolving character of behaviorist thought. In the past decade, numerous researchers, some formerly of a strict behaviorist persuasion, have begun to apply cognitive concepts such as

memory structures, internal representations, expectancies, and cognitive maps to instances of animal behavior that were previously treated simply as the effects of conditioning on essentially passive organisms.[1] As a result, there seems at present to be an attenuation of the traditional antagonism between behaviorist and cognitive approaches to psychology.[2]

But this recent development is by no means an unprecedented one. In this context, it is worth recalling that these two approaches were reconciled and united in the "purposive behaviorism" developed during the 1920s and 1930s—the very heyday of behaviorism—by the influential American psychologist, Edward Chace Tolman.[3] In fact, the new theorists of animal cognition have borrowed from Tolman a number of specific concepts and have adopted his general conception of organisms as active and purposeful processors of information. For one who is interested in the conceptual evolution of behaviorism,[4] this state of affairs raises a provocative question: how was Tolman able to develop a viable cognitive behaviorism which not only anticipated recent developments but also helped sustain cognitive psychology during a period in which the stricter

Adapted from Smith, L. D. (1982). Purpose and cognition: The limits of neorealist influence on Tolman's psychology. *Behaviorism, 10,* 151–163. Copyright © 1982 by Behaviorism. Adapted and reprinted by permission of the publisher and the author.

forms of behaviorism enjoyed hegemony over psychological theorizing? Because Tolman's theory was a highly eclectic one which interwove behaviorism with cognitive and Gestalt approaches to psychology, there can be no simple answer to this question, but a central thread of the story involves Tolman's belief that a conceptually adequate behaviorism permits and even *requires* a role for the concepts of purpose and cognition.

Tolman acquired this belief during his years as a graduate student at Harvard (1911–1915), where he fell under the influence of the New Realism espoused by his teachers, Edwin B. Holt and Ralph Barton Perry. Contrary to Watsonian behaviorism, the neorealism of these philosopher-psychologists involved the conviction that the purposive and cognitive features of behavior are amenable to treatment in non-idealistic scientific terms. With this notion, Holt and Perry set Tolman on the road to a highly molar (non-physiological) behaviorism. As Tolman himself later put it, his Harvard teachers taught him "to be complicated but to remain naturalistic."[5]

In this paper, I will trace the development of the concepts of purpose and cognition as they were transmitted from the neorealist to Tolman and as Tolman later elaborated them. The paper will examine the neorealist background of Tolman's psychology, the intellectual tensions which led to the demise of the philosophical movement, and the subsequent developments in Tolman's thought which enabled him gradually to escape the conceptual pitfalls into which neorealism's influence had led him. Through his continual refinement of the concepts of purpose and cognition, the conceptual scheme for his molar behaviorism became increasingly coherent and workable.

The developments described here show the impact of philosophy on the formulation of an important "system" of behavioral psychology at precisely the time when most psychologists eschewed any relation to or dependence on philosophy.[6] Throughout the first third of this centu-

ry, largely because of behaviorism's rising influence, increasing numbers of psychologists self-consciously rejected intellectual and institutional ties with philosophy. This trend, which coincided with a general shift of interest from ontological to methodological issues,[7] culminated in psychology's embrace of logical positivism in the late 1930s. Although Tolman was sensitive to these trends and adapted the concepts of purpose and cognition accordingly, the conceptual apparatus of his purposive behaviorism was clearly rooted in his philosophical background.

THE HARVARD BACKGROUND (1901–1918)

The Neorealist Interpretation of Purpose and Cognition

The adherents of neorealism[8] viewed the oscillations of nineteenth century philosophy as ample demonstration of the inadequacies of the idealist, dualist, and materialist traditions. Their primary aim was to steer a course through these traditions leading directly to a thorough-going naturalism, one which would sacrifice inclusiveness for a more compatible relationship with the special sciences. The movement initially arose as a critique of idealism, first expressed in America in Perry's and W. P. Montague's attacks on the Harvard idealist Josiah Royce in 1901 and 1902.[9] Voicing a theme that would often be repeated, these authors assaulted the idealist notion that the world is constituted by the preeminent act of cognition. Rather than decisively conditioning the world, cognition was to take its place *within* the natural world and provide the basis for the more complex derivative phenomena of value and ethics.

Although the neorealist program was first and foremost a criticism of idealism, it quickly broadened into a further critique of dualism and materialism. Perry in particular argued against the dualist view that "one's own mind, or the mind at home, must be preferred as more genuine than the mind abroad" and that mind is a private entity "encased in a non-mental and impenetrable shell.[10] The New Realists held that the world is *presented* to an observer rather than being *represented* by "invisible pawns" in the perceiver's private sphere, a dualist fiction regarded as "concretely intolerable" for psychology.[11] To the neorealists, materialism was an equally fallacious doctrine primarily because it erred in "denying the *facts,* as well as the theory, of consciousness."[12] Materialism's assignment of mental events to the realm of epiphenomena collided with the New Realists' insistence that the things of thought be given the same ontological status as physical entities.

The American neorealist movement was formally proclaimed in a statement coauthored by Holt, Perry, and four collaborators just a year before Tolman's arrival at Harvard in 1911.[13] An elaboration of the neorealist position appeared two years later in a manifesto entitled *The New Realism.* During this heyday of the movement, Tolman was introduced to and "excited by" the New Realism through a seminar taught by Holt.[14] Around this time, Perry and Holt began extending the neorealist program to psychology by formulating a behaviorism which gave the mentalistic concepts of purpose and cognition an objective status in the natural world.

Holt's seminal paper on "Response and Cognition" and his book *The Freudian Wish* both appeared in 1915. These works criticized the adoption of the materialist's "bead theory" of causality in the realm of behavior. True behavior differs from mere reflex, Holt contended, in being an integrated and novel synthesis which exhibits "objective reference" to environing objects. The immediate stimulus (e.g., light on the retina) which governs the isolated reflex "recedes" in importance as behavior becomes more highly organized until the environing object itself controls the response. Holt's notion of the recession of the stimulus enabled him to define the art of cognition as simply the "objective reference" of an integral response to an object. The putative and suspect relation between the subject and object of consciousness is, according to

Holt, just this objective relation between behavior and object. To ignore the functional reference of behavior is to succumb to the dualist superstition that "ideas" in the "sensorium" somehow represent the environment.

At about this time, Perry was pursuing a similar analysis of the concept of purpose. In "Purpose as Systematic Unity" (1917), he argued against the idealistic notion that purpose is a global characteristic underlying the universe and advocated a behavioral interpretation of concrete instances of purposiveness. In "Purpose as Tendency and Adaptation" (1917), he examined mechanistic biological treatments of purpose as tendencies and homeostatic adjustments and found them too limited to account for the purposive nature of highly organized plastic behavior. In its most general case, purpose must be identified with *adaptability* rather than mere adaptation, a crucial insight which Perry developed in his 1918 essay "Docility and Purposiveness." Purpose was to be found, according to Perry, in that "margin of modifiability" which characterizes the activity of a docile or corrigible organism.[15]

By 1918, Holt and Perry had thus arrived at their shared conception of behavior as a highly integrated, synthetic, and modifiable pattern of responses. This conception was motivated philosophically by their desire to objectify and naturalize the metaphysically charged concepts of purpose and cognition rather than consign them to oblivion in a materialistic world-view. In a sense, the neorealists' conception of behavior was a natural extension of the doctrine of external relations to the realm of behavior. Both purpose and cognition involved the observable actions of an organism *in relation to* gross objective features of the environment. Any narrowly physiological definition of behavior would necessarily fail to acknowledge this crucial relatedness of response and environment.

Although Tolman was exposed to this orientation during his Harvard years, it was not until after his arrival in Berkeley in 1918 that he worked it into the full-blown research program which he came to designate as "molar behaviorism."[16] Tolman's early theoretical papers leading up to the publication in 1932 of his *Purposive Behavior in Animals and Men* often cited Holt and Perry as important early proponents of a nonphysiological behaviorism. Tolman also repeatedly acknowledged having borrowed from Perry the idea that a molar behaviorism must recognize the purposive or docile character of behavior.

Pitfalls of Neorealism

While the influence of Holt and Perry on Tolman is relatively direct and well-known, the role played by their neorealist philosophy in this influence has gone unrecognized by historians. As we have seen, the New Realism shaped the general conception of behavior adopted by these three thinkers. However, the neorealist program involved further philosophical positions which inhibited the development of that conception into a practicable behaviorism. It is to these problematic features of New Realism that we now turn.

In their eagerness to reject the idealistic claim that the cognitive act constitutes the world, the New Realists were unwilling to admit that anything experienced depends for its existence on the fact of being experienced. The English neorealist T.P. Nunn had already in 1909 pursued this stance to the point of asserting that even pain is external to the mind—it is an objective experience to be reckoned with just as any material object. Holt followed suit by arguing that such allegedly nonveridical perceptions as illusions, hallucinations, and mirror images likewise reside outside the mind and that one's behavior can exhibit objective reference to them. Since contents of experience do not come tagged as "real" or "unreal," Holt simply assigned all experiences to the ontological realm of neutral "subsistents."

In the neutral monism to which Holt and Perry subscribed, subsistents were neutral in the sense of having "being" without any connotation of reality or unreality. According to Holt, "every content...subsists of its own right in the all-inclusive universe of being."[17] A content could thus occur in consciousness without depending on it. Whereas the idealists had claimed that direct knowledge is possible only if the known depends on the knower, the neorealists asserted "the independence of the immanent" as their cardinal tenet. Subsistents were both immanent, i.e., directly presented in experience, *and* independent of that experience.[18]

In denying that the act of knowing involves any constructive activity on the part of the knower, the neorealists were led to the further important position of denying the distinction between primary and secondary qualities. Holt was especially willing to educe the bolder implications of this rather extreme view. Secondary qualities such as color subsist, according to him, out there in the thing which consciousness selects and are therefore just as objective as primary qualities. The neorealists had maintained all along that "the knower...is homogeneous with the environment...and may itself be known as are the things it knows."[19] In conjunction with the contention that qualities are presented, not represented, in perception, this claim meant that the psychologist who studies cognition in another organism has rather direct access to another mind. Taken literally in its strongest form, the New Realism implied that the mental qualities of another organism are just as objective as its bodily qualities and are therefore directly presented to, rather than being constructed or inferred by, the observer. Being of equal stature on the objective plane of subsistence, mind and body were viewed as equally manifest to the observer of behavior.

Invoking a realm of subsistence, however, proved to be a philosophically awkward maneuver which lent little support to the program of objectifying mental contents. As a consequence, both Perry and Holt frequently fell back on neurophysiological interpretations in their pursuit of objectivity, especially in those cases in which mental events were not so clearly revealed in behavior. They spoke of expectations, for instance, as nascent physiological adjustments and of ideas as centrally stimulated signs. But in resorting to such interpretations, they not only compromised their anti-materialist position, but also undercut their view that mind is directly presented in behavior.

As a movement, the New Realism began as a reaction against the excesses of idealism and ended as a victim of its own excesses. Although its radical implications were drawn out with audacity and ingenuity, they were soon recognized as untenable overreactions. By 1920 the Critical Realism of Arthur O. Lovejoy and others had reasserted the activity of the observer in conditioning the known, the representational character of knowledge, the philosophical import of nonveridical experience, and the need for an ontology of greater complexity than simple subsistence.[20] Holt and Perry themselves abandoned neorealism, the former pursuing instead a materialistically inclined philosophical behaviorism and the latter developing a theory of value.[21]

PURPOSIVE BEHAVIORISM AT BERKELEY (1918–1938)

Just as the New Realism was collapsing under its own intellectual tensions, Tolman was beginning to elaborate his molar behaviorism from a neorealist basis. Like his mentors, Tolman was concerned to avoid the extremes of idealism and mechanistic materialism, but in adopting the conceptual outlook of his Harvard teachers, he inherited the risk of being drawn into its untoward exaggerations. Specifically, he was faced with the risks of viewing purpose and cognition as primary-like qualities of behavior, of invoking questionable ontologies for them, and of giving them unwarranted physiological interpretations.

In what follows, I will show that from 1918 to 1938 the development of purpose and cognition in Tolman's thinking represented a move away from their philosophical parentage. An examination of Tolman's early views suggests that he had

indeed absorbed the inconsistencies of the New Realism and, although he was not explicitly reacting to neorealism's excesses,[22] the resolution of these inconsistencies in his later work required freeing the concepts of purpose and cognition from their association with neorealism's shortcomings. Tolman's articulation of a molar behaviorism went hand in hand with his reformulation of the concepts of purpose and cognition as he continually strove during this period to make the concepts viable in the context of experimental psychology. This reformulation transpired in the form of three closely related developments: the transition from viewing purpose and cognition as characteristics which are read directly from behavior to viewing them as characteristics which are read into behavior; the adoption of an instrumentalistic view of scientific theories; and the modification of the presumed relation between the concepts of molar behaviorism and those of physiology.

From Subsistents to Intervening Variables

In his early theoretical papers of the 1920s, Tolman often spoke of mental characteristics— as would a consistent neorealist—as if they were presented directly to the observer of behavior. Purpose, for example, was viewed simply as a "descriptive phenomenon" which when adequately conceived "is itself but an objective aspect of behavior." As such, purpose was considered to be identical with a set of behaviors which exhibit a certain "persistence until" character, but was not to be inferred from behavior. To infer purpose from behavior was, according to Tolman, to eschew behaviorism in favor of a mentalism of the sort advocated by William McDougall. Tolman wrote that "the fundamental difference between him and us arises in that he, being a 'mentalist', merely *infers* purpose from these aspects of behavior; whereas we, being behaviorists, *identify* purpose with such aspects."[23]

By 1925, Tolman was referring to purpose and cognition both as "descriptive aspects" of behavior and as "determiners" of behavior.[24] This equivocal treatment of the concepts as having both manifest-descriptive and underlying-explanatory roles persisted in Tolman's thought for a period of ten years. In 1926, Tolman was again emphasizing that purpose and cognition are presented to an observer in the observed behavior itself. Purpose, he said, could be "pointed to" and "discovered by looking *at* another organism." In Tolman's words,

> It is a descriptive feature immanent in the character of the behavior *qua* behavior. It is not a mentalistic entity supposed to exist parallel to, and to run along side of, the behavior. It is *out there in* the behavior; of its descriptive warp and woof.[25]

In this statement, we see a recapitulation of the neorealists' assertion of the "independence of the immanent": the purpose of another organism is directly presented in the observer's experience and yet is independent of it.[26]

But in his efforts to make purpose objective, Tolman was expressing a viewpoint which was as difficult to defend as the extreme New Realism of his teachers. In 1928, the criticisms of the Chinese behaviorist Z.Y. Kuo forced Tolman to admit that purpose "has to be inferred from its effects and cannot be directly sensed." Even so, Tolman followed this concession with the qualifying assertion that purpose is a "perfectly objective feature which appears in behavior" and is therefore neither mentalistic nor introspectionistic.[27] The conceptual advantage of construing purpose as an immediate feature of behavior was apparently difficult for Tolman to forgo.

Tolman's thinking on this issue vacillated through the appearance in 1932 of his classic *Purposive Behavior in Animals and Men.* The eminent historian of psychology, E.G. Boring, has remarked that the concepts employed by Tolman in this work "show how necessarily indeterminate is the line between the direct observation of datum, on the one hand, and the not-fully-conscious inference of function, on the other."[28] Nowhere was the fuzziness of this line clearer than in the case of Tolman's most fundamental concepts, purpose and cognition. Within a single paragraph of *Purposive Behavior,* Tolman described purposes and cognitions on the one hand as "immanent" in behavior, "in-lying," "immediate," and "discovered" by observers, and on the other hand as "determinants" and "causes" of behavior which are "invented" or "inferred" by observers.[29]

Tolman later wrote that he was struggling during this period toward definitions of purpose and cognition as intervening variables in equations relating environmental variables to behavioral variables.[30] In *Purposive Behavior,* he construed purpose and cognition as "immanent determinants" of behavior in the sense that they referred to the shapes of the functions connecting antecedent determiners and dependent behavior. Shortly thereafter, Tolman began to break up each function into a series of two or more functions and to insert variables representing purposes and cognitions between the successive steps. While these variables were loosely conceptualized as states of the organism, they were known only through the functional relationships between observable variables.

Thus, after two decades of conceptual development, the concepts of purpose and cognition which Tolman had borrowed from the neorealists finally found in 1935 a methodological status as intervening variables. In that year, he first unambiguously applied the language of intervening variables to purpose and cognition in a paper entitled "Psychology vs. Immediate Experience."[31] This paper completed the difficult transition from assigning purpose and cognition an ontological status of subsistence-in-behavior to giving them an instrumental status of intervening-in-equations.

Instrumentalism and Molar Behaviorism

The key to the developments described above lay in Tolman's acquisition of a frankly instrumentalistic view of scientific theories. This view was articulated in the final chapter of *Purposive Be-*

havior, wherein Tolman contended that science provides, not a replica of reality, but a map or a "symbolic compendium by means of which to predict and control."[32] Purpose and cognition were regarded as logical constructs which, like those of physics, aid in predicting and controlling immediate experience without trying to describe or relive it. In the tradition of William James, Tolman denied that immediate experience is more subjective than objective, more private than public, and more properly in the domain of psychology than of physics. In their purely logical status as intervening variables, purpose and cognition were thus for Tolman decisively freed of any subjectivist taint and could serve as explanatory devices without fear of mentalism. This instrumentalistic view also enabled Tolman to eschew the ontological distinctions of mind-body dualism in favor of the methodological distinction between theory and experience. He wrote:

> There is, if you will, still left in my universe a dichotomy, but it is a dichotomy not between physical entities, and mental entities, but between both of these as mere logical constructs, on the one hand, and immediate experience as the actually given, rich, qualified, diffuse, matrix from which both sciences [physics and psychology] are evolved, on the other.[33]

By functionally defining his intervening variables in terms of molar independent and dependent variables and their connecting equations, Tolman was also able to escape the temptation of physiologizing the concepts of purpose and cognition. The development of his views on the relationship between molar behavior and physiology reveals once again the declining influence of neorealism and the avoidance of its pitfalls. Tolman's first theoretical paper, "Nerve Process and Cognition" (1918), attempted a physiological interpretation of cognition much like those of his neorealist teachers. In it, Tolman sought "a definition of cognition which naturally and of itself provides its own neurological explana-

tion."[34] Cognition was defined as an internal neurological sorting of qualities which would result in a system of interconnected neural paths; a path for an idea like "finance" would have connections with paths for the ideas of "commerce" and "industry" as well as with paths for sensory qualities such as "dollar signs."

By 1922, however, Tolman had given up such speculation and was clearly seeking a conceptual framework for a *non*physiological behaviorism. In that year, he even criticized Perry for being unaware of the "essential difference between such a true behaviorism and a mere physiology."[35] But Tolman was still admitting in 1925 that the concepts of a nonphysiological behaviorism would eventually be reduced to the more accurate and general concepts of physiology. Not until after his formulation of intervening variables did he arrive at the fully molar behaviorism which, augmented with Gestalt concepts, led him to claim in 1938 that the laws of physiology may actually depend on those of behavior.[36] Tolman's development of a truly molar behaviorism was thus essentially complete in 1938: behaviorism could now be viewed as a science of behavior *qua* behavior with no necessary tie to physiology.[37] The last vestiges of the molecular definition of the response, which Tolman had earlier caricatured as Watsonian Muscle Twitchism, were now finally laid to rest.

CONCLUSION

Embedding purpose and cognition within an instrumentalistic theory of behavior enabled Tolman to retain the sound lessons of his neorealist teachers while circumventing the exaggerated epistemological views of neorealism which brought about its demise. Molar behaviorism provided a conception in which purpose and cognition remained objective, naturalistic, and nonphysiological, without being viewed simplistically as primary-like qualities of the cognizing organism, and above all without being assigned a contrived ontological status such as subsistence. Even though Tolman later tried to interpret his intervening variables in topological terms,[38] purpose and cognition remained essentially methodological in character, a situation which obviated the need for philosophically nettlesome questions of ontology.

While Tolman's reshaping of the notions of purpose and cognition represented a move away from their neorealist formulations, it would be rash to conclude that the neorealist influence on his thought ended with this transition. Although Tolman's later writings cited Holt and Perry mainly for their molar conception of behavior, it is likely that his attribution of "hypotheses" to rats reflected the neorealist conviction that knowledge must be formulated as propositions.[39] It is also likely that the version of neutral monism that he espoused in 1935 was influenced by Holt's earlier neutral monism.[40] Tolman was even assigning *The New Realism* to his Berkeley students as late as the early 1930s.[41] These facts suggest that the full extent and nature of neorealist influence on Tolman remains a complex historical problem to which this paper has posed only a partial solution.

In adopting and adapting the concepts of purpose and cognition from his neorealist teachers, Tolman helped preserve and shape the tradition of cognitive psychology during a time when it was nearly eclipsed by the ascendency of classical behaviorism. He was able to do so by demonstrating that such concepts were compatible with a behaviorism of a more sophisticated—clearly non-Watsonian—variety. Yet the purposive behaviorism he developed was a complex system, and shortly before his death, Tolman expressed despair over the immense practical difficulty of determining intervening variables and their interactions.[42] Although the point cannot be argued here, I would suggest that it was just this sort of difficulty that became tractable with the realization by psychologists in the 1960s that computer programs are highly suited for expressing complex interactions in models of cognitive

processing. If Tolman's theoretical innovations suffered from the limitations of the technology available in his time, they would seem to suffer no longer. In the words of a major text in learning theory, "the sort of program Tolman envisioned seems now to be coming to fruition in modern cognitive psychology."[43]

NOTES

(1) Several examples are contained in Stewart H. Hulse, Harry Fowler, and Werner K. Honig, eds., *Cognitive Processes in Animal Behavior* (Hillsdale, N.J.: L. Erlbaum Associates, 1978).

(2) Thomas H. Leahey has argued that there is no such antagonism, because cognitive psychology as it is commonly practiced today *is* behaviorism in all important respects. See his "The Revolution Never Happened: Information Processing *Is* Behaviorism," presented at the Eastern Psychological Association. New York, N.Y., 23 April 1981. The conceptual continuity between behaviorism and cognitive psychology has been discussed by Daniel C. Dennett. "Why the Law of Effect Will Not Go Away," in *Brainstorms: Philosophical Essays on Mind and Psychology* (Montgomery, Vermont: Bradford Books, 1978), pp. 71–89.

(3) Tolman was one of the three major neobehaviorists who followed in Watson's wake (along with Clark L. Hull and B. F. Skinner). An excellent brief account of all four of these behaviorists is provided by Richard J. Herrnstein. "Introduction to John B. Watson's Comparative Psychology," in Mary Henle, Julian Jaynes, and John J. Sullivan, eds., *Historical Conceptions of Psychology* (New York: Springer Publishing Co., 1973), pp. 98–115. This essay was written as the introduction to Watson's *Behavior: An Introduction to Comparative Psychology* (1914), reissued in 1967 by Holt, Rinehart & Winston.

(4) The term "evolution" is used here because it connotes the possibility of progression in a given line of development but without implying the existence of any final state toward which the progression moves. Like any other approach to a scientific subject matter, behaviorism (or any of its

sub-varieties) can defensibly be said to progress, but *not* without reference to the (necessarily relative) corpus of presuppositions and problems which guide its development. The present account of Tolman's conceptual development is intended to reveal a context-bound progression which has in part led to contemporary cognitive psychology. Whether Tolman's solutions to Tolman's conceptual difficulties represented progress in some broader sense is another (possibly unanswerable) question. Much the same can be said of the evolution of contemporary cognitive psychology in general. For a compelling, but largely neglected, argument for a scientific pluralism, see Arne Naess, *The Pluralist and Possibilist Aspect of the Scientific Enterprise* (Oslo: Universitetsforlaget, 1972).

(5) Edward C. Tolman, "Edward Chace Tolman," in Edwin G. Boring, ed., *A History of Psychology in Autobiography,* vol. IV (Worcester, Mass.: Clark University Press, 1952), pp. 323–339, on p. 339.

(6) See Laurence D. Smith, "Psychology and Philosophy: Toward a Realignment, 1905–1935," *Journal of the History of the Behavioral Sciences,* 1981, *17:* 28–37.

(7) See Jerome S. Bruner and Gordon W. Allport, "Fifty Years of Change in American Psychology," *Psychological Bulletin,* 1940, *37:* 757–776.

(8) Neorealism (or equivalently New Realism) was inspired by the works of Franz Brentano and Alexius Meinong on the Continent, and William James in America. It was developed in England by G. E. Moore, T. P. Nunn, and Bertrand Russell. Holt and Perry, who were students and devoted followers of James, were two of its leading exponents in America. For brief expositions of neorealism, see John Passmore, *A Hundred Years of Philosophy,* rev. ed. (New York: Basic Books, 1966). pp. 259–280, and *The Encyclopedia of Philosophy,* s.v. "New Realism," by Thomas Robischon. A critical account of New Realism may be found in Arthur O. Lovejoy. *The Revolt against Dualism* (Chicago: Open Court, 1930).

(9) Ralph B. Perry, "Professor Royce's Refutation of Realism and Pluralism," *The Monist,* 1901–1902, *12:* 446–458; William P. Montague, "Professor Royce's Refutation of Realism," *Philosophical Review,* 1902, *11:* 43–55. Although Royce was the specific target of these assaults, the New Realists were generally critical of idealism, which was still powerful in American academic philosophy during this decade.

(10) Ralph B. Perry, *Present Philosophical Tendencies* (New York: George Braziller, Inc., 1955), pp. 273–274. Originally published in 1912.

(11) Edwin B. Holt, Walter T. Marvin, William P. Montague, Ralph B. Perry, Walter B. Pitkin, and Edward G. Spaulding, *The New Realism* (New York: Macmillan Co., 1912), pp. 38, 39.

(12) Edwin B. Holt, "Response and Cognition," *Journal of Philosophy, Psychology, and Scientific Method,* 1915, *12:* 365–373, 393–409; reprinted in Holt, *The Freudian Wish and Its Place in Ethics* (New York: Henry Holt and Co., 1915), p. 207.

(13) Edwin B. Holt, Walter T. Marvin, William P. Montague, Ralph B. Perry, Walter B. Pitkin, and Edward G. Spaulding. "The Program and First Platform of Six Realists," *J. Phil.,* 1910, *7:* 393–401.

(14) Tolman, "Edward Chace Tolman," p. 325

(15) Ralph B. Perry, "Purpose as Systematic Unity," *The Monist,* 1917, *27:* 352–375; "Purpose as Tendency and Adaptation," *Phil. Rev.,* 1917, *26:* 477–495; "Docility and Purposiveness," *Psychol. Rev.,* 1918, *25:* 1–20.

(16) Tolman adopted C.D. Broad's expression "molar behaviorism" to emphasize the distinction between his brand of nonphysiological behaviorism and "molecular" versions which rely heavily on physiology and a reflex model of behavior.

(17) Edwin B. Holt, "The Place of Illusory Experience in a Realistic World," in Holt, et al., *The New Realism,* p. 366.

(18) In adopting subsistence rather than existence or reality as a fundamental mode of being, the New Realists divorced themselves decisively from naive realism and what Holt referred to as the "singularly crude brick bat notion of physical object." The ambiguity of the term "realism" was admitted by Holt: "for realism by no means everything is real; and I grant that the name realism tends to confuse persons who have not followed the history of the term" (Holt, "Illusory Experience," pp. 371, 359). Holt's neutral mo-

nism derived from William James's doctrine of pure experience, as did Bertrand Russell's a decade later. See Edwin B. Holt, *The Concept of Consciousness* (New York: Macmillan Co., 1914). This exposition of neutral monism was completed in 1908.

(19) Holt, et al., "Introduction," in *The New Realism*, p. 35.

(20) Durant Drake, Arthur O. Lovejoy, James B. Pratt, Arthur K. Rogers, George Santayana, Roy W. Sellars, and C.A. Strong, *Essays in Critical Realism* (London: Gordian Press, 1920).

(21) For an incisive overview of the infighting at Harvard which hastened the decline of neo-realism, see Bruce Kuklick, *The Rise of American Philosophy* (New Haven, Conn.: Yale University Press, 1977), pp. 347–350.

(22) Tolman rarely made explicit reference to the New Realism, and in his later writings cited Holt and Perry mainly for their molar conception of behavior.

(23) Edward C. Tolman, "Behaviorism and Purpose," *J. Phil.*, 1925, *22:* 36–41, on p. 37. Tolman's strategy of identifying traditionally mentalistic phenomena with types of responding constituted an early form of operationism. Unlike the operationism of the thirties, which was often invoked as a means of *avoiding* metaphysics, Tolman's early operationism had a neorealist metaphysical backing. McDougall's purposivism had only an indirect influence on Tolman. McDougall came to Harvard in 1920, five years after Tolman had left. Tolman noted that his purposive system was "a sibling of the systems of Perry and Woodworth, and only a first cousin of that of McDougall." See *Purposive Behavior in Animals and Men* (New York: Century & Co., 1932), p. 423.

(24) Edward C. Tolman, "Purpose and Cognition: The Determiners of Animal Learning." *Psychol. Rev.*, 1925, *32:* 285–297.

(25) Tolman, "A Behavioristic Theory of Ideas," p. 355 (italics in the original). The neorealist view of perception revealed in this passage finds perhaps its closest contemporary counterpart in the perceptual theory of James J. Gibson. Gibson was in fact a student of Holt at Princeton after Holt left Harvard. As he recorded in his autobio

graphical sketch, Gibson took to Holt's ideas "with enthusiasm." See "James J. Gibson" in Edwin G. Boring and Gardner Lindzey, eds., *A History of Psychology in Autobiography,* vol. V (New York: Appleton-Century-Crofts, 1967), p. 129.

(26) The present account emphasizes philosophical influences on the development of Tolman's thought, but his philosophical views did not operate in a vacuum independently of his experimental research. As is widely known, Tolman's research from 1918 on was conducted with mazes. Of all the types of apparatus in use at that time by psychologists, the maze was probably the type most appropriate for a neorealist because it made the objective reference of the investigator toward the rat's purposes and cognitions a matter of visible spatial relations. The rat's cognitions were directly perceivable as its sequences of turns toward the goal box. Its purposes were presented as gettings-away-from the start box and gettings-toward the goal. Any investigator who merely observed these patterned behaviors was immediately privy to cognitions and purposes qua objective relations in physical space. Tolman's philosophical views and his chosen experimental method were thus mutually reinforcing aspects of his research program.

(27) Edward C. Tolman, "Purposive Behavior," *Psychol. Rev.*, 1928, *35:* 524–530, on pp. 524, 525. Kuo's criticisms were expressed in Z.Y. Kuo, "The Fundamental Error of the Concept of Purpose and the Trial and Error Fallacy," *Psychol. Rev.*, 1928, *35:* 414–433.

(28) Edwin G. Boring, *A History of Experimental Psychology*, 2nd rev. ed. (Englewood Cliffs, N.J.: Prentice-Hall, Inc., 1950), p. 721.

(29) Tolman, *Purposive Behavior,* p. 19.

(30) Tolman, "Edward Chace Tolman," p. 333.

(31) Edward C. Tolman, "Psychology vs. Immediate Experience," *Philosophy of Science*, 1935, *2:* 356–380. Although intervening variables were Tolman's invention, they quickly became a popular methodological device among many neobehaviorists, including Clark Hull. For a review of the concept, see Paul Lazarsfeld, "Concept Formation and Measurement in the Behavioral Sciences: Some Historical Observations," in Gordon DiRenzo, ed., *Concepts, Theory, and Explanation in*

the Behavioral Sciences (New York: Random House, 1966), pp. 144–202. The extent to which Tolman actually clarified his concepts of purpose and cognition has been questioned by Richard F. Kitchener, "Behavior and Behaviorism," *Behaviorism,* 1977, *5:* 11–71, on pp. 32–41. Tolman's concept of purpose and its relationship to the concepts of Perry and Holt have been discussed, without reference to neorealism, by Margaret Boden, *Purposive Explanation in Psychology* (Cambridge, Mass.: Harvard University Press, 1972), pp. 73–85.

(32) Tolman, *Purposive Behavior,* p. 425. Tolman cited the Berkeley philosopher Stephen C. Pepper in connection with the notion of theories as "maps." Tolman and Pepper had been graduate students together under Perry at Harvard and maintained close personal and intellectual ties throughout their careers. Tolman's interest in operationism and logical positivism also reinforced his instrumentalistic view of theories. In any case, his views were representative of a widespread shift of attention from ontological questions to methodological issues.

(33) Tolman, "Psychology vs. Immediate Experience," pp. 359–360. Paul Tibbetts has argued that the doctrine of pure experience espoused by Tolman in this paper requires an instrumentalistic view of theories; see Tibbetts, "The Doctrine of 'Pure Experience': The Evolution of a Concept from Mach to James to Tolman," *J. Hist. Behav. Sci.,* 1975, *11:* 55–66.

(34) Edward C. Tolman, "Nerve Process and Cognition," *Psychol. Rev.,* 1918, *25:* 423–442, on p. 423.

(35) Edward C. Tolman, "A New Formula for Behaviorism," *Psychol. Rev.,* 1922, *29:* 44–53, on p. 47.

(36) Edward C. Tolman, "Physiology, Psychology, and Sociology," *Psychol. Rev.,* 1938, *45:* 228–241.

(37) B. F. Skinner was also pursuing a nonphysiological behaviorism during the 1930s. See his "The Concept of the Reflex in the Description of Behavior," *Journal of General Psychology,* 1931, *5:* 427–458, and "The Generic Nature of the Concepts of Stimulus and Response," *J. Gen. Psych.,* 1935, *12:* 40–65. After having read the former paper, Tolman wrote Skinner in 1931: "I do of course agree with the disposal of physiology which you suggest." This letter appears in B. F. Skinner, *The Shaping of a Behaviorist* (New York: Alfred A. Knopf, 1979), pp. 364–365. The direction of influence between Tolman and Skinner remains a point of some contention. See Robert C. Bolles, "Scholar's Progress," review of Skinner's *The Shaping of a Behaviorist, in Science,* 1979, *204:* 1073–1074.

(38) Tolman, "Edward Chace Tolman," p. 335.

(39) W. M. O'Neil, "Realism and Behaviorism," *J. Hist. Behav. Sci.,* 1968, *4:* 152–160, on p. 159.

(40) Compare Tolman's "Psychology vs. Immediate Experience" with Holt's *Concept of Consciousness.*

(41) Edward C. Tolman, Bibliographies, File M133, Archives of the History of American Psychology, University of Akron, Akron, Ohio.

(42) Edward C. Tolman. "Principles of Purposive Behavior," in Sigmund Koch, ed., *Psychology: A Study of a Science,* vol. II (New York: McGraw-Hill, 1959), pp. 92–157.

(43) Ernest Hilgard and Gordon Bower, *Theories of Learning,* 4th ed. (Englewood Cliffs, N.J.: Prentice-Hall, Inc., 1975), p. 151. In his autobiographical sketch of 1952, Tolman noted that his concept of the sign-gestalt-expectation "seems to have been the source . . . of the now widely current term 'expectancy' " ("Edward Chace Tolman," p. 331). Since that time, his concept of the cognitive map has also come into widespread use.

On Skinner and Hull
A Reminiscence and Projection

Norman Guttman

Earlier this year Professor Hiroshi Imada of Kwansei Gakuin University and Professor Masaya Sato of Keio University invited a number of American psychologists to contribute to a symposium on "The Hullians and Skinnerians in Psychology" to be held at the annual meeting of the Personality and Behavior Disorders Society of Japan on September 26, 1976. They wrote:

> Please be free to be frank and not to be bound by formal style of your paper. In Japan we have words HONNE (literally meaning "true voice") and TATEMAE (appearance to the public). We would like to know your HONNE, or what you truly think of the topic, freed from your loyalty (if any,) to your former teachers.

What follows is my response to that invitation.

The thoughts I am privileged to offer the Personality and Behavior Disorders Society are, in the first place, an attempt to answer the questions you have put to your American colleagues: First, why has the Skinnerian approach become so very popular in the United States in the last generation, while the Hullian view—which seems in many fundamentals to resemble it so closely—lost ground? Second, how does one assess the atheoretical, Skinnerian, descriptive approach versus the highly theoretical, highly formal, Hullian approach which refers to many intervening variables? These are both, by themselves, very large questions, which to answer properly would require as many pages as an ordinary book and the first of which alone would entail the writing of a sizable part of the recent history of Amer-

Guttman, N. (1977). On Skinner and Hull: A reminiscence and projection. *American Psychologist, 32,* 321–328. Copyright © 1977 by the American Psychological Association. Reprinted by permission of the publisher.

ican psychology, the rise of the far-flung Skinner movement and its counterreactions. But in the second place, I shall endeavor to go beyond even these important and interesting questions to give my impressions of the situation that prevails in systematic psychology, for it appears to me, as to other observers, that no version of neobehaviorism occupies the predominant intellectual position shared by Hull and Skinner (along with Tolman, Guthrie, Spence, Mowrer, and others) only a few years ago. Different elements have entered or reentered the scene and have qualified and modulated behaviorism so that the behaviorist family of theories no longer occupies, and may never again occupy, the center and forefront of the stage to the extent it once did. That remark is part fact, but also part wish, and both aspects are expanded in the last section of this essay.

The first question posed involves assumptions of fact also, and before one seeks to explain any fact it is provident to ascertain whether the fact is really true. While it is unlikely that anyone who has followed recent American psychology would doubt the dual fact of the rise of Skinner and the decline of Hull, some hard data may add conviction. If one tabulates references in the *Journal of Experimental Psychology* to Clark L. Hull, together with references to his closest systematic collaborator Kenneth W. Spence, one finds the following enumeration by decades: In 1940, 4 percent of the 107 papers published refer to one or the other of these men. By 1950, 7 years after the publication of Hull's *Principles of Behavior,* the figure is a remarkable 39 percent of 86 papers. By 1960 the peak influence has passed and the figure is 24 percent ($N = 131$), and in 1970 it is back to 4 percent ($N = 196$). Twenty years ago or less, the pages of American journals were filled with experiments inspired by the postulates and theorems of the Hull-Spence system, and there were numerous essays and reviews that sought either to repair and extend, or on the contrary to demolish, this grand construction. But the fame and notoriety of the development, which for all its prominence was entirely an academic glory, have now passed, having scarcely outlasted the lifetimes of its two architects, also now both deceased. *Sic transit gloria mundi;* obviously, no small part of the answer to why any system of psychology loses hold resides in human mortality.

B. F. Skinner, happily, is still with us, and his later years have been very productive and influential, but if we were to look through the *Journal of Experimental Psychology* for indications of his prominence, we would find that, in none of the volumes sampled, is he referenced more than a couple of times per year; his channels to fame bypassed the mainstream of the American psychological establishment. Skinner and his followers, as we shall relate, made their own media and have formed their own establishment. While there are today countless persons, inside psychology and outside, who would call themselves followers of Skinner, I am really not acquainted with a psychologist who would say he is simply a Hullian. It is incidentally revealing that in the latest edition of Chaplin and Krawiec's *Systems and Theories of Psychology* (1974), Hull's hypothetico-deductive theory is presented in the chapter "Learning II: Miniature Theories." I should say at once that this same chapter also includes Skinner, Tolman, and Guthrie, and it is a significant commentary on the neobehaviorist theories of the last generation that they should have diminished in stature to the point where any or all of them should be called miniature. It scarcely needs to be pointed out that Chaplin and Krawiec have missed the proper meaning of the term *miniature,* which should really be applied to distinguish such formulations of the scope of the Estes (1959) statistical theory, the Bush and Mosteller

(1955) theory, or many others of yet smaller range from the comprehensive, ambitious general formulations of the 1930s and 1940s. In experimental psychology today, where it advances, we have passed from the age of competing theories to the stage of alternative mathematical models, which aim to account for determinate laboratory findings and are not concerned with behavior at large and in toto but usually with selected aspects of performance and learning. Current models tend to concentrate on phenomena that the laboratory itself has generated and to leave aside certain large, difficult areas of previous interest, such as emotion and motivation. Today's mathematical psychology owes part of its genesis to Hull's influence, but the style and scope of analytical thought has undergone a change toward modesty and specification, and toward improved precision and greater sophistication. Current research generally employs basic concepts far outside the vocabulary of earlier conditioning theory, and much of it is foreign to the spirit of both Hull and Skinner, especially insofar as it concerns itself with cognitive and perceptual processes and structures and other things of like "mentalistic" character.

The later developments of which I have spoken are not such as the larger world takes much into account, but it certainly takes Skinner into account. B. F. Skinner was numbered among *The 100 Most Important People in the World Today* (Robinson, 1970); perhaps he would be in a yet smaller group in 1976. A survey in 1975 showed Skinner to be the best known scientist in the United States (just above Margaret Mead), and surely not more than a very tiny fraction of the American public would recognize Clark Hull's name, since only a few psychology majors can now identify him. Fame and influence are not the same, and influence upon psychology is different from social influence; but Skinner's effect on the discipline is, I think, connected with his world fame. The latter is of such magnitude that it is difficult to grasp it in full, though I shall try to give some concrete indications of it in order to summarize where his impact falls and what his position seems to be in the world thought of our times.

Skinner has become a symbol; he has become more than himself. Skinner is, as it were, the leading figure in a myth, a myth already made in the popular imagination and awaiting a new occupant. He has succeeded to the role of the scientist-hero, the Promethean fire-bringer, the master technologist and instructor of technologists. Also, his is the role of the chief iconoclast, the image-breaker who liberates our thoughts from ancient restrictions. To this composite role Skinner adds the unique personal element of encouragement, reinforcement, kindness, love— which he presents as a universal message based, at long last, on a scientific foundation. To several audiences before (e.g., Krantz, 1972), I have suggested that Skinner could be characterized as a unique combination of the figures of Thomas A. Edison, Jesus Christ, and Bertrand Russell, and I stand by that characterization here, intending no disrespect for any of the four parties named. But it should be added that the scientist-hero image usually has a dark side, and this sinister aspect Skinner has also managed to acquire, despite his efforts to be seen in a positive light. To rectify his image, and in order to change men's thoughts, he has vigorously argued that what men commonly regard as bad—being controlled—is really good. This argument, I estimate, has been as unsuccessful as it is wrong-headed, for Skinner has failed to understand that what people usually mean by control of behavior is different from what he means. The ordinary meaning of having one's behavior controlled is being subjected to the will (the wishes, desires, and values) of another person, but Skinner means the much more general fact that any organism's actions and state always depend upon antecedent and surrounding conditions. Control in Skinner's sense is no more than a metaphysical or scientific platitude, a commonplace, almost a banality, but he appears to argue that a widespread acceptance of the determinist proposition is somehow the essential step toward the betterment of human life and society. He has written in this vein with a persistence which reflects the depth of his concern for the survival of the human species and the quality of its culture. I am unable to apprehend the connection between the acceptance of the determinist thesis and the cure of the world's ills; the whole idea of the argument strikes me as intellectualist in the extreme. It seems to me that the world is maintained and grows better through a million good deeds and good thoughts that have their root in no particular metaphysics but in the living substance of civilization itself, actualized by uncounted nameless and reasonable men.

But at any time in history, the world seizes upon one or a few figures who are eligible to symbolize for that generation the best of its hopes and who have become so known through their accomplishments and expressions. Let us adequately understand that there has been alive in the world for many generations a considerable sentiment in favor of the scientific, naturalistic perspective on things. This philosophy is opposed to mysticism, superstition, and animism, and it includes such doctrines as determinism, materialism, physicalism, and also the epistemological attitudes of empiricism, positivism, pragmatism, and the like. It does not far misrepresent the situation to say that in the last decade Skinner has risen to the position of the most conspicuous symbol of these allied beliefs. Skinnerism is the banner around which such ideas have rallied; and he has intended that it be so through the philosophical writings (Skinner, 1971, 1974) to which he has devoted most of his recent energies.

Skinner stands not just for the scientific type of world view but even more prominently for the type of social philosophy that is its natural accompaniment. *Walden Two* (1948) was the first expression of his utopianism; and underlying this expression is a form of social and political criticism that finds many sympathizers among those distressed or horrified by the contemporary social scene and seeking an avenue for the realization of their resilient hopes for the perfectibility of man. Skinner's utopianism is rather antipolitical and antieconomist—it is an alternative to contemporary Marxism in its politicized, governmentalized form. But Skinner's utopianism is as optimistic and progressive in spirit as it is regressive in content, envisioning as it does something of a return to a happier state of nature, the recreation of a simpler, face-to-face culture of villages, towns, or scientifically-ruled secular monasteries. How very appealing is this vision, with its embodiment of positive morality through positive reinforcement, its affirmation of cultivated hedonism through the reinforcement principle, its sponsorship of the liberal ideal of individual development and its utter rejection of punishment, coercion, and worse. And this is a goal, furthermore, to which one can devote one's active, intentional energies, one's preparedness to control the environment for one's *own* purposes. Here is the very essence and meaning of *operant* behavior, in contrast to respondent behavior, which is merely and abjectly reactive to the blind events in the surround. Thus, to understand the influence of Skinner, I propose that one take adequate account of the moral forces and ideals that his philosophy so perfectly captures.

To obtain an accurate measure of Skinner's effect upon the contemporary world beyond the areas of general philosophy and social philosophy, attention must be paid to the fields of education and psychotherapy. It was in these fields that he gained his credentials, so that his philosophy was listened to. The programed learning movement was started by Skinner single handedly; it has grown into a thing of immense proportions involving literally thousands of practitioners and further developers whose applications of the concept have by now been felt by untold millions of students. UNESCO surveys (see Spaulding, 1967; UNESCO, 1973) have revealed that in no fewer than 72 nations (capitalist, socialist, and "third world") there are active developments in programed instruction. At least a dozen new journals contain the phrase "programed instruction" in their titles, and many dozens more are devoted to the field. No really sufficient account of this massive educational phenomenon of the 20th century has to my knowledge been written, probably because a historian of education would be engulfed by the available materials and because we are still too close to the events to see their total shape and eventual result. The vocabulary of the educator has been drastically altered; the way he thinks and talks about the learning process and the teacher's task has been transformed. Learning is now conceived as the reinforcement of behavior. The environment of which the teacher is a part is now an apparatus of reinforcement, a system of contingencies. The notion of teacher accountability, which includes the explicit statement of behavioral objectives and the firm measurement of behavioral outcomes, has grown out of the broad conception of educational technology. The technology of teaching presently includes many other components (such as computer-assisted instruction), but Skinner started us off with teaching machines, auto-tutoring, and individualized instruction based upon the shaping of operant behavior. An indication of the change in what educators talk and write about is given in the accompanying graph (Figure 1), which shows the number of entries in the *Education Index* from 1950 through 1975 under *reinforcement* and similar categories. The interest increases over the 25 years by a factor of 100, from 2 articles to more than 200 per year. REINFORCEMENT becomes a separate heading in 1967–1968, joined in 1971–1972 by BEHAVIOR MODIFICATION. Clearly, educational leaders are of the belief that Skinnerian procedures and concepts promise a solution to the massive problems of the schools in the 20th century, though a careful reading of the titles of what they write suggests a growing skepticism.

One can give only a few indications of the burgeoning of the behavior modification movement. I think it is a correct opinion that Skinner's ideas

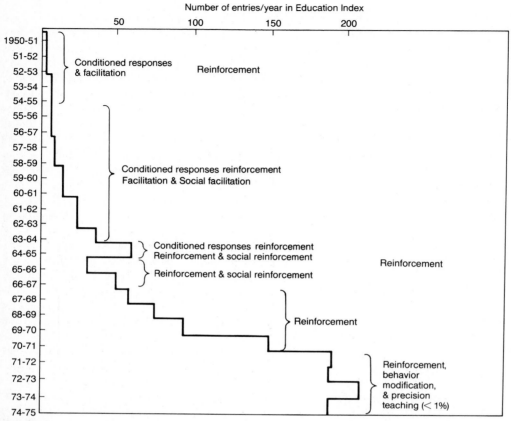

FIGURE 1
Illustration of the rise in interest in reinforcement and related topics in the American educational literature.
(Note the changes in classification. *Facilitation* drops out by 1964–1965. *Reinforcement* (undifferentiated)
is the inclusive heading from 1967 through 1970. *Behavior modification* enters as a major heading in
1971–1972.)

have been the chief stimulus for this development, which I see as the main competitor of psychoanalysis at the present time. Conditioning principles from the very beginning have been applied by many workers in the mental health professions, but the operant-conditioning approach has become perhaps the chief conceptual underpinning of current practice. Wolpe (1969) credits Skinner and Lindsley (Note 1) with coining the expression *behavior therapy,* but more recently a highly diverse set of methods and concepts has been included under the behavior mod-

ification heading (e.g., Sherman, 1973). There are now four English-language journals concerned with behavior modification and therapy, including the *Journal of Applied Behavior Analysis,* founded in 1968 by a group that was mainly Skinnerian in origin and affiliation. Ten years earlier the *Journal of the Experimental Analysis of Behavior* was established to provide an outlet for the research reports of workers in the Skinnerian tradition, toward whose products the existing journals were not receptive. One should note that Division 25 of the American Psychological Association (Division for the Experimental Analysis of Behavior) is exclusively a Skinnerian organization, the only section of APA identifiable with an individual psychologist. Division 25's members are as often behavior modifiers as laboratory workers, and these are frequently the same persons. Before we leave organizations and publications, we should mention the lively new journal *Behaviorism,* whose content is reflective of the type of philosophical and psychological theoretical issues generated by Skinner's writings.

I cannot adequately begin to discuss the numerous moral, practical, or theoretical questions that surround behavior modification and its offshoots. Nor can I give more than passing mention to other whole major developments on which Skinner's effect has been exerted. The latter would include on the active side token economies in hospitals and prisons as well as the technology of infant care associated with the notorious baby-tender of the late 1940s. On the research scene, countless laboratories of psychopharmacology and behavioral neurology (as well as psychology) employ operant conditioning apparatus and methods. And the study of language has become, in important measure, a special branch of the study of operant behavior, as the result of Skinner's (1938, 1957) thesis that language produced and language responded to can be described, analyzed, and understood in the terms requisite for any other instrumental behavior, though at a higher degree of elaboration. Finally, by taking in language, the Skinnerian approach begins to encompass in its fashion the domains of thinking, reasoning, and knowing, which are psychology's most ancient and sacred precincts.

Now, having documented in the most sketchy fashion the extent of Skinner's reach, I turn more directly to the questions with which I began. Part of the explanation of the phenomenon of Skinner has already been given, by reference to the state of preparedness of the intellectual community to absorb Skinner's values, conceptions, and methods. My review has reminded us of the sheer bulk and range of the work Skinner has accomplished in his lifetime, entering field after field of important concern to a degree no other behaviorist has approached. He has repeatedly addressed the wider public audience in preference to the exclusively academic. No reader can fail to be affected by his style of expression, which is exceptionally lucid, modest, and confident. The artfulness of Skinner's rhetoric seems to me to be born of an inner confidence in the conceptions propounded, and nothing could be more persuasive.

Still, these are secondary considerations, and I have not reached the heart of the matter, not yet shown wherein Skinner surpassed Hull. It comes down to the reiterated application of a single, graspable, eminently teachable idea, an evidently true and general formula: There is a situation, and the organism does something, and the situation changes, and lo and behold the state of the organism changes, toward greater or less activity of a certain kind. The formula goes by many names: reinforcement, operant conditioning, operant behavior, contingency of stimulus upon response, shaping, reward and punishment, law-of-effect, feedback. There are far too many names to list, but what is described is exactly the same in essence and basic form. Something is added to the basic stimulus-response formula that one already knows, and as a result one knows something better and truer, even though the added something may also be what one already knows. But it is just this accomplishment of having reduced the matter to such a highly graspable and very extensible formula that Skinner brought about, and then he went on with the extensions. One is reminded here of Isaiah Berlin's famous observation about hedgehogs and foxes: The fox knows many things, while the hedgehog knows only one thing, but he knows it exceedingly well. The Skinnerians are like the hedgehogs of psychology, and reinforcement is the thing they know exceedingly well. Reinforcement has endless exemplifications, shapes, sizes, and colors, and by means of the principle one is supposed to comprehend most of learning, motivation, and performance.

Clark L. Hull knew about the reinforcement principle, but for him it was buried amidst a multitude of other ideas and themes. He was unable to give it emphatic expression because, while he claimed to espouse a molar behaviorism, his understanding of the molar-molecular distinction was quite hazy and his attachment to the molar approach was manifestly ambivalent and wavering. He wanted explanations as well as descriptions. Hull's system, as elaborated in his *Principles of Behavior* (1943) and its successor volumes (1951, 1952), was composed of many principal elements and many principles, both methodological and substantive. The theory's most distinctive feature was its intention to cast objective, behavioristic psychology into the form of an explicit hypothetico-deductive system—a system, moreover, of precise quantitative laws of great generality. It is well known that the Hullian system drew its psychological substance from Pavlov and Thorndike. Hull assumed that conditioning was the basic, indeed the only, type of learning, and he proposed that conditioning was dependent on the reduction of primary organic needs, drives, or tensions. There is just a single learning mechanism, and this associative process is rooted deep within the soil of motivation. Here, one may notice, Hull made a certain underlying, almost invisible connection with Freud and psychoanalysis, because Freud also taught that mental association is determined by pleasure, pain, and satisfaction. Here Hull joined hands, though not dramatically, with other irrationalists who put feeling above reason, and conation ahead of cognition, in the scheme of things. Yet much as Hull was attached to the drive-reduction idea (among other principles), the propelling power behind his work was supplied by his admiration of formal systems in mathematics and science. His intellectual ideals were Euclid, Newton, Whitehead, and Russell, as he indicates in the *Principles of Behavior*. Visibly he aspired to write the *Principia* of psychology

and become the Newton of behavior. But above and beyond this personal goal, he was convinced that psychology could become a definite, clear, universally agreed-upon science only if it resolved to state its laws in the form of explicit postulates. These postulates had to be knitted together to comprise a tight deductive system, and the entire structure of propositions had to produce unambiguous quantitative predictions pertaining to quantitative experimental findings.

More than anything else, Hull desired that psychology should become a progressive scientific discipline capable of linear movement and visible advance. He wished to see all of the basic problems of psychology settled decisively by experimentation rather than remaining matters of endless circular debate and argumentation. The answer to stagnation and intellectual chaos was to be the construction of formal hypothetico-deductive systems, and such systems could work only if all the concepts they employed referred directly or indirectly to measurable properties of environment and organism, to aspects of stimulus and response. The latter requirement is the requirement for operational definition, and the application of the operationalist philosophy of science to psychology amounts to an acceptance of the basic tenets and viewpoint of behaviorism. It was Hull's opinion that Gestalt psychology, like any version of mentalism or subjectivism (or, for that matter, vitalism), was too vague to meet the demand for scientific rigor, and he hoped that through an insistence on operationism, formalism, and quantification, Gestalt theory would be exposed and dissipated.

What Hull held in his mind was the image of a certain kind of science, a style, an atmosphere, an intrinsic character. It was not to any extent an image of what this style of scientific psychology was to be used for, and what is more remarkable is that the image did not consist of any firm, experienced conception of phenomena of behavior. It was not so much an image of reality as of the proper science of these realities. No single Hullian proposition was more than tentative, and the whole was a somewhat arbitrary carrying forward of a rather obvious line of thought. Its empirics lay mostly in the future; only here and there did it draw upon past experience, and even then rather selectively. The system offered a form of expression, but to anyone already familiar with the behavioristic way of thinking and with the myriad phenomena of conditioned behavior—say, to one who was by then a Skinnerian—Hull's system offered very little that was not already within reach. To such a one, the Hullian form of words appeared superfluous, extravagant, pretentious, and inappropriate to the state of knowledge. I well remember in 1943 sitting for many hours with B. F. Skinner and other laboratory co-workers going over the galley proofs of *Principles of Behavior,* which had been sent to Skinner for review. Our reaction, frankly, was one of amusement, for how was it possible that anyone who had any actual laboratory experience with animal behavior in a couple of species could deal with the available data so seriously, so precisely, so pontifically? A scientific worker stands amidst certain facts that he knows, or thinks he knows somewhat, and he confronts these facts with a certain attitude, but if his attitude is wrong, then all of his efforts toward a superior establishment of fact will not avail. There seemed to us, who were Skinnerians 30-odd years ago, glaring flaws, even dangers, in Hull's appraisal of where the experimental investigation of behavior then stood and in his sentiments about how it should be advanced. Skinner's ironically titled essay "Are Theories of Learning Necessary?" (1950) was aimed at Hull, and opposition arose from other quarters. The critique by Lashley & Wade (1946) was nearly scornful, and Koch's long, meticulous analysis (1954) was devastating on all counts. In a brief but closely reasoned review, Cotton (1955) showed that Hull's system could not yield testable predictions.

While Hull advertised that he was offering psychology a set of axioms and postulates from which theorems could be deduced, the logical character of the system was in fact nothing like Euclidean geometry. Its propositions are largely restatements of various experimental findings that are logically unconnected and independent, and from which further "theorems" cannot be deduced. This attempted axiomatic construction stands side by side with a second formalized development of a wholly different sort, which is an attempt to trace from stimulus impingement, completely through the organismic system, to certain response measures as the final output. Here is to be found Hull's famous, long chain of "intervening variables." Each variable is conceived as a real number on some scale—in each case a wholly invented scale except possibly the input and output scales—and the numbers are combined by algebraic relations into a single formula. The algebraic and axiomatic developments in Hull's theory have no obvious relationship to one another, except that each may be seen from a distance as an attempt to endow the theory with some kind of logical unity and coherence. The algebraic treatment should be understood as Hull's answer to the basic explanatory problem of scientific psychology: What happens between stimulus and response? This problem has been around since before the reflex, before Descartes, and even before Aristotle. Leaving aside genetic and evolutionary problems, it is possibly the *only* problem of explanatory psychology, under which all specific problems can be subsumed. For myself, I do not believe the problem has a single answer or a general answer, but an answer only for any particular species in a particular type of situation. In specific cases, everything we can possibly know about the organism inwards or outwards makes a contribution, and there can no more, I believe, be a complete answer in a given case than there can be a general answer at any chosen level of precision for all cases, that is, for all acts of all organisms. When I strive to understand what Hull was attempting to achieve in constructing his sequence of intervening variables, I have to conclude that it amounts to encompassing, preempting, and indeed displacing every other (partial) analysis of psychological phenomena before or since. Here, on the one hand we have Skinner, who tells us nothing about what happens between stimulus and response (and tells us not to be interested), and on the other hand we have Hull, who without adequate consciousness of what he is postulating, in effect wants to tell us everything, and, moreover, tell it in quantitative terms. It is hard to say which of these approaches does greater violence to common sense and to ordinary psychological understanding. Is it less self-defeating to advocate the generalized empty organism as one's official thesis or to fill the empty organism with just six or seven or ten artificial variables in order to account for its astronomical complexity, its astounding subtlety and variation of function?

Fortunately, as we all know and should be quite willing to declare, no one who is in full possession of his powers of judgment is obligated to accept either Skinner's or Hull's radical ideas about psychology. For the most part, without making a great fuss about it, the majority of psychologists now active understand, for example, that there is a great deal more to human and animal learning than reinforcement of overt behavior or conditioning more generally. What people acquire through experience consists of more than respondents and operants; they learn concepts, rules, schemata, attitudes, and roles, and they learn these thousand things through observation, imitation, deliberate instruction, inference, and so on. It is once again becoming widely recognized that human psychological organization and dynamics simply cannot be encompassed by the limited range of descriptive and explanatory concepts afforded by either of the neobehaviorisms we have been considering. The basic question actually is whether any single system can ever encompass the full rich range of psychological fact. Can the thoughts, the general principles, of any one distinctive school even provide a sufficient initial orientation to these facts? Yet, if all that is demanded of a system is just an orientation (and the prominent neobehaviorisms have prom-

ised a great deal more), then the generic behaviorist approach operates under such severe self-imposed restrictions that it very quickly fails to meet even that modest demand. In my view (and mine is far from an original opinion), the failure is grounded in the behaviorist's or the neobehaviorist's narrow perception of what a psychological phenomenon is. Less important is his predilection for a certain kind of explanation of phenomena—that is, associationist, environmentalist, peripheralist, elementarist, etc. The behaviorist starts out by seeing fewer types and levels of psychological phenomena than the man in the street sees without any formal instruction whatever. The common man can recognize that this thing he is considering is an image, this is a dream, this is a belief, or a hypothesis, an attitude, an inference, or any one of a hundred other sorts of psychological formation or process.

The ability to perform these recognitions and to use psychological concepts with some efficiency and accuracy is a very elaborate ability everyone absorbs from the culture by various routes that no analyst of cognition has as yet sufficiently described. It ought to be appreciated that every more formal, developed scientific psychology is erected upon the platform of the concepts embodied in ordinary language and is engaged in carrying such understandings to a higher level of differentiation and perfection. But the business of the behavioristic theorist consists to a large extent of dedifferentiating the ordinary store of psychological concepts and dismantling the apparatus of common sense; he wishes to substitute a fewer number of very general and actually quite vague ideas (such as operant behavior, reinforcement, response strength, etc.) for a much greater number of more specialized ones that have evolved through eons of cultural experience. I am not sure that contemporary psychologists are clearly and articulately aware of the nature of the cognitive maneuver that behavioristic theory requires them to execute, nor of its intellectual cost; but in the practice of psychology, whether in the laboratory or the field, they resiliently continue to employ the essential concepts that the phenomena demand. Such a very active field as memory, for example, has been enriched by new concepts about stages and types of memorial structures built upon old ideas made more precise by probing research; this example could be endlessly multiplied. Each field acquires an array of principles exactly appropriate to it, while the sweeping methodological strictures of operationistic molar behaviorism continue to lose their once persuasive force. Nothing holds back the various authentic analyses of behavior that have been proceeding since the dawn of psychology.

Skinner's analysis of behavior is a special analysis, not a general one; it focuses on certain kinds of relations between action and environment that had not been adequately attended to in previous investigations, and thereby it makes a significant and permanent contribution to the understanding of the whole. The distinctive aspects of Hull's theoretical work similarly cannot be judged as valueless, for they include a number of primordial exercises in the quantitative analysis of behavior. It is probably a safe prophecy that Skinner's influence upon psychological thought and theory will, for many reasons, outlast that of Hull, but it is a much safer prediction that Skinner's influence will be felt in the active affairs of civilization long after the Skinnerian phase of psychology has ended and long after scientific psychology as a whole has accommodated the special contributions of Skinnerian science.

REFERENCE NOTE

1 Skinner, B. F., & Lindsley, O. R. *Studies in behavior therapy. Status reports II and III* (Contract NS-ORI-7662). Arlington, Va.: Office of Naval Research, 1954.

REFERENCES

Bush, R. R., & Mosteller, F. *Stochastic models for learning.* New York: Wiley, 1955.

Chaplin, J. P., & Krawiec, T. S. *Systems and theories of psychology* (3rd ed.). New York: Holt, Rinehart & Winston, 1974.

Cotton, J. W. On making predictions from Hull's theory. *Psychological Review,* 1955, *62,* 303–314.

Estes, W. K. The statistical approach to learning theory. In S. Koch (Ed.), *Psychology: A study of a science* (Vol. 2). New York: McGraw-Hill, 1959.

Hull, C. L. *Principles of behavior.* New York: Appleton-Century, 1943.

Hull, C. L. *Essentials of behavior.* New Haven, Conn.: Yale University Press, 1951.

Hull, C. L. *A behavior system.* New Haven, Conn.: Yale University Press, 1952.

Koch, S. Clark Hull. In W. K. Estes et al., *Modern learning theory; A critical analysis of five examples.* New York: Appleton-Century-Crofts, 1954.

Krantz, D. L. Schools and systems: The mutual isolation of operant and non-operant psychology as a case study. *Journal of the History of the Behavioral Sciences,* 1972, *8,* 86–102.

Lashley, K. S., & Wade, M. The Pavlovian theory of generalization. *Psychological Review,* 1946, *53,* 72–87.

Robinson, D. B. *The 100 most important people in the world today.* New York: Putnam, 1970.

Sherman, A. R. *Behavior modification, theory and practice.* Monterey, Calif.: Brooks/Cole, 1973.

Skinner, B. F. *The behavior of organisms.* New York: Appleton-Century, 1938.

Skinner, B. F. *Walden two.* New York: Crowell-Collier-Macmillan, 1948.

Skinner, B. F. Are theories of learning necessary? *Psychological Review,* 1950, *57,* 193–216.

Skinner, B. F. *Verbal behavior.* New York: Appleton-Century-Crofts, 1957.

Skinner, B. F. *Beyond freedom and dignity.* New York: Knopf, 1971.

Skinner, B. F. *About behaviorism.* New York: Knopf, 1974.

Spaulding, S. (Ed.). *Programmed instruction: An international directory.* Pittsburgh: International Education Clearinghouse, University of Pittsburgh, 1967. (Paris: UNESCO, 1967)

UNESCO. *International directory of programmed instruction.* Paris: UNESCO, 1973.

Wolpe, J. *The practice of behavior therapy.* New York: Pergamon, 1969.

CHAPTER 15

PSYCHOANALYSIS

As Clark University in Worcester, Massachusetts, approached its twentieth anniversary, its president, G. Stanley Hall, was busy planning an academic gathering that is unique in the history of psychology (see Cromer & Anderson, 1970; Evans & Koelsch, 1985). Hall had wanted Wundt to visit the United States and give a special anniversary lecture, but Wundt declined, saying that he was committed to speaking at his own university in Leipzig, which would celebrate its five hundredth anniversary that same year. Even without Wundt, the 1909 gathering at Clark was an impressive one. William James was there, as was E. B. Titchener. Other dignitaries included William Stern, Franz Boaz, Joseph Jastrow, James McKeen Cattell, Carl Seashore, and Carl Gustav Jung. The featured speaker at the conference was a 53-year-old physician from Vienna in his only visit to the United States—Sigmund Freud (1856–1939). Freud gave five public lectures at that conference, which were published later in the *American Journal of Psychology* (Freud, 1910). In those lectures he traced the intellectual history of his theory and method of psychoanalysis, giving initial credit to the work of another Viennese physician, Joseph Breuer (1842–1925), whose most famous case Freud described to his American audience:

> Dr. Breuer's patient was a girl of twenty-one, of a high degree of intelligence. She had developed in the course of her two years' illness a series of physical and mental disturbances which well deserved to be taken seriously. She had a severe paralysis of both right extremities, with anesthesia, and at times the same affection of the members of the left side of the body, disturbance of eye-movements, and much impairment of vision; difficulty in maintaining the position of the head, an intense *Tussis nervosa,* nausea when she attempted to take nourishment, and at one time for sev-

eral weeks a loss of the power to drink, in spite of tormenting thirst. Her power of speech diminished, and this progressed so far that she could neither speak nor understand her mother tongue; and finally, she was subject to states of "absence," of confusion, delirium, alteration of her whole personality. (Freud, 1910, p. 184)

This case history belongs to the most renowned patient in the history of psychoanalysis, a woman called "Anna O." Breuer had treated Anna during the period 1880–1882, at one time seeing her every day for a year. The hysterical symptoms described above were, according to Breuer, eliminated one by one until Anna was totally cured. This cure had been brought about by having Anna relive the experiences that had led to her symptoms, either by talking about them naturally or while in a hypnotic state. For example, she noted that her aversion to drinking water was similar to an aversion she had experienced as a child when she saw a dog drinking water from a glass. Once she had discussed this earlier incident with Breuer, the drinking aversion disappeared. Breuer referred to these cures as *cathartic*—the symptoms were reduced or eliminated through the release of the patient's pent-up anxiety.

Breuer had discussed this case with Freud, who viewed the cathartic method as an important tool in treating hysteria. Their friendship grew, and eventually they collaborated on a book published in 1895, entitled *Studies in Hysteria,* a book that some historians regard as the beginning of psychoanalysis (e.g., Kendler, 1987; Schultz & Schultz, 1987). The book contained five case studies, including that of Anna O. The importance of that case cannot be overstated; it was viewed as "the prototype of a cathartic cure and one of the basic occurrences that led Freud to the creation of psychoanalysis" (Ellenberger, 1972, p. 267).

Breuer was not the only important influence on Freud in the latter part of the nineteenth century; recall from Chapter 5 that Jean Martin Charcot exerted substantial influence in the four and one-half months that Freud studied with him in late 1885 and early 1886. Using nonhysterical patients, Charcot was able to demonstrate that under hypnosis, they could be made to exhibit the convincing physical symptoms of hysteria. That meant that conditions of the body could definitely be altered by conditions of the mind, an important realization for Freud's growing interest in psychiatry. Charcot's other principal influence on Freud was the result of a casual remark suggesting that sexual problems were the underlying cause of hysteria. Freud's emphasis on sex as a causative agent of paramount importance in neuroses led to the dissolution of his friendship with Breuer (Sulloway, 1979).

In developing his method of therapy, Freud eventually abandoned hypnosis, a technique that had figured prominently in the work of both Breuer and Charcot. He found that some subjects were very difficult to hypnotize and that, in fact, he was able to get valuable insights into a patient's behavior simply by having the patient talk spontaneously about anything that came to mind, a technique we know as *free association*. The free associations of Freud's patients were often shocking to him, as they frequently described sexual seductions by their parents, usually the father, when they were very young. Freud decided that sexual abuse of children by their parents was much more common than anyone had imagined, and these patient revelations reinforced his belief in sex as a principal cause of neurosis. But then he had an insight that was to alter radically his interpretation of those events; the stories of sexual seduction revealed by his patients were, for the most part, just that—stories! They were fantasies of desired but not actual encounters (a fact disputed by at least one contemporary writer—see Masson, 1984).

Freud's emphasis on sex as an etiologic agent was not altered by this new interpretation. It made him even more aware of the powerful role of unconscious processes as determinants of behavior. He understood that for his patients, fantasy and reality were not easily distinguished. When reality was too difficult to face, the mind would create its own version of that reality, which Freud called *psychic reality*. The chief goal of psychoanalysis was to expose the psychic reality for the distortion that it was and to help the patient understand and accept the actual reality. These insights led to the development of Freud's view of personality, as well as to the refinement of his therapeutic technique of psychoanalysis, ideas that were defined more fully in what Freud and many historians regard as his most important book, *The Interpretation of Dreams* (1900).

The impetus for that book was Freud's own self-analysis, which he began in 1896. Realizing that he could not use the technique of free association for such an analysis, he began to make a record of his dreams to use in that task. A year earlier Freud began to argue for the significance of dreams as wish fulfillments. He regarded that insight as so important that he recorded the date of its occurrence: "In this House on July 24, 1895 the Secret of Dreams was revealed to Dr. Sigmund Freud" (E. Freud, 1960). He understood the value of dreams as the "royal road to the unconscious" and had used dream analysis with his patients.

The dream as told by the patient and Freud's recall of his own dreams were called the *manifest content* of the dream. But such content was the subject of dream recall in the waking state, when a person's defenses would be fully operative. The real meaning of the dream lay in what Freud called its *latent content*. It was there that the repressed wishes would be found. One of the repressed wishes first discussed in this famous book was the Oedipus complex, an idea that generated considerable controversy.

Freud's masterpiece on dreams was followed by the publication of *The Psychopathology of Everyday Life* (1901), a book that illustrated how slips of the tongue (*Freudian slips*), simple mistakes, and temporary losses of memory were actually revelations of unconscious conflicts. Thus, like the latent content of dreams, these everyday "errors" could give important insight into a person's personality. Four years later Freud published *Three Essays on the Theory of Sexuality* (1905), a book that further defined his ideas on psychoanalysis as a theory of personality, with particular emphasis on his growing realization of the nature of infantile sexuality.

In the brief introduction to this chapter it is simply not possible to cover much of the complexity and diversity of Freud's contributions in a life that spanned

83 years. No person since Darwin has so radically affected our intellectual world. Freud's ideas have found expression not only in psychology and psychiatry but also in art, literature, drama, education, and the actions of everyday life. He was in his time, and continues to be, a figure of substantial controversy. Some of his ideas have been discarded in the light of contemporary psychological knowledge, but many contributions remain. Through his work he (1) focused awareness on unconscious processes in behavior, (2) defined a variety of defense mechanisms, such as repression, and showed how those are used as coping responses, (3) made the world cognizant of the importance of early experiences as determinants of later personality and adjustment, (4) helped to bring human sexuality out of its Victorian darkness, and (5) generated great public interest in the questions of psychology, an interest that continues today.

The readings in this chapter have been chosen to focus on the origin of psychoanalysis as theory and method. The initial selection is from Freud's *Interpretation of Dreams* and deals with the method of dream interpretation and dreams as wish fulfillments.

The next selection concerns the reaction to that book by the educated German public. In that article, Hannah S. Decker, a historian of medicine and psychoanalysis, describes her research in the archives and newspaper files of Germany. She refutes earlier claims about the disinterested reception of Freud's famous book, arguing instead that the public reaction was largely an appreciative one.

The final selection, an example of historical detective work at its best, is authored by H. F. Ellenberger, whose work on Charcot is included in Chapter 5. In this article Ellenberger dramatically revises the interpretation of the case of Anna O, relying heavily on a newly discovered document—a case report on Anna O written by Breuer in 1882. That report and Breuer's later account in the book he coauthored with Freud give very different versions of the case. Ellenberger concludes that in the treatment of Anna O both the catharsis and the cure are questionable.

Collectively the articles in this chapter illustrate the beginning formalization of psychoanalytic thought and how the history of those ideas continues to change in the light of new evidence. But they are only a beginning to the richness of that history. For those readers interested in additional material, two sources are recommended: the biography of Freud by his disciple Ernest Jones (1961) and a more recent Freud biography by Frank J. Sulloway (1979) that documents the great influence of Darwin on Freud's thinking.

REFERENCES

Breuer, J., & Freud, S. (1895). *Studien über Hysterie*. Vienna: Franz Deuticke.

Cromer, W., & Anderson, P. A. (1970). Freud's visit to America: Newspaper coverage. *Journal of the History of the Behavioral Sciences, 6,* 349–353.

Ellenberger, H. F. (1972). The story of "Anna O": A critical review with new data. *Journal of the History of the Behavioral Sciences, 8,* 267–279.

Evans, R. B., & Koelsch, W. (1985). Psychoanalysis arrives in America: The 1909 psychology conference at Clark University. *American Psychologist, 40,* 942–948.

Freud, E. (1960). *The letters of Sigmund Freud.* New York: Basic Books.

Freud, S. (1900). *The interpretation of dreams.* Available from Avon Books, New York, 1968.

Freud, S. (1901). *The psychopathology of everyday life.* Available from Avon Books, New York, 1965.

Freud, S. (1905). *Three essays on the theory of sexuality.* Available from Avon Books, New York, 1962.

Freud, S. (1910). The origin and development of psychoanalysis. *American Journal of Psychology, 21,* 181–218.

Jones, E. (1961). *The life and work of Sigmund Freud.* New York: Basic Books.

Kendler, H. H. (1987). *Historical foundations of modern psychology.* Chicago: Dorsey Press.

Masson, J. M. (1984). *The assault on truth: Freud's suppression of the seduction theory.* New York: Farrar Straus Giroux.

Schultz, D. P., & Schultz, S. E. (1987). *A history of modern psychology* (4th ed.). San Diego: Harcourt Brace Jovanovich.

Sulloway, F. J. (1979). *Freud: Biologist of the mind.* New York: Basic Books.

The Method of Dream Interpretation

Sigmund Freud

I shall...select one of my own dreams for the purpose of elucidating my method of interpretation. Every such dream necessitates a preliminary statement; so that I must now beg the reader to make my interests his own for a time, and to become absorbed, with me, in the most trifling details of my life; for an interest in the hidden significance of dreams imperatively demands just such a transference.

PRELIMINARY STATEMENT

In the summer of 1895 I had treated psychoanalytically a young lady who was an intimate friend of mine and of my family. It will be understood that such complicated relations may excite manifold feelings in the physician, and especially the psychotherapist. The personal interest of the physician is greater, but his authority less. If he fails, his friendship with the patient's relatives is in danger of being undermined. In this case, however, the treatment ended in partial success; the patient was cured of her hysterical anxiety, but not of all her somatic symptoms. At that time I was not yet quite sure of the criteria which denote the final cure of an hysterical case, and I expected her to accept a solution which did not seem acceptable to her. In the midst of this disagreement we discontinued the treatment for the summer holidays. One day a younger colleague, one of my most intimate friends, who had visited the patient—Irma—and her family in their country residence, called upon me. I asked him how Irma was, and received the reply: "She is better, but not quite

well." I realize that these words of my friend Otto's, or the tone of voice in which they were spoken, annoyed me. I thought I heard a reproach in the words, perhaps to the effect that I had promised the patient too much, and—rightly or wrongly—I attributed Otto's apparent "taking sides" against me to the influence of the patient's relatives, who, I assumed, had never approved of my treatment. This disagreeable impression, however, did not become clear to me, nor did I speak of it. That same evening I wrote the clinical history of Irma's case, in order to give it, as though to justify myself, to Dr. M., a mutual friend, who was at that time the leading personality in our circle. During the night (or rather in the early morning) I had the following dream, which I recorded immediately after waking:

DREAM OF JULY 23–24, 1895

A great hall—a number of guests, whom we are receiving—among them Irma, whom I immediately take aside, as though to answer her letter, and to reproach her for not yet accepting the "solution." I say to her: "If you still have pains, it is really only your own fault."—She answers: "If you only knew what pains I have now in the throat, stomach, and abdomen—I am choked by them." I am startled, and look at her. She looks pale and puffy. I think that after all I must be overlooking some organic affection. I take her to the window and look into her throat. She offers some resistance to this, like a woman who has a set of false teeth. I think, surely, she doesn't need them.—The mouth then opens wide, and I find a large white spot on the right, and elsewhere I see extensive grayish-white scabs adhering to curiously curled formations, which are evidently shaped like the turbinal bones of the nose.—I quickly call Dr. M., who repeats the examination and confirms it....Dr. M. looks quite unlike his usual self; he is very pale, he limps, and his chin is clean-shaven. . . . Now my friend Otto, too, is standing beside her, and my friend Leopold percusses her covered chest, and says: "She has a dullness below, on the left," and also calls attention to an infiltrated portion of skin on the left shoulder (which I can feel, in spite of the dress). . . . M. says: "There's no doubt that it's an infection, but it doesn't matter; dysentery will follow and the poison will be eliminated." . . . We know, too, precisely how the infection originated. My friend Otto, not long ago, gave her, when she was feeling unwell, an injection of a preparation of propyl . . . propyls . . . propionic acid . . . trimethylamin (the formula of which I see before me, printed in heavy type). . . . One doesn't give such injections so rashly. . . . Probably, too, the syringe was not clean.

This dream has an advantage over many others. It is at once obvious to what events of the preceding day it is related, and of what subject it treats. The preliminary statement explains these matters. The news of Irma's health which I had received from Otto, and the clinical history, which I was writing late into the night, had occupied my psychic activities even during sleep. Nevertheless, no one who had read the preliminary report, and had knowledge of the content of the dream, could guess what the dream signified. Nor do I myself know. I am puzzled by the morbid symptoms of which Irma complains in the dream, for they are not the symptoms for which I treated her. I smile at the nonsensical idea of an injection of propionic acid, and at Dr. M.'s attempt at consolation. Towards the end the dream seems more obscure and quicker in tempo than at the beginning. In order to learn the significance of all these details I resolve to undertake an exhaustive analysis.

ANALYSIS

The hall—a number of guests, whom we are receiving. We were living that summer at *Bellevue,* an isolated house on one of the hills adjoining the Kahlenberg. This house was originally built as a place of entertainment, and therefore has unusually lofty, hall-like rooms. The dream was dreamed in *Bellevue,* a few days before my wife's birthday. During the day my wife had mentioned that she expected several friends, and among them Irma, to come to us as guests for her birthday. My dream, then, anticipates this situation: It is my wife's birthday, and we are receiving a number of people, among them Irma, as guests in the large hall of *Bellevue.*

I reproach Irma for not having accepted the "solution," I say, "If you still have pains, it is really your own fault." I might even have said this while awake; I may have actually said it. At that time I was of the opinion (recognized later to be incorrect) that my task was limited to informing patients of the hidden meaning of their symptoms. Whether they then accepted or did not accept the solution upon which success depended—for that I was not responsible. I am grateful to this error, which, fortunately, has now been overcome, since it made life easier for me at a time when, with all my unavoidable ignorance, I was expected to effect successful cures. But I note that in the speech which I make to Irma in the dream I am above all anxious that I shall not be blamed for the pains which she still suffers. If it is Irma's own fault, it cannot be mine. Should the purpose of the dream be looked for in this quarter?

Irma's complaints—pains in the neck, abdomen, and stomach; she is choked by them. Pains in the stomach belonged to the symptom-complex of my patient, but they were not very prominent; she complained rather of qualms and a feeling of nausea. Pains in the neck and abdomen and constriction of the throat played hardly any part in her case. I wonder why I have decided upon this choice of symptoms in the dream; for the moment I cannot discover the reason.

She looks pale and puffy. My patient had always a rosy complexion. I suspect that here another person is being substituted for her.

I am startled at the idea that I may have overlooked some organic affection. This, as the reader will readily believe, is a constant fear with the specialist who sees neurotics almost exclusively, and who is accustomed to ascribe to hysteria so many manifestations which other physicians treat as organic. On the other hand, I am haunted by a faint doubt—I do not know whence it comes—whether my alarm is altogether honest. If Irma's pains are indeed of organic origin, it is not my duty to cure them. My treatment, of course, removes only hysterical pains. It seems to me, in fact, that I wish to find an error in the diagnosis; for then I could not be reproached with failure to effect a cure.

I take her to the window in order to look into her throat. She resists a little, like a woman who has false teeth. I think to myself, she does not need them. I had never had occasion to inspect Irma's oral cavity. The incident in the dream reminds me of an examination, made some time before, of a governess who at first produced an impression of youthful beauty, but who, upon opening her mouth, took certain measures to conceal her denture. Other memories of medical examinations, and of petty secrets revealed by them, to the embarrassment of both physician and patient, associate themselves with this case.—''She surely does not need them,'' is perhaps in the first place a compliment to Irma; but I suspect yet another meaning. In a careful analysis one is able to feel whether or not the *arrière-pensées* which are to be expected have all been exhausted. The way in which Irma stands at the window suddenly reminds me of another experience. Irma has an intimate woman friend of whom I think very highly. One evening, on paying her a visit, I found her at the window in the position reproduced in the dream, and her physician, the same Dr. M., declared that she had a diphtheritic membrane. The person of Dr. M. and the membrane return, indeed, in the course of the dream. Now it occurs to me that during the past few months I have had every reason to suppose that this lady too is hysterical. Yes, Irma herself betrayed the fact to me. But what do I know of her condition? Only the one thing, that

like Irma in the dream she suffers from hysterical choking. Thus, in the dream I have replaced my patient by her friend. Now I remember that I have often played with the supposition that this lady, too, might ask me to relieve her of her symptoms. But even at the time I thought it improbable, since she is extremely reserved. She *resists,* as the dream shows. Another explanation might be that *she does not need it;* in fact, until now she has shown herself strong enough to master her condition without outside help. Now only a few features remain, which I can assign neither to Irma nor to her friend; pale, puffy, false teeth. The false teeth led me to the governess; I now feel inclined to be satisfied with bad teeth. Here another person, to whom these features may allude, occurs to me. She is not my patient, and I do not wish her to be my patient, for I have noticed that she is not at her ease with me, and I do not consider her a docile patient. She is generally pale, and once, when she had not felt particularly well, she was puffy.* I have thus compared my patient Irma with two others, who would likewise resist treatment. What is the meaning of the fact that I have exchanged her for her friend in the dream? Perhaps that I wish to exchange her; either her friend arouses in me stronger sympathies, or I have a higher regard for her intelligence. For I consider Irma foolish because she does not accept my solution. The other woman would be more sensible, and would thus be more likely to yield. *The mouth then opens readily;* she would tell more than Irma.†

* The complaint of pains in the abdomen, as yet unexplained, may also be referred to this third person. It is my own wife, of course, who is in question; the abdominal pains remind me of one of the occasions on which her shyness became evident to me. I must admit that I do not treat Irma and my wife very gallantly in this dream, but let it be said, in my defence, that I am measuring both of them against the ideal of the courageous and docile female patient.

† I suspect that the interpretation of this portion has not been carried far enough to follow every hidden meaning. If I were to continue the comparison of the three women, I should go far afield. Every dream has at least one point at which it is unfathomable; a central point, as it were, connecting it with the unknown.

What I see in the throat: a white spot and scabby turbinal bones. The white spot recalls diphtheria, and thus Irma's friend, but it also recalls the grave illness of my eldest daughter two years earlier, and all the anxiety of that unhappy time. The scab on the turbinal bones reminds me of my anxiety concerning my own health. At that time I frequently used cocaine in order to suppress distressing swellings in the nose, and I had heard a few days previously that a lady patient who did likewise had contracted an extensive necrosis of the nasal mucous membrane. In 1885 it was I who had recommended the use of cocaine, and I had been gravely reproached in consequence. A dear friend, who had died before the date of this dream, had hastened his end by the misuse of this remedy.

I quickly call Dr. M., who repeats the examination. This would simply correspond to the position which M. occupied among us. But the word "quickly" is striking enough to demand a special examination. It reminds me of a sad medical experience. By continually prescribing a drug (sulphonal), which at that time was still considered harmless, I was once responsible for a condition of acute poisoning in the case of a woman patient, and hastily turned for assistance to my older and more experienced colleague. The fact that I really had this case in mind is confirmed by a subsidiary circumstance. The patient, who succumbed to the toxic effects of the drug, bore the same name as my eldest daughter. I had never thought of this until now; but now it seems to me almost like a retribution of fate— as though the substitution of persons had to be continued in another sense: this Matilda for that Matilda; an eye for an eye, a tooth for a tooth. It is as though I were seeking every opportunity to reproach myself for a lack of medical conscientiousness.

Dr. M. is pale; his chin is shaven, and he limps. Of this so much is correct, that his unhealthy appearance often arouses the concern of his friends. The other two characteristics must belong to another person. An elder brother living abroad occurs to me, for he, too, shaves his chin, and if I remember him rightly, the M. of the dream bears on the whole a certain resemblance to him. And some days previously the news arrived that he was limping on account of an arthritic affection of the hip. There must be some reason why I fuse the two persons into one in my dream. I remember that, in fact, I was on bad terms with both of them for similar reasons. Both had rejected a certain proposal which I had recently made them.

My friend Otto is now standing next to the patient, and my friend Leopold examines her and calls attention to a dullness low down on the left side. My friend Leopold also is a physician, and a relative of Otto's. Since the two practise the same speciality, fate has made them competitors, so that they are constantly being compared with one another. Both of them assisted me for years, while I was still directing a public clinic for neurotic children. There, scenes like that reproduced in my dream had often taken place. While I would be discussing the diagnosis of a case with Otto, Leopold would examine the child anew and make an unexpected contribution towards our decision. There was a difference of character between the two men like that between Inspector Brasig and his friend Karl. Otto was remarkably prompt and alert; Leopold was slow and thoughtful, but thorough. If I contrast Otto and the cautious Leopold in the dream I do so, apparently, in order to extol Leopold. The comparison is like that made above between the disobedient patient Irma and her friend, who was believed to be more sensible. I now become aware of one of the tracks along which the association of ideas in the dream proceeds: from the sick child to the children's clinic. Concerning the dullness low on the left side, I have the impression that it corresponds with a certain case of which all the details were similar, a case in which Leopold impressed me by his thoroughness. I thought vaguely, too, of something like a metastatic affection, but it might also be a reference to the patient whom I should have liked to have in

Irma's place. For this lady, as far as I can gather, exhibited symptoms which imitated tuberculosis.

An infiltrated portion of skin on the left shoulder. I know at once that this is my own rheumatism of the shoulder, which I always feel if I lie awake long at night. The very phrasing of the dream sounds ambiguous: "Something which I can feel, as he does, in spite of the dress." "Feel on my own body" is intended. Further, it occurs to me how unusual the phrase "infiltrated portion of skin" sounds. We are accustomed to the phrase: "an infiltration of the upper posterior left"; this would refer to the lungs, and thus, once more, to tuberculosis.

In spite of the dress. This, to be sure, is only an interpolation. At the clinic the children were, of course, examined undressed; here we have some contrast to the manner in which adult female patients have to be examined. The story used to be told of an eminent physician that he always examined his patients through their clothes. The rest is obscure to me; I have, frankly, no inclination to follow the matter further.

Dr. M. says: "It's an infection, but it doesn't matter; dysentery will follow, and the poison will be eliminated." This, at first, seems to me ridiculous; nevertheless, like everything else, it must be carefully analysed; more closely observed it seems after all to have a sort of meaning. What I had found in the patient was a local diphtheritis. I remember the discussion about diphtheritis and diphtheria at the time of my daughter's illness. Diphtheria is the general infection which proceeds from local diphtheritis. Leopold demonstrates the existence of such a general infection by the dullness, which also suggests a metastatic focus. I believe, however, that just this kind of metastasis does not occur in the case of diphtheria. It reminds me rather of pyaemia.

It doesn't matter is a consolation. I believe it fits in as follows: The last part of the dream has yielded a content to the effect that the patient's sufferings are the result of a serious organic affection. I begin to suspect that by this I am only trying to shift the blame from myself. Psychic treatment cannot be held responsible for the continued presence of a diphtheritic affection. Now, indeed, I am distressed by the thought of having invented such a serious illness for Irma, for the sole purpose of exculpating myself. It seems so cruel. Accordingly, I need the assurance that the outcome will be benign, and it seems to me that I made a good choice when I put the words that consoled me into the mouth of Dr. M. But here I am placing myself in a position of superiority to the dream; a fact which needs explanation.

But why is this consolation so nonsensical? *Dysentery.* Some sort of far-fetched theoretical notion that the toxins of disease might be eliminated through the intestines. Am I thereby trying to make fun of Dr. M.'s remarkable store of far-fetched explanations, his habit of conceiving curious pathological relations? Dysentery suggests something else. A few months ago I had in my care a young man who was suffering from remarkable intestinal troubles; a case which had been treated by other colleagues as one of "anaemia with malnutrition." I realized that it was a case of hysteria; I was unwilling to use my psychotherapy on him, and sent him off on a sea-voyage. Now a few days previously I had received a despairing letter from him; he wrote from Egypt, saying that he had had a fresh attack, which the doctor had declared to be dysentery. I suspect that the diagnosis is merely an error on the part of an ignorant colleague, who is allowing himself to be fooled by the hysteria; yet I cannot help reproaching myself for putting the invalid in a position where he might contract some organic affection of the bowels in addition to his hysteria. Furthermore, dysentery sounds not unlike diphtheria, a word which does not occur in the dream.

Yes, it must be the case that with the consoling prognosis, "Dysentery will develop, etc.," I am making fun of Dr. M., for I recollect that years ago he once jestingly told a very similar story of a colleague. He had been called in to consult with him in the case of a woman who was very seriously ill, and he felt obliged to confront his colleague, who seemed very hopeful, with the fact that he found albumen in the patient's urine. His colleague, however, did not allow this to worry him, but answered calmly: "*That does not matter,* my dear sir; the albumen will soon be excreted!" Thus I can no longer doubt that this part of the dream expresses derision for those of my colleagues who are ignorant of hysteria. And, as though in confirmation, the thought enters my mind: "Does Dr. M. know that the appearances in Irma's friend, his patient, which gave him reason to fear tuberculosis, are likewise due to hysteria? Has he recognized this hysteria, or has he allowed himself to be fooled?"

But what can be my motive in treating this friend so badly? That is simple enough: Dr. M. agrees with my solution as little as does Irma herself. Thus, in this dream I have already revenged myself on two persons: on Irma in the words, "If you still have pains, it is your own fault," and on Dr. M. in the wording of the nonsensical consolation which has been put into his mouth.

We know precisely how the infection originated. This precise knowledge in the dream is remarkable. Only a moment before this we did not yet know of the infection, since it was first demonstrated by Leopold.

My friend Otto gave her an injection not long ago, when she was feeling unwell. Otto had actually related during his short visit to Irma's family that he had been called in to a neighbouring hotel in order to give an injection to someone who had been suddenly taken ill. Injections remind me once more of the unfortunate friend who poisoned himself with cocaine. I had recommended the remedy for internal use only during the withdrawal of morphia; but he immediately gave himself injections of cocaine.

With a preparation of propyl...propyls... propionic acid. How on earth did this occur to me? On the evening of the day after I had written the clinical history and dreamed about the case, my wife opened a bottle of liqueur labelled

"Ananas,"* which was a present from our friend Otto. He had, as a matter of fact, a habit of making presents on every possible occasion; I hope he will some day be cured of this by a wife.† This liqueur smelt so strongly of fusel oil that I refused to drink it. My wife suggested: "We will give the bottle to the servants," and I, more prudent, objected, with the philanthropic remark: "They shan't be poisoned either." The smell of fusel oil (amyl...) has now apparently awakened my memory of the whole series: propyl, methyl, etc., which furnished the preparation of propyl mentioned in the dream. Here, indeed, I have effected a substitution: I dreamt of propyl after smelling amyl; but substitutions of this kind are perhaps permissible, especially in organic chemistry.

Trimethylamin. In the dream I see the chemical formula of this substance—which at all events is evidence of a great effort on the part of my memory—and the formula is even printed in heavy type, as though to distinguish it from the context as something of particular importance. And where does trimethylamin, thus forced on my attention, lead me? To a conversation with another friend, who for years has been familiar with all my germinating ideas, and I with his. At that time he had just informed me of certain ideas concerning a sexual chemistry, and had mentioned, among others, that he thought he had found in trimethylamin one of the products of sexual metabolism. This substance thus leads me to sexuality, the factor to which I attribute the greatest significance in respect of the origin of these nervous affections which I am trying to cure. My patient Irma is a young widow; if I am required to excuse my failure to cure her, I shall perhaps do best to refer to this condition, which her admirers would be glad to terminate. But in what a singular fashion such a dream

---

* "Ananas," moreover, has a remarkable assonance with the family name of my patient Irma.

† In this the dream did not turn out to be prophetic. But in another sense it proved correct, for the "unsolved" stomach pains, for which I did not want to be blamed, were the forerunners of a serious illness, due to gall-stones.

is fitted together! The friend who in my dream becomes my patient in Irma's place is likewise a young widow.

I surmise why it is that the formula of trimethylamin is so insistent in the dream. So many important things are centred about this one word: trimethylamin is an allusion, not merely to the all-important factor of sexuality, but also to a friend whose sympathy I remember with satisfaction whenever I feel isolated in my opinions. And this friend, who plays such a large part in my life: will he not appear yet again in the concatenation of ideas peculiar to this dream? Of course; he has a special knowledge of the results of affections of the nose and the sinuses, and has revealed to science several highly remarkable relations between the turbinal bones and the female sexual organs. (The three curly formations in Irma's throat.) I got him to examine Irma, in order to determine whether her gastric pains were of nasal origin. But he himself suffers from suppurative rhinitis, which gives me concern, and to this perhaps there is an allusion in pyaemia, which hovers before me in the metastasis of the dream.

One doesn't give such injections so rashly. Here the reproach of rashness is hurled directly at my friend Otto. I believe I had some such thought in the afternoon, when he seemed to indicate, by word and look, that he had taken sides against me. It was, perhaps: "How easily he is influenced; how irresponsibly he pronounces judgment." Further, the above sentence points once more to my deceased friend, who so irresponsibly resorted to cocaine injections. As I have said, I had not intended that injections of the drug should be taken. I note that in reproaching Otto I once more touch upon the story of the unfortunate Matilda, which was the pretext for the same reproach against me. Here, obviously, I am collecting examples of my conscientiousness, and also of the reverse.

Probably too the syringe was not clean. Another reproach directed at Otto, but originating elsewhere. On the previous day I happened to meet the son of an old lady of eighty-two, to whom I am obliged to give two injections of morphia daily. At present she is in the country, and I have heard that she is suffering from phlebitis. I immediately thought that this might be a case of infiltration caused by a dirty syringe. It is my pride that in two years I have not given her a single infiltration; I am always careful, of course, to see that the syringe is perfectly clean. For I am conscientious. From the phlebitis I return to my wife, who once suffered from thrombosis during a period of pregnancy, and now three related situations come to the surface in my memory, involving my wife, Irma, and the dead Matilda, whose identity has apparently justified my putting these three persons in one another's places.

I have now completed the interpretation of the dream. In the course of this interpretation I have taken great pains to avoid all those notions which must have been suggested by a comparison of the dream-content with the dream-thoughts hidden behind this content. Meanwhile the "meaning" of the dream has dawned upon me. I have noted an intention which is realized through the dream, and which must have been my motive in dreaming. The dream fulfils several wishes, which were awakened within me by the events of the previous evening (Otto's news, and the writing of the clinical history). For the result of the dream is, that it is not I who am to blame for the pain which Irma is still suffering, but that Otto is to blame for it. Now Otto has annoyed me by his remark about Irma's imperfect cure; the dream avenges me upon him, in that it turns the reproach upon himself. The dream acquits me of responsibility for Irma's condition, as it refers this condition to other causes (which do, indeed, furnish quite a number of explanations). The dream represents a certain state of affairs, such as I might wish to exist; *the content of the dream is thus the fulfilment of a wish; its motive is a wish.*

This much is apparent at first sight. But many other details of the dream become intelligible when regarded from the standpoint of wish-fulfilment. I take my revenge on Otto, not merely for too readily taking sides against me, in that I accuse him of careless medical treatment (the injection), but I revenge myself also for the bad liqueur which smells of fusel oil, and I find an expression in the dream which unites both these reproaches: the injection of a preparation of propyl. Still I am not satisfied, but continue to avenge myself by comparing him with his more reliable colleague. Thereby I seem to say: "I like him better than you." But Otto is not the only person who must be made to feel the weight of my anger. I take my revenge on the disobedient patient, by exchanging her for a more sensible and more docile one. Nor do I pass over Dr. M.'s contradiction; for I express, in an obvious allusion, my opinion of him: namely, that his attitude in this case is that of an ignoramus ("Dysentery will develop, etc."). Indeed, it seems as though I were appealing from him to someone better informed (my friend, who told me about trimethylamin), just as I have turned from Irma to her friend, and from Otto to Leopold. It is as though I were to say: Rid me of these three persons, replace them by three others of my own choice, and I shall be rid of the reproaches which I am not willing to admit that I deserve! In my dream the unreasonableness of these reproaches is demonstrated for me in the most elaborate manner. Irma's pains are not attributable to me, since she herself is to blame for them, in that she refuses to accept my solution. They do not concern me, for being as they are of an organic nature, they cannot possibly be cured by psychic treatment.—Irma's sufferings are satisfactorily explained by her widowhood (trimethylamin!); a state which I cannot alter.—Irma's illness has been caused by an incautious injection administered by Otto, an injection of an unsuitable drug, such as I should never have administered.—Irma's complaint is the result of an injection made with an unclean syringe, like the phlebitis of my old lady patient, whereas my injections have never caused any ill effects. I am aware that these explanations of Irma's illness, which unite in acquitting me, do not agree with one another;

that they even exclude one another. The whole plea—for this dream is nothing else—recalls vividly the defence offered by a man who was accused by his neighbour of having returned a kettle in a damaged condition. In the first place, he said, he had returned the kettle undamaged; in the second place it already had holes in it when he borrowed it; and in the third place, he had never borrowed it at all. A complicated defence, but so much the better; if only one of these three lines of defence is recognized as valid, the man must be acquitted.

Still other themes play a part in the dream, and their relation to my non-responsibility for Irma's illness is not so apparent: my daughter's illness, and that of a patient with the same name; the harmfulness of cocaine; the affection of my patient, who was traveling in Egypt; concern about the health of my wife; my brother, and Dr. M.; my own physical troubles, and anxiety concerning my absent friend, who is suffering from suppurative rhinitis. But if I keep all these things in view, they combine into a single train of thought, which might be labelled: concern for the health of myself and others; professional conscientiousness. I recall a vaguely disagreeable feeling when Otto gave me the news of Irma's condition. Lastly, I am inclined, after the event, to find an expression of this fleeting sensation in the train of thoughts which forms part of the dream. It is as though Otto had said to me: "You do not take your medical duties seriously enough; you are not conscientious; you do not perform what you promise." Thereupon this train of thought placed itself at my service, in order that I might give proof of my extreme conscientiousness, of my intimate concern about the health of my relatives, friends and patients. Curiously enough, there are also some painful memories in this material, which confirm the blame attached to Otto rather than my own exculpation. The material is apparently impartial, but the connection between this broader material, on which the dream is based, and the more limited theme from which emerges the wish to be innocent of Irma's illness, is, nevertheless, unmistakable.

I do not wish to assert that I have entirely revealed the meaning of the dream, or that my interpretation is flawless.

I could still spend much time upon it; I could draw further explanations from it, and discuss further problems which it seems to propound. I can even perceive the points from which further mental associations might be traced; but such considerations as are always involved in every dream of one's own prevent me from interpreting it farther. Those who are overready to condemn such reserve should make the experiment of trying to be more straightforward. For the present I am content with the one fresh discovery which has just been made: If the method of dream-interpretation here indicated is followed, it will be found that dreams do really possess a meaning, and are by no means the expression of a disintegrated cerebral activity, as the writers on the subject would have us believe. *When the work of interpretation has been completed the dream can be recognized as a wish-fulfilment.*

The Interpretation of Dreams: Early Reception by the Educated German Public

Hannah S. Decker

It is a commonly accepted notion that when Sigmund Freud's *The Interpretation of Dreams* first appeared it was barely noticed and, when noticed, regarded unappreciatively or even contemptuously.[1] But, by presenting some new evidence, I would like to show that, as far as the educated German[2] public was concerned, this is, on the whole, an erroneous belief. I shall also discuss the problem of why the initial enthusiastic response was not sustained.

I

Freud anticipated the worst and hoped for the unusual when his *Interpretation of Dreams* appeared in November, 1899. The week after its publication he wrote to his friend Wilhelm Fliess in Berlin: "the critics will find nothing better to do than to fasten on these pieces of carelessness"[3]— by which he meant his errors in identifying Schiller's birthplace and in naming Hannibal's father.

What he had actually hoped for was an immediate and resounding acclamation, though book reviews appeared no more promptly in 1900 than they do today. Six weeks after the publication of his dream book, Freud complained to Fliess that "the book has had just one notice, in the *Gegenwart*. As criticism it is empty and as a review inadequate. It is just a bad patchwork of my own fragments, but I forgive it everything because of the one word 'epoch-making.'" Obviously, Freud wanted no mere book review. Only a searching and intensive article would meet his criteria for a proper review. A week into the new year, Freud impatiently wrote that the new century had brought him nothing but "a stupid review in the *Zeit*." Two weeks after that he mentioned there were no new reviews.[4]

Two months later (March, 1900) Freud wrote to Fliess that "not a leaf has stirred to show that the interpretation of dreams meant anything to anyone." Twelve more days passed and Freud was equally gloomy:

> ...the reception it has had so far has not given me any pleasure. It has met with the most meagre understanding, any praise that has been bestowed has been as meagre as charity, most people clearly dislike it, and I have not yet seen any trace that anyone has detected what is important in it.[5]

Decker, H. S. (1975). *The Interpretation of Dreams:* Early reception by the educated German public. *Journal of the History of the Behavioral Sciences, 11,* 129–141. Copyright © 1975 by the Clinical Psychology Publishing Company. Reprinted by permission of the publisher.

July brought no change in Freud's outlook. He "[bewailed] the fate" of his book. "I have not heard of any more reviews, and the nice things said to me from time to time by people I meet annoy me more than the general silent condemnation."[6]

In October the subject rated only a postscript: "There was a review of the dream book in the *Münchner Allgemeine Zeitung* of October 12th."[7] Freud did not bother to elaborate that the review was enthusiastic and appreciative.

When Ernest Jones published the first volume of his definitive biography of Freud, he not only confirmed the dismal picture Freud had painted for Fliess, but darkened it. Where Freud had written "I was astonished to find a really friendly *feuilleton* article in a newspaper, the *Wiener Fremdenblatt* ..."[8] Jones merely said that a "short article" had been published. Jones listed five reviews of *The Interpretation of Dreams* in nonscientific periodicals in 1900 and 1901, summarily concluding "and that was all.... It was simply ignored."[9]

But a careful investigation of the German lay literature reveals quite another side to the reception accorded Freud's theories on dreams. For one thing, German reception of psychoanalysis must not be confused with its Viennese counterpart. Freud remained generally unaware of what was happening outside of Vienna and often had an inaccurate picture of his reception in the German-speaking world as a whole. Jones, at all times, not just in his discussion of the dream books, always underscored the negative aspects of Freud's reception.[10]

Actually, what happened was almost the reverse of what Freud and Jones said. And therein lies an historical problem. There was a satisfactory and appreciative response in the German lay literature to Freud's work on dreams. And in the period from 1893–1907,[11] the articles on dreams in German periodicals reached a high point in 1902.[12] This sudden spate of articles strongly suggests that an interest in dreams was stimulated by Freud's publications of 1900 and 1901. But the interest was not sustained and dropped off very

quickly after 1902. The question inevitably occurs: Why, in spite of the adequate and appreciative notice in many general periodicals to Freud's ideas about dreams, was there no continued attention to them afterwards? In my concluding remarks, I will suggest some possible answers to this question.

II

On the whole, scientific authorities of Freud's day believed that in dreams human mental activity is in a lower and less efficient state and that the higher intellectual faculties are suspended or gravely impaired. These scientists variously regarded dreams as psychic anarchisms, confusions of ideational life, crazy activity or degradations of the thinking and reasoning faculty. They used such adjectives as incoherent, absurd, nonsensical or senseless to describe dreams. A dream was considered by most scientists to be a somatic and not a psychic process; it was a bodily reaction to some somatic stimulus that had succeeded in disturbing sleep.[13]

But these ideas were not always shared by educated laymen. For one thing, laymen were more likely than scientists to have remained influenced by age-old popular ideas which ascribed meanings to dreams. For generations, dreams had been interpreted through fixed explanations: to dream of losing a tooth always meant the loss of a friend; dreams of funerals always meant forthcoming marriages.[14] Moreover, nonscientists did not have the same commitment to organic explanations of human functions as did scientists of the day. Romantic ideas (ca. 1780–1840) about the relationship between the psyche and dreams continued to influence many laymen, although physicians and psychologists who were Freud's contemporaries often harshly condemned these ideas.

As a result, Freud's dream theories received, on the whole, a much better reception at the hands of laymen than at the hands of doctors and psychologists (though there are important exceptions to this generalization as far as physicians are concerned). And it was not only those laymen who had read Freud who agreed with him. A basic agreement with Freud's outlook can be seen in essays on dreams written by laymen who seem to have had no knowledge of Freud's works.[15]

Because of these circumstances, it is not surprising that 80 percent of the lay response to Freud's theories about dreams was enthusiastic. This response was most usually either to *The Interpretation of Dreams* (issued in November, 1899 with a title page date of 1900) or to *On Dreams* (1901, published as a monograph in Leopold Löwenfeld's series, *Grenzfragen des Nerven- und Seelenlebens)*. When discussing "lay" reception of Freud's ideas on dreams, it is useful to make a distinction between reaction and exposure. When a physician reviewed Freud's work under the heading "Medicine" in a popular publication, the public was being *exposed* to psychoanalytic ideas. So too when Freud's followers presented their views. Actual *reaction* can only be gauged in the articles and reviews by laymen unaffiliated with medicine or psychoanalysis. At any rate, reaction far outshadowed exposure in the attention given to Freud's theories about dreams.

Not surprisingly, the theory that received the most attention was Freud's very basic premise that a dream is a fulfillment of a wish. Only one commentator disagreed with Freud's explanation. In his "Report on the Sciences" for the readers of the *Deutsche Revue,* the psychiatrist C. M. Giessler conceded that children's dreams are often wish dreams since the "feelings and aspirations of children generally push them towards the satisfaction of needs which mainly consist of wishes; but this is not the case with adults." Giessler strove to convince his lay readers that the dream is an "event that in all cases is unnecessary and in many cases is pathological." The dream state signified psychic decay, the retrogression of psychic and physiologic elements to earlier epochs of the life of individuals and of the species.[16] Obviously, if the dream

demonstrated "psychic decay," it could not be for Giessler the fulfillment of the mature adult's wish.

But Wilhelm Weygandt, also considered a medical expert on dreams, wrote that in many dream analyses Freud had made it "plausible" that dreams are the fulfillments of wishes.[17] Dr. Carl Oppenheimer in the weekly *Umschau* refrained from an opinion since he had not conducted his own studies and tests, but he concluded that Freud's views were "very ingenious [*geistvoll*] and the whole book very much worth reading." In the monthly *Türmer,* a public health specialist, Georg Korn, presented Freud's theory along with several others in a noncommittal review article.[18]

But not all doctors proffered Freud's views to their lay audiences in such reserved manner. Otto Lubarsch (1860–1933), one of Germany's most outstanding pathologists, reported to *Die Woche's* readers that "Freud's conception...is extraordinarily fruitful for the understanding of dreams. We will have to wait to see if it fits all cases or whether it needs some corrections as to particular cases. But as far as I am concerned, after reading Freud's pamphlet [*Ueber den Traum*] many of my own dreams, which previously had been incompletely understood, became clear."[19]

Professor Lubarsch's enthusiastic acceptance of Freud's wish fulfillment hypothesis was frequently echoed by lay writers. In rich prose, the poet and dramatist, Jacob Julius David, explained Freud's theory for the readers of the Berlin weekly, *Nation*.[20] Freud had shown "an uncommonly honest search for truth," and *Die Traumdeutung* radiated "the great joyousness a discoverer derives from his work." Because Freud had sought "to bring law and unity to the senseless, childish images with which dreams try to mock us," concluded David, it was necessary to call attention to his work. It is noteworthy that David's article appeared just two months after *Die Traumdeutung*. Freud complained about the lack of immediate notice of his work, but he was frequently unaware of or unduly deprecated the attention paid to it.

A teacher of zoology, botany and chemistry, Ludwig Karell, "happily" greeted Freud's "searching and critical" theory in the daily supplement to the Munich *Allgemeine Zeitung*. In the weekly *Gegenwart,* Eduard Sokal, a writer of nontechnical articles on psychological matters, announced the arrival of the "Columbus of dream research...the famous Viennese neurologist Sigmund Freud [who] with great acumen demonstrates the common roots of dream phenomena in individual cases." An anonymous author in *Gaea,* a long-established, serious journal devoted to science and geography, proclaimed "Freund" [*sic*] the first to have established the laws that governed dreams.[21] Naturally, Freud's theory of dreams as fulfillments of wishes was also publicized for lay audiences by his followers.[22]

As regards specific aspects of the wish fulfillment theory, the majority of commentators were most impressed with Freud's enunciation of the "dream work." These are the processes of condensation, displacement, etc., utilized by the dreamer. All the physicians except Giessler called attention to these aspects of Freud's theory. Weygandt felt Freud's detailed analysis of dream work was one of the most noteworthy parts of his book. Lubarsch provided his readers with a full discussion of the relationship between manifest and latent dream content, characterizing Freud's work with the usual sobriquet: "extremely ingenious" (*geistreich*).[23]

Among the lay writers, the science teacher Karell praised Freud for the "rich material" which he had compiled on condensation and displacement, both of which Karell carefully explained and illustrated. A Catholic pastor, Ceslaus M. Schneider, also was impressed by the "comprehensive material" Freud had gathered in support of his method of dream interpretation. The anonymous author in *Gaea* completely accepted Freud's "very important studies" of how

dream work produces an imposing condensation of the basic elements.... That dream work utilizes the ambiguity of words is an important discovery of the Viennese investigator; it will probably be a departure point for further disclosures about certain obscure areas of psychic life.[24]

Sigmar Mehring, the Berlin poet and *feuilletoniste,* appreciated the significance of Freud's discovery that the very same processes that existed in dreams also manifested themselves in wit and in the everyday act of forgetting. These "primary" processes all arose from the same source: the user's unconscious. Freud had thus opened "a very important perspective into the phenomena of thought."[25]

Mehring presents us with the curious case of a poet and humorist who completely accepted the one psychoanalytic book he had read, *Jokes and Their Relation to the Unconscious,* and then declared himself unable to agree with an idea that had originated in a book he had not read, *The Interpretation of Dreams.* Mehring (1) adopted the view that dreams and wit both originate in the unconscious, (2) agreed that the phenomenon of condensation existed in wit, dreams and in everyday slips, (3) favored Freud's ideas on fantasy over those of a rival theorist (Scherer) on the sources of poetic creation, (4) but then declared that a dream "is nothing but a chaotic, goalless game!" It seems probable that if Mehring was so won over by the book on jokes, he would have been equally won over by the book on dreams—if he had read it. Mehring's case suggests that, at least among poets and writers, psychoanalysis in the early years did not so much face the problem of a hostile audience as of an audience that was, quite simply, tiny. It seems clear that Freud's ability to convince people with literary interests was never in doubt. But for a number of years Freud was not particularly interested in lay reaction; it was medical acceptance that he at first craved.[26]

Whether Freud's work was of a scientific nature was always an urgent question. Many psychiatrists and most experimental psychologists attacked psychoanalysis on this ground, since they had very definite criteria for what constituted "science" and "scientific method." Weygandt was typical of this group, taking Freud to task for basing his investigations only on his own dreams and those of documented neurotic patients.[27] The pathologist Lubarsch, on the other hand, whose work and reputation met every definition of turn-of-the-century science, did not deem that Freud's subjects had invalidated his conclusions. Clearly not every German scientist lost his flexibility of thought and succumbed to rigid methodological definitions of knowledge. As a result of Freud's work, Lubarsch concluded that the dream possessed "great psychological worth so that through its exact analysis, we can obtain insight into the innermost recesses of our heart. And as Freud emphasizes, it is of priceless significance for the understanding of many symptoms of psychic disturbances and perhaps also for their treatment."[28]

Lubarsch's reaction was shared by most laymen who came into early contact with Freud's discoveries about dreams. David began his review by announcing that he was going to discuss a book that was of "great importance" for psychologists. Several months later, the zoologist and botanist Karell declared that Freud "easily succeeds" in proving that dreams have the character of a wish "by producing experimental evidence." Reverend Schneider reported that Freud's book "does not lose itself—and that is its excellent quality—in aimless psychological speculation that lacks a goal." Freud had "scientifically assimilated" his material, and his "manner of expression was sober, positive and clear."[29]

The titles of two articles explicitly summed up their authors' outlook: the one by Sokal, quite simply, "Scientific Dream Interpretation"; the other, for the lay scientific periodical *Gaea,* "The Dream in the Light of Scientific Investigation." The author of this latter essay concluded that earlier hypotheses "must be contradicted" because Freud had discovered that "the world of dreams has its own causality." Freud had arrived at his conclusions only after "deep and basic investigations." The author was moved to "recognize how greatly the result of deep scientific investigation contradicts immediate naive experience."[30]

Other writers were more concerned with Freud's theory of the sources of dreams. In this matter no one contested Freud's conclusion that all dreams are a combination of childhood experiences and impressions, as well as subjects of current interest. It is worth noting in this regard how eagerly David and Karell embraced Freud's explanation of dreams about the deaths of family members. If dreams were wish fulfillments, did one really wish the death of a parent or sibling? Yes—but this was based on angry feelings one had as a child and rested on a child's conception of death as a temporary separation, *i.e.,* the child's inability truly to understand the word "forever." This is why, explained both authors, dreams of death were often unaccompanied by the painful feelings adults associate with death. An adult dreams about death in the manner a child conceives of it.

But some of Freud's reviewers found themselves severely tested as to the *extent* of their agreement with him on the sources of dreams. If one accepted that early life experiences were a fertile source of dreams, then how else to account for sexual dreams except that children had sexual thoughts and feelings? Most reviewers circumvented the problem by accepting the *general* childhood etiology of dreams but not mentioning the *specific* sexual experiences that Freud had discussed.

Yet not all shied away from the provocative issue. Weygandt, at one extreme, was openly shocked at the "extraordinary" relationships to parents described by Freud: hatred of father and sexual inclination towards mother. Freud had gone "so far" as to connect the tragedy of Oedipus with Oedipus' marrying of his mother.[31] The usual response, however, was simply to acknowledge Freud's hypothesis but take no position on it. The undisguised openness of Weygandt's recoil from the notion that childhood sexuality was a source of dreams was a rare reaction; and equally uncommon was David's wholehearted recognition of it. First sexual impulses occurred very early. Sensuality grows between father and daughter, mother and son. It manifests itself very early in a kind of jealousy and in caressing. A little girl gladly takes the place of her mother when the mother is absent. Wishes for the fulfillment of sexual relationships between parents and children "lie in all of us," said David.[32]

Not surprisingly, the two authors who dealt explicitly with sexuality were the same two who took stands on Freud's use of symbolism. Weygandt, the scientist, "confessed that the [*Interpretation of Dreams*] offers well observed material and goes into the endeavor of analyzing this material farther, or, said better, deeper than anyone up to now has tried to do. But there can be too much of a good thing, and the false paths of an unfruitful symbolism are not avoided." To David the poet, however, it did not seem odd that to understand the nature of dreams

> one must peel off several layers, clarify the manifold ramifications, be strong and honest towards oneself, before one can advance to this powerfully masked core.... Sometimes [sexuality] appears in the clearest of symbols. At other times it disguises itself in the most remarkable manner. [Freud's interpretation] is strange but enlightening.[33]

There was one author, a Munich philologist and scholar of mythologies and fairy tales, whose immediate interest in *The Interpretation of Dreams* prompted him to write an article with underlying themes cutting across several of the psychoanalytic theories already mentioned:[34] that dreams are meaningful because they are a direct continuation of thoughts, wishes and fears held during the waking state; that early life wishes,

including sexual ones, find a place in dreams; and that symbolism plays a vital role in dreaming and waking states.

The scholar, Friedrich von der Leyen (1873–1966), composed an essay for the short-lived *Der Lotse (The Pilot)* an ambitious, avant-garde cultural weekly published in Hamburg. In the same volume as von der Leyen's article, there appeared pieces by Lou Andreas-Salomé, Max Dessoir, Hugo Münsterberg, Rainer Maria Rilke, Georg Simmel, Ferdinand Tönnies, and an article about Stefan George. Because of the pioneering nature of *Der Lotse,* there is a strong possibility that some of the above authors, as well as other *Lotse* contributors, read von der Leyen's essay, thus coming into contact with Freud's work seven months after its appearance.

Von der Leyen demonstrated that dreams stem from life experiences. Dreams are enlarged and explicit versions of what people wish for and what they worry about. Fairy tales, myths and legends are also magnified accounts of life, which explains their universal appeal. Many fairy tales actually stem from dreams; they are oft-told dreams which have entered the literature and traditions of a people, first verbally and then in writing.

Von der Leyen pointed out that an earlier, forgotten scholar, Ludwig Laistner, had attempted to prove the connection between dreams and fairy tales in his book, *The Riddle of the Sphinx* (1889). But Laistner's work, in spite of its comprehensiveness, had not been well received by scholars because Laistner was not able to prove his conclusions with the help of a consistent methodology. However, von der Leyen hoped that in the future the "riddle" would receive more sympathetic consideration since "strict science" had now arrived at similar conclusions to Laistner's, *i.e., Die Traumdeutung* of the learned Viennese doctor, "Siegmund" [*sic*] Freud.[35]

Von der Leyen demonstrated the similarity between many legends and fairy tales and common dreams: the martyrdom of Sisyphus, the trials of Hercules and Odysseus, the myth of the sword of Damocles, the tales of the Arabian nights, the saga of Oedipus, the tale of the emperor's new clothes. For the last two, von der Leyen cited Freud in detail to prove his contentions.[36]

In a letter to Fliess (July 4, 1901), Freud remarked that von der Leyen had sent him a copy of the *Lotse* article. Ernst Kris has reported that Freud and von der Leyen corresponded for a while and that the philologist seems to have drawn others' attention to Freud's work, but that "Leyen regarded Freud's subsequent works with reserve and scepticism."[37]

Only two reviewers, Lubarsch and David, publicly applied Freud's dream theories to themselves. Lubarsch presented two of his own dreams to show how one was the fulfillment of a wish, and how the other, though appearing senseless, really had a meaning. David wrote that he knew from his own experience how suppressed and troubled childhood memories, long forgotten, make their appearance in dreams.[38]

III

The lay reaction to psychoanalytic dream theories clearly illustrates a common early response to psychoanalysis. This response is seen also in the medical reception, but never as distinctly expressed as by some of the lay commentators.[39] Indeed, in the reaction of physicians it is more a thing sensed than expressed. More than a few of Freud's reviewers and even his outspoken critics revealed a feeling of awe at Freud's conclusions, but indicated their helplessness in not knowing quite what to make of them. These men clearly recognized they had read something brilliant, something unusual, but they were unable to define and categorize it in terms of their past experience. The recurrent use of the adjectives *geistreich* and *geistvoll* to characterize both Freud and his theories is an example of this reaction. For "ingenious" is not altogether a complimentary word. It has implications of cleverness without a foundation, of some sleight-of-hand that the viewer senses, even though he has seen no evidence of it.

Partly, Freud's style of writing accounts for this response. It was unusual for scientific literature of the day to be written as vividly and compellingly as Freud's often was. Also, his habit of arguing by analogy was very suspect in certain scientific circles. The extraordinary occurrence of Freud's receiving the Goethe prize for literature in 1930 shows that his literary style was indeed a prominent part of his work. This style always affected his readers, either positively or negatively.[40]

The label "ingenious" was also a reaction to the substance of psychoanalysis. Freud logically, step by step, brought his readers to conclusions that at the outset many of them would never have thought possible. When all was done, they stepped back in wonderment, quite unable to realize how they had arrived where they were, unable to find flaws, yet with a feeling of having been misled. They could do no other than to praise Freud for his conclusions. But these conclusions often left them uncomfortable, thus the frequent use of "ingenious." The word was either an escape hatch or a hiding place of last resort.

Sometimes a commentator put his feelings into more precise language. Thus Sigmar Mehring noted: "One follows him without strong contradiction, to some extent seduced by pleasure in the numerous, very funny proofs.... After the tense expectation comes a startling disclosure."[41] Following a wholly favorable review of *Die Traumdeutung,* J. J. David's closing words were that he owed to Freud's work "much stimulation, both in agreement and *rejection* [italics mine]."[42] The word "rejection" comes like a shot out of the blue. Parenthetically, we may note here that "stimulating" was another favorite adjective of Freud's reviewers, a word by which they consciously praised and unconsciously refrained from a total commitment. It was Eduard Sokal, in his "*Scientific* [italics mine] Dream Interpretation," who most clearly enunciated the problem.

Sokal could not praise Freud enough: "Columbus ...famous...great acumen...." Yet in the middle of one of the most appreciative discussions of those "two excellent works" on dreams, Sokal wrote: "In the analysis of such particular examples of dreams, Freud shows himself to be a true master of psychological observation, though just this virtuosity of his interpretive artistry may arouse in some a doubt as to the scientific worth of the theory."[43] In an age where science was measured by the dispassionateness of its facts, "interpretive artistry" was a damning indictment.

Now let us attempt to explain the lack of continued interest in the dream theories. The observations just expressed provide some clue. More specifically, we can ask who could have served as promulgators of Freud's hypotheses, and then we can examine their actual response.

The foremost candidates were the psychologists, the only scientists who, as a group, had mapped out for their province the study of the normal phenomena of the human mind. But by 1900 it was the experimental—the physiological—psychologists who were in the ascendancy in German psychology. The experimental psychologists were preoccupied exclusively with the study of the conscious and slavishly devoted to the laboratory as the only place where a truly scientific psychology could emerge. This was the discipline William James called "brass instrument" psychology. Its influential and authoritarian leader was Wilhelm Wundt, who did not die until 1920 and who called the concept of the unconscious "mythological."[44]

The experimentalists saw "conscious processes" as ubiquitous. Oswald Külpe (1862–1915), one of Wundt's leading followers, pointed out that these processes even appear in sleep in the form of dreams. William Stern (1871–1938), who had trained with the physiological psychologist Hermann Ebbinghaus, was worried about the "mystical and chaotic" implications of Freud's theories for the new field of experimental psychology, struggling to gain acceptance as a modern science.[45]

Wundt himself spoke out with great incisiveness about the explanation of dreams. External irritants and stimulations, he stressed, are the effective agents of dreaming. For example, lying in an uncomfortable position causes a dream about hard physical labor. Slight intercostal pain is responsible for a dream that one is being stabbed by an enemy.[46]

Since the ideas in dreams came from sensations, Wundt said they were "mostly illusions of fancy." Therefore, it was "a *physiological* problem to formulate a theory of sleep, dreams, and hypnosis." That it was a physiological problem was an assumption, but it seemed the most likely scientific one. Yet often "mystical and fanciful hypotheses" were applied to dreams and hypnosis. One such was that there was increased mental activity in dreams. "In reality all that can stand the light of thorough examination in these phenomena is in general readily explicable on psychological and physiological grounds; what is not applicable in this way has always proved on closer examination to be superstitious self-deception or intentional fraud."[47]

The reactions of the experimentalists to *The Interpretation of Dreams* were not based solely on hostility to psychoanalysis. The basic interests and theoretical commitments of the early physiological psychologists were so far distant from those of Freud's as to preclude any possibility of a rapprochement between their science and psychoanalysis.

The next likely promulgators of Freud's ideas were the physicians, who might have been expected to make some use of the significance Freud's dream theories had for mental disturbances. But they fought off dream interpretation as a throwback to the fixed explanations of dreams which were such an integral part of folk medicine. For Freud also offered fixed explanations, declaring, for instance, that in a dream of flying the dreamer was always reexperiencing certain types of movements from childhood—either being lifted, rocked or tossed by an adult, or a romping game. A dream of being naked or insufficiently dressed was a repetition of a time in childhood when one ordinarily appeared before others inadequately clothed. And to all dreams, Freud ascribed the common character of a wish. To many physicians, Freud's interpretations seemed similar to popular superstitions which were the stock-in-trade of local folk healers.

To psychiatrists these were important considerations. True, the psychiatrists were not as insecure as the psychologists about their place in turn-of-the-century science. But they were still only fifty years away from the time when German psychiatry was regarded by the Western world as riddled with mysticism. Moreover, Freud had openly admitted that he had taken large parts of his evidence from the dreams and associations of his neurotic patients. Physicians three-quarters of a century ago, much like others of their day, almost always saw health and sickness as two polarities, easily open to distinction, and never linked. Again, as with the psychologists, more was involved than inherent hostilities toward psychoanalysis—which is not to deny the existence of these hostilities.

Freud was well aware that it was not only his sexual interpretations, his Viennese Jewish background or the personal neurotic resistances of his critics that was to prevent sustained interest in his work. "There can be no doubt," he emphatically stated in the opening chapter of *The Interpretation of Dreams,*

> that the psychical achievements of dreams received readier and warmer recognition during the intellectual period which has now been left behind, when the human mind was dominated by philosophy and not by the exact natural sciences. . . . The introduction of the scientific mode of thought has brought along with it a reaction in the estimation of dreams. Medical writers in especial tend to regard psychical activity in dreams as trivial and valueless; while philosophers and non-professional observers—amateur psychologists—. . . have (in closer alignment with popular feelings) retained a belief in the psychical value of dreams. Anyone who is inclined

to take a low view of psychical functioning in dreams will naturally prefer to assign their source to somatic stimulation. . . .[48]

Thus, Freud in 1899 predicted with deadly accuracy what would be the initial response to his book: "non-professional observers" would give it a much better reception than scientists and physicians. Unfortunately, historians have paid more attention to Freud's letters to Fliess than to this revealing passage in *The Interpretation of Dreams.* In his book Freud described with cool detachment the contemporary scientific attitude. But once his masterwork was in print, his objectivity vanished. When his unrealistic expectations of immediate professional acclamation were not met, he despaired of any recognition.[49]

But recognition came immediately from the *literati,* though at first they were few in number. Eventually the few became many. The years after World War I saw the flowering of psychoanalytic dream interpretation in German intellectual circles. But people of literary interests in 1900 were also creatures of the age of materialistic science. Though this orientation had already begun to lose its special dominance among the avant-garde before the war, it still provided, by far, the favorite *Weltanschauung* for those who considered themselves "modern."

Moreover, Freud was not eager to court this group; indeed, with only two exceptions during his entire psychoanalytic career, he never entered into any public debate or defense of his hypotheses. A good example of Freud's idiosyncratic attitudes concerning publicizing his work occurred four months after the publication of *The Interpretation of Dreams.* Having learned from his friend Fliess that a leading intellectual periodical, the *Neue Rundschau,* had decided not to review the book, Freud rebelled against Fliess' suggestion that he write an article about it as an alternative to its being reviewed. He wrote Fliess that he had five reasons for not submitting such an article, the fifth obviously being the emotional reaction of a man hurt by rejection:

I want to avoid anything that savours of advertisement. I know that my work is odious to most people. So long as I behave perfectly correctly, my opponents are at a loss. If I once start doing the same as they do, they will regain their confidence that my work is no better than theirs....So I think the most advisable course is quietly to accept the *Rundschau's* refusal as an incontrovertible sign of public opinion.[50]

As we well know, authors are not always so prideful, and their desire to spread their ideas is not usually held against them. But Freud seemed more concerned with "correct" behavior before his medical colleagues than in convincing a generally educated audience. "Odious" was certainly not to be the response in lay periodicals to psychoanalytic dream theories. And equally certainly, publication in the *Rundschau* was not seeking a mass audience of the commonest denominator.

At any rate, Freud himself bears a small measure of responsibility for the fact that five years later the *Rundschau* published a laudatory article hailing the significance of Freud's work on dreams, but with nary a mention of his name.[51] Without question, the author, Jentsch, was referring to Freud's work. The clearest proofs of this are Jentsch's acknowledgement that dreams are the fulfillment of wishes (p. 882) and his entitling his article "*Traumarbeit*"—Freud's very own phrase for the dream mechanisms he had discovered. Jentsch praised the dream studies and interpretations as being "serious...scientific... legitimate and rational" and, inevitably, "ingenious." The work had been carried out with "virtuosity and acumen." He envisioned that the studies would probably lead to the "important, practical elucidation of both general and specific psychological theories about people."

It remains to be noted that it was often the nonmedical aspects of psychoanalysis that attracted those men and women who became the second generation of Freudians—those young doctors and smaller number of laymen who became psychoanalysts in Germany in the 1920's. One of the foremost of these nonmedical aspects was the reliance of psychoanalysis upon symbolism, which figures so prominently in dream interpretation. Many German psychoanalysts have reported having a strong literary interest in their adolescent years, which was immensely gratified by reading Freud.[52] These men and women savored Freud's style, shared his introspective interests, and appreciated the importance he attached to symbols. Here, of course, were the chief promulgators of Freud's dream theories.

This paper has dealt with two main issues:

(1) I have sought to demonstrate that the German lay exposure to and reception of Freud's dream books was not scanty and not mainly unfavorable. Freud's complaints and Jones' reechoing of them have been uncritically accepted. But further investigation has shown that Freud, expecting an immediate response to his book on dreams, never appreciated or realized the extent to which they were reviewed in Germany during the first few years after their publication. This research has been strengthened by the discovery of additional references, seemingly unknown to historians of psychoanalysis. The articles in lay periodicals by Giessler, Jentsch, Korn, Lubarsch, Sokal, and the anonymous author in *Gaea* all fall into this category.

(2) In demonstrating the existence of this appreciative audience, I have thereby raised an historical problem. It is perfectly true, as earlier historians have shown, that the early response of the educated German public to psychoanalytic dream theories was limited. But this occurred *in spite of,* and not because of, an enthusiastic, early lay exposure and reaction to *The Interpretation of Dreams.* It is undeniable that psychoanalytic theories always faced resistance because of their sexual content and Freud's Viennese Jewish background. But there are additional explanations for the delay in the acceptance of the dream theories: the unconscious reservations of

reviewers as exhibited in their continual use of the word "ingenious"; a scientific climate that discouraged educated lay interest; and Freud's own initial reluctance to court intellectuals with literary interests. It was the latter group which eventually produced many of the most eloquent proponents of the value of psychoanalysis as well as many of its most dedicated practitioners.

NOTES

1 Some correction of this view has already been made by Ilse Bry and Alfred H. Rifkin, "Freud and the History of Ideas: Primary Sources, 1886–1910," *Science and Psychoanalysis,* 1962, *5,* 6–36; and by Henri F. Ellenberger, *The Discovery of the Unconscious: The History and Evolution of Dynamic Psychiatry* (New York: Basic Books, 1970).

2 I am using the word "German" in its strict geographical sense.

3 Sigmund Freud, *The Origins of Psychoanalysis: Letters to Willhem Fliess, Drafts and Notes: 1887–1902 by Sigmund Freud,* ed. by Marie Bonaparte, Anna Freud and Ernst Kris; trans. by Eric Mosbacher and James Strachey (New York: Basic Books, 1954), p. 303 [hereafter *OPA*].

4 *OPA,* pp. 306, 307, 309.

5 *OPA,* pp. 311, 313–314.

6 *OPA,* pp. 323–324.

7 *OPA,* p. 325. This was Ludwig Karell's favorable review. See pp. 6, 7, 8, 9 below.

8 *OPA,* p. 311.

9 Ernest Jones, *The Life and Work of Sigmund Freud* (New York: Basic Books, 1955), Vol. 1, pp. 360–361.

10 I have pointed out Jones' distortion of Freud's reception by German physicians in "The Medical Reception of Psychoanalysis in Germany, 1894–1907: Three Brief Studies," *Bulletin of the History of Medicine,* 1971, *45,* 461–481.

11 These dates encompass the initial period of reception of psychoanalysis in Germany. In 1893 Breuer's and Freud's "Preliminary Communication" on hysteria appeared, and in 1907 Karl Abraham, Freud's first "official" German disciple, opened his practice in Berlin.

12 I base this statement on the entries under "Dreams" in the *Bibliographie der deutschen Zeitschriften-Literatur* and my examination of these entries from 1893 through 1908.

13 Sigmund Freud, *The Interpretation of Dreams,* in *Standard Edition of the Complete Psychological Works of Sigmund Freud,* trans. by James Strachey (London: Hogarth Press, 1958), Vol. 4, pp. 48–65 [hereafter *SE*].

14 Walter Bromberg, *The Mind of Man: The Story of Man's Conquest of Mental Illness* (New York and London: Harper, 1937), p. 247.

15 Two such essays of especial interest are those by Timotheus Fabri, "Das Traumleben—als Erzieher," *Die Woche,* 1905, *7,* 154; and Alb. Gruhn, "Zur Psychologie des Traumes," *Pädagogisches Archiv,* 1907, *49,* 263–265.

16 Carl Marx Giessler, "Die Bedeutung der Träume," [review article] *Deutsche Revue,* 1906, *31,* 245–246. In choosing Giessler to write a review article on the significance of dreams, the editor of the *Deutsche Revue* picked a man who had previously expressed his strong belief in the importance of dream research for investigations in related fields of hypnotism, child psychology, psychiatry, as well as the psychology of normal life. It was Giessler's opinion that dreams could give doctors important clues about both physical and mental illnesses. See "Die Grundtatsache des Traum zustandes, *Allgemeine Zeitschrift für Psychiatrie,* 1901, *58,* 182.

17 "yg," [Wilhelm Weygandt], Review of *Die Traumdeutung* in *Literarisches Zentralblatt für Deutschland,* 1901, *52,* col. 1495 [hereafter *LZD*]. Weygandt was asked to do this review because of his own investigations which appeared in 1893 as *Entstehung der Träume.*

18 Carl Oppenheimer, Review of *Die Traumdeutung* in *Die Umschau,* 1900, *4,* 219; and Georg Korn, "Neuere Forschungen über Schlaf und Traumleben" [review article], *Der Türmer,* 1902, *4,* 441. Freud called Oppenheimer's review "short, friendly and uncomprehending." (Freud's May 16, 1900 letter to Fliess in *OPA,* p. 320.)

19 O. Lubarsch, "Schlaf und Traum" [review article], *Die Woche,* 1902, *4,* 17. See also the first installment of this article in *Die Woche,* 1901, *3,* 2246. *Die Woche* was a mass oriented weekly. Lubarsch

had become famous at twenty-eight for first rec-ognizing carcinoids, relatively benign abdominal tumors, with the microscopic picture of malignan-cy. He was honored on his sixtieth and seventieth birthdays with *Festschrifts* in *Virchows Archiv*.

20 J. J. David, Essay based on *Die Traumdeutung* in *Die Nation*, 1900, *17*, 239, *Die Nation* was a well established Berlin weekly with articles on politics, economics, literature, the theater, as well as short book reviews.

21 Ludwig Karell, Review of *Die Traundeutungen* [*sic*] in *Beilage zur Allgemeinen Zeitung*, Munich, Oct. 12, 1900, No. 234, p. 4 [hereafter *BAZ*]; Eduard Sokal, "Wissenschaftliche Traumdeu-tung," *Die Gegenwart*, 1902, *61*, 84–85; "Der Traum im Lichte der wissenschaftliche Unter-suchung," *Gaea: Natur und Leben*, 1902, *38*, 44.

22 See Wilhelm Stekel, "Typische Träume" in the *Beilage, Berliner Tageblatt*, 1906, No. 37; and Hugo Friedmann, "Die Bedeutung des unbe-wussten Seelenlebens und eine Methode ze dessen Aufstellung," *BAZ*, Oct. 15, 1907, No. 183, pp. 67–68.

23 Oppenheimer, *Die Umschau*, *4*, 218; Korn, *Der Türmer*, *4*, 441; "yg," *LZD*, col. 1495; Lubarsch, *Die Woche*, *4*, 17.

24 Karell, *BAZ*, p. 5; C. M. Schneider, Review of *Die Traumdeutung* in *Jahrbuch für philo-sophische und spekulative Theologie*, 1901, *15*, 476; "Der Traum...," *Gaea*, *38*, 46–47.

25 Sigmar Mehring, "Das Wesen des Witzes," *Die Nation*, 1906, *23*, 284. David's article had also ap-peared in *Die Nation*.

26 Freud was a physician, an exceptionally well trained and bright neurologist; from 1893–1905, all of Freud's psychoanalytic papers were published in medical journals; psychoanalysis and its prede-cessor, the cathartic method, were initially devel-oped in response to deeply puzzling medical prob-lems of the late nineteenth century. Also see below, pp. 140–141.

27 "yg," *LZD*, col. 1495.

28 Lubarsch, *Die Woche*, p. 19.

29 David, *Nation*, p. 238; Karell, *BAZ*, pp. 4–5; Schneider, *Jahrbuch*, pp. 475–476.

30 Sokal, *Gegenwart*, p. 84; "Der Traum...," *Gaea*, pp. 45, 46, 48. This raises the question of whether scientists are always the best judges of what is "sci-entific." Probably they are. But it seems also ob-vious that at particular moments, a scientist's com-mitment to certain principles interferes with his ability to appreciate a new way of looking at an old problem.

31 "yg," *LZD*, col. 1495.

32 David, *Nation*, p. 239.

33 "yg," *LZD*, col. 1495; David, *Nation*, p. 239. Nat-urally, when Freud's followers wrote for popular audiences, they were quite informative about the role of symbolism. See for example C. G. Jung, "Cryptomnesia" [1905], *Collected Works*, Vol. 1 (New York: Pantheon Books, 1957), p. 99. Jung's article originally appeared in Maximilian Harden's prestigious periodical, *Die Zukunft*. See also Friedmann, *BAZ*, pp. 66–68 and Stekel, *Berliner Tageblatt*, 1906, No. 37.

34 Friedrich von der Leyen, "Traum und Märchen," *Der Lotse*, 1901, *1*, 382–390.

35 *Ibid.*, pp. 383–384.

36 *Ibid.*, pp. 387–388.

37 See *OPA*, p. 332. Some psychoanalysts' (though not necessarily Kris's) distorted interpretation of such responses to psychoanalysis evokes my great curiosity about the details of von der Leyen's ac-tual later reaction. I have been unable, however, to learn more about the events behind Kris's state-ment.

38 Lubarsch, *Die Woche*, 1901, p. 2246, and 1902, pp. 17–18; David, *Nation*, p. 239.

39 See Hannah S. Decker, "The Reception of Psy-choanalysis in Germany, 1893–1907" (Unpub-lished Ph.D. dissertation, Columbia University, 1971), especially chapters III–V. To be published by International Universities Press, New York.

40 After writing this, I learned that this observation is also made by Walter Schönau, *Sigmund Freuds Prosa* (Stuttgart: Metzlersche Verlags buchhandlung, 1968). I am indebted for the ref-erence to William G. Niederland, "Freud's Lit-erary Style: Some Observations," *American Imago*, 1971, *28*, 23.

41 Mehring, *Nation*, p. 284.

42 David, *Nation*, p. 239.

43 Sokal, *Gegenwart*, p. 84.

44 Wilhelm Wundt, *Grundzüge der physiologishen Psychologie*, Vol. 3 (5th ed.; Leipzig: Verlag von Wilhelm Engelmann, 1903), p. 514.

45 William Stern, Review of *Die Traumdeutung* in *Zeitschrift für Psychologie und Physiologie der Sinnesorgane*, 1901, *26*, 131–133.

46 Wundt, *Physiologischen Psychologie*, 3, p. 653.

47 Wundt, *Outlines of Psychology*, trans. by C. H. Judd (2nd rev. English ed.; Leipzig: Wilhelm Engelmann, 1902), pp. 303–307.

48 Freud, *The Interpretation of Dreams, SE, 4*, pp. 63–64.

49 Perhaps the insistent and repetitive nature of Freud's complaints about the reaction to *The In-terpretation of Dreams* was partly determined by Freud's filial-like relationship to Fliess and were unconscious requests for paternal concern and comfort from Fliess. This observation stems from comments made by Dr. Peter Wilson of the Department of Psychiatry, Cornell University Medical College.

50 *OPA*, p. 316.

51 Ernst Jentsch, "Traumarbeit," *Neue Rundschau*, 1905, *16*, 875–882.

52 Personal interviews.

The Story of "Anna O": A Critical Review with New Data

H. F. Ellenberger

To this day, the most elementary account of psychoanalysis begins with the story of a mysterious young woman, "Anna O", whose numerous hysterical symptoms disappeared one by one as Josef Breuer was able to make her evoke the specific circumstances that had led to their appearance. The patient herself called this procedure "talking-cure" or "chimney sweeping," but Breuer termed it "catharsis." Anna O's cure took place in 1880–1882, but the case history was published thirteen years later, that is, in 1895 in Breuer and Freud's *Studies in Hysteria*. From that time on, Anna O's story was given as the prototype of a cathartic cure and one of the basic occurrences that led Freud to the creation of psychoanalysis.

Today, the veil of legend surrounding the foundation of psychoanalysis has been only partly lifted up by objective research. In the following we will examine Anna O's story in the light of the historical-critical method in order to ascertain what can be considered historically certain, possible but doubtful, definitely legendary.

Ellenberger, H. F. (1972). The story of "Anna O": A critical review with new data. *Journal of the History of the Behavioral Sciences, 8*, 267–279. Copyright © 1972 by the Clinical Psychology Publishing Company. Reprinted by permission of the publisher.

After a brief summary of Breuer's original report of 1895, we will make a survey of all subsequent researches about Anna O, following the chronological sequence of the investigations. We will bring two newly discovered documents, one being a hitherto unknown case history of the patient, written by Breuer himself in 1882, and the second one a follow-up written in the Sanatorium Bellevue, Kreuzlingen, where Anna O was transferred in July 1882. We will try to see what new light these documents throw upon Anna O's story.

BREUER'S ORIGINAL REPORT OF 1895

According to Breuer, Anna O was 21 years old at the time when she fell ill, that is, in 1880. She belonged to a well-to-do family. She was very intelligent, attractive, kind, charitable, but moody and stubborn. The family was extremely puritanical and, Breuer says, "the sexual element was surprisingly undeveloped" in Anna. There was, he added, a marked contrast between the refined education she had received and the monotonous home life she led. This brought her to escape into long daydreams that she called her "private theater." However these daydreams did not interfere with her daily activities and her family were not aware of them.

Her illness, as described by Breuer in 1895,[1] went through four chronologically sharply delimited periods.

1) The *period of latent incubation,* from July 1880 to December 10, 1880. The starting-point was a severe physical illness of her beloved father. She gave him intensive care, staying up during the night and resting in the afternoon. But she became exhausted and had to be kept away from the sick father. Thereupon she began to suffer from an intensive coughing and she had long episodes of sleepiness and agitation in the afternoon. According to Breuer, Anna O had at that time all kinds of hidden symptoms that neither her family nor she herself suspected. But Breuer did not see her during that period; his description of her symptoms—overt or hidden—was a later reconstruction.

2) The *period of manifest psychosis,* went from December 1880 to April 1881. During that period Anna O was under Breuer's care and she remained in bed from December 11, 1880 to April 1, 1881. A great variety of symptoms appeared within a short time, beginning with ocular disturbances, followed with paralyses, contractions, zones of tactile anesthesia, and linguistic disorganization. She spoke an agrammatical jargon composed of a mixture of four or five languages. Her personality, now, was split into one "normal," conscious, sad person, and one morbid, uncouth, agitated person who had hallucinations of black snakes. It happened that for two weeks she remained completely mute, but Breuer knew that this had followed a certain painful incident; and after he could bring her to talk about this incident, the patient started to speak again. Now, however, she talked only in English, though still understanding what people told her in German. On late afternoons she had what she called (in English) her "clouds," that is a kind of drowsiness; then she could be easily hypnotized. Breuer usually visited her in these moments; she told him her daydreams; they were

mostly stories of an anxious girl around sick persons. During the month of March there came a gradual improvement and she left her bed for the first time on April 1, 1881.

3) The *period of "continuous somnambulism alternating with more normal conditions"* went from April 5 to December 1881. The death of her father, on April 5, 1881, was a severe shock. After two days of deep stupor, a new set of severe symptoms appeared. She manifested a "negative instinct" against her close relatives and recognized no one, except Breuer; he had to feed her for some time. She spoke nothing but English, and now, apparently she was unable to understand what was told or written in German.

About ten days after her father's death, a consultant was called. She manifested "negative hallucinations" toward him; in other words she behaved as if she did not perceive his presence. The consultant tried to force her attention by blowing some smoke toward her face. This attempt was followed by a terrific attack of anger and anxiety. On the same evening, Breuer had to leave for a journey. When he came back he found that Anna O's condition was much worse. During his absence she had refused to eat, she had fits of intense anxiety and ghastly hallucinations. Breuer began to hypnotize her again on the evening; she told him about her recent hallucinations, whereupon she was relieved. The personality contrast was now between the disturbed mind of the daytime and the clear mind of the night.

Because Anna O had manifested suicidal impulses, it was felt that she could no longer be kept at home, and—much against her will—she was transferred into a country-house near Vienna, on June 7, 1881. After three days of great agitation, she quieted down. Breuer visited her every three or four days. Her symptoms now appeared in a regular cycle and were relieved by Breuer's hypnotic sessions. She remained quiet after Breuer's visits; but during the intervals had to be given fairly high amounts of chloral.

It was found that no one but Breuer could practice what she now called her "talking cure" or "chimney sweeping." While Breuer was on a vacation trip, one of his colleagues attempted to give her the same treatment but failed. Nevertheless her condition gradually improved. She played with a Newfoundland dog and visited a few poor people in the neighborhood. In the fall, she went back to Vienna, where her mother had moved to another house. However her condition became worse in December 1881, so that she had to be taken back to the country-house.

4) The *fourth period,* extended from December 1881 to June 1882. A very remarkable, two-fold change occurred in the illness. First, a difference in regard to the multiple personality. There still were the "normal" and "sick" personalities, but the main feature was that the sick personality lived 365 days earlier than the healthy one. Thanks to the diary her mother had kept about her illness, Breuer was able to check that the events she hallucinated had occurred, day by day, exactly one year earlier. She sometimes shifted spontaneously and rather abruptly from one personality to the other; Breuer could provoke the shifting by showing her an orange. The second modification concerned the nature and content of the talking-cure. Once, under hypnosis, she told Breuer how her difficulties in swallowing water had started after she had seen a dog drinking from a glass. Having told Breuer this, the symptom disappeared. This initiated a new kind of treatment. She told Breuer, in reverse chronological order, each appearance of a given symptom with exact dates, until she reached the original manifestation and initial event, and then the symptom disappeared. Obviously, this was an extremely time-consuming procedure. Breuer gives as an example one of the symptoms, the patient's transient states of deafness; he found seven subforms of this symptom and each one of them constituted one of the "series" that Breuer had to treat separately. The first subform, "not hearing when someone came in" had occurred 108 times, and the patient had to tell the detail of each one of these 108 occurrences in reverse chronological order, until Breuer reached

the first manifestation: she once had not heard her father coming in. But the six other subforms of the "not hearing" symptom as well as each other symptom had to be treated for itself with a similar procedure. Breuer eradicated each symptom in that tedious way. Finally, the last symptom was traced back to a specific incident: while nursing her sick father she had had a hallucination of a black snake, had been upset, had muttered a prayer in English, the only one that came to her mind. As soon as Anna had recovered that memory, the paralysis left her arm and she was able to speak German. The patient had decided and announced in advance that she would be cured in June 1882, on the anniversary of her transfer to the country-house, and in time for her summer vacation. Then, Breuer says, "she left Vienna for a trip, but needed much time until she recovered her psychic equilibrium. Since then she enjoys a fully good health."

The current accounts of Anna O's illness do not emphasize the unusual features of that story, such as the peculiar form of multiple personality during the fourth period (one person living in the present and the other 365 days earlier). Above all, it is absolutely not so that "it sufficed to recall the circumstances under which the symptom had appeared" (this point is explicitly stated by Breuer): Anna had to recall each instance when the symptom had occurred, whatever the number, in the exact reverse chronological order. Anna O's illness was not a "classical case of hysteria" but a unique case of which, to the author's knowledge, no other instance is known, either before or after her.

FROM BREUER TO JONES

Anna O's story remained for a long time an anonymous case history which psychoanalysts and non-psychoanalysts faithfully copied from book to book, with a certain tendency to oversimplification. It was proclaimed as being the prototype of a cathartic cure. Janet's claims to priority, based on his cases of Lucie (1886), Marie

(1889) and a few other ones after 1890 were rejected on the ground that he had been anticipated by Breuer. At times, a few doubts were expressed about the diagnostic. Goshen,[2] in 1952, contended that Anna, as well as the other patients described in the *Studies in Hysteria* had been schizophrenics.

For many years, very few new details emerged about Anna O's case. In 1924 Freud[3] suggested that Breuer had been the unaware victim of "transference love." In a seminar given in Zurich in 1925, Jung[4] revealed that Freud had told him that the patient had actually not been cured. Jung stated that this famous first case "so much spoken about as an example of brilliant therapeutic success, was in reality nothing of the kind. . . . There was no cure at all in the sense of which it was originally presented." And yet, Jung added, "the case was so interesting that there was no need to claim for it something that did not happen."

In 1953, Ernest Jones revealed—much to the family's displeasure—the true name of the patient: Bertha Pappenheim. In his biography of Freud, Jones[5] published a new version of the story. Unfortunately it is not clear to what extent Jones documented himself in Freud's unpublished correspondence, or simply reported from memory details which he had heard many years earlier. According to Jones's version, Freud had told him that Breuer had developed a strong "counter-transference" toward his patient so that Mrs. Breuer became jealous and Breuer decided to bring the treatment to its end. But on that same evening he was called to the patient to find her in the throes of an hysterical childbirth, the logical termination of a phantom pregnancy that had slowly developed without Breuer's awareness; Breuer hynotized her and then "fled the house in a cold sweat." On the next day he left with his wife for Venice to spend a second honeymoon which resulted in the conception of a daughter, Dora. The patient was removed to an institution in Gross Enzersdorf and remained very sick for several years. In the sanitarium she inflamed the heart of the psychiatrist in charge,

so that her mother came from Frankfurt and took her back there. Later she recovered, developed a remarkable social activity, and devoted her life to the cause of the emancipation of women and the care of orphan children.

Jones's version is in many points incompatible with that of Breuer, but owing to the revelation of the patient's true identity it could be expected that new tracks were open toward objective biographical research.

WHO WAS BERTHA PAPPENHEIM?

Bertha Pappenheim was not an unknown figure among Jewish circles. A short biographical note on her was already to be found in the *Grosse Jüdische National Biographie,* edited by S. Winiger. Her death in 1936 was commemorated with a 40-page special issue of a journal she had founded, the *Blätter des Jüdischen Frauen bundes,*[6] with introductory notes from Martin Buber and Max Warbi and substantial accounts of her life, writings, and social activities. Material toward her biography had been gathered but was destroyed during World War II. A number of biographic details were collected by Mrs. Ellen Jensen[7] in Denmark, and a little monograph was published by Mrs. Dora Edinger in 1963.[8]

Bertha Pappenheim belonged to a distinguished old Jewish family. Her grandfather, Wolf Pappenheim, a prominent personality of the Pressburg ghetto, had inherited a great fortune. Her father, Siegmund Pappenheim, was a well-to-do merchant in Vienna. The family belonged to the strictly orthodox Jewish community. Little is known of her childhood and youth. She spoke English perfectly, read French and Italian. According to her own account, she led the usual life of a young lady of high Viennese society, with outdoor activities including horseback riding, and doing a great deal of needlework. It was reported that after her father's death in 1881 she and her mother left Vienna and settled in Frankfurt on the Main. In the later 1880's Bertha devoted herself fully to philanthropic activities. For about twelve years she was the director of an orphanage in Frankfurt. She traveled in the Balkan countries, the Near East, and Russia, to inquire into prostitution and white slavery. In 1904 she founded the *Jüdischer Frauenbund* (League of Jewish Women), and in 1907 she founded a teaching institution affiliated with that organization. Among her writings are travel reports, studies on the condition of Jewish women and on the criminality among Jews, and a number of short stories and theatricals (which reveal more concern with social problems than true literary talent). In her late years she re-edited ancient Jewish works into modernized form, including a history of a prominent ancestor. Toward the end of her life she was depicted as a deeply religious, strict and authoritarian person, utterly selfless and devoted to her work, who had retained from her Viennese education a lively sense of humor, a taste for good food, and the love of beauty, and who possessed an impressive collection of embroideries, china, and glassware. When Hitler seized power and began to persecute the Jews she discouraged their emigration to Palestine or other countries. She died in March 1936, perhaps too early to realize that she had been mistaken in that regard. After World War II she was remembered as an almost legendary figure in the field of social work, to the extent that the government of Western Germany honored her memory by issuing a postage stamp with her picture.

In the biographic notices of 1936 there was no mention of a nervous illness in Bertha's youth. Bertha was said to have left Vienna for Frankfurt with her mother after the father's death in 1881. There is a wide gap indeed between the descriptions of the philanthropist and pioneer social worker, Bertha Pappenheim, and of Breuer's hysterical patient, Anna O.

One means for filling this gap could have been to replace the person into the context of Viennese life of the early 1880's. Obviously Bertha Pappenheim had nothing in common with the "sweet girl" *(das süsse Mädel)* of Schnitzler's theaticals and novels. Many Jews of the higher social strata kept the strict puritanical mores that had been those of their parents or grandparents in the ghetto. However they had access to the privilege and pleasures of the Austrian wealthy bourgeoisie. Bertha had received a fine education, she enjoyed outdoor activities and theater, but all this could not lead her to an independent or professional life; universities were still closed to women. We thus find in her situation a contrast between the ambitions and the obstacles set to ambitions; the same contrast is found in the story of several prominent hysterical women of that time.[9]

It is Juan Dalma[10] who showed the connection between Anna O's cure and the widespread interest in catharsis that followed the publication in 1880 of a book on the Aristotelian concept of catharsis by Jacob Bernays[11] (the uncle of Freud's future wife). For a time catharsis was one of the most discussed subjects among scholars and one of the topics of conversation in sophisticated Viennese salons. A historian of literature complained that, following the treatise by Bernays, there had been such a craze for the topic of catharsis that few people remained interested in the history of drama.[12] The time was ripe for catharsis to become a psychotherapeutic procedure.

THE AUTHOR'S OWN RESEARCH

During the preparation of my book, *The Discovery of the Unconscious,* I conducted in Vienna an inquiry about Bertha Pappenheim. The first task was to exactly identify the characters of the story. In the *Heimat-Rolle* (in the Community Archives) I found the following indications. Bertha's father, Siegmund Pappenheim, merchant, was born in Pressburg on June 10, 1824; he died in Vienna on April 5, 1881 (this is exactly the date given by Breuer as that of the death of Anna O's father, thus a confirmation of the identity between Anna O and Bertha Pappenheim). Her mother, Recha Goldschmidt, was born in

Frankfurt on the Main on June 13, 1830. They had three children, all of them born in Vienna: Henriette, born on September 2, 1849, Bertha, born on February 27, 1859, Wilhelm, born on August 15, 1860. Henriette, who was ten years older than Bertha, died in early youth. The family lived for many years in the Jewish quarter of Leopoldstadt, but moved to Liechtensteinerstrasse in 1880 (incidentally this street was near to the Berggasse where Freud was to live from 1891 to 1938).

A few details about Pappenheim can be found in the *Memoirs* of Sigmund Mayer.[13] He had been acquainted in the ghetto with old Wolf Pappenheim, a man of a rather humble condition who, following an unexpected inheritance had been metamorphosed into a wealthy patrician. All the Pappenheims were distinguished people, Mayer says. Mayer was well acquainted with Wilhelm (Bertha's brother), whom he depicts as an accomplished gentleman, strongly identified with the Jewish tradition but open to all modern ideas, who owned perhaps the most complete library on socialism to be found in Europe.

Bertha Pappenheim was related to prominent Jewish families from her mother's side too. This is shown in an extremely rare book that she and her brother Wilhelm published in private print in 1900. It is a German translation of the memoires of an illustrious ancestor, Glückel von Hameln (1645–1724).[14] The translation is supplemented with a series of genealogical tables. One sees the connections of the Goldschmidts with numerous well-known Jewish names (such as the families Gomperz, von Portheim, Homburger, Friedländer, Oppenheim, etc.).

Coming now to Jones's version of Bertha's illness, we find difficulty reconciling it with the facts. First, Breuer's last child, Dora, was born on March 11, 1882 (as evidenced by the *Heimat-Rolle* in Vienna). Thus she could not possibly have been conceived after the supposed terminal incident of June 1882. The approximate time of Dora's conception (June 1881) would rather coincide with the date of Bertha's transfer to the country-house, but there is no evidence that Breuer interrupted the treatment at this time. (It was the beginning of the period when he went to visit her every few days, when her symptoms developed in the form of a regular cycle.) Second, there was never a sanitarium in Gross-Enzersdorf. Mr. Schramm, who wrote a history of the locality, told the author that it must have been confused with Inzersdorf, where there was a fashionable sanitarium. Upon inquiry, the author learned that it had been closed, and its medical archives transferred to the Viennese Psychiatric Hospital. No case history of Bertha Pappenheim could be found there.[15]

In Dora Edinger's biography of Bertha Pappenheim there was a photograph of Bertha with the date 1882, showing a healthy-looking, sporting woman in riding habit, in sharp contrast to Breuer's portrait of a home-bound young lady who had no outlets for her physical and mental energies. Thanks to the help of Mrs. Dora Edinger, I received the authorization to examine the original of that picture. As was usual in that time, the picture was stuck on a piece of card-board. The date 1882 had been embossed by the photographer. The name and address of the photographer could no longer be deciphered. However, when the picture was examined under special light in the laboratory of the Montreal City Police, the name of the town, *Constanz*, appeared, with a part of the address.[16] This discovery led to the question: What was Bertha doing in riding habit in Konstanz, Germany, at the time when she was supposed to be severely sick in a sanitarium near Vienna? Mrs. Edinger suggested that she could have been treated in one of the sanitariums which existed in that part of Europe. Actually, there was one famous sanitarium, in the little Swiss town of Kreuzlingen, quite close to Konstanz: the Sanatorium Bellevue. I asked the present director, Dr. Wolfgang Binswanger, if the medical archives contained a case history of Bertha Pappenheim. I learned from him that Bertha Pappenheim had actually sojourned there as a patient from July 12 to October 29, 1882. The patient's file contained two documents: a copy of a case history written by Breuer himself in 1882, and a follow-up written by one of the doctors of the Sanatorium Bellevue.

BREUER'S UNKNOWN REPORT OF 1882

The name of Breuer does not appear in the document, but it quite obviously originates from him: it is the story of the same patient told by the same physician; whole sentences are almost identical with those of the *Studies in Hysteria*. It is a manuscript of $21\frac{1}{2}$ pages of large size, manifestly a copy written by a lay person; a number of difficult words were misunderstood, left blank, or corrected by another hand.

The report of 1882 contains numerous details which were left out in the later version, but it ends rather abruptly at the end of the "third period" of Bertha's illness. The time has not yet come for a publication of the complete document, but we will give a cursory view of the early case history, stressing the points where it gives new information or differs from the 1895 report.

The 1882 report provides a more complete picture of the family constellation. Bertha had difficulties with her "very serious" mother. Her brother (never mentioned in the *Studies in Hysteria*) plays a certain role; she sometimes had quarrels with him. There are several mentions of her "passionate love for her father who pampered her."[17] Breuer confirms that the sexual element was "astonishingly undeveloped" in Bertha and says that he had never found it represented in the immense amount of her hallucinations. She had never been in love, "insofar her relationship to her father did not replace it, or rather was replaced by it."[18] Two other features in Bertha's character are stressed: her stubborn, childish opposition against medical prescriptions; and her opposition against religion: "She is thoroughly unreligious.... Religion played a role in her life only as an object of silent struggles and silent opposition,"[19] although, for her father's sake, she outwardly followed all the religious rites of her strictly orthodox Jewish family.

As early as in the spring of 1880, we learn, Bertha began to suffer from facial neuralgia and muscular jerks. What Breuer called the "first period of the illness" went from July 17 to December 10, 1880. Breuer states that he did not see her during that time. All of what he related about her symptoms during that period, he learned later from the hypnotized patient, and the patient herself, in her conscious state, knew only what Breuer told her about it. To these hypnotic revelations belong the story of the initial symptom. During the night of July 17 to 18, while the father was sick and the family waited for the arrival of a surgeon from Vienna, it happened that Bertha had a hallucination of a black snake crawling out of the wall to kill her father. She wanted to drive it away, but could not move her right arm; she saw her fingers as transformed into as many little snakes with tiny skulls, instead of the nails. She was filled with anguish, tried to pray, but could not speak until she found an English sentence. At this point the spell was interrupted by the whistling of an engine: it was the train that brought the surgeon from Vienna. A great number of other symptoms are described; many of them occurred during a peculiar state of absentmindedness which she termed (in English) "time-missing." Her visual perceptions were strangely distorted. Looking upon her father, she saw him as a skeleton and his head as a skull. After having once been shaken by her brother she became momentarily deaf but from that time on a transient deafness always appeared whenever she was shaken. A great number of other symptoms appeared, but, Breuer says, no one around her ever noticed anything of them.

At the beginning of September 1880, the family went back to Vienna (it is not stated where they were before). Bertha devoted herself to nursing her sick father. Her symptoms were aggravated, a "nervous cough" appeared. Breuer saw her for the first time at the end of November on account of an "hysterical cough"; he recognized at once that she was mentally sick—something that had escaped her family's notice.

The second period (the "manifest illness" of Breuer's report of 1895), thus began shortly after Breuer's first visit. Bertha remained in bed from December 11, 1880, to April 1, 1881. Breuer gives a lengthy description of that period of the disease, which does not add very much to what he reported in 1895. In 1882, however, he laid more emphasis upon Bertha's "truly passionate love for her father."[20] The period when she remained mute for two weeks (in 1882 Breuer called it an "aphasia") occurred, Breuer says, after she had once been hurt (*gekränkt*) by her father. After being excluded from seeing her father, she felt a longing (*Sehnsucht*) for him. During that period of the illness Breuer was concerned with an anatomical diagnosis; he considered the possibility of a tubercle in the felt *fossa Sylvii* with a slowly expanding chronic meningitis. However, the "nervous" character of her cough, and the tranquillising effect of Breuer's listening to the stories she told him evenings led him to think of a "purely functional ailment."[21]

Breuer's report of 1882 gives a great number of hitherto unknown data about the third period of Bertha's illness. First, we learn why her father's death was such a shock to her. During the previous two months she had not been allowed to see him and had continuously been told lies about his condition. In spite of her lasting anxiety, there had been some improvement in Bertha's illness and she had got up for the first time on April 1. On April 5, at the moment when her father was dying, she called her mother and asked for the truth, but was appeased and the lie went on for some time. When Bertha learned that her father had died, she was indignant: she had been "robbed" of his last look and last word. From that time on, a marked transformation appeared in her condition: anxiety replaced by a kind of dull insensitivity with distortions in her visual perceptions. Human beings appeared to her as wax figures. In order to recognize someone she had to perform what she called (in English)

a "recognizing work." The only person she immediately recognized was Breuer. She manifested an extremely negative attitude toward her mother and to a lesser degree, toward her brother.

We learn that the consulting psychiatrist who came about ten days after the father's death was none other than Krafft-Ebing. The story of his intervention is related with the same details (save that we learn the fact that the smoke he blew into her face was from a burning piece of paper!). Unfortunately nothing is said of Krafft-Ebing's diagnosis and recommendations.

In view of the difficulty of keeping Bertha at home and because of several suicidal attempts, it was decided to transfer her to Inzersdorf. However it was not in the fashionable sanitarium of the Drs. Fries and Breslauer,[22] but in a kind of cottage close to the sanitarium (Breuer called it in 1882 a *Villa*, in 1895 a *Landhaus*), so that she could be kept under the daily care of the psychiatrists of that institution, while still visited by Breuer every few days. The transfer was performed "without deceit, but by force" on June 7, 1881.

Bertha's illness had reached its acme in that month of June, and from that time on there were periods of slow improvement and relapses. Breuer, as we know, came frequently; he was able to soothe her by listening to her stories. But his task was not always easy; he had to use much persuasion and to introduce the story with the sentence (in English): "And there was a boy..." and she had to feel his hands to make sure of his identity. Dr. Breslauer did not enjoy the same success and had to give her chloral.

Breuer tells of a five-week vacation from whence he came back in the middle of August (whether he went to Venice is not mentioned in the report). On his return, he found Bertha in a pitiful condition: "emotionally very bad, disobedient, moody, nasty, lazy."[23] It also looked as if her fantasy was exhausted. She gave distorted accounts of what had irritated her during the last days. There was an unexpected development at this point. Breuer's report of 1882 brings a new, more complete version of the discovery of the "talking-cure." He found that certain of the patient's whims or fancies (he called them by the French word *caprices*) could disappear when traced back to the "psychic incitements" (*psychische Reize*) which had been at their origin. (Let us recall that even earlier Bertha's "aphasia" had disappeared when Breuer could get the patient to tell that it started after having been offended by her father.) But the patient had taken to quite a few other "fancies." Thus, she went to bed with her stockings on; sometimes she woke up at 2 or 3 in the morning and complained that she had been left to go to bed in her stockings. One evening she told Breuer that while her father was sick and she had been forbidden to see him, she used to get up in the night, put her stockings on and go to listen at his door, until one night she was caught by her brother. After she told Breuer of this incident, the stockings "fancy" disappeared. The following occurrence (described as being the first one in the *Studies in Hysteria*) was the story of the little dog: for six weeks Bertha refused to drink water and quenched her thirst with fruits and melons; she told Breuer that it had started after seeing her lady companion's dog drinking water from a glass; she had been disgusted but had said nothing. Five minutes after telling Breuer the story she was able to drink water and the "drinking inhibition" (*Trink hemmung*) disappeared forever. Breuer found that certain "caprices" could be traced back, simply to some "fantastic thought" which the patient had imagined; such was her refusal to eat bread. The next step in the progress of the treatment was Breuer's discovery that not only "caprices," but also seemingly neurological symptoms could be made to disappear in the same way.

The end of the case history is disappointing. Breuer tells in a few lines that Bertha came back to her mother in Vienna at the beginning of November 1881, so that he was able to give her her talking-cure every evening. However "for unaccountable reasons" her condition became worse

in December. At the end of December, during the period of the Jewish Holidays, she was agitated; during that whole week she told Breuer every evening the fantastic stories that she had imagined at the same period of the preceding year; they were, day by day, the same stories.

The report contains nothing about the "fourth period" of the illness, although it is stated at the beginning of the report that it extended from December 1881 to the middle of June 1882. It ends with that enigmatic sentence: "After termination of the series great alleviation."[24] It should also be noted that there is nowhere any mention of a hysterical pregnancy and that the word catharsis appears nowhere in the 1882 report.

THE FOLLOW-UP OF THE SANITORIUM BELLEVUE

The copy of Breuer's long report is immediately followed on its last page by the beginning of a 2½ page follow-up, obviously written at the end of Bertha's sojourn by one of the doctors of the Sanitorium Bellevue. It bears the title: "Evolution of the illness during the sojourn in Bellevue from July 12, 1882, to October 29, 1882."

This follow-up is in many regards very instructive, in other regards disappointing. Someone who would know of Anna O only what Breuer related in the *Studies in Hysteria* would hardly guess that it is a follow-up of the same patient just after she had undergone Breuer's "cathartic cure." The follow-up consists of a long enumeration of medications given to the patient on account of a severe facial neuralgia. We learn that the facial neuralgia had been exacerbated during the past six months (that is, the "fourth period" of her illness) and that during that period high amounts of chloral and of morphine had been prescribed. On her admission the amount of morphine was reduced to 7 to 8 centigrams of morphine in two daily injections. But the pains were at times so intolerable that one had to give her 10 centigrams. When she left the sanitarium, she still received injections amounting to a total of 7 to 10 centigrams *pro die*. The follow-up, however, contains mention of "hysterical features" (*hysterische Merkmale*) in the patient, of her "unpleasant irritation against her family,[25] of her "disparaging judgments against the ineffectiveness of science in regard to her sufferings,"[26] of her "lack of insight into the severity of her nervous condition."[27] She often remained for hours under the picture of her father and told of visiting his tomb in Pressburg. In the evening, she regularly lost the use of the German language as soon as she had put her head on the pillow; she would even terminate in English a sentence that she had begun in German. The follow-up ends with this sentence: "Here, she did understand and speak French, though it was difficult to her on certain evenings." There is no mention of where the patient went after leaving Bellevue.

COMMENTARY

The time has not yet come for a complete and truly objective appraisal of Anna O's story. The two newly discovered documents may however shed some light upon a few points.

We know, now, that when Breuer published Anna O's story in 1895 he had under his eyes a previous report he had written in 1882 (whole lines are sometimes almost identical). This report, however, relates the story of the patient up to December 1881 and leaves out the "fourth period" of her illness. On the other hand, it seems that during the period when Breuer treated his patient he did not write daily notes about her. There are good reasons to think that the 1882 report was written from memory: there are no precise dates, aside from those of the father's death and of Bertha's transfer to the country-house. (Breuer does not even mention the date of his first visit to Bertha, nor that of the consultation with Krafft-Ebing). This might also be the reason why Breuer tells in 1895 of his "incomplete notes," when referring to the "fourth period" of the illness.

Breuer's report of 1882 brings a more complete picture of the patient's family and environment. Breuer draws a connection between the fact that Bertha had never been in love and her "truly passionate love to her father." We learn of her difficulties with her "very serious mother" and her quarrels with her brother. There is also a passing mention of an aunt.

Bertha's stubborn character is emphasized in the 1882 report, with her "childish opposition" to the doctors. Unexpected is the fact that Bertha was "thoroughly unreligious" in the midst of her strictly orthodox Jewish family. One would wish to know how and when she returned to the faith of her ancestors and became the ardent religious personality of the later years. We also learn of Bertha's visits to the theater and her interest in Shakespeare's plays.

The problematic features of the "first period" of Bertha's illness appear more clearly in the 1882 report than in the 1895 case history. Breuer did not see Anna during that first period and he emphasizes that her illness was completely unnoticed by her family. She did not remember her symptoms of that period and knew about them only what Breuer had learned from her under hypnosis and told her afterwards. One may wonder how Breuer could take at face value all the revelations of the hypnotized patient, whereas he expressly notes that—on the conscious level—she "gave distorted accounts of what had irritated her during the last days."

In the 1882 report the course of Bertha's illness appears as having been somewhat more stormy than in the narrative of 1895. We learn why the father's death was such a severe psychic trauma for the patient. We see more clearly that there was a succession of ups and downs, with at least four periods of worsening: (1) after the father's death; (2) after the transfer to the country-house; (3) during Breuer's vacation of July-August 1881; (4) and "for unaccountable reasons" in November 1881. We see more clearly the origin and development of the what was called later "cathartic" treatment: at first and for a long time the "chimney-sweeping" merely meant that Bertha unburdened her mind from the stories she had imagined during the past days. But there came a time (in August 1881) when her fantasy was exhausted, and then she started to tell about the events that had been the starting-point of her (quite conscious and voluntary) "caprices." Later, she extended this procedure to the more serious, seemingly neurological symptoms. It is also noteworthy that the neurological symptoms, particularly the facial neuralgia, stand out more clearly in the 1882 report than in the 1895 case history. Breuer's concern with the brain-anatomical seat of the illness is noted in two places in the 1882 report.

Unfortunately the "fourth period" of Bertha's illness keeps its mystery entirely. The case history of 1895 tells of a strange, indeed unique, condition, and of two personalities, one living exactly 365 days before the other, and of the extraordinary therapeutic method of curing the illness by having the patient tell in reverse chronological order all occurrences of a given symptom, whatever the number, until one came to the first manifestation with the circumstances of its appearance. But Breuer's report of 1882 is almost completely silent about these strange facts. The Kreuzlingen follow-up does not mention anything of all this and merely refers to the fact that the patient had gotten used to taking high doses of chloral and morphine. In this follow-up the patient is depicted as a neurological case of a rather unpleasant person showing some hysterical features.

Thus, the newly discovered documents confirm what Freud, according to Jung, had told him: the patient had not been cured. Indeed, the famed "prototype of a cathartic cure" was neither a cure nor a catharsis. Anna O had become a severe morphinist and had kept a part of her most conspicuous symptoms (in Bellevue she could no longer speak German as soon as she had put her head on the pillow). Jones's version of

the false pregnancy and hysterical birth throes cannot be confirmed and does not fit into the chronology of the case.

In *The Discovery of the Unconscious* I proposed the hypothesis that Anna O's illness was similar to one of those great "magnetic diseases" of the early 19th century such as that of the "Seeress of Prevorst." This would mean that the illness was a creation of the mythopoetic unconscious of the patient with the unaware encouragement and collaboration of the therapist. However, there must have been in Bertha's case more than just a "romance of the subliminal self" (to use Frederick Myers' terminology). Anna O's illness was the desperate struggle of an unsatisfied young woman who found no outlets for her physical and mental energies, nor for her idealistic strivings. It needed much time and effort before she succeeded in sublimating her personality into the respectable figure of a pioneer of social work, fighter for the rights of women and the welfare of her people—Bertha Pappenheim.

NOTES

1 Joseph Breuer und Sigmund Freud: *Studien über Hysterie,* Leipzig und Vienna, Deuticke, 1895, pp. 15–37.

2 Charles E. Goshen: The Original Case Material of Psychoanalysis. *American Journal of Psychiatry,* vol. 108, 1951–1952, pp. 830–834.

3 Sigmund Freud: *Medizin in Selbstdarstellung,* IV, 1924, p. 15.

4 *Notes on the Seminar in Analytical Psychology Conducted by C. G. Jung,* Zurich, March 23–July 6, 1925. Arranged by Members of the Class, Zurich, 1926 (unpublished typescript).

5 Ernest Jones: *The Life and Work of Sigmund Freud,* vol. I. New York, Basic Books, 1953, pp. 223–226.

6 *Blätter des Jüdischen Frauenbundes für Frauenarbeit und Frauenbewegung,* vol. XII, no. 7/8, July-August, 1936.

7 Ellen Jensen: Anna O. Ihr späteres Schicksal. *Acta psychiatrica et neurologica scandinavica,* vol. 36,

no. 1, 1961, pp. 119–131. See also: Allen M. Jensen: Anna O.—A Study of Her Later Life. *Psychoanalytic Quarterly,* vol. 39, no. 2, 1970, pp. 269–293.

8 Dora Edinger (Ed.): *Bertha Pappenheim: Leben und Schriften.* Frankfurt-am-Main, Ner-Tamid-Verlag, 1963.

9 See the stories of Catherine Muller and of Helene Preiswerk in the author's book, *The Discovery of the Unconscious,* New York, Basic Books, 1970, pp. 315–317, 689–691.

10 Juan Dalma: La catarsis en Aristoteles, Bernays y Freud. *Revista de Psiquiatría y Psicología Medical,* vol. 6, 1963, pp. 253–269. Reminiscencias Culturales Clásicas en Algunas Corrientes de Psicologia Moderna, *Revista de la Facultad de Medicina de Tucuman,* vol. 5, 1964, pp. 301–332.

11 Jacob Bernays: *Zwei Abhandlungen über die Aristotelische Theorie des Drama.* Berlin, Wilhelm Hertz, 1880.

12 Wilhelm Wetz: *Shakespeare vom Standpunkt der vergleichenden Literaturgeschichte.* Hamburg, Haendeke, Lehmkübe, 1897, vol. 1, p. 30.

13 Sigmund Mayer: *Ein jüdischer Kaufmann, 1831 bis 1911. Lebenserinnerungen.* Leipzig, Duncker und Humblot, 1911, pp. 49–50.

14 *Die Memoiren des Glückel von Hameln... Autorisierte Uebertragung nach der Ausgabe des Prof. Dr. David Kaufman von Bertha Pappenheim.* Wien, 1910. Verlag von Dr. Stefan Meyer und Dr. Wilhelm Pappenheim.

15 For assistance in the author's inquiries he is indebted to Mr. Schramm, of Gross Enzersdorf, Mr. Karl Neumayer, Mayor of Inzersdorf, and Dr. W. Podhajsky, Director of the Viennese Psychiatric Hospital.

16 Thanks are due to Dr. Jörg Schuh-Kuhlmann who performed that investigation and to the Montreal City Police Laboratory for this valuable contribution to a point of psychiatric history.

17 "*...in leidenschaftlicher Liebe zu dem sie verhätschelnden Vater.*"

18 "*...soweit nicht ihr Verhältnis zum Vater dieses ersetzt hat oder vielmehr damit ersetzt war.*"

19 "*Sie ist durchaus nicht religiös....Eine Rolle in ihrem Leben spielte Religion nur als Gegenstand stiller Kämpfe und stiller Opposition.*"

20 "*...ihre wahre leidenschaftliche Liebe.*"

21 "*...dass es sich doch um rein funktionnelles Leiden handle.*"

22 Details about the Inzersdorf sanitarium may be found in Heinrich Schlöss (Ed.): *Die Irrenpflege in Oesterreich in Wort und Bild.* Halle, Carl Marhold, 1912, pp. 241–253. The institution had been founded in 1872 by Hermann Breslauer (a former assistant of Prof. Leidensdorf) and Dr. Fries. The main building was the former castle of a noble family; there was a large English park. All kinds of psychotic and neurotic patients were treated.

23 "*...moralisch recht schlecht, unfügsam, launisch, boshaft, träge.*"

24 "*Nach Beendigung der Serie grosse Erleichterung.*"

25 "*...geradezu unliebenswürdigen Gereiztheit gegen Angehörige.*"

26 "*So beurtheilte sie in abfälliger Weise die Unzulänglichkeit der Wissenschaft gegenüber ihren Leiden.*"

27 "*Die fehlende Einsicht in die Schwere ihres Stat. nervosus.*"

CHAPTER 16

GESTALT PSYCHOLOGY

In 1912, Edward L. Thorndike was delivering his presidential address in Cleveland, Ohio, before the twenty-first annual meeting of the American Psychological Association; G. Stanley Hall's student, Henry Herbert Goddard, was publishing his famous book on the Kallikak family showing the relationship between heredity and feeblemindedness; William Stern was introducing the concept of the intelligence quotient (IQ) to mental testing; and John B. Watson was writing his Behaviorist Manifesto. In that same year, a German journal of psychology published an article entitled "Experimentelle Studien über das Sehen von Bewegung" (experimental studies on the perception of movement). That article was to signal the beginning of a new school of thought in psychology, a system known as *Gestalt psychology*.

The author of that 1912 paper was Max Wertheimer (1880–1943), a German psychologist who is viewed as the founder of Gestalt psychology. The source of those studies on the perception of movement is the subject of one of the most famous anecdotes in the history of modern psychology. The idea came to Wertheimer when he was traveling on a train in 1910 during his vacation. He got off the train in Frankfurt, purchased a toy stroboscope (a device that presents a series of successive pictures producing apparent motion), and tested his ideas in his hotel room. He continued his research at the Frankfurt Psychological Institute, where he was joined in his efforts by two recent doctoral graduates from the University of Berlin: Kurt Koffka (1886–1941) and Wolfgang Köhler (1887–1967). These three would become the triumvirate of Gestalt psychology, launching their fight against a German psychology whose atomistic approach was antithetical to their views of consciousness.

Wertheimer's initial experiments in Frankfurt involved a type of apparent movement he labeled the *phi phenomenon*. Two black lines were stroboscopically presented against a white background. The first line was vertical, the second horizontal, and the two were positioned so that if they were seen simultaneously they would form a right angle. The first line would appear briefly and then disappear, followed by the appearance of the second line. The position of the lines was held constant, as was their time of exposure. Only the temporal interval between the offset of the first line and the onset of the second line was varied. When the interval was approximately 30 milliseconds, the observer reported that the lines appeared and disappeared simultaneously. If the interval was increased to 60 milliseconds, the observer reported seeing movement; that is, the observer saw a single line moving from the vertical position to the horizontal position, rather than two separate lines appearing in succession (Max Wertheimer, 1912).

This form of apparent movement was not new to the scientific world. What was new was Wertheimer's interpretation of the movement; he viewed it as an experience that was not reducible to its component elements. Not only was it impossible to make such a reduction by even the most deliberate of introspections, but the seen movement could not be readily explained by describing the appearance and disappearance of the two static lines. There was something *more* to the experience than was evident in those line stimuli (see O'Neil & Landauer, 1966). This awareness is indicated in the Gestalt maxim that "the whole is different from the sum of its parts"; that is, there is a quality of experience that is often independent of the collection of stimulus elements that make up that experience—an idea anticipated by Christian von Ehrenfels (1859–1932), with whom Wertheimer had studied.

Ehrenfels was at Graz University in Austria in 1890 when he published his criticism of the incompleteness of Wundt's atomistic psychology. His objection was not to the study of elements; rather it was that Wundt's analysis was ignoring important elements—elements that were beyond the mere sensory elements. He called these elements form qualities (*Gestalt qualitäten*) and described their existence with the example of a musical melody. A melody, he argued, is more than just the collection of individual notes; it is also the patterning or configuration of those notes. Thus a melody played at either end of a piano keyboard would be recognizable as the same melody, even though each version would consist of entirely different sound frequencies. For Ehrenfels, the configuration of the notes (the form quality of the melody) was one more element to be added to the individual elements (notes) in the conscious experience of a melody.

Wertheimer built on Ehrenfels's work, but with an interesting and insightful twist:

> The whole quality is not just one more added element. The qualities of the whole determine the characteristics of the parts. . . . the nature of the parts is determined by the whole rather than vice versa; therefore analysis should go "from above down"

rather than "from below up." One should not begin with elements and try to synthesize the whole from them, but study the whole to see what its natural parts are. (Michael Wertheimer, 1987, p. 136)

Thus, for Wertheimer, Wundt's approach was not just incomplete, it was wrong. Its reductionism produced a view of consciousness that was distorted, artificial. The Gestalt psychologists argued for the study of immediate experience, which they defined very differently from Wundt. Immediate experience consists of wholes, usually segregated wholes seen against a background, not the batches of sensations they saw as artificially created by the methods of the Wundtians: "analysis destroys the very reality it seeks to explain;...to reduce a thing to its elements and study it piecemeal is to lose sight of the thing itself" (Heidbreder, 1933, p. 373).

The holistic approach of the Gestalt psychologists was in direct opposition to the prevailing view of German psychology at the beginning of the twentieth century. They struggled to gain their place, and what began as a foothold eventually supplanted Wundtian psychology, as perhaps best indicated by the ascendancy of Wolfgang Köhler to German psychology's premier position as head of the Psychological Institute at Berlin University in 1921.

For most American psychologists initial exposure to Gestalt psychology came from an article published by Kurt Koffka in a 1922 issue of the *Psychological Bulletin*. The article, entitled "Perception: An Introduction to Gestalt-Theorie," led many American psychologists to see Gestalt psychology as a perceptual theory. But Gestalt theory was in fact much broader, emphasizing particularly the areas of thinking and learning. The reason for much of the early work on perception was that Wundt and his followers had focused on perception. Thus the Gestalt psychologists attacked the older theory in its stronghold (Michael Wertheimer, 1987).

In the 1920s and early 1930s, Gestalt psychology enjoyed considerable success in Germany. But all that would come to a sudden, and sometimes tragic, end when the Nazis came to power in 1933. Koffka had already left Germany, taking a position at Smith College in Northampton, Massachusetts, in 1927. Wertheimer, who was Jewish, fled Germany in 1933, taking a university position at the New School for Social Research in New York City. Two years later, after tense confrontations with the Nazis, Köhler followed him to the United States, accepting a position at Swarthmore College in the Philadelphia area.

Wertheimer and Köhler were two of many German and Austrian émigré-psychologists who came to the United States to escape the Nazis. They left prestigious professorships in the best German universities to take lesser positions in the United States. The 1930s were hard times in the United States, the era of the Great Depression; jobs were scarce for American doctorates, much less for the wave of European immigrants. For these newly arrived psychologists the culture was unfamiliar, the language was a problem, and the dominant psychology of behaviorism was as objectionable as that of the Wundtians.

In behaviorism the Gestalt psychologists found another atomistic approach to psychology—complex behaviors were the result of combinations of simple reactions. Behaviorism was just one more molecular approach, filled with the artificiality inherent in such approaches. Its artificiality was clearly indicated by its denial of consciousness as a valid topic for scientific study. On the other side, the Americans, too, were dismayed by this foreign psychology that espoused the study of consciousness using introspective methods. It sounded too much like the mentalism they had so recently discarded.

Although Gestalt psychology did not displace behaviorism, tenets of Gestalt theory found their way into the psychology of perception and learning (recall the comments on Edward C. Tolman in Chapter 14). Its greatest influence, however, was evident in the emergence of the cognitive revolution in American psychology beginning in the 1950s. Much of the contemporary work on thinking, problem solving, language, and information processing has antecedents in Gestalt psychology.

The philosophy and history of Gestalt psychology are surveyed in the three articles in this chapter. The first selection, by Wolfgang Köhler, was written shortly before his death—his last scientific paper. It represents an intellectual history of the Gestalt movement and a defense against its German and American critics. In it Köhler describes the early work in Germany as well as the continuation of the research in the United States. The reader should be aware that this article benefits from the first-hand experiences of Köhler as part of Gestalt psychology's origin, but it also represents recollections of events that sometimes happened more than 50 years ago. Although some historians would question its accuracy on grounds of personal bias and possible memory distortions, this history according to Köhler is a lucid and interesting account.

The second selection is by Mary Henle, whose work the reader has encountered in Chapters 1 and 8. In this article she tells the fascinating story of the final days of the Psychological Institute at Berlin University and how Köhler fought to keep it going in the face of growing Nazi pressures. It is a tale of great human courage and an example of archival research and storytelling at their best.

The final selection is by Michael M. Sokal, whose work on James McKeen Cattell appears in Chapter 10. In this selection, Sokal describes the treatment of Gestalt psychology in the behaviorist America, arguing that understanding the outcome of the intellectual migration requires a differentiation of reactions to Gestalt psychology, the Gestalt movement, and the Gestalt psychologists themselves. He concludes that American psychology was more open to Gestalt ideas and the Gestalt psychologists than many previous histories have implied. That view is not without its opponents (see Henle, 1977).

Personalities often play an important role in shaping any discipline, including the science of psychology. This chapter probably illustrates that more clearly than any other chapter in this book. All three selections demonstrate how personalities have affected the history of Gestalt psychology on both sides of the Atlantic Ocean. That personalistic lesson is an important one to learn and an appropriate ending for this book.

REFERENCES

Heidbreder, E. (1933). *Seven psychologies*. New York: Appleton-Century-Crofts.

Henle, M. (1977). The influence of Gestalt psychology in America. *Annals of the New York Academy of Sciences, 291*, 3–12.

Koffka, K. (1922). Perception: An introduction to Gestalt-theorie. *Psychological Bulletin, 19*, 531–585.

O'Neil, W. M., & Landauer, A. A. (1966). The phi-phenomenon: Turning point or rallying point. *Journal of the History of the Behavioral Sciences, 2*, 335–340.

Wertheimer, Max (1912). Experimentelle studien über das Sehen von Bewegung. *Zeitschrift fur Psychologie, 61*, 161–265. English translation appears in T. Shipley (Ed.), *Classics in psychology*. New York: Philosophical Library, 1961.

Wertheimer, Michael (1987). *A brief history of psychology* (3d ed.). New York: Holt, Rinehart and Winston.

Gestalt Psychology

Wolfgang Köhler

What we now call Gestalt psychology began to develop in 1910. At the time, there was not much psychology anywhere in Germany. People were doing experiments on memory, with the technique introduced by Ebbinghaus, and on the problems of psychophysics. Fechner, a physicist-philosopher, somewhat optimistically regarded difference limens, as investigated by Weber, and the quantitative relation between stimulus and sensation from his own studies, as the beginning of a real science of the mind. Max Wertheimer, in 1910, was disturbed by the narrowness of such enterprises. He tried to study more interesting psychological facts and, as a first example, he chose apparent movement, the movement seen when two objects appear in fairly rapid succession, one in one place and another in a different location.

Apparent movement as such was known; but many psychologists regarded it as a mere cognitive illusion. Since no real objective movement occurs under these conditions, it was believed that apparent movement could not be a real perceptual fact. Rather, it was felt, it must be a product of erroneous judging. The explanation went like this. First, I see one object; immediately afterwards I see an object of the same kind in a somewhat different place. Naturally, I regard this second object as identical with the first, and conclude that the first has simply moved from the one place to the other.

This is a tranquilizing explanation. No longer need we worry about apparent movement. But this is also what we would now call a case of "explaining away." A striking perceptual fact is observed which we cannot immediately explain. Then we invent an explanation for which there

is no factual evidence, an explanation according to which there simply is no perceptual fact that has to be explained, but only a curious cognitive blunder.

"Explaining away" has not entirely disappeared from psychology even now, although such extraordinary constructions as the one just mentioned are no longer used for the purpose. The procedure may kill important problems. When tempted to do this kind of thing, we therefore ought immediately to test our proposed explanation in experiments.

This is what Wertheimer did. He studied the conditions under which apparent movement is seen. He varied the spatial locations of the objects involved, and the rate at which they followed each other; he observed the variations of the movement itself which occurred under such conditions, and so on. He also showed his subjects optimal apparent movement and similar movement of a real object, side by side and simultaneously. He found that the two could not be distinguished by the observer. Eventually he added a most important test which, it was afterwards discovered, had once before been done by a physiologist. First, a great many repetitions of apparent movement are shown in a given place. Later, when a stationary pattern is shown in the same place, subjects clearly see a negative afterimage of the apparent movement, just as negative afterimages are seen after repeated presentations of a physically real movement.

Wertheimer's was a masterpiece of experimental investigation in the field of perception. It was also the beginning of extremely fruitful studies in general Gestalt psychology. Much thinking and many discussions followed. The number of basic questions which Wertheimer now began to consider increased rapidly. At the time, he did not publish what he found; rather, he told Koffka about his questions and his tentative answers, and Koffka in turn began to tell his students what he had learned from Wertheimer and about further ideas that he himself had developed in the same productive spirit. These students investigated one interesting possibility after another in the new field. For a brief time I was able to take part in this development. It was Koffka who, realizing that Wertheimer hesitated to write down what he was thinking, formulated first principles of Gestalt psychology in an excellent article which was published in 1915.

Similar questions had begun to be discussed in Austria. Years before Wertheimer began his work, von Ehrenfels had called attention to a serious omission in the customary treatment of perceptual facts. We are accustomed, he said, to regard perceptual fields as collections of local sensations whose qualities and intensities are determined by corresponding local physical stimuli. This simple assumption, he added, cannot explain a large number of particularly interesting perceptual phenomena. For, quite apart from such local sensations, we often find in perceptual fields phenomena of an entirely different class—Gestalt qualities such as the specific shapes of objects, the melodic properties of this or that sequence of tones, and so forth. These Gestalt qualities remain practically unaltered when the stimuli in question are transposed. They seem to depend upon relations among the stimuli rather than upon the individual stimuli as such.

From these, and other obvious perceptual facts, the Austrian psychologists developed an interpretation of perception which differed radically from the views developed by Wertheimer. Since the Gestalt qualities could not be derived from the properties of individual sensations, the psychologists in Austria felt that they must be products of higher mental operations which the mind constantly imposes on mere sense data. This theoretical approach, the so-called production theory, did not seem particularly inviting to Wertheimer and Koffka. Nevertheless one has to admit that at least one member of the Austrian

School, Benussi, sometimes seemed to forget the curious production theory, and then invented most original experiments.

At this point, I have to say a few words about my own experiences during this period. I was aware of what Wertheimer was trying to do and found it not only objectively interesting but also most refreshing as a human endeavor. He observed important phenomena regardless of the fashions of the day and tried to discover what they meant. I had a feeling that his work might transform psychology, which was hardly a fascinating affair at the time, into a most lively study of basic human issues. My own work, however, was not yet related to Wertheimer's investigations, although I did write a fairly energetic paper against the tendency of others to invent explanations which served to get rid of many most interesting facts. Just when Wertheimer's work came near its most decisive stage, I became separated from my friends in Germany when I was sent to Spanish Africa by the Prussian Academy of Science. They wanted me to study a group of chimpanzees, just captured for the purpose in western parts of the African continent.

The chimpanzees proved to be extremely interesting creatures. I studied their sometimes strangely intelligent behavior and also the curious restrictions to which such achievements were often subject. Somewhat later, I occasionally interrupted these studies and investigated the perception of chimpanzees and, for the sake of comparison, that of chickens. It soon became clear that in the visual field of both species constancies of size and of brightness are almost as obvious as they are in humans. In further experiments these animals, particularly the chimpanzees, learned to choose between two objects of different size or brightness. I was able to show in tests of transposition that what they had learned was relationally determined. (I later discovered that experiments of the same kind had been done, a short time before, by American psychologists.)

I was kept in Africa for more than six years

by the First World War. During that long period I did not always feel inclined to continue my work in animal psychology. Ideas with which I had become acquainted in Europe would come back to me, most often the changes in psychological thinking which Wertheimer had just introduced. But I was also very much aware of what I had learned as a student of Max Planck, the great physicist. He had just discovered the quantum of electromagnetic radiation, but at the time taught us mainly what physicists called field physics. Under Planck's influence I had dimly felt that between Wertheimer's new thinking in psychology and the physicist's thinking in field physics there was some hidden connection. What was it? I now began to study the important works on field physics. The first discovery I made was that, fifty years before Wertheimer, some of his basic questions had already been asked not by psychologists but by physicists, first of all by Clerk Maxwell, the greatest physicist of that period. The Gestalt psychologists, we remember, were always disturbed by a thesis which was widely accepted by others. One psychologist, strongly influenced by traditional convictions, had formulated it in the following words: "I do not know whether perceptual fields actually consist of independent local elements, the so-called sensations. But, as scientists, we have to proceed as though this were true." An extraordinary statement—an a priori general conviction about the right procedure in science is assumed to be more important than the nature of the facts which we are investigating.

From its very beginning, Gestalt psychology ignored this thesis and began its work with simple and unbiased observations of facts. Independent local sensations? Consider again what happens in apparent movement. After a first visual object has appeared in one place, a second visual object does not appear in its normal location but nearer the place where the first has just disappeared, and only then moves towards what I just called its normal location. Clearly, therefore, the process corresponding to the second ob-

ject has been deflected, has been attracted by a remnant of what has just happened in another place, the place of the first object, and has only then approached its "normal" location. Consequently, under the conditions of such experiments, the second object does not behave as though it were an independent local fact at all. The statement, quoted earlier, that perceptual fields must be assumed to consist of independent local sensations, is therefore at odds with the behavior of percepts even under such fairly simple conditions. Or take any of the well-known perceptual illusions, say the Müller-Lyer illusion. Can there be any doubt that in this case two lines of objectively equal length become lines of different length under the influence of the angles added at the ends of the distances to be compared? And so on, in a long list of examples, all of them incompatible with the statement about the nature of perceptual fields.

Ours was an uphill fight. I felt greatly relieved, as mentioned above, to find so fundamentally similar an approach from the side of physics. In his great treatise, *Electricity and Magnetism,* Clerk Maxwell had remarked that we are often told that in science we must, first of all, investigate the properties of very small local places one after another, and only when this has been done can we permit ourselves to consider how more complicated situations result from what we have found in those elements. This procedure, he added, ignores the fact that many phenomena in nature can only be understood when we inspect not so-called elements but fairly large regions. Similarly, in 1910, Max Planck published lectures which he had just delivered in New York. In one of these, when discussing the second principle of thermodynamics, the entropy principle, the author states emphatically that those who try to build up physics on the assumption that a study of local elements has to precede any attempt to explain the behavior of larger systems will never understand the entropy principle, the principle which deals with the direction of physical processes. Or take Eddington, the astronomer, who once wrote the following sentences: "In physics we are often invited to inspect all tiny elements of space in succession in order to gain a complete inventory of the world." But, the author objects, if we were to do this, "all properties of the physical world would be overlooked which cannot be found or understood as matters of tiny elements in space."

I was greatly surprised by these statements of eminent scientists which so obviously agreed with statements made by Gestalt psychologists. Did these great physicists merely add further mysteries to the mysteries in which, according to many critics, the Gestalt psychologists were mainly interested? Actually, these physicists did not refer to mysteries at all. Rather, they studied a great many specific physical situations and did so in an extraordinarily clear fashion. They handled these situations as wholes rather than as collections of small, local, independent facts; they had to because of the nature of such situations, the parts of which are all functionally related (or interdependent) so that what happens at a given moment at a place happens only so long as conditions and events everywhere else in the system are not altered, so long, that is, as all interactions within the whole system remain the same.

Most of us are probably familiar with Kirchhoff's laws which describe the distribution of a steady electric flow in a network of wires. When looking at the fairly simple expression which indicates what occurs within a particular local branch of the network, we see at once that this expression refers to the conditions of conduction not only in this particular local branch but also to conditions in all other branches. This is, of course, necessary because, in the steady state, the local currents throughout the network must balance one another—which means that, while a current develops in the local branch, its flow is influenced by the flow in all other branches as much as by the condition in the interior of its branch. What could be more natural when function is balanced everywhere within the system

as a whole? Obviously, there is no mystery in this behavior of physical systems. And there would be no mystery either if the same kind of thing happened in a brain rather than in a network of wires. To be sure, networks of wires are exceptionally simple examples; other systems in which functional interrelations determine local facts in a far more radical fashion are not so easy to handle.

I was much impressed by such facts in physics. They offered a striking lesson to psychology in general and seemed to give Gestalt psychology a most welcome justification. I wrote, in Africa, a book about this part of exact physics and its possible application to psychology and to the understanding of brain function. The book has remained practically unknown in this country, partly, I think, because it uses the language and the logic of field physics, a part of physics with which not all of us are familiar.

When the book was published in 1920, both Wertheimer and Koffka greatly enjoyed its content. It showed that the alleged mysteries of Gestalt psychology agreed with perfectly clear procedures and facts in natural science. In a sense, Gestalt psychology has since become a kind of application of field physics to essential parts of psychology and of brain physiology.

When I was able to return to Germany, I found a most lively group of students just appearing at the Psychological Institute of the University of Berlin. They were attracted by Wertheimer, by Kurt Lewin, and, to a degree, by what I had discovered when experimenting with chimpanzees and reading physics in Africa. Not all our work referred to Gestalt psychology. For instance, we managed to prove that the famous moon illusion is by no means restricted to situations in which the sky and the moon play the decisive role. But Gestalt psychology remained the central issue. A few simple examples. One student, Scholz, examined the distance between two successively shown parallel lines when the rate of their succession was varied. He found that the second line appeared clearly too near the first line long before the rate of the succession approached that needed for apparent movement. Hence, the second line was attracted by some remnant of the first, just as Wertheimer had said. Or again: in an attempt to investigate time errors in the comparison of shapes, and the connection of such errors with the fate of young memory traces, Lauenstein did some beautiful experiments. Also, just about the same time, von Restorff and I applied Gestalt principles of perception to problems of memory, and in doing so discovered the so-called isolation effect. Kurt Lewin, too, did experiments in memory. But his main achievements were experiments in which he boldly transferred psychological situations from ordinary life to the laboratory and thus enlarged the range of psychological investigations in a highly productive fashion.

The most important person of our group, however, remained Wertheimer, who at the time was completing his most significant study in perception, his investigation of the way in which objects, figures, and patches are segregated from their environment as circumscribed entities. Perhaps it was not emphasized at the time, but for most of us it became the main result of his observations that, in this fashion, he gave a perfectly clear meaning to the term "perceived wholes" which, before, had sounded so mysterious to many colleagues. Obviously, the appearance of wholes of this kind is just as much a matter of division or separation within the visual field as it is of their coherence, their unitary character.

So long as Wertheimer's observations referred only to well-known unitary things, many authors were inclined to believe that it was merely learning ("previous experience") which makes them appear as firm units detached from their environment. But Wertheimer continued his investigation of perceptual wholes when the units in question were unitary groups of individual objects rather than simple things. In such situations one can often demonstrate that the formation of specific group units is not a matter of prior learning. Wertheimer did not deny that

sometimes past experience does influence perceptual grouping. But, on the other hand, one should not forget what Gottschaldt once demonstrated: that, in many cases, purely perceptual organization is too strong to be affected by past experience, even when this past experience is, as such, most powerful.

In the meantime, several European and American psychologists who were not members of the Gestalt group became intensely interested in its work. They had begun independently to work on similar problems. One such person was Edgar Rubin who concentrated on what he called the relation of "figure" and "ground" in perception. For instance, even when an object is part of a large frontal-parallel plane, this object appears slightly separated from the ground and stands out in the third dimension. We now know that this separation is not only a qualitative curiosity but a real perceptual depth effect which can easily be varied in a quantitative fashion, and may then establish quite specific shapes in three dimensional space.

Other psychologists who turned in the same direction were David Katz and Albert Michotte in Europe, Lashley, Klüver and, to a degree, Gibson in America. I wish more people would study Michotte's marvelous publications, and also a lecture which Lashley delivered in 1929, when he was president of the American Psychological Association. The spirit of this lecture was throughout that of Gestalt psychology; later, it is true, Lashley became a bit more skeptical. Once, when we discussed the main tenets of Gestalt psychology, he suddenly smiled and said, "Excellent work—but don't you have religion up your sleeve?"

Time is too short for a discussion of the great achievements of Wertheimer and Duncker in the psychology of thinking. Their work in this field may be regarded as the last great development in Gestalt psychology that occurred in those years. Since then almost all members of the old school have died, and only a few younger psychologists are left whose investigations are clearly related to those of the earlier period: Asch, Arnheim, Wallach, Henle, Heider—all of whose work is well known to us.

When the Nazi regime became intolerable, I emigrated to the United States which I knew well from earlier visits. In America, I tried to continue the investigations which had been started in Berlin. For instance, when actual perceptions have disappeared, traces of them must be left in the nervous system. They are supposed to be the factual condition which makes recall of those perceptions possible. My first question was: traces of what in perception? Perceptual fields contain not only individual objects but also other products of organization such as segregated groups, sometimes groups which contain only two members. Grouping of this kind may be just as obvious in perception as are the individual members of the groups. Now, this means a perceptual unification or connection within the group, and there is no reason why, in the realm of memory traces, this connection or unification should not be just as clearly represented as are the members of the group. Consequently, when the group has only two members, we must expect these members to be connected not only in perception but also as traces. How would this fact manifest itself in memory?

Among the concepts used in the psychology of memory, the concept "association" may mean, for instance, that two items in a perceptual field are functionally so well connected that, when one of them is reactivated, the same happens also to the other item. This is precisely what one has to expect if, in perception, the two items form a pair-group, and if the unitary character of the perceived pair is represented as a correspondingly unitary entity in the realm of traces. If this were true, the concept of association would be directly related to the concept of organization as applied to pairs in perception.

This assumption can be tested in simple experiments in the following manner. The formation of pairs in perception depends upon the characteristics of the objects involved; it is, for instance, most likely to occur when these objects resemble each other—or when both belong to the same class of objects. Consequently, if association is an aftereffect of pair formation in perception, association must be most effective precisely when the objects are similar or at least obviously members of the same general class. Tests of this conclusion could be quite easily arranged and showed, for instance, that association of members of a given class is far more effective than association of objects dissimilar in this sense. I fully realize—and some, Postman in particular, have emphasized—that this result may still be explained in another fashion; therefore, I have just begun to do further experiments which ought to tell us whether or not the organizational interpretation of our results is correct. Work in a young science is an exciting affair. It becomes particularly exciting when new functional possibilities have just been introduced. I am grateful to those who make the present issue even more exciting by their objections. They force me to do further experiments which will decide whether the concept of organization is applicable to basic facts in memory.

Objections have also been raised against the Gestalt psychologist's organizational explanation of the isolation effect, or the Restorff effect. Here again, some investigators, including Postman, believe that the intrusion of dangerous concepts developed in the study of perception may be avoided and replaced by older, well-known, and therefore (according to them) healthier ideas. I recently constructed sets of experiments which had to have one result if the Restorff effect can be understood in the conservative way, but just the opposite result if this effect must be interpreted as a consequence of organization in perception and in memory. The results prove that, in this case, the unhealthy organizational explanation is undoubtedly correct.

Another more recent investigation referred to a problem in perception. Wallach and I tried to discover whether, after prolonged presentation of visual objects in a given location, these objects (or others) show any aftereffects such as changes of size or of shape. When numerous objects and combinations of objects had been used for the purpose, it became perfectly clear that prolonged presence of a visual object in a given place causes not only distortion of this object but also displacements of other test objects, displacements away from the previously seen inspection objects. Practically any visual objects may serve as inspection objects in such experiments. Eventually it became obvious that the well-known distortions observed by Gibson in the case of some particular figures such as curves and angles were special examples of a veritable flood of what we now call figural aftereffects.

When we had studied the figural aftereffects which occur in a frontal-parallel plane before the observer, Wallach and I asked ourselves whether there are not similar distortions and displacements in the third dimension of visual space. These experiments clearly showed that there are displacements of test objects in the third dimension, and that these are often even more conspicuous than the displacements which occur in the first two dimensions. Next, I tried another perceptual modality, namely kinesthesis, where Gibson had already observed a figural aftereffect. We could not only corroborate Gibson's findings, but could also observe such effects in further kinesthetic situations. Again, not only in the kinesthetic modality, but also in simple touch were examples of figural aftereffects immediately observable. Once, when I tried auditory localization, displacements of the same kind seemed to occur. Obviously, then, figural aftereffects can be demonstrated in most parts of the perceptual world. This made us look with some suspicion at facts in perception which had generally been regarded as facts of learning. The Müller-Lyer illusion, for instance, can be abolished or greatly reduced when the pattern is shown repeatedly. This fact had previously always been regarded as a matter of learning how to observe the pattern better and better. But one look at this pattern suggests that it is most likely to develop considerable aftereffects, effects which would surely reduce the size of the illusion under conditions of continued or often repeated observation. Fishback and I found that such aftereffects, not learning in the usual sense, were probably the right explanation of the reduction of the illusion so often found by other psychologists.

Now, what kind of change in the nervous system is responsible for all these aftereffects? Or, what kind of process occurs in so many parts of the nervous system and always has about the same result? This question I regarded as particularly important because it seemed probable that the very process which is responsible for normally organized perception also causes the figural aftereffects when perception continues to occur in a given place for some time.

The nature of figural aftereffects in the visual field made it fairly easy to discover a good candidate for this fundamental role. The candidate must be able to explain the following facts:

1 The figural aftereffects are the result of an obstruction in the nervous system. Why else should test objects recede from the places where inspection objects have been seen for some time?

2 The process in question and the obstruction which it causes cannot be restricted to the circumscribed area in which the inspection object is seen. Otherwise, why does even a fairly remote test object recede from that area?

3 The intensity of the process which causes the obstruction has to be particularly great near the boundary between the inspection object and its background. For simple observations show that the displacements of test objects are particularly conspicuous just inside and outside this contour, in both cases, of course, away from the contour.

These simple statements almost tell the physiologist what kind of process occurs in the brain when we see visual objects, and which then produces the figural aftereffects. Among the processes possible in the brain, only steady electrical currents spreading in the tissue as a volume conductor have the functional characteristics just mentioned. Such currents would originate when a circumscribed area with certain characteristics is surrounded by a larger area with different properties. The current would pass through the circumscribed area in one direction, and would then turn and pass through its environment in the opposite direction, so that a closed circuit and current result. Consequently all together just as much current would pass through the environment as flows through this circumscribed area, a behavior which fits our condition 2. The current would be most intense near the boundary of the two regions, because here the lines of flow will be shortest and thus the resistance lowest— a behavior which fits our condition 3. Condition 1, the fact that the processes in question must cause an obstruction in the tissue, is satisfied by any currents which pass through layers of cells. In fact, the flow has several kinds of effects on the tissue, all of them well known to the electrophysiologists. When the flow continues for some time, these effects are obstructions. Physiologists in Europe call these obstructions electrotonus, a name which (for unknown reasons) has not become popular in the United States. The term means that where currents enter cells, a kind of resistance or, better, obstruction develops in the surface layers of the cells, and this reduces the local flow—whereupon the current is forced to change its own direction and distribution. Thus the current has precisely the effects which appear in perception as distortions and displacements, in other words, as figural aftereffects.

We have now returned to field physics, but field physics applied to the neural medium. I need not repeat what I explained in the beginning of my report. What happens locally to a current that flows in a volume conductor is not an independent local event. What happens locally is determined and maintained within the total distribution of the flow.

Although this explanation seemed plausible enough, could we be sure that the brain is really pervaded by quasi-steady currents when we perceive? We could not, and therefore I tried to record such brain currents when visual objects appeared before human subjects or animals. This was not an easy task. To be sure, several physiologists (in England) had recorded steady currents from other active parts of the nervous system, but not from the striate area, the visual center of the brain. After initial attempts made in order to discover optimal conditions for what we planned to do, we did succeed, and could record many such currents not only from the visual, but also from the auditory cortex. I am surprised to see that, so far, no physiologists have repeated or continued our work. Too bad: the microelectrode inserted in an individual cell seems to have abolished all interest in more molar functions of the nervous system.

Our observations lead to one question after another. For instance, how do currents of the visual cortex behave when the third dimension of visual space is conspicuously represented in what we see? Or also, are currents of the brain capable of establishing memory traces in the brain? And so forth. The situation is exciting. What we now need more than anything else are people who get excited. Sooner or later there will be some people who enjoy the atmosphere of adventure in science, the atmosphere in which we lived when Gestalt psychology just began its work. If that could develop in Germany, why should it not also happen in America, the country which once produced so many pioneers?

One Man against the Nazis—Wolfgang Köhler

Mary Henle

In the 1920s and early 1930s, psychology was flourishing at the Psychological Institute of Berlin University under the direction of Wolfgang Köhler. There was truly an all-star cast of characters. In addition to the director, Max Wertheimer had been there from about 1916 until 1929, when he left to accept the chair at Frankfurt. Kurt Lewin, too, came to Berlin after World War I and remained until his resignation in 1933. Köhler's last assistants in Berlin are still known, although all of them died young: Karl Duncker, whose studies of problem solving and of induced movement remain classics; von Lauenstein, who is known mainly for his theory and investigation of time errors—an important problem, since time errors offer a good opportunity to study the behavior of young memory traces; von Restorff, whom we know for her work with Köhler on the isolation effect (sometimes called the Restorff effect) and on theory of recall. The Chief *Assistent* at the institute, Hans Rupp, chief by virtue of seniority, will hardly figure in our story.*

Berlin, with Köhler and Wertheimer, was the seat of Gestalt psychology in those days, along with another highly productive seat at Giessen under Koffka until 1924, when Koffka came to America. Berlin had seen the publication of major theoretical and experimental contributions to Gestalt psychology. Wertheimer published, among others, major papers on Gestalt theory, including the paper on perceptual grouping. Köhler's *Die physischen Gestalten in Ruhe und im stationären Zustand* appeared in 1920. His work on chimpan-

zees was still appearing, and there were numerous papers, both theoretical and experimental, many of them in perception but also in other fields. His translation of his book, *Gestalt Psychology,* into German was published in 1933. Lewin's early papers on perception and on association appeared, and then the long and influential series, published with his students, on *Handlungs- und Affektpsychologie.*

Among the students at the institute, I will mention only a few, mainly names we know today. Rudolf Arnheim and later Werner Wolff worked in the field of expression; Metzger's work on visual perception was under way, including the work on the *Ganzfeld.* Gottschaldt's studies on the influence of past experience on visual form perception came out of the institute; his figures are still in use in the Embedded Figures Test. Hans Wallach did his first work there. Kopfermann's beautiful experiments on depth perception, Ternus's on phenomenal identity, von Schiller's on stroboscopic movement, and much, much more excellent work were all products of the Psychological Institute. A number of young American PhDs came to study and work at the institute, for example, Robert B. MacLeod, Donald K. Adams, Karl Zener, Carroll Pratt, Leonard Carmichael, and others.

On January 30, 1933, the Nazis came to power. The first effects on German universities were dismissals of Jewish professors and others considered to be hostile to the new regime. This story is well known. The dismissals ranged from Nobel laureates (including Einstein, Haber, Franck, Hertz) to *Assistenten.* Hartshorne relates an anecdote which he says was widely believed—that Max Planck, the great physicist, petitioned Hitler to stop the dismissal of scientists for political reasons; he stressed the importance of science for the country. Hitler is said to have replied, "Our national policies will not be re-

Henle, M. (1978). One man against the Nazis: Wolfgang Köhler. *American Psychologist, 33,* 939–944. Copyright © 1978 by the American Psychological Association. Reprinted by permission of the publisher and the author.

* It should be mentioned that at that time an *Assistent* in a German university already had the PhD but was not yet *habilitiert,* that is, had not yet the so-called right to teach, which was conferred after a second dissertation.

voked or modified, even for scientists. If the dismissal of Jewish scientists means the annihilation of contemporary German science, then we shall do without science for a few years!'' (Hartshorne, 1937, pp. 111–112).

About the dismissed scholars, their university colleagues kept silent. As Köhler remarked years later, ''Nothing astonished the Nazis so much as the cowardice of whole university faculties, which did not consist of Nazis. Naturally this corroborated the Nazis' contempt for the intellectual life'' (Köhler, Note 1).

The future of an independent professor was, of course, uncertain. As early as April 1, 1933, Köhler, briefly outside of Germany, wrote to Ralph Barton Perry:

Nobody in Germany with any decency in his bones... knows very much about his near future. If nothing happens, I shall be in Chicago for the meeting of the American Association....

As to myself, my patriotism expects the Germans to behave better than any other people. This seems to me a sound form of patriotism. Unfortunately it is very different from current nationalism which presupposes that the own people are right and do right whatever they are and do. However, there will still be some fight during the next weeks. Don't judge the Germans before it is over.

With the dismissal of James Franck, the great experimental physicist, Köhler made public his stand. The fight had begun. On April 28, 1933, he wrote, for the *Deutsche Allgemeine Zeitung,* the last anti-Nazi article to be published openly in Germany under the Nazi regime, ''Gespräche in Deutschland'' (Conversations in Germany). The courage of such an act may be indicated by the fact that everybody expected Köhler to be arrested for it.

Why, ask the powerful men who rule Germany, have many valuable people not joined the Nazi party? Of them Köhler comments, ''Never have I seen finer patriotism than theirs.'' Regarding the wholesale dismissal of Jews from universities and other positions, he continues,

During our conversation, one of my friends reached for the Psalms and read: ''The Lord is my shepherd, I shall not want....'' He read the 90th Psalm and said, ''It is hard to think of a German who has been able to move human hearts more deeply and so to console those who suffer. And these words we have received from the Jews.''

Another reminded me that never had a man struggled more nobly for a clarification of his vision of the world than the Jew Spinoza, whose wisdom Goethe admired. My friend did not hesitate to show respect, as Goethe did. Lessing, too, would not have written his *Nathan the Wise* unless human nobility existed among the Jews?...It seems that nobody can think of the great work of Heinrich Hertz without an almost affectionate admiration for him. And Hertz had Jewish blood.

One of my friends told me: ''The greatest German experimental physicist of the present time is Franck; many believe that he is the greatest experimental physicist of our age. Franck is a Jew, an unusually kind human being. Until a few days ago, he was professor at Göttingen, an honor to Germany and the envy of the international scientific community.''

Perhaps the episode of Franck's dismissal

shows the deepest reason why all these people are not joining [the Party]: they feel a moral imposition. They believe that only the quality of a human being should determine his worth, that intellectual achievement, character, and obvious contributions to German culture retain their significance whether a person is Jewish or not.

Expecting arrest, the Köhlers and members of the institute spent the night of April 28 playing chamber music. But the Nazis did not come.

Four months later, reprints of this article were still being circulated. Letters poured in, for the most part from strangers, occasionally critical, but the overwhelming majority was full of admiration for Köhler's courageous stand. Warm thanks were expressed by Jew and non-Jew alike. The following letter, as a single example, was signed only ''A German Jew'':

Today I read your article, "Conversations in Germany." I am not ashamed to admit that, despite my 65 years, I was deeply moved by it and tears came to my eyes. I asked myself: Are there really Germans in Germany who can still muster such courage?

I am a Jew, born in Germany as were my father and grandfather. I am a simple merchant, not a politician, who formerly for many years employed hundreds of Christian workers of all parties and religions and who enjoyed the greatest respect and recognition from them.

These lines are simply intended to express to you my respect for your straightforward, fearless way of thinking.

I omit my name since it is not relevant. I feel that in spirit I want to shake your hand, since I have children who now may no longer look upon Germany as their homeland.

On November 3, 1933, the government decreed that professors must open their lectures with the Nazi salute. Köhler flipped his hand in a caricature of the salute and said:

Ladies and gentlemen, I have just saluted you in a manner that the government has decreed. I could not see how to avoid it.

Still, I must say something about it. I am professor of philosophy in this university, and this circumstance obligates me to be candid with you, my students. A professor who wished to disguise his views by word or by action would have no place here. You could no longer respect him; he could no longer have anything to say to you about philosophy or important human affairs.

Therefore I say: the form of my salute was until recently the sign of very particular ideas in politics and elsewhere. If I want to be honest, and if I am to be respected by you, I must explain that, although I am prepared to give that salute, I do not share the ideology which it usually signifies or used to signify.

The National Socialists among you will particularly welcome this explanation. Nobility and purity of purpose among the Germans are goals for which the National Socialists are working hard. I am no National Socialist. But out of the same need to act nobly and purely, I have told

you what theGerman salute means in my case and what it does not mean. I know you will respect my motives.

A witness reports that the audience of 200 greeted these remarks with thunderous applause, despite the presence of numerous brownshirts and many Nazi sympathizers (Crannell, 1970).

There was no real interference with the work of the institute until one evening in the beginning of December 1933, when Köhler gave the psychological colloquium. The doors to the colloquium room were guarded by troops, some in uniform, others in civilian clothes. When the students and assistants wanted to leave after the colloquium, they were stopped and their student cards examined.

Köhler did not then interfere with the inspection. When it was over, he telephoned the rector of the university, Eugen Fischer, protesting the unannounced raid. A discussion was arranged: The rector, who admitted that the procedure had been incorrect, agreed to exempt the Psychological Institute from further inspections of this kind. He had no objection to Köhler's informing the psychological colloquium of this agreement, and Köhler did so.

In the rector's absence, on February 26, 1934, Deputy Rector Bieberbach ordered another inspection of the institute. In accordance with his agreement with the rector, Köhler refused permission, and the inspection was not carried out. The rector was informed and offered no objection.

But trouble was ahead. A trip to Norway the next month gave Köhler another opportunity to write freely to Perry:

I am trying to build up a special position for myself in which I might stay with honour. As yet it seems to work, but the end may come [any] day. Quite exciting sometimes, not a life of leisure, occasionally great fun. The art is not to act in passion, but to make at once use of any occasion when the others make a mistake; then it is time to push a foot forward or to hit without serious danger for oneself. You will say that such is the method of cowards. But think of the difference in strength!...

Good work is being done in Berlin, as though we had to do what the emigrants are no longer able to do in Germany. Unfortunately my assistants have been in serious danger several times because of political denunciations—a denunciation a month is more or less our current rate; as yet, however, it has always been possible to save them.

Again the rector left town, and on April 12, 1934, Bieberbach ordered a new inspection "despite the agreement between Rector Fischer and Professor Köhler." The search of the institute was carried out under the leadership of a law student named Hennig, who submitted a report full of suspicions, innuendoes, and accusations but no more hard evidence than the discovery of a couple of foreign newspapers in an office (newspapers not banned by the regime) and the smell of cigarette smoke in an unoccupied room. His impertinent report insulted Professor Köhler and ended with the recommendation that two assistants, Drs. Duncker and von Lauenstein, as well as three employees, be dismissed. He recommended that the institute be moved to new quarters which would be easier to supervise and even suggested the need for another structure of the institute "which corresponds better to our time and our spirit."

Köhler angrily informed the rector on April 13 that he was, for the time being, unable to continue to direct the institute and that he had therefore transferred the directorship to his chief assistant, Professor Rupp. He reminded Rector Fischer that the agreement between them had been violated and that his authority as director had been seriously undermined; only when the situation was rectified would he resume his duties as director.

Bieberbach, the deputy rector, replied (April 14), reaffirming his "self-evident right" to inspect every part of the university. Köhler telephoned the Minister of Science, Art, and Education, Dr. Achelis, and on April 18 sent him a copy of the whole correspondence, including Hen-

nig's report along with his own detailed reply. He requested an immediate end to a situation which he could not regard "as compatible with the dignity of the University of Berlin."

On the same date, Rector Fischer replied to Köhler's letter of April 13, denying that there had ever been any agreement that the Psychological Institute be exempted from inspections. He expressed the desire to settle the disagreement without the intervention of the Ministry and requested an oral reply from Köhler.

Köhler's reply was *written* (April 20, 1934). In his letter he assures the rector that he welcomes an oral discussion when clarification has been achieved on the earlier one in which the agreement had been made, but he makes it altogether clear that the rector's account does not correspond with the facts:

> With the greatest astonishment I read in your letter the sentence: "Of an agreement between us that there would be no inspection of students in your Institute there was obviously never any question," as well as the further one: "I have only said to you that the inspecting student had to announce himself to the Director of the Institute on his appearance." ... Something of value is to be expected from an oral discussion with you only when you recall how we came to this agreement and how, until a short time ago, it was taken for granted by both of us.

Köhler concludes that as soon as the rector and he agree again about that earlier agreement, he will welcome an oral discussion.

Two weeks later, May 3, Fischer expresses his disagreeable surprise that Köhler attaches a condition to an oral discussion to try to settle the issues between them. He asserts that it is "a matter of one opinion against another."

Köhler's reply on May 8, even less than the others in this series, hardly corresponds to the kind of communication normally expected from a professor to the rector of his university.

> I can give the following explanation: If another person, in a discussion with me, makes a detailed and

completely unmistakable agreement with me, if for months afterwards this agreement is carried out on both sides, but one day the other declares that the agreement was never made, then prudence forbids me to have another discussion with this person before he has corrected his mistake in a manner that produces confidence again. For who would protect me from a mistake of the same kind which could result from a further discussion? This holds for discussions with the Rector Magnificus exactly as for anyone else.

He points out that the rector has simply continued to renounce his agreement without giving any thought to the actual facts of the case.

This cannot continue....It is...extremely important, even if it has until now been taken for granted, that the administration make no error in memory which concerns matters of morals. I therefore ask you to communicate with me in writing by May 19 whether you have, in the meantime, recalled our agreement. I assume that in the meantime you will also find words of reproach and regret about the behavior of Hennig as authorized by the Rectorate and about his incredible report.

Thus Köhler is again in effect calling the Rector Magnificus of his university a liar, he makes clear that a matter of morals is involved, and he delivers what can only be called an ultimatum.* A copy of this letter and of Fischer's letter of May 3 was sent to the minister with the following remark:

It is unusual for a professor to behave in this way toward the Rector. But the behavior of the Rector which leads me to do so is much more unusual. The dilatory handling of the matter I can no longer permit, and I must therefore insist that an untenable situation come to an end in a reasonable time.

Apparently no reply was received, either from the rector or from Dr. Achelis. On May 21, after the expiration of the ultimatum, Köhler (now in Scotland on a brief lecturing tour) sent to the

* The letters lose something in translation. For example, the form of address to the rector was not simply "you," but, "your Magnificence."

Ministry and to the Dean of the Philosophical Faculty a request for retirement.

On the same day he wrote to Perry:

My resignation is most likely to be final. Since most of the serious workers in psychology had to leave before, and since my excellent assistants would not stay without me, this means the abolition of German psychology for many years. I do not regard myself as responsible. If only 20 professors had fought the same battle, it would never have come so far with regard to German universities.

The reply to Köhler's request for retirement was a letter from an official of the Ministry to the effect that the transfer of civil service personnel to retirement status cannot simply be done upon request. Köhler is asked to discuss the matter with Dr. Achelis.

Meanwhile, the situation was deteriorating at the institute. A handyman, one Herr Schmidt, whose denunciation was apparently responsible for the dismissal of von Lauenstein, refused to carry out instructions, claiming the protection of the rector. Representatives of the German Student Organization (Nazis, of course) interfered in the administration of the institute, and the rector did nothing about it. In June 1934 a torchlight procession planned by students at the institute to honor Professor Köhler was forbidden. Students were called to the Department for Political Education and threatened when they tried to defend the institute. Two students, in an interview with the leader of the German Student Organization, heard Köhler attacked as a man who does not "stand on the ground of National Socialism" and who "identifies with the Jew Wertheimer." They learned that Duncker's habilitation would be prevented and that the attack on Köhler and his assistants was just the beginning.

In July 1934, matters had temporarily improved: The Ministry had intervened. On July 21, after a morning meeting, Köhler wrote to thank the *Ministerialdirektor* for his "intervention and benevolent justice." He assured him that he would withdraw his resignation as soon as the following conditions were met: the reinstatement of von Lauenstein, the granting of leave and subsequent transfer of the handyman Schmidt, the dismissal of the leader of psychology students of the German Student Organization, and a public statement from the Ministry.

It was not until September 24, 1934, that the Ministry, represented by Vahlen, wrote to the rector of the University of Berlin the conclusions of his investigation of the Psychological Institute. Vahlen expresses his conviction that the personal attacks on Professor Köhler were unjustified, nor can he approve of the measures taken, with the Rector's permission, by the student organization. No action was taken against Hennig, the student leader of the raid on the institute, only because he had been removed from his position for other reasons. The Ministry considered justified Köhler's objections to the methods used by the leader of the student group.

On the other hand, Vahlen finds reason to criticize Köhler's refusal to discuss matters with the rector as well as the tone of his letters. He disapproves in particular of Köhler's interruption of his duties as director of the institute and of his activities there. He assures the rector that Professor Köhler has his confidence, and he expects all measures aimed at discrediting the institute to stop immediately.

The public statement made by the Ministry is the following:

> Accusations which have been raised against the Psychological Institute force me to point out that Professor Köhler has the confidence of the Minister. I expect from the Student Organization that no more cases of hostile behavior take place against Professor Köhler, his Institute, and his students.

A copy of this letter was sent to Köhler, along with a repetition of criticisms of Köhler's behavior toward the rector, with whom Vahlen asks him to cooperate in the future.

A month later Köhler was in the United States, delivering the William James Lectures at Harvard. Here he received a letter from Bieber-bach, the deputy rector, asking him to sign an oath of loyalty to Adolf Hitler. The letter went unanswered until February. In the meantime, on January 7, 1935, Vahlen wrote to Köhler that the vacancy created by the departure of Professor Kurt Lewin had been filled. Dr. Keller of Rostock had been appointed in December, although Köhler had not been consulted. Vahlen assumes that Köhler will give his consent retroactively, and he is reassured by the opinion of the acting director, Rupp, that Köhler would have no objection. The minister asks for Köhler's opinion and wants to know whether, under these circumstances, Köhler's request to resign still holds.

On February 2, Köhler wrote that the law requiring a loyalty oath does not apply to him, since he has submitted his resignation to the Ministry. On the next day he replied to Vahlen's communication of January 7. He refers to the minister's earlier criticisms of the intrusions into the administration of the institute, for which he is grateful. But that same letter had contained reference to the "peculiar composition" of the circle close to Professor Köhler and had criticized the manner in which he had defended himself against the rector. He takes exception to both points, and on the basis of them had been considering for some time whether to renew his request to resign. Then he received the news of Dr. Keller's appointment. He can only see this as a continuation of the measures that first led him to request retirement: It is totally impossible for him to direct the institute when, time after time, important decisions are made without even consulting him. He can therefore not withdraw his request for resignation. For this, as he writes to the minister, he would need a most dramatic and binding assurance that he could be Director of the Psychological Institute of the University of Berlin "without repeatedly being subjected to the kind of treatment that only a weakling with no sense of honor could tolerate."

Apparently Köhler again requested reinstatement of his assistants, and this request was denied. Accordingly, a new request to resign was addressed to the minister on August 22, 1935,when Köhler was again in Germany. In it he points out that it is impossible for him to continue his work without these assistants, who represent new points of view now beginning to spread to all countries.

And so ended the great days of the Psychological Institute of the University of Berlin. Even before his final resignation, Köhler wrote an obituary notice to an American friend, Donald K. Adams:

> I feel obliged to announce to all those who have taken a friendly interest in the Psychological Institute at Berlin that this institute does not exist any more—though the rooms and the apparatus and Mr. Rupp are still there. The government has decided in May to dismiss all the assistants who were trained by me and in June, during the term, they were suddenly forbidden to continue their work and their teaching: Duncker, von Lauenstein and von Restorff. Since, at my last visit in Berlin, I had expressly stated orally and in official documents that I could not possibly remain as director without the help of my young friends and since this is a clear case of their modern brutality (another man uses this method in order to push *me* out), the measure is morally equivalent to my own dismissal too. I shall have a last interview with the Nazi authorities in August. But there is not one chance in a hundred for my staying on in Germany.... We were depressed for some days but have come back to the fighting spirit once more. Personally, I shall be glad when I have no contact with the official Germany of today, and I have so many good friends in this country, more indeed than over there. My deepest anxiety refers to the assistants. I am not yet sure whether I shall be able to place them somewhere.

The new Nazi director of the institute would not allow Köhler's students to remain (Wallach, Note 2); and of course his assistants were gone. A few went to other universities, some emigrated, some died. The young generation of Gestalt psychologists was effectively wiped out.

It is difficult to guess what would have been the effect on psychology in Germany, and indeed in the world, if the Psychological Institute had been allowed a few more productive years. It was perhaps the outstanding psychological institute of its time. Max Planck, in a letter to Köhler in the midst of the struggle, speaks of the importance of its preservation "in its unique significance for science and for our university." The institute attracted students from many countries; and the ideas of Gestalt psychology were respected and were spreading in Germany and in other countries. It is possible that our science would be different today if that institute had been able to continue its work.

The courageous struggle of Wolfgang Köhler against the Nazis could not save the Psychological Institute. Was that struggle in vain? I think not. For as we look back on it, it shows us once more what a human being can be.

REFERENCE NOTES

1 Köhler, W. *Peace and education*. Unpublished lecture given during World War II. In the Library of the American Philosophical Society, Philadelphia, Pennsylvania.
2 Wallach, H. Personal communication, September 10, 1973.

REFERENCES

Crannell, C. W. Wolfgang Köhler. *Journal of the History of the Behavioral Sciences,* 1970, *6,* 267–268.
Hartshorne, E. Y. *The German universities and National Socialism.* Cambridge, Mass.: Harvard University Press, 1937.
Mandler, J. M., & Mandler, G. The diaspora of experimental psychology: The Gestaltists and others. *Perspectives in American History,* 1968, *2,* 371–419.

The Gestalt Psychologists in Behaviorist America

Michael M. Sokal

To many people in the United States, . . . Gestalt psychology in the 1920s and early 1930s meant primarily the work of Wolfgang Köhler, and the history of his interaction with American psychologists through the mid-1930s reveals much about the way in which Gestalt ideas and the Gestalt psychologists were received. . . . This fact, as well as the many rumors that still circulate concerning Köhler's relations with several American psychologists, especially those at Harvard, justifies an extensive treatment of his role. It is not generally known that Köhler had contacts with American psychology as early as 1914, when he was working with chimpanzees at Tenerife. Early that year, Robert M. Yerkes, then a young assistant professor at Harvard, wrote to Köhler, expressing interest in his work, asking for further information about it, and hoping to be able to join the German professor off the coast of Africa. The outbreak of the European war and Köhler's internment on Tenerife ended Yerkes's travel plans. But the two psychologists soon began to exchange offprints, and the American even asked John B. Watson to send Köhler a set of his articles. Yerkes also had Köhler's motion picture films of his chimpanzee experiments processed in the United States when this became impossible on the islands. But this friendly and mutually profitable exchange was marred in 1916, when Yerkes published *The Mental Life of Monkeys and Apes* and did not cite Köhler's work. And with American entry into the war in 1917, the relationship came to a temporary close.[1]

Shortly after the war, Yerkes used his temporary position with the National Research Council to try to re-establish contact with Köhler. He accomplished this by 1921, and soon the two psychologists exchanged books, offprints, and congratulations on each other's appointments: Köhler's at Berlin and Yerkes's at Yale. Yerkes even offered to send money to Köhler to cover the cost of the books and offprints, in view of the deterioration of the economic situation in Germany and "the unfairness of the exchange situation," but Köhler would not accept. By 1923, the two men were again learning much from a correspondence they both apparently enjoyed. And in 1924, Yerkes reviewed Köhler's *Mentality of Apes* most positively, writing that both its "observations and conclusions . . . are important" and hoping "that it may also achieve wide influence."[2]

Later in 1924 Carl Murchison at Clark University arranged for Köhler to serve as visiting professor at the Worcester institution during 1925, and the reaction of many American psychologists was enthusiastic. Terman, a Clark alumnus who had been bemoaning the condition of psychology at his alma mater, was especially pleased. As he wrote to a Clark official, "It was a splendid stroke to get Dr. Köhler to come over." Boring and Yerkes congratulated Köhler on his appointment and were among the first to welcome him to America. Boring, of course, had been studying Gestalt psychology at the time, and his welcome was particularly enthusiastic. "The psychological stock of America took a jump upward as soon as I heard you were safely on shore."[3] Once Köhler was at Worcester, Boring and Yerkes saw him regularly, and the visitor spoke at least once at both Harvard and Yale. Boring even attended weekly seminars led by Köhler at Clark, which he described as "great fun," at least in part because the meetings included extensive discussions of Köhler's experimental work. These seminars in turn led to Köhler's influential chapters in *Psychologies of 1925*, published by Clark University Press.[4] Meanwhile, Köhler met with other members of the American psychological commu-

Adapted from Sokal, M. M. (1984). The Gestalt psychologists in behaviorist America. *American Historical Review, 89*, 1240–1263. Copyright © 1984 by the American Historical Association. Adapted and reprinted by permission of the publisher and the author.

nity and impressed most of them. He and Koffka attended a meeting of the Society of Experimental Psychologists as guests, two of the few ever so honored....During a later visit to Stanford, Köhler impressed Terman as "an intellectually active man" with "youth and vigor." Yerkes also recommended Köhler and Koffka to the home secretary of the National Academy of Sciences as "two of the foremost German psychologists" in an effort to get for them a place on the academy's programs. In 1926 Ogden sought the translation and publication in English of other books by Köhler. Although unsuccessful, the attempt shows how important to American psychology Köhler's ideas had become.[5]

Soon after Köhler started lecturing at Clark in January 1925, Boring and James H. Woods, chairman of the joint Department of Philosophy and Psychology at Harvard, proposed to invite Köhler to Cambridge the following fall as visiting professor. The idea had the support of Harvard philosophers—Ralph Barton Perry was then reviewing favorably *Mentality of Apes,* and Woods even told the Harvard administration that he himself would raise the funds to pay for Köhler's salary. As director of the Harvard Psychological Laboratory, Boring exchanged letters with Köhler about the position. Köhler was interested, for he wanted to work with Harvard graduate students.[6]

But in late April 1925 Köhler spoke at Cambridge under the auspices of the Harvard Philosophical Club, and his talk disappointed Boring greatly. He later described it as being full of "general theoretical analogies [and] unformulated psychological events [with] not [one] bit of experimentation." In another letter, he expressed dissatisfaction with the "vagueness of [Köhler's] speculation." He had hoped to find in Köhler the experimentalist that he strongly believed the Harvard department needed, only to discover that the Gestaltist was moving away from the laboratory.[7]

Personal concerns may also have figured in Boring's reversal. He was a moody and over-sensitive man, highly conscious of his status as Harvard's leading psychologist, which would have been threatened by Köhler's appointment. But at the same time he was jealous of Harvard's position in the American psychological community and knew that it would be generally enhanced if Köhler lectured at the university.[8] His continuing correspondence with Köhler mirrors Boring's ambivalence. In June he listed in detail the facilities available at Harvard, and added, "I am very anxious for you to come." And yet he stressed the space and financial limitations at Harvard and feared Köhler might "be disappointed" at not having "what you could have had at Berlin." In response Köhler began to express doubts about the visiting appointment and finally begged off in the summer of 1925, citing his responsibilities to his colleagues in Berlin that prevented an extension of his leave. "Just about the time that Köhler got an inkling that Harvard might do something to get him here," Boring wrote several years later, "he stiffened up towards me."[9]

Köhler's relations with Boring were undoubtedly "stiff." Boring's ambivalence probably set him on edge, but more than Boring's attitude was involved. Köhler was a difficult man to get to know, and he, too, enjoyed status as a professor at Germany's leading university. He believed his psychology vastly superior to any yet developed and urged its merits on Americans with a confidence that some saw as arrogance. He had high standards of propriety and was easily put off by anything he considered improper. According to an American student in Berlin, even his German friends thought him "a little too temperamental" and inclined to be rigidly formal on even informal occasions. Before transcending the formal "Sie" to the intimate "Du," Köhler had to know somebody socially for ten years or more. American friends attributed Köhler's constraint to discomfort in speaking English, his unbending need to do the proper thing socially, and his basic shyness. Whatever its cause, it did "put off" many Americans and complicated his relations with many people in this country, especially Boring, whose own personality did not ease the situation. The two men apparently never understood one another and found the negotiations difficult. Both tried to be cordial and conciliatory throughout their correspondence, and their letters to each other were always polite. But Boring, at least, disliked Köhler and felt disliked in turn. The depth of his feelings bothered him, however, and Boring once even wrote of them to his colleague, Perry, describing his letter as "the confession of a divided neurotic soul."[10] But neurotic or not, the relationship between the two men affected the history of American psychology.

Despite the personal feelings involved, Köhler did not close the door in the summer of 1925 to a visiting position at Harvard and hinted that he would welcome an invitation to Cambridge in the future. Boring and Woods apparently discussed this possibility with Abbot Lawrence Lowell, Harvard's president. Köhler's fame in America in the mid-1920s was such that he had already been recommended strongly to Lowell by a member of the university's Board of Overseers. Henry Osborn Taylor, the New York philosopher and historian, had described Köhler in a letter to Lowell as "a light in a dark night." Lowell, intrigued by these recommendations, made inquiries of his own, writing to Edward Bradford Titchener, the leading structuralist. Titchener responded that he had been impressed by Köhler's experimental work in Germany before World War I but found his later theoretical work so disappointing that he feared "Köhler's health may have been seriously impaired by his four years' residence on Tenerife." Furthermore, Köhler in person impressed Titchener even less favorably, appearing "apathetic and uninspiring," a reaction shared, he said, by other Americans. The Cornell psychologist warned Lowell against offering Köhler a permanent chair but thought that a one-year visiting professorship would be a good test of the Gestaltist's health and ability.[11] Boring was not the only psychologist of the mid-1920s who believed that Köhler's major scientific achievements lay behind him.

Lowell apparently did not tell Boring and Woods of Titchener's opinion, and in January 1926 the two men again made plans to approach Köhler about a visiting professorship. Although these plans fell through,[12] a possibility appeared in December for a permanent appointment. In that month William McDougall, the English psychologist who had been teaching at Harvard since 1920, resigned his position and left Cambridge for Duke University. Woods immediately thought of Köhler as McDougall's successor and was supported by Perry and other Harvard philosophers. Boring, however, told his colleagues that what Harvard psychology required was a leading experimentalist and that Köhler, having left the laboratory for theoretical exploration, did not fill this need. He strongly favored the appointment of an American, such as Lashley or Tolman. He also told Perry, and perhaps others, of his personal feelings about Köhler. But he still believed that the Gestaltist's appointment at Harvard would do much for the university's standing in psychology, and, as he phrased it, he did not "think that [Köhler's] dislike of me... [was] a reason for not calling him, but [was] rather sorry to have this personal reaction to render me unsure of my other professional judgment." He therefore went along with Woods and Perry and agreed to ask Köhler to join the Harvard faculty, at least on a temporary basis.[13]

Köhler, however, did not respond to two of Boring's letters on the subject. A third letter from Boring, and one from Woods, did bring a reply, but it did not clarify the situation. To be sure, some of the correspondence between these three men has apparently been lost or destroyed, so the details of the episode are unclear. Those letters that survive are polite and even friendly, and yet those who saw all the correspondence were not sure of what Köhler, who hated financial negotiations connected with jobs, intended. Boring wrote to Terman, "My own interpretation of the correspondence is that he will not accept... [but] some at Harvard interpret the same letters as meaning that he is coming." The one letter from Köhler to Boring that survives illustrates the problem of determining the former's intentions. "When I think of you and my other friends at Harvard the choice looks simple. But when I look at the economic situation and the number of lectures to which an American Professor tends to be obligated, then my face drops."[14] Not until the fall of 1927 did Köhler definitely notify Harvard that he would stay in Berlin. Apparently he apologized to Boring for the long suspense. In reply Boring tried to be conciliatory, but his annoyance is evident. "After all what is Harvard against Berlin?...That you have left us in the lurch and we are still limping along is certainly not your fault, but is entirely our responsibility." It is no wonder then that he later described this period as "the summer that Köhler blew up on us."[15]

Harvard still had to appoint a successor to McDougall, and the philosophers continued to urge that a European be chosen for the position. They kept hoping that Köhler might be persuaded to come to Cambridge. But Boring still argued for an American and an experimentalist, and he found that other American psychologists shared his, and Titchener's, low opinion of Köhler's post-1920 work, which was too grandly speculative for their tastes. Terman noted, "I doubt ...he will ever do much more experimenting." Boring complained to his philosophical colleagues about their preference for European psychologists, who performed "the scissors and cardboard kind of experiments that do not reflect favorably upon Harvard's psychology in America." His concern for Harvard's reputation meshed with his antipathy toward Köhler's work. He cited the "criticism from the men whose opinion I respect and in whose judgment I concur." In the spring of 1928 Köhler's name was again mentioned for the position at Harvard, and Boring blew up. "American psychologists who felt that Harvard had made a mistake with both [Hugo] Münsterberg and McDougall would feel that it again erred."[16] But Boring's outburst got him nowhere, since many Harvard philosophers wanted Köhler. In the fall of 1928 he analyzed the situation:

> The issue is out in the open. It is between A and B.
> A. Breadth of interest, vision and imagination.
> B. Technical skill and knowledge within a given field.
> We want both. We can not have them. Actually they are negatively correlated....
> Hocking, Perry and Woods are for A and thus for a renewal of the offer to Köhler.
> I am for B and thus can not conscientiously agree to Köhler.[17]

Boring was also annoyed that philosophers were trying to tell psychologists how to manage their own affairs. His protests over the way in which the entire situation had been handled were later a major reason why philosophy and psychology at Harvard were reorganized in the mid-1930s as separate departments within a joint division.[18]

Meanwhile, Boring had been devoting all of the time that he could spare from Harvard matters to the study of the history of psychology, in preparation for the writing of his well-known book, *History of Experimental Psychology,* published in 1929. This research, his quarrels with his Harvard colleagues, and his feelings about Köhler's experimental work, all led him to reconsider his early enthusiasm for Gestalt psychology, which he had never expressed in print. Several of his friends—for example, Margaret Floy Washburn—had always been critical of the school, and Boring had always been sensitive to the opinions of other psychologists. Some thought highly of the work of individual Gestaltists but criticized that of others. Terman, for example, found Lewin's work exciting but had qualms about Koffka's and Köhler's. He described a talk by Koffka at Stanford as "piffle" and, though somewhat impressed by Köhler's early writings, thought little of Köhler's future as an experimental psychologist. Terman felt that propagandizing by Gestalt psychologists detracted from the merit of their ideas, and Boring began to be concerned about this aspect of his relationships with Koffka and Köhler.[19]

Gestaltists were not the only psychologists of the 1920s to argue that the school to which they belonged possessed the only valid approach to psychology. And yet American psychologists were especially bothered by the attitude of the Gestaltists. As shown earlier, some felt that the Gestaltists had come to the United States almost as intellectual missionaries, spreading a new gospel. And Köhler's stiffness did nothing to ease the situation. Recently the term "Mandarin" has been used to characterize the attitudes and behavior of many of the German university professors of the period. In some ways the entire Gestalt movement represented a revolt against traditional German university culture, but in other, deeper ways the Gestaltists shared many traits typical of the faculties of German universities.[20] Although they never heard the term "Mandarin" applied to the Gestaltists, many American psychologists would have easily recognized the characterization.

When Boring's *History of Experimental Psychology* appeared, his ten-page discussion of Gestalt psychology was negative in tone. Apparently he felt that he had tried to be fair. "It is a question as to whether I have been favorable or unfavorable." But friends of Gestalt psychology like Ogden had little doubt about Boring's actual opinion. His analysis of the school continually stressed its origins as a "psychology of protest" against the older, atomistic theories of psychology. Although he admitted that, "if this negative element were all that there is to *Gestalt* psychology, it would never have become an important movement," most of his discussion revolved around its criticisms of older ideas. Furthermore, he emphasized the continuity of Gestalt ideas with older theories and criticized the Gestaltists because they "made little effort to show the antiquity of the[ir] objection."[21] One can readily see why Ogden felt attacked.

The year 1929 also saw the publication of Köhler's *Gestalt Psychology,* which he wrote in English and intended as a general introduction to his science for American psychologists. To show his readers what Gestalt psychology was not, he opened his presentation with a long critique of behaviorism. But the psychology that these chapters attacked was almost a caricature of the American science, since they neither mentioned (with one exception in a single sentence) any behaviorist nor included a detailed discussion of any behaviorist study, even by way of example. (A bibliography did list three works by behaviorists, but only one by Watson, and that a short article.) The book also included chapters on sensory organization, association, recall, and insight, which explained quite clearly the Gestalt perspective on these topics.[22] The volume was at least partially successful, but it did not win many friends for the Gestalt school.

Although not a behaviorist, Boring believed that he had to respond to the book, and he criticized Köhler's vague and slanted account of the American school. But he made sure to comment favorably on the most substantive chapters. Boring's review was entitled "The *Gestalt* Psychology and the *Gestalt* Movement," and it praised the former, while criticizing the latter. But despite his belief that Köhler's book required his response, he felt uneasy about it and attempted, before it was published, to soften its impact. He asked a friend to read a draft to make sure it was not too "violent." He sent galley proofs of the note to Köhler in Berlin and tried in a cover letter to explain his ambivalence. "Sometimes I seem to be so enthusiastic about it and sometimes so negative." He wrote of his "enthusiasm for the research that has come out under this label" but admitted, "I get very angry about the label of *Gestalt* psychology and its solidarity as a new movement."[23]

If Köhler responded to Boring's letter or to the review, his answer has been lost, but Koffka's reaction was calm, reasoned, and cordial. He argued "that the Gestalt *movement* has been created not by the Gestalt psychologists but by their opponents" and claimed that "many misunderstandings may have been caused by the fact that Köhler and I were invited to give so many public lectures," from which "concrete details" had to be omitted. There was some validity to Koffka's points, especially in view of the long list of papers criticizing Gestalt psychology that Boring presented in his history, and Koffka's attitude toward his public lectures might certainly explain why Terman thought the one he heard was "piffle." Boring found at least some truth in Koffka's rebuttal. But at the same time he harked back to the talk that Köhler had given in 1925 at the Harvard Philosophical Club, which had impressed him so unfavorably. Boring made sure to stress that these specific criticisms did not apply to Koffka, but, though cordial, Boring clearly was unhappy with Gestalt psychology, or at least with the Gestalt school.[24]

Boring's note was not the only response to Köhler's book critical of the Gestalt movement. The *New Republic,* for example, published an article by Edward S. Robinson, a Yale psychologist, on "A Little German Band," which was subtitled "The Solemnities of Gestalt Psychology." The essay was important in that it apparently marked the first time that Köhler and Koffka were referred to in print as Gestaltists. Previously Americans called them Gestalt psychologists or Gestalt theorists, but after its appearance in this article "Gestaltist" passed into general usage, analogous to behaviorist or structuralist and usually, despite Robinson's intent, without disparaging implications. But Köhler and other Gestalt psychologists always saw the term as an insult to them and their work and decried its use. Boring avoided it, at least partly in deference to their feelings. But even today, when many psychologists speak fondly of their teachers as Gestaltists, those still annoyed by the term blame its coinage on Boring.[25]

By clarifying Gestalt psychology and its concepts for an American audience, Köhler's *Ge-*

stalt Psychology made it easier for behaviorists and other non-Gestalt psychologists to attack his point of view. And in the following years, such attacks multiplied. For example, an article on "The Phantom of the Gestalt" concluded that "the Gestalt...has no assignable value in psychological description nor any real existence within the experimental sequence." Similarly, in "Materializing the Ghost of Köhler's Gestalt Psychology," an American psychologist argued that Gestalt concepts, if reinterpreted within the framework of Washburn's motor theory of consciousness, would be immediately subsumed within the mainstream of American psychology. These critiques and others like them are difficult to interpret, but all indicate a growing familiarity with, if not a deep understanding of, Gestalt ideas among American psychologists. By 1933, when it was included as one of the *Seven Psychologies* in Edna Heidbreder's classic survey of American schools of psychology, Gestalt psychology was clearly a part of the American psychological scene.[26]

Meanwhile, Koffka remained at Smith, Boring at Harvard, and Köhler at Berlin. These three men continued to correspond regularly with each other, and all went on with their scientific work. Boring drifted toward behaviorism and published *The Physical Dimensions of Consciousness,* an attack on dualism that he later admitted was "immature" and a friendly colleague called a "silly little thing." Koffka began work on his very influential book, *Principles of Gestalt Psychology,* which went far beyond Köhler's introduction. In Germany, the rise of Hitler did not immediately affect Köhler, as he was an "Aryan," but he greatly disliked the Nazis and what they stood for and was one of the few non-Jewish scientists in Germany to oppose the regime actively.[27] In the mid-1930s developments at Harvard led to another invitation to Köhler. The Division of Philosophy and Psychology sponsored the William James lectures and decided—after hearing two distinguished American philosophers, John Dewey and Arthur O. Lovejoy—to invite a foreign, or at least foreign-born, psychologist as the next lecturer. After considering Carl Gustav Jung, the faculty soon focused on Koffka and Köhler. In comparing the two, the Harvard psychologists found that each had different strengths; they had to determine just what they wanted. As Boring summarized their deliberations, the Harvard professors decided "that the most distinguished and appropriate appointment that could be made at the present time would be Köhler and that the most useful appointment in the effect it would have upon the atmosphere of the laboratory would be Koffka. I have lent my support to the view that we must in such an appointment weight distinction very heavily, and that we ought therefore to ask Köhler."[28]

In December 1933, Harvard invited Köhler to be the third William James lecturer, to deliver a course of ten or twelve public lectures, and to conduct a seminar for graduate students. Boring wrote to Köhler that *both* the philosophers and the psychologists in the division wanted the Gestaltist to accept the appointment and that he was especially hopeful of hearing Köhler again. Köhler responded as he had to so many previous invitations from Harvard, writing that he would love to accept "this invitation, which I regard as an unusual honour," and stressing that "it should have been impossible for me to accept without knowing about your point of view." He did not agree to the proposal immediately, citing the difficult problems he faced at the University of Berlin with regard to the Nazi-controlled administration.[29]

But Köhler soon afterwards accepted and arrived at Cambridge in September 1934. Boring attended the lecture series and, burying his misgivings, apparently hoped to see a good deal of Köhler, arranging at least one social event for the visitor and his wife. But on the whole he was greatly disappointed; Köhler spent most of his time with Harvard's distinguished philosophers, especially Perry. In planning for Köhler's visit, Boring assumed that the Gestaltist would not need an office near the psychology laboratory,

but his colleagues in philosophy convinced him otherwise. Once in Cambridge, Köhler hardly used the office, and the two psychologists rarely met. By November, the situation became so bad that Boring felt he had to write to Köhler, if he was to have an opportunity to discuss some points raised in the lectures. "Things are so disposed that we are not thrown together for conversation."[30] In all, Boring seems to have come across as a pushy American, and Köhler seems to have retreated into his personal shell. Both psychologists acted with the best intentions, but neither knew how to improve the relationship.

Boring had other reasons to be annoyed. The lectures that Köhler gave—published four years later as *The Place of Value in a World of Fact*—extended various philosophical implications of Gestalt theory into the realm of ethics and aesthetics and focused much attention on epistemological and metaphysical problems. Köhler's English was good, but the lectures were not as easily followed as were the substantive chapters of *Gestalt Psychology,* which perhaps merely reflected the complexity of the topics on which he spoke. Later reviews in philosophy journals and the popular press praised the book as, for example, "keen, wide-ranging, and original." But most reviews of it by psychologists—especially those taking some sort of behaviorist perspective—were extremely negative.[31] And Boring was one who decried what Köhler had done. He knew that the lectures would not focus on experimental studies and their implications, but apparently he had expected Köhler to talk about psychology, even if from a theoretical perspective. Instead, Köhler spoke on epistemology and metaphysics, and Boring was angry. At issue, too, was more than a simple tension between philosophy and psychology. In 1934, at least one psychologist wrote to Boring that the single lecture by Köhler that he had heard did not impress him, and Boring's reply reveals much. "You commented on being disappointed in a lecture which you heard recently. I can say only that I heard the whole series and am terribly disappointed, and a little humiliated at the knowledge that I took the time to go to them. The content was not well informed nor related to current knowledge. The ideas were not important or clear. Most of the argument was childishly elementary, although I caught suggestions of something sinister behind the scenes once in a while—but I was never sure. The vocal presentation was dull and tiresome, although the literary was, if you could grasp it, exceptionally able. This then is what we applaud so heartily!''[32]

To be sure, Boring was at a critical point in his life and about to undergo psychoanalysis in an attempt to free himself from the despondency that plagued him throughout the mid-1930s.[33] But his criticisms of Köhler were as much intellectual as personal. Apparently, soon after Köhler completed his William James lectures, the philosophers at Harvard urged that he be appointed professor at the university, and, with the situation in Germany worsening, Köhler was more open to such an appointment than ever before. But Boring, as director of the psychological laboratory and head of the Department of Psychology within the Division of Philosophy and Psychology, adamantly opposed the appointment. This position also gave Boring easier access to James B. Conant, a chemist who was Harvard's new president, and he was, at last, able to convince the Harvard administration to close the door permanently to Köhler. In all, Boring's opposition was final, and in 1935 he was able to appoint Lashley to a Harvard professorship, thus bringing to Cambridge the type of experimentalist he always wanted. (An earlier offer to Tolman fell through, in part because the Californian "loved[d] Berkeley and dislike[d] Cambridge.'')[34] Despite this success, Boring's despondency grew, as his role in this incident apparently cost him several friends at Harvard. Even in the 1980s rumors still circulate about the feud between Boring and Köhler, and how it cost Köhler a Harvard professorship.[35] In any event, by the end of 1935 Köhler had settled at Swarthmore College, where he established an institu-

tional base for his work comparable to Koffka's at Smith. There he was a major influence on the development of such distinguished psychologists as Mary Henle, Solomon Asch, and Robert B. MacLeod. Within a year or two Boring and Köhler were again corresponding cordially, and after World War II Boring readily admitted Köhler's great influence on American psychology. In the 1950s Köhler was honored by election to the National Academy of Sciences—in fact, he was elected as soon as he became eligible through naturalization[36]—and to the presidency of the American Psychological Association.

The transmission of Gestalt psychology was a complicated affair, but several points are especially striking. One major conclusion is that, like the transit of the new physics to America,[37] the diffusion of Gestalt psychology from Germany to the United States began long before Hitler came to power. Americans were too interested in German ideas and Germans too interested in American opportunities to wait until political events forced them into contact. By 1930 Gestalt psychology was firmly established in the United States as a psychological school, and graduate students interested in a Gestalt-focused education in psychology knew where to study. The rise of the Nazis certainly contributed to the completion of the migration, but it did not determine the direction in which American psychology developed. Another point worth noting is that Americans found that they had to react to at least three different factors—Gestalt psychology, the Gestalt movement, and the Gestalt psychologists themselves. They responded differently to each. Some, like Boring, were attracted by Gestalt experimental work but reacted negatively to Gestalt theory. And clearly, despite Koffka's disclaimer, the protagonists of Gestalt theory constituted a movement that tried to convert Americans to their view of the world. Americans quite naturally resented their missionary efforts.

The personalities of the psychologists involved—both German and American—also helped shape the course of the migration. Certainly Köhler's formality, Boring's oversensitivity, and the concern for status that both men shared affected their interactions. And yet, despite the dominance of behaviorism, American psychology was open to Gestalt ideas, and today many Gestalt interpretations of psychological phenomena have joined the mainstream of modern American psychology. Certainly perception is an area of research molded by Gestalt ideas. Even in the 1920s and 1930s, the experimental work of leading American psychologists strongly exhibited the influence of the Gestalt approach to their science. Lashley's stress on basic neural mechanisms and, especially, Tolman's "Purposive Behaviorism"—one of the most influential approaches to psychology in the 1930s—clearly owed much to Gestalt theory. That both were offered positions at Harvard at a time when Köhler's suitability for such a position was being debated further illustrates how Americans differentiated between the psychologists and the ideas. In other areas of psychology, too, Gestalt concepts have been influential. Lewin's work, for example, with its stress on an individual's interaction with his or her "life space" or social field, has done much to shape modern social psychology.

Finally, and perhaps most controversially, I think we can conclude that the Gestalt psychologists themselves were well received in the United States. To be sure, the few who still define themselves as Gestalt psychologists argue that America did not give their teachers what it should have. But in many ways, this attitude is reminiscent of the situation of the 1920s and early 1930s when Koffka and Köhler allowed their movement to get the better of their ideas and preached to the Americans, trying to convert the heathen to the true gospel. In any event, all major Gestalt psychologists found positions in America in the middle of the depression and were able to carry on with the work they had started in Germany. This work enriched American psychology greatly and did much to counter the attractions of extreme behaviorism. If

Gestalt psychology has today lost its identity as a school of thought—and very few of Koffka's, Köhler's, Wertheimer's, or Lewin's students call themselves Gestalt psychologists—it is not because the mainstream of American psychology has swamped their ideas. Rather, their work has done much to redirect this mainstream, which adopted many of their points of view. Few other migrating scientific schools have been as successful.[38]

NOTES

(1) Yerkes to Köhler, March 27, May 20, 1914, July 17, October 10, December 21, 1916, January 10, 1917; Köhler to Yerkes, April 17, 1914, February 15, May 19, 1916, September 10, 1917, December 13, 1916, March 2, 1917, Yale University Archives, New Haven, Robert M. Yerkes Papers [hereafter, Yerkes Papers].

(2) Yerkes to U.S. Department of State, February 14, 1921; Yerkes to Köhler, April 13, October 8, 1921, March 6, 1922, November 6, 1923; Köhler to Yerkes, May 19, October 23, 1921, January 29, 1922, Yerkes Papers; and Yerkes, review of Köhler's *Mentality of Apes,* in *International Book Review,* June 1925, p. 461.

(3) Terman to C. H. Thurber, May 26, 1924, Stanford University Archives, Stanford, CA, Lewis Terman Papers [hereafter Terman Papers]; Boring to Köhler, June 9, 1924, February 6, 1925, Harvard University Archives, Cambridge, MA, Edwin G. Boring Papers [hereafter Boring Papers]; and Yerkes to Köhler, October 22, 1924, January 26, 1925, May 7, 1924; Köhler to Yerkes, February 8, 1924, February 15, 1925, Yerkes Papers.

(4) Boring to Yerkes, October 28, 1925; Yerkes to Köhler, May 7, 1925, Yerkes Papers; Boring to Köhler, March 31, 1925; Köhler to Boring, April 2, April 20, 1925, Boring Papers; and Köhler, "An Aspect of Gestalt Psychology," and "Intelligence in Apes," in Carl Murchison, ed., *Psychologies of 1925* (Worcester, Mass., 1926), 129–43, 145–61.

(5) Terman to Boring, January 26, 1927, Terman Papers; Yerkes to David White, March 5, 1925, Yerkes Papers; Kegan Paul Trench Trubner and Company to Köhler, November 16, 1926, Janu-

ary 19, February 15, June 14, July 22, October 11, 1927, American Philosophical Society Library, Philadelphia, Wolfgang Köhler Papers [hereafter, Köhler Papers]; and Boring, "The Society of Experimental Psychologists, 1904–1938," *American Journal of Psychology*, 51 (1938): 410–21. . . . The Society of Experimental Psychologists, [an] exclusive group, first brought together in 1904 by Edward B. Titchener of Cornell and not formally organized until after his death in 1927, limited attendance at its meetings to the directors of American university psychological laboratories and their entourages of junior colleagues and graduate students. Attendance in 1925 was higher than at any previous meeting; American psychologists came both to celebrate the dedication of Eno Hall, the new psychological laboratory at Princeton, and to meet with and hear Köhler and Koffka, the honored guests.

(6) Woods to Abbot Lawrence Lowell, March 17, 1925, Harvard University Archives, Cambridge, Mass., Abbot Lawrence Lowell Papers [hereafter, Lowell Papers]; and Boring to Woods, April 15, April 16, 1925; Boring to Köhler, March 25, March 31, 1925; Köhler to Boring, April 2, 1925, Boring Papers.

(7) Boring to Koffka, April 23, 1930; Boring to Raymond H. Wheeler, March 3, 1927, Boring Papers.

(8) Boring, *Psychologist at Large: An Autobiography and Selected Essays* (New York, 1961); and Julian Jaynes, "Edwin Garrigues Boring, 1886–1968," *Journal of the History of the Behavioral Sciences,* 5 (1969): 99–112.

(9) Boring to Köhler, June 4, 1925; Köhler to Boring, July 12, 1925; Boring Papers; Boring to Yerkes, October 28, 1925, Yerkes Papers; Boring to Wheeler, March 3, 1927, Boring Papers; and Köhler to Woods, [July 10, 1925], Köhler Papers.

(10) Jean M. Mandler and George Mandler, "The diaspora of experimental psychology: The Gestaltists and others." In D. Fleming & B. Bailyn (Eds.), *The Intellectual Migration: Europe and America, 1930–1960,* Cambridge, MA, 1969, pp. 371–419; interview with Edwin B. Newman, October 3, 1979; and Carroll C. Pratt to Boring, April 19, 1931, as quoted in Boring to Terman, July 31, 1931; Boring to Perry, [1928], Boring Papers.

(11) Taylor to Lowell, February 28, 1926; Lowell

toTaylor, March 2, 1926; Lowell to Titchener, April 17, 1926, Lowell Papers; and Titchener to Lowell, April 19, 1926, Cornell University Archives, Ithaca, N.Y., Edward Bradford Titchener Papers [hereafter, Titchener Papers].

(12) Boring to Woods, January 6, January 21, March 18, 1926, Boring Papers; and Köhler to Woods, March 15, 1926, [April 1926], Köhler Papers.

(13) Boring to Perry, [1928], Boring Papers; Woods to Boring, December 17, 1926; Boring to Woods, December 27, 1926, Boring Papers; Boring to Terman, January 17, 1927, Terman Papers; and Boring to Clarence I. Lewis, August 14, 1927, December 4, April 4, 1928, Harvard University Archives, Cambridge, Mass., Department of Philosophy Papers [hereafter, Department of Philosophy Papers].

(14) Boring to Terman, July 11, 1927, Terman Papers; and Boring to Woods, January 13, 1927; Köhler to Boring, May 13, 1927 (my translation from the German), Boring Papers.

(15) Boring to Köhler, January 6, 1928, Boring Papers; and Boring to Terman, August 9, December 14, 1927, Terman Papers. Also see Boring to Lewis, August 2, August 14, 1927, Department of Philosophy Papers.

(16) Terman to Boring, January 26, 1927, Terman Papers; and Boring to Lewis, December 4, December 7, 1927, April 4, October 30, 1928, Department of Philosophy Papers.

(17) Boring to Lewis, October 30, 1928, Department of Philosophy Papers.

(18) Boring to Perry, November 15, 1928, Department of Philosophy Papers.

(19) Terman to Boring, August 3, January 26, 1927, Terman Papers; Washburn, "Gestalt Psychology and Motor Psychology," *American Journal of Psychology,* 37 (1926): 516–20; and Washburn to Boring, September 16, 1925; Boring to Carl E. Seashore, June 25, August 21, 1928, Boring Papers.

(20) Fritz K. Ringer, *The Decline of the German Mandarins: The German Academic Community, 1890–1933* (Cambridge, Mass., 1969); and Mitchell G. Ash, "The Emergence of Gestalt Theory: Experimental Psychology in Germany, 1890–1920 (Ph.D. dissertation, Harvard University, 1982).

(21) Boring to Köhler, February 27, 1930, Boring Papers, and *A History of Experimental Psychology* (New York, 1929), 570–80, 591–93.

(22) Köhler, *Gestalt Psychology* (New York, 1929).

(23) Boring to Joseph Peterson, January 13, 1930; Boring to Köhler, February 27, 1930, Boring Papers, and E. G. Boring, "The *Gestalt* Psychology and the *Gestalt* Movement," *American Journal of Psychology, 42* (1930): 308–15.

(24) Koffka to Boring, April 22, 1930; Boring to Koffka, April 23, 1930, Boring Papers; and Boring, *History of Experimental Psychology,* 593.

(25) Robinson, "A Little German Band," *New Republic,* November 27, 1929, pp. 10–14. James R. Angell, president of Yale and a psychologist, apparently criticized Robinson sharply for the tone of his review; see Robinson to Angell, December 10, 1929, Yale University Archives, New Haven, Conn., James R. Angell Presidential Papers. Also see Grace Heider to Jean and George Mandler, December 21, 1927, Archives of the History of American Psychology, Akron, Ohio, Jean Matter Mandler and George Mandler Papers [hereafter Mandler Papers].

(26) Frederick H. Lund, "The Phantom of the Gestalt," *Journal of General Psychology,* 2 (1929): 307–23; F. M. Gregg, "Materializing the Ghost of Köhler's Gestalt Psychology," *Psychological Review,* 39 (1932): 257–70; and Edna Heidbreder, *Seven Psychologies* (New York: Appleton-Century-Crofts, 1933). Also see William McDougall, "Dynamics of Gestalt Psychology," *Character and Personality,* 4 (1930): 232–44, 319–34; and S. C. Fisher, "A Critique of Insight in Köhler's Gestalt Psychology," *American Journal of Psychology,* 43 (1931): 131–35.

(27) Boring, *The Physical Dimensions of Consciousness* (New York, 1933); Jaynes, "Edwin Garrigues Boring"; Mary Henle, "One Man against the Nazis—Wolfgang Köhler," *American Psychologist,* 33 (1978): 939–44; and Ash, "The Struggle against the Nazis," *ibid.,* 34 (1979): 363–64.

(28) Boring to Perry, March 22, October 14, 1933, Boring Papers.

(29) Köhler to Boring, January 22, 1934; Boring to Köhler, December 7, 1933; Boring to Koffka, December 13, 1933, Boring Papers.

(30) Boring to Köhler, March 19, October 2, November 7, 1934; Boring to Perry, April 13, 1934, Boring Papers; and Boring to Jean and George Mandler, February 14, 1968, Mandler Papers.

(31) See *Journal of Philosophy,* 36 (1939): 107–08; *New York Times,* February 5, 1939, p. 6; Harry L. Hollingworth, review of Köhler's *Place of Value in a World of Facts,* in *American Journal of Psychology,* 53 (1940): 146–52; and J. R. Kantor, review of Köhler's *Place of Value in a World of Facts,* in *Psychological Bulletin,* 36 (1939): 292–96; and Köhler, *The Place of Value in a World of Facts* (New York, 1938).

(32) Boring to Leonard Carmichael, [December 20, 1934]; Carmichael to Boring, December 15, December 22, 1934, American Philosophical Society Library, Philadelphia, Leonard Carmichael Papers.

(33) Boring, *Psychologist at Large,* 53–54; and Jaynes, "Edwin Garrigues Boring," 107. Also see Boring and Hanns Sachs, "Was This Analysis a Success?" *Journal of Abnormal and Social Psychology,* 35 (1940): 4–16.

(34) Boring to Terman, March 27, 1928, Terman Papers; and Frank A. Beach, "Karl Spencer Lashley," in National Academy of Sciences *Biographical Memoirs, 35* (1961): 163–204.

(35) Harry Helson to Jean and George Mandler, February 27, 1968, Mandler Papers; Boring to Perry, November 28, 1933; Perry to Boring, October 28, December 1, 1933, Boring Papers; and Jaynes, "Edwin Garrigues Boring," 107.

(36) Boring to Terman, March 7, 1947, Terman Papers; and Boring to Jean and George Mandler, February 14, 1968, Mandler Papers.

(37) Stanley Coben, "The Scientific Establishment and the Transmission of Quantum Mechanics to the United States, 1919–32," *AHR,* 76 (1971): 442–66.

(38) Several distinguished scholars will disagree with most of these conclusions and have, in fact, drawn others directly opposed to them. For example, see Mary Henle, "The Influence of Gestalt Psychology in America," in R. W. Reiber and Kurt Salzinger, eds., *The Roots of American Psychology: Historical Influences and Implications for the Future* (New York, 1977), 3–12.

INDEX